OXFORD MANAGEMENT READERS

INTANGIBLE ASSETS

The OXFORD MANAGEMENT READERS series reflects the inter-disciplinary nature of much teaching of management. The aim of the series is to bring together carefully selected contributions on particular issues. The volumes will be based around either key themes or topics on the management curriculum.

INTANGIBLE ASSETS

Values, Measures, and Risks

Edited by
John R. M. Hand
Baruch Lev

OXFORD
UNIVERSITY PRESS

OXFORD
UNIVERSITY PRESS

Great Clarendon Street, Oxford OX2 6DP

Oxford University Press is a department of the University of Oxford.
It furthers the University's objective of excellence in research, scholarship,
and education by publishing worldwide in

Oxford New York

Auckland Bangkok Buenos Aires Cape Town Chennai
Dar es Salaam Delhi Hong Kong Istanbul Karachi Kolkata
Kuala Lumpur Madrid Melbourne Mexico City Mumbai
Nairobi São Paulo Shanghai Taipei Tokyo Toronto

Oxford is a registered trade mark of Oxford University Press
in the UK and in certain other countries

Published in the United States
by Oxford University Press Inc., New York

© The various contributors 2003

The moral rights of the authors have been asserted

Database right Oxford University Press (maker)

First published 2003

British Library Cataloguing in Publication Data

Data available

Library of Congress Cataloging in Publication Data

Intangible assets / edited by John R.M. Hand and Baruch Lev.
p. cm. – (Oxford management readers)
Includes bibliographical references
1. Intellectual capital—Management. 2. Intangible property—Management.
I. Hand, John R. M., 1960– II. Lev, Baruch III. Series.
HD53 .1575 2003 338–dc21 2002038146
ISBN 0-19-925693-4 (hbk.)
ISBN 0-19-925694-2 (pbk.)

1 3 5 7 9 10 8 6 4 2

Typeset by Newgen Imaging Systems (P) Ltd., Chennai, India
Printed in Great Britain
on acid-free paper by
Biddles Ltd., Guildford & King's Lynn

Foreword

When historians look back at the turn of the century, they will note one of the most profound economic shifts of the era: The rise of the Intangible Economy.

What remains a mystery still is how they will judge our reaction and response to this shift. Those who insisted that the shift was merely fad—the recent dot com boom and bust being their proof—will obviously be proven wrong. The Intangible Economy is here to stay. But will the pace of change of the infrastructure of our economy—our disclosure laws, our management techniques and our measurement capabilities that inform our resource allocation choices—have been sufficient to avoid growing pains during this transformation? Will the pace of change be so slow that productivity is undermined and our future standard of living adversely affected? Or will we, as a society, have realized the tremendous beneficial import of the shift and moved forthrightly to adjust our policies and business practices to accommodate the change, allow it to flourish and reap the advantages?

Clearly, the subject matter of the essays presented here could not be timelier. The world economy and financial system is increasingly driven not by traditional hard assets—plants, warehouses, and the like—but by intangibles. Few can deny the importance of knowledge-based assets—be they software algorithms or intellectual property or global securities trading systems. Yet our economic and financial policies seem to have clear trouble keeping pace with this accelerating new reality.

As an example of the kind of thorny issues raised by the Intangible Economy, consider our financial reporting and disclosure system.

As a lawyer, regulator, and now entrepreneur, I have come to the firm belief that our disclosure system—which is no doubt the finest and most transparent on the planet—is increasingly incapable of capturing the effect of intangibles on a company. The system was conceived and developed in a bricks-and-mortar economy, not an Intangible Economy. I wonder at what point disclosure and reporting becomes so ill suited to the intangible economy that it no longer facilitates transparency and openness. If the disconnect worsens substantially, I fear it will become much more difficult for people to understand how companies operate, generate profits, and compare to other companies here and abroad. We have, just recently, seen the spectacular collapse of a company that branded itself as the harbinger of the new economy—a company whose collapse calls into question in the minds of some the adequacy of auditor independence. But it also calls into question, more obviously and more importantly, the question of the adequacy of financial reporting generally for new economy and intangible-rich companies. It is far easier to believe financial disclosures that might otherwise seem unbelievable if there is no real basis for belief or disbelief because the public disclosures are increasingly useless, not only because they may be opaque, but also because they are quite simply not very useful. They just don't measure what it is that investors rely on to determine value. Similarly, it is far easier to bid up the market value of dot coms when there is no good measurement system to verify a perhaps more reasonable counter judgment, and far easier to bid them down to levels that seem wholly unjustified when, again, there are no good measurement systems to suggest a different value. A return to the 'traditional metrics' works fine with traditional companies, but as many of the articles contained in this volume note, the workings of intangible-rich companies are not traditional, and their drivers of wealth production are not so easily measured.

The disconnect between the old and the new could ultimately stagger the bedrock confidence the entire world has had in our financial system. The result would be an increase in the cost of capital for all, and an underallocation of resources to the new while favouring the old, not because the old is necessarily better (which in some cases it obviously may be), but because it is familiar and more easily measurable. That would be a shame for all of us. We have already seen the short-term effects of a capital famine regarding new economy companies. Imagine the impact, and the tremendous loss, if the famine becomes permanent.

Hopefully, we can peer some into the future and adjust our current course by reacting forthrightly to the issues posed by intangibles. It starts with awareness, across the economic spectrum, regulators, government officials, academicians, corporate executives, and laymen alike of the issues, and of the potential solutions.

I can think of no better place to begin than right here.

Steve Wallman,
(ex-Commissioner of the SEC; founder
and CEO of FOLIOfn)

Intangibles have grown to become a far larger part of firm valuations and national wealth in the last twenty years. As the papers in this volume document, human knowledge is the source of much of this intangible capital.

Sometimes the fruits of human knowledge are fixed in intellectual property, brand identity, and other legal and accounting artifacts. But, in many cases, human knowledge is part of the general organizational capital of firms.

Sometimes the knowledge exists in physical form, written down in operations manuals, but often it is tacit knowledge: the unverbalized knowledge about how to get things done.

Knowledge about how to get things done, verbalized or unverbalized, is particularly important when technology is changing rapidly. Firms that learn, explicitly or implicitly, how to utilize new technology have an edge over those that do not. But as knowledge about what works and what does not diffuses in the economy, the competitive advantage of knowing how to effectively use technology erodes.

When Ford Motor Company implemented the assembly line in the second decade of this century, it gained a huge competitive advantage, due to its mastery of a superior method of manufacture. Its competitors struggled to adopt Ford's techniques and, eventually, succeeded, making the whole economy more productive.

Fifteen years ago, some companies could gain a competitive edge by using fax machines effectively. Five years ago, some companies gained a competitive edge by using email effectively. Two years ago, it was the Internet.

Perhaps as knowledge about how to use information technology becomes more widespread, intangibles will end up being a smaller part of firm valuations. When everyone effectively uses an assembly line, or a fax machine, or email, then these technologies no longer offer competitive advantage and supra-normal returns.

Maybe, but do not count on it. Technology continues to march on. Companies that learn how to use existing technologies effectively today will continue to learn new technologies tomorrow. As long as there is technological change, there will be tangible rewards for intangible knowledge.

Hal R. Varian,
Dean of the School of Information Management
and Systems at the University of California, Berkeley

Acknowledgements

Leonard Nakamura, 'A Trillion Dollars a Year in Intangible Investment and the New Economy'. Developed from an earlier article of the same title in *Business Review* (Philadelphia Federal Reserve Bank). Reprinted by permission of the Philadelphia Federal Reserve Bank.

Carl Shapiro and Hal Varian, 'The Information Economy'. Reprinted from *Information Rules: A Strategic Guide to the Network Economy* by Carl Shapiro and Hal Varian (1999: 1–18) by permission of Harvard Business School Press, Boston MA. Copyright © 1999 by the Harvard Business School Publishing Corporation; all rights reserved.

Paul Romer, 'The Soft Revolution: Achieving Growth by Managing Intangibles', *Journal of Applied Corporate Finance*, vol. 11, No. 2 (Summer 1998), pp. 8–14. Reprinted by permission of Stern Stewart Europe Limited.

Stephen R. Bond and Jason G. Cummins, 'The Stock Market and Investment in the New Economy: Some Tangible Facts and Intangible Fictions'. Developed from an earlier article of the same title in *Brookings Papers on Economic Activity*, 1 (2000), pp. 61–108.

Baruch Lev and Theodore Sougiannis, 'The Capitalization, Amortization, and Value-Relevance of R&D', *Journal of Accounting and Economics*, vol. 21 (1996), pp. 107–38. Copyright © 1996 Elsevier Science. Reprinted by permission.

Mary Barth, Michael Clement, George Foster, and Ron Kasznik, 'Brand Values and Capital Market Valuation', *Review of Accounting Studies*, vol. 4, pp. 41–68. Reprinted by permission of Plenum.

Lynne G. Zucker, Michael R. Darby, and Marilynn B. Brewer, 'Intellectual Human Capital and the Birth of the Biotechnology Enterprise', *American Economic Review*, vol. 88, No. 1 (1988), pp. 290–306. Reprinted by permission of the American Economic Association.

Zhen Deng, Baruch Lev, and Francis Narin, 'Science and Technology as Predictors of Stock Performance', *Financial Analysts Journal*, May/June (1999). Copyright © 1999 Association for Investment Management and Research. Reprinted by permission. All Rights Reserved.

Jeff Boone and K. K. Raman, 'Off-Balance Sheet R&D Assets and Market Liquidity', *Journal of Accounting & Public Policy*, vol. 20, No. 2 (2001), pp. 97–128. Copyright © 2001 Elsevier Science. Reprinted by permission.

David Aboody and Baruch Lev, 'Information Asymmetry, R&D, and Insider Gains', *Journal of Finance*, vol. 55, No. 6 (2000), pp. 2747–66. Reprinted by permission of Blackwell Publishing Ltd.

Acknowledgements

Louis Chan, Josef Lakonishok, and Theodore Sougiannis, 'The Stock Market Valuation of Research and Development Expenditures', *Journal of Finance*, vol. 56 (2001), pp. 2431–56. Reprinted by permission of Blackwell Publishing Ltd.

Joan Luft and Michael Shields, 'Why Does Fixation Persist? Experimental Evidence on the Judgment Performance Effects of Expensing Intangibles', *The Accounting Review*, October (2001). Copyright © 2001 the American Accounting Association. Reprinted by permission.

Margaret Blair and Steven Wallman, 'The Growing Intangibles Reporting Discrepancy'. Reprinted from *Unseen Wealth: Report of the Brookings Task Force on Intangibles* by permission of The Brookings Institution. Copyright © 2001 Brookings Institute Press.

Wayne Upton, Jr., 'Challenges from the New Economy for Business and Financial Reporting'. Reprinted from *Business and Financial Reporting, Challenges from the New Economy* (FASB Special Report) by permission of the Financial Accounting Standards Board. Copyright © FASB.

Baruch Lev and Paul Zarowin, 'The Boundaries of Financial Reporting and How to Extend Them'. An abbreviated version of a paper with the same title that appeared in the *Journal of Accounting Research*, vol. 37, No. 2 (Autumn 1999). Reprinted by permission.

Baruch Lev, 'What Then Must We Do?' An abbreviated version of Chapter Five of *Intangibles: Management, Measurement, and Reporting* by Baruch Lev (2001) by permission of The Brookings Institution. Copyright © 2001 Brookings Institute Press.

Contents

I. INTANGIBLES IN THE MODERN ECONOMY

Contents

Contents

List of Contributors

David Aboody — Associate Professor of Accounting, The Anderson School, UCLA

Mary E. Barth — Atholl McBean Professor of Accounting, Stanford Graduate School of Business

Margaret Blair — Research Director of the Sloan-GULC Project of Business Institutions, and Visiting Professor, Georgetown University Law Center

Stephen R. Bond — Gwilyn Gibbon Research Fellow in Public Economics, Nuffield College, Oxford University

Jeff P. Boone — Assistant Professor of Accounting, Mississippi State University

Marilynn B. Brewer — Professor, Department of Psychology, Ohio State University

Louis K.C. Chan — Professor of Finance, University of Illinois

Michael B. Clement — Assistant Professor of Accounting, University of Texas at Austin

Jason G. Cummins — Federal Reserve Board

Michael R. Darby — Warren C. Cordner Professor of Money and Financial Markets, The Anderson School, UCLA

Zhen Deng — Ph.D. student, New York University

George Foster — Foundation Professor of Management and Director of the Executive Program for Growing Companies, Stanford Graduate School of Business

John R. M. Hand — Professor and Chairman, Accounting Faculty, Kenan-Flagler Business School, UNC Chapel Hill

Ron Kasznik — Associate Professor of Accounting, Stanford Graduate School of Business

Josef Lakonishok — William G. Karnes Professor of Finance, University of Illinois

Baruch Lev — Philip Bardes Professor of Accounting and Finance at Stern School of Business, New York University, and Director of the Vincent C. Ross Institute for Accounting Research and the Project for Research on Intangibles

Joan L. Luft — Associate Professor, Michigan State University

Randall Morck — Professor, Stephen A. Jarislowsky Distinguished Chair in Finance, University of Alberta

List of Contributors

Leonard Nakamura	Economic Advisor, Federal Reserve Bank of Philadelphia, USA
Francis Narin	President, CHI Research
K.K. Raman	Professor of Accounting, University of North Texas
Paul Romer	STANCO 25 Professor of Economics in the Graduate School of Business at Stanford University and a Senior Fellow of the Hoover Institution
Chandrakanth Seethamraju	Assistant Professor of Accounting, Olin School of Business, University of Washington, St. Louis
Carl Shapiro	Transamerica Professor of Business Strategy in the Economic Analysis and Policy Group at the Walter A. Haas School of Business at the University of California at Berkeley
Michael D. Shields	Eli Broad Professor of Accounting, Michigan State University
Theodore Sougiannis	Associate Professor of Accounting, University of Illinois
Wayne S. Upton, Jr	Financial Accounting Standards Board
Hal R. Varian	Dean of the School of Information Management and Systems at the University of California at Berkeley
Steven Wallman	Founder and CEO of FOLIOfn, and formerly a commissioner of the Securities and Exchange Commission
Bernard Yeung	Krasnoff Professor of International Business at Stern School of Business, New York University
Paul Zarowin	Associate Professor, Stern School of Business, New York University
Lynne G. Zucker	Professor of Sociology, UCLA

Introduction and Overview

....

John R. M. Hand and Baruch Lev

Wealth and growth in modern economies are driven primarily by *intangible assets*, defined as claims to future benefits that do not have a physical or financial form. Patents, bioengineered drugs, brands, strategic alliances, customer lists, a proprietary cost-reducing Internet-based supply chain—these are all examples of intangible assets. The more traditional physical and financial assets are rapidly becoming commodities, since they are equally accessible to competitors, and consequently yield at best a competitive return on investment. Dominant market positions, abnormal profits, and even temporary monopolistic advantages are today most effectively achieved by the sound deployment of intangible assets.

As a result, intangibles are increasingly taking center stage in firms' business strategies and the valuation calculus performed by investors. Responding to the intensified competition brought about by the globalization of trade, far-reaching deregulation, and ever faster technological changes, firms are radically changing their business models. Many of these changes involve or create intangibles. Firms are substituting intangibles for physical assets and accelerating the pace at which they innovate by exploiting investments in intangible assets. Intangibles are also playing a major macroeconomic role, changing the growth and cyclical dynamics of national economies, as recently observed by Federal Reserve Chairman Alan Greenspan:

From one perspective, the ever-increasing proportion of our GDP that represents conceptual—as distinct from physical—value added may actually have lessened cyclical volatility. In particular, the fact that concepts cannot be held as inventories means a greater share of GDP is not subject to a type of dynamics that amplifies cyclical swings.[1]

The importance of intangible assets is magnified by the fact that they are not restricted to the high technology sector, but are instead dominant in every well-run enterprise. A recent ranking of the fifty US companies with the largest intangible capital (Fortune magazine, April 2001) contained not just 'new-economy' firms, such as Microsoft, Intel, America Online, and Cisco Systems, but also twenty-eight 'old-economy' companies such as General Electric, Wal-Mart, DuPont, Coca-Cola, and Alcoa. Examples of other non-tech companies with valuable intangibles are British Petroleum, Goldman Sachs, and Unilever. In today's economy, intangible assets are pervasive across virtually all business sectors and in every major industrial country.

Although managers and financial analysts intuitively perceive the importance of intangibles to business success, they currently lack knowledge about the systematic findings of research into the economic attributes of intangibles, particularly regarding measurement and valuation. As a result, the management of intangibles and the investment valuation of intangibles-intensive companies tends to be haphazard. For example, there are no widely accepted tools available with which a manager might assess the return on investments in intangibles (R&D, brands, employee training). Similarly, investor valuations of intangible-intensive firms are inadequate, leading to systematic mispricing of securities and excessive stock price volatility.

The recent collapse of many Internet and telecom companies, the bursting of the NASDAQ bubble, and the contagion effect on other high-tech markets around the world—along with the demise of Enron, Winstar, Global Crossing, and other leading new-economy companies—focused the attention of observers on the vulnerabilities of intangibles. It is important not to lose sight of the strengths of intangibles and instead to realize that, even in the post-Enron and post-NASDAQ bubble era, intangibles created by R&D, brand enhancement, and unique organizational designs and processes still remain the major value creators at both the corporate and national levels. However, the fact that property rights on intangibles are not fully secured ('partial excludability' in economists' parlance), that there are no transparent and competitive markets in intangibles (absence of ready exit strategies for owners of intangibles and 'comparables' for investor valuations), and the deficient accounting for intangible assets (no early warning signals about impairment of intangibles) render owners of intangibles and investors in intangibles-intensive enterprises vulnerable to unexpected changes in business conditions.[2] These vulnerabilities highlight the need for an in-depth understanding of the economics of intangibles and the development of tools to better manage and evaluate intangible assets.

The speed with which intangibles have risen to global prominence also creates a demand for careful scholarship about these major value drivers. The papers contained and reviewed in this volume bring together for the first time the best research in the exciting and rapidly emerging area of intangibles. Although academic work on intangibles is distributed across a wide array of disciplines, important and promising conceptual and empirical inroads have recently been made that are worthy of communication to a broad audience of business people,

MBA and PhD students, and researchers across the world. This *Reader* seeks to gather the best of a rapidly growing research base into one volume so that the next generation of questions can be asked and answered from a solid foundation.

The concepts and empirical findings contained in the papers presented below are directly relevant to business people who seek to maximize shareholder value in the intangible-intensive economy of the new century. The scope of business applications includes the following:

- grasping the sheer scale and economic impact of corporate investments in intangibles
- managing the unique aspects of the economics of information for business advantage
- appreciating how scientific discovery, technological change, and innovation create and sustain growth
- capitalizing on the geographic clustering of intellectual human capital when forming new high-technology businesses
- adding value through branding
- understanding how and why science and technology indicators predict stock performance
- valuing trademarks
- making sense of seemingly perverse relations between reported corporate losses and market value for intangible-intensive companies
- deciding how to diversify across industries and geography to optimize corporate success
- exploiting economies of scale in intangibles (i.e. the fact that investments in intangibles tend to be more profitable the larger they are)
- recognizing the wide range of adverse effects of the informational deficiencies caused by both the accounting for intangibles and the fundamental properties of intangibles
- being apprised of the changes in financial reporting and disclosure rules that are likely to come about because of the growing importance of intangibles
- using a new information system—the *value-chain blueprint*—to assess the effectiveness of the innovation activities of the enterprise.

While these insights and applications are of great concern to corporate executives, they are equally relevant to investors and financial analysts striving to fathom and value intangibles-intensive companies, as well as to public policymakers engaged in the promotion of national growth and welfare.

The articles in the *Reader* are the original works of scholars and policymakers in accounting, economics, finance, and information technology. Many of the authors are internationally renowned scholars working at top universities. Their work is highly contemporary, being largely researched and written during the past five years.

The intended audience of the *Reader* comprises primarily MBA and PhD students in business, graduate students in economics, and faculty in the fields of accounting, economics, finance, and management. However, the empirical rather than mathematical orientation of the articles, and the introductory notes we provide, render the *Reader* accessible to motivated business people and financial analysts with a rudimentary knowledge of business and economics.

The *Reader* has four sections: Part I explains why most scholars and business people believe that intangibles have become so important—both in terms of size and economic potential—in the modern economy. The view is not uniformly held, however, thus Part I contains one article arguing against our viewpoint. The papers in Part II investigate the impact of specific kinds of intangibles on firm performance and equity market values, while the papers in Part III document the frequently severe adverse effects of the informational deficiencies that are created by the accounting and financial reporting rules that govern intangibles. Finally, the papers in Part IV conclude by calling for improved disclosure and measurement of intangibles in financial statements, as well as by making concrete suggestions for what such solutions should look like.

....

The Readings

Part I: Intangibles in the Modern Economy

Intangibles are not new. Whenever ideas have been put to use in households, fields, and workshops—such as the invention of the wheel, the windmill, or the printing press—intangibles (also known as intellectual capital or knowledge assets) have been created. Breakthrough inventions, such as electricity and transportation, have created waves of intangibles throughout history.

What *is* new is the dramatic surge in the size and importance of corporate intangibles since the early 1980s. While indirect evidence of this appears in the mounting value of the mean market-to-book ratio of the S&P 500 companies over the course of the last twenty years—increasing from 1.0 to about 5.0 during the period ending in 2002—we begin the *Reader* with the direct evidence contained in Leonard Nakamura's paper 'A Trillion Dollars a Year in Intangible Investment and the New Economy'. Nakamura uses three different approaches to empirically demonstrate that private US firms invested at least $1 trillion in intangibles in 2000, a level of investment that roughly equals the gross investment in corporate tangible assets. He further computes that the capital stock of US intangibles has an equilibrium market value of at least $5 trillion, approximately equal to one half the market value of all US corporations. Such massive numbers strongly suggest that academics, business people, and policy-makers should take intangibles very seriously.

The major driver behind the recent surge in intangibles is the unique combination of three related economic forces: intensified business competition brought about by the globalization of trade; the far-reaching deregulation in key economic sectors, such as telecommunications, transportation, energy, and financial services; and the acceleration of information technologies, most recently exemplified by the Internet. Carl Shapiro and Hal Varian crisply outline the unique economic attributes of information in the chapter 'The Information Economy'. On the supply side of the equation, they note that information is costly to produce but very cheap to reproduce. On the demand side, information technology and infrastructure have dramatically leveraged economies of scale inherent in information goods by lowering the cost of accessing and using them. The result has been an explosion in the use of information and the associated consumer surplus, aided at times by the positive-feedback loops inherent in the network externalities that characterize some kinds of information goods. The authors also discuss the challenges in assigning prices to information products and securing ownership over them.

In his insightful yet easy-to-comprehend article 'The Soft Revolution: Achieving Growth by Managing Intangibles', Paul Romer reinforces and adds to the issues discussed by Shapiro and Varian. Romer argues that intangibles are the primary reason for economic growth and ascending standards of living. He defines intangibles as the instructions, formulas, recipes, and methods of doing things that together constitute the process of rearranging matter. We are wealthier today than our ancestors were 100 years ago, he proposes, because we have taken the fixed quantity of raw materials available on planet Earth and rearranged them in increasingly novel ways that have made the materials more productive and valuable. He illustrates this point using the PC. Although the typical PC has about the same amount of raw materials today that it had five years ago (copper, iron, silicon, plastic, etc.), those same resources are now rearranged in ways that make today's PC up to thirty times more powerful than PCs were five years ago. In Romer's view, business is undergoing a 'soft revolution' in which the intangibles defined above are transforming companies and national economies from the inside out.

Not everyone views the world with such enthusiasm concerning intangibles. To provide balance on scholars' views on intangibles, we conclude Part I with the dissenting view of Stephen Bond and Jason Cummins, entitled 'The Stock Market and Investment in the New Economy: Some Tangible Facts and Intangible Fictions'. Bond and Cummins critically examine whether the increase in stock market valuations, particularly those of high-technology firms in the second half of the 1990s, reflected the growing role of intangible capital in generating profits,

5

or whether the increase instead reflected a persistent and broad-based overvaluation of firms relative to their fundamental values. The authors do this by examining the investment patterns of tangible and intangible capital. Their conclusion: while a limited role for intangible investments in improved equity market values is observed, no evidence is found that it accounts for the spectacular rise that in fact occurred. As such, their work provides a valuable counterweight to those who would attribute the entirety of the massive increases in equity prices over the course of the 1990s to intangible assets. Bond and Cummins' arguments are consistent with the collapse of the high tech stock price bubble during 2000 and 2001.

Part II: The Impact of Specific Intangibles on Firm Performance and Market Value

There are three major classes of intangibles: those created primarily through innovation and discovery, those that underlie organizational practices, and those related to human resources. For example, the bulk of Merck & Co.'s intangibles arose from Merck's massive and highly successful innovation effort ($2.34 billion of R&D in 2000), which was conducted internally and in alliance with other entities. Alternatively, Wal-Mart's and Dell Computer's major value drivers reside in their unique organizational designs, which were implemented through innovative supply chains, or through direct customer marketing of built-to-order computers via the telephone and Internet. Finally, the value of human resources-related intangibles is demonstrated by Xerox's Eureka system, which effectively shares information among the company's 20,000 maintenance personnel and thereby increases employee productivity.

Part II of the *Reader* is devoted to laying out the rich set of empirical findings that have been uncovered by researchers as they examine the economic attributes of a broad range of intangible assets. Collected here are what we consider to be the leading examples of research into understanding the value created for firms by their investments in R&D, brands, intellectual human capital, science and technology, and trademarks. The studies provide evidence of the extent to which spending on different types of intangibles is associated with increases in the future profitability or current equity market values of the firms involved. The dominant theme of the selected works is the establishment of empirical linkages between inputs (e.g. investment in R&D or branding) and outputs (earnings, productivity, or shareholder value). The studies uniformly show that there are strong and economically consequential empirical relations between a wide scope of input measures of intangibles and a variety of outputs, particularly corporate profitability and equity market values.

An example of the insights provided by the authors in this section is the paper by Baruch Lev and Theodore Sougiannis entitled 'The Capitalization,

Amortization, and Value-Relevance of R&D'. There, Lev and Sougiannis examine the validity of concerns embedded within Generally Accepted US Accounting Principles (GAAP) about the reliability, objectivity, and value-relevance of recognizing R&D as an asset. They do this by estimating the R&D capital—which of course is not presented on corporate balance sheets—of a large sample of US public companies. Their conclusion: such estimates are statistically reliable and economically meaningful. When they further adjust the reported earnings and book values of sample firms for the R&D capitalization, they find that those adjustments enhance investors' information. A significant association over time between firms' R&D capital and *subsequent* stock returns is documented as well, suggesting either a systematic mispricing of the shares of R&D-intensive companies (a theme we return to in Part III), or a compensation for an extra-market risk factor associated with R&D.

Brands, a major intangible prevalent in consumer products—electronics (Sony), food and beverages (Coca-Cola), and more recently in Internet companies (AOL, Yahoo!, and Amazon)—are often created by a combination of innovation and organizational structure. Coke's highly valuable brand is the result of a secret formula and exceptional marketing savvy. The unique products created and acquired by AOL during the 1990s are responsible for its brand, along with massive marketing (customer acquisition) expenditures. In *'Brand Values and Capital Market Valuation'*. Mary Barth, Michael Clement, George Foster, and Ron Kasznik examine whether brand values can be quantified, and, if so, whether such values are taken into account by investors. They do this for a set of firms whose brand values are estimated by Interbrand Ltd. (a consultancy) and find that the estimated brand values are positively and significantly related to firms' equity market values and stock returns, over and above the effect on market values of advertising expenses, operating margins, market share, and analyst earnings forecasts.

Intellectual human capital is also a powerful intangible asset, as illustrated by the paper *'Intellectual Capital and the Birth of US Biotechnology Enterprises'* by Lynne Zucker, Michael Darby, and Marilynn Brewer. These researchers investigate the relationships between the intellectual human capital of 'star' scientists making frontier discoveries, the impact of great university bioscience programs, and the presence of venture capital in the founding of US biotech enterprises during the period 1976–89. They find that the founding and location of new biotech firms are determined primarily by measures of intellectual capital, particularly by the number of the firm's star scientists actively publishing genetic sequence discoveries. They conclude that—at least early in the firm-founding process—star scientists are scarce, immovable factors of production whose intellectual capital enables them to capture supranormal economic returns.

Patents and innovations (new products, services) are key outcomes of R&D activities. Zhen Deng, Baruch Lev, and Francis Narin, in their paper *'Science and*

Technology as Predictors of Stock Performance', examine the ability of patent-based citation measures to predict the subsequent stock returns and market-to-book ratios of public companies. Citations or references to a firm's patents included in subsequent patent applications ('forward citations') offer a reasonably reliable measure of R&D value, because such citations are an objective indicator of the firm's technological capabilities and the impact of its innovations and research on the subsequent development of science and technology. The authors find that three measures possess predictive ability: the number of patents granted to the firm in a given year; the intensity of citations to a firm's patent portfolio by subsequent patents; and a measure based on the number of citations in a firm's patents ('backward citations') to scientific papers (in contrast with citations to previous patents). This latter measure reflects the 'scientific intensity' of a patent and may provide a proxy for the extent of basic research conducted by the company. The fact that patent indicators were found to be associated with *subsequent* stock prices and returns suggests that investors are not fully aware of the ability of these measures to convey useful information about firms' innovation processes and capabilities. This, of course, is not surprising given the relative novelty of patent-related measures as indicators of enterprise value.

In his study '*The Value-Relevance of Trademarks'*, Chandra Seethamraju focuses the research on brands by concentrating on trademarks. He demonstrates in multiple ways that the values of internally developed trademarks are measurable, material, and value-relevant to investors. He tests the value relevance of trademarks within a production function framework and finds that trademarks augment the information conveyed by sales. The empirical association between trademarks and sales is then used as a basis for assigning value to the new trademarks registered by sample firms in 1997. Seethamraju estimates that the mean value of registered trademarks for his sample firms is $580 million. Then, using an accounting-based equity valuation framework, he shows that the estimated values of new trademarks are associated with the market values of firms and reaches the conclusion that such estimates represent value-relevant information that is reflected in share prices. This raises the possibility that firms might improve financial reporting by providing increased disclosures about trademarks in their financial statements. Finally, Seethamraju shows that the stock market reacts swiftly and positively to announcements of trademark acquisitions, most likely because investors believe that the purchased trademark will generate synergies from the firm's existing product line. Moreover, firms making quantitative disclosures about trademarks enjoy, on average, a size-adjusted return of 2.9 per cent greater than firms making just qualitative disclosures, in all likelihood because quantitative disclosures reduce the uncertainty associated with future profit projections.

The accounting for intangibles in the United States is highly conservative, because virtually all expenditures made on intangibles are required to be written off against net income in the year in which they are incurred. Only in very rare instances (e.g. software development) are expenditures on intangibles allowed to be capitalized and then amortized into net income over time. In 'Profits, Losses, and the Nonlinear Pricing of Internet Stocks', John Hand shows that when the level of a firm's expenditures on intangibles becomes large enough, seemingly perverse and counterintuitive correlations emerge between firms' net incomes and equity market values. He demonstrates this phenomenon using Internet firms, whose expenditures on brand and R&D intangibles averaged more than 70 per cent of their revenues. For these firms, Hand finds that the pricing of accounting variables is sharply nonlinear in two ways. First, losses are negatively priced (namely, they add market value), because such losses primarily reflect large investments in intangible marketing and R&D assets, not poor operating performance. Second, intangibles are priced as assets when income is negative, but not when income is positive, and intangibles are dominant in the firm's business strategy. These pricing nonlinearities are found to change steadily over time, with the pricing of profits becoming less positive and the pricing of losses less negative. These findings indicate that the conventional assumption that accounting information maps into equity value in a linear and inter-temporally constant way is inappropriate for young, growing, intangible- and/or technology-intensive companies.

In their intriguing paper 'Why Firms Diversify: Internalization vs Agency Behaviour'. Randall Morck and Bernard Yeung show that corporate diversification—both across industries and countries—enhances the value of an enterprise in the presence of intangibles, but destroys value without intangibles. The former part of this evidence appears to run counter to the mantra 'Focus on core operations, and spin off unrelated activities' that is often voiced by managers and consultants. This view is supported by the evidence of a 15–20 per cent discount in the shares of diversified firms relative to similar pure-play companies. In fact there is no inconsistency here, because Morck and Yeung's findings about the positive contribution of diversification to value relate only to companies that possess substantial intangibles. As the authors point out, while diversification across unrelated operations often detracts from enterprise value, diversification aimed at scaling intangibles results in considerable value added. Such leveraging of intangibles across industries and countries obviously requires considerable organizational capital, such as the knowledge systems of pharmaceutical and chemical companies aimed at sharing information among R&D personnel, or the capacity to acquire resources and identify potential buyers/licensees or Internet-based supply chains. These forms of organizational capital are potent resources that enable firms to create value via diversification.

The economics of intangible assets are typically quite different from those of their tangible counterparts. For example, investments in intangibles are far riskier than equivalent expenditures on tangible or financial assets, in the sense that the formers' payoffs are asymmetrical and likely to result in extreme outcomes. That is, whereas the value created by tangible and financial assets usually clusters more or less symmetrically around some mean value determined by competition, the value created by intangible assets is asymmetric, having a high likelihood of zero value and a small likelihood of hugely positive value. Moreover, intangible assets are also infrequently traded in markets, and often possess property rights that are not fully securable by the company—further increasing their riskiness.

Counterbalancing these risks is the considerable upside potential that intangibles offer. Successful intangibles can lead to rapid market dominance and increasing returns-to-scale through a potent combination of supply-side economies of scale and/or demand-side network effects. Supply-side economies of scale arise because intangibles are generally nonrival assets, meaning that they can be deployed at the same time in multiple uses and that a given deployment does not detract from the usefulness of the asset in other situations (negligible opportunity costs). On the demand side, intangibles may often benefit from positive-feedback loops or network effects, which are prevalent where users particularly value large networks, such as in computer, software, telecommunications, and consumer electronics markets. In such situations the benefits of being part of a network increase with the number of people connected to the network. As a result, a firm's existing customers may beget new customers without any significant expenditure on the part of the firm.

Related to the above, John Hand explores the extent to which R&D, advertising, and personnel intangibles exhibit increasing returns-to-scale in 'The Increasing Returns-to-Scale of Intangibles'. Hand uses data on all publicly traded US firms over the period 1980–2000 for two purposes. First, he measures the average net present value or fundamental profitability of expenditures made on R&D, advertising, and personnel intangibles over the past twenty years. Then he tests whether greater magnitudes of expenditures lead to greater fundamental profitability. Consistent with the view that intangibles yield increasing returns-to-scale, Hand finds that R&D and advertising are more profitable, on average, the larger the expenditures made on those intangibles. Moreover, the increasing returns-to-scale phenomenon was more pronounced in the 1990s than in the earlier economy of the 1980s.

Part III: The Adverse Consequences of Intangibles' Information Deficiencies

Economic models and theories are generally structured around costs and benefits. Investments in intangibles are no exception. While the studies included in

Part II of the *Reader* largely explore the benefits associated with intangibles, the questions addressed by the papers in Part III are cost oriented. Specifically, these papers investigate the extent of the private and social harms resulting from deficiencies in the valuation and reporting of intangibles.

The major culprit turns out to be the paucity of internally collected and externally reported information about intangible assets. This information deficiency adversely impacts the sophistication with which intangibles are managed and valued. While information deficiencies may seem to be the result of accounting shortcomings (e.g. expenditures on intangibles are expensed, while those on physical and financial assets are capitalized), they are in fact deeply rooted in the unique economic attributes of intangibles—high risk, lack of full control over benefits, and the absence of transparent markets in intangibles. When combined with the fact that corporate executives and auditors currently have few, if any, incentives to expand the information available about intangibles, serious private and social harms can and do arise. In this section we therefore highlight scholarship that has explored the nature, extent, and consequences of the problems due to information deficiency endured by intangibles.

In a paper entitled '*Off-Balance Sheet R&D Assets and Market Liquidity*', Jeff Boone and K.K. Raman investigate whether the information asymmetry (namely, managers know more about their intangible assets than investors and lenders) arising from the unrecorded, off-balance sheet nature of R&D assets detrimentally affects the market liquidity of such firms' stocks, thereby increasing their cost of capital. Boone and Raman find that it does. In particular, they examine the impact of changes in R&D expenditures on stocks' bid–ask spread, which is a measure of liquidity. Relating R&D changes to bid-ask spreads is an effective way to examine the consequences of the information asymmetries created by R&D. This is true because the bid–ask spread reflects investors' transaction costs (the cost of buying then selling a security), which in turn affect companies' cost of capital since, if spreads widen, investors will require a compensation for the higher transaction costs. Boone and Raman report a statistically significant association between increases in R&D expenditures and both the widening of securities' bid–ask spreads and the 'depth' of trade (i.e. the quantity of securities the market maker is willing to commit for a given quoted spread). This evidence establishes a link between deficiencies in R&D reporting and the consequent increase in cost of capital, which in turn impedes firms' investment and growth. This suggests a social harm.

Compelling evidence on the existence of a unique, intangibles-related information asymmetry between managers and investors, and the exploitation of such asymmetry by some executives comes from a study of insider gains by David Aboody and Baruch Lev entitled '*Information Asymmetry, R&D, and Insider Gains*'. Corporate executives' compensation packages are heavily weighted with stock and stock options, particularly in technology and science-based companies. These executives are allowed to trade in the shares of their companies (insider trading), but they are prohibited from trading on material 'inside information', which is loosely defined as information that would have affected investors' decisions, once disclosed. Aboody and Lev examine all trades by corporate officers in the stocks of their companies over the 1985–98 period and form the following conclusions. First, gains to insiders in companies with R&D activities are, on average, three to four times larger than insiders' gains in companies without R&D. Second, when insiders' trades in R&D companies are publicly disclosed through the SEC filings—on average, twenty five days after the trades were executed—investors react to the information by buying shares when insiders' purchases are reported, and selling upon being informed that insiders unloaded shares. Such reactions by investors suggest that R&D creates significant information asymmetries between managers and investors, such as managers knowing about a drug failing clinical tests, or a software program successfully passing a beta test, and that much of this information is kept from investors until the disclosure of insiders' trades. Not only are the private and social harms of such information deficiencies obvious (insiders' gains come at the expense of outside investors), but excessive insider gains erode investors' confidence in the integrity of capital markets, leading to thin trades and a decrease in the social benefits from large, transparent capital markets. The concerns of investors in mid-2002 with the ethical conduct of executives and the integrity of markets are echoed in this study.

Louis Chan, Josef Lakonishok, and Theodore Sougiannis document another significant adverse consequence of the informational deficiencies of intangibles in their paper 'The Stock Market Valuation of Research and Development Expenditures'. The authors examine whether stock prices fully reflect the value of firms' R&D expenditures. They propose that since intangible assets are not reported on financial statements under current US accounting standards, the valuation problem facing investors may be especially challenging. The authors report that the stock of companies with high R&D relative to market value (generally firms that tend to have poor past returns) show strong signs of underpricing. The market apparently fails to give sufficient credit for firms' R&D investments, suggesting that such firms face an unduly high cost of capital. The harmful social consequences are obvious: companies that invest consistently in intangibles (technology, knowledge), yet are still not stellar performers, tend to have a high cost of capital imposed on them by capital markets, thereby impeding their investment and growth. Once more, a link seems to be established between reporting deficiencies related to intangibles and real, harmful consequences.

Last in Part III is the study 'Why Does Fixation Persist? Experimental Evidence on the Judgment Performance Effects of Expensing Intangibles' by Joan Luft and Michael Shields. This paper demonstrates in an experimental setting—which is different from the large-scale empirical studies summarized above—that when individuals use information on intangible expenditures to predict future profits, expensing (in contrast to capitalizing) the expenditures significantly reduces the accuracy, consistency, consensus, and self-insight of the individuals' subjective profit predictions. Consistent with psychological theories of learning, subjects participating in the experiment did not learn the exact magnitude of the effect of intangibles on future profits as well when the intangibles were expensed, compared with capitalized intangibles, which led to the above-mentioned deficiencies. This study suggests that managerial decisions based on traditional accounting information (intangibles expensed) may lead to adverse consequences. An experimental design, such as that used in this study, overcomes the limitation of empirical studies, given that capitalization of intangibles is rarely observed in financial reports.

Part IV: The Need for Solutions: Improved Measurement and Disclosure of Intangibles

In a July 2000 hearing of the Senate Committee on Banking, Housing, and Urban Affairs devoted to 'Adapting a 1930s Financial Reporting Model to the 21st Century', each of the five testifying experts primarily ascribed the deficiencies of information in corporate financial reports to the growth of intangible assets and the inadequate treatment of these assets by the traditional accounting system.[3] Intangible assets, they argued, surpass physical assets in most business enterprises, both in value and contribution to growth, yet they are routinely expensed in the financial reports, thereby remaining absent from corporate balance sheets. The problem, however, is not limited to corporate balance sheets. Financial reports and other corporate disclosures rarely provide relevant information (in footnotes or other articulations) on important aspects of intangibles, such as amounts spent on software, employee training, brand enhancement, and other intangibles. This leads to biased and deficient reporting of firms' performance and value and the harms documented by the research presented in Part III.

What then should be done? We conclude the *Reader* by presenting eloquent and powerful calls to action that have been made by key policy-makers, as well as outlining some innovative and concrete solutions.

The first broad and succinct call to action comes in '*The Problem*', the first Chapter in '*Unseen Wealth: Report of the Brookings Task Force on Intangibles*' written by Margaret Blair and Steven Wallman. This *Report* notes that, although intangibles have historically not been treated in the national accounts as part of national wealth, nor accounted for as part of the assets of firms, intangibles are very large and becoming more important over time in modern economies.[4]

John R. M. Hand and Baruch Lev

The *Report* focuses on how accurate and useful information about intangible inputs into the modern economy could be provided—namely, information about the ideas, special skills, organizational structures and capabilities, brand identities, mailing lists and data bases, and the networks of social, professional, and business relationships that make it possible for people to exchange services, experiences, technology, and knowledge in the creation of goods and services.

The second paper in this section is Chapter 1 of a *Special Financial Accounting Standards Report* written by Wayne Upton, Jr, entitled '*Business and Financial Reporting, Challenges from the New Economy*'. The *Special Report* examines issues and implications posed by three propositions about what many see as accounting's failure to keep pace with a changing economy. The three propositions are as follows: (1) Traditional financial statements are largely backward looking and focused on the ability to realize value from physical and financial assets and liabilities. A new financial reporting paradigm is needed to capture and report on where and how the firm creates value. (2) The important value drivers in the modern economy are largely nonfinancial and do not lend themselves easily to presentation in financial reports. However, a set of measures could be developed that would allow investors and creditors to evaluate and compare business entities. (3) Intangibles are the distinguishing feature of a modern economy. Accounting standard-setters should develop a basis for the recognition and measurement of internally generated intangible assets such as R&D and brands, rather than only recognizing them when they are acquired from others.[5]

Upton stresses that the problems presented by intangibles for business and financial reporting are global and not specific to the United States. He notes that over and above the attention paid to the issues by the American Institute of Certified Public Accountants, the Financial Accounting Standards Board, and the Securities and Exchange Commission, notable efforts to come to grips with the problems have been made by the Canadian Institute of Chartered Accountants, the Danish Agency for Development of Trade and Industry, the Netherlands Ministry of Economic Affairs, the Institute of Chartered Accountants in England and Wales, and the Organization for Economic Cooperation and Development. Intangibles are thus a worldwide concern.

The last two papers of the *Reader* make concrete suggestions for how financial reports could be improved in dealing with intangibles. Several of the papers outlined above advocate the capitalization of intangibles in financial reports—'recognition' of intangibles, in the accounting jargon. But capitalization is only a partial solution to the intangibles-related information deficiencies. First, capitalization reflects the historical cost of investments in intangibles, rather than the more relevant current values (although costs are, of course, generally correlated with current values); second, capitalized values reflect only the financial aspects of intangibles, abstracting from important nonfinancial attributes, such as citations to patents, employee turnover, or customer satisfaction. It is important, therefore, to extend the scope of solutions to the information problems of intangibles beyond capitalization. The last two papers in the *Reader* attempt to do that.

In '*The Boundaries of Financial Reporting and How to Extend Them*', Baruch Lev and Paul Zarowin use a large sample of firms to empirically establish the important linkage between changes in firms' intensity of R&D and the documented deterioration over the past twenty years in the informativeness of financial statement items, such as earnings, cash flows, and equity (book) values. Worth noting is that it is primarily the change in the rate of expenditures on intangibles that creates informational problems, not merely the level or magnitude of intangibles.

In the second part of the paper, Lev and Zarowin propose a new accounting procedure—continuously restated financial reports—to overcome the major objection to the recognition of intangible assets: the relatively high uncertainty (low reliability) surrounding the outcomes of intangibles. Restated reports, akin to the continuous restatement of key macroeconomic data (e.g. quarterly GDP), will revise the values of intangibles and the consequent earnings as new information about the likelihood of outcomes (e.g. an FDA drug approval) becomes available. Restated reports thus provide data of increasingly higher quality and informativeness.[6]

The last article in the *Reader* is based on a chapter from Baruch Lev's book on intangibles.[7] A different approach to improving the information on intangibles is taken here. Rather than deal with *individual* intangibles (patents, brands, etc.), a comprehensive system that reflects the innovation activities of companies—the value-chain blueprint—is proposed. The view here is that intangibles interact with other corporate assets in the major activity of business enterprises, which is value creation. The proposed value-chain blueprint, accordingly, provides detailed information on the three major stages of value creation: Investment (in R&D, brand enhancement, IT, etc.), product/service development (e.g. results of clinical tests for drugs), and commercialization (revenues from recently introduced products). Major emphasis is placed on establishing input/output linkages, such as between employee training and turnover, thus allowing information users to compute return on investments (ROI of intangibles) and thereby assessing managerial ability and technological capabilities.

Postscript

Wealth and growth in modern economies and corporations are driven primarily by the astute deployment of intangible assets. Indeed, abnormal profits, dominant market positions, and even temporary monopolies are most effectively achieved by the sound deployment of intangible assets along with other resources. While this reality is intuitively understood and acted on by business people, it has only recently become the subject of sustained academic attention. The goal of this *Reader* is to bring together the very best research and advocacy in the exciting and rapidly emerging area of intangible assets. The papers in the *Reader* provide a comprehensive tableau of rigorous perspectives and empirical evidence that encapsulate the best thinking about intangible assets by scholars and policy makers in accounting, economics, finance, and information technology, thereby creating a solid foundation for the business use of intangibles, as well as for further research in this area.

Notes

1. Testimony before the Committee on Financial Services, US House of Representatives, 27 February 2002.
2. See B. Lev, Intangibles: Management, Measurement, and Reporting (Brookings Institution Press, 2001: ch 2) for a discussion of intangibles' vulnerabilities ('value detractors').
3. Hearing held on 19 July 2000. Testifying experts were: Robert Elliott (KPMG), Baruch Lev (New York University), Steve Samek (Arthur Andersen), Peter Wallison (American Enterprise Institute), and Michael Young (Willkie Farr & Gallagher).
4. The US Bureau of Economic Analysis has been accounting for software development and acquisition costs since 1998 as an asset (investment) in the national accounts.
5. In recognition of these needs, the Financial Accounting Standards Board (FASB) formally added to its agenda in January 2002 the Intangibles Disclosure Project.
6. These proposed restatements are, of course distinct from the current (mid-2002) avalanche of restated earnings in the United States that results from reporting errors and fraud.
7. B. Lev, Intangibles: Management, Measurement, and Reporting, ibid. ch. 5.

I. INTANGIBLES IN THE MODERN ECONOMY

1

A Trillion Dollars a Year in Intangible Investment and the New Economy[1]

Leonard Nakamura

1. Introduction

The US economy is often called a new economy. One reason is that newly developed products are everywhere: Microsoft's Windows2000, AOL/Time Warner's movie 'Harry Potter and the Sorcerer's Stone', Pfizer's Viagra, and Gillette's Mach3 razor blades are four prominent examples. Developing each product required its corporate sponsor to invest hundreds of millions of dollars. For example, Gillette invested $700 million to develop the Mach3 razor blade from 1990 to 1998. AOL/TimeWarner spent over $150 million to bring J. K. Rowling's vision of 'Harry Potter and the Sorcerer's Stone' to the screen.

These investment expenditures gave rise to economically valuable, legally recognized *intangible assets*, including copyrights ('Harry Potter' and Windows2000) and patents (Viagra and Mach3) that give the investing firms the exclusive right for a certain period to sell the newly developed products. These assets can be extremely valuable. Pfizer sold over $1 billion worth of Viagra in 1999 after its introduction in April of the previous year; 'Harry Potter' sold nearly $100 million in movie-theater tickets in its first weekend, and Gillette's Mach3 razor blade was the top seller in the United States by the end of 1998, having secured more than 10 per cent of the razor blade replacement market in less than a full year.

Patents and copyrights on new consumer products are not the only types of intangible assets. New processes for making existing goods, such as the process for coating cookie wafers with chocolate, and new producer goods, like PC servers and fibre optic telephone cables, can also be patented or copyrighted or, perhaps, protected as trade secrets. Other intangible assets are brand names and trademarks. These can help a firm certify the quality of an existing product or introduce new products to potential purchasers. Not only can a reputation for quality persuade shoppers to try an item for the first time, but a clever use of advertisements can go a long way towards targeting precisely those who will gain the most from the product and thereafter become loyal, repeat customers.

Yet, because they are not investments in tangible assets, most expenditures on intangible assets are not recognized as investments in either US companies' financial accounts or the US national income and product accounts. This practice may have been reasonable when investment in such assets was a negligible portion of our total investment, but that is no longer the case—corporate investments in intangible assets have risen to equal or surpass those in tangible assets.

In this article, we will look at two key consequences of these accounting conventions. First, not only are reported corporate profits understated, they are understated more than they used to be because corporations are investing more of their cash flow in intangible assets. As a result, US price/earnings ratios are overstated and the market value of stocks has risen relative to their tangible net worth. Second, US national income, saving, and investment are understated because a larger proportion of output is invested in intangibles. As we shall see, growing investment in intangibles also helps explain how the measured US personal saving rate can be near zero even as US wealth has grown considerably. The US economic and financial performance is less puzzling when we take this intangible investment into account.[2]

....

2. Rising Investment in Research and Development and Other Intangibles

2.1. Research and Development

Research and development (R&D) expenditures to create new products have certainly been rising. Looking at the long sweep of US data since 1953, we see that R&D expenditures have more than doubled as a proportion of corporate gross domestic product (GDP) (Table 1 and Fig. 1).[3] By contrast, we see that tangible investment in plant and equipment (as a proportion of GDP) was no higher in the 1990s than in the 1950s and 1960s (Table 1 and Fig. 2). During the

Table 1. Tangible and Intangible Investment as Percentage of GDP

Period	Tangible Investment	R&D	Tangible Plus R&D	Advertising	Software	Total Measured Investment
1953–59	9.5	0.7	10.2	2.2	0.0	12.4
1960–69	9.7	0.9	10.6	2.1	0.1	12.8
1970–79	10.0	1.0	11.8	1.8	0.3	13.9
1980–89	11.6	1.3	12.9	2.2	0.6	15.6
1990–99	10.0	1.6	11.6	2.2	1.2	14.9
2000	11.2	1.8	13.1	2.4	1.9	17.3

Source: Flow of Funds, US NIPA, National Science Foundation and McCann-Erickson.

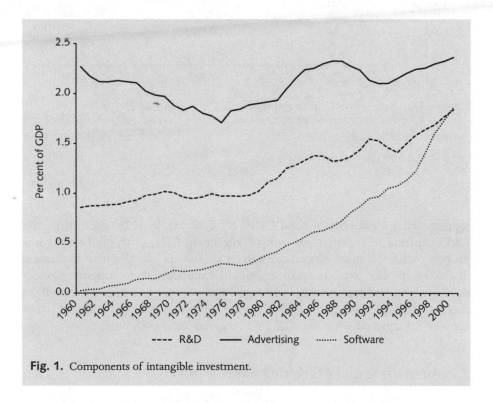

Fig. 1. Components of intangible investment.

postwar period, investment spending, including R&D, rose 1.4 per cent points as a proportion of GDP, from 10.2 per cent in the 1950s to 11.6 per cent in the 1990s. Most of this increase was due to R&D expenditures. Looking at the third column in Table 1, we can see that if we count R&D as investment, the years since the 1970s have been ones of strong investment.

According to National Science Foundation (NSF) estimates, in 2000, US corporations spent $181 billion of their own funds on R&D. This expenditure

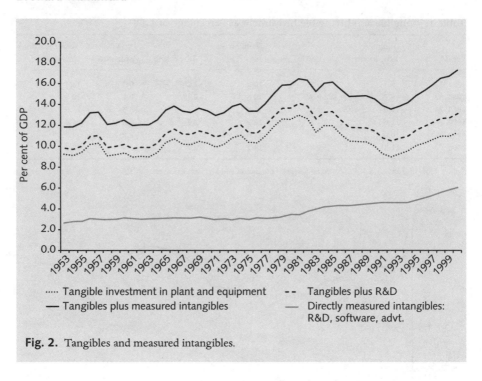

Fig. 2. Tangibles and measured intangibles.

represented 1.8 per cent of total GDP.[4] By contrast, in 1978, such corporate R&D expenditures were 1 per cent of aggregate GDP. Both of these figures probably underestimate expenditures to create new products. Firms that invest in R&D typically have to make additional expenditures to support product development, including marketing, consumer testing, and executive decision making, that are not part of the engineering and scientific expenses that account for most of what the NSF calls research and development.

2.2. Advertising and Marketing Expenditures

Advertising and marketing expenditures are often a crucial cost of selling new goods, and at least some of these expenditures might well be considered investments.[5] The US advertising expenditures were high in the 1950s in the consumer boom after the Second World War, as households caught up with purchases postponed by the war. Then, advertising expenditures slipped through the mid-1970s as the consumer boom slowed. Since bottoming out at 1.6 per cent of GDP in 1975, these expenditures have generally risen modestly (Table 1 and Fig. 1).

According to advertising agency McCann-Erickson (2000), firms spent $233 billion on advertising in 2000. This expenditure represents 2.3 per cent of GDP, up from 1.9 per cent in 1978. However, McCann-Erickson's data reflect the market for advertising agencies; they do not include many other marketing expenses that firms incur, such as the sales forces of pharmaceutical companies or fees paid to public relations firms and athletes—marketing expenses that have been rising faster than agency fees. To the extent that firms spend this money to inform consumers about new products, advertising and marketing expenditures should be counted as investments in intangible assets because the information supplied to consumers through these avenues will generate profits over a sustained period.

One might further argue that the executive time spent in support of investment decisions should be included in investment costs. Certainly, employment in executive occupations has grown in the past two decades, rising from less than 9 per cent of US employment in 1950, 1960, and 1970, to more than 10 per cent in 1980 and more than 14 per cent in 1997. (A parallel rise has occurred for manufacturing industries alone.) The rise in R&D expenditures in the 1980s and 1990s has been accompanied by increases in advertising expenditure and executive employment, some part of which were necessary investments in new products.

2.3. Software

One area in which the national income accounts have come to grips with measuring investment in intangibles is software. According to the Bureau of Economic Analysis (BEA), in 2000, private businesses invested $183 billion in software, or 1.8 per cent of GDP, compared with 0.3 per cent in 1978 (Table 1 and Fig. 1). This software investment comes in three types: prepackaged software, custom software, and own-account software.

Prepackaged software ($61.4 billion in 2000) is sold at arm's length, that is, the company that invests in the software is different from the company that makes it. Sales of prepackaged software to consumers have always been counted as consumer expenditures. But such sales to firms were counted as expenses, not investment, until the BEA changed its method in 1998. Note that as part of the investment in new software, firms must also train their employees in the use of the software.[6] Thus, purchases of software underestimate the total resources firms must allocate when they invest in new software.

The software investments of firms that purchase prepackaged software do not include the intangible investments made by the makers of the software. A company's investment in creating software is separate from the buyer's investment in software. For example, Microsoft's investments in producing the Windows operating system and in the Microsoft Office suite of products are separate from the investments that corporations make when they buy licenses to use these same programs. Microsoft's value as an ongoing concern resides primarily in the intellectual property rights it holds for the software it has created and is separate from the value created by other firms' investments to acquire licenses to use Microsoft Windows and Microsoft Office.

Custom software is also purchased, but like custom clothing, it is uniquely adapted for the buyer ($57 billion in 2000). In some of these cases, the rights to the software are sold to the buyer. In other cases, a substantial proportion of the software rights remain with the software producer. When property rights remain with the producer, custom software sales data may understate the value of the producer's investment.

Own-account software is made by employees of the user ($64 billion in 2000). To measure investment in own-account software, the BEA examines how many programmers are employed at firms that do not sell software and estimates how much of their work goes into developing new software (investment) vs. maintenance and repair of existing software (expense). The most recent study of this division, which was published in 1982, found that 62 per cent of programmers' time was spent on creating new programs.[7] The BEA estimates that since then, programmers have become more involved in repair and maintenance. Therefore, the BEA counts 50 per cent of programmers' time as new software investment, a figure it describes as underscoring the arbitrariness of such measures.

2.4. Other Industries' Intangibles

Expenditures on R&D, advertising, and software do not exhaust firms' expenditures on intangibles by any means. For example, most financial corporations do not report their expenditures to develop new products as R&D expenses. Yet financial corporations have been making a large and growing investment in financial innovations, including investment vehicles like derivatives and mutual funds, electronic payment systems, ATMs, and credit and debit cards. They have also invested large sums in customer databases and in customer relationships associated with these new instruments.

Almost no data are collected on financial corporations' expenditures on intangibles.[8] However, financial corporations' noninterest expenditures have been rising rapidly. For example, in 2000, noninterest expenditures for commercial banks were $215.5 billion, or 2.1 per cent of GDP, up from 1.6 per cent of GDP in 1978. Noninterest expenditures include commercial banks' innovations and marketing expenses, but they are only an *indicator* of banks' investment in intangibles because they also include expenditures for tellers and bank branches. The market value of financial institutions has recently averaged more than 20 per cent of the market value of nonfinancial corporations, compared with around 11 per cent in 1978. If financial corporations spend proportionally as much on R&D as nonfinancial corporations report spending, this would add another $50 billion to R&D. Commercial banks alone have added more than $50 billion in noninterest expenditures in this same period. And that neglects the innovative expenditures of mutual funds, insurance companies, real estate firms, other depositories, or investment banks.

Writers, artists, and entertainers make additional investments in intangibles, and these investments are not recorded as part of R&D. In 1997, according to the US economic census, the publishing, motion picture, and sound recording industries had a total revenue of $221 billion. Associated with this stream of revenues are investments in creativity and in finding, developing, and publicizing artists and their work (Caves, 2000).

Much of the investment in movies, television, and other media pays off quickly because it shows up in movie-theater ticket sales or videotape rentals. Other programming costs, such as many television network broadcasts, are paid for by advertising. However, as Richard Caves points out, television series are produced at a loss—the network's payment for first broadcast rights does not cover the production costs of the series. What producers hope for is that the series will run long enough (three to five seasons have usually been the minimum) so that reruns can be profitably syndicated. Syndication will sometimes pay substantially more than the initial broadcast rights. Similarly, a movie series like 'Star Wars' can become a multibillion dollar property, since sequels, video games, toys, and clothes based on the series can be sold.

3. A Trillion Dollars in Intangible Investment

In my paper, 'What Is the US Gross Investment in Intangibles? (At Least) One Trillion Dollars a Year!' I use a variety of sources to estimate a reasonable middle ground for total US investment of intangibles. Each of my estimates for intangible investment is based on incomplete data, but all of them point to an estimate that is at least half a trillion dollars, and almost assuredly twice that amount. My methodology is to attempt to capture estimates from three separate aspects of intangible investing: expenditures (how much users pay for investments), labour inputs (what workers' occupations are and how much they are being paid), and corporate operating margins (as viewed through their tax accounts and their public financial reports).

Specifically, the first estimate is based on the expenditures of those that use intangibles in production just discussed: the NSF's data on industrial expenditures

Table 2. Median Pay of Full-time Workers in 2000

Category of Workers	Number	Median Pay	Estimated Payroll	Estimated Payroll as % of Total
Engineers, architects, etc.	2156	1098	2,367,288	4.0
Mathematicians and computer scientists	1890	992	1,874,880	3.2
Natural scientists	490	913	447,370	0.8
Social scientists	296	826	244,496	0.4
Writers, artists, athletes, and entertainers	1377	727	1,001,079	1.7
Creative professionals	6209	911	5,935,113	10.0
Service professionals	9878	754	7,449,271	12.6
Professional specialty	16,087	832	13,384,384	22.6
Executive	15,368	840	12,909,120	21.8
Technicians	3652	648	2,366,496	4.0
Sales	10,133	550	5,573,150	9.4
Administrative support	14,468	469	6,785,492	11.5
Service	11,020	355	3,912,100	6.6
Precision production	12,163	613	7,455,919	12.6
Operators	15,411	446	6,873,306	11.6
Farming, forestry, and fishing	1616	334	539,744	0.9
Total	99,918	593	59,259,967	

on research and development, the US BEA's estimates of software investment, and McCann–Erickson's estimates of expenditures on advertising media. These together were 6 per cent of the size of US GDP in 2000 (Fig. 2). For the reasons stressed earlier, this seems a reasonable minimum for intangible investment.

The second estimate is based on inputs that are identifiable as contributing to the production of intangibles. I use occupational statistics to determine the proportion of labour income going to workers whose occupations are creative—engineers, scientists, writers, artists, etc. These are estimated to represent 10.0 per cent of payrolls in 2000, using data from the Bureau of Labour Statistics' Current Population Statistics on full-time workers and the median pay they receive (Table 2). If creative workers represent nearly 10 per cent of wages and salaries, it would appear that estimating that 10 per cent of US output is for intangibles is low and that 15 per cent might not be out of the question, since other workers, including executives and knowledge workers like teachers and doctors, also provide inputs into intangible investments.

The third estimate is based on operating margins. If firms are spending a substantial amount on intangibles, and have been doing so for some years, the successes of this expenditure should permit firms on average to increase markups. I argue in my paper that intangible investment accelerated in the late 1970s. The change in markups since then can be estimated using corporate expense statements, as a shift of expenditures away from direct production

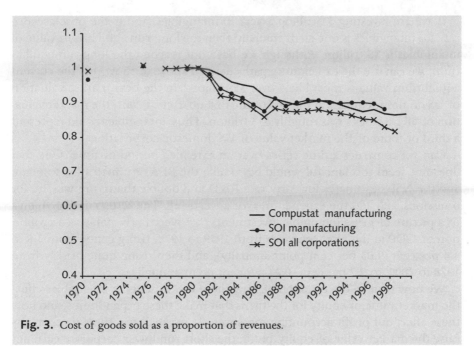

Fig. 3. Cost of goods sold as a proportion of revenues.

costs, which Compustat and the US Treasury's Statistics of Income label 'cost of goods sold', to research and development, administrative, marketing, and general expenses. These series show that cost of goods sold, relative to revenues, fell about 10 per cent points after 1980 (Fig. 3). That suggests that intangible investments permitted firms to raise markups by 10 per cent of output, which is consistent with an estimate that such investments account for more than 10 per cent of corporate expense.

All these estimates suggest strongly, if imprecisely, that at least 6–10 per cent of US GDP is spent annually on intangibles, and possibly substantially more. It turns out that it is possible to use an indirect method to arrive at a surprisingly precise lower bound on the gross investment in intangibles. The ratio of consumption to true gross domestic product, including both tangible and intangible investments, should be relatively stable. If so, then the rise in the ratio of consumption to measured gross domestic product will provide a relatively precise estimate of the increase in unmeasured intangible investment. This ratio suggests that unmeasured intangible investment was $910 billion in 2000, with a 5 per cent confidence interval of plus or minus $200 billion. Adding in the $183 billion in software investment that was measured in that year, we arrive at a lower bound estimate of US gross investment in intangibles of $1.1 trillion. This estimate is a lower bound in that it measures the increase in investment in intangibles after 1977 (Nakamura, 2001*b*).

If we are investing $1 trillion a year in intangibles, and if the obsolescence rate for intangibles is one-sixth annually, then the long-run equilibrium value of intangibles is $6 trillion. Although we have not reached the long-run equilibrium, we can use the expenditure paths derived above to show that the current equilibrium value is most likely over $5 trillion.[9] In the bear market valuation of US domestic equities at the end of the first quarter of 2001, the market valuation of all US stocks was roughly $13 trillion. Thus, intangibles could represent a third or more of the market value of US domestic corporations.

Can we construct a time series over an extended period of time? One that does not seem too fanciful would be to take the BEA's estimates for software and the NSF's estimates for corporate R&D and double them, to make up for omissions, and add the expenditures for advertising. The results, in Fig. 4, give us a picture of gross intangible investments that were fairly stable as a proportion of GDP in the nineteen years from 1959 to 1978, rising gently from 3.8 to 4.4 per cent (0.03 per cent point annually), and then rising quite briskly from 1978 to 2000, to 9.7 per cent (0.24 per cent point annually).

We now turn to the question of how these investments in intangibles affect the market value of equity for the firms that make these expenditures, and how these affect our profit accounting measures. As we shall see, these investments raise the market value of equity, but in the short run lower corporate earnings estimates.

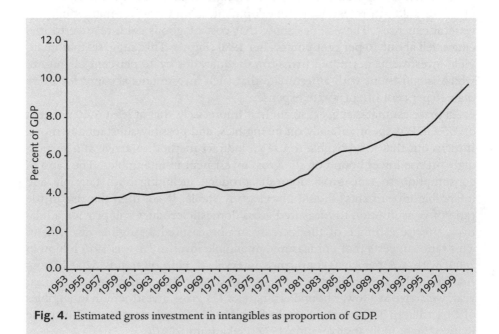

Fig. 4. Estimated gross investment in intangibles as proportion of GDP.

4. Rising Intangible Investment Leads to Rising Stock Market Values of Firms

One surprising aspect of the US economy has been the rapid growth in the value of corporations' stock market equity. The Dow Jones Industrial Average of share prices rose from 933 in 1981 to 9879 at the end of the first quarter of 2001. This tenfold increase contrasts with the performance of nonfinancial corporations' after-tax reported profits, which went up fivefold, and with the growth of nonfinancial GDP, which went up less than 2.5 times.[10] The swift rise in share prices has led to a rise in the ratio of stock prices to current after-tax profits (called the price/earnings ratio) to a level that is unprecedented in the postwar period (Table 2 and Fig. 5). This turn of events has worried many observers and has raised the possibility that stockholders have become excessively optimistic about the value of US corporations.

Other things equal, the price/earnings ratio should be high when the expected growth rate of profits (and thus of earnings per share) is high relative to the rate of return that stockholders require on the shares they own. That can happen when profits are temporarily low and expected to bounce back, as was the case during the 1990–91 recession. It can also happen when profits are high, as during the second half of the 1990s, if they are expected to grow rapidly in the future.

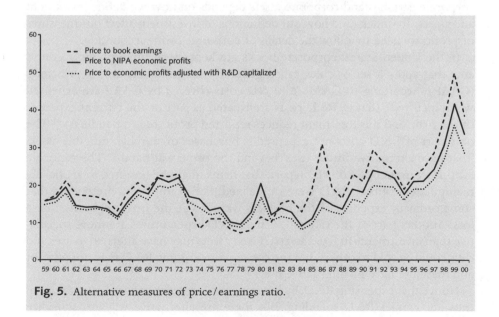

Fig. 5. Alternative measures of price/earnings ratio.

But over the long run, profits have tended to grow at the same rate as the economy as a whole. Is there any rational reason to believe that profits should grow strongly in the future and thereby justify the high valuations placed on shares? In fact, there is. As we shall show, rising investment in intangible assets reduces measured current profits and raises expected future profits. Thus, rising new product development can help explain the high price/earnings ratio. To see how investment in intangibles affects reported price/earnings ratios, we first need to think about how we measure profits.

4.1. Financial Accounting

The accurate measurement of profit is fundamental to financial accounting. Profit tells us two things: how much revenues exceeded costs (a measure of the economic value of current operations of the firm) and how much the assets of the corporation have increased (before any cash distributions to shareholders). Formally, accountants define profit as 'the excess of revenues over all expenses'. Expenses are 'the costs of goods, services, and facilities used in the production of current revenue' (Estes, 1981). To the extent that a firm buys things that are not used up in production, those additional costs are investments, not expenses, and are capitalized, that is, considered assets. A capital asset gives rise to an expense only to the extent that the capital asset's value falls while in use, a process called depreciation or capital consumption. The intertwining of the measurement of corporate earnings and corporate assets depends on how we define investment and assets. To understand how our definitions of investment affect our measures of profit, we need to follow the details of corporate profit accounting.

In the United States, corporate books are kept by certified public accountants that apply a set of rules called generally accepted accounting principles (GAAP). According to GAAP, 'All R&D costs covered by GAAP are expensed when incurred'; that is, R&D costs are treated as part of the current expenses of the firm, and this treatment reduces reported profit (see Appendix A).[11] The only part of R&D costs not expensed is purchases of durable, tangible assets 'that have alternative future uses' beyond the project at hand.[12] The rationale for this treatment of R&D is, in part, that firms might be tempted to artificially manipulate profits if R&D were capitalized. For example, by pretending that some ordinary expenses of the business were R&D, the firm might disguise a loss. Another part of the rationale is that R&D expenditures are more speculative than investments in fixed assets. (Fixed assets may have alternative uses and thus could be sold to others, but the concept undergoing R&D may not pan out and therefore have no alternative use.)

Notice that expensing R&D, by lowering profits, reduces corporate taxes and thus encourages R&D spending. But there are alternative ways to subsidize

R&D, if that is what we wish to do. Indeed, the federal government already provides additional subsidies to R&D through the research and experimentation tax credit.

4.2. Revised Measures of Profit

Over the years, studies have relatively consistently shown that a firm's R&D expenditures raise the stock market valuation of that firm by at least an equal amount.[13] This finding suggests that the book value of assets would be a better guide to the true value of a corporation if R&D expenditures were capitalized, that is, treated as long-term investments and depreciated over time.[14] Indeed, in some industries creativity expenditures are treated just this way. For example, in the film industry, the expenses of making a movie are capitalized and depreciated over the commercial life of the property.[15] So the investing groups that produced 'Titanic' had to forecast the revenues expected from movie theaters, pay-per-view broadcasts, cable TV rights, and video sales and depreciate the expenses of making the movie over the period in which these revenues were expected to be earned. If investments as risky as films can be capitalized and depreciated, there seems little reason to believe that an acceptable estimate cannot be made for R&D expenditures.

4.3. Intangible Investments: Hard to Measure, But not Impossible

One factor that makes measuring tangible investments easier than measuring intangible investments is that the firm that makes tangible capital goods is typically different from the firm that will use it. For example, the firm that will use—that is, invest in—computers will generally buy them from another firm rather than making them itself. This makes the investment highly visible: a transaction has occurred, and money has changed hands to attest to the investment's value.

By contrast, intangible investment is generally done in-house: Intel's chips are designed by its engineers, Microsoft's software is designed by its programmers, and Eli Lilly's drugs are developed by its biochemists. So the outlay made to create intangibles is harder to verify. Moreover, while some expenses are clearly aimed at creating intangible assets, other expenses are harder to determine. For example, it is difficult to know how much of a chief executive's time is devoted to producing intangibles and how much to coordinating production.

But it is not impossible. Some corporations attempt to allocate expenses to current production or to future projects. Such corporations require their employees to report work hours on a project-by-project basis. These projects can be classified into those that contribute to current production and those that produce intangible assets. Thus, it might be possible for a corporation to divide money spent on sales and general and administrative needs into expenses for current production and intangible asset production. Doing so might well provide a corporation with a measure of the resources that go into intangible investment that would be of substantial value to its shareholders. If this practice became widespread, statistical analysis would then be possible to evaluate which proportion of these expenditures result in the creation of an intangible asset.

There are cases in which the intangible investment yields a salable asset. When Chrysler designs a new car, or Eli Lilly develops a new drug, or J. K. Rowling writes a new Harry Potter novel, the design, or the drug, or the novel is a product that could be sold to the highest bidder for a fixed sum. Indeed, this sometimes happens. A design firm such as Pininfarina can design a car for a manufacturer; a small biotech start-up may sell a new drug to a major pharmaceutical company; and a writer may be commissioned to ghostwrite a book. In these cases, there is no real problem in classifying each of the sales as either income or output.

But with intangible assets it's more difficult. Most of the time, there is no direct transaction to tell us what the intangible asset is worth. Transactions that do tell us about the value of intangible assets are capital transactions: the buying and selling of the equity shares of firms that have invested in and produced the intangible assets. So our only way to measure the success of the vast majority of investment in intangible assets is changes in the stock-market value of firms—which are highly volatile.

Fortunately, under GAAP, accountants are required to record R&D expenditures separately so that shareholders and others can be aware of them. Thus, we have data to empirically estimate what corporate profits would be if R&D expenditures were treated the same way as tangible investment expenditures.

Can expensing R&D, rather than capitalizing and depreciating it, make an important difference in how we assess the profitability of US firms over the past half century? Consider Table 4. The first column represents after-tax profits of corporations as they are normally reported, the so-called 'book profits', from Table 3. These book profits show that profitability as a proportion of corporate product has generally declined. True, earnings in the 1990s are higher than the low earnings of the 1980s, but both are well below earnings in the three other postwar decades. And the price/earnings ratio based on book profits averages 28.4 from 1990 to 1999 compared with only 17.7 in the 1960s. And in 2000, the price/earnings ratio is a steep 38.5, more than double the 1960–69 ratio.

However, book profits are somewhat deceptive. Economic profits are a better measure (Table 4). For one thing, economic profits correct for the fact that during the 1970s, corporate earnings were bloated by inventory 'profits' that

Table 3. Profits and Stock-Market Value of Nonfinancial
Corporations (As a Proportion of Nonfinancial
Corporate Gross Domestic Product)

Period	After tax Book Profits	Stock-Market Value (%)	Price–Earnings Ratio
1953–59	8.8	110	12.7
1960–69	8.3	146	17.7
1970–79	7.8	99	13.6
1980–89	5.2	85	17.5
1990–99	6.1	174	28.4
2000	5.9	228	38.5

Notes: Book profits are after-tax nonfinancial corporate profits. Stock-market value is market value of nonfinancial corporate equity. Price/earnings ratio equals stock-market value divided by after-tax book profits.

Source: Bureau of Economic Analysis and Flow of Funds.

Table 4. Profits and Stock-Market Value of Nonfinancial Corporations (As a Proportion of Nonfinancial Corporate Gross Domestic Product)

Period	Profits				Price–Earnings Ratios		
	After-tax Book Profit (%)	After-tax Economic Profit[a] (%)	R&D Adjusted Economic Profit[b] (%)	Stock-Market Value (%)	After-tax Book Profits[c]	After-tax Economic Profits[d]	R&D-adjusted Adjusted Economic Profits[e]
1960–69	8.3	9.4	10.0	146	17.7	15.7	14.7
1970–79	7.8	6.3	6.9	99	13.6	15.8	14.4
1980–89	5.2	6.1	7.0	85	17.5	14.4	12.3
1990–99	6.1	7.0	8.0	174	28.4	24.4	21.4
2000	5.9	6.8	8.0	228	38.5	33.7	28.5

[a] After-tax nonfinancial corporate profits with inventory valuation and capital consumption adjustments.
[b] After-tax nonfinancial corporate profits with inventory valuation and capital consumption adjustments were further adjusted as R&D expenditures were capitalized and depreciated as described in the text.
[c] Equals stock-market value divided by after-tax book profit.
[d] Equals stock-market value divided by after-tax economic profit.
[e] Equals stock-market value divided by R&D adjusted economic profit.

corporations earned because inventories they were holding rose in price along with everything else.[16] Furthermore, economic profits also adjust depreciation rates to reflect more accurately the economic lives of corporate tangible assets.[17] Even economic profits, however, treat R&D as an expense rather than as an investment.

How different would profit measures be for nonfinancial corporations if we included R&D expenditures as investments and capitalized and depreciated them? Suppose we use a geometric depreciation rate of one-sixth, a figure suggested by the work of Dennis Chambers *et al.* (1998). The third column in Table 4 shows what happens when we capitalize and gradually depreciate R&D expenditures, rather than expensing them.

The R&D-adjusted profits are higher than economic profits. On average during the 1990s, R&D-adjusted profits have been 14 per cent higher than economic profits and nearly 31 per cent higher than book profits. More important, the amount by which R&D-adjusted profits exceed economic profits has been growing. The gap has nearly doubled from the 1960s to the 1990s, rising from 0.6 per cent of corporate product to 1 per cent. While this adjustment somewhat reduces the gap between earlier price-earnings ratios and today's, the gap remains substantial.

Although other factors are undoubtedly important in explaining stock prices and earnings, treating R&D in a way that parallels treatment of tangible investment expenditures takes a step toward improving our understanding of current stock-market equity values (Fig. 5). The low stock-market valuations of the 1970s and the relatively high valuations of the 1960s and 1990s are easier to understand.[18] And R&D is just one example of investment in intangible assets. Adjustments to account for other intangibles would further narrow the gap.

4.4. The Value of the Stock Market

An alternative route can be taken to estimate the value of the stock market, using James Tobin's idea that the equilibrium market value of corporations should be the replacement cost of their assets, less net debt. The standard version of this theory emphasizes investments in tangibles. If markets are competitive, then the current value of tangible investments net of debt will, in long-run equilibrium, equal the market value of equities.

Figure 6 shows the net worth of US nonfinancial corporations, scaled by US gross domestic product, and the market value of their corporate equities, using data from the US flow of funds accounts, showing end-of-year ratios from 1952 to 2000. It also shows the market value of all domestic corporate equities, financial and nonfinancial. The net worth of financial corporations is difficult to estimate, and the flow of funds accounts do not report a total net worth for this group. As shown, there are two periods—the mid-1960s and the mid-1990s—in which the stock market was approximately at its long-run equilibrium value under the view that tangibles are the sole source of stock-market equity value.

According to this theory of the stock market, the net worth of nonfinancial corporations is a smaller proportion of GDP today than it was during the three decades from 1960 to 1990. In this view, stock-market investors have been grossly misled since at least 1995 about the value of their holdings. At the end

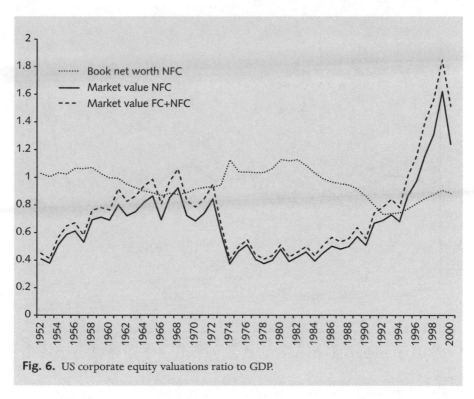

Fig. 6. US corporate equity valuations ratio to GDP.

of the first quarter of 2001, the market value of nonfinancial corporations (using the S&P Industrials as a guide) had probably fallen to about $11 trillion. If only tangible assets have value, then the stock market has still to fall another 25 per cent.

Figure 7 shows the net worth of all US corporations, financial, and nonfinancial, scaled by gross domestic product, under the assumption that intangible investments create value in much the same way that tangible investments do. For nonfinancial corporations, I assume here the electronics revolution wiped out all existing intangible assets in 1978 and that effective investment in intangibles began to occur in 1978. I assume that effective investment in intangibles has increased steadily, in line with the estimates developed in my paper, to about $1 trillion annually. For financial corporations, I assume that financial net worth is equal to nonfinancial net worth times the ratio of the stock-market values of financial to nonfinancial corporations.

For nonfinancial corporations, I use the expenditure estimates shown in Fig. 4 and assume that obsolescence takes place at an annual rate of 16 per cent. Counting intangibles, stock-market valuations began to catch up with reality only in 1996, and since then, at least by past standards, the stock market has

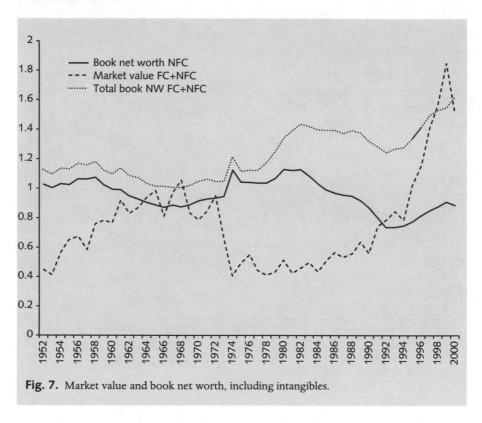

Fig. 7. Market value and book net worth, including intangibles.

been near equilibrium. In this calculation, the end-of-year net worth of US domestic corporations includes roughly $5 trillion in intangible assets. The last data point marked on the figure is year end 2000. In this view, the bear market of the first quarter of 2001 drove the value of the stock market significantly below its long-run equilibrium value.

5. National Income Accounting and Intangibles: Rising Wealth, Falling Saving

The difference in accounting treatment of tangible and intangible assets affects the US national income and product accounts as well as corporate financial statements. By not counting spending on R&D and other intangible assets as investment, our national accounts understate not only investment but also national income and national saving.

Our national income accounts need not use the same investment definitions as do financial accountants; indeed, it is economic profits and not book profits that fit into our measures of national income. Nevertheless, the national income accounts have traditionally not treated spending on intangible assets as investment. Why?

5.1. Two Types of Wealth: Tangible and Intangible

Peter Hill (1999), of the Organization for Economic Cooperation and Development and one of the chief modern architects of national accounting systems, has traced the exclusion of intangible assets back to the distinction between goods and services. He argues persuasively that as far back as Adam Smith, goods were material and could be stored while services were immaterial and transitory. This transitory nature meant services could not be counted as assets, but goods could. Logically, then, things that are counted as investment must be tangible. The role of immaterial assets, such as patents or the goodwill of brand names, was easily downplayed or ignored, given this basic dichotomy. Irving Fisher, the Yale Economics professor who invented the chain-weighted index now used to construct quantity and price indexes in the US national income accounts, began his 1920 classic, *The Purchasing Power of Money*, by defining economics as 'the science of wealth' and wealth as 'material objects owned by human beings'. This definition—that only what is material, and therefore tangible, can constitute wealth—underlies the national income accounting conventions we use to determine asset value, profit, saving, and investment. But as we have seen, tangible assets—equipment, structures, and land—are not the only assets of lasting economic value. Indeed, investment in intangible assets represents a growing proportion of our economy.[19]

If we look at national accounts from the income side, the failure to count expenditures on intangible assets as investment reduces corporate profits, which in turn reduces corporate saving. As we have argued, the paper reduction in profits has a counterpart in rising capital gains—the values of corporate equities has risen together with increased corporate investment in intangibles. In turn, these capital gains cause households to be wealthier.

Thus the statistical omission should not fool households, who will consume based not on their statistical income, which omits part of their investment, but on their incomes as they perceive them. In addition to not recognizing intangible investment, there is another convention in the US income accounts that makes a good deal of sense that causes household income to be understated. Because capital gains are so volatile, the national income accounts include only part of investment income: dividends and interest payments.[20] Capital gains are excluded, yet capital gains from the stock market have been responsible for about half of the increase in the net worth of American households in the past two decades.[21]

The official measures of household income include dividend payments but not stock-market capital gains. The measured personal saving rate has been low for the past decade because stock-market capital gains have been high and dividends are low. Personal saving in the United States was low throughout the 1990s, but the net worth of Americans increased from $20 trillion to $41 trillion from the end of 1989 to the end of 2000. Adjusting for inflation, this figure represents a real increase, in 1996 dollars, of $14 trillion (from $24 trillion to $38 trillion).[22] During the three decades before 1990, the US personal saving rate (the ratio of personal saving to disposable personal income) averaged 9 per cent. From 1952 to 1989, the annual personal saving rate never fell below 6.9 per cent (Fig. 8).

By contrast, in the 1990s, the saving rate averaged much less, 6 per cent, and fell during the course of the decade, from 7.8 per cent in 1990 to 2.4 per cent in 1999. In 2000, it was 1 per cent. But during the earlier period of relatively high saving rates, Americans did not become rich, and as measured saving fell during the 1990s, Americans' wealth increased dramatically. This puzzle remains whether we measure savings and wealth in nominal terms or in real terms.[23]

During the 1960s and 1970s, stock-market capital gains were 0.4 per cent of GDP. During the 1980s they were 3.7 per cent of GDP, and in the 1990s, 16.0 per cent.[24] If we use these averages over decades to smooth growth, then from the 1970s to 1980s, the nominal and real growth of the economy, including

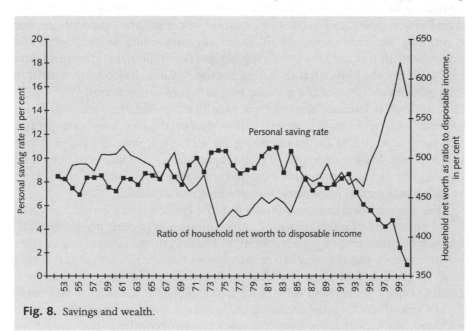

Fig. 8. Savings and wealth.

stock-market capital gains, may have been 0.3 per cent higher than reported, and from the 1980s to the 1990s, about 1.2 per cent higher.[25]

If we attribute this rate of capital gains to intangible investment, intangible investment must have been quite large. As measured by inputs, investments in intangibles add up to $1 trillion a year.[26] If so, this can help explain why capital gains have been so large.

5.2. Some Consequences of Excluding Capital Gains

Excluding capital gains from our measures of household and national income has several disquieting consequences. First, the household saving rate is very low and likely to remain so as long as stock-market capital gains remain strong. Since these capital gains are founded on very large investments in intangible assets, there is little reason to think they will not continue, on average. Of course, volatility will continue, as the recent stock market downturn reminds us.

Second, if stock options continue to rise in importance as a form of reward to employees, employee compensation will increasingly depend, at least in part, on stock-market capital gains. This compensation can be measured in terms of the market value of the option when issued or in terms of the realized value of the option when it is exercised. How to properly measure this compensation in our accounts is a question that is yet unanswered. At present, most employee stock options are included in personal income when they are exercised, not when they are granted. Recently, personal income for 2000 was revised upward, in large part because the amount of stock options exercised was larger than initially anticipated. As a result, measured personal saving rose from a negative to a low positive number.

Third, when stock options are exercised or when stocks are sold and capital gains are realized, tax obligations are accrued. These capital gains taxes have been an important element of the surge in personal income tax payments in the late 1990s that has continued into the new millennium. As a consequence, tax payments as a proportion of measured household income have risen. Thus, even if we ignore capital gains in our income and compensation measures, they have an important impact on government finance and measured household saving, since increased personal tax payments raise government saving and lower household saving.

Finally, the income of financial intermediaries often feeds off capital gains. For example, firms that manage investment funds often earn a proportion of the capital gains they accrue on behalf of clients, and an investment bank may make a substantial fraction of its income from capital gains. How to include such earnings in the national accounts is not easily determined, but since such corporations account for a fifth of all stock-market equity, they are an important part of

the economy. Changes in the US economy have made US economic developments inherently more difficult to analyse. In particular, production becomes
riskier as more of our efforts are devoted to producing intangible assets.
Measuring this effort is hard, and measuring its outcome is even harder. Yet
making the effort to measure these investments is surely preferable to ignoring
them, even though the outcome is not entirely satisfactory.

If we were to include increases in households' net worth in GDP, the variability of these capital gains would overwhelm that of the rest of income. In
1999, real household net worth rose by $4 trillion (in 1996 dollars); in 2000 it fell
about $2 trillion. Since real GDP was roughly $9 trillion in 1999, real GDP
including these capital gains was about $13 trillion; in 2000, it tumbled to $7 trillion.[27] Thus GDP growth measured this way was negative by more than 40 per
cent! That decline is the amount we would generally associate with an economic catastrophe like the Great Depression. Yet the unemployment rate
scarcely changed between 1999 and 2000; in fact, it fell slightly from an average
of 4.2–4.0 per cent.

It may well turn out that excluding capital gains from our measures of
national income and living with a spuriously low personal saving rate may be the
best alternative. However, we might wish to add another measure of household
income and saving that does include capital gains. Indeed, we might want to
have one measure that includes capital gains that have been realized, that is,
where the investor has taken the profit by actually selling the stock, and another
one that includes all stock-market capital gains, realized and unrealized.

It may not be possible to use a single standard of GDP as our sole measure
of US economic progress. Nevertheless, we should continue to improve our
measures of GDP. The BEA has taken an important step by including software
investment in GDP. Other items the BEA should consider in the future include
R&D and advertising.

6. Conclusion: A New Paradigm?

This article has explored how investment, profit, and saving are understated in
our corporate and national accounts, particularly since the mid-1970s, because
of our accounting treatment of intangible assets.[28] In fact, the US economy is
in better condition than statistics suggest. Rising investment in intangible assets
helps explain the rising value of US equities. That explanation, in turn, suggests
that continued strong economic growth and strong profit growth in the
future are not so implausible. The economic growth that ensues from rapid

development of new products has largely been hidden from economists because our accounting framework does not reveal this linkage clearly.

However, there can be no guarantee that investment in intangibles will grow as it has in the past two decades. The growth of intangible investment depends on the continuing belief that new products are waiting to be discovered, invented, and created, and the accompanying belief that such products will prove to be profitable. If the expected rate of return to intangible investment were to decline, such investment would slow.

R&D creates risks as well as opportunities. The popularity of new products can cause old product lines to be abandoned and existing businesses to become outmoded. Economist Joseph Schumpeter referred to this process as 'creative destruction'. In an ideal world, creativity would run ahead of destruction, keeping workers employed and consumption rising at a steady pace. In the real world, the disruptive forces sometimes gain the upper hand, and we encounter widespread unemployment, declines in asset values, and slowdowns in investment in intangibles. In either case, in good times or in bad, we need to recognize the increasing importance of intangible investment for our economy. Otherwise, statistical conventions can cause us to misread the fundamental forces propelling economic activity.

Appendix A: Are All R&D Projects Lemons?

Accountants use balance sheets and income statements to illustrate the interrelationship of income, expenses, profits, and assets. Balance sheets present the assets of the firm, such as cash and inventory, and its liabilities, or debts. The excess of assets over the firm's debts is called the book value of equity. (This equity is listed as a liability, since it is 'owed' to the owners of the business, so total liabilities, including equity, are equal to total assets.) Income statements present the income and expense flows that determine whether a profit has been made. The difference between book value of equity at the start of an accounting period and at the end of the period equals the profit shown on the income statement for that period.

Take as an example my son, Moses, setting up a lemonade stand. He starts with $5 on hand; at this point his 'firm' has a book value of equity of $5 (Balance Sheet 1a). Assume, for the sake of simplicity, that the only cost of production for the lemonade stand is lemons.[29] Lemons cost 25 cents each, so the $5 is used to purchase twenty lemons, which are in turn used to produce lemonade, which is then sold for $10. Revenues were $10 and expenses were $5, so profit was $5 (Income Statement 1). This $5 profit is reflected in the asset balance sheet, because Moses now has $10 cash-in-hand to prove that his firm's net worth has gone up $5 (Balance Sheet 1b).

Now suppose that Moses had started with $10 on hand (Balance Sheet 2a). This purchases forty lemons, twenty of them used to make $10 worth of lemonade, and twenty stored for the next day's business. Again there is a $5 profit, for although $10 was spent on lemons,

Balance Sheet 1a (Beginning of day)		Income Statement 1		Balance Sheet 1b (End of day)	
Assets		Revenues		Assets	
Cash	$5	Lemonade	$10	Cash	$10
		Expenses			
Liabilities	$0	Lemons	$5	Liabilities	$0
Book value of equity	$5	Profit	$5	Book value of equity	$10

Balance Sheet 2a (Beginning of day)		Income Statement 2		Balance Sheet 2b (End of day)	
Assets		Revenues		Assets	
Cash	$10	Lemonade	$10	Cash	$10
		Expenses		Lemon inventory	$5
Liabilities	$0	Lemons used	$5	Liabilities	$0
Book value of equity	$10	Profit	$5	Book value of equity	$15

Balance Sheet 3a (Beginning of day)		Income Statement 3		Balance Sheet 3b (End of day)	
Assets		Revenues		Assets	
Cash	$10	Lemonade	$10	Cash	$10
		Expenses		Lemon inventory	$4
Liabilities	$0	Lemons used	$5	Liabilities	$0
Book value of equity	$10	Spoilage	$1	Book value of equity	$14
		Profit	$4		

Balance Sheet 4a (Beginning of day)		Income Statement 4		Balance Sheet 4b (End of day)	
Assets		Revenues		Assets	
Cash	$10	Lemonade	$10	Cash	$10
		Expenses			
Liabilities	$0	Lemons used	$5	Liabilities	$0
Book value of equity	$10	Design costs	$5	Book value of equity	$10
		Profit	$0		

only $5 worth was used to produce current revenue (Income Statement 2). Twenty lemons went into inventory, the technical term for goods owned by the firm that are available for future use or sale. So the lemonade firm is now worth $15, consisting of $10 cash and $5 in lemon inventory (Balance Sheet 2b).

When a firm invests in *tangible* assets—in this case twenty lemons—there is no deduction from profit until the assets either are used in production or begin to depreciate or spoil.

If assets depreciate, a portion of the initial expense is deducted. The principle is that the facilities used to produce current revenue are a cost only to the extent that their value has declined during use. For example, if four of Moses' lemons spoil, his $5 inventory will decline in value to $4. In this case, the firm's accounts would show spoilage of $1, profits of $4, and a lemonade firm worth $14 (Income Statement 3 and Balance Sheets 3a and 3b).

So far, we have said nothing about intangible investment. Again, let us suppose Moses starts with $10 cash-in-hand (Balance Sheet 4a), but let's suppose he is also a designer, who spends $5 developing a lemonade-pitcher design and sells $10 worth of lemonade using $5 worth of lemons. According to standard accounting principles, his firm's total revenue is $10, and the cost of the R&D to design the lemonade pitcher is expensed, that is, counted as a cost of current operations, not as an investment. In other words, the investment in the design of the lemonade pitcher is treated as an additional cost of making the lemonade. The day's profits are zero (Income Statement 4). The accounting value of the lemonade firm is $10, the proceeds from the sale of lemonade (Balance Sheet 4b). Until Moses sells the lemonade-pitcher design, the design's accounting value is zero. If Moses can later sell the lemonade-pitcher design for $10, the firm will recognize a capital gain of $10 and an extraordinary profit of $10. The profit, in accounting terms, will appear out of nowhere. Put another way, accounting procedures treat all R&D efforts as if they are destined to be failures—they produce zero assets until proven otherwise.

....

Notes

1. This article is an update of Nakamura (1999*b*) and also includes material from Nakamura (2001*a,b*). The views expressed here are those of the author and do not necessarily reflect those of the Federal Reserve Bank of Philadelphia or of the Federal Reserve System.
2. In Nakamura (1997, 1998, 1999*a*) I have explored the consequences of new products and new retail practices for the measurement of inflation and output growth.
3. The data we are discussing are stated in nominal terms, rather than being adjusted for inflation (i.e. in real terms). This distinction is important because prices of some investment goods—such as computers—have been declining rapidly, so firms are able to obtain a lot more computational power for their dollars today than in the past. On the other hand, these rapid technological improvements are not, by and large, reflected in the published deflators for R&D expenditures. Indeed, how to properly deflate R&D expenditures is a substantial, unsolved research question.
4. In addition, the NSF estimates that governments in the United States, mainly the federal government, spent $72 billion on research and development in 2000, while universities, colleges, and other nonprofit organizations spent an additional $12 billion. In all, $265 billion is estimated to have been spent on research and development, or roughly 2.6% of aggregate US GDP. Expenditures by private industry are counted here because all of this

expenditure has as its purpose the creation of private intangible assets. Moreover, the public expenditure on research and development is already included in gross domestic product as part of government expenditures. It is also the case, however, that, increasingly, universities, colleges, and other organizations and individuals take advantage of research sponsored by the federal government or nonprofits to license new product development, thereby creating intangible assets.

5. New goods, unlike existing goods, are by definition unfamiliar to consumers. Educating consumers about a new good's existence and how to use it raises the value of the corporation's product (so it is an investment in a corporate asset) and raises the benefit received by consumers (so it is a social asset generating consumer surplus). An example is the sales force of a pharmaceutical company that rapidly disseminates information about a new drug.

6. This point was emphasized by Shinkyu Yang and Erik Brynjolfson (2001).

7. Thus this study comes from the era before the widespread use of personal computers and computer networks.

8. For more on intellectual property and financial innovation, see Hunt (2001).

9. For alternative calculations that suggest similarly large magnitudes of intangible capital, see Hall (1999) and McGrattan and Prescott (2001).

10. The growth of the market value of nonfinancial corporate equity, the S&P 500, and the Dow Jones Industrials has been approximately equal over this period.

11. See Jan R. Williams (1998, ch. 41, pp. 41–4). This treatment was formalized in 1974. Before that, most companies followed 'the conservative procedure of expensing such costs as incurred, rather than capitalizing any part of them' (Johnson and Gentry 1974: 443).

12. That is, a computer purchased for an R&D project can be capitalized to the extent that after its current use, it will retain value because it can be used in future projects. But durable lab equipment whose only use is the project at hand should be expensed.

13. See, for example, Hall (1993).

14. Although ideas need not deteriorate over time, they do tend to lose their economic value. In particular, patents and copyrights give their owners monopoly rights over the assets for a limited time (twenty years in the case of patents).

15. Note that even though these creativity expenses are treated as investments and capitalized under GAAP, they are not treated as investments in the national accounts, as discussed earlier.

16. This adjustment, called the inventory valuation adjustment, removes the part of inventory profit due strictly to inflation and also adopts a uniform convention for the valuation of inventories.

17. This adjustment, called the capital consumption adjustment because capital consumption is a synonym for depreciation, is necessary because depreciation charges allowed by tax law often do not match true depreciation.

18. Still, the 1980s appear somewhat out of line, since stock-market valuation in general was very low then.

19. The BEA has recently published a statistical accounting of R&D investment and assets (a 'satellite' account) but has neither incorporated these data into its regular accounts nor kept the data up to date (Carson *et al.* 1994).

20. See Peach and Steindel (2000) for an interesting discussion of this problem and the importance of realized capital gains (capital gains that investors have received by selling their investments and, thus, can be used to pay for consumption).

21. The market value of domestic corporate equities rose $12 trillion, from $2 trillion at the end of 1979 to $14 trillion at the end of 2000, in 1996 dollars. During that time, the total net worth of US households (which hold almost all of domestic equities) rose $23 trillion, from $15 trillion to $38 trillion. By contrast, real estate holdings of US households rose by about $6 trillion during this period.

22. Specifically, we have used the GDP deflator to eliminate the effects of inflation.

23. In nominal terms, during the three decades before 1990, the net worth of American households as a proportion of after-tax income actually fell slightly, from 493 to 504%. So with the lower saving rate of the 1990s, we might have expected a still lower net worth. Instead, net worth rose to 620% of after-tax income at the end of 1999, before falling to 579 by the end of 2000. Alternatively, in real terms, net worth, measured in 1996 dollars, rose from $8.4 trillion at the end of 1959 to $23.4 trillion at the end of 1989—a $15.0 trillion increase over thirty years and a compound annual growth rate of 3.5%. By the end of 1999, net worth rose to $38.1 trillion—a $14.7 trillion increase in just ten years and a compound annual growth rate of 4.8%. Thus, whether we compare increases in wealth with nominal incomes or with consumer price inflation, households' wealth grew more rapidly in the 1990s than in previous decades.

24. From the end of 1959 to the end of 1979, capital gains on equities of domestic corporations, according to the Flow of Funds accounts, averaged just $12.8 billion a year in 1996 dollars, while real GDP averaged $3.6 trillion. From the end of 1979 to the end of 1989, yearly stock-market capital gains averaged $209 billion while real GDP averaged $5.6 trillion. From the end of 1989 to the end of 1999, annual stock-market capital gains averaged $1.2 trillion while real GDP averaged $7.6 trillion.

25. Thus if we add capital gains to output, much of the productivity slowdown after the mid-1970s may disappear.

26. For details, see Nakamura (2001*b*).

27. To be more precise, if we use the GDP deflator to convert net worth into 1996 dollars, in 1999 households' net worth rose $4.2 trillion and in 2000 it fell $1.9 trillion. In 1999, real GDP without capital gains was $8.9 trillion, and in 2000 it was $9.2 trillion. Thus, including capital gains, real GDP was $13.1 trillion in 1999, and $7.3 trillion in 2000, a decline of 44%.

28. Additional discussion of how mismeasurement of inflation has contributed to the underestimation of output since the mid-1970s can be found in Nakamura (1997).

29. Thus to avoid cluttering up the analysis, we assume that the sugar, water, cups, and labour normally used in selling lemonade are not necessary in this case or, perhaps more realistically, are supplied free by Moses' dad.

References

Carson, Carol S., Bruce T. Grimm, and Carol E. Moylan (1994), 'A satellite account for research and development', *Survey of Current Business*, 74: 37–71.

Caves, Richard (2000), *Creative Industries: Contracts Between Art and Commerce* (Cambridge MA: Harvard University Press).

Chambers, Dennis, Ross Jennings, and Robert B. Thompson (1998), 'Evidence on the usefulness of capitalizing and amortizing research and development costs', mimeo, University of Texas.

Estes, Ralph (1981), *Dictionary of Accounting* (Cambridge, MA: MIT), pp. 81–105.

Fisher, Irving (1920), *The Purchasing Power of Money*, 2nd edn (New York: Macmillan), 1.

Hall, Bronwyn (1993), 'The stock market value of R&D investment during the 1980's', *American Economic Review*, 83: 259–64.

Hall, Robert E. (1999), 'The stock market and capital accumulation', NBER Working Paper 7180.

Hill, Peter (1999), 'Tangibles, intangibles, and services: A new taxonomy for the classification of output', *Canadian Journal of Economics*, 426–46.

Hunt, Robert M. (2001), 'You can patent that? are patents on computer programs and business methods good for the new economy?', Federal Reserve Bank of Philadelphia *Business Review*, First Quarter 2001.

Johnson, Glenn L. and James A. Gentry Jr. (1974), *Finney and Miller's Principles of Accounting, Intermediate* (Englewood Cliffs, NJ: Prentice-Hall).

McCann-Erickson World Group (2000), *Bob Coen's Insider's Report*. http://www.mccann.com/html/coenreport.html

McGrattan, Ellen R. and Edward C. Prescott (2001), 'Is the stock market overvalued?', NBER Working Paper No. 8077.

Nakamura, Leonard (1997), 'Is the US economy really growing too slowly? Maybe we're measuring growth wrong', Federal Reserve of Philadelphia *Business Review*.

——(1998), 'The retail revolution and food-price measurement', Federal Reserve of Philadelphia *Business Review*.

—— (1999a), 'The measurement of retail output and the retail revolution', *Canadian Journal of Economics*, 408–25.

—— (1999b), 'Intangibles: What put the *New* in the new economy?', Federal Reserve Bank of Philadelphia *Business Review*.

—— (2001a), 'Investing in intangibles: Is a trillion dollars missing from GDP?' Federal Reserve Bank of Philadelphia *Business Review*.

—— (2001b), 'What is the US gross investment in intangibles? (At Least) one trillion dollars a year!' Federal Reserve Bank of Philadelphia Working Paper 01-15.

National Science Foundation (2000), *National Patterns of R&D Resources: 2000 Data Update*. http://www.nsf.gov/sbe/srs/nsf01309/pdf/tabd.pdf.

Peach, Richard and Charles Steindel (2000), 'A nation of spendthrifts? An analysis of trends in personal and gross saving', Federal Reserve Bank of New York *Current Issues in Economics and Finance*, 6.

Williams, Jan R. (1998), *1999 Miller GAAP Guide* (New York: Harcourt Brace).

Yang, Shinkyu and Erik Brynjolfsson (2001), 'Intangible assets and growth accounting: Evidence from computer investments', paper presented at New York University's fourth Intangibles Conference.

## 2

The Information Economy

Carl Shapiro and Hal R. Varian

As the century closed, the world became smaller. The public rapidly gained access to new and dramatically faster communication technologies. Entrepreneurs, able to draw on unprecedented scale economies, built vast empires. Great fortunes were made. The government demanded that these powerful new monopolists be held accountable under antitrust law. Every day brought forth new technological advances to which the old business models seemed no longer to apply. Yet, somehow, the basic laws of economics asserted themselves. Those who mastered these laws survived in the new environment. Those who did not, failed.

A prophecy for the next decade? No. You have just read a description of what happened a hundred years ago when the twentieth century industrial giants emerged. Using the infrastructure of the emerging electricity and telephone networks, these industrialists transformed the US economy, just as today's Silicon Valley entrepreneurs are drawing on computer and communications infrastructure to transform the world's economy.

The thesis of this book is that durable economic principles can guide you in today's frenetic business environment. Technology changes. Economic laws do not. If you are struggling to comprehend what the Internet means for you and your business, you can learn a great deal from the advent of the telephone system a hundred years ago.

Sure, today's business world is different in a myriad of ways from that of a century ago. But many of today's managers are so focused on the trees of technological change that they fail to see the forest: the underlying economic forces that determine success and failure. As academics, government officials, and consultants we have enjoyed a bird's-eye view of the forest for twenty years, tracking industries, working for high-tech companies, and contributing to an ever-growing literature on information and technology markets.

In the pages that follow, we systematically introduce and explain the concepts and strategies you need to successfully navigate the network economy. Information technology is rushing forward, seemingly chaotically, and it is difficult to discern patterns to guide business decisions. But there is order in the chaos: a few basic economic concepts go a long way toward explaining how today's industries are evolving.

Netscape, the one-time darling of the stock market, offers a good example of how economic principles can serve as an early warning system. We are not sure exactly how software for viewing Web pages will evolve, but we do know that Netscape is fundamentally vulnerable because its chief competitor, Microsoft, controls the operating environment of which a Web browser is but one component. In our framework, Netscape is facing a classic problem of interconnection: Netscape's browser needs to work in conjunction with Microsoft's operating system. Local telephone companies battling the Bell System around 1900 faced a similar dependency upon their chief rival when they tried to interconnect with Bell to offer long-distance service. Many did not survive. Interconnection battles have arisen regularly over the past century in the telephone, the railroad, the airline, and the computer industries, among others. We wonder how many investors who bid Netscape's stock price up to breathtaking heights appreciated its fundamental vulnerability.

We examine numerous business strategies on both the information (software) and the infrastructure (hardware) sides of the industry. Software and hardware are inexorably linked. Indeed, they are a leading example of complements, one of the key concepts explored in our book. Neither software nor hardware is of much value without the other; they are only valuable because they work together as a system.

....

1. Information

We use the term *information* very broadly. Essentially, anything that can be digitized—encoded as a stream of bits—is information. For our purposes, baseball scores, books, databases, magazines, movies, music, stock quotes, and Web pages are all *information goods*. We focus on the value of information to different consumers. Some information has entertainment value, and some has business value, but regardless of the particular source of value, people are willing to pay for information. As we see, many strategies for purveyors of information are based on the fact that consumers differ greatly in how they value particular information goods.

Of course, information is costly to create and assemble. The cost structure of an information supplier is rather unusual. Since the very nature of competition in information markets is driven by this unusual cost structure, we begin our overview of information strategy there.

1.1. The Cost of Producing Information

Information is costly to *produce* but cheap to *reproduce*. Books that cost hundreds of thousands of dollars to produce can be printed and bound for a dollar or two, and 100-million dollar movies can be copied on videotape for a few cents.

Economists say that production of an information good involves *high fixed costs* but *low marginal costs*. The cost of producing the first copy of an information good may be substantial, but the cost of producing (or reproducing) additional copies is negligible. This sort of cost structure has many important implications. For example, cost-based pricing just does not work: a 10 or 20 per cent markup on unit cost makes no sense when unit cost is zero. You must price your information goods according to consumer value, not according to your production cost.

Since people have widely different values for a particular piece of information, value-based pricing leads naturally to differential pricing. We explore strategies for differential pricing in detail in Chapters 2 and 3. Chapter 2 is concerned with ways to sell an information good to identifiable markets; Chapter 3 examines ways to 'version' information goods to make them appeal to different market segments which will pay different prices for the different versions.

For example, one way to differentiate versions of the same information good is to use *delay*. Publishers first sell a hardback book and then issue a paperback several months later. The impatient consumers buy the high-priced hardback; the patient ones buy the low-priced paperback. Providers of information on the Internet can exploit the same strategy: investors now pay $8.95 a month for a Web site that offers portfolio analysis using 20-minute delayed stock market quotes but $50 a month for a service that uses real time stock market quotes.

We explore different ways to version information in Chapter 3 and show you the principles behind creating profitable product lines that target different market segments. Each version sells for a different price, allowing you to extract the maximum value of your product from the marketplace.

1.2. Managing Intellectual Property

If the creators of an information good can reproduce it cheaply, others can copy it cheaply. It has long been recognized that some form of 'privatization' of information helps to ensure its production. The US Constitution explicitly grants Congress the duty 'to promote the progress of science and useful arts, by securing, for limited times, to authors and inventors, the exclusive right to their respective writings and discoveries'.

But the legal grant of exclusive rights to intellectual property via patents, copyright, and trademarks does not confer complete power to control information. There is still the issue of enforcement, a problem that has become even more important with the rise of digital technology and the Internet. Digital information can be perfectly copied and instantaneously transmitted around the world, leading many content producers to view the Internet as one giant, out-of-control copying machine. If copies crowd out legitimate sales, the producers of information may not be able to recover their production costs.

Despite this danger, we think that content owners tend to be too conservative with respect to the management of their intellectual property. The history of the video industry is a good example. Hollywood was petrified by the advent of videotape recorders. The TV industry filed suits to prevent home copying of TV programs, and Disney attempted to distinguish video sales and rentals through licensing arrangements. All of these attempts failed. Ironically, Hollywood now makes more from video than from theater presentations for most productions. The video sales and rental market, once so feared, has become a giant revenue source for Hollywood.

When managing intellectual property, your goal should be to choose the terms and conditions that maximize the *value* of your intellectual property, not the terms and conditions that maximize the protection. In Chapter 4 we will review the surprising history of intellectual property and describe the lessons it has for rights management on the Internet.

1.3. Information as an 'Experience Good'

Economists say that a good is an *experience good* if consumers must experience it to value it. Virtually any new product is an experience good, and marketers have developed strategies such as free samples, promotional pricing, and testimonials to help consumers learn about new goods.

But information is an experience good *every* time it's consumed. How do you know whether today's *Wall Street Journal* is worth 75 cents until you've read it? Answer: you do not.

Information businesses—like those in the print, music, and movie industries—have devised various strategies to get wary consumers to overcome their reluctance to purchase information before they know what they are getting. First, there are various forms of browsing: you can look at the headlines at the news-stand, hear pop tunes on the radio, and watch previews at the movies. But browsing is only part of the story. Most media producers overcome the experience good problem through *branding* and *reputation*. The main reason that we read the *Wall Street Journal* today is that we have found it useful in the past.

The brand name of the *Wall Street Journal* is one of its chief assets, and the *Journal* invests heavily in building a reputation for accuracy, timeliness, and relevance. This investment takes numerous forms, from the company's Newspapers in Education program, to the distinctive appearance of the paper itself, and the corporate logo. The look and feel of the *Journal's* online edition testifies to the great lengths designers went to carry over the look and feel of the print version, thereby extending the same authority, brand identity, and customer loyalty from the print product to the online product. The *Wall Street Journal* 'brand' conveys a message to potential readers about the quality of the content, thereby overcoming the experience good problem endemic to information goods.

The computer scientists who designed the protocols for the Internet and the World Wide Web were surprised by the huge traffic in images. Today more than 60 per cent of Internet traffic is to Web sites, and of the Web traffic, almost three-fourths is images. Some of these images are *Playboy* centerfolds, of course—another brand that successfully made the move to cyberspace—but a lot of them are corporate logos. Image is everything in the information biz, because it's the image that carries the brand name and the reputation.

The tension between giving away your information—to let people know what you have to offer—and charging them for it to recover your costs is a fundamental problem in the information economy.

1.4. *The Economics of Attention*

Now that information is available so quickly, so ubiquitously, and so inexpensively, it is not surprising that everyone is complaining of information overload. Nobel prize-winning economist Herbert Simon spoke for us all when he said that 'a wealth of information creates a poverty of attention'.

Nowadays the problem is not information access but information overload. The real value produced by an information provider comes in locating, filtering, and communicating what is useful to the consumer. It is no accident that the most popular Web sites belong to the search engines, those devices that allow people to find information they value and to avoid the rest.

In real estate, it is said that there are only three critical factors: location, location, and location. Any idiot can establish a Web presence—and lots of them have. The big problem is letting people know about it. Amazon.com, the online bookstore, recently entered into a long-term, exclusive agreement with America Online (AOL) to gain access to AOL's 8.5 million customers. The cost of this deal is on the order of $19 million, which can be understood as the cost of purchasing the *attention* of AOL subscribers. Wal-Mart recently launched the Wal-Mart Television Network, which broadcasts commercials on the television sets lined up for sale at the company's 1,950 stores nationwide. Like AOL,

Wal-Mart realized that it could sell the attention of its customers to advertisers. As health clubs, doctors' offices, and other locations attempt to grab our valuable attention, information overload will worsen.

Selling viewers' attention has always been an attractive way to support information provision. Commercials support broadcast TV, and advertisement is often the primary revenue source for magazines and newspapers. Advertising works because it exploits statistical patterns. People who read *Car and Driver* are likely to be interested in ads for BMWs, and people who read the *Los Angeles Times* are likely to be interested in California real estate.

The Internet, a hybrid between a broadcast medium and a point-to-point medium, offers exciting new potentials for matching up customers and suppliers. The Net allows information vendors to move from the conventional broadcast form of advertising to one-to-one marketing. Nielsen collects information on the viewing habits of a few thousand consumers, which is then used to design TV shows for the next season. In contrast, Web servers can observe the behaviour of millions of customers and immediately produce customized content, bundled with customized ads.

The information amassed by these powerful Web servers is not limited to their users' current behaviour; they can also access vast databases of information about customer history and demographics. Hotmail, for example, offers free e-mail service to customers who complete a questionnaire on their demographics and interests. This personal information allows Hotmail to customize ads that can be displayed alongside the user's e-mail messages.

This new, one-to-one marketing benefits both parties in the transaction: the advertiser reaches exactly the market it wants to target, and consumers need give their attention only to ads that are likely to be of interest. Furthermore, by gathering better information about what particular customers want, the information provider can design products that are more highly customized and hence more valuable. Firms that master this sort of marketing will thrive, while those that continue to conduct unfocused and excessively broad advertising campaigns will be at a competitive disadvantage.

2. Technology

We have focused so far on the information side of 'information technology'. Now let us turn to the technology side—that is, the infrastructure that makes it possible to store, search, retrieve, copy, filter, manipulate, view, transmit, and receive information.

Infrastructure is to information as a bottle is to wine: the technology is the packaging that allows the information to be delivered to end consumers. A single copy of a film would be of little value without a distribution technology. Likewise, computer software is valuable only because computer hardware and network technology are now so powerful and inexpensive.

In short, today's breathless pace of change and the current fascination with the information economy are driven by advances in information technology and infrastructure, not by any fundamental shift in the nature or even the magnitude of the information itself. The fact is, the Web is not all that impressive as an information resource. The static, publicly accessible HTML text on the Web is roughly equivalent in size to 1.5 million books. The UC Berkeley Library has eight million volumes, and the average quality of the Berkeley library content is much, much higher! If 10 per cent of the material on the Web is 'useful', there are about 150,000 useful book-equivalents on it, which is about the size of a Borders superstore. But the actual figure for 'useful' is probably more like 1 per cent, which is 15,000 books, or half the size of an average mall bookstore.

The value of the Web lies in its capacity to provide immediate access to information. Using the Web, information suppliers can distribute up-to-date information dynamically from databases and other repositories. Imagine what would happen if the wine industry came up with a bottle that gave its customers easier, quicker, and cheaper access to its wine. Sure, the bottle is only infrastructure, but infrastructure that can reduce cost and increase value is tremendously important. Improved information infrastructure has vastly increased our ability to store, retrieve, sort, filter, and distribute information, thereby greatly enhancing the value of the underlying information itself.

What is new is our ability to manipulate information, not the total amount of information available. Mom-and-pop hardware stores of yesteryear regularly checked their inventories. The inventory information now captured by Home Depot, while surely more accurate and up-to-date, is not vastly greater than that of a generation ago. What is truly new is Home Depot's ability to reorder items from suppliers using electronic data interchange, to conduct and analyse cross-store demand studies based on pricing and promotional variations, and to rapidly discount slow-moving items, all with minimal human intervention.

Indeed, in every industry we see dramatic changes in technology that allow people to do more with the same information. Sears Roebuck popularized catalog sales more than a century ago. Lands' End does not have that much more raw information than Sears did. Like Sears, it has a catalog of products and a list of customers. What is new is that Lands' End can easily retrieve data on customers, including data on previous purchases, that allows it to engage in targeted marketing. Furthermore, Lands' End can use the telecommunications and banking infrastructure to conduct transactions in real time over the telephone and online.

Content providers cannot operate without infrastructure suppliers, and vice versa. The information economy is about both information *and* the associated technology.

2.1. *Systems Competition*

Systems show up everywhere in information technology: operating systems and applications software, CPUs and memory chips, disk drives and controller cards, video cassette recorders and the videotapes themselves. Usually, one firm cannot hope to offer all the pieces that make up an information system. Instead, different components are made by different manufacturers using very different production and business models. Traditional rules of competitive strategy focus on competitors, suppliers, and customers. In the information economy, companies selling complementary components, or *complementors*, are equally important. When you are selling one component of a system, you cannot compete if you are not compatible with the rest of the system. Many of our strategic principles are specifically designed to help companies selling one component of an information system.

The dependence of information technology on systems means that firms must focus not only on their competitors but also on their collaborators. Forming alliances, cultivating partners, and ensuring compatibility (or lack of compatibility!) are critical business decisions. Firms have long been faced with make/buy decisions, but the need for collaboration, and the multitude of cooperative arrangements, has never been greater than in the area of infotech.

The history of the Microsoft–Intel partnership is a classic example. Microsoft focused almost exclusively on software, while Intel focused almost exclusively on hardware. They each made numerous strategic alliances and acquisitions that built on their strengths. The key for each company has been to commoditize complementary products without eroding the value of its own core strengths. For example, Intel has entered new product spaces such as chipsets and motherboards to improve the performance of these components and thereby stimulate demand for its core product: microprocessors. Intel has helped to create a highly competitive industry in component parts such as video cards, sound cards, and hard drives as well as in the assembly and distribution of personal computers.

Microsoft has its following of independent software vendors (ISVs), and both companies have extensive licensing programs with original equipment manufacturers (OEMs). And they each have each other, an extraordinarily productive, if necessarily tense, marriage. It's in the interest of each company to create multiple sources for its partner's piece of the system but to prevent the emergence of a strong rival for its own piece. This tension arises over and over again in the information technology sector; Microsoft and Intel are merely the most visible, and profitable, example of the complex dynamics that arise in assembling information systems.

Apple Computer pursued a very different strategy by producing a highly integrated product consisting of both a hardware platform and the software that ran on it. Their software and hardware was much more tightly integrated than the Microsoft/Intel offerings, so it performed better. (Microsoft recognized this early on and tried to license the Apple technology rather than investing in developing its own windowing system.) The downside was that the relative lack of competition (and, later, scale) made Apple products more expensive and, eventually, less powerful. In the long run, the 'Wintel' strategy of strategic alliance was the better choice.

2.2. Lock-In and Switching Costs

Remember long-playing phonograph records (LPs)? In our lexicon, these were 'durable complementary assets' specific to a turntable but incompatible with the alternative technology of CDs. In plain English: they were durable and valuable, they worked with a turntable to play music, but they would not work in a CD player. As a result, Sony and Philips had to deal with considerable consumer *switching costs* when introducing their CD technology. Fortunately for Sony and Philips, CDs offered significant improvement in convenience, durability, and sound quality over LPs, so consumers were willing to replace their music libraries. Quadraphonic sound, stereo AM radio, PicturePhones, and digital audiotape did not fare as well. We will see how the new digital video (or versatile) disks (DVDs) will do in the next few years.

As the impending problem of resetting computers to recognize the year 2000 illustrates, users of information technologies are notoriously subject to switching costs and lock-in: once you have chosen a technology, or a format for keeping information, switching can be very expensive. Most of us have experienced the costs of switching from one brand of computer software to another: data files are unlikely to transfer perfectly, incompatibilities with other tools often arise, and, most important, retraining is required.

Switching costs are significant, and corporate information officers (CIOs) think long and hard about changing systems. Lock-in to historical, legacy systems is commonplace in the network economy. Such lock-in is not absolute—new technologies do displace old ones—but switching costs can dramatically alter firms' strategies and options. In fact, the magnitude of switching costs is itself a strategic choice made by the producer of the system.

Lock-in arises whenever users invest in multiple complementary and durable assets specific to a particular information technology system. You purchased a library of LPs as well as a turntable. So long as these assets were valuable—the albums were not too scratched and the turntable still worked—you had less reason to buy a CD player and start buying expensive CDs. More generally, in replacing an old system with a new, incompatible one, you may find it necessary to swap out or duplicate *all* the components of your system. These components typically include a range of assets: data files (LP records, COBOL programs, word processing documents, etc.), various pieces of durable hardware, and training, or human capital. Switching from Apple to Intel equipment involves not only new hardware but new software. And not only that, the 'wetware'—the knowledge that you and your employees have built up that enables you to use your hardware and software—has to be updated. The switching costs for changing computer systems can be astronomical. Today's state-of-the-art choice is tomorrow's legacy system.

This type of situation is the norm in the information economy. A cellular telephone provider that has invested in Qualcomm's technology for compressing and encoding the calls it transmits and receives is locked into that technology, even if Qualcomm raises the price for its gear. A large enterprise that has selected Cisco's or 3Com's technology and architecture for its networking needs will find it very costly to change to an incompatible network technology. Whether the enterprise is locked in to proprietary Cisco or 3Com products or to an 'open' standard with multiple suppliers can make a big difference.

Lock-in can occur on an individual level, a company level, or even a societal level. Many consumers were locked into LP libraries, at least in the sense that they were less inclined to purchase CD players because they could not play LPs. Many companies were locked into Lotus 1–2–3 spreadsheets because their employees were highly trained in using the Lotus command structure; indeed, Lotus sued Borland for copying the 1–2–3 command structure in its spreadsheet product, Quattro Pro, a dispute that went all the way to the Supreme Court. Today, at a societal level, most of us are locked into Microsoft's Windows desktop operating environment.

2.3. Positive Feedback, Network Externalities, and Standards

For many information technologies, consumers benefit from using a popular format or system. When the value of a product to one user depends on how many other users there are, economists say that this product exhibits *network externalities*, or *network effects*. Communications technologies are a prime example: telephones, e-mail, Internet access, fax machines, and modems all exhibit network externalities.

Technologies subject to strong network effects tend to exhibit long lead times followed by explosive growth. The pattern results from *positive feedback:* as the installed base of users grows, more and more users find adoption worthwhile. Eventually, the product achieves critical mass and takes over the market. Fax machines illustrate nicely the common pattern. The Scottish inventor Alexander Bain patented the basic technology for fax machines in 1843, and AT&T introduced a wire photo service in the United States in 1925, but faxes remained a niche product until the mid-1980s. During a five-year period, the demand for and supply of fax machines exploded. Before 1982 almost no one had a fax machine; after 1987, the majority of businesses had one or more.

The Internet exhibited the same pattern. The first e-mail message was sent in 1969, but up until the mid-1980s e-mail was used only by techies. Internet technology was developed in the early 1970s but did not really take off until the late 1980s. But when Internet traffic did finally start growing, it doubled every year from 1989 to 1995. After the Internet was privatized in April 1995, it started growing even faster.

But network externalities are not confined to communications networks. They are also powerful in 'virtual' networks, such as the network of users of Macintosh computers: each Mac user benefits from a larger network, since this facilitates the exchange of files and tips and encourages software houses to devote more resources to developing software for the Mac. Because these virtual networks of compatible users generate network externalities, popular hardware and software systems enjoy a significant competitive advantage over less popular systems. As a result, growth is a strategic imperative, not just to achieve the usual production side economies of scale but to achieve the *demand side* economies of scale generated by network effects.

We explore the implications of network externalities for business strategy in Chapter 7. The key challenge is to obtain critical mass—after that, the going gets easier. Once you have a large enough customer base, the market will build itself. However, having a superior technology is not enough to win. You may need to employ marketing tools such as penetration pricing to ignite the positive feedback.

The company that best understands information systems and complementary products will be best positioned to move rapidly and aggressively. Netscape grabbed the Web browser market early on by giving away its product. It lost money on every sale but made up for it in volume. Netscape was able to give away its browser and sell it, too, by bundling such critical components as customer support with the retail version and by selling complementary goods such as server software for hefty prices.

In competing to become the standard, or at least to achieve critical mass, consumer *expectations* are critical. In a very real sense, the product that is *expected* to become the standard *will* become the standard. Self-fulfilling expectations are one manifestation of positive-feedback economics and bandwagon effects. As a result, companies participating in markets with strong network effects seek to convince customers that their products will ultimately become the standard, while rival, incompatible products will soon be orphaned.

Competitive 'pre-announcements' of a product's appearance on the market are a good example of 'expectations management'. In the mid-1980s, when Borland released Quattro Pro, a new spreadsheet, Microsoft was quick to counter with a press release describing how much better the next release of its comparable program, Excel, would be. It did not take long for the press to come up with the term *vaporware* to describe this sort of 'product'. Microsoft played the same game IBM had played in an earlier generation, when IBM was accused of using pre-announcements to stifle competition. When network effects are strong, product announcements can be as important as the actual introduction of products.

Product pre-announcements can be a two-edged sword, however. The announcement of a new, improved version of your product may cut into your competitors' sales, but it can also cut into your own sales. When Intel developed the MMX technology for accelerating graphics in the fall of 1996, it was careful not to advertise it until *after* the Christmas season. Likewise, sales of large-screen TV sets in 1997 declined as consumers waited for digital television sets to arrive in 1998.

Because of the importance of critical mass, because customer expectations are so important in the area of information infrastructure, and because technology is evolving so rapidly, the *timing* of strategic moves is even more important in the information industry than in others. Moving too early means making compromises in technology and going out on a limb without sufficient allies. Japan's television network NHK tried to go it alone in the early 1990s with its own high-definition television system, with disastrous consequences: not only has NHK's analog MUSE system met with consumer resistance in Japan, but it has left the Japanese behind the United States in the development and deployment of digital television. Yet moving too late can mean missing the market entirely, especially if customers become locked into rival technologies.

Whether you are trying to establish a new information technology or to extend the lifetime of technology that is already popular, you will face critical compatibility decisions. For example, a key source of leverage for Sony and Philips in their negotiations with others in the DVD alliance was their control over the original CD technology. Even if Sony and Philips did not develop or control the best technology for DVD, they were in the driver's seat to the extent that their patents prevented others from offering backward-compatible DVD machines. Yet even companies with *de facto* standards do not necessarily opt for backward compatibility: Nintendo 64 machines cannot play Nintendo game cartridges from the earlier generations of Nintendo systems.

Another method for achieving critical mass is to assemble a powerful group of strategic partners. For this purpose, partners can be customers, complementors, or even competitors. Having some large, visible customers aboard can get the bandwagon rolling by directly building up critical mass. In November 1997 Sun took out full-page ads in the *New York Times* and other major newspapers reciting the long list of the members of the 'Java coalition' to convey the impression that Java was the 'next big thing'.

Having suppliers of complements aboard makes the overall system more attractive. And having competitors aboard can give today's and tomorrow's customers the assurance that they will not be exploited once they are locked in. We see this strategy being used with DVD today; Sony and Philips, the original promoters of CD technology, have teamed up with content providers (that is, customers) such as Time Warner and competitors such as Toshiba to promote the new DVD technology. Both player manufacturers and disk-pressing firms are on board, too. The same pattern occurs in the emergence of digital television in the United States, where set manufacturers, who have the most to gain from rapid adoption of digital TV, are leading the way, with the Federal Communications Commission (FCC) dragging broadcasters along by offering them free spectrum for digital broadcasts.

Very often, support for a new technology can be assembled in the context of a formal standard-setting effort. For example, both Motorola and Qualcomm have sought to gain competitive advantages, not to mention royalty income, by having their patented technologies incorporated into formal standards for modems and cellular telephones.

If you own valuable intellectual property but need to gain critical mass, you must decide whether to promote your technology unilaterally, in the hope that it will become a *de facto* standard that you can tightly control, or to make various 'openness' commitments to help achieve a critical mass. Adobe followed an openness strategy with its page description language, PostScript, explicitly allowing other software houses to implement PostScript interpreters, because they realized that such widespread use helped establish a standard. Nowadays, participation in most formal standard-setting bodies in the United States requires a commitment to license any essential or blocking patents on 'fair, reasonable, and non-discriminatory terms'.

A go-it-alone strategy typically involves competition to *become* the standard. By contrast, participation in a formal standard-setting process, or assembling allies to promote a particular version of technology, typically involves competition *within* a standard. Don't plan to play the higher-stakes, winner-take-all battle to become the standard unless you can be aggressive in timing, in pricing, and in exploiting relationships with complementary products. Rivalry to achieve cost leadership by scale economies and experience, a tried and true strategy in various manufacturing contexts, is tame in comparison. Just ask Sony about losing out with Beta in the standards war against VHS, or the participants in the recent 56 k modem standards battle. We explore effective strategies for standards battles in Chapter 9.

------

3. Policy

The ongoing battle between Microsoft and the Justice Department illustrates the importance of antitrust policy in the information sector. Whether fending off legal attacks or using the antitrust laws to challenge the conduct of competitors or suppliers, every manager in the network economy can profit from understanding the rules of the game.

Microsoft's wishes to the contrary, high-tech firms are not immune to the antitrust laws. Competitive strategy in the information economy collides with antitrust law in three primary areas: mergers and acquisitions, cooperative standard setting, and monopolization. We explore the current legal rules in each of these areas in Chapter 10.

Overall, we do not believe that antitrust law blocks most companies from pursuing their chosen strategies, even when they need to cooperate with other industry members to establish compatibility standards. Now and then, companies are prevented from acquiring direct rivals, as when Microsoft tried to acquire Intuit, but this is hardly unique to the information sector.

The Sherman Anti-Trust Act was passed in 1890 to control monopolies. Technology has changed radically since then. As we have stressed, the underlying economic principles have not. As a new century arrives, the Sherman Act is flexible enough to prevent the heavy hand of monopoly from stifling innovation, while keeping markets competitive enough to stay the even heavier hand of government regulation from intruding in our dynamic hardware and software markets.

## 3

The Soft Revolution: Achieving Growth by Managing Intangibles

Paul Romer

Donald Lessard: Good afternoon, and, on behalf of our hosts Jerry Fair and Mike Murray of Bank of America, let me welcome you all to this discussion of the role of soft, or intangible, assets in driving corporate growth in the new global economy. I am Don Lessard, Professor of International Management at MIT's Sloan School of Management, and I will be serving as moderator of the discussion.

Our main subject, then, is corporate growth: How does it happen, and how can corporate executives promote and sustain it? We have an interesting view of the growth process that we want to explore today with Paul Romer. Paul is Professor of Economics at Stanford University's Graduate School of Business. He has written extensively on the subject of economic growth, and his views have been widely cited by the likes of Peter Drucker, Michael Porter, Paul Krugman, and Alvin Toffler. In fact, Paul's work has received so much attention that he is already, at age forty considered to be in the running for a Nobel Prize. His accomplishment has been to develop what amounts to a new theory of economic growth—one that moves the factors of scientific discovery, technological change, innovation, and productivity back to the centre of economic analysis.

What we would like to do is to start by having Professor Romer spend 20 minutes or so outlining his theory of growth. Then, after a short break, Paul will be joined in a panel discussion by the chief executives of three large public corporations. And, before turning to Paul, let me briefly introduce the three CEOs in the order in which they will be speaking:

Lawrence Perlman is Chairman and Chief Executive Officer of Ceridian Corporation, a leading US information services company that serves the human resources, transportation, and electronic media markets. Larry has done a remarkable job in building the company's businesses—which include

Ceridian Employer Services, Comdata Corporation, and The Arbitron Company—out of the remains of the old Control Data. In less than six years, he has taken a company on the verge of Chapter 11 and created a new set of businesses that are today worth about $4.5 billion.

Stan Shih is Chairman, Chief Executive Officer, and co-founder of the Acer Group, which is based in Taiwan. With 1997 sales of $6.5 billion, Acer is the world's third largest manufacturer of personal computers, and a leading supplier of brand name PC products worldwide. In addition to its technological accomplishments, the company also has an innovative organizational structure—one that has created an entrepreneurial culture through extensive use of managerial and employee stock ownership in Acer's five separate, publicly traded business units.

Michael Volkema is President and Chief Executive Officer of Herman Miller, a leading US manufacturer of office furniture. Since May of 1995, the year Mike assumed his current position, the company has achieved an unbroken string of records in quarterly sales, orders, and earnings. Like Acer, Herman Miller has a tradition of innovative gain-sharing with employees, first with its Scanlon Plan developed in the 1950s and, more recently, with its adoption of Economic Value Added, or EVA, as a performance and incentive measure for all of the company's 7500 employees.

With these introductions behind us, I will now turn the floor over to Paul Romer.

1. The Theory Behind the Soft Revolution

Paul Romer: Thanks, Don, for the kind words. And let me also thank Jerry Fair for the chance to meet with this group of CEOs. The ideas that we will be talking about today are on the cutting edge of both research and corporate practice. I'm looking forward to learning from you, the practitioners, in the panel session and in the informal discussions that follow.

I want to start with what might sound like an odd question: How can it be that we are wealthier today than people were 100 years ago? Or, to take it to an extreme, think back 100,000 years ago when our ancestors all lived in hunter–gatherer societies. How could it be that we are wealthier now than people were then? The question is puzzling because, if you add up all the things that we own, it is clear that the underlying quantity of raw materials has not changed over time. To put the point in extreme form, the total physical mass here on earth is the same that it is ever been, and now we have to divide this up among a much larger group of people. So how could it be that we have more total wealth per person than we have ever had before?

When you think about this in the very broad sweep of things, there's only one explanation for this increase in wealth. We took this raw material that was available to us and rearranged it in ways that made it more valuable. We took stuff that was not very valuable and made it much more valuable. So it is not the raw material, or the mass of the things here on earth, that really lies behind economic success and high standards of living; it is this process of rearrangement. And what lies underneath this process of rearrangement are instructions, formulas, recipes, methods of doing things—the things that accountants classify as *intangible* assets if they recognize them at all. They tell us how to take something that is not very valuable and rearrange it into a new configuration that is more valuable.

In recent years, this perspective has changed how economists think about economic growth. We no longer think about the accumulation of more things—machines, factories, and natural resources—as the key to increases in standards of living. Current thinking in economics has even moved beyond the popular concept of investing in human capital. Starting in the 1970s, many economists began to say that 'it is not really physical capital that matters, it is human capital that really drives increases in wealth'. But what we are recognizing now is that there is a different way of thinking about growth that goes beyond thinking about either physical or human capital. The essence of this new way of thinking can be understood in terms of the ideas and formulas that we use to increase the value of raw material. The most important lesson from this new approach is that growth takes place when companies and individuals discover and implement these formulas and recipes. What I want to do today is to convince you that this insight about the growth of nations help us better understand the growth of individual companies as well.

Now, to make my claim a little more precise, let me give you just a couple of examples of these formulas and recipes. Let us start by taking the 100,000-year perspective and ask what we used to do to entertain ourselves. Back in prehistory, the only thing we could do with iron oxide—ordinary rust—was to use it as a pigment in painting cave walls. Over time people learned slightly different formulas, different ways to rearrange and use the rust; we learned to put the pigment in an oil base, spread it on canvas, and thus achieved much more interesting forms of visual stimulation.

Today we take that same iron oxide and spread it on videotape, combine it with some aluminum, plastic, copper, and other things that go into making a VCR—and use the iron oxide to entertain ourselves with images on a television screen. Or we can take the same iron oxide, put it on a disk, put the disk inside a computer, and store all kinds of interesting software that enables you to play games or do work in your office. So, those same basic raw materials—things like iron oxide and copper and steel—can be arranged in ways that are dramatically more valuable than they were before.

We see this same process operating in 'real time' in the new high-tech economy. Think about a typical PC. A PC has about the same raw materials in it today that it had about five years ago—that is, about thirty or forty pounds of copper, iron, silicon, and so forth if it is a desktop PC. But those elements are now arranged in slightly different ways that allow today's PCs to be anywhere from ten to thirty times more powerful than they were just five years ago.

So the driving process in these increases in value, these increases in GDP and in wealth, is the discovery of new and better formulas, recipes, instructions for rearranging things. Of course, it is not just the *discovery* of these formulas and processes that creates value; it is also the carrying out of those instructions, the reworking of that knowledge into physical forms that allow for practical application, I am putting this emphasis on the discovery phase of this two-part process of value creation because it is the second, or implementation, stage that usually gets all of our attention.

When they think about economic activity, most people picture a factory with raw materials and workers going in one side, with some transformation going on inside, and with valuable outputs coming out the other side. That image focuses attention on the second phase, the carrying out of the instructions. The problem with this picture, however, is that it does not help you think about the really deep part of economic activity, which is discovering the instructions in the first place.

If you think back to what a company like US Steel looked like at the turn of the century, you will see that most people who worked there were engaged in the second part of the process—carrying out the instructions. There were people who were transporting ore, feeding fuel into blast furnaces, shaping the steel, and so on. But, at the same time, there were also a few people who were looking for slightly different ways to fuel the blast furnace, trying different types of ore and other raw materials to see what would happen. To be sure, that was a fairly small part of economic activity. But it was clearly there, it was important, and it drove growth back then as it drives growth today. It just was not very visible back then.

Now, let us consider another kind of company operating today. Think about a company like Merck. If you walked around inside Merck and tried to classify what everybody was doing, you would find that almost everyone would be engaged in trying to find new formulas, new instructions, better ways to arrange very simple raw materials—organic molecules. They would be looking for one particular formula that, when implemented, would become the basis for some new pharmaceutical product that would have great value.

Now, who are the present-day analogues at Merck of those people at US Steel who a century ago dug the ore out of the mine, transported it, and fed the blast furnace? These are the people who are actually stamping out the pills at Merck, putting them into bottles, and then shipping them around the country.

But those people are really a very small part of the employment picture of a company like Merck.

This contrast between the present-day Merck and the old US Steel is really a microcosm for the transformation of the entire US economy—and for much of the global economy as well. What has happened over the past 100 years or so is that the entire economy has shifted from looking more like US Steel to looking increasingly like Merck. Although many people are recognizing that this new high-tech, knowledge economy differs in important ways from the old economy, there is still lots of confusion—among economists and businessmen alike—about exactly how to characterize these changes. And since most people don't really understand what is fundamental about the changes, they are having some difficulty learning how to take these lessons from the economy as a whole—and the lessons about long-run growth of nations—and put those lessons to work within the individual business firm.

This change is what I have called the *Soft Revolution*. Economists and businessmen are going through a fundamental change in their conception of the economy. We are now focusing on these soft assets like knowledge, instructions, recipes, formulas. In my own writings, I have used the word *software* as a catch-all term to talk about all of those kinds of inputs into economic activity.

To help you think about these soft assets, I want to borrow a typology that comes from Silicon Valley. There people do not think of the world in terms of, say, land and labour—the way people thought of economies 200 or 300 years ago. They also do not think of capital and labour as the key inputs. What they think of instead are *software*, *hardware*, and *wetware*.

What they mean by the first two terms should be fairly clear. Software is the set of these instructions that I have been talking about—the formulas and processes that we follow when we create value. Hardware includes the tangible assets, the *physical* capital that we use to carry out our transformations. Wetware, the final category, derives its name from the fact that humans have a brain which people in Silicon Valley think of as a 'wet' computer. Wetware represents the *human* input into economic activity. Although some people might find it a little too cute or high-tech, this distinction between software and wetware is meant to remind us that human assets and human capital are fundamentally different from the formulas and processes that I have been calling software. That is really the message that I hope you will take away from my talk, and I hope this message provides a set of issues that we will be able to focus our panel discussion on: What are the key soft assets within a company? How does a firm manage them? How does it produce them? How does management capture economic value from those soft assets?

Now, let me give you just a couple of examples to remind you that software in this sense is much broader than just literal computer software. In the process, I will drive home this distinction between wetware and software.

I once read a story about a company that supplied parts to auto firms. This company owned a factory that stamped out gears. One of the workers operating a press had die on the press that lasted about 30 or 40 per cent longer than the dies on everybody else's presses. When the workers in this part of the factory looked into this issue, they eventually realized that there was just a very small difference in how this worker organized his day. He came in and turned on his press at the beginning of the day, then went to assemble all of his materials, and then started stamping gears. All of the other workers would come in, assemble all their materials first, and then turn on the press and go to work. So, this particular worker was preheating his die without knowing it—and no one else was. And this operation of preheating the die turned out to have the effect of making the die last significantly longer. Other workers began doing the same thing and thereby reduced costs for the firm.

So what happened in this operation? There was a piece of wetware— something that was in this worker's head that he did not even realize the importance of. He and his co-workers turned this into software. Once people realized what the key was here, they could articulate it, they could codify it, they could write it down or explain it to someone else. This meant that it could be translated to every other die-press operator in the factory. So instead of management having to say, 'Gee, there is something terrific about Joe, we wish we had a whole lot more workers just like him', it now had a formula, an instruction that could be used for every press operator in the company. The workers took wetware and converted it into software that could be used over and over again. In so doing, they created a lot of value.

Let me give you another example of the interaction between software and wetware—one that illustrates a different kind of software. I assume most of you have heard of EVA, or Economic Value Added, which is a system for evaluating and rewarding managerial performance. EVA can be thought of as a piece of software that a company can use to structure its reporting and incentive compensation systems to improve the efficiency of it operations.

Now that piece of software, after it gets written down in some instruction manuals and described in seminars, does not by itself lead to increases in economic value. You have got to take that software, teach it to people, convert the software back into wetware that is in somebody's brain. But once you have done that, that software embodied in somebody's brain can change how each worker in the firm carries out his or her activities.

I was talking at lunch with Mike Volkema about how this process took place at Herman Miller, and Mike may talk about this later in the panel. They have had great success with EVA. It is a good illustration of how abstract ideas, codified formulas, can create value in a company.

So, again, there is something distinctive about software. If software were really just like hardware or wetware, there would not really be much point in making a big fuss about it. And this Soft Revolution that we seem to be going through—where intangibles are suddenly coming to the forefront in everybody's thinking about economic activity—really would not amount to very much. We would just put a slightly different label on the things we were managing and then we would proceed on down the road. But it turns out that this potential for reuse makes software really a very different kind of asset from all of the other hard assets and human assets.

There are actually two key differences. The first is that there there is *no scarcity* in the realm of software. There is in fact an incomprehensibly large set of instructions, formulas, recipes, ideas, that we can discover. This is very important for those of us who think about growth at the level of the nation or the world because it helps explain why people who have worried about 'limits to growth' have turned out to be so wrong.

This view was much more common in the 1970s than it is today, but there is still an important fraction of the general intellectual community who thinks that the prospects for growth are very limited. The kind of thing you hear is, 'As soon as income increases in Asia and people in China and India try and consume at the same level as people in the US, then we will all be in big trouble', When you take this view, you are effectively relying on the kind of thinking that I tried to invoke at the beginning of the lecture—the notion that 'there is a fixed amount of mass here on earth and, once everybody else wants their share of it, we are all going to have to get by with less'.

This is just profoundly misleading as a way of thinking about prospects for the future. In effect, there is unlimited scope for discovering new ideas, new pieces of software, new recipes. I am quite confident when I say that there is no reason—looking out 100 years, 500 years, or even 1000 years—that we have to reach a point where there is no more opportunities for growth for the nation as a whole.

And this same lesson applies just as much to the individual firm as it does to the nation. Let me go back to my earlier story about the gears. Think about what a particular gear press operator does as just a sequence of instructions that he carries out every day: First step, collect your materials; second step, turn on your gear press, and so on. Now suppose there are twenty discrete activities that that press operator engages in. (And, if you do not like the press operator example, you can think of this as a problem of, say, taking twenty parts that you are assembling to make a PC.) The relevant piece of instruction here, the relevant piece of software, is simply the list of the order in which the worker carries out these different activities. Another piece of software might say, 'Start instead with the old step seven, then attach part one, and next fourteen'.

Now ask yourself, how many possible sequences are there for ordering those twenty steps? How many different ways are there to order those in a sequence? Well, that number turns out to be ten to the nineteenth power—that is one followed by nineteen zeroes. That number is larger than the total number of seconds that have elapsed since the Big Bang created the universe. If you had been trying all of the possible arrangements to see which ones work best—and if you had been doing a new one every second since the Big Bang—you still would not be all the way through.

So, even something as mundane as stamping out gears or a simple assembly operation admits an enormous amount of variation. And many firms have realized that when they have people producing physical objects, they can also get them to start producing software. If you tell those workers, 'Watch what you are doing. If you see a small variation—if you do something different and something good happens—let us know about it. Find some way to feed that up the organization so that we can ensure that everybody else throughout the organization can do it, too'. Of course, this is what the Japanese have called *continuous improvement*. In the language I am suggesting here, we can see that, in order to accomplish continuous improvement, a firm must take every worker and turn him or her into a potential knowledge worker. Every worker then has the potential to produce software. And, as I suggested a minute ago, there is no sense in which any firm or any country or the world as a whole is going to run out of room to find better ways to do things.

So that scope for unlimited discovery is one important distinguishing feature of software. There is a second important difference between software and other assets—one that appears related, but is actually quite distinct. In contrast to hard assets, the number of people who can use any given piece of software is effectively infinite. For example, take the case I mentioned earlier where the operator turns on the press before gathering his materials. It is not only that one operator who can use that piece of software, that set of instructions, but anyone else in the factory. In fact, anyone else in the world who runs a stamping press can use that same piece of information without taking anything away from the first worker.

This is very different from the economics of a barrel of oil. If I have a barrel of oil and want to use it to run my car, you can not use it at the same time; one of us gets it but not both. If I have a piece of land, either I can build my house on it or you can build your house on it—but we cannot both do it. But a piece of software can be used by everybody at the same time.

This feature of software has two implications. The first is that you can generate enormous value for the world by taking good pieces of software and replicating them, thereby allowing anybody who could potentially benefit from them to use them. From the point of view of the world economy as a whole, this is a very optimistic and encouraging prospect. It says, in effect, that we can take all of the poor people in the world right now, let them use all of the knowledge, all of the discoveries, that we already take advantage of—and we can raise their standard of living without reducing our own. So, from a global economic perspective, this new perspective on value and wealth is much more optimistic than the traditional one—the one based on scarce physical resources that gave economics its nick-name 'the dismal science'.

Now what does all this mean for the people in this audience—for the CEOs of large companies? Once you have got one of these pieces of software, the value to you as a CEO or a shareholder is proportional to the size of the market in which you can sell it. As Mike Murray was just telling us about Bank of America's investment in information technology, once you invest in literal software to run your operations—or in the more figurative kinds of software that literal software makes possible—the return you can capture from that investment grows strictly in proportion to the size of the market where you can use it. Think about what kind of potential that means in a world with five billion people and growing; the potential gains for individuals who can capture good pieces of software and use them over and over again are enormous.

Let me just run through a few examples to help us think about how this process works. If George Eastman had been able to use the formula for Kodachrome only in New York State, it would not have been very valuable, and Eastman Kodak would have never have attained its current size. But Eastman took the same formula and used it with people throughout the entire United States—and then later throughout the world—and enriched both himself and the community of Rochester, New York in the process.

The same thing would apply for literal computer software. If Bill Gates had been able to sell DOS or Windows only in Washington State, he would not be a multibillionaire. When he can sell that same code throughout the US and the rest of the world, the value he can capture for himself and for his shareholders is much larger.

So this process of globalization that we are seeing is just starting. And the kind of consolidation that is going on in the banking industry, with its reuse of many different kinds and levels of software, is still at a very early stage. In many ways, this consolidation designed to realize economies of scale and scope—economies that are made possible in part by new software—may be the dominant driving force in economic activity in decades to come. We will keep discovering new software and improving technology the way we have in the past century. But at the same time we are going to see an enormous expansion in the rate at which valuable software gets translated to the rest of the world in years to come. And that will be good for people everywhere in the world. It will also have spectacular benefits for those firms that manage to get ahead of this process; they will end up capturing a small part of the large value that they create for the world as a whole. And, as the software business has convincingly shown, capturing a small fraction of a huge amount of social value can be very rewarding for shareholders.

Now, let me mention some other characteristics of software that matter for a business firm. First, a fundamental difference between software and wetware is that software is an asset that you can *own*. You can only *rent* the wetware, you never really own it.

The flipside of this observation, however, is that software is very hard to *control*. In some cases you can protect it with copyrights or patents or secrecy, but in most cases you cannot. Managing property rights and capturing value from software is a much more complicated proposition than capturing value from a piece of land or a building or a piece of equipment. So, although there is this enormous potential from capturing value associated with software, management will have to exercise a lot of creativity and subtlety in finding ways to control its software and extract value from it. Again, the literal software industry illustrates how counter-intuitive this process may be. In some cases, the best way to establish control over a valuable piece of software may be give some other piece of software away for free and lock your users in.

Another important implication for business stems from the inexhaustible scope for discovering new things. There is considerable potential for creating value by carefully staking out a part of software 'space' that you own or that you are particularly good at exploring. I like to think of this software space— this set of all possible formulas—as a virtually infinite piece of geography where different firms can go out and stake claims. In deciding on a strategy for your firm, you might say to yourself, 'This is a part of knowledge or formula space that we are particularly good at exploiting. The space of ideas is so large that nobody else is in exactly this same territory trying to compete on exactly the same grounds'. This gives you a potential advantage. Not only can you exploit any particular pieces of software that you own right now, but you can also get a headstart over everybody else in finding the nearby pieces of software, the small changes in the formulas, the small improvements in how things are done. So there is a potential for firms to identify their real competence in terms of the knowledge space that they specialize in—not just in controlling that space, but in using it to extend the frontiers of knowledge.

Let me just conclude with one final observation. When we think about countries, the most important pieces of software are ideas about how to generate more ideas.

For a nation, one example of this kind of software would be its patent system. In the nineteenth century, Britain had a patent system that was essentially a piece of software, a set of ideas about how to manage the discovery process that was incorporated into the British legal and regulatory framework. Britain's patent system was not very effective. It was very expensive, it did not allow small inventors to participate, and it restricted transfers of patents so you could not actually have markets in patents.

In the United States, we created a different regulatory and legal system, a different set of ideas about how to manage patents. And by creating that different system, we unleashed the enormous potential that existed in this country to make new inventions. Ultimately we surpassed the British both in terms of our total standard of living and our level of technological expertise. Today the average income of US citizens is about $6000 higher than that of their British counterparts. And this difference can be attributed in no small measure to having the right kind of software for managing the production of software, the right kind of legal or environmental framework.

That change suggests something about the kind of potential that I think exists within a firm to find not just a single formula like Kodachrome, but a system for managing a discovery process in your area of expertise—one that could unleash the power of the people who work for you. By improving your own ability to manage this process of discovery and idea generation, you have the potential to generate enormous value for your shareholders, just as the US patent system generated enormous value for people living in this country.

You may not have thought of it this way, but the success of the business you run depends critically on how well you manage your soft assets. As they say in Silicon Valley, 'Everybody is now in the software business'. Increasingly, we will all find that although software is where all the risk is, it is also where all the returns are.

2. The Case of Ceridian

Don Lessard: Thanks, Paul. Now let us turn to the three CEOs whom I introduced earlier. As I mentioned, we have three quite different firms represented at this table—and the differences among them do a nice job of illustrating this transformation from hard to soft assets. For example, the Ceridian Corporation, which used to be called Control Data before Larry Perlman created Ceridian out of it in 1992, is a company that once was a hardware company, but now makes almost nothing physical. That was Larry's vision when he took over as CEO. Ceridian thus represents a transformation of a company almost completely from hard to soft.

Stan Shih's company, Acer, is one that I have followed with interest for some time. Acer seems to be several years ahead of the general evolution of Taiwan's economy. As Taiwan progresses from being primarily a subcontractor to a skilled manufacturer to a product designer to a general integrator, you see Acer a couple of years ahead of that general shift. So, you can almost see the change of a country just by watching what is happening at Acer.

Of the three companies represented at this table, Herman Miller would appear to be the most like a traditional hardware company. It makes furniture— something we can all see and touch. But, as Mike Volkema is going to tell us, his company too has gone a long way towards becoming a 'software' company since he took over in 1995.

So, let me start the second part of this panel discussion by asking Larry Perlman a question that I will also put to the other two CEOs. And that is: 'Where would you position your firm on this continuum from US Steel to Merck that Paul Romer described earlier? Are you more like Merck? Or are you more like US Steel'?

Larry Perlman: Well, if I was talking to our shareholders, I would certainly tell them that we were like Merck and not like US Steel. But, although we are clearly moving in that direction all the time, we are not all the way there. To help you understand my answer I need to give you a little background on the growth of Ceridian.

It has been only about five and a half years since we created Ceridian. Ceridian is the successor to what used to be Control Data, which, as many of you know, was a large mainframe computer company. Control Data also had a large defense electronics business and was a major producer of hard disk drives. It made a lot of things that Paul Romer would classify as hard.

At the end of the 1980s, the company got into a great deal of difficulty. And at the beginning of the 1990s, I became CEO. That is when I had the pleasure of meeting the Bank of America people—people like Jerry Fair and Dan Boote and Tim Bottoms. The bank was a substantial creditor at the time. And I will tell you—and this is an unsolicited commercial—that working with them through that process of keeping the company from going into Chapter 11 and then building Ceridian has been a very satisfying experience.

But there have been some obstacles along the way. And, it now seems more like ten or twelve years than five. At its peak, Control Data's computer business had about $4 billion in revenue and 50,000 employees. Ceridian today has about $1.2 billion in revenue and 9000 employees. But this year, Ceridian will again make more money from operations than Control Data's computer business ever did in any one year with four times the revenue and five times the number of employees.

We no longer make anything you can drop on your foot. We are a diversified services company. We are in three primary markets—marketing information services, transportation services, and human resources services. We built two of these three businesses out of operations that existed in Control Data but were not central to the company. We acquired the third.

The development of Ceridian in the past few years really serves to reinforce Paul Romer's comments. The model that I have tried to create in each business is to take a core product or capability and build additional services around it. Our core human resources product is payroll. We are the second largest provider today of payroll service—a business that, although it is been around for a long time, has recently become part of an electronic delivery system. What we did was to take our basic payroll product—the processing of a company's payroll data and the production and delivery of the paycheck—and added to it a tax filing product. We are now a large processor of withholding tax payments for companies around the country; we process over $200 billion a year in tax payments.

Next we surrounded these payroll and tax filing businesses with another ring of businesses, such as a time and attendance product—what most of you would recognize as the old time-clock service. Then we added a benefit administration service and a human resources information service business, and we are regularly adding new services. We also developed, from an internal service, an employee advisory resource business, where we do everything from telephone servicing of employee problems to workplace dispute resolution for large companies. To telephone counselling we have added a work-life advisory business that includes consulting on elder care and child care services for companies.

To help understand the business model, visualize a target. The bull's-eye is the core product—in this case paychecks—and the other businesses are each concentric rings around that bull's-eye. And these are all businesses that we have added since the early 1990s.

We have followed this same business model in the two other business areas— transportation services and marketing information services. In the transportation services business, we started as a service that enabled trucking companies to control costs by using a proprietary system to pay for fuel on the road. That core product is the bull's-eye of this target. We have added rings around the fueling product. These include fuel tax reporting, permits, logistics for transportation companies, routing services, and driver support. Each ring is a separate service that we charge for. In the marketing information services business, we started with the radio ratings product of Arbitron and have recently added a number of other products around that core such as demographic data, software for internal management of radio stations, and marketing services and training—all services that produce revenue.

Besides expanding the range of products around these three different cores, we have also been able to grow by expanding geographically, by taking existing products into new markets. For example, in the human resources business, we are now the largest provider of those services in Canada and the United Kingdom. As another example, we are now doing total payroll outsourcing for companies, where we take over the customer's payroll department and take care of all their payroll-related services. In the transportation business, we are moving the services we provide to long haul customers to the local market. The marketing information business is moving outside the United States with the Arbitron 'brand' as the core. And in each new geographic location we will follow the model of leading with core product and building rings around that product.

So, success in finding new ways to apply our fundamental skillset has enabled us to achieve considerable growth and increases in shareholder value.

Starting with a total market capitalization of about $300 million in mid-1991, Ceridian now is a company with a value over $4 billion. To create that kind of shareholder value in a company that sells many related services, you have to replicate and transfer your technology, your know-how. Or, to use Paul Romer's term, you have to find ways to extend the use of your 'software'.

We are in the software business, as Paul describes it, even though we do not think of ourselves as a software company. We are continually creating processes that we can use over and over again. Anybody can do something well once in one location. But to do the same thing well in a lot of locations, and to be able to move out in those concentric circles from payroll processing to, say, time and attendance reporting, has been the key to Ceridian's profitable growth. Finding new ways to use the skillsets of the people in the organization is the challenge. It is not easy. But to be able to do that successfully is, I think, the key to growth in any services business.

Lessard: Larry, where did this idea of concentric circles spreading from a central core come from? Is this a nice, tidy, after-the-fact rationalization of a largely unplanned process, or is it a growth strategy that was formulated and articulated fairly early on in this process?

Perlman: Well, I've been drawing those bull's-eyes and circles for about six years now. But that's not what we did right at the beginning in 1990 and 1991. The first job was just to keep the company from going under. So we were not drawing any targets then; the targets were on our own backs. But ever since we have had enough breathing room to begin thinking about future growth, the company's strategic plan has been guided by this model.

3. The Case of Acer

Lessard: Stan, can you tell us a little bit about where Acer lies on this continuum from Merck to US Steel, and how that has changed over the years?

Stan Shih: I not exactly sure how to answer that question. But perhaps you can answer it for me after I have told you a little about the founding of the company and the vision behind it.

Twenty-two years ago we had a vision of a company that we wanted to create in my home country of Taiwan. We did not want to do what most companies in Taiwan were then doing—that is, serve as manufacturing subcontractors for products designed by US and European and Japanese multinationals. We wanted to participate more directly in the high-tech revolution that was going on in the developed economies.

But, in so doing, we were running against the conventional wisdom about the comparative advantage of lesser developed countries, and about their expected role in the emerging global economy. According to the conventional thinking of the time, Taiwan was not supposed to be involved in that kind of high-tech enterprise. And the business environment in Taiwan certainly did not seem to encourage the start-up of high-tech ventures. There was no local capital market ready to fund such an operation, and there was no established model to pattern the company after.

So I had to come up with a formula, a new approach to doing business. And I had to come up with some capital. The company that is today known as Acer was started with $25,000 that my wife and I put together along with a small group of colleagues. In part because of our limited capital, we were also forced to devise an unusual organizational structure—one that is quite different from both the family-owned businesses that predominate in Asia and Europe and the large public US companies with their dispersed shareholdings. One of the important features of our new organizational structure is managerial and employee stock ownership. But, before I describe that ownership, I need to mention one other aspect of our corporate structure.

Acer today is not a single company, but rather what I like to call a 'global confederation of companies'. We now have five business units with publicly traded shares—and we expect to take as many as another eighteen units public in the next five years. In each of these five business units, our managers and employees own from 10 to 30 per cent of the equity, depending on how 'people-intensive' we judge each business to be. The way it typically works is that, for each of our business units, we allow the managers of that unit to buy shares at book value—generally an amount equal to two or three times their annual salary—while the units are still private. Then, if the unit goes public, the managers have a chance to earn a very high rate of return—in some cases it has been as much as seven or eight times their initial investment.

Because of our managers' large share of equity ownership and considerable decision-making authority, we have been practising things like 'empowerment' and 'intrapreneurship' long before they were given those names. So decentralization combined with managerial and employee ownership is our key piece of organizational 'software', if you will. It has been one of our most important formulas for success, for enabling us to become a $6.5 billion company. The entrepreneurial culture encouraged by this structure has helped us to create innovations in hardware and hardware production in the past, and it is now playing a major role as we transform ourselves into a software company.

So, we have developed a number of technological innovations that have become the standard for high-tech business in Taiwan. Our approach has also enabled us both to move into a number of different high-tech industries in Taiwan and Asia, and to diversify geographically into South America and

Europe as well as the United States. In fact, Acer's success has been one of the main reasons for the currently high level of Taiwan's participation in the global high-tech economy. And the Taiwanese economy is being transformed in the process. Although Taiwan has only recently gone through its own equivalent of the European Industrial Revolution, the Soft Revolution described by Professor Romer is already pushing us toward a new paradigm. With the rise of multimedia and the Internet, many Taiwanese companies are starting to plan for growth based not on tangible goods, as in the past, but on R&D and other intangibles.

As Don Lessard suggested, we have attempted to anticipate these changes by continually repositioning the company. Originally Acer was a hardware company; our business was manufacturing personal computers. Over time, we have been transforming ourselves into a software company. In the future, our strategic plan is make Acer a company that specializes in the development and management of *intellectual properties*.

Why do we want to become an 'IP' company? To the extent that we can innovate and then secure intellectual property rights in our innovations, we can make more money and add value for our shareholders. Up until now, we have not been able to copyright our formulas because of weak protection of intellectual property in Taiwan, and in Asia generally. Our success has created a lot of competitors for us in Asia. And, as a consequence, our shareholder returns, although high, have not been high enough.

So, our plan for Acer in the twenty-first century is to become an IP company. But our fundamental challenge is essentially the same as it's been since we started the company in 1976: how to ensure that all our people are continually making full use of their energy and imaginative powers to create valuable intellectual property. As I said earlier, we have a formula for success that we have relied on the past; and although we cannot copyright that formula, we can use it to keep building and sustaining the corporate culture that has gotten us to this point. The educational system in Taiwan is an effective one—it is an important source of our employees' human or intellectual capital. And the structure of society in Taiwan is more open than in most Asian nations and so affords people more opportunity for innovation. These are both important advantages that we are counting on to contribute to our future development.

And, as I said, at Acer we have attempted to build on these advantages by creating an entrepreneurial culture inside the company. By combining greater decision-making autonomy with significant employee ownership, we have created an environment where people have both the freedom and the incentives to innovate. And this ability and incentive to innovate is critical not only for Acer, but for Taiwan and all of Asia. Although there may be many reasons why Asian economies are struggling today, I like to emphasize the lack of innovation. While American companies are continuously moving toward soft or intangible goods, the Japanese or Asian economic systems continue to be based primarily on the production of tangible goods. Because of our lack of innovation, we are falling behind. The challenge facing Asian companies today is finding ways to participate more directly in the Soft Revolution. Thank you.

Lessard: Thanks, Stan. Before we turn to Mike Volkema, let me ask you one follow-up question. Acer is now in the process acquiring the hardware assets of Siemens Nixdorf in the PC business. When those two companies come together, what differences do you foresee between a German-based engineering firm and a Taiwanese firm in terms of their relative focus on ideas or software as opposed to tangible goods?

Shih: Right now we are very competitive in producing computers. But American companies have already moved into other areas, transforming themselves into the so-called 'computerless' computer companies and 'fabless' semiconductor companies—that is, designers or manufacturers of semiconductors that have no fabrication facilities. So, in the short term we have to focus on increasing our efficiency by reducing costs. But, in the long run, we need, to create more and more software—both literal software, and the kind Paul Romer was talking about. Eventually, we will have to turn ourselves into a software company.

So, although the immediate attraction of acquiring SNI is to provide us with access to the German or European market, the acquisition also plays a role in our long-range plan. By allowing us to combine our R&D efforts in Europe with our R&D in Taiwan and Silicon Valley, the acquisition of SNI will add to our global research capability. In this sense, it is part of our long-term plan to transform Acer into a software company.

4. The Case of Herman Miller

Lessard: Now let us turn to Mike Volkema, CEO of Herman Miller. At first glance, I would say this company looks more like US Steel than Merck. But, Mike, I assume you are going to try convince us that your company looks more like Merck.

Mike Volkema: Herman Miller is a company with a rich heritage. It is about seventy-five years old, and it is responsible for almost every important innovation in the office furniture business in the past fifty years. For example, office furniture systems—you know those 'Dilbert' cubicles that at least some of your people sit in—were invented by the company. The company also invented ergonomic seating for office workers. And although this chair I am now sitting in is not one of ours, I take solace in the thought that this office-type chair is much more comfortable than the banquet chairs you are sitting in.

So, the success of Herman Miller has long been based in large part on its inventive capability—and not only on product innovation, but also on innovation in organizational structure as well. In the 1950s, long before employee participation came into vogue, Herman Miller developed what was known as a Scanlon plan that encouraged employee participation through gain-sharing programs.

But companies, like human beings, go through lifecycles, through periods of decline as well as growth. In the mid-1990s, we hit a period where our profitability began to suffer. The economy was great, our industry was growing in double digits for the first time in about a decade, and our revenues were growing at about the industry rate. The only problem was that our margins on the products that we were selling were eroding. Our operating expenses had gotten out of control, and there had been a whole array of things that the company had tried that did not work and that we had had to write off. The net effect was that in 1995, what should have been a very good year turned out to be, for all practical purposes, just a breakeven year.

That's when someone on the Board of Directors kind of tapped me on the shoulder. Now, we were not in quite as bad a shape as Larry says Control Data was in when they started Ceridian. But it was a time when we had to sit down, organize a new leadership team, and then think hard about what business we are really in.

So, like Ceridian and Acer, we at Herman Miller felt that we were entering into a new era—one that we believed was going to be as radically different from the past as when we moved from an agrarian society to the Industrial Age. We realized that the rapid deployment of technology into the work environment was changing the nature of work and the places where people work. And the change was so great that all of a sudden our old concept of furnishing offices did not sound like a great business to us. It no longer looked like a growth industry. During the 1970s and 1980s, the business was very stable and predictable. Even though we were in a business that everybody liked to classify as 'cyclical', the industry was able to grow steadily at about 4 per cent per year, which was a little above the Gross Domestic Product. And we were a reasonable-size company; our market cap was about $500 million at that time.

So, we as a leadership team began the process of change by saying to ourselves, 'We have got to wake up and realize that the office furniture business is not just about having the best products anymore. It is about services as well as products'. Or, to put it another way, our business is about how to package all of our knowledge about work environments and make it available to our clients. For example, we do strategic facility plans on a consulting basis for some of our larger corporate clients—and these plans reflect our accumulated knowledge. But the design of our products also embodies that organizational knowledge. If it is one of our chairs you are sitting in, we would argue that that chair contains as much packaged knowledge as one of our facility plans.

Then, after rethinking the nature of our business and our sources of competitive advantage, we started deploying new techniques and aligning our organizational structure in order to add value for our clients and our shareholders. Our ideas were by no means all home-grown; we borrowed shamelessly from anybody else we thought had an idea that we could use. For example, we deployed Toyota production system methodology and Q9000 on the shop floor. We are also a big user of economic value added, or EVA, for evaluating performance and as the basis for incentive pay. Within a one-year period, we put literally every single one of our 7500 employees through our EVA 101 course. Both of these pieces of organizational 'software', if you will, have really paid off for us. They have encouraged our employees to develop value-adding practices and then replicate them throughout the organization.

The net effect of this rethinking and changes by the new leadership team is that, after my first three years on the job (and I am celebrating that third anniversary, by the way, because someone reminded me when I took the job that the average life expectancy of a CEO is three years), our market cap is up about 400 per cent. Although we are using no more capital today than we used in 1995—thanks in part to our EVA program—our sales have grown from $1 to $1.7 billion. And I attribute a lot of that success to a whole group of leaders who got together and decided what packaged knowledge we were to employ—not only internally but also as we tried to reach out to customers to figure out new and better ways to serve them.

Lessard: Mike, one point that came up both in your comments and in Larry's is this question of how knowledge is captured by the organization. It starts out as wetware, a better idea in some employee's brain. For example, somebody in one of the plants figures out how to do something better. My question is this: What do you do to increase the probability that somebody in your organization recognizes promising new things when they happen—and, perhaps just as important, that when such things are recognized, they are then transformed into software that can be used throughout the company? How do you organize this discovery and transformation process?

Volkema: We are dealing with clients, and we are dealing with products. But let me focus on the product side. The first thing that we tried to do with our product design and development was to figure out what our commercialization process was—and, having figured it out, then to codify it in such a way that everyone would understand and follow it. So, you first have to identify your product innovation process, and then subject the process itself to a continuous-improvement kind of monitoring on an ongoing basis.

Especially with some of the lean-thinking kinds of principles, the real challenge is how to get the new information into the system. The danger is that if you do not get people to adhere to a process that you have determined is the right one, then you can end up taking one step forward and two steps backward. So, although I am a believer in continuous change and improvement,

I also believe in developing and communicating a procedure for making changes that everyone understands and follows. In some instances, we have been good at that and in others we have not been so good.

Perlman: I agree that the process for making changes is important. But to me the real challenge has been to develop the ability to recognize a valuable innovation—the ability to determine that somebody really is carrying out a process better than somebody else and then capturing that practice and replicating it throughout the organization. To do that effectively requires measurement systems that measure the right things.

In services businesses like ours, I think people often measure the wrong things. For example, there tends to be a focus on minimizing transaction costs while ignoring customer satisfaction and retention. When business is good, as it is now, everybody gets excited about getting new customers. And the trend toward outsourcing has been a great source of revenue growth for Ceridian's businesses. But I keep saying, 'Wait a minute, you guys are not spending enough time thinking about retaining the customers that you have and selling additional services to them'. I am now insisting on measuring and tracking the number of separate billable services we provide to existing customers.

5. Protecting Intellectual Property (and the Issue of Microsoft)

Lessard: Now that each of our three CEOs has told us a little about his company, I want to focus the rest of the discussion on some specific issues that arise in managing soft assets. And perhaps we can start with this challenge of protecting intellectual property that is now facing Stan Shih at Acer. Paul, what advice would you give Stan?

Romer: Perhaps one way to start thinking about this issue is to envision another continuum with Merck, which has always insisted on having very strong protection of its intellectual property, at one end, and this time with Xerox at the other end—and let us call it Xerox PARC, in particular, because it used to have a very open policy in sharing its intellectual property. In the case of Xerox PARC, a lot of people have gotten a free ride and made money off of its discoveries.

So, Stan, in terms of your business processes and your business model, I would say that you are a little closer to Xerox PARC than maybe you want to be. You seem to be trying to move a bit in the direction of Merck.

Shih: Yes, that is right. But it might help you to understand my position if I tell you a little about Chinese culture or history. Intellectual property rights is a relatively new concept in Asian societies. The customary assumption is that innovations and intellectual property belong to society and not to the individual or company who discovers them. This, of course, is in direct contrast to the Western notion that individuals or enterprises can actually own and protect intellectual property.

And, because the Chinese system effectively makes all ideas common property, it discourages innovation. It also discourages people from sharing their innovations inside companies, which they might do if they had the protection of a patent. In the Chinese culture, it is customary for the master to pass down his knowledge only to his successor, not to outsiders. And the strength of this tradition can be explained, at least in part, as a result of the absence of legal protection of intellectual property. Without such protection, secrecy may be the only way to benefit from a new idea.

But when I started our company, I said to myself that the Chinese view of intellectual property is wrong. We must find a way to create a culture of shared knowledge. We should make sure that the master transfers his know-how to all the people—or at least to all his colleagues inside the company. The disadvantage of our open approach at Acer, however, is that there is no means of protecting our intellectual property. As I said earlier, our competitors in Taiwan and Asian quickly imitate our ideas and cut into our profits.

So, that is my first point. My second point has to do with the small size of the Asian markets. And the small size of these markets, together with the absence of legal protection of intellectual property rights in Taiwan or Asia, has resulted in a situation where there are many duplicates of the same product—many more than in the United States, where you have a big market and where if you own something, you copyright it. In the United States, you can become rich just by writing a book. No one in Taiwan can become rich by writing a book. If I write a book all I do is share my knowledge with people who will become my competitors.

And that is why I am positioning my company to become an intellectual property company in the twenty-first century. One of our aims of investing in the United States and Europe is to get copyright protection for some of our intellectual properties. This is an important part of our plan to create the software that we can use to achieve higher returns for our shareholders.

Lessard: Looking at these different property rights systems is a useful exercise, if only because very often we do not notice what parts of our own systems work well. The US system encourages innovation by allowing companies some protection for their discoveries, while the companies themselves encourage sharing of information inside the firm. By contrast, Taiwanese firms as a rule seem to have limited information sharing *within* firms and no legal protection against transfers of trade secrets *among* firms. To recognize a useful innovation, sometimes you have to look at something that is quite different.

Romer: I agree, and I think there is a very interesting message behind Stan's story. We cannot have an economy based on ideas if a firm cannot capture some of the value from the ideas it develops. But there is another side to this issue of intellectual property rights—something that can be illustrated from one of Mike Volkema's recent experiences. Property rights over ideas and software are much more complicated than property rights over physical objects. Property rights over land are conceptually very simple. In that case the optimal system is to have sharp, unambiguous, absolute boundaries—property rights with infinite lives—and that is really the end of the story.

But when you get into intellectual properties, it is much more complicated. You clearly need some forms of intellectual property protection or nobody will write the book, nobody will create the software. Mike Volkema at Herman Miller had a recent experience with patent litigation where, as I understand it, the claim on the other side was not so great, but our system for protecting property rights is so expensive that Herman Miller settled rather than try to get a resolution.

When we think about property rights, however, it is important to remember that we cannot only have a system that is too expensive to operate, but also one that could ultimately give protection that is too strong. If we had given AT&T an infinite-lived patent on the transistor, everybody in the world who wanted to do something new with the transistor would have had to negotiate a contract with the people at AT&T first. This could have significantly slowed down the development of the whole digital electronics industry.

So, as all countries move ahead, I think we have got to believe that nobody has as yet got exactly the right set of systems, or the right national software, for protecting intellectual properties. Just as China and Taiwan need to move toward a little bit stronger protection, I think we in the United States need to do two things: first, we need to rationalize our system to make it less costly to operate; second, we need to differentiate a little more explicitly between some types of software that really should have very long patents or intellectual property protection, and other forms where perhaps we should not give as much protection as we do.

Lessard: That begs the question: What do you think about the current controversy over Microsoft? Do you agree with the Justice Department's case, or should Microsoft be viewed as a national treasure and be allowed to proceed unfettered?

Romer: That case falls just exactly in the context of this trade-off I was just describing. Let me start with what I think is the case for allowing Microsoft to operate without intervention. Microsoft has been able to expropriate the value from a lot of new inventions in the software industry and then bring them all in-house either by buying them or copying them. Then it has put these innovations in a package that is very inexpensive. So there's a sense in which

Microsoft has provided a very inexpensive product to consumers precisely by weakening intellectual property rights in the software industry.

Lessard: This is the Robin Hood theory of Microsoft.

Romer: Think about Postscript, for example. Postscript had some intellectual property and some software for managing the screen and the printer. And they wanted to charge a very high license fee for it. But Microsoft essentially said, 'We are going to drive you out of business or we are going to invent around you. Either way, we are not going to pay the kind of licensing fees that you want'. But if Adobe had gotten its way and charged maybe $100 for its part of the license, the $1000 PC would never have been possible. So there is a good side to having a single monopolist like Microsoft that can keep overall costs for software down.

Now, what is the bad side? The bad side is that when they can extract the value from a new inventor like Postscript, or from a new operation like Netscape, then you run the risk that there is going to be too little left on the table for anybody who is a new inventor. So there are areas in software now where the venture capitalists will say, 'Even if you have got an extremely good idea, we are not going to fund you because you are too close to Microsoft. We know that the best-case outcome for us is that we get into negotiations with Microsoft and they buy us out; in the worst case, they just steal the ideas and we get nothing'.

So, in a sense, letting Microsoft run free is a bit like having very weak intellectual property rights protection for everybody else in the software industry. That keeps prices low, but it could stifle innovation. Even without extremely strong patent protection or legal protection, because of the nature of the market forces, such companies could end up in a position that is so strong that they prevent new firms from entering the market. There may no longer be any scope for a company like Intuit to bring into existence a new application like Quicken.

So the way I would judge how to proceed on a policy basis is to ask the question: What should we do to keep innovation proceeding as rapidly as possible? The point I was trying to suggest is that sometimes you can slow innovation down if you make intellectual property rights too strong. At the same time, though, it is also important to keep in mind Stan's case, where intellectual property rights are too weak. In that case, governments need to strengthen property rights, to get more innovation—and that is a very important message for some parts of the world.

What we need to do in the United States is to stay somewhere in the middle where we get the benefits of sharp competition and low prices, on the one hand, but where there is still enough room and incentive for new firms to come in and innovate. But let me also say that trying to resolve this pretty complicated trade-off using antitrust law is like using a blunt axe to do some very subtle surgery.

Perlman: I agree with Paul that the courtroom is the wrong place to deal with that issue. After all, Microsoft did not achieve the kind of market dominance they now have simply by using the intellectual property laws that we have been talking about. I think it is a pretty good lesson for all of us that the only reliable protection against competition is the ability to build a strong market position and to keep moving forward with it. The best defense is a good offense—and Microsoft's done an extraordinary job of this.

Paul, you earlier mentioned the example of the ownership of land. I think a more relevant legal analogy for this discussion are all the legal problems that surround water and riparian rights. After all, everybody is entitled to the water but nobody owns it. The answer to this problem has always been to be as far upstream as you can get. I think that that is what Microsoft has been able to do and I think that is what the competitive battle is really about—it is about how you get upstream.

I also believe that over time the solution to this legal problem is going to come from market forces. Long before this antitrust case gets resolved other competitors are going to find ways to get access to that water.

Volkema: I recently gave a speech to my son's graduating class at college. And when I told him I was going to mention Microsoft, he said to me, 'Dad, you may get some questions about when profit becomes *too much* profit?' My response was, 'Microsoft is a great example of value pricing'. As Paul was saying earlier, if a lot of individual firms were to try and develop their own software with the same functions as Windows 98, those firms could not afford to do what Microsoft does for anywhere near the price that Microsoft charges. As a consequence, most of us are more than willing to pay them their 80 per cent margins.

---

6. Software and Mass Customization

Lessard: The main point emerging from this discussion seems to be that a great deal of value can be created by transforming wetware into software, by taking an insight or discovery by an employee or group of employees and then implementing that discovery by replicating it on a larger scale. But this focus on scale and standardization would seem to be at odds with another broad trend—namely, consumers' growing demand for more choices, for customized solutions, particularly in the service industries. So how do you resolve this apparent contradiction?

Romer: You can see from the cost, or supply, side how powerful this dynamic is. You incur the costs once; and if you can sell it many times over, then there are very big returns to you. Your costs just do not scale with your sales. The question is how to take advantage of this opportunity. What you face on the demand side of this is a lot of people with very different situations and very different demands. The big successes I think have been organizations that have been able to figure out ways to standardize while still achieving a wide variety of product offerings.

I know it sounds like an oxymoron, but there is more than an element of truth in the term *mass customization*. What this really comes down to is that you can standardize certain pieces of the process, and then allow either your customers or other producers to customize the last piece. This way, you get the benefits of the standardization. There is a whole lot of work that Lotus can do in putting together the spreadsheet for you, or that Microsoft now does now in putting together the spreadsheet for you. But they really just give you the tool which you then must adapt or customize to solve your particular problems.

So I think a lot of this software—replicable, general-purpose stuff—that is getting developed is actually a kind of tool rather than a completely specified final solution. And I suspect that this is a central element in what Larry Perlman does at Ceridian because every company he goes to must have slightly different requirements in terms of how it runs its human resources systems. There are general systems that you must be able to customize.

Perlman: Your point is a very important one. For example, we have done a good job of differentiating our payroll service from competitors who have been successful at offering a relatively standardized solution. Ceridian focuses on customizing the payroll service for customers. The downside of this customization approach is that it costs money, and Ceridian's margins have been historically much lower than those of the competitors. But the strategy of adding new services around the payroll core that I described earlier is important to improving margins because, by creating value for customers through this broad idea of software, margins have been improving.

But there are limits to this kind of customization. We do not want a significant portion of revenues to come from consulting. Consultants can not replicate themselves very effectively. Looked at as a business that charges purely for the services of individuals on a one-off basis, it is not a business where we could create the kind of software that allows us to leverage resources and develop repetitive revenue.

So, what we have to do in Ceridian's businesses—and in the marketing, information business in particular—is to avoid falling into the trap of becoming a consulting firm. The more you get into consulting, the farther away you get from the advantages of standardization—the ability to use software over and over again. And that is one of the keys to success in these services businesses. It is achieving a balance between customization and standardization—providing customers with customized solutions that produce repetitive, predictable revenue without getting dragged into a resource-intensive consulting service.

Shih: We are now working on the customization of our PCs. To accomplish this, I came up with a concept called the 'X-computers'. The X signifies that the product will have multiple applications, many of them not yet invented or discovered. We believe that, as the PC becomes a tool for daily use in homes as well as offices, customization will become very important.

These new applications will be based on the Internet and the PC open standard. So, the infrastructure is already well established. Our task is to repackage these applications in a form to make it simple. It is not only a cost issue, it is simplicity, too. If we can produce a simpler product, more people will buy it, and we can reduce the total cost of ownership by spreading our investment costs over a much large customer base.

But the key in this is reducing costs and the time required for the customization. Of course, our new X computer will still have standard features, parts in common with our older machines. And it is by reusing the common technology—whether it is software, hardware, or the whole service infrastructure—that we are able to lower costs.

Romer: Let me just elaborate on that last point. This concept of reusable components is really fundamental to how you achieve reusability while still allowing for customization. That shows up in hardware, as Stan just told us. But it is also increasingly showing up more in the creation of literal software. It is been promised over and over again by people in computer-aided software engineering, though without results. But we may really see it some day.

Lessard: Notice the range we have achieved with our definition of reusability. We have gone from reusability of specific components in different products to the reusability of Larry's strategic planning concept of concentric circles surrounding a target core competence. Larry, do you have other examples of how you reuse specific aspects of one of your products or services?

Perlman: To reuse a process you must be able to understand your customers' needs and respond with innovations. Take Ceridian's marketing information services business. We measure radio listenership and transform raw information into a data service that we sell to radio stations. Those ratings serve as their currency when they sell advertising. Through a joint venture, we now have access to a lot of demographic information about magazines and newspapers readership. And this has enabled us to take the same data that we sell to radio stations, combine it with the new data from the joint venture and from other sources, and develop a product for advertisers that will allow them to use media much more effectively.

That is an example of taking the same data, modifying it or combining it with something, and reusing it. In so doing, we have created a whole new market that was not available before. Part of the key to this was new technology that allowed us to do data mining—and this in turn has allowed us to combine different databases from different sources.

And there are applications of this example in many other business situations. For example, take Mike Volkema's business. If it ranges from selling somebody a chair to figuring out the whole office system, it seems to me there have got to be lots of interesting ways to repackage services to attract different customers.

Volkema: I agree with you, Larry. What we are both experiencing is part of a radical shift away from a 'product-push' society—one in which companies figured out what products they could produce, and then pushed them in the market. Of course, there was always some effort to determine what markets wanted, but it was a static kind of analysis; it was a fixed target that was designed primarily to make things easier for the production people.

Today we are turning into what I call a 'Federal Express' society—one that places two major demands on producers: One, we are addicted to speed; and, two, we want lots of options. And the key to success in this new world is using the new technology in a systematic and intelligent way to understand the customer need—and then modifying our products to meet that need.

Let me give one example of that process. In dealing with large organizations, we have something that we call 'tailored product solutions'. In such cases, the companies often begin with the view that they have certain special requirements, but they want the solution in standard lead times. We accommodate this by aligning all of our capabilities— right down to the shop floor—to support one-of-a-kind solutions.

And, as Larry said, one of the real surprises in all of this is the information that we get from just going through the process of designing solutions for our clients. In particular, we often gain new information about best practices that becomes resellable, or reusable, in a different setting. For example, we have found ways to lower our clients' churn rate—that is, their cost of moving furniture around during organizational changes—from $600 to $300 per white collar worker per year by making some simple changes in the product configuration and supporting services. All of a sudden you realize that somebody can be twice as productive as somebody else at managing the same task. So, you capture that insight, package it, and then find ways to use it to help other customers lower the cost of operating their offices.

---

7. Software and Organizational Innovation

Mike Murray: Paul, how do you prevent replication from becoming calcification? When large organizations find a successful way of doing something, a bureaucracy tends to grow up that says, 'This is the way we do it here because, by God, that is what has gotten us where we are today. So, yes, we will let you customize, but only within a very narrow band'. It usually takes an outside competitor to come in with a new way of doing things.

Romer: Let me tell you another story that I hope you will remember. It is somewhat like the gear stamping story but it goes in the other direction.

Some mechanics operating in the American Airlines maintenance facility in Chicago found a slightly different procedure for taking engines on and off DC-10s. And although it appeared to be more efficient, the new procedure ultimately led to a case where the engine fell off a plane in flight and a lot of people were killed. The lesson here is that although you often see cases where a little bit of deviation from existing practices can be very productive and lead to extra value, there are other cases in economic life where we have to adhere very strictly to what's known as the best practice and be very careful when we deviate from that.

So, as a business leader, what that leaves you with is a very constrained trade-off. You would like people to experiment, to come up with different ways to do their jobs. But in many cases you have got to constrain their freedom. The key, perhaps, is having the flexibility to be able to shift back and forth quickly between two apparently contradictory positions. On the one hand, you have to have a set of best practices and make sure everybody adheres to it. But, at the same time, you have to be constantly in search of new best practice—and when you find it, you have to be prepared to promulgate that quickly throughout the firm.

Now, from the point of view of someone who is a macroeconomist, I think individual firms are typically better at finding one good practice, instilling it, and then having their workers stay with that than they are at substituting new ones. How we solve the problem of getting new practices implemented in the economy is by letting inflexible firms collapse and die. So, you have a firm that is very good at one task—say, IBM's expertise with mainframes; and from the economy-wide point of view, if IBM cannot handle the switch to PCs that is okay. We will just let IBM shrink and we will let a whole new kind of organization come up—one that revolves around firms like Acer and Intel and Microsoft, and that does things in a very different way. So, from the economy-wide perspective, a lot of entry of new firms and a lot of competition from new entrants is part of how we deal with the risk of calcification.

Now, that does not help you as a business leader thinking about the future of one of the biggest banks in the world. There might be ways to simulate a little bit of that within the organization. For example, think about what Stan has done at Acer, or the structure of Thermo Electron in Cambridge. Both of these companies have sold minority interests in several of their subsidiaries to the public, thereby setting up small, related organizations—each with a high degree of autonomy. By so doing, you can sometimes create a kind of competition within the organization where a new unit can grow up and displace an old one if the new unit finds a better way to do things.

So I suspect that we will see more of this model of having competition between organizations, in part to increase companies' ability to shift resources fairly quickly from parts of the organization that are no longer productive to new ones at the cutting edge. But it frankly is not something we have seen a whole lot of success with in the past. To avoid the kinds of problem that arose with the airline engine, most organizations create strong pressures towards uniformity and consistency. In so doing, they leave enough power for the existing entrenched interests to kill off the new divisions. For example, the mainframers at IBM were apparently able to hamstring the PC division. So, I think this is one of these meta-ideas—an idea about how to manage ideas—that will be very important moving ahead. Perhaps Stan's structure with a lot of different organizations that are linked through equity ownership but still actually have different shares will prove to be the model of the future.

8. Accounting for the Value of Intellectual Property

Cheryl Francis: Up to this point, we have talked in broad conceptual terms about continuous improvement and best practices. But, as Larry mentioned earlier, we need better measures of performance to tell us whether what we have discovered is really a better practice than the status quo. In fact, it seems as if economists' definition of productivity is itself in a state of continuous flux. So, my question is: How can we use our accounting and measurement systems to determine when we have a valuable innovation? And how do we measure the gains from developing new kinds of software?

Romer: I will respond by saying what I think economists should say more often, which is 'Gee, I do not know'. And let me underscore this point. There is a lot of talk right now about 'intellectual capital', talk that suggests that we could treat what I was calling software as a kind of capital asset. It also goes on to suggest that we can use standard accounting procedures—essentially standard measures like historical cost and transfer prices—and apply them to soft assets.

But the differences between software and other assets mean that a lot of this accounting machinery would be inappropriate. For example, if you have got someone in a firm who has got a really good piece of software, a good idea, it would be a big mistake to have a transfer price on that idea within the firm. As soon as it is working in one place, you ought to get it working throughout the whole firm. You should not let a price impede that process.

So, I think that, at a fundamental level, we do not yet know what are the analogues of cost measures, transfer prices, and so forth that will work. And, again, I think this is one of those levels of metasoftware, or metaideas, where we are going to see a lot of experimentation out into the next century.

Lessard: A number of people have already commented briefly on this issue. Larry mentioned the importance of using measures of customer satisfaction and customer retention, as well as measures of cost and efficiency, as a guide to evaluating the sustainable, long-run profitability of a company's services. And Mike Volkema suggested that EVA could be an improvement over the conventional accounting measurement model because it makes employees consider the amount of capital they are using in their activities.

What can each of the three of you say about how you have had to change your financial discipline to accommodate this change? And is there any common denominator in these changes? Although we academics may not have the answers to these questions, you have to deal with them every day, so let us find out what you do.

Perlman: I would never venture an opinion after an economist said he did not have an answer.

But, in all seriousness think about how long it has taken us—and about how far away we still are—from getting accurate measurements on the manufacturing floor. We are still using standard cost systems; it is very hard to get people to use the input/output kinds of measurements that are now being proposed by activity-based costing advocates. As a consequence, we really do not yet know how profitable each individual manufacturing activity and process is. We know how profitable the company is as a whole, but we do not really know how to measure the profitability of the components.

I have been involved in the disk drive business for a long time. One of the big challenges in financial planning for that business is to determine when to switch a production line from product A to product B. It is in part a difficult financial measurement problem, and I do not see people spending enough time thinking about it, much less providing a solution.

From my perspective, I think the answer to these kind of measurement problems is more decentralization. I know it is really hard for a big organization to move in this direction. But I believe that the key to responsiveness and profitability in many service businesses is much greater reliance on decentralization, whether it is a human resources services business that is operating out of a lot of different offices or a bank that has to break itself up into a number of smaller geographic units as well as product lines to try and figure out what's working well and what is not working well. I do not know how else you get the flexibility within an organization unless you try to break it down into smaller pieces and measure how well some things are working.

But, as both Paul and Mike Murray suggested earlier, that goes against human nature—the natural desire of top management to retain as much control as possible. Decentralizing also means that we must have a lot more tolerance for failure and mistakes. The first time somebody makes a bad loan because the bank's senior management gave them a lot of flexibility, and you say, 'Okay, you are now working for the local savings & loan association as a teller', that consequence is quickly learned by people throughout the organization. After something like that, it is very hard to get people to try new things and take risks.

So, my view is that you should decentralize, you should develop good measures for the decentralized activities, and then you must react quickly to what the measurements are telling you. And I think that organizations that follow this prescription eventually learn how to do it well. But it takes time—and a few mistakes—to reach that point.

Volkema: In the context of this measurement issue, let me just say a brief word about our EVA program. EVA may be able to help address a number of measurement issues because it is both a financial framework and an incentive system.

EVA has enabled Herman Miller not just to conserve capital, but to stretch the capital that we have as far as we can—and in productive ways. As I mentioned earlier, in the past three years, we have increased sales from $1 billion to $1.7 billion without any increase in capital employed. Our managers and employees have found ways to reduce our companywide inventories by $17 million, or 24 per cent. Our accounts receivable have been reduced 22 per cent from fifty-five days in 1995 to forty-three days at the end of 1997. At the same time, our total building space has been reduced by 15 per cent. And, again, all of these efficiencies have been achieved while growing sales at almost 15 per cent a year. In the process, as I said, our market cap has quadrupled—and the value of our employees' ownership stake in Herman Miller has risen by over $300 million.

So, like Larry, I too think there is a lot to be said for empowering people, provided your managers and employees have strong incentives to create value—and, as I said earlier, provided your people stick to your established process for making changes.

Shih: I too agree with Larry's point about decentralization, and that is reflected in the organizational structure of our company—in our participative management style and employee stock ownership. But we do not really rely much on *internal* measurement systems for performance evaluation or for incentive purposes. As I mentioned earlier, five of our business units are now publicly traded. In each of those cases, we have effectively let the market take care of our measurement and incentive problems. When one of our business units is doing something extraordinarily well, we take it public and then let the market tell us whether or not it is continuing to perform—and our managers are rewarded according to its judgements. And, as I also said earlier, our plan in the next five years is to take eighteen more business units public—as many as we can.

---

9. In Closing

Romer: I do not want to get into a fight with Larry about who is more ignorant about this measurement issue, but I cannot let him have the last word on this. My belief is that business people are usually way out ahead of the economists. It is business people like Larry who will have to make choices on questions like how to manage intangible assets. The innovations in this area will come from them, not from economists who solve these problems in the ivory tower. Economists will come along afterwards and just codify the results after you have worked them all out.

Lessard: I think that is a nice note to end on. The Soft Revolution clearly has a lot of resonance with recent global developments in business and finance. And I would like to thank all of the panelists for taking part in this. They were responding in real time. They heard Paul's talk and ten minutes later they were back here responding to questions. Thank you all very much.

4 The Stock Market and Investment in the New Economy: Some Tangible Facts and Intangible Fictions[1]

Stephen R. Bond and Jason G. Cummins

'In the Old Economy, the value of a company was mostly in its hard assets—its buildings, machines, and physical equipment. In the New Economy, the value of a company derives more from its intangibles—its human capital, intellectual property, brainpower, and heart. In a market economy, it is no surprise that markets themselves have begun to recognize the potent power of intangibles. It's one reason that net asset values of companies are so often well below their market capitalization'.

(Vice President Al Gore, Microsoft CEO Summit. May 8, 1997)

'I think there is such an overvaluation of technology stocks that it is absurd . . . and I'd put our company's stock in that category'.

(Steve Ballmer (President, Microsoft), Wall Street Journal (p. C1) September 24, 1999)

1. Introduction

Broadly characterizing, there are two opposing views about the relationship between the stock market and the New Economy. According to one view—expressed in the quotation from Vice President Al Gore—intangible investment helps to explain why companies' market values are so much larger than the values of their tangible assets. According to the other view—expressed, ironically, by the President of Microsoft, the company that is one of the premier representatives of the New Economy—stock market valuations have become unhinged from fundamentals. Even though Gore and Ballmer may have ulterior motives, their perspectives frame the debate about the relationship between the stock market and the New Economy.

One way to start thinking about this relationship is in terms of the theory of stock market efficiency. When the stock market is strongly efficient, the market value of a company is, at every instant, equal to its fundamental value, defined as the expected present discounted value of future payments to shareholders. If we abstract from adjustment costs and market power, then we can highlight the central role strong efficiency plays: it equates the company's market value to its enterprise value—that is, the replacement cost of its assets. However, the most readily available measure of the enterprise value in company accounts data, the book value of tangible assets, is typically just a fraction of the market value—and for New Economy companies it is an even smaller fraction because they rely on intangible assets more than do Old Economy companies. Hence, the rest of the enterprise value must come from adjusting for the replacement cost of tangible assets and including intangible assets. When price inflation, economic depreciation, and technical progress are modest, the difference between the replacement cost and the book value of tangible assets is relatively small. This means that intangibles account for the remaining difference.

Unfortunately, it is difficult to gauge whether intangibles do, in fact, make up the difference because they are, by their very nature, difficult to measure. As a result, the accounting treatment of them by the Financial Accounting Standards Board (FASB) is conservative—which means that companies must select methods of measurement that yield lower net income, lower assets, and lower shareholders' equity in earlier years. Thus expenditures for R&D, advertising and the like are expensed even though they represent expected future profits.[2] The stock market forms expected values of these future profits but the assets generating them will *never* show up on the balance sheet. Consequently, it is argued by many researchers that the fundamental accounting measurement process of periodically matching costs with revenues is seriously distorted, adversely affecting the informativeness of financial information.[3]

The practical appeal of thinking in terms of strong efficiency is that the purported growth of intangible capital that characterizes the New Economy provides a ready explanation for the stock market expansion. Some researchers—Hall (1999), for example—have even argued that the value of intangible assets can then be inferred from the gap between market capitalization and the measured value of tangible assets. The practical drawback, however, is that this makes the inferred valuation of intangible capital the critical determinant of market efficiency. At a basic level then the logic of this approach is circular: accounting principles for intangible assets are unsatisfactory and, as a result, it is difficult for market participants to value companies; but strong stock market efficiency is assumed in order to assign a value to intangibles.[4] In essence, intangibles are the New Economy version of 'dark matter' in cosmology. The fundamental question in the two fields is the same: can an elegantly simple model be justified based on what we cannot easily measure?

When the stock market is not strongly efficient the firm's market value can differ from its fundamental value. This formulation sidesteps the question whether intangibles account for the missing value of companies, only to point up another one that is just as thorny. If the stock market fails to properly value intangibles, then what do market prices represent? One perspective is that the stock market is efficient in the sense that prices reflect all information contained in past prices (called weak efficiency), or that they reflect not only past prices but all other publicly available information (called semistrong efficiency). These weaker concepts of market efficiency are not necessarily inconsistent with deviations of market prices from fundamental prices that are caused, for example, by bubbles. Another perspective eschews efficiency in favour of behavioural or psychological models of price determination. For our purposes we focus only on whether market prices deviate from fundamentals, not why, so we use the term 'noisy' share prices as synecdoche for any of the potential reasons for mispricing.

Another way to begin thinking about the relationship between the stock market and the New Economy is purely empirical. Tobin's average q—which is defined, in its simplest form, as the ratio of the stock market value of the firm to the replacement cost of its assets—provides the empirical link. Under conditions familiar from the q theory of investment, average q equals unity when the stock market is strongly efficient and we ignore taxes, debt and adjustment costs. This means that the market value of the firm is just equal to the replacement cost of its tangible and intangible assets. Since intangible capital is difficult to measure, in practice average q is computed using tangible capital. This is why average q can exceed unity and why it must increase as intangible assets become a larger fraction of total assets.

To take specific examples, consider two companies that are intangible-intensive, Coca-Cola and Microsoft. Most of the market value of Coke consists of the value of its secret formula and marketing know-how, neither of which are recorded on its balance sheet.[5] Similarly, according to Chairman Bill Gates, Microsoft's 'primary assets, which are our software and our software development skills, do not show up on the balance sheet at all'. www.microsoft.com/BillGates/Speeches/03-26london.htm. Hence average q, constructed using only the replacement cost of tangible capital, should exceed unity for these companies.

In panel A of Fig. 1, we plot, as a dashed segment, the annual averages of Coke's average q, denoted as q^E, where the superscript indicates that we construct the variable using equity price data. In 1982, at the start of the sample we

Stephen R. Bond and Jason G. Cummins

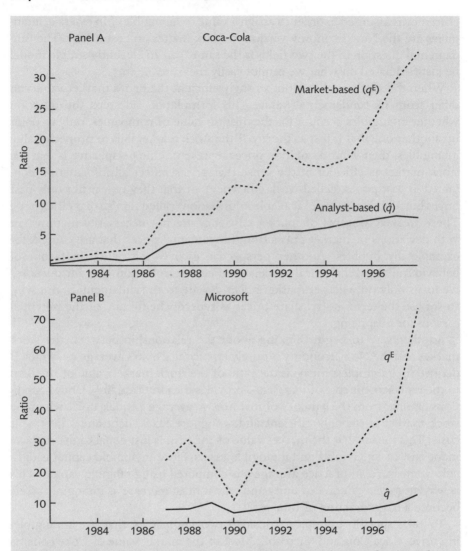

Fig. 1. Market-based and analyst-based q ratios for Coca-Cola and Microsoft, 1982–98.[a]

Note:
[a] q^E is the ratio of the market valuation of the firm's equity to the replacement cost of its tangible capital; $\hat{q}$ is the ratio of the present discounted value of analysts' consensus earnings forecasts to the replacement cost of tangible capital. Both q ratios adjust for debt, taxes, and current assets. Microsoft first issued public equity in 1986.

Source: Authors' calculations based on Compustat and I/B/E/S data.

use in our empirical work, Coke's q^E is 1.[6] If we assume for the sake of argument that we constructed the replacement cost value of tangible assets without error, this indicates that the market under-valued the intangible assets of Coke—indeed, it gave them no value at all. In 1998, at the end of our sample, Coke's q^E exceeds 34. If we assume strong efficiency, then this means that the value of Coke's intangible assets increased from zero to thirty-three times the value of Coke's tangible assets. In other words, according to the market, Coke's intangibles are now worth thirty-three times what its tangible assets are worth, whereas they used to be worth nothing.

We can benchmark q^E by comparing it to a measure of fundamentals that is based on the profits that Coke is expected to generate. We do so using earnings forecasts made by the professional securities analysts, supplied by I/B/E/S and also contained in our dataset. In panel A of Fig. 1 we plot, as a solid segment, the annual averages of Coke's $\hat{q}$, which replaces the equity valuation of the firm contained in q^E with the present discounted value of the analysts' consensus earnings forecasts for the firm. The construction uses the one- and two-year ahead forecasts and the five-year growth forecast.[7] We discount expected earnings over the next five years using the current interest rate on the thirty-year US Treasury bond, plus an 8 per cent risk premium, and include a terminal value correction to account for the value of the company after our forecast horizon. We choose the timing of the forecasts so that $\hat{q}$ is based on the same information set as q^E. By choosing this timing, the market-based measure already incorporates the information contained in the forecasts. In all other respects $\hat{q}$ is identical to q^E. The time-series comparison between Coke's $\hat{q}$ and q^E suggests that Coke's intangible asset growth (as inferred using the assumption of strong efficiency) is not expected by professional analysts to generate similar profit growth.

In panel B of Fig. 1, we plot, as a dashed segment, the annual averages of Microsoft's q^E. When Microsoft enters our sample in 1987, having first issued public equity in 1986, its q^E is equal to 24. By the end of the sample, it has risen to 74. The volatility is perhaps even more notable than the threefold increase. Consider these two facts: in 1990 Microsoft's q^E dropped by more than 50 per cent only to increase more than 100 per cent in the following year; nearly half the total increase over the sample period occurred from 1997, when the value of q^E is 39. We can benchmark these changes by comparing them with changes in Microsoft's $\hat{q}$. When the 50 per cent drop occurred, $\hat{q}$ also dropped, but by about 30 per cent. While q^E recovered dramatically in the following year, $\hat{q}$ increased by less than 15 per cent. Finally, when q^E doubled from 1997 to 1998, $\hat{q}$ grew by about one-third that amount. This comparison suggests that the change in the value of Microsoft's intangibles (as inferred using the assumption of strong efficiency) is not closely associated with changes in what the analysts expect Microsoft to earn in the future.

While we have chosen these companies because they are widely familiar and because their experience has been remarkable, they are, by no means,

Stephen R. Bond and Jason G. Cummins

unusual examples. Rather the increase in the level of q^E—illustrated by Coke's example—and the volatility of q^E—illustrated by Microsoft's example—are microcosms of the broader experience of the more than 1100 companies in our sample. In panel A of Fig. 2, we plot, as a dashed segment, the unweighted

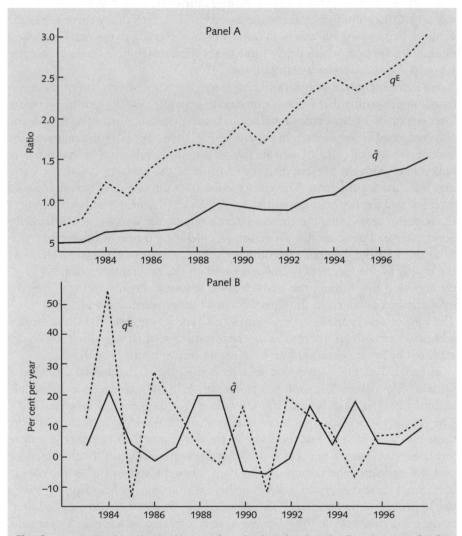

Fig. 2. Average levels and growth rates of market-based and analyst-based q ratios for the entire sample of firms, 1982–98.[a]

Note:
[a] Sample size grows from about 300 in 1982 to more than 1100 in 1998.

Source: Authors' calculations based on Compustat and I/B/E/S data.

average of q^E in each year for the entire sample of companies we observe in each year. In 1982, there are about 300 companies in the sample and the average of q^E is about 0.7. By the end of the sample there are more than 1000 firms and q^E is about 3.0, a 330 per cent increase. Our sample is an unbalanced panel of firms so the increase could reflect entry and exit, but it does not: The average value of q^E increases by about 300 per cent for those firms that are in the sample from 1982 to 1998.

In panel A of Fig. 2 we also plot, as a solid segment, the average annual values of $\hat{q}$. The average value of this new variable is about 0.50 in 1982 and about 1.5 in 1998, for a 200 per cent increase.[8] In every year the standard deviation across firms of q^E is greater than $\hat{q}$. We can further measure the difference between q^E and $\hat{q}$ by defining a new variable called $QDIF = (q^E - \hat{q})/\hat{q}$. The median value of $QDIF$ in 1982 is 0.15 and in 1998 it is 0.75, indicating that a wide gap has opened over time for the median firm in the sample.

In panel B of Fig. 2 we plot the average annual growth rates of q^E and $\hat{q}$. There are a number of years in which the two move together. Notably, the two rise and fall dramatically at the start of the sample and the two track each other through the one recession in our sample, in 1991. But overall the striking feature of the two series is that they are only loosely correlated—the correlation coefficient is only 0.14. Hence, there seems to be limited agreement between the market valuation and the analyst-based valuation of companies. One way for those who believe that we have entered a New Economy to rationalize this finding is to argue that the market is more far sighted than the analysts who cover the firms. Returning to the metaphor of intangibles as 'dark matter' this is akin to saying that the average person who looks up into the sky is better able to measure the missing mass of the universe than the professional astronomer.

To put the issue simply, q^E can increase in two ways: its denominator increasingly omits assets that generate value, or its numerator increasingly over-values assets. While the comparison between q^E and $\hat{q}$ seems to support the latter interpretation we cannot conclusively distinguish between these explanations by examining just q^E and $\hat{q}$. But we can distinguish between them by focusing on the relationship between our measures of q and investment behaviour. Under certain assumptions—detailed in Section 2 where we formally derive the model—average q is a sufficient statistic for total investment. This means that it embodies all the relevant information about investment opportunities.

To understand why studying investment behaviour is helpful, consider the first reason q^E can increase. If the firm's assets increasingly consist of intangibles, then it would be unsurprising to find that q^E is only loosely related, or perhaps even unrelated, to tangible investment behaviour. Turning to Fig. 3, we find that this possibility is not inconsistent with the data. In panel A of Fig. 3, we plot the annual averages of q^E and the tangible investment rate, denoted as I/K, where I is tangible investment and K is the stock of tangible capital.

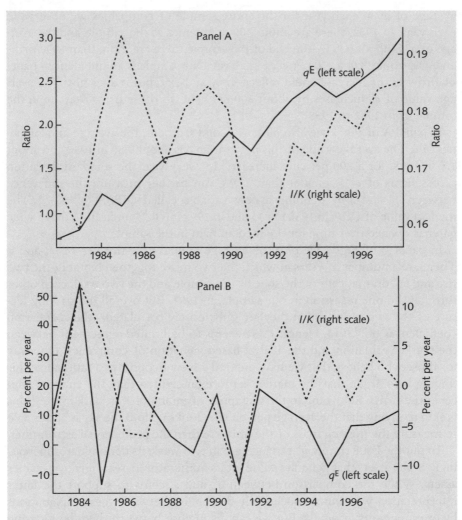

Fig. 3. Average levels and growth rates of market-based q ratios and investment–capital ratios for the entire sample, 1982–98.[a]

Note:

[a] I/K is the ratio of tangible investment to the stock of tangible capital. The sample is the same as in Fig. 2. The correlation coefficient between the growth rates of q^E and I/K is 0.25.

Source: Authors' calculations based on Compustat data.

In panel B we compare the growth rates of I/K and q^E. The correlation coefficient between the two series is positive, but I/K does not closely track q^E—notice that the growth rate of I/K follows the growth rate of q^E during the 1991 recession but that the correlation is actually negative since 1994.

This is the basic puzzle about investment that has been confirmed time and again in empirical studies (see, e.g. Chirinko, 1993a). The disconnect between I/K and q^E results in econometric estimates of the coefficient on q^E that are small in magnitude and/or imprecise, which implies that investment is subject to enormous adjustment costs.[9] This has sparked a number of active research inquiries. The most prominent of these focus on whether capital market imperfections or nonconvex adjustment costs help rationalize this finding (for surveys of these respective literatures see, Hubbard, 1998; Caballero, 1999).

In contrast, we believe that previous results may be spurious because: (1) the underlying model ignores intangibles which are an important part of total investment; (2) share prices are noisy signals of fundamentals; or (3) some combination of both. These possibilities have not been considered because intangibles and fundamentals are difficult to measure.[10] There are two steps in our strategy to deal with these measurement problems. The first step is to develop a model that requires data on only the flow of intangible capital, not its stock. There is no practical way to calculate the stock of intangible assets for the companies in our sample—indeed there is an active debate we already alluded to about whether such an endeavour would be feasible even with new accounting regulations. But no one disputes that intangible investments are observable as advertising, R&D, and the like—these items are expensed on the income statement. We show how to use this information in the following section where we introduce our model.

The second ingredient is the analysts' earnings expectations we have already introduced. Cummins *et al.* (1999) first showed that there is a close time-series link between investment and analysts' forecasts. Although we use the earnings forecasts in a different way, we confirm this finding. In Fig. 4 we plot I/K from Fig. 3 along with $\hat{q}$. Panel B shows the close correlation between the two series. What is particularly striking is that the *turning points* of the growth of I/K are predicted by the growth of $\hat{q}$. Of course, this finding is meant only to be suggestive. Tobin's average q, whether it is constructed with equity price data or analysts' earnings expectations, is an endogenous variable. News—like a new product invention—affects investment as well as the stock market price and analysts' forecasts. The econometric approach we discuss in detail in Section 4 can correct for this endogeneity. In addition, in constructing our measures of fundamentals we have almost surely introduced measurement error. This is likely to be particularly acute in the case of $\hat{q}$ because we have to make a number of assumptions to calculate the present discounted value of expected future profits. However, under certain conditions our econometric approach can also control for this type of measurement error. In our empirical work, we show that the close association between tangible investment and $\hat{q}$ is robust to controlling for these econometric issues.

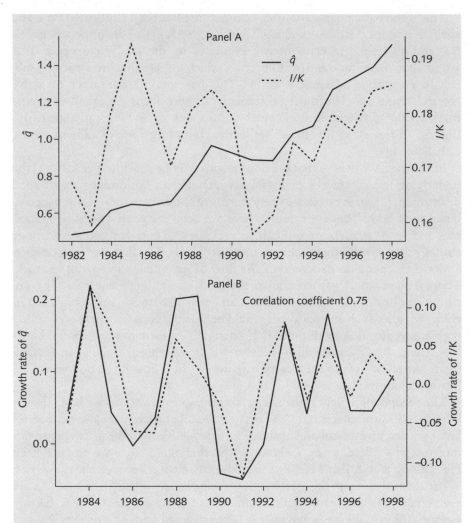

Fig. 4. Average levels and growth rates of analyst-based q ratios and investment–capital ratios for the entire sample, 1982–98.[a]

Note:

[a] I/K is the ratio of tangible investment to the stock of tangible capital. The sample is the same as in Fig. 2. The correlation coefficient between the growth rates of $\hat{q}$ and I/K is 0.75.

Source: Authors' calculations based on Compustat data.

The figures in this introduction set the stage for our investigation. In Figs 1 and 2, we showed using the specific examples of Coke and Microsoft and using our entire sample of firms that there is a great deal of action in the level and variance of the measure of fundamentals based on the stock market that has nothing to do with the measure based on expected earnings. In Figs 3 and 4, we showed that while it is conceivable that more and more capital has gone missing from the balance sheet, a compelling alternative is that share prices are noisy. In our formal empirical work we confirm these findings. While we find a limited role for intangibles in our model of tangible investment, we nevertheless find a strong relationship between tangible investment and $\hat{q}$ that is not mirrored in the relationship between tangible investment and q^E. The puzzle in the relationship between stock prices and investment can be explained by the importance of noisy share prices, and the story of the New Economy as it relates to the stock market rise appears to be largely a fiction.

2. Model

We use the neoclassical model of investment as the basis for our investigation. In the first subsection we set up the model and present the empirical investment equation that relates Tobin's Q and the demand for fixed capital when there is a single capital good. In the second subsection we show how this empirical model can be modified to incorporate the key feature of the New Economy—that we should distinguish between two different types of capital, only one of which can be measured. In the final subsection we show how to modify the model to incorporate the key feature of noisy share prices—that the value of the firm is mismeasured because asset prices deviate from their fundamental value.

2.1. The Q Model of Investment

In each period, the firm chooses investment in each type of capital good: $I_t = (I_{1t}, \ldots, I_{Nt})$, where j indexes the N different types of capital goods and t indexes time.[11] Given (1) below, this is equivalent to choosing a sequence of capital stocks $K_t = (K_{1t}, \ldots, K_{Nt})$, given K_{t-1}, to maximize V_t, the cum-dividend value of the firm, defined as:

$$V_t = E_t \left\{ \sum_{s=t}^{\infty} \beta_s^t \Pi \left(K_s, I_s, \varepsilon_s \right) \right\}, \tag{1}$$

where E_t is the expectations operator conditional on the set of information available at the beginning of period t; β_s^t discounts net revenue in period s back to time t; Π is the revenue function net of factor payments, which includes the productivity shock ε_s as an argument. We assume that Π is linear homogeneous in (K_s, I_s) and that the capital goods are the only quasi-fixed factors—or, equivalently, that variable factors have been maximized out of Π. For convenience in presenting the model, we also assume that there are no taxes and the firm issues no debt, although we incorporate taxes and debt in our empirical work when we construct q.

The firm maximizes (1) subject to the series of constraints:

$$K_{j,\,t+s}=(1-\delta_j)\,K_{j,\,t+s-1}+I_{j,\,t+s}, \quad s\geq 0, \tag{2}$$

where δ_j is the rate of economic depreciation for capital good j. In this formulation, investment is subject to adjustment costs but becomes productive immediately. Furthermore, current profits are assumed to be known, so that both prices and the productivity shock in period t are known to the firm when choosing I_{jt}. Other formulations—such as one where there is a production and/or a decision lag—are possible but we choose this, the most parsimonious specification, because the results we highlight in this study are insensitive to these alternatives.

We follow the approach introduced by Hayashi (1982) to derive an empirical investment equation based on Tobin's q for the case of a single homogeneous capital good subject to quadratic adjustment costs:[12]

$$\left(\frac{I}{K}\right)_{it}=a+\frac{1}{b}\left(q_{it}-1\right)\frac{p_t}{g_t}+\varepsilon_{it}$$

$$=a+\frac{1}{b}\left(\frac{V_{it}}{p_t(1-\delta)K_{i,t-1}}-1\right)\frac{p_t}{g_t}+\varepsilon_{it}$$

$$=a+\frac{1}{b}\,Q_{it}+\varepsilon_{it}, \tag{3}$$

where p_t and g_t are the price of the investment good and the price of output, respectively; and a and b are the technical coefficients of the adjustment cost technology. The goal of the econometric procedure is to estimate these structural parameters.

The productivity shock in (3) affects I_{it} since ε_{it} is known when I_{it} is chosen. It also affects Π and is therefore correlated with V_{it}. As a result, this model is unidentified without further assumptions. To estimate it we need to control for the endogeneity of Q. We turn our attention to this task in Section 4.

2.2. A Model of the New Economy

The key idea behind the story of the New Economy is that capital is composed of a tangible and an intangible component. The tangible part is what is easiest to measure—property, plant, and equipment—while the intangible part is more difficult to measure since it depends on how advertising, R&D, and the like create assets for the firm. For practical reasons this intangible component has been ignored in most studies of investment.

It is possible to estimate a very general model with two types of capital using two interrelated Euler equations. This is a common approach in the literature on dynamic factor demand—for example, Cummins and Dey (2000) estimate the dynamic demand for equipment and structures using firm-level panel data. Such an approach is ill-suited to our investigation for two reasons. First, even though intangible investment is observable, as we pointed out in the introduction, it is impractical to construct intangible capital stocks firm-by-firm. Second, the Euler equation approach eschews the information contained in share prices so it is unsuitable for studying whether share prices are noisy. Rather we take an approach based on Tobin's q which nests both the multiple capital goods of the New Economy and noisy share prices.

In the mathematical appendix of our original publication, we consider the case of two capital goods subject to additively separable adjustment costs.[13] Denoting tangible investment and the stock of tangible capital by I_1 and K_1, and intangible investment and the stock of intangible capital by I_2 and K_2, we derive an equation for investment in tangible capital as:

$$\left(\frac{I_1}{K_1}\right)_{it} = a_1 + \frac{1}{b_1}\left(\frac{V_{it}}{p_{1t}(1-\delta_1)K_{1i,t-1}} - 1\right)\frac{p_{1t}}{g_t} - \frac{b_2}{b_1}\left(\frac{1-\delta_2}{1-\delta_1}\right)\left(\frac{I_2}{K_1}\right)_{it}$$
$$+ \frac{a_2 b_2}{b_1}\left(\frac{1-\delta_2}{1-\delta_1}\right)\left(\frac{K_2}{K_1}\right)_{it} - \frac{1}{b_1}\left(\frac{1-\delta_2}{1-\delta_1}\right)\left(\frac{p_{2t}}{p_{1t}}\right)\left(\frac{K_2}{K_1}\right)_{it} + \varepsilon_{it}. \tag{4}$$

This equation cannot be estimated without data on the stock of intangible capital (K_2), which we have argued is difficult, if not impossible, to measure. However, we can notice that so long as the ratio of intangible capital to tangible capital (K_2/K_1) is stable over time for a given firm, and the ratio of the price of intangible capital to the price of tangible capital (p_2/p_1) is similarly stable, then the last two terms in (4) will be well approximated by a firm-specific effect (e_i). While these assumptions are certainly restrictive, they are not ruled out by a model with multiple capital goods, and they allow us to proceed in the absence of data on the stock of intangibles. Maintaining these assumptions, we obtain an estimable equation for tangible investment as:

$$\left(\frac{I_1}{K_1}\right)_{it} = a_1 + \frac{1}{b_1}\left(\frac{V_{it}}{p_{1t}(1-\delta_1)K_{1i,t-1}} - 1\right)\frac{p_{1t}}{g_t} - \frac{b_2}{b_1}\left(\frac{1-\delta_2}{1-\delta_1}\right)\left(\frac{I_2}{K_1}\right)_{it} + e_i + \varepsilon_{it}. \tag{5}$$

This equation differs in a number of important ways from the standard setup in (3). Notice that the tangible investment-capital ratio—not the total investment–capital ratio which we have argued is unobservable—is related to Tobin's q and the ratio of intangible investment to tangible capital. The coefficient on this latter ratio is a function of the adjustment cost parameters and depreciation rates for tangible and intangible capital. This shows that the basic Q model that ignores intangible capital is misspecified unless b_2 is zero or $\delta_2 = 1$, or the covariance between Tobin's Q and intangible investment is zero. Based on *a priori* reasoning these conditions are unlikely to be satisfied: intangible capital surely has at least some adjustment costs and does not depreciate completely in each period; and presumably intangible investment is undertaken because it affects the average return to capital and hence V_t. The negative coefficient on I_2/K_1 is easy to interpret. For companies making intangible investments, $V_{it}/[p_{1t}(1 - \delta_1)K_{i,t-1}]$ will tend to be high. But, in part, this is just a signal to the company to invest in intangibles rather than tangible capital. So in modelling tangible investment specifically we need to correct the high value of $V_{it}/[p_{1t}(1 - \delta_1)K_{i,t-1}]$, which is what the negative coefficient on the I_2/K_1 term achieves.

2.3. A Model with Noisy Share Prices

Under the assumption that stock market prices are strongly efficient, the firm's equity valuation (V_t^E) coincides with its fundamental value (V_t), and the empirical investment equations in (3) or (5) can be estimated consistently—if the endogeneity of average q is controlled for by using suitable instrumental variables—by using the equity valuation to measure V_t. We relax this strong efficiency assumption to allow for the possibility that $V_t^E \neq V_t$, and consider the implications of the resulting measurement error in average q for the estimation of the investment models. We illustrate the approach using the basic empirical investment equation in (3) since the application to the New Economy investment equation (5) is immediate, but notationally more cumbersome.

We first write

$$Q_t = \frac{V_t}{g_t(1-\delta)K_{t-1}} - \frac{p_t}{g_t}, \tag{6}$$

$$V_t^E = V_t + m_t, \tag{7}$$

where m_t is the measurement error in the equity valuation V_t^E, regarded as a measure of the fundamental value V_t. The measure of Q_t that uses the firm's equity valuation then has the form

$$Q_t^E = \left(\frac{V_t + m_t}{p_t(1-\delta)K_{t-1}} - 1\right)\frac{p_t}{g_t}$$

$$= (q^E - 1)\frac{p_t}{g_t}$$

$$= Q_t + \frac{m_t}{g_t(1-\delta)K_{t-1}}$$

$$= Q_t + \mu_t, \tag{8}$$

where μ_t is the corresponding measurement error induced in Q_t^E. Substituting Q_t^E for Q_t in (3) then gives the empirical investment equation when there are noisy share prices

$$\left(\frac{I}{K}\right)_{it} = a + \frac{1}{b}Q_{it}^E + \left(\varepsilon_{it} - \frac{\mu_{it}}{b}\right). \tag{9}$$

When the measurement error (μ_{it}) is persistent and correlated with the kinds of variables that are used as instrumental variables, there is no way to identify this model. This scenario seems particularly plausible if one's prior is that the stock market is prone to certain types of noisy share prices, like bubbles.[14] Consider a bubble that is related to observable measures of the fundamentals—for example, current cash flow. To take a specific example, consider Coke again. When Coke announces its current cash flow, this news affects the bubble in its share price today and in the future since the bubble is persistent. If we roll forward, say, three years and think about using cash flow from three years back as an instrumental variable for the current measure of Q_{it}^E, it is immediately obvious that this lagged cash flow variable is correlated with μ_{it} when μ_{it} is persistent. Hence, lagged variables that are correlated with firm performance are inadmissible instruments when there is persistent measurement error in share prices that is correlated with firm performance. This form of measurement error simply cannot be dealt with using conventional techniques.

To breach this impasse, we need another way to measure fundamentals that does not suffer from this problem. We propose to use securities analysts' consensus forecasts of future earnings as a measure of $E_t[\Pi_{t+s}]$. Combining these forecasts with a simple assumption about the discount rates β_{t+s}^t, we can construct an alternative estimate of the present value of current and future net revenues as

$$\hat{V}_t = E_t\left(\Pi_t + \beta_{t+1}^t\Pi_{t+1} + \cdots + \beta_{t+s}^t\Pi_{t+s}\right). \tag{10}$$

We then use this estimate in place of the firm's stock market valuation to obtain an alternative estimate of average q, and hence

$$\hat{Q}_t = \left(\frac{\hat{V}_t}{p_t(1-\delta)K_{t-1}} - 1 \right) \frac{p_t}{g_t}$$

$$= (\hat{q}_t - 1) \frac{p_t}{g_t}. \tag{11}$$

Clearly our estimate of $\hat{V}_t$ will also measure the firm's fundamental value V_t with error. The potential sources of measurement error include truncating the series after a finite number of future periods, using an incorrect discount rate, and the fact that analysts forecast net profits rather than net revenues. Letting $v_\tau = \hat{Q}_t - Q_t$ denote the resulting measurement error in our estimate of Q_t, the econometric model is then

$$\left(\frac{I}{K} \right)_{it} = a + \frac{1}{b}\hat{Q}_{it} + \left(\varepsilon_{it} - \frac{v_{it}}{b} \right). \tag{12}$$

The measurement error v_{it} may also be persistent. Identification will depend on whether this measurement error is uncorrelated with suitably lagged values of instruments, for example, sales, profits, or investment. We regard this as an empirical question that will be investigated using tests of overidentifying restrictions.

....

3. Data

The Compustat dataset is an unbalanced panel of firms from the industrial, full coverage, and research files. The variables we use are defined as follows.

The replacement cost of the tangible capital stock is calculated using the standard perpetual inventory method with the initial observation set equal to the book value of the firm's first reported net stock of property, plant, and equipment (data item 8) and an industry-level rate of economic depreciation constructed from Hulten and Wykoff (1981). Gross tangible investment is defined as the direct measure of capital expenditures in Compustat (data item 30). Cash flow is the sum of net income (data item 18) and depreciation (data item 14). Both gross investment and cash flow are divided by the current period replacement cost of the tangible capital stock. The measures of fundamentals, Q^E and $\hat{Q}$, both contain a variety of adjustments to account for debt, taxes, inventories, and current assets. We discuss these adjustments and the construction of $\hat{V}$ in detail in the appendix of our original publication. The implicit price deflator (IPD) for total investment for the firm's three-digit Standard Industrial Classification (SIC) code is used to deflate the investment and cash flow variables and in the perpetual inventory calculation of the replacement value of the firm's capital stock. The three-digit IPD for gross output is used to form the relative price of capital goods.

In order to understand the different measures of intangible investment we use, it is helpful to review some basic accounting. The income statement contains information about expenditures internal to the firm that generate intangible assets. Accountants highlight two types of information about intangible investment that are available on the income statement, advertising (data item 45) and R&D (data item 46). There are also intangible expenditures that are included in selling, general, and administrative expenses. But that category of expenses is so broad it is unlikely to be useful as a measure of intangible investment. Both of these measures of intangible investment are deflated using the sectoral IPD for total investment and divided by the current period replacement cost of the firm's tangible capital stock. Using alternative deflators did not affect the empirical results.

We employ data on expected earnings from I/B/E/S International Inc., a private company that has been collecting earnings forecasts from securities analysts since 1971.[15] To be included in the I/B/E/S database, a company must be actively followed by at least one securities analyst, who agrees to provide I/B/E/S with timely earnings estimates. According to I/B/E/S, an analyst actively follows a company if he or she produces research reports on the company, speaks to company management, and issues regular earnings forecasts. These criteria ensure that I/B/E/S data come from well-informed sources. The I/B/E/S earnings forecasts refer to net income from continuing operations as defined by the consensus of securities analysts following the firm. Typically, this consensus measure removes from earnings a wider range of nonrecurring charges than the 'extraordinary items' reported on firms' financial statements.

For each company in the database, I/B/E/S asks analysts to provide forecasts of earnings per share over the next four quarters and each of the next five years. We focus on the annual forecasts to match the frequency of our Compustat data. In practice, few analysts provide annual forecasts beyond two years ahead. I/B/E/S also obtains a separate forecast of the average annual growth of the firm's net income over the next three to five years—the so-called 'long-term growth forecast'. To conform with the timing of the stock market valuation we use to construct Q^E, we construct $\hat{Q}$ using analysts' forecasts issued at the beginning of the accounting year.

We abstract from any heterogeneity in analyst expectations for a given firm-year by using the mean across analysts for each earnings measure (which I/B/E/S terms the 'consensus' estimate). We multiply the one-year-ahead and two-year-ahead forecasts of earnings per share by the number of shares outstanding to

Stephen R. Bond and Jason G. Cummins

yield forecasts of future earnings levels. Forecasts of earnings for subsequent periods are obtained by increasing the average of these two levels in line with the forecast long-term growth rate. We discount expected earnings over the next five years using the current interest rate on the 30-year Treasury bond plus an 8 per cent risk premium, and use a terminal value correction to account for earnings in later years. Further details are provided in the appendix of our original publication.

The sample we use for estimation includes all firms with at least four consecutive years of complete Compustat and I/B/E/S data. We require four years of data to allow for first differencing and the use of lagged variables as instruments. We determine whether the firm satisfies the four-year requirement after deleting observations that fail to meet a standard set of criteria for data quality.

4. Empirical Specification

Following Blundell *et al.* (1992), our empirical specification allows for the productivity shock (ε_{it}) for firm i in period t to have the first-order autoregressive structure

$$\varepsilon_{it} = \rho \varepsilon_{i,t-1} + \eta_{it}, \tag{13}$$

where η_t can further be allowed to have firm-specific and time-specific components. Allowing for this form of serial correlation in (9) gives the dynamic specification

$$\left(\frac{I}{K}\right)_{it} = a(1-\rho) + \frac{1}{b}Q^E_{i,t-1} - \frac{\rho}{b}Q^E_{i,t-1} + \rho\left(\frac{I}{K}\right)_{i,t-1}$$
$$+ \left[\eta_{it} - \frac{1}{b}(\mu_{it} - \rho\mu_{i,t-1})\right] \tag{14}$$

and a similar dynamic specification based on the model defined by (12), where $\hat{Q}$ replaces Q^E; and for the model defined by (5), where we include $(I_2/K_1)_{it}$ and $(I_2/K_1)_{I,t-1}$ as additional regressors. We allow for time effects by including year dummies in the estimated specifications. Estimation allows for unobserved firm-specific effects by using first-differenced generalized method of moments (GMM) estimators with instruments dated $t-3$ and earlier. This is implemented using DPD98 for GAUSS.

We report four diagnostic tests for each model we estimate. We test the validity of our instrument set in three ways. First, we report the p-value of the m_2 test proposed by Arellano and Bond (1991) to detect second-order serial correlation in the first-differenced residuals. The m_2 statistic, which has a standard normal distribution under the null, tests for nonzero elements on the second

112

off-diagonal of the estimated serial covariance matrix. Second, we also test whether the first off-diagonal has nonzero elements. Since first-differencing should introduce an MA(1) error we expect that the null of no first-order serial correlation should be rejected in virtually every case. Third, we report the p-value of the Sargan statistic (also know as Hansen's J-statistic), which tests the joint null hypothesis that the model is correctly specified and that the instruments are valid (for further details see Arellano and Bond 1991; Blundell et al., 1992).[16] Unfortunately, it is not possible to test either hypothesis separately. Thus, considerable caution should be exercised in interpreting why the null is rejected—the instruments may be invalid due to serial correlation in the residuals, the model may be misspecified, or both problems may be present. The final diagnostic test we report is the p-value for the common factor restriction that we impose, which is not rejected in any of the specifications we consider.

5. Empirical Results

Table 1 presents the GMM estimates of the first-differenced New Economy and noisy share price investment equations for the full sample of companies using our different controls for fundamentals and intangible investment. We implement GMM with an instrument set that contains the period $t-3$ and $t-4$ values of I/K and CF/K, as well as a full set of year dummies.

We first discuss the results based on the noisy share price investment equations (9) and (12). The coefficient on Q^E (shown in column 1) is small and statistically insignificant at the five-per cent level. The p-value of the Sargan test, reported with the other diagnostic tests below the estimate, decisively rejects the joint test of the model and instrument validity. These results are consistent with the presence of an important measurement error component in share prices that is both persistent over time and correlated with our instruments. In contrast, the coefficient on $\hat{Q}$ (shown in column 5) is ten times greater than that on Q^E and precisely estimated. More important than the magnitude of the estimate is that there is no evidence from the diagnostic tests that the model containing $\hat{Q}$ is misspecified. These results are consistent with orthogonality between the measurement error in our measure of $\hat{q}$ constructed from analysts' earnings forecasts, and the lagged investment and cash flow variables used as instruments.

If intangibles are important, and are not captured by the fixed effects, these results should be viewed with skepticism. So we move to the New Economy investment equation where we introduce sequentially the two measures of intangible investment (scaled, as dictated by the model, by tangible capital). We then include both of the variables together.

Table 1. GMM Estimates of First-differenced Dynamic Investment Equations with Intangibles

Regressor	(1)	(2)	(3)	(4)	(5)	(6)	(7)	(8)	(9)	(10)	(11)	(12)
Q_t^E	0.011	0.014	0.011	0.014					-0.007	-0.006	-0.008	-0.007
	(0.007)	(0.007)	(0.007)	(0.007)					(0.009)	(0.010)	(0.009)	(0.010)
$\hat{Q}_t$					0.110	0.136	0.104	0.135	0.119	0.139	0.112	0.137
					(0.021)	(0.022)	(0.022)	(0.022)	(0.024)	(0.024)	(0.025)	(0.024)
ADV_t/K_{it}		-0.745		-0.679		-1.260		-1.238		-1.249		-1.206
		(0.366)		(0.362)		(0.510)		(0.496)		(0.547)		(0.525)
RD_t/K_{it}			-1.540	-1.504			-0.454	-0.082			-0.358	-0.118
			(0.618)	(0.625)			(0.642)	(0.724)			(0.665)	(0.746)
ρ	0.340	0.381	0.387	0.420	0.176	0.169	0.215	0.175	0.168	0.210	0.209	0.228
	(0.057)	(0.059)	(0.049)	(0.055)	(0.059)	(0.061)	(0.055)	(0.060)	(0.058)	(0.070)	(0.054)	(0.069)
Diagnostic tests (p-values)												
First-order serial correlation	0.000	0.000	0.000	0.000	0.000	0.001	0.000	0.001	0.000	0.000	0.000	0.000
Second-order serial correlation	0.765	0.531	0.345	0.261	0.227	0.185	0.427	0.212	0.221	0.270	0.387	0.337
Sargan test	0.003	0.022	0.012	0.042	0.323	0.932	0.310	0.897	0.257	0.923	0.259	0.900
Common factor restriction	0.222	0.595	0.325	0.475	0.436	0.785	0.529	0.906	0.743	0.782	0.739	0.849

Notes: The dependent variable is the first difference of the ratio of tangible investment to tangible capital, I_{it}/K_t. Year dummies are included (but not reported) in all regressions. Robust standard errors on coefficients are in parentheses. The sample contains the firms with at least four years of complete Compustat and I/B/E/S data. The number of firms in this sample is 1114, for a total of 7484 observations. The estimation period is 1986–98.

Instrumental variables are the period $t-3$ and $t-4$ values of I/K and CF/K. The instrument sets also contain year dummies. The test for first- and second-order serial correlation in the residuals is asymptotically distributed as $N(0,1)$ under the null of no serial correlation. The test of the overidentifying restrictions, called a Sargan test, is asymptotically distributed $\chi^2(n-p)$, where n is the number of instruments and p is the number of parameters.

Source: Authors' calculations using Compustat and I/B/E/S data.

When Q^E is used as the control for fundamentals the coefficients on the ratio of advertising to tangible capital and the ratio of R&D to tangible capital are negative and statistically significant (columns 2 and 3), as predicted by our model. When both measures are included together (column 4), they are both statistically significant at the ten-per cent level and jointly significant at the five-per cent level (this F-test is not reported in the table). The coefficient on Q^E is little affected when any or all of the measures are included, although it is more precisely estimated in two of the four cases. The Sargan test rejects the model at the five-per cent level in all four cases.

The investment equations that use $\hat{Q}$ and the measures of intangible investment are not rejected by the Sargan test; but only the estimate on advertising is statistically significant from zero (column 6). The coefficient on R&D is negative but not significant (column 7).

When both measures are included the estimate on advertising is still significant, but that on R&D remains insignificant (column 8)—the two are jointly significant at the five-per cent level (this Wald test is not reported in the table). When the advertising variable is included, the estimated coefficient on $\hat{Q}$ increases, consistent with the prediction that including this flow measure of investment in intangibles will correct the measure of average q for the presence of intangible assets.

In the final four columns of the table, we use both measures of fundamentals in the investment equation. The estimated coefficients on $\hat{Q}$ are about the same as when Q^E is not included, while the estimated coefficients on Q^E lose significance. In all cases, when $\hat{Q}$ is included in the model the Sargan test is not rejected, nor are the other key diagnostic tests. This is a surprising result: conditional on $\hat{Q}$, there is no additional information relevant for tangible investment in the conventional share price measure of average q. Recall that the timing of the variable construction is such that the market-based measure incorporates the analysts' forecasts and both measures are instrumented using lagged publicly available information. Hence, our results mean that the part of Q^E that is uncorrelated with $\hat{Q}$ has no explanatory power for investment. In other words, the part of the stock market valuations that is uncorrelated with analysts' earnings forecasts is a sideshow for investment. Whether or not we account for intangibles does not affect this conclusion.

....

6. Conclusion

The fundamental issue we address is whether the increase in the stock market relative to the measured stock of tangible capital reflects the growing role of intangible capital in generating profits—that is, the birth of the New Economy—or whether it reflects noisy share prices—that is, a persistent and broadly based increase in the market valuation of companies relative to their fundamental value. We introduce a new approach based on the Q model of investment that is rich enough to encompass both these possibilities. We then study investment behaviour—in both tangible and intangible capital—and assess whether it is consistent with one or both explanations. While we can identify a limited role for intangible investment, there is no evidence that this factor alone can account for the spectacular rise in the stock market valuation of firms. Our evidence points to serious anomalies in the behaviour of share prices.

Our findings suggest that even when we account for the role of intangible investment, there is a wide, and growing, gap between the market valuation of firms and a valuation based on expected future profits. The latter is demonstrably more informative about these firms' tangible investment behaviour. Perhaps most surprisingly, we find that there is no information about investment behaviour contained in stock prices once we control for fundamentals using expected future profits. Hence, fluctuations in share prices that are unrelated to earnings' forecasts appear to be both pervasive and a sideshow for investment. While this is found to be true for intangible intensive or New Economy companies, our results are not limited to these firms. Our findings suggest that persistent deviations of equity values from firms' fundamental valuations are an important feature of US stock markets in the past seventeen years, and that this can account for the weak observed relationship between share prices and investment. Our findings further suggest that managers make investment decisions to maximize the present value of expected future profits, and are not influenced by the seemingly anomalous behaviour of share prices. One implication is that monetary policy makers need not be unduly concerned about the impact of 'irrational exuberance' on business investment, although there may be other reasons, such as wealth effects on consumption, why they will nevertheless be interested in the behaviour of the stock market.

Notes

1. We thank participants at the Brookings Panel on Economic Activity and Tor Jakob Klette for helpful comments and suggestions. We thank Haibin Jiu for his super research assistance. Stephen Bond gratefully acknowledges financial support from the ESRC Centre for Fiscal Policy at the Institute for Fiscal Studies. The data on earnings expectations are provided by I/B/E/S International Inc.

2. The difficulty of measuring the future benefits is the reason usually advanced for expensing these items. Generally Accepted Accounting Principles (GAAP) require that internal R&D, advertising and other such costs be written off to expense when incurred. In contrast, purchases of intangibles from outside the firm—for example, patents, trademarks, formulas, and brands—are recorded as assets because market prices are available. The only exception to this asymmetric treatment is the capitalization of some software development costs (FASB 1985).

3. Baruch Lev and his collaborators' seminal research on intangibles forms much of the empirical basis for those who advocate fundamental reform of accountancy. For an overview of this research see Lev and Zarowin (1999).

4. The perspective of Blair and Wallman (www.stern.nyu.edu/ross/ProjectInt/about.html), who head up the Brookings Institute's Intangible Assets research project (which is spearheading an effort to reform the accounting for intangibles), is so remarkable in this regard that it is worth quoting at length: 'Currently, less than half (and possibly as little as one-third or less) of the market value of corporate securities can be accounted for by "hard" assets—property, plant and equipment... The rest of the value *must, necessarily*, be coming from organizational and human capital, ideas and information, patents, copyrights, brand names, reputational capital, and possibly a whole host of other assets, for which we do not have good rules or techniques for determining and reporting value' (italics added). Only under a number of strong assumptions, of which strong efficiency is just one, must intangibles make up the rest of the market value of the company. But Blair and Wallman believe that accountancy fails to convey crucial information about intangibles so the assumption of strong efficiency would seem to be questionable. Of course, one need not take such an extreme position to justify efforts to collect better data.

5. Coke divested itself of most of its physical assets when it spun-off Coca-Cola Enterprises. In the calculations that follow we use Compustat data, which provides consistent time series data that relate only to what is now Coca-Cola Co.

6. We discuss in greater detail the composition of our broader sample and the construction of the variables in it, including the ones we introduce in this section, in Section 3. In particular, the two measures of fundamentals that we introduce in this section contain all the usual adjustments for debt, taxes, and so forth.

7. There is a large literature about the properties of earnings forecasts. The consensus in the finance and accounting literature is that analysts are too optimistic about the near-term prospects of companies (see, e.g. Fried and Givoly, 1982; Brown, 1996). Keane and Runkle (1998) show, however, that the studies in this literature suffer for material econometric deficiencies. When they are corrected, Keane and Runkle find that analysts' quarterly forecasts are rational expectations forecasts.

8. The comparable increase for the firms in the sample from 1982 to 1998 is 150 per cent, indicating that new entrants do have an appreciable effect on the growth in the annual average of $\hat{q}$. This is perhaps not surprising since part of the entry in our sample comes from analysts' initiating coverage of firms with high potential growth opportunities.

9. The consensus view seems to be that this result remains even when the underlying firm data are used in conjunction with an estimator that attempts to address the endogeneity of q^E. A number of papers by Cummins and his collaborators argue that this

consensus is premature. Cummins *et al.* (1994, 1996, 1999) all recover more economically significant estimates of the effect of fundamentals when they control for the endogeneity and/or measurement error that likely plague empirical investment equations.

10. The techniques used by Blundell *et al.* (1992) and Hayashi and Inoue (1991) correct for measurement error in average q when it is serially uncorrelated by using lagged values of average q as instrumental variables. We argue below that the measurement error in q^E is serially correlated which explains why using lagged values of average q does not successfully control for measurement error.

11. The firm index i is suppressed to economize on notation except when we present the empirical investment equations, where it clarifies the variables that vary by firm.

12. We use lowercase q_{it} to denote the valuation ratio $V_{it}/[p_{1t}(1 - \delta_1)K_{i,t-1}]$ and capital Q_{it} to denote the function of this ratio that enters the investment equation.

13. For previous treatments of the Q model with multiple capital inputs see, Chirinko (1993*b*) and Hayashi and Inoue (1991).

14. Shiller (1981), among others, has suggested that equity valuations are excessively volatile compared to fundamental values. Blanchard and Watson (1982) and Froot and Obstfeld (1991) have developed models of rational bubbles that do not violate weaker concepts of market efficiency. Campbell and Kyle (1993) have analysed models with noise traders that have similar empirical implications.

15. This discussion draws on joint work with Steve Oliner and Kevin Hassett.

16. Formally, the Sargan statistic is a test that the overidentifying restrictions are asymptotically distributed χ^2_{n-p}, where n is the number of instruments and p is the number of parameters.

References

Arellano, Manuel and Stephen Bond (1991), 'Some tests of specification for panel data: Monte Carlo evidence and an application to employment equations', *Review of Economic Studies*, 58(2): 277–97.

Blanchard, Olivier I. and Mark W. Watson (1982), 'Bubbles, rational expectations, and financial markets', in Paul Wachtel (ed.) *Crises in the Economic and Financial Structure*. (Lexington, MA: Lexington Books).

Blundell, Richard, Stephen Bond, Michael Devereux, and Fabio Schiantarelli (1992), 'Investment and tobin's q: Evidence from company panel data', *Journal of Econometrics*, 51(1–2): 233–57.

Brown, Lawrence D. (1996), 'Analyst forecasting errors and their implications for security analysis: An alternative perspective', *Financial Analysts' Journal*, 52(January/February): 40–7.

Caballero, Ricardo I. (1999), 'Aggregate investment', in John Taylor and Michael Woodford (eds) *Handbook of Macroeconomics, Volume 1b* (Amsterdam: Elsevier Science).

Campbell, John Y. and Albert S. Kyle (1993), 'Smart money, noise trading and stock price behaviour', *Review of Economic Studies*, 60(1): 1–34.

Chirinko, Robert S. (1993a), 'Business fixed investment spending: Modeling strategies, empirical results, and policy implications', *Journal of Economic Literature*, 31(4): 1875–911.

——(1993b), 'Multiple capital inputs, Q, and investment spending', *Journal of Economic Dynamics and Control*, 17(5–6): 907–28.

Cummins, Jason G. and Matthew Dey (2000), 'Taxation, investment, and firm growth with heterogeneous capital', Unpublished paper, New York University.

——Kevin A. Hassett, and Glenn Hubbard (1994), 'A reconsideration of investment behavior using tax reforms as natural experiments', *BPEA*, 2: 1–74.

————(1996), 'Tax reforms and investment: A cross-country comparison', *Journal of Public Economics*, 62(1–2): 237–73.

——and Stephen D. Oliner (1999), 'Investment behavior, observable expectations, and internal funds', Unpublished paper, New York University.

Financial Accounting Standards Board (1985), *Status of Statement No. 86, Accounting for the Costs of Computer Software to be Sold, Leased, or Otherwise Marketed* (Stamford, Conn.: Financial Accounting Standards Board).

Fried, Dov and Dan Givoly (1982), 'Financial analysts' forecasts of earnings: A better surrogate for market expectations', *Journal of Accounting and Economics*, 4(2): 85–107.

Froot, Kenneth A. and Maurice Obstfeld (1991), 'Intrinsic bubbles: The case of stock prices', *American Economic Review*, 81(5): 1189–214.

Hall, Robert E. (1999), 'The stock market and capital accumulation', NBER Working Paper 7180, Cambridge, MA: National Bureau of Economic Research (June).

Hayashi, Fumio (1982), 'Tobin's marginal q and average Q: A neoclassical interpretation', *Econometrica*, 50(1): 213–24.

Hayashi, Famio and Tohru Inoue (1991), 'The relation between firm growth and Q with multiple capital goods: Theory and evidence from panel data on Japanese firms', *Econometrica*, 59(3): 731–53.

Hubbard, R. Glenn (1998), 'Capital market imperfections and investment', *Journal of Economic Literature*, 36(1): 193–225.

Hulten, Charles R. and Frank Wykoff (1981), 'The measurement of economic depreciation', in Charles R. Hulten (ed.) *Depreciation, Inflation, and the Taxation of Income from Capital* (Washington: Urban Institute).

Keane, Michael P. and David E. Runkle (1998), 'Are financial analysts' forecasts of corporate profits rational?' *Journal of Political Economy*, 106(4): 768–805.

Lev, Baruch and Paul Zarowin (1999), 'The boundaries of financial reporting and how to extend them', *Journal of Accounting Research*, 37(2): 353–85.

Shiller, Robert J. (1981), 'Do stock prices move too much to be justified by subsequent changes in dividends'? *American Economic Review*, 71(3): 421–36.

II. THE IMPACT OF SPECIFIC INTANGIBLES ON FIRM PERFORMANCE AND MARKET VALUE

5 The Capitalization, Amortization, and Value-relevance of R&D

Baruch Lev and Theodore Sougiannis

1. Introduction

A direct relationship between research and development costs and specific future revenue generally has not been demonstrated, even with the benefit of hindsight. For example, three empirical research studies, which focus on companies in industries intensively involved in research and development activities, generally failed to find a significant correlation between research and development expenditures and increased future benefits as measured by subsequent sales, earnings, or share of industry sales.

(Statement of Financial Accounting Standards No. 2, p. 14)

The presumed absence of a relation between R&D expenditures and subsequent benefits was a major reason for the FASB's decision in 1974 to require the full expensing of R&D outlays in financial reports of public corporations. The last twenty years have witnessed an unprecedented growth of R&D investment in the United States and other developed economies and the emergence of new, science-based industries (e.g. software, biotechnology, and telecommunications). Nevertheless, the requirement for full R&D expensing in the United States—based on the assertion that 'a direct relationship between research and development costs and specific future revenue generally has not been demonstrated...'—is still in effect.[1] Apparently, US standard-setters are concerned with the reliability and objectivity of the estimates required for R&D capitalization, and with the associated audit risk. The specter of providing managers with additional opportunities for earnings management must also weigh heavily on regulators.

The main objective of this study is to address the issues of reliability, objectivity, and value relevance of R&D capitalization. We do this by first estimating the relation between R&D expenditures and subsequent earnings for a large cross-section of R&D-intensive firms. This estimation allows us to compute firm-specific R&D capital and its amortization rate, as well as the measurement of the periodic R&D amortization (in contrast with the GAAP expense, which equals the R&D outlay). We then adjust reported earnings and book values of the sample firms for the R&D capitalization and show that the adjusted values are significantly associated with stock prices and returns, indicating the value relevance to investors of the R&D capitalization process developed here. Finally, we demonstrate in an intertemporal context that R&D capital is reliably associated with *subsequent* stock returns. This intriguing finding may be due to a systematic mispricing of the shares of R&D-intensive firms (market inefficiency), or to the R&D capital proxying for an extra-market risk factor (equilibrium returns). Taken together, the evidence presented here indicates that the association between R&D expenditures and subsequent earnings is, in general, both statistically significant and economically meaningful, in clear contradiction to a major premise of FAS No. 2—the absence of an association between R&D expenditures and subsequent benefits.

R&D research in economics and related areas (e.g. organizational behaviour) is extensive and growing (see Cohen and Levine, 1989, for a survey), stimulated primarily by the major role of innovation in the theory of economic growth and social welfare. In contrast, this important subject is only infrequently examined in the accounting literature, as indicated by the following brief research survey. Dukes (1976) examined investors' perceptions of R&D and concluded that they adjust reported earnings for the full expensing of R&D. Similarly, Ben-Zion (1978) showed that firms' market minus book values are cross-sectionally correlated with R&D and advertising expenditures. Hirschey and Weygandt (1985) demonstrated that Tobin's Q values (the ratio of market value to replacement cost of assets) are cross-sectionally correlated with R&D over sales ratios (R&D intensity). A different approach to assess R&D relevance was pursued by Woolridge (1988) and Chan et al. (1990). Using an event methodology they documented a positive investor reaction to firms' R&D announcements. Similar evidence, derived from analysts' forecast errors, was provided by Bublitz and Ettredge (1989). Finally, several studies were aimed at evaluating the economic consequences of FAS No. 2. While some researchers detected a decline in the R&D intensity of small firms subsequent to FAS No. 2 enactment (e.g. Horwitz and Kolodny, 1981; Wasley and Linsmeier, 1992), others failed to observe significant changes in managerial R&D decisions (e.g. Elliott et al., 1984). Overall, while documenting investors' cognizance of the capital aspects of R&D, the accounting research on innovation is sparse indeed. Compared with ours, the above studies generally used *proxies* for R&D investment, such as the R&D to sales ratio, while we estimate firm-specific R&D capital and adjust reported earnings for the full R&D expensing. Furthermore, while we examine whether investors fully adjust for the R&D expensing (market efficiency), previous studies have not investigated this issue.

In the next section we present our methodology for estimating the relation between R&D and earnings, followed by an outline of the R&D capitalization process in Section 3. Section 4 describes the adjustment of reported earnings and book values for R&D capitalization, while Section 5 presents the contemporaneous analysis, relating stock prices and returns to the R&D-adjusted financial variables. Section 6 reports the intertemporal analysis, relating R&D capital to subsequent stock returns, while Section 7 concludes the study.

2. Estimating the R&D–earnings Relation

Our estimation of R&D capital and its amortization rate is derived from the fundamental relation between the value of assets and the earnings generated by them. Accordingly, we define the earnings of firm i in period t, E_{it}, as a function of tangible, TA_{it}, and intangible assets, IA_{it}, where the latter includes the R&D capital:[2]

$$E_{it} = g(TA_{it}, IA_{it}). \tag{1}$$

While the values of earnings and tangible assets (at historical costs) are reported in financial statements, the intangible capital, IA, is not reported and therefore has to be estimated.

Given our focus on R&D, we single it out of intangible assets and define its value, RDC_{it}, as the sum of the *unamortized* past R&D expenditures. Those are the expenditures that are expected to generate current and future earnings:

$$RDC_{it} = \sum_k \alpha_{i,k} RD_{i,t-k}, \tag{2}$$

where α_{ik} is the contribution of a dollar R&D expenditure in year $t - k$ ($k = 0, \ldots, N$) to subsequent earnings (i.e. the proportion of the R&D expenditure in year $t - k$ that is still productive in year t).

Substituting expression (2) into (1) yields:

$$E_{it} = g\left(TA_{it}, \sum_k \alpha_{i,k} RD_{i,t-k}, OIA_{it}\right), \tag{3}$$

where OIA_{it} are other (than R&D) intangible assets. (E_{it} is the R&D-adjusted earnings, namely reported earnings plus current R&D expenditures minus the amortization of R&D capital.)

Note that we derive the value of R&D capital from the firm's earnings. An alternative is to estimate that value from the difference between the firm's market and book (or replacement cost) values (e.g. Cockburn and Griliches, 1988; Hall 1993a).[3] We prefer to derive R&D capital from its direct benefits—earnings—over its estimation from market values, since the former avoids the notorious circularity in the use of market prices to estimate values of assets or liabilities. This circularity arises from the general presumption that market prices are *determined* by reported financial variables, and therefore such prices cannot be logically used to determine the values of financial variables. Furthermore, the estimation of fundamental variables (e.g. R&D capital or an environmental liability) from market values precludes one from investigating the extent of market efficiency with respect to the examined variables. Such an investigation is conducted below.[4]

2.1. Estimation of Expression (3) and Data Sources

The variables in relation (3) are defined thus. Earnings, E_{it}, is measured as operating income before depreciation and the expensing of R&D and advertising. Operating income is used as a measure of R&D benefits, since R&D investment and its consequences seem largely unrelated to nonoperating items, such as administrative expenses and financing charges. Depreciation, R&D, and advertising expenses were excluded from (added back to) operating income since they represent, largely *ad hoc*, writeoffs of the independent variables in (3)—tangible and intangible assets.[5]

Tangible assets, TA_{it} in (3), consist of three components: plant and equipment, inventories, and investment in unconsolidated subsidiaries and purchased intangibles. Each of these asset items has been separately adjusted for inflation in the data source we use (to be described below). Across our sample firms and years examined (1975–91), the average shares of tangible assets, inventories, and other investments are: 0.70, 0.23, and 0.07, respectively. The major intangible asset, R&D capital, is represented here by the lag structure of annual R&D expenditures, expression (2), where these expenditures, $RD_{i,t-k}$, are adjusted for inflation to reflect current-year dollars.

Advertising expenditures on product promotion and brand development may create an additional intangible asset for some sample firms. This may raise an omitted variable problem in expression (3), if R&D capital were the only intangible asset included. Conceptually, advertising capital can be estimated from its lag structure, similarly to the procedure applied to R&D (2). However, inspection of our data source, which focuses on R&D firms, revealed that annual advertising expenditures were occasionally missing for many sample firms, straining the requirement for a reasonable length of lag structure for reliable estimation. We therefore employed a procedure frequently used by economists (e.g. Hall, 1993b), in which the advertising intensity (advertising expenses over sales) is substituted for advertising capital. Empirical evidence (e.g. Bublitz and Ettredge, 1989; Hall, 1993b), indicates that, in contrast to R&D, the effect of advertising expenditures on subsequent earnings is short-lived, typically one to two years only. Accordingly, an advertising proxy based on annual expenditures may account reasonably well for the omitted variable in expression (3).[6]

The estimated expression, scaled by total sales to mitigate heteroscedasticity is,

$$(OI/S)_{it} = \alpha_0 + \alpha_1 (TA/S)_{i,t-1} + \sum_k \alpha_{2,k} (RD/S)_{i,t-k}$$

$$+ \alpha_3 (AD/S)_{i,t-1} + e_{it}, \tag{4a}$$

OI = annual operating income, before depreciation, advertising, and R&D expenses, of firm i in year t,
S = annual sales,
TA = the value of plant and equipment, inventory, and investment in unconsolidated subsidiaries and goodwill, in current dollars, measured at the beginning-of-year values,
RD = annual R&D expenditures in current dollars,
AD = annual advertising expenses, measured at the beginning-of-year values.

Note that if expression (4a) is subject to correlated omitted variables problem, then the estimated values of the α coefficients may be overstated.

Three data bases are used in this study: (1) the 1993 CRSP daily file, (2) the 1993 COMPUSTAT file, and (3) the NBER's R&D Master File (described in detail in Hall et al., 1988).[7] The R&D Master File was constructed from consecutive COMPUSTAT tapes, starting with the 1978 tape. Accordingly, the earliest data on the Master File relate to the year 1959. The COMPUSTAT tapes used as sources for the R&D Master File are: the Industrial (NYSE, AMEX, and large OTC firms), OTC (the remaining OTC firms), Full Coverage (non-NASDAQ firms), and the Research (deleted firms) tapes. The R&D Master File includes about 2600 manufacturing companies which reported R&D expenditures. It is thus subset of merged COMPUSTAT tapes, focusing on R&D firms. This file has several attractive features for our study. In particular, asset values and expenses (e.g. R&D) are adjusted to current dollars, and given the frequent use of this data base in time-series analyses, key variables (e.g. plant, sales, R&D expenditures) were scanned to identify large yearly jumps in the data and locate missing values. In such cases, the original annual reports and 10-Ks were examined and the data were completed and corrected when possible (for a detailed discussion of these quality checks, see Hall et al., 1988).[8]

2.2. Simultaneity

Models, such as (4a), relating output to capital, generally raise simultaneity issues. Specifically, when a shock to the regression residual affects both the dependent (output) and one or more independent variables (capital), the latter will be correlated with the residual term, leading to inconsistent regressions estimates. For example, an exogenous shock enhancing demand for the firm's products will generally increase both current earnings and the marginal return to capital, the latter leading to increased investment in R&D. In this case, R&D expenditures cannot be considered an exogenous variable, and OLS estimation of (4a) will yield inconsistent estimates. This calls for estimating expression (4a) in a simultaneous equation context.

To account for simultaneity, we use the instrumental variable method, where an instrument (another variable) is chosen to substitute for the explanatory variable [RD_{it} in expression (4a)] which may be correlated with the residual. A successful instrument is one which is correlated with the substituted explanatory variable, yet is uncorrelated with the residual. We chose as the instrument for firm i the average level of R&D expenditures (deflated by sales) of the *other* firms in its four-digit SIC code.[9] The industry R&D instrument is appealing on both theoretical and empirical grounds. Industry R&D level is obviously unaffected by firm idiosyncratic shocks (e.g. a specific managerial strategy or a corporate control change affecting the firm's cost of capital), thereby considerably limiting its correlation with the original regression (4a) residual. At the same time, there are strong reasons to believe that the correlation between a given firm's R&D expenditures (the original variable) and the industry average (the instrument) is generally high. Corporate activities are often evaluated by investors and financial analysts against industry norms, deterring managers from significantly deviating from them.

More fundamentally, an association between a firm's R&D expenditures and those of the industry is induced by the well-known 'spillover' phenomenon, namely by firms' efforts to learn of and benefit from the innovative activities of other firms. Obviously, in order to benefit from others' knowledge, one has to develop a capacity to exploit that knowledge, achieved by increasing one's own R&D (e.g. hiring scientists who will follow other firms' activities). Indeed, economists have observed that firms that invest more in their own R&D are better able to exploit externally generated knowledge than firms with lower R&D expenditures (e.g. Evenson and Kislev, 1973; Mowery, 1983). Cohen and Levinthal (1989) found that firms invest in R&D for two purposes: to generate

Table 1. The Association Between the Instrumental Variable (Industry R&D) and the Substituted Variable (Firm R&D)

Industry	N^a	$\hat{a}$	$\hat{b}$	Adj. R^2
Chemicals and Pharmaceutics (28)[b]	74	0.029	0.458	0.20
		(2.00)	(11.81)	
Machinery and Computer Hardware (35)	118	0.009	0.677	0.34
		(9.00)	(26.54)	
Electrical and Electronics (36)	98	0.012	0.616	0.16
		(9.60)	(13.84)	
Transportation Vehicles (37)	54	0.008	0.613	0.30
		(6.40)	(13.11)	
Scientific Instruments (38)	69	0.015	0.680	0.16
		(7.50)	(24.50)	
Other R&D Industries	412	0.030	0.328	0.14
		(5.64)	(7.28)	

Notes:
[a] Average number of firms in the yearly regressions, 1975–91.
[b] Two-digit SIC code.
$(RD/S)_{it}$ = Ratio of R&D expenditures to sales of firm i in year t and $(IRD/S)_{it}$ = Industry R&D expenditures to sales ratio (four- or three-digit SIC codes), excluding firm i.
Mean coefficient estimates of yearly cross-sectional regressions (1975–91) of individual firms' annual R&D expenditures scaled by sales (RD/S) on their four-digit industry average R&D (IRD/S). T-values are presented in parentheses.
Regression is $(RD/S)_{it} = a + b(IRD/S)_{it} + u_{it}$.

new knowledge and to develop 'absorptive capacity'—the ability to recognize, assimilate, and exploit others' knowledge. R&D spillover will thus contribute to a positive association between a firm's R&D expenditures and those of related firms (the industry).

The positive association between firm-specific R&D expenditures and those of the industry (the instrument) is corroborated by the data in Table 1. These are mean coefficient estimates, over the years 1975–91, from regressing cross-sectionally individual firms' R&D expenditures on the corresponding four-digit industry R&D level (both variables scaled by sales). Note that the regressions are estimated by pooling over firms in two-digit industries (e.g. SIC codes 28, 35 . . .), where each of those two-digit industries includes multiple four-digit industry means.[10] For example, the two-digit industry No. 28 (Chemicals and Pharmaceutics) includes twelve four-digit industry groups. Moreover, for each observation of the dependent variable, $(RD/S)_{it}$, we exclude the firm's R&D expenditure from the corresponding four-digit industry average (independent variable). Accordingly, in each cross-section of two-digit industry, the independent variable takes a different value for each observation. It is evident from Table 1 that for all industries, the industry R&D level coefficient, $\hat{b}$, is positive, highly statistically significant, and quite stable (around 0.65 for four of the six industries). There thus exists the desired association between our instrumental variable—the industry R&D—and the substituted explanatory variable, RD_{it}, in expression (4a).[11]

We apply the instrumental variable method by running a two-stage least squares regression. In the first stage, for every year and two-digit industry, firms' scaled R&D expenditures, $(RD/S)_{it}$, are cross-sectionally regressed on the four-digit industry R&D level, $(IRD/S)_{it}$,

$$(RD/S)_{it} = a + b(IRD/S)_{it} + u_{it}. \tag{4b}$$

In the second stage, expression (4a) is estimated with the fitted value of $(RD/S)_{it}$ from (4b), substituting for the actual value of $(RD/S)_{it}$.

2.3. Other Estimation Issues

The system of equations (4a) and (4b), relating operating earnings to tangible capital, advertising intensity, and the R&D lag structure, is *cross-sectionally* estimated for each two-digit industry and sample year. The reason for the cross-sectional estimation of (4a) is that data limitations preclude an efficient estimation from individual firms' time series. Our estimates of R&D amortization rates [derived from the α_{2k} coefficients in expression (4a)] are thus industrywide estimates which are then applied to individual firms.

A multicollinearity problem is encountered in the estimation of the R&D lag structure, $\sum_k \alpha_{2,k}(RD/S)_{i,t-k}$, in expression (4a), since annual R&D expenditures for most companies are relatively stable over time. A frequently used approach to address this problem, which is particularly serious in relatively short time series, is 'reduced parameterization', namely the estimation of fewer parameters than the number of lags, k, in the time series. This is achieved by assuming a priori that the lag coefficients, $\alpha_{2,k}$, reflecting the R&D benefits, behave according to some general structure, such as a polynomial. The increased efficiency results from the need to estimate a small number of parameters, relative to the number of lags in the series. The efficiency comes, of course, at the expense of assuming an a priori structure of coefficients. The specific estimation technique we used is the Almon lag procedure (for details see, e.g. Johnston, 1984: 352–8; Maddala, 1992: 424–9). The Almon procedure has a flexibility advantage over several competitors (e.g. the Koyck lag or the binomial lag), since it allows experimentation with polynomials of various degrees and the consequent fitting of a suitable polynomial to the data. In contrast, the Koyck lag imposes a strictly declining pattern on the coefficients, while the binomial and Pascal lag procedures impose quadratic patterns.

3. The R&D Capitalization

The system of equations (4a) and (4b), relating earnings to assets, was run cross sectionally, with the instrumental variable (industry R&D level) and the Almon lag procedure, for each two-digit sample industry and year. Table 2 provides an example of the estimation procedure for industry 36—Electrical and Electronics Manufacturers—covering the early part of the sample period: 1975–81. These estimates are used to adjust reported earnings and book values of the sample companies in the *subsequent* year, 1982. Similarly, the 1983 reported earnings and book values were adjusted from R&D capitalization estimates based on data of the preceding years 1975–82. This is an important feature of our analysis: the adjustment of reported earnings and book values in any sample year is based on estimates derived from expression (4a) run over the preceding years, starting with 1975 (the year FAS No. 2 came into effect).[12] Thus, all information used in the R&D adjustment process was ex ante known.

In the industry-wide estimates from expression (4a) we ignore the statistically insignificant R&D lag coefficient estimates, $\hat{a}_{2,k}$. For example, in the first row of Table 2 (year 1975), the coefficients of lags 6–10, $\hat{a}_{2,6}$ to $\hat{a}_{2,10}$, were insignificant and therefore not reported in the table, while in 1980 and 1981, the lags 6 and 7 coefficients were significant (perhaps due to the larger sample size in those years or to a shift in R&D benefits). The horizontal sum of the significant R&D coefficients, $\Sigma \hat{a}_{2,k}$ (second column from the right), reflects the total (undiscounted) effect of $1 invested in R&D on current and future operating income. For example, based on the 1975 estimation (first row in Table 2), the average contribution to operating income of $1 invested in R&D by Electrical and Electronics manufacturers was $2.328. While total benefits of $2.328 from $1.00 R&D expenditure may appear to be large, it should be recalled that these benefits refer to operating income before R&D amortization, and before major expense items, such as selling, general and administrative expenses, as well as financing expenses and income taxes. Furthermore, these benefits accrue over five years but are not discounted.

The estimated regression coefficients for each of the years 1975–81 are averaged and reported in the second to bottom row in Table 2. These averages are used to compute a key R&D capitalization parameter—the annual amortization rates of the R&D capital, δ_k (reported in the bottom line of Table 2),

$$\delta_k = \hat{\alpha}_{2,k} / \sum_k \hat{\alpha}_{2,k}. \tag{5}$$

The R&D amortization in year k is thus the ratio of that year's benefits *expired*, $\hat{\alpha}_{2,k}$, to total benefits, $\Sigma_k \hat{\alpha}_{2,k}$. For example, the amortization rate of current (year 0) R&D expenditures, δ_0, is $0.268/2.348 = 0.114$. Thus, on average, in the

Table 2. Example: Derivation of Annual Amortization Rates of R&D for 1982. Industry 36 (Electrical and Electronics)

Year	No. of Firms	α_0	α_1	α_3	$\alpha_{2,0}$	$\alpha_{2,1}$	$\alpha_{2,2}$	$\alpha_{2,3}$	$\alpha_{2,4}$	$\alpha_{2,5}$	$\alpha_{2,6}$	$\alpha_{2,7}$	$\sum_{k=0}^{7} \hat{\alpha}_{2,k}$	Adj. R^2
1975	44	0.266	0.136	1.833	0.361	0.536	0.561	0.471	0.304	0.095	—	—	2.328	0.91
		(0.73)	(6.01)	(1.61)	(4.19)	(3.74)	(3.73)	(3.21)	(2.41)	(2.04)				
1976	49	−0.346	0.181	0.856	0.342	0.514	0.547	0.476	0.331	0.146	—	—	2.356	0.91
		(−0.84)	(7.40)	(0.69)	(5.18)	(5.24)	(5.26)	(5.28)	(4.94)	(2.86)				
1977	52	−1.143	0.191	1.543	0.356	0.543	0.593	0.535	0.402	0.226	0.037	—	2.692	0.89
		(−4.50)	(7.51)	(2.06)	(5.08)	(5.22)	(5.54)	(6.08)	(7.30)	(5.14)	(2.13)			
1978	66	−0.943	0.236	0.048	0.293	0.451	0.498	0.458	0.356	0.218	0.067	—	2.341	0.86
		(−3.14)	(7.92)	(0.08)	(3.66)	(3.75)	(3.89)	(4.08)	(4.23)	(3.63)	(2.36)			
1979	69	−1.074	0.249	0.527	0.318	0.490	0.542	0.501	0.393	0.244	0.082	—	2.570	0.88
		(−3.41)	(7.88)	(0.87)	(3.74)	(3.82)	(3.98)	(4.17)	(4.41)	(4.06)	(2.94)			
1980	68	−1.069	0.189	1.303	0.099	0.180	0.243	0.289	0.316	0.325	0.302	0.269	2.023	0.82
		(−2.52)	(6.53)	(1.57)	(4.95)	(5.00)	(5.06)	(5.07)	(5.01)	(5.07)	(4.79)	(4.71)		
1981	70	−0.387	0.217	0.906	0.104	0.188	0.254	0.301	0.330	0.339	0.316	0.287	2.119	0.85
		(−0.89)	(7.40)	(1.78)	(4.00)	(4.08)	(4.03)	(4.06)	(4.07)	(4.03)	(3.90)	(3.87)		
Mean		−0.671	0.200	1.002	0.268	0.415	0.463	0.433	0.347	0.228	0.115	0.079	2.348	0.87
R&D amortization, δ_k^a					0.114	0.177	0.197	0.184	0.148	0.097	0.049	0.034		

Note:

[a] The R&D annual amortization rates are calculated from the mean R&D coefficients $\alpha_{2,k}$ ($k = 0, \ldots, 7$) as follows: $\delta_k = \hat{\alpha}_{2,k} / \sum_{k=0}^{7} \hat{\alpha}_{2,k}$.

Coefficient estimates of regression (4), run cross-sectionally for each of the years 1975–81, using instrumental variables and the Almon lag procedure (t-values in parentheses):

Regression is $(OI/S)_{lt} = \alpha_0 + \alpha_1 (TA/S)_{l,t-1} + \sum_k \alpha_{2,k}(RD/S)_{lt-k} + \alpha_3(AD/S)_{l,t-1} + e_{lt}$, where $(OI/S)_{lt}$ = operating income (before depreciation, R&D amortization, and advertising expenses) over sales, of firm i in year t, $(TA/S)_{l,t-1}$ = tangible assets (plant and equipment, investment in unconsolidated subsidiaries, and inventory), in current dollars, over sales, $(RD/S)_{l,t-k}$ = annual R&D expenditures over sales, in current dollars, of firm i for k lag years, $(AD/S)_{l,t-1}$ = advertising expenses over sales, of firm i. The instrumental variable for the $(RD/S)_{l,t}$ term is the four-digit industry-average R&D over sales, expression (4b).

Electrical and Electronics industry (over the period 1975–81), the amortization rate of current R&D expenditures was 11.4 per cent. The amortization rate of the preceding year's (year 1) R&D expenditures was 17.7 per cent. Accordingly, the amortization of the R&D capital in 1982 (the proper R&D expense, rather than the GAAP expense) consists of 11.4 per cent of the 1982 R&D expenditure, plus 17.7 per cent of the 1981 R&D expenditure, plus 19.7 per cent of the 1980 R&D expenditure, and so on back in time over all R&D vintages that are still contributing to year t earnings. The annual amortization rates, bottom line of Table 2, are used to compute both the R&D capital and its amortization for 1982, as will be demonstrated in Section 4. Note that prior to 1975 (the year FAS No. 2 came into effect) some firms capitalized part of their R&D expenditures. This introduces noise into our data and increases measurement error, particularly in the early sample years (the 1970s) which rely heavily on pre-FAS No. 2 data. This may explain the apparent shift (nonstationarity) of the R&D coefficients ($\hat{\alpha}_{2,0}$; $\hat{\alpha}_{2,1}$; ...) in Table 2, occurring in 1980.

Table 2 demonstrates the estimation of the R&D amortization rates for firms in the Electrical and Electronics industry in 1982. Similar estimations were made for all sample years and industries, allowing the adjustment of reported earnings and book values of all sample firms and years (1975–91). An overview of these estimates is provided in Table 3 which reports for each sample industry the mean coefficients of the yearly regressions. The amortization rates, δ_k, in Table 3, were computed from the sixteen yearly regressions, 1975–90, and were used in the earnings and book value adjustments made for the last sample year, 1991. Note that in Table 3, the coefficients of tangible capital, α_1, indicating the contribution of the beginning-of-year tangible assets to operating income, range from 0.084 (Other Industries) to 0.155 (Electrical and Electronics). These values indicate the industry-average annual return on tangible assets, and they are in line with the estimates of Griliches and Mairesee (1990), ranging from 0.11 to 0.15. The coefficients of advertising intensity, α_3 (a flow variable), range between 0.906 (Transportation Vehicles) and 1.639 (Scientific Instruments). Thus, a $1 advertising expenditure is associated with an operating income (before advertising) increase of roughly $1.00–1.60.

The length of the statistically significant lagged R&D coefficients, $\alpha_{2,k}$, in Table 3 indicates the average *duration* of R&D benefits (useful life of R&D capital). Thus, in Chemicals and Pharmaceutics, the average useful life of R&D is the longest—nine years ($\alpha_{2,8}$ is the last significant coefficient), while in Scientific Instruments the average R&D life is the shortest—five years. These results are generally consistent with Nadiri and Prucha (1992), whose estimates of the useful life of R&D range between seven and nine years. The different durations of R&D capital are mainly related to the ability of innovators to *appropriate* the benefits of innovations, namely to prevent others from copying or imitating them. Benefit appropriation is primarily achieved by patents, but industries

Table 3. R&D Amortization Rates of All Sample Industries For 1991

Industry	Chemicals and Pharmaceutics (28)		Machinery and Computer Hardware (35)		Electrical and Electronics (36)		Transportation Vehicles (37)		Scientific Instruments (38)		All other R&D Industries	
No. of Firm-years	1106		1751		1375		757		990		5653	
Coefficient	α	δ_k^a	α	δ_k	α	δ_k	α	δ_k	α	δ_k	α	δ_k
$\hat{\alpha}_0$	0.812		−0.658		−0.517		1.487		0.278		−0.517	
$\hat{\alpha}_1$	0.137		0.135		0.155		0.109		0.132		0.084	
$\hat{\alpha}_3$	1.234		1.493		1.055		0.906		1.639		1.015	
$\hat{\alpha}_{2,0}$	0.215	0.082	0.177	0.106	0.224	0.114	0.146	0.072	0.232	0.135	0.201	0.110
$\hat{\alpha}_{2,1}$	0.350	0.133	0.279	0.168	0.347	0.176	0.249	0.123	0.355	0.207	0.322	0.176
$\hat{\alpha}_{2,2}$	0.415	0.158	0.319	0.192	0.386	0.196	0.313	0.155	0.413	0.240	0.376	0.205
$\hat{\alpha}_{2,3}$	0.424	0.161	0.309	0.186	0.360	0.183	0.344	0.170	0.419	0.244	0.376	0.205
$\hat{\alpha}_{2,4}$	0.387	0.147	0.262	0.157	0.288	0.146	0.347	0.171	0.299	0.174	0.324	0.177
$\hat{\alpha}_{2,5}$	0.317	0.121	0.192	0.115	0.186	0.095	0.327	0.162			0.233	0.127
$\hat{\alpha}_{2,6}$	0.226	0.086	0.125	0.076	0.098	0.050	0.298	0.147				
$\hat{\alpha}_{2,7}$	0.158	0.060			0.079	0.040						
$\hat{\alpha}_{2,8}$	0.136	0.052										
$\sum_{k=0}^{N}\hat{\alpha}_{2,k}$	2.628		1.663		1.968		2.024		1.718		1.832	
Adj. R^2	0.89		0.68		0.73		0.73		0.80		0.59	

Notes:

[a] Annual R&D amortization rate = $\delta_k = \hat{\alpha}_{2,k} / \sum_k \hat{\alpha}_{2,k}$.

Mean coefficient estimates of regression (4a), over the years 1975–90, using instrumental variables and the Almon lag procedure.

All the α coefficients, except for the intercept, are statistically significant at the 0.05 level or better (two-tail t-test).

differ widely in the effectiveness of patent protection. Both Mansfield (1986) and Levin *et al.* (1987) argue that patents are highly effective in appropriating returns in the chemicals and drug industries, moderately effective for mechanical equipment and machinery manufacturers, and least effective (i.e. it is relatively easy for competitors to 'invent around' the patents) in instruments and motor vehicles.[13] This ranking generally accords with Table 3 estimates regarding the cross-industry differences in the useful life of the R&D investment.

The estimated total benefits of \$1 investment in R&D, $\sum_k \hat{\alpha}_{2,k}$, are reported on the next to bottom line of Table 3. These benefits range from \$2.628 for Chemicals and Pharmaceutics to 1.663 in Machinery and Computer Hardware.[14] Note that these undiscounted benefits accrue over a relatively long period of time—five to nine years. Based on the estimated flow of benefits (the $\alpha_{2,k}$ in Table 3), assumed to accrue at year-end, the annual internal rate of return of a \$1 R&D investment in chemicals and pharmaceutics is 28 per cent. Similarly computed, the estimated annual rates of return on a \$1 investment in R&D in the remaining industries are: Machinery and Computer Hardware—15 per cent, Electrical and Electronics—22 per cent, Transportation Vehicles—19 per cent, Scientific Instruments—20 per cent, and Other Industries 20 per cent. Recall, that these are benefits in terms of operating income, namely before depreciation and amortization, general expenses, and taxes. In terms of after tax net income, our return estimates accord well with the Grabowski and Mueller (1978) return estimates of 16.7 per cent for chemicals and pharmaceutics and 11.7 per cent over all R&D industries, as well as with the Lichtenberg and Siegel (1989) more recent estimates of 13 per cent return on R&D investment across all industries (for the period 1972–85).

---

4. Adjusting Reported Earnings and Book Values

The industry-wide amortization rates, δ_k, are used to compute for each sample firm the annual R&D *amortization*, RA_{it},

$$RA_{it} = \sum_k \delta_k RD_{i,t-k}. \qquad (6)$$

The periodic R&D amortization (different, of course, from the GAAP expense, which is the current R&D outlay—RD_{it}) is thus the sum of current and past R&D outlays, $RD_{i,t-k}$, each multiplied by the appropriate amortization rate, δ_k.

Earnings adjusted for the R&D capitalization, X_{it}^C, are equal to reported (GAAP) earnings, X_{it}^E, plus the expensed R&D outlay, RD_{it}, minus the R&D amortization(6):

$$X_{it}^C = X_{it}^E + RD_{it} - RA_{it}. \tag{7}$$

To avoid complicating the analysis, we do not adjust earnings under R&D capitalization, X_{it}^C, for deferred taxes.[15] The association documented below between returns and the R&D-adjusted data would have been strengthened by adding deferred taxes.

The *R&D capital* at year-end, RDC_{it}, of each sample firm is obtained by cumulating for each year, starting with 1975 (the year FAS No. 2 became effective), the unamortized portion of the annual R&D expenditures:

$$RDC_{it} = \sum_{k=0}^{N-1} RD_{i,t-k} \left(1 - \sum_{j=0}^{k} \delta_j \right), \tag{8}$$

where N is useful life or duration of R&D (e.g. nine years in the chemicals and pharmaceutics industry). The R&D capital is thus the sum of the unamortized portion of the current year R&D outlay, $RD_{i,t} \times (1 - \delta_0)$, plus the unamortized portion of last year's R&D outlay which is amortized twice, $RD_{i,t-1} \times (1 - \delta_0 - \delta_1)$, and so on back to the end of the useful R&D life. A detailed example of the computation of earnings under R&D capitalization (X_{it}^C), the R&D amortization (RA_{it}), and the R&D capital (RDC_{it}), for Merck & Co. is provided in the Appendix.

The impact of the above adjustments on the sample firms' reported data is substantial. The average (over firms and years) understatement of reported earnings due to R&D expensing (i.e. the percentage difference between adjusted, X_{it}^C, and reported, X_{it}^E, earnings) ranges from 26.8 per cent in Electrical and Electronics to 9.7 per cent for 'Other Industries'. The average earnings understatement for all sample firms and years is 20.55 per cent. The understatement of reported equity, resulting from the absence of the R&D capital, ranges from 24.6 per cent for both Scientific Instruments and Machinery and Computer Hardware to 12.3 per cent in 'Other Industries'. The mean book value understatement for all sample firms and years is 22.2 per cent.

The relation between adjusted and reported return on equity (ROE) is more complicated, being a function or the growth rate in R&D expenditures, the amortization rate of the R&D capital, and its duration. Holding other things equal, ROE based on R&D capitalization will be higher than reported ROE for firms with a sufficiently high growth rate of R&D expenditures. This is corroborated by a regression run across all sample firms and years, of the difference between capitalized and reported ROE on the five-year geometric growth rate of R&D expenditures, which yielded a coefficient 0.115 (t-value = 6.49) for the R&D growth rate.

5. Contemporaneous Analysis: Stock Prices, Returns, and R&D Capitalization

We wish to examine the value relevance of the variables derived from the R&D capitalization process described above. This can be done by examining, in a *contemporaneous* setting, the association between stock prices (or returns) and the R&D capitalization estimates, as well as evaluating the *intertemporal* association between R&D-adjusted variables and subsequent stock returns. The former, contemporaneous analysis, indicates the extent of current recognition of R&D relevance by investors, while the intertemporal analysis may suggest market inefficiency (i.e. investors failing to fully recognize the value relevance of R&D).

Kothari and Zimmerman (1995) evaluate the adequacy of price and return models for accounting research and conclude that the 'use of both return and price models has the potential to yield more convincing evidence'. We adopt this recommendation and examine the following return and price models.

5.1. Definition of Variables and Models

P_{it} = share price of firm i three months after fiscal year-end,

R_{it} = annual stock return from nine months before fiscal t year-end through three months after it,

X_{it}^E, X_{it}^C = reported (GAAP) and adjusted (7) earnings-per-share (before extraordinary items), respectively,

$X_{it}^C - X_{it}^E$ = 'error' or misstatement in reported earnings due to the R&D expensing; this misstatement is equal to $RD_{it} - RA_{it}$, namely the annual R&D outlay minus the R&D amortization, which in turn is equal to the *net* (amortized) investment in R&D during t,

$X_{it}^B =$ $X_{it}^E + RD_{it}$ is reported earnings before the R&D expensing.

Return Models

$$R_{it} = \alpha_1 + \beta_1 X_{it}^E + \gamma_1(X_{it}^C - X_{it}^E) + u_{it}, \tag{9}$$

$$R_{it} = \alpha_2 + \beta_2 X_{it}^E + \gamma_2 \Delta X_{it}^E + \delta_2(X_{it}^C - X_{it}^E) + \Omega_2 \Delta(X_{it}^C - X_{it}^E) + u_{it}, \tag{10}$$

$$R_{it} = \alpha_3 + \beta_3 X_{it}^B + \gamma_3 \Delta X_{it}^B + \delta_3(X_{it}^C - X_{it}^E) + \Omega_3 \Delta(X_{it}^C - X_{it}^E) + u_{it}. \tag{11}$$

All right-hand variables in (9)–(11) are deflated by beginning of fiscal year share price, $P_{i,t-1}$. Annual differencing is indicated by Δ.

Model (9) is the basic returns–earnings relation: stock returns regressed on the price-deflated level of earnings. We single out for examination of value relevance the estimated 'error' or misstatement in reported earnings, $X_{it}^C - X_{it}^E$.

Model (10) incorporates the first differences in reported earnings, ΔX_{it}^{E}, and in the earnings misstatements, $\Delta(X_{it}^{C} - X_{it}^{E})$, because differencing often yields a stationary series (Christie, 1987). Model (11) substitutes X_{it}^{B}, reported earnings *before* R&D expensing, for the after R&D earnings, X_{it}^{E}. The reason: when X_{it}^{E} is the explanatory variable (model (10)), the R&D expenditure (RD$_{it}$) is a component of all four independent variables, and thus may be associated with different estimated coefficients. In model (11), on the other hand, the R&D expenditure is only present in the two right-most independent variables.

Price models

$$P_{it} = \alpha_4 + \beta_4 X_{it}^{E} + \gamma_4 (X_{it}^{C} - X_{it}^{E}) + u_{it}, \tag{12}$$

$$P_{it} = \alpha_5 + \beta_5 X_{it}^{E} + \gamma_5 (X_{it}^{C} - X_{it}^{E}) + \Omega_5 (BV_{it}^{C} - BV_{it}^{E}) + u_{it}. \tag{13}$$

Expression (12) is the parsimonious price model, with the 'error' in reported earnings singled out. Model (13) accounts for both the misstatements in reported earnings and in book value. The latter, $BV_{it}^{C} - BV_{it}^{E}$, equals the total capitalized value of R&D, RDC$_{it}$ in (8). Since the price regressions are not deflated, we applied White's correction for heteroscedasticity. We expect positive values for all the coefficients (except the intercepts) in both the returns and price regressions. The reason: earnings are expected to be positively correlated with stock prices and returns, while the misstatements in reported earnings and book value, which equal the net annual investment in R&D and the total R&D capital, respectively, should on average be associated with market value increases (assuming managers follow the net present value rule in their R&D decisions).

5.2. Findings

Table 4 presents estimates of the contemporaneous price and return regressions outlined above. Specifically, for each sample firm and year we adjusted earnings, book values, and R&D capital (expressions (6)–(8)), from data publicly available prior to the year of adjustment. For example, the 1982 adjusted earnings, book values, and R&D capital of the sample firms are based on R&D amortization rates computed from 1975–81 data, as demonstrated in Table 2 for the Electric and Electronics industry. The values reported in Table 4 are mean regression coefficients and corresponding t-values derived from the sixteen individual-year regressions, 1976–91.[16]

It is evident from Table 4 that in all the return and price configurations (except for rows 5 and 9), our adjustment to reported earnings, $X_{it}^{C} - X_{it}^{E}$ (the difference between earnings under R&D capitalization and GAAP earnings), is as expected positive and highly statistically significant.[17] Furthermore, the coefficients of the earnings misstatement, $X_{it}^{C} - X_{it}^{E}$ are substantially larger than

Table 4. Contemporaneous Analysis: Prices (returns)—Financial Variables, 1976–91

Dependent Variable	Independent Variables								Adj. R^2
	Intercept	X_{it}^E	ΔX_{it}^E	$(X_{it}^C - X_{it}^E)$	$\Delta(X_{it}^C - X_{it}^E)$	X_{it}^B	ΔX_{it}^B	$(BV_{it}^C - BV_{it}^E)$	
1. Return (R_{it})—All firms	0.969 (17.38)	1.114 (11.11)	—	2.030 (4.14)	—	—	—	—	0.09
2. Return—Upper quartile[a]	0.425 (4.21)	1.197 (8.79)	—	2.207 (5.68)	—	—	—	—	0.09
3. Return (R_{it})	−0.004 (−0.07)	0.805 (6.17)	0.854 (7.41)	2.286 (4.48)	0.091 (0.16)	—	—	—	0.12
4. Return—Upper quartile[a]	−0.031 (−0.53)	0.586 (4.29)	0.767 (5.23)	2.576 (4.70)	−0.928 (−1.13)	—	—	—	0.11
5. Return (R_{it})	−0.036 (−0.59)	—	—	0.746 (1.30)	−0.100 (−0.18)	0.884 (7.13)	0.690 (6.11)	—	0.13
6. Return—Upper quartile[a]	−0.087 (−1.35)	—	—	2.622 (4.21)	−0.777 (−0.75)	0.718 (7.54)	0.757 (5.86)	—	0.13
7. Price (P_{it})—All firms	9.425 (22.25)	6.240 (11.28)	—	10.612 (14.37)	—	—	—	—	0.44
8. Price—Upper quartile	7.882 (12.93)	6.335 (16.21)	—	8.760 (8.31)	—	—	—	—	0.46
9. Price (P_{it})	9.025 (10.73)	5.193 (8.25)	—	0.953 (0.92)	—	—	—	2.368 (16.11)	0.46
10. Price—Upper quartile[a]	5.453 (6.50)	4.701 (16.94)	—	2.460 (2.55)	—	—	—	2.070 (11.68)	0.55

Note:

[a] These regressions were run for firms in the upper quartile of the R&D capital to reported book value ratio, (RDC/BV)$_{it}$, namely firms with a relatively large estimated R&D capital. X_{it}^C and BV_{it}^C are earnings and book values adjusted for R&D capitalization. X_{it}^B is reported earnings before R&D expensing. X_{it}^E and BV_{it}^E are reported earnings and equity, respectively. Mean coefficient estimates from stock price and return regressions run on reported earnings (X_{it}^E), the misstatement in reported earnings ($X_{it}^C - X_{it}^E$), and the misstatement in equity ($BV_{it}^C - BV_{it}^E$). T-values in parentheses.

those of reported earnings. For example, in row 1, the mean coefficient of $X_{it}^C - X_{it}^E$ is 2.030, almost twice as large as the earnings level coefficient, 1.114. In the price regressions (rows 7 and 8), the coefficients of $X_{it}^C - X_{it}^E$ are roughly 50 per cent larger than the earnings coefficients. Since $X_{it}^C - X_{it}^E$ is equal to the net (of amortization) annual investment in R&D, the large regression coefficients attest to the high value placed on this investment by investors. Such a high value accords with a major theme of this study, namely that R&D investment contributes, on average, to future earnings and cash flows. When the estimated R&D capital ($RDC_{it} = BV_{it}^C - BV_{it}^E$) is included in the price regressions (rows 9–10), it too is highly statistically significant. Thus, both the annual net investment in R&D and the cumulated R&D capital are value relevant to investors.[18]

Our sample is large (about 1300 companies in Table 4) and therefore contains a fair number of firms with relatively small R&D expenditures, potentially distorting the above findings. Accordingly, we add a focus on firms with relatively large R&D investment by ranking all sample firms in every year by their R&D capital-to-equity values (i.e. RDC_{it}/BV_{it}^E), and running the price and return regressions over firms in the upper quartile of this ranking. Estimates of these regressions are reported in rows 2, 4, 6, 8, and 10 in Table 4. It is evident that, in the returns regressions (rows 2, 4, 6), the coefficients of the earnings misstatement, $X_{it}^C - X_{it}^E$, for intensive R&D capital firms are larger and more significant than the corresponding total sample coefficients. Furthermore, in the two cases where the coefficient of $X_{it}^C - X_{it}^E$ for the total sample are statistically insignificant (regressions 5 and 9), the coefficients of the same variable for firms with large R&D capital (rows 6 and 10) are highly significant.

5.3. A Survivorship Bias?

Can the positive and statistically significant association between the R&D capitalization values and both stock prices and returns (Table 4) be driven by a sample selection bias? Could these results be due to our sample consisting of firms which were ex post successful in their R&D activities? We think not.

First, our main source of data, the R&D Master File (Section 2) was compiled from successive COMPUSTAT tapes, starting with 1978. Accordingly, firms which were included in earlier tapes, yet were subsequently dropped because of bankruptcies or mergers, are included in the R&D Master File and in our sample. Moreover, the R&D Master File includes the COMPUSTAT Research File which contains, among others, failed firms. This inclusion in our sample of failed and merged companies mitigates a possible survivorship bias.

We nevertheless wished to examine directly the existence of a survivorship bias, and therefore computed 'Jensen's (1968) alphas' for the sample firms (see also Ball and Kothari, 1991, for use of Jensen's alphas). This parameter, reflecting *abnormal returns*, is derived from the following monthly time-series regression:

$$R_{RD,t} - R_{Ft} = \alpha + \beta(R_{Mt} - R_{Ft}) + e_t, \qquad (14)$$

where

$R_{RD,t}$ = value-weighted return on the sample firms in month t (192 months during 1976–91),

R_{Ft} = risk-free return, measured as the average ninety-day rate on Treasury bills, in month t,

R_M = CRSP value-weighted market return in month t.

Regression (14) was run over the 192 months in 1976–91. The estimated α coefficient reflects the average abnormal return of the sample firms relative to the market. Accordingly, if our sample is characterized by unusually good performers (a survivorship bias), then the estimated α should be positive and statistically significant.

The estimated coefficients of expression (14), with t-values in parentheses, are

$$\alpha = -0.0003, \quad \beta = 0.842, \quad \text{Adj. } R^2 = 0.86.$$
$$(-0.25) \qquad (33.81)$$

The estimated Jensen's alpha is thus insignificantly different from zero.[19] Accordingly, the value relevance of the R&D adjustment to earnings as well as that of the estimated R&D capital, apparent from Table 4, do not appear to be driven by a survivorship bias in our sample.

6. Intertemporal Analysis: R&D Capital and Subsequent Stock Returns

The contemporaneous analysis (Section 5), indicating the value relevance of the R&D capitalization estimates, leaves open a most intriguing and important question: Do investors fully recognize the value relevance of R&D information, when reported or do they only adjust partially for the R&D expensing under GAAP? Such partial adjustment is analogous to the 'post earnings announcement drift' (e.g. Bernard and Thomas, 1990), indicating that while investors generally react to unexpected earnings at the announcement date, such reaction is incomplete (an underreaction), as evidenced by the systematic return drifts subsequent to the earnings announcements. The extent (completeness) of investor reaction to new information bears on the efficiency of capital markets and may also have important regulatory implications. For example, if investors are found to over- or underreact to current R&D information, a case can be made for changing the disclosure environment to improve investors' comprehension of the information.

The extent of investors' reaction to R&D information can be examined in an *intertemporal* setting, where R&D capitalization estimates based on currently available information are associated with subsequent stock returns. A significant association may suggest an incomplete contemporaneous adjustment to R&D information. We examine this association within a model recently used by Fama and French (1992), where stock returns were regressed on *lagged* values of the following fundamentals: systematic risk (β), firm size (market capitalization), the book-to-market ratio, financial leverage, and the earnings-to-price ratio. We add to these fundamentals the firm's estimated R&D capital scaled by its market value. Evaluating the relation between returns and lagged R&D capital within this model assures that the R&D variable does not proxy for other risk or mispricing variables (e.g. the book-to-market or the price-to-earnings ratios) present in the analysis. Accordingly, we estimate the following cross-sectional regression:

$$R_{i,t+j} = c_{0,j} + c_{1,j}\beta_{i,t} + c_{2,j}\ln(M)_{i,t} + c_{3,j}\ln(B/M)_{i,t} + c_{4,j}\ln(A/B)_{i,t}$$
$$+ c_{5,j}(E(+)/M)_{i,t} + c_{6,j}(E/M \text{ dummy})_{i,t}$$
$$+ c_{7,j}\ln(\text{RDC}/M)_{it} + e_{i,t+j}, \tag{15}$$

where

$R_{i,t+j}$ = *returns*: monthly stock returns of firm i, starting with the seventh month after fiscal t year-end, $j = 1, \ldots, 12$,

$\beta_{i,t}$ = *risk*: CAPM-based beta of firm i, estimated from sixty monthly stock returns up to month t (one month preceding the return calculation); a minimum of twenty-four months is required,

$M_{i,t}$ = *size*: market value of firm i, calculated as price times number of shares outstanding at t,

$(B/M)_{i,t}$ = *book-to-market*: ratio of book value of common equity plus deferred taxes to market value of equity of firm i at fiscal year-end,

$(A/B)_{i,t}$ = *leverage*: ratio of book value of total assets to book value of common equity of firm i at fiscal year-end,

$[E(+)/M]_{i,t}$ = *earnings/price ratio*: ratio of positive earnings before extraordinary items (plus income-statement deferred taxes, minus preferred dividends), to the market value of equity of firm i at fiscal year-end; this variable is set equal to 0 when earnings are negative,

$(E/M \text{ dummy})_{i,t}$ = 1 if earnings of firm i for fiscal t are negative, and 0 otherwise,

$(\text{RDC}/M)_{i,t}$ = *R&D capital*: estimated R&D capital (expression (8)) over market value of equity at year-end.

The following time-line clarifies the intertemporal regressions:

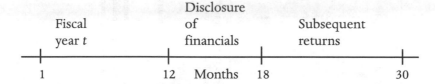

The accounting fundamentals—book value, earnings, total assets, and R&D capital (RDC)—pertain to fiscal year t (months 1–12). Six months (13–18) are then allowed for the public disclosure of fiscal t annual financial statements by all sample firms, followed by twelve monthly stock returns, $R_{i,t+j}$ (months 19–30). For each of the fifteen fiscal years examined in this analysis (1975–89), we run regression (15) cross-sectionally for each of the subsequent twelve return months.[20] In total, 180 cross-sectional regressions were computed (15 years × 12 regressions per year).[21]

Table 5 reports mean coefficient estimates of expression (15) over the 180 months, for the total sample (top panel) and for the firms in the upper quartile of the R&D capital-to-total assets ranking (i.e. firms with a relatively large R&D investment). The first row of coefficients in each panel is generated by a replication of the Fama–French (1992) analysis, namely regression (15) *without* the R&D variable. This was aimed at examining the conformity of our sample of R&D firms with the COMPUSTAT population (Fama–French sample), with respect to the returns–fundamentals' relation. It is evident from Table 5 that a close conformity indeed exists: as in Fama–French, the only two variables that are statistically significant are size and the book-to-market ratio. The systematic risk, β, is in each regression statistically insignificant, as are the remaining fundamentals. Our results are close to Fama–French's in terms of coefficient sizes. For example, Fama and French report that the average risk premium for the book-to-market factor (the premium per unit of the regression slope of book-to-market), is 0.40 per cent per month, while our estimated book-to-market (B/M) coefficient (upper panel of Table 5) is 0.33 per cent. Thus, in terms of the returns-fundamentals relation, our sample of science-based companies does not differ much from the total COMPUSTAT sample.

When the R&D capital-to-market (RDC/M) ratio is included in the regression (second row of each panel), its coefficient is positive and statistically significant (0.0015, $t = 3.10$) at better than the 0.01 level. This finding is even more pronounced for firms in the upper quartile of the R&D capital-to-total assets ratio, namely those with relatively large R&D capital. The coefficient of R&D capital, 0.0114 (Table 5 bottom row), is about eight times larger than the R&D coefficient for the total sample (0.0015). Given the mean value RDC/M, 0.327, the regression coefficient of 0.0114 (monthly) translates to an annual return of

Table 5. Intertemporal Analysis: R&D Capital and Subsequent Stock Returns

Regressions	Intercept	β	Size	B/M	A/B	E(+)/M	E(−)/M dummy	RDC/M	Adj. R^2
Total sample									
Without R&D[a]	0.0251	−0.0012	−0.0014	0.0033	−0.0007	0.0022	−0.0030	—	0.036
	(5.95)	(−0.66)	(−2.74)	(2.90)	(−0.52)	(0.02)	(−1.46)	—	
With R&D[a]	0.0286	−0.0014	−0.0013	0.0002	−0.0013	0.0022	−0.0031	0.0015[b]	0.042
	(6.32)	(−0.79)	(−2.61)	(1.91)	(−1.00)	(0.27)	(−1.58)	(3.10)	
Upper quartile[c]									
Without R&D	0.0303	−0.0009	−0.0019	0.0043	0.0021	−0.0181	−0.0072	—	0.053
	(5.12)	(−0.30)	(−2.76)	(2.44)	(0.70)	(−0.87)	(−1.60)	—	
With R&D	0.0474	−0.0011	−0.0014	−0.0051	−0.0082	−0.0231	−0.0102	0.0114[d]	0.056
	(5.91)	(−0.41)	(−1.99)	(−1.52)	(−2.12)	(−1.09)	(−2.25)	(3.88)	

[a] 'Without R&D' and 'With R&D' refers to regression (15) run *without* the R&D capital, that is, the construct used by Fama and French (1992), and *with* the R&D capital, respectively.

[b] When R&D capital is scaled by financial variables rather than market value, the coefficient estimates and *t*-values (in parentheses) of R&D capital over total assets = 0.0015 (3.10), and R&D capital over book value of equity = 0.0014 (2.95). These regressions were run on firms in the upper quartile of the R&D capital-to-total assets ratio, namely firms with a large R&D capital.

[c] These regressions were run on firms in the upper quartile of the R&D capital-to-total assets ratio, namely firms with a large R&D capital.

[d] The coefficient estimates and *t*-values (parentheses) of R&D capital over total assets are: 0.0114 (3.88), and R&D capital over book value of equity = 0.0075 (3.41).

Mean coefficient estimates of cross-sectional regressions (15) of monthly stock returns on lagged values of fundamental variables. The returns are for the twelve months after fiscal year-end (plus six months). The means are computed over 180 regressions run for each month in 1975–89. *T*-statistics are reported in parentheses.

Regression: $R_{i,t+j} = c_0 + c_1\beta_{it} + c_2\ln(M)_{it} + c_3\ln(B/M)_{it} + c_4\ln(A/B)_{it} + c_5(E(+)/M)_{it} + c_6(E/M \text{ dummy})_{it} + c_7\ln(RDC/M)_{it} + e_{i,t+j}$,

with $R_{i,t+j}$ = twelve monthly stock returns of firm *i* from the seventh month after fiscal year-end, β_i = CAPM beta of firm *i*, estimated from sixty monthly stock returns (minimum of twenty-four) up to month *t*, $(M)_{it}$ = market value of equity of firm *i* at *t*, $(B/M)_{it}$ = book-to-market ratio of firm *i* at fiscal year-end, $(A/B)_{it}$ = ratio of book value of total assets of firm *i* to book value of equity, at fiscal year-end, $(E(+)/M)_{it}$ = ratio of positive earnings to the market value of equity at fiscal year-end and equal to 0 when earnings are negative, $(E/M \text{ dummy})_{it}$ = 1 if earnings are negative and 0 otherwise, $(RDC/M)_{it}$ = R&D capital-to-market value of firm *i* at fiscal year-end.

4.57 per cent. This is our estimate of the average market mispricing of R&D capital in R&D-intensive companies.

Note that for the upper-quartile firms, the statistical significance of the book-to-market ratio vanishes with the introduction of the R&D capital, while leverage (A/B) and the negative earnings dummy, $E(-)/M$, become significant. It should also be noted that the association between R&D capital and subsequent returns does not depend on the scaling of the R&D variable by *market* value. As footnotes b and d to Table 5 indicate, when we scale R&D capital by *book* value of total assets (A), or by the *book* value of equity (B), the regression coefficients of R&D capital and their significance level are remarkably close to those in the table.[22]

Summarizing, firms' R&D capital was found to be associated with subsequent stock returns. Given the analysis and discussion of Section 5.3, this association does not appear to be due to a survivorship bias. Similarly to other findings of this type (e.g. the book-to-market association with returns in Fama and French, 1992), this association may result from a mispricing of securities, namely investors' underreaction to R&D information, or it may reflect an extra-market risk factor associated with R&D capital (i.e. equilibrium returns). Disentangling these alternative explanations is a major endeavour, obviously beyond the boundaries of this study. Whether the R&D association with subsequent returns indicates mispricing or the existence of an extra-market risk factor, it enhances our conclusion concerning the value relevance of R&D capitalization.

---

7. Summary

The following major conclusions can be drawn from the evidence presented above:

1. The R&D capitalization process developed here yields statistically reliable estimates of the amortization rate of the R&D capital. These amortization rates are used to compute firm-specific R&D capital and adjust reported earnings and equity (book) values to reflect the capitalization of R&D.

2. The major outcomes of these adjustments—the corrections to reported earnings and book values for R&D capitalization—were found to be strongly associated with stock prices and returns, indicating that the R&D capitalization process yields value relevant information to investors.

3. The estimated R&D capital does not appear to be fully reflected contemporaneously in stock prices, since R&D capital is associated with subsequent

Table 6. Merck & Co.: The Adjustment of Reported Earnings and Book Values for R&D Capitalization (in $ millions)

	Reported Data				Adjusted Data				
Year	Earnings*	R&D Expenditures*	Equity*	ROE	R&D Amortization[a]	R&D Capital[b]	Earnings[c]	Equity[d]	ROE
1975	228.78	124.51	947.00	0.28	80.54	334.11	272.76	1281.11	0.25
1976	255.48	136.35	1099.22	0.27	91.06	379.40	300.77	1478.62	0.23
1977	277.52	144.90	1275.03	0.25	102.38	421.92	320.04	1696.95	0.22
1978	307.33	161.35	1452.82	0.24	114.72	468.55	354.17	1921.38	0.21
1979	381.78	188.07	1663.45	0.26	128.63	527.99	441.22	2191.44	0.23
1980	415.40	233.90	1863.32	0.25	146.49	615.40	502.80	2478.72	0.23
1981	398.26	274.17	2001.46	0.21	168.61	720.95	503.82	2722.41	0.20
1982	415.14	320.16	2203.99	0.21	193.78	845.33	539.51	3049.31	0.20
1983	450.85	356.04	2434.61	0.20	227.04	974.33	579.86	3408.95	0.19
1984	492.97	393.12	2544.16	0.20	261.12	1106.34	624.97	3650.50	0.18
1985	539.90	426.26	2634.00	0.21	297.03	1235.56	669.12	3869.56	0.18
1986	675.70	479.80	2569.10	0.26	335.50	1379.86	820.00	3948.96	0.21
1987	906.40	565.70	2116.70	0.35	379.31	1566.25	1092.79	3682.95	0.28
1988	1206.80	668.80	2855.80	0.57	431.53	1803.52	1444.07	4659.32	0.39
1989	1495.40	750.50	3520.60	0.52	491.43	2062.59	1754.47	5583.19	0.38
1990	1781.20	854.00	3834.40	0.51	560.52	2356.07	2074.68	6190.47	0.37
1991	2121.70	987.80	4916.20	0.55	640.81	2703.06	2468.69	7619.26	0.40

Notes:

* Earnings = Compustat item #18, R&D expenditures = Compustat item #46, Book value of equity = Compustat item #60.

[a] The R&D amortization, RA_{it}, for 1991 ($640.81 million), is calculated as follows:

$$RA_{it} = \sum_k \delta_k RD_{t,-k}$$

$= 0.082 \times 987.8 + 0.133 \times 854 + 0.158 \times 750.5 + 0.161 \times 668.8 + 0.147 \times 565.7 + 0.121 \times 479.8 + 0.086 \times 426.3 + 0.06 \times 393.1 + 0.052 \times 356$

$= 640.81$ million.

[b] R&D capital, RDC_{it}, for 1991 ($2,703.06 million), is calculated as follows:

$$RDC_{it} = \sum_{k=0}^{N-1} RD_{it-k} (1 - \sum_{j=k}^{k} \delta_j)$$

$= (1 - 0.082) \times 987.8 + (1 - 0.082 - 0.133) \times 854 + (1 - 0.082 - 0.133 - 0.158) \times 750.5 + (1 - 0.082 - 0.133 - 0.158 - 0.161) \times 668.8 + (1 - 0.082 - 0.133 - 0.158$
$- 0.161 - 0.147) \times 565.7 + (1 - 0.082 - 0.133 - 0.158 - 0.161 - 0.147 - 0.121) \times 479.8 + (1 - 0.082 - 0.133 - 0.158 - 0.161 - 0.147 - 0.121 - 0.086) \times 426.3$
$+ (1 - 0.082 - 0.133 - 0.158 - 0.161 - 0.147 - 0.121 - 0.086 - 0.06) \times 393.1 + (1 - 0.082 - 0.133 - 0.158 - 0.161 - 0.147 - 0.121 - 0.086 - 0.06 - 0.052)$
$\times 356 = \$2,703$ million.

The coefficients 0.082, 0.133 ... in footnotes a and b are the amortization rates, δ_k, for the Chemical and Pharmaceuticals industry presented in Table 3.

[c] Income under capitalization (X_{it}^C) = reported net income (X_{it}^E) + reported R&D expenditures (RD_{it}) − R&D amortization (RA_{it}).

[d] Equity under capitalization (BV_{it}^C) = reported equity (BV_{it}^E) + R&D capital (RDC_{it}).

stock returns. This suggests either a systematic mispricing of the shares of R&D-intensive firms (underreaction to R&D information), estimated at an annual rate of 4.57 per cent, or that the subsequent excess returns are compensating for an extra-market risk factor associated with R&D.

Taken together, these findings suggest that R&D capitalization yields statistically reliable and economically relevant information, contradicting a major tenet of FASB Statement No. 2: 'A direct relationship between research and development costs and specific future revenue generally has not been demonstrated'.

Appendix: Merck & Co.: Example of the Adjustment of Earnings and Book Values for R&D Capitalization

Table 6 presents Merck's reported (GAAP) and R&D-adjusted values for the years 1975–91. The four left-hand columns are derived from Merck's annual financial reports, while the five columns on the right are the adjusted values reflecting R&D capitalization. These adjustments are based on the procedures described in Sections 2–4 above, and are detailed in the footnotes to Table 6. The detailed computation of Merck's 1991 R&D amortization and its R&D capital, using the Chemicals and Pharmaceutics amortization rates (δ_k in Table 3) is presented on the bottom part of Table 6.

As expected, Merck's reported earnings and equity values are in every year lower than the corresponding R&D-adjusted values. However, Merck's return on equity (ROE) based on the capitalized numbers (right column) is substantially lower than its reported ROE (e.g. 0.40 vs 0.55 in 1991). This is mainly due to Merck's relatively low growth rate of R&D expenditures—less than 20 per cent a year during 1987–91—compared with about 35 per cent average annual growth rate in earnings over that period. In general, R&D-adjusted ROE will be higher than reported (GAAP) ROE when the growth rate of R&D expenditures is sufficiently large.

Notes

1. In 1985 the FASB made an exception to the full expensing requirement for some software development costs, see FAS No. 86 (Eccher, 1995). In several other countries, R&D capitalization is allowed and even required. For example, in the United Kingdom, SSAP 13 requires that expenditures on pure and applied research should be written off as incurred, but development expenditures may, in certain defined circumstances, be deferred to future periods. The Canadian Standard (section 345 of the CICA

Handbook) goes further to require the deferment of certain development expenditures. The International Accounting Standard, IAS 9, is generally in line with the Canadian standard with respect to R&D capitalization.

2. This formulation accords with production function estimations (e.g. Mairesse and Sassenou, 1991; Hall, 1993a), where gross output (e.g. sales) is related to labour and material inputs, as well as to the stocks of physical and intangible capital. Our dependent variable, earnings, proxies for output minus labour and material inputs, leaving the values of tangible and intangible assets as the independent variables.

3. Market values were also used in prior accounting research (e.g. Ben-Zion, 1978; Hirshey and Weygandt, 1985) to estimate R&D amortization rates.

4. It should also be noted that we estimate the value of R&D capital by relating an input measure (R&D expenditures) to an output indicator—earnings. There are various attempts in the economic literature to estimate the value of R&D capital by other output measures, such as the number of patents granted, the number of inventions resulting from the R&D process, or the frequency of citations in scientific publications and in patent requests (e.g. Pakes, 1985).

5. Replication of our estimates with net income (before extraordinary items) as the dependent variable yielded very similar results to those based on operating income.

6. Peles (1970), in one of the earliest studies on advertising amortization, also documents the short life (impact on subsequent sales) of advertising capital. His estimated annual amortization rates for advertising were: 100% for the car industry, 40–50% for beer advertising (i.e. roughly two-year life), and 35–45% for cigarettes.

7. The Master File was updated to 1991.

8. In addition to the checks made in the R&D database we eliminated from the sample firms that had large mergers (those contributing 50% or more to annual sales), since such mergers seriously disrupted the time series examined. The total number of firms eliminated due to mergers was 121.

9. We require at least four other firms in the four-digit SIC group. If less than four firms are available, the industry is defined at the three-digit level in which firm i is classified.

10. The industry classification in Table 1 (two-digit codes 28, 35, 36, 37, 38, and 'Other R&D Industries') is also used in the rest of the study. The individual two-digit industries resulted from our requirement that each one will have at least twenty firms in each year examined (1975–91). All industries with less than twenty firms in at least one year were grouped into 'Other R&D Industries'. We also required that each sample firm has at least ten annual lags of R&D data and its R&D/Sales ratio is at least 2%.

11. The industry R&D was also found by Berger (1993) to be the most significant variable in explaining firm-specific R&D expenditures (the other variables were: cash flow, GNP, Tobin's Q ratio, last year's R&D expenditures, and the R&D tax credit).

12. 1975 was the first year for the estimation of expression (4a). Note, however, that the R&D lagged data for the 1975 regression (as well as those for succeeding years) extend back to 1959, the first year on the R&D Master File.

13. Levin et al. (1987) suggest that patents are particularly effective in the chemical and drug industries because of the clear standards that can be applied to assess a patent's validity, e.g. a specific molecular structure. In contrast, it is more difficult to demonstrate and

defend the novelty of a new component of a mechanical system. Patents are the major, but not the only means of appropriating R&D benefits. Investment in complementary sales and service efforts and secrecy of the innovative process are other appropriability means (Cohen and Levin, 1989, section 4.3).

14. When expression (4a) was run without the instrumental variable (industry level R&D), the estimated lagged R&D coefficients were, in general, smaller and somewhat less significant. For example, for the Chemicals and Pharmaceutics industry (SIC code 28), the total R&D benefits of $1.00 investment estimated without the instrumental variable was $2.383, while the estimate with the instrumental variable was $2.628 (Table 3).

15. Note, however, Daley's (1995) finding that the deferred tax component of the reported tax expense is considered an expense by investors.

16. We estimate R&D amortization rates for every industry and year, 1975–90. These estimates enable us to adjust reported data from 1976 (1975 is 'lost' in the differencing of earnings) to 1991, the year subsequent to the end of amortization rate estimation.

17. The change in this variable, $\Delta(X_{it}^{C} - X_{it}^{E})$, is not significant, probably due to the relative stability for most firms of R&D expenditures in successive years. Indeed, the standard deviation of $X_{it}^{C} - X_{it}^{E}$ is about 50% larger than that of $\Delta(X_{it}^{C} - X_{it}^{E})$.

18. To examine whether the earnings and book value adjustments for R&D capitalization just proxy for expected growth, we reran the regressions in Table 4, adding to the independent variables the beginning-of-year market-to-book ratio, which reflects investors' expected growth (used by Collins and Kothari, 1989). The addition of this ratio decreases to some extent the coefficient of the earnings misstatement, $X_{it}^{C} - X_{it}^{E}$, but the latter remains statistically significant (at the 0.01 level). For example, in regression 1 (Table 4), the earnings misstatement coefficient is 2.030 ($t = 4.14$). When the market-to-book ratio is added to that regression, the earnings misstatement coefficient is 1.294 ($t = 3.07$).

19. When we ran regression (14) on annual rather than monthly returns, the estimated α coefficient was 0.0248 ($t = 0.85$), namely statistically insignificant. The annual β coefficient was 1.152 ($t = 6.569$), which appears more reasonable than the monthly β of 0.842 (above).

20. In the preceding analyses we examined the years 1975–91. Here we stop in 1989, since we need stock returns for $1\frac{1}{2}$ years subsequent to each fiscal year.

21. Note that these regressions are not run on overlapping months. For example, for the fiscal year ending in December 1980, the returns range from July 1981 to June 1982. The following fiscal year, ending December 1981, is associated with the nonoverlapping returns starting in July 1982 and ending in June 1983. The numbers of sample firms in each-sectional regression ranges between roughly 900 in the earlier sample years (the 1970s) to 1500 in the latter period.

22. The R&D capital in expression (15) is based on our estimation procedures described in Sections 2–4. As a comparison, we replaced in (15) that estimate with the *sum* of R&D outlays in the current and the preceding two years (i.e. $RD_{it} + RD_{i,t-1} + RD_{i,t-2}$). Over our entire sample and time period, this substitution made little difference with respect to the estimated R&D capital (RDC/M) coefficient and its statistical significance. However, when we focus on firms with relatively large R&D capital we obtain substantial differences.

For example, for the firms in the upper quartile of the R&D capital-to-total assets ratio, the estimated RDC/M coefficient based on the sum of the recent three years R&D is 0.0078 ($t = 3.01$), while the RDC/M coefficient based on the capitalization procedure (Table 5) is 0.114 ($t = 3.88$). When we focus on the firms in the top decile of the R&D capital-to-total assets ratio, the difference is even more striking. The RDC/M coefficient based on the three-year R&D is statistically insignificant (0.0105, $t = 1.20$), while that based on the capitalization procedure is large and significant (0.0165, $t = 1.85$). It appears, therefore, that our R&D estimation procedure yields different and improved results, compared with a mechanistic capitalization, such as the sum of R&D expenditures in the last three years.

References

Ball, R. and Kothari, S. P. (1991), 'Security returns around earnings announcements', *The Accounting Review*, 66: 718–38.

Ben Zion, U. (1978), 'The investment aspect of nonproduction expenditures: An empirical test', *Journal of Economics and Business*, 30: 224–9.

Berger, P. (1993), 'Explicit and implicit tax effects of the R&D tax credit', *Journal of Accounting Research*, 31: 131–71.

Bernard, V. and Thomas, J. (1990), 'Evidence that stock prices do not fully reflect the implications of current earnings for future earnings', *Journal of Accounting and Economics*, 13: 305–40.

Bublitz, B. and Ettredge, M. (1989), 'The information in discretion outlays: Advertising, research and development', *The Accounting Review*, 64: 108–24.

Chan, S., Martin, J., and Kensinger, J. (1990), 'Corporate research and development expenditures and share value', *Journal of Financial Economics*, 26: 255–76.

Christie, A. (1987), 'On cross-sectional analysis in accounting research', *Journal of Accounting and Economics*, 9: 231–58.

Cockburn, I. and Griliches, Z. (1988), 'Industry effects and appropriability measures in the stock market's valuation of R&D and patents', *American Economic Review*, 78: 419–23.

Cohen, W. and Levin, R. (1989), 'Empirical studies of innovation and market structure', in R. Schmalensee and R. Willig (eds), *Handbook of Industrial Organization*, Vol. II (Amsterdam: Elsevier Science B.V.)

——and Levinthal, D. (1989), 'Innovation and learning: The two faces of R&D—Implications for the analysis of R&D investment', *Economic Journal*, 99: 569–96.

Collins, D. W. and Kothari, S. P. (1989), 'An analysis of intertemporal and cross-sectional determinants of earnings response coefficients', *Journal of Accounting and Economics*, 12: 143–81.

Daley, M. (1995), *The Impact of Deferred Tax Allocation on Earnings as a Measure of Firm Performance*, Ph.D. Dissertation (Rochester, NY: University of Rochester).

Dukes, R. (1976), 'An Investigation of the Effects of Expensing Research and Development Costs on Security Prices,' in: Proceedings of the Conference on Topical Research in Accounting (New York, NY: New York University).

Eccher, E. (1995), *The Value Relevance of Capitalized Software Development Costs* (Evanston, IL: Northwestern University, Kellogg School of Management).

Elliott, J., Richardson, G., Dyckman, T., and Dukes, R. (1984), 'The impact of SFAS No. 2 on firm expenditures on research and development: Replications and extensions', *Journal of Accounting Research*, 22: 85–102.

Evenson, R. and Kisley, Y. (1976), 'A stochastic model of applied research', *Journal of Political Economy*, 84: 265–81.

Fama, E. and French, K. (1992), 'The cross-section of expected stock returns', *Journal of Finance*, 47: 427–65.

FASB (Financial Accounting Standards Board) (1974), 'Accounting for research and development costs', Statement of Financial Accounting Standards No. 2.

—— (1985), 'Accounting for the costs of computer software to be sold, leased, or otherwise marketed, Statement of Financial Accounting Standard No. 86.

Grabowski, H. and Mueller, D. (1978), 'Industrial research and development, intangible capital stocks, and firm profit rates', *Bell Journal of Economics*, 9: 328–43.

Griliches, Z. and Mairesse, J. (1990), 'R&D and productivity growth: comparing Japanese and U.S. manufacturing firms', in: C. Hulten (ed.) *Productivity Growth in Japan and the United States* (Chicago, IL: University of Chicago Press), 317–48.

Hall, B. (1993a), *New Evidence on the Impacts of Research and Development* (Berkeley, CA: University of California).

—— (1993b), 'The stock market value of R&D investment during the 1980s', *American Economic Review*, 83: 259–64.

—— Cummins, C., Laderman, E., and Mundy, J. (1988). 'The R&D master file documentation', NBER technical working paper no. 72, updated to 1990 in NBER working paper no. 3366, May 1990.

Hirschey, M. and Weygandt, J. (1985), 'Amortization policy for advertising and research and development expenditures', *Journal of Accounting Research*, 23: 326–35.

Horwitz, B. and Kolodny, R. (1981), 'The FASB, the SEC and R&D', *Bell Journal of Economics*, 12: 249–62.

Johnston, J. (1984), *Econometric Methods*, 3rd ed. (New York, NY: McGraw-Hill).

Kothari, S. and Zimmerman, J. (1995), 'Price and return models', *Journal of Accounting Economics*, 20: 155–92.

Lev, B. and Thiagarajan, R. (1993), 'Fundamental information analysis', *Journal of Accounting Research*, 31: 190–215.

Levin, R., Klevorick, K., Nelson, R., and Winter, S. (1987), 'Appropriating the returns from industrial R&D', *Brookings Papers on Economic Activity*, 3: 783–820.

Lichtenberg, F. and Siege, D. (1989), 'The impact of R&D investment on productivity: New evidence using linked R&D–LED data', NBER working paper no. 2901.

Maddala, G. (1992), *Introduction to Econometrics*, 2nd ed. (New York, NY: Macmillan).

Mairesse, J. and Sassenou, M. (1991), 'R&D and productivity: A survey of econometric studies at the firm level', NBER working paper no. 3666.

Mansfield, E. (1986), 'Patents and innovation: An empirical study', *Management Science*, 32: 173–81.

Mowery, D. (1983), 'The relationship between intrafirm and contractual form of industrial research in American manufacturing, 1900–1940', *Explorations in Economic History*, 20: 351–74.

Baruch Lev and Theodore Sougiannis

Nadiri, I. and Prucha, I. (1992), *Estimation of the Depreciation Rate of Physical and R&D Capital in the U.S. Total Manufacturing Sector* (New York, NY: New York University).

Pakes, A. (1985), 'On patents, R&D, and the stock market rate of return', *Journal of Political Economy*, 93: 390–409.

Peles, Y. (1970), 'Amortization of advertising expenditures in the financial statements', *Journal of Accounting Research*, 8: 128–37.

Wasley, C. and Linsmeier, T. (1992), 'A further examination of the economic consequences of SFAS No. 2', *Journal of Accounting Research*, 30: 156–64.

Woolridge, R. (1998), 'Competitive decline and corporate restructuring: Is a myopic stock market to blame'?, *Journal of Applied Corporate Finance*, 1: 26–36.

6 Brand Values and Capital Market Valuation

Mary E. Barth, Michael B. Clement, George Foster, and Ron Kasznik

There is growing recognition that intangible assets are important determinants of firm value. Examples of intangible assets include brands, technology, customer loyalty, and the human capital and commitment of employees. US Generally Accepted Accounting Principles (GAAP) do not consistently recognize such intangible assets as accounting assets. A major reason for not according these assets financial statement recognition is concern about whether their values are reliably estimable. This study tests hypotheses relating to whether brand values estimated and published by a well-respected financial magazine reflect valuation relevant information and are sufficiently reliable and timely to be reflected in share prices and returns.

In 1992, *Financial World* (FW) began publishing an annual survey of brand values estimated using a methodology developed by an established brand valuation consulting firm, Interbrand, Ltd., and described in the Appendix. The inaugural survey published in 1992 reported fiscal year 1991 values for forty-two brands. By 1997, the survey included over 330 brands, owned by firms in a variety of industries. The estimated values indicate that brands are large assets of many sample firms; the estimates represent approximately forty per cent of market value of equity and recognized assets for the median sample firm.

This paper examines the association between FW's brand value estimates and equity share prices of firms owning the brands. We test the joint hypothesis that brand values are relevant to equity valuation of firms owning brands and FW's brand value estimates are sufficiently reliable to be associated with share prices and returns. To test this hypothesis, we estimate the association between the brand value estimates and share prices, controlling for equity book value and net income, and the association between year-to-year changes in brand value estimates and annual share returns, controlling for net income and changes in net income. Our sample extends from 1991 to 1996. We find consistent evidence that the brand value estimates are significantly associated with equity market values in both specifications, providing evidence in support of our hypothesis.

Estimates from a system of simultaneous equations provide evidence that our primary findings are not attributable to estimates of brand values being based on share prices. This analysis also reveals that, as predicted, the brand value estimates are significantly positively associated with advertising expense, brand operating margin, and brand market share. However, contrary to predictions, the estimates are not significantly positively related to sales growth. Additional analyses reveal that brand value estimates provide significant explanatory power for share prices incremental to advertising expense, operating margin, growth, and market share. Brand value estimates also are significantly positively related to share prices after controlling for recognized brand assets and analysts' earnings forecasts. Several sensitivity checks indicate that our findings are robust.

Taken together, our findings indicate that the FW brand value estimates capture information that is relevant to investors and are sufficiently reliable to be reflected in share prices and returns.[1] Because our priors are that brand values are relevant to equity investors, these findings call into question concerns of those who believe that brand value estimates are too unreliable to be the basis for recognition as an intangible accounting asset.

The remainder of the paper proceeds as follows. Section 1 discusses institutional background relating to brand values and related research. Section 2 describes the data and presents descriptive statistics. Section 3 outlines our research design and Section 4 presents our empirical findings. Section 5 offers some additional analyses and Section 6 summarizes and concludes the study.

1. Institutional Background and Related Research

1.1. Institutional Background

Although definitions of brands differ (see, e.g. Aaker, 1991, 1996; Keller, 1997), the underlying notion is that of a distinctive name with which the consumer has a high level of awareness and a willingness to pay either higher than otherwise average prices or make higher than otherwise purchase frequency. Keller (1997) lists the following benefits of a brand name: greater loyalty from customers, less vulnerability to competitive marketing actions, less vulnerability to marketing crises, larger margins, more inelastic consumer response to price increases, more elastic consumer response to price decreases, greater trade cooperation and support, increased marketing communication effectiveness, possible licensing opportunities, and additional brand extension opportunities. The net effect of these benefits is that a branded product potentially provides a firm with a higher level of operating earnings over time than does an otherwise unbranded product. However, although cost incurred is a potential measurement alternative for brands, not all expenditures made in promoting a brand result in increases in brand value. For example, an expensive advertising program that misfires may, at best, have a minimal effect on sales and, at worst, turn away existing or potential customers. It is an empirical issue whether the potential benefits listed above are realized for a given brand, thereby translating into increased firm value.[2]

US GAAP for brands has at least three features that are the subject of debate. First, recognition of brands is inconsistent across firms. Internally developed brands are not recognized as assets whereas acquired brands, for example, through a purchase business combination, typically are recognized and amortized against net income over the brand's estimated useful life, which cannot exceed forty years. Second, even though brand values can change markedly from period to period, changes in brand values largely are unaccounted for, even for brands recognized as assets. Although US GAAP requires write-downs for impaired recognized brand assets, US GAAP does not permit recognition of increases in brand values. Third, expenditures that increase brand values, such as advertising, are expensed in the period incurred rather than capitalized. This can result in firms that invest in brand name development reporting depressed earnings while brand values are increasing.[3]

US GAAP requires disclosure, and the Financial Accounting Standards Board (FASB) is considering requiring recognition, of fair values of all financial instruments. Although currently there is no US proposal to disclose or recognize non-financial assets at fair value, fair values of all assets likely are relevant to financial statement users. One reason the FASB distinguishes financial and non-financial assets is the belief that values are not reliably estimable for nonfinancial assets, especially intangible assets such as brands. However, GAAP in countries other than the United States for example, Australia, permits recognition of the value of internally developed intangible assets, such as those associated with brand names (see, e.g. Barth and Clinch, 1998).

1.2. Related Research

The marketing and management literatures include several empirical studies linking brand attributes and security prices and/or returns. Simon and Sullivan (1993) outline a technique for estimating a firm's brand equity, based on firms' market value. In their technique, the replacement cost of tangible assets is first subtracted from the firm's market capitalization to estimate the value of intangible assets. Second, this value of intangible assets is apportioned into a brand value component, a nonbrand value component, for example, research and development and patents, and an industry component, for example, regulation. Simon and Sullivan use their intuition to validate Wall Street's cognizance of marketing factors. They find, as one might expect, that industries and firms with commonly known brand names have high estimates of brand equity.

Aaker and Jacobson (1994) examine associations between measures of brand quality and security returns, using the EquiTrend measure of brand quality. The EquiTrend brand quality measure is based on a study by Total Research Corporation, which surveyed a nationally representative sample of consumers from 1991 to 1993 to evaluate the quality of 100 major brands. Aaker and Jacobson examine whether returns in the twelve months preceding each annual survey reflect the unexpected change from one survey to the next in the brand's quality measure. They find that the relation between brand quality and returns is positive, as predicted, and statistically significant.

Related studies in the accounting literature, for example, Abdel-khalik (1975), and Hirschey and Weygandt (1985), investigate whether advertising expenses are value-relevant, which one would expect if advertising expense is a proxy for the development of valuable brand names. These studies find evidence consistent with this conjecture. However, Bublitz and Ettredge (1989) conclude that benefits from advertising expenditures are short-lived, consistent with recognizing them as current-period expenses. More recently, Barth and Clinch (1998) provide evidence that recognized revalued intangible assets of Australian firms, a substantial proportion of which relate to brand names, are value-relevant. Some studies also investigate firms' and analysts' actions associated with nonrecognition of intangible assets, such as brand names. In particular, Barth and Kasznik (1998) find that firms' decisions to repurchase shares on the open market and the market's reaction to the repurchase announcement are significantly positively related to proxies for unrecognized intangibles, including brand names. Also, Barth et al. (1998) find that unrecognized intangible assets, including brand names, are significantly positively related to analyst coverage and the effort analysts expend to cover firms.

2. Data and Descriptive Statistics

We obtain estimated brand values from FW's 1992–97 annual surveys of brands that relate to brand values for fiscal years from 1991 to 1996 (*Financial World*,

1992–97). FW reports value estimates, sales, and operating margins for individual brands, by industry. It also reports the percentage change in the brand value estimate from the previous year. The Appendix describes the methodology FW uses to estimate brand values, which is designed to estimate the increased firm value associated with the firm's brand names. Our sample comprises 1204 brands with value estimates reported by FW during the sample period. To obtain estimated brand value for a particular firm-year observation, we sum the estimated values of the brands owned by a particular firm and reported by FW in that year.[4] This results in 595 sample firm-year observations, relating to 183 publicly traded US firms.[5] We obtain data for other variables from the 1996 Full Coverage Compustat and CRSP databases.

Table 1 presents selected descriptive statistics relating to brand value estimates. Panel A presents statistics relating to the temporal distribution of sample firms and brand names and reveals that, over the sample period, FW expanded coverage of brands and firms. The 1991 sample includes thirty-seven brands owned by twenty-six firms, whereas the 1996 sample includes 299 brands owned by 152 firms. Panel B presents statistics relating to the number of FW reported brands owned by each sample firm and reveals that in each sample year, the median (mean) firm has approximately one (two) brand(s). However, the number of brands owned by a particular firm ranges up to seventeen in 1995. Panel C of Table 1 presents descriptive statistics relating to values of individual brands. It shows that, over the sample period, the mean (median) brand values ranges from $1538 ($541) million in 1993 to $4098 ($1454) million in 1991. The large brand values in 1991 are primarily attributable to the inaugural survey focusing on major brand names, for example, Marlboro, Coca-Cola, Budweiser, and Pepsi-Cola.

Figure 1, Panel A, graphs the distribution of one-year changes in estimated brand values for the 1083 brands of 520 firms for which we have brand value estimates in two consecutive years.[6] It indicates that brand values in our sample have, for the most part, increased over time, although many have decreased. Figure 1, Panel B, shows that the one-year change in estimated brand values at the firm-level also varies considerably. Untabulated statistics indicate that the mean (median) year-to-year changes in brand values at the brand- and firm-levels are 6.7 per cent (6.0 per cent) and 8.3 per cent (7.0 per cent), respectively. They also indicate that 67.2 and 71.5 per cent year-to-year changes in brand values at the brand- and firm-level are increases, 30.2 and 28.1 per cent are decreases, and only 2.6 and 0.4 per cent are unchanged.

Figure 2 presents multi-year changes in estimated brand values for the 1993–96 period, over which FW brand value estimates are available for a substantial number of brands. We base the figure on brands for which FW reports estimated values each year in this period, enabling us to calculate a sequence of three successive brand value changes.[7] Figure 2, Panel A, first partitions the

Table 1. Summary of 1204 Brand Value Estimates, for 595 Firm-Year Observations From 1991 to 1996 Surveys, Reported in *Financial World* (1992–97)

Panel A: Number of sample firms and brand names

Year	Number of Firms	Number of Brand Names	% of Total Brand Names
1991	26	37	3
1992	58	95	8
1993	108	240	20
1994	106	229	19
1995	145	304	25
1996	152	299	25
Total	595	1204	100

Panel B: Number of brands per firm

Year	Firms	Mean	Median	Std Dev.	Min.	Max.
1991	26	1.4	1.0	0.9	1.0	4.0
1992	58	1.6	1.0	1.2	1.0	5.0
1993	108	2.2	1.0	2.5	1.0	12.0
1994	106	2.1	1.0	2.4	1.0	12.0
1995	145	2.1	1.0	2.7	1.0	17.0
1996	152	2.0	1.0	2.3	1.0	14.0
Pooled	595	2.0	1.0	2.3	1.0	17.0

Panel C: Brand values (in $ million)

Year	Number	Mean	Median	Std Dev.	Q1	Q2
1991	37	4098	1454	6524	582	3732
1992	95	2696	1058	5644	436	2378
1993	240	1538	541	3612	185	1434
1994	229	2091	739	4416	256	1900
1995	304	1900	633	4388	222	1651
1996	299	2267	880	4898	328	1994
Pooled	1204	2085	745	4591	256	1879

1993–94 estimated brand value changes into those that are positive and those that are negative or zero. For each of these partitions, we repeat the sign-partitioning for 1994–95 estimated value changes, and repeat the entire process for 1995–96 changes. This results in eight portfolios representing different combinations of the sign of successive annual estimated brand value changes. For each portfolio, we set the 1993 estimated brand value equal to 100 and then compute the mean estimated brand value of each portfolio in 1996 relative to the normalized 1993 value. Thus, brands that increase in value after 1993 have calculated amounts greater than 100. Panel B presents analogous statistics for year-to-year changes at the firm level.

Consistent with Fig. 1, Fig. 2, Panel A, reveals a substantial proportion of brands with three consecutive years of increased value, 47.3 per cent of the sample brands. These brands have a 1996 mean normalized value of 147.9, which means that, on average, these brands increased in value 47.9 per cent over the 1993–96 period. The 3.3 per cent of sample brands with a sequence of three negative changes in brand value have a 1996 mean normalized value of 76.7 per cent, which means that, on average, these brands decreased in value 23.3 per cent. Panel B reveals a similar pattern for firm-level brand value estimates, although there are no firms with three consecutive years of total brand value decreases.

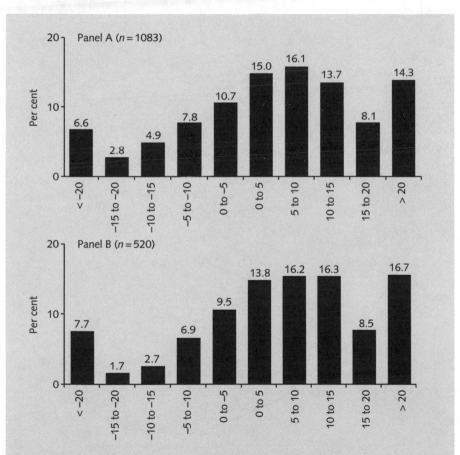

Fig. 1. Frequencies of one-year percentage changes in estimated individual and firm brand values, based on one-year changes in estimated brand values at the brand (Panel A) and firm (Panel B) levels, from 1992 to 1996.

Mary E. Barth et al.

Figures 1 and 2 highlight several features of estimated brand values that are pertinent to existing financial reporting rules. First, a policy of assuming brand values do not increase over time, absent a change in brand ownership, is inconsistent with the evidence; the average one-year sample brand value increase is more than 6 per cent. Second, there is considerable variation in the sign and magnitude of brand value changes over time. This variation is not

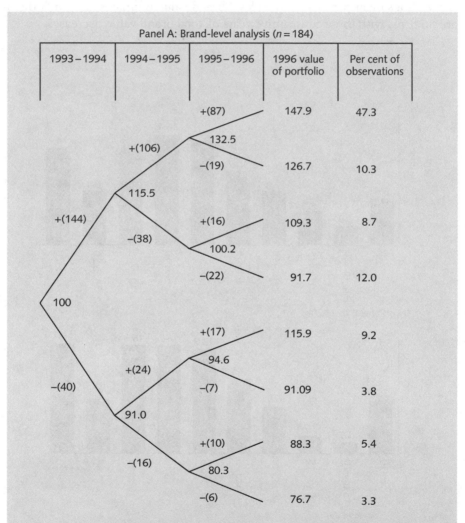

Fig. 2. Sequence of changes in estimated individual and firm brand values over the period 1993–96 (values are normalized by setting 1993 brand value estimates to 100). Based on brands with value estimates for each of the years 1993–96.

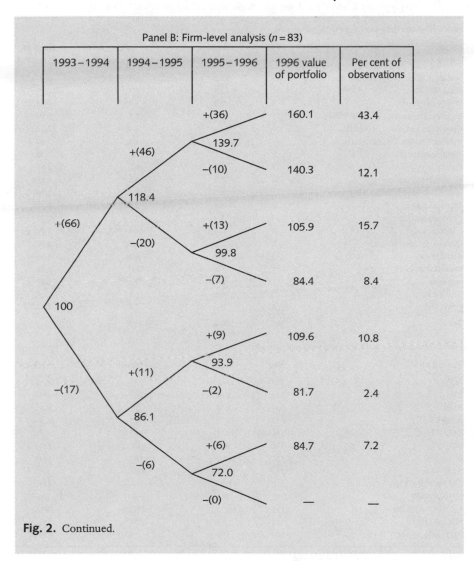

Fig. 2. Continued.

surprising given the diverse factors that can affect brand values, including factors beyond the control of the firm owning the brand, such as actions by competitors.[8]

Table 2 presents descriptive statistics relating to sample firms, for firm-year observations with available data. The industry statistics in Panel A are based on two-digit SIC codes. The last column in the panel reports the ratio of sample firms' industry membership percentage to the Compustat population percentage. A ratio greater than 1.00 means that the industry has greater than average

Table 2. Descriptive Statistics for 595 Firm-Year Observations for 183 Firms, from 1991 to 1996 Surveys, with Brand Value Estimates Reported in *Financial World* (1992–97)

Panel A: Industry classification of the 183 sample firms

Industry	No.	Frequency in Sample (% (1))	Frequency in Compustat (% (2))	Ratio of (1) and (2)
Mining, Oil and Gas, Construction	3	1.6	6.4	0.25
Food, Tobacco	42	22.9	2.1	10.90
Textile, Apparel	5	2.7	1.4	1.93
Lumber, Furniture, Paper, Printing	5	2.7	3.3	0.82
Chemicals and Allied Products	30	16.4	6.4	2.56
Rubber, Plastics, Leather, Glass	14	7.7	2.1	3.67
Metal Industries	2	1.1	2.8	0.39
Machinery	13	7.1	6.2	1.15
Electrical Equipment	14	7.7	6.5	1.18
Miscellaneous Manufacturing	15	8.2	8.4	0.98
Transportation	8	4.4	2.3	1.91
Communications	8	4.4	3.2	1.38
Utilities	0	0.0	3.4	0.00
Durable goods wholesale	0	0.0	4.1	0.00
Retail trade	4	2.2	6.2	0.35
Financial services	3	1.6	19.0	0.08
Software	11	6.0	7.3	0.82
Real Estate	0	0.0	1.1	0.00
Others	6	3.3	7.8	0.42
Total	183	100.0	100.0	

Panel B: Size and performance measures for sample firm-years

Variable	No.	Mean	Median	Std Dev.
MV	515	13673	6777	19,581
BV	536	3682	1700	4936
M/B	504	4.75	3.38	4.91
ASSETS	537	12789	5050	26,340
SALES	536	10631	5897	14,930
NI	536	697	310	1143
MARGIN	536	4331	2507	5645
ADV	536	344	120	572
SALES_GRWTH	530	10%	8%	12%
NI/AVG_MV	497	5%	6%	6%
NI/AVG_ASSETS	531	8%	7%	9%
NI/AVG_BV	511	22%	20%	22%
RETURN	506	1%	−2%	31%

MV is market value of equity at fiscal year end.
BV is book value of equity at fiscal year end.
M/B is market-to-book ratio, for firms with positive book value of equity.
ASSETS is total assets at fiscal year end.
SALES is total sales.
NI is income from continuing operations.
MARGIN is sales minus cost-of-goods-sold.
ADV is advertising expense.
SALES_GRWTH is sales growth, measured as $(\text{sales}_{t-1}/\text{sales}_{t-(1+i)})^{1/i}$, where $3 \le i \le 5$.
AVG_MV, AVG_ASSETS, and AVG_MV reflect the average of beginning and ending balances.
RETURN is year t stock return, measured from three months after end of year $t-1$ to three months after the end of year t, minus the CRSP value-weighted return.
For purposes of this table, all variables are expressed in $ million, except for variables expressed in percentage form. As regression variables, they are deflated by number of shares outstanding.

representation in this study. Panel A reveals that the sample includes more food and tobacco, chemicals and allied products, and rubber, plastic, leather, and glass firms than one would expect based on the Compustat population. The industry group with a markedly lower representation in our sample relative to the Compustat population is financial services, 1.6 per cent in the sample vs 19 per cent in Compustat.

The size and performance measure statistics in Panel B reveal that sample firms are relatively large; the mean (median) market value of equity, MV, is $13,673 ($6777) million. The book value of equity, BV, for these firms is substantially lower, with mean (median) value of $3682 ($1700) million. The sample firms' mean (median) market-to-book ratio is 4.75 (3.38), which compares with an untabulated mean (median) of 3.18 (1.83) for all Compustat firms. These statistics are consistent with the notion that, on average, sample firms have substantial unrecognized net assets, presumably such as brand names. Untabulated statistics reveal that adjusting book value of equity by adding the brand value estimates results in mean and median market-to-book ratios that are closer to, but still greater than, unity; that is, 1.91 and 1.43, respectively.

Table 2 also reveals that sample firms are, on average, profitable, with mean (median) net operating income, NI, of $697 ($310) million, or 5 per cent (6 per cent) of mean market value of equity. The ratio of net income to book value of equity is substantially higher, with mean (median) ratio of 22 per cent (20 per cent). The table also indicates that the sample firms, on average, have 10 per cent annual sales growth. Untabulated tests reveal that the 1 per cent (−2 per cent) mean (median) annual market-adjusted return for sample firms is not significantly different from zero.

Table 3 presents summary statistics associated with sample firms' brand values (Panel A) and annual changes in these values (Panel B). The statistics reveal that the mean (median) firm-year has brand values estimated at $4220 ($1748) million, and that these unrecognized assets represent a significant portion of sample firms' recognized assets. For example, the mean (median) ratio of estimated brand values to market value of equity is 44 per cent (37 per cent). Moreover, the mean (median) ratio of estimated brand values to recognized assets is 70 per cent (42 per cent), and the mean (median) ratio of estimated brand values to book value of equity is 209 per cent (105 per cent). Thus, including estimated brand values on the balance sheet could have a significant effect on reported financial statement amounts.[9] Consistent with Figs 1 and 2, the statistics in Panel B suggest that the average one-year change in sample firms' brand value is positive. Specifically, the mean (median) one-year change in brand values is $278 ($68) million, which represents 1 per cent (2 per cent) of market value of equity and 11 per cent (5 per cent) of book value of equity.

Table 3. Estimated Values of Brand Names, for 595 Firm-year Observations from 1991 to 1996
Surveys, Reported in *Financial World* (1992–97)

Variable	No.	Mean	Median	Std Dev.
Panel A: Firms' brand value estimates				
BRANDS	595	4220	1748	7855
BRANDS/MV	515	44%	37%	43%
BRANDS/ASSETS	537	70%	42%	85%
BRANDS/BV	520	209%	105%	335%
Panel B: One-year changes in firms' brand value estimates				
ΔBRANDS	520	278	68	1587
ΔBRANDS/AVG_MV	439	1%	2%	13%
ΔBRANDS/AVG_ASSETS	462	4%	2%	18%
ΔBRANDS/AVG_BV	450	11%	5%	41%

BRANDS is the firm's total estimated value of brand names.
ASSETS is total assets at fiscal year end.
MV is market value of equity at fiscal year end
BV is book value of equity at fiscal year end
Δ BRANDS is the one-year change in the firm's total estimated value of brand names.
AVG_MV, AVG_ASSETS, and AVG_MV reflect the average of beginning and ending balances.
BRANDS and ΔBRANDS are expressed in $ million.

....

3. Research Design

Our objective is to assess whether FW's brand value estimates are associated
with share prices and returns. Finding that they do is evidence that brand
names are relevant for equity valuation of firms owning brand names and that
FW's brand value estimates are sufficiently reliable to be reflected in share
prices.[10] Because our priors are that brand values are relevant to investors, we
interpret failure to detect a significant relation as evidence that error in estimating brand values is substantial. Thus, we interpret a significant relation as
evidence that brand value estimates are sufficiently reliable to be reflected in
share prices. We test our predictions using two specifications, one relating
brand values to share prices, and one relating one-year changes in brand values
to annual share returns.

3.1. Brand Values and Share Prices

The first set of tests examines the association between market value of
equity and brand value estimates. Specifically, we estimate the following

cross-sectional regression:

$$MV_{it} = \sum_{Y=91}^{96} \alpha_{0Y}YR_{Yit} + \alpha_1 BV_{it} + \alpha_2 NI_{it} + \alpha_3 BRANDS_{it} + \varepsilon_{1it}, \qquad (1)$$

where MV is share price at fiscal year end; BV is book value of equity per share; NI is earnings per share from continuing operations; BRANDS is the total of the firm's FW brand value estimates per share, that is, the sum of the individual brand value estimates, deflated by number of shares outstanding; and YR_Y is an indicator variable that equals one if the observation is from fiscal year Y, and zero otherwise.[11] i and t denote firms and years, respectively. We permit the regression intercept to vary across years to control for mean calendar time-specific effects. We also estimate equation (1), excluding YR_Y, separately for each year, thereby effectively permitting all coefficients to vary across years.

One can interpret equation (1) using the Ohlson (1995) valuation model. For example, one can interpret BRANDS as an 'other information' variable in Ohlson's model. Thus, observing $\alpha_3 > 0$ is evidence that estimated brand values capture valuation-relevant information not reflected in BV or NI. Alternatively, focusing on the possibility of recognizing brand values on the balance sheet, one could interpret (BV + BRANDS) as an 'as if' book value of equity. This interpretation suggests testing whether α_1 and α_3 are equal.[12] Equation (1) also can be viewed as deriving from an asset-based valuation equation, where earnings is included as a proxy for unrecognized net assets (Barth and Landsman, 1995). All interpretations of the equation lead to predicting a positive α_3. Based on prior research, we also predict the coefficients on book value of equity per share and earnings per share, α_1 and α_2, to be positive.

3.2. Brand Value Changes and Returns

One also can examine value-relevance of estimated brand values by investigating the association between annual changes in brand values and contemporaneous annual share returns. Another motivation for estimating a returns specification is to investigate the timeliness of changes in brand value estimates, where timely means that the change in BRANDS from one year to the next reflects changes in the value of the firm's brands during that year. If FW's brand value estimates capture valuation relevant information, but are not timely, we can observe a significant relation in the price specification, but not in the returns specification. Thus, observing a significant relation in both specifications is evidence that brand value estimates are timely. Estimating a returns specification also permits us to investigate effects on our inferences of potential specification problems, such as omitted variables. If the omitted variables and coefficients are constant (change) over time, then the price (returns) regression can be misspecified (Landsman and Magliolo, 1988).

The following cross-sectional estimation equation specifies our returns regression:

$$\text{RETURN}_{it} = \sum_{Y=92}^{96} \beta_{0Y}\text{YR}_{Yit} + \beta_1\text{NI}_{it} + \beta_2\Delta\text{NI}_{it} + \beta_3\Delta\text{BRANDS}_{it} + \varepsilon_{2it}, \quad (2)$$

where RETURN_{it} is the firm i's year t share return, measured from three months after year end for $t-1$ to three months after year end for year t. ΔNI_t is NI_t minus NI_{t-1}, and ΔBRANDS_t is BRANDS_t minus BRANDS_{t-1}. Because the number of brands covered by FW increases over time, for purposes of estimating equation (2), we measure BRANDS_{t-1} by applying FW's reported value change percentage to BRANDS_t.[13] Other variables are as previously defined and all independent variables, except YR, are deflated by market value of equity at the beginning of year t. As with (1), we also estimate equation (2) separately for each year.

Assuming FW's brand value estimates provide at least some timely value-relevant information, we predict a positive association between annual changes in brand value estimates and contemporaneous returns, incremental to income and changes in income. Thus, we predict β_3 to be positive. Following Easton and Harris (1991), among others, we include in equation (2) NI and ΔNI and predict their coefficients, β_1 and β_2, to be positive.

3.3. Simultaneous Equations Estimation

Our hypothesis is that market value of equity reflects firms' brand values. Thus, we view brand values as 'causing' observed share prices, incremental to other value-relevant variables, such as book value of equity and net operating income. However, our estimation equations use a proxy for brand values, rather than the 'true' value of brand names. It is possible that FW bases its brand value estimates, at least in part, on observed share prices. That is, it is possible that brand value estimates and share prices are jointly endogenously determined. This possibility raises concerns about whether any relation we document using (1) and (2) is attributable to simultaneity bias.

To address this issue, we discussed with FW personnel the process that they use to estimate brand values. They emphasized that their focus is on the brand strength and profitability factors which comprise the Interbrand brand valuation model, as described in the Appendix, and that the valuation process does not involve consideration of the market value of equity of the brand-owner firms.

However, to ensure that our inferences are unaffected by possible simultaneity bias, we also test our hypothesis about value-relevance of the FW brand value estimates using the following system of simultaneously estimated equations. The first is (1), which specifies market value of equity as a function of brand values and the second, (3), specifies brand values as a function of market value of equity.

$$MV_{it} = \sum_{Y=91}^{96} \alpha_{0y} YR_{Yit} + \alpha_1 BV_{it} + \alpha_2 NI_{it} + \alpha_3 BRANDS_{it} + \varepsilon_{1it}, \qquad (1)$$

$$BRANDS_{it} = \sum_{y=91}^{96} \delta_{0y} YR_{yit} + \delta_1 FACTORS_{it} + \delta_2 MV_{it} + \varepsilon_{3it}, \qquad (3)$$

where **FACTORS** is a vector of exogenous variables that reflect factors likely considered by FW in estimating brand values. These variables serve to identify (3) and thus, ideally, are significantly associated with brand values, but not significantly associated with the error in its estimation. In our implementation, **FACTORS** comprises advertising expense, ADV, brand operating margin as reported by FW, BR_MARGIN, firm sales growth, SALES_GRWTH, and brand market share, MKT_SHARE. SALES_GRWTH is measured as $(sales_{t-1}/sales_{t-(1+i)})^{1/i}$, where $3 \le i \le 5$ and sales are obtained from Compustat. MKT_SHARE is measured as the weighted average of the firm's sales from brands in a given industry divided by sales of all brand sales in that industry, as reported by FW, with weights equal to the firm's sales relating to brands in a particular industry compared with total firm sales from brands.[14] ADV and BR_MARGIN are deflated by number of shares outstanding.[15]

To estimate the system of equations, we use two-stage least squares (2SLS). In the first stage, we regress BRANDS on all of the exogenous variables in (1) and (3), that is, BV, NI, ADV, BR_MARGIN, SALES_GRWTH, and MKTSHARE. In the second stage, we estimate equation (1) using the fitted value of BRANDS from the first stage, BRANDS_PRD, in place of BRANDS. By construction, the fitted value does not reflect the association between the estimation error in BRANDS, relative to brand value, and market value of equity and, thus, using ordinary least squares in the second stage yields a consistent estimator of α_3. We perform the analogous estimation procedure for (3). As explained in Section 4.2, we also estimate a simultaneous estimation equation system for the relation between changes in brand values and returns.

4. Findings

4.1. Value-Relevance of Brand Value Estimates

Table 4 presents summary statistics from estimating equation (1), which provide evidence that brand value estimates are value-relevant. Findings from the fixed-effects pooled regression in the first set of columns indicate that, as predicted, the coefficient on BRANDS is significantly positive, incremental to net income and book value of equity (t-statistic $= 5.57$). This finding is consistent with the brand value estimates capturing valuation-relevant information and being sufficiently reliable to be reflected in share prices. The second set of columns presents summary statistics for the separate-year estimation of (1), including two Z-statistics that test coefficient estimate significance across years. The first, Z1, assumes residual independence, and the second Z2, relaxes this assumption.[16] The Z1 (Z2) statistic of 5.22 (5.49) for the separate-year regressions corroborates the pooled regression findings of significance in the predicted direction for the coefficient on BRANDS. Also, as predicted, the coefficients on book value of equity, BV, and net income, NI, are significantly positive in the pooled and separate-year estimations.[17]

Table 4. Summary Statistics from Regression of Market Value of Equity on Book Value of Equity, Net Operating Income, and Brand Value estimates. Sample of Firms with Brand Value Estimates from 1991 to 1996 Surveys, Reported in *Financial World* (1992–97)

Variable	Prediction	Pooled Fixed Year Effects Coefficient	t-statistic	Separate-Year Estimation Coefficient Mean	Std Dev.	t-statistic Mean	Std Dev.	Z1	Z2
Intercept	−	−	−	17.77	4.77	5.50	1.79	13.27	6.87
BV	+	0.64	8.84	0.26	0.74	2.57	2.80	6.24	2.05
NI	+	5.23	12.78	8.92	5.17	6.70	2.42	16.13	6.19
BRANDS	+	0.29	5.57	0.25	0.08	2.16	0.88	5.22	5.49
Number obs.		508		84.17	44.38				
Adjusted R^2		0.56		0.66	0.14				

BV is book value of equity at fiscal year end.
NI is income from continuing operations.
BRANDS is the firm's total estimated value of brand names.
All variables are deflated by number of shares outstanding.
Fixed-effects refers to estimation with fixed-year effects. The year-specific intercepts are untabulated.
Z1 equals $(1/\sqrt{T}) \sum_{j=1}^{T} (t_j/\sqrt{k_j/(k_j - 2)})$ where t is t-statistic, T is number of years, and k is degrees of freedom for regression in year j.
Z2 equals mean t/(std dev. $t/\sqrt{5}$).

The coefficient on BRANDS, 0.29, is significantly less than on BV, 0.64, in the pooled specification, consistent with BRANDS containing more estimation error than the average component of book value of equity. However, in the separate-year estimation, the mean BRANDS coefficient is almost the same as that for the coefficient on BV, 0.25 vs 0.26, consistent with BRANDS and BV being assessed similarly by investors.[18]

Table 5 presents summary statistics from estimating equation (2). The table reveals that, consistent with predictions, one-year changes in brand value estimates are significantly positively associated with contemporaneous returns. The evidence is consistent between the pooled fixed effects estimation (t-statistic $= 5.55$) and the aggregate separate-year estimation statistics ($Z1 = 5.17$ and $Z2 = 3.47$). Untabulated findings indicate that inclusion in the pooled estimation of ΔBRANDS increases the adjusted R-squared of the model from 0.12 to 0.18. These findings are consistent with those of the price specification and provide evidence that the finding of value-relevance for estimated brand values is not attributable to effects of omitted correlated variables. Finding that changes in brand value estimates are significantly positively related to contemporaneous returns also indicates that at least some of the change in brand value estimates is timely. Also consistent with predictions, net income and changes in net income are significantly positively associated with contemporaneous returns in both estimation specifications.

Table 5. Summary Statistics from Regression of Returns on Net Operating Income, Change in Net Operating Income, and Changes in Brand Value Estimates. Sample of Firms with Brand Value Estimates from 1992 to 1996 Surveys, Reported in *Financial World* (1993–97)

| | | | | Separate-year Estimation | | | | | |
| | Pooled Fixed Year Effects | | | Coefficient | | t-statistic | | | |
Variable	Prediction	Coefficient	t-statistic	Mean	Std Dev.	Mean	Std Dev.	Z1	Z2
Intercept	—	—	—	−0.09	0.12	−1.94	2.30	−4.29	−1.69
NI	+	1.37	4.79	1.18	2.31	1.92	2.59	4.24	1.48
ΔNI	+	0.35	1.68	1.17	1.14	1.26	0.71	2.78	3.55
ΔBRANDS	+	0.54	5.55	0.58	0.34	2.36	1.36	5.17	3.47
Number obs.		412		82.20	35.41				
Adjusted R^2		0.18		0.24	0.03				

Returns are market-adjusted returns for the 12-month period beginning three months after the beginning of year t.
Δ BRANDS is the one-year change in the firm's total value of brand names.
Fixed-effects refers to estimation with fixed-year effects. The year-specific intercepts are untabulated.
Independent variables are deflated by beginning of period price.
Z1 equals $(1/\sqrt{T}) \sum_{j=1}^{T}(t_j/\sqrt{k_j}/(k_j - 2))$ where t is t-statistic, T is number of years, and k is degrees of freedom for regression in year j.
Z2 equals mean $t/$(std dev. $t/\sqrt{4}$).

4.2. Evidence on Lack of Simultaneity Bias

Table 6 presents summary statistics from estimating the price specification as part of a system of simultaneous equations. Panel A presents findings relating to the brand value estimation equation (3) and Panel B presents findings relating to the market value estimation equation (1) where BRANDS is an explanatory variable.

The first set of results in Panel A relates to the OLS regression of BRANDS on market value of equity and the four variables we use to identify the brand value equation. It reveals that, as predicted, advertising expense, ADV, brand operating margin, BR_MARGIN, and brand market share, MKTSHARE, all have significantly positive relations with estimated brand values. These findings indicate that brands of firms that spend more on advertising and brands that have larger margins and market share have larger estimated brand values. The relation between BRANDS and SALES_GRWTH is insignificant. Also, as predicted, we observe a significantly positive relation between BRANDS and market value of equity, MV, which is consistent with market value of equity explaining brand value estimates.[19]

The second set of summary statistics in Table 6, Panel A, is from estimating the second-stage regression using the fitted value from the first stage, MV_PRD, in place of market value of equity, MV. The results are consistent with the OLS estimates for all of the variables except MV_PRD, which, as explained below, we obtain from an analogous two-stage estimation procedure. Interestingly, the coefficient on MV_PRD is not significantly different from zero, indicating that after controlling for potential simultaneity bias, market value of equity does not explain estimated brand values.

Table 6, Panel B, presents findings related to the effects of potential simultaneity on our primary regression equation (1). The first set of results relates to OLS estimation using the 487 observations for which we have complete data for estimating equation (3). The results are similar to those in Table 4 for the entire sample. The second set of results reveals that inferences from Table 4 are not attributable to effects of simultaneity bias. Specifically, findings from estimating equation (1) after replacing BRANDS by BRANDS_PRD, the fitted brand value variable based on a first-stage regression of BRANDS on all of the exogenous variables in the system, and, thus, not on market value of equity, are similar to those in Table 4. The coefficient on BRANDS_PRD is significantly positive, as predicted.

Consistent with measurement error reduction via the two-stage procedure, the coefficient on BRANDS_PRD is somewhat larger than on BRANDS in the OLS estimation, 0.34 vs 0.29. This increase in BRAND's estimated coefficient is sufficient to prevent us from rejecting the null hypothesis that the coefficients on BRANDS_PRD and BV in Table 6, Panel B, are equal. Although failure to

Table 6. Summary Statistics from Simultaneous Equation Estimation Treating Market Value of Equity and Brand Value Estimates as Jointly Determined Endogenous Variables. Fixed Year Effects Estimation for Sample Firms with Brand Values Estimates from 1991 to 1996 Surveys, Reported in *Financial World* (1992–97)

	Ordinary Least Squares				2nd Stage of 2-Stage Least Squares		
Variable	Prediction	Coefficient	*t*-statistic	Variable	Prediction	Coefficient	*t*-statistic

Panel A: $\text{BRANDS}_{it} = \sum_{y=91}^{96} \delta_{0y} \text{YR}_{yit} + \delta_1 \textbf{FACTORS}_{it} + \delta_2 \text{MV}_{it} + \varepsilon_{3it}$

ADV	+	1.70	6.40	ADV	+	1.73	6.43
BR_MARGIN	+	3.58	17.34	BR_MARGIN	+	3.75	15.93
SALES_GRWTH	+	−2.03	−0.47	SALES_GRWTH	+	−1.47	−0.34
MKT_SHARE	+	13.94	4.03	MKT_SHARE	+	14.55	4.14
MV	+	0.06	2.89	MV_PRD	?	0.02	0.65
Number obs.	487			Number obs.	487		
Adjusted R^2	0.58			Adjusted R^2	0.58		

Panel B: $\text{MV}_{it} = \sum_{y=91}^{96} \alpha_{0y} \text{YR}_{yit} + \alpha_1 \text{BV}_{it} + \alpha_2 \text{NI}_{it} + \alpha_3 \text{BRANDS}_{it} + \varepsilon_{1it}$

BV	+	0.63	8.64	BV	+	0.62	8.33
NI	+	5.35	12.95	NI	+	5.23	12.05
BRANDS	+	0.29	5.49	BRANDS_PRD	+	0.34	4.54
Number obs.	487			Number obs.	487		
Adjusted R^2	0.57			Adjusted R^2	0.56		

BRANDS is the firm's total estimated value of brand names.
BRANDS_PRD is fitted value from estimation of BRANDS on all exogenous variables in the system of equations consisting of the equations in Panels A and B.
FACTORS comprises advertising expense, ADV, brand operating margin as reported by FW, BR_MARGIN, firm sales growth, SALES_GRWTH, measured as $(\text{sales}_{t-1}/\text{sales}_{t-(1+i)})^{1/i}$, where $3 \le i \le 5$ and sales are obtained from Compustat, and brand market share, MKT_SHARE, calculated as the weighted average of the firm's sales from brands in a given industry divided by sales of all brand sales in that industry, as reported by FW, with weights equal to the firm's sales relating to brands in a particular industry compared with total firm sales from brands.
MV is market value of equity measured at fiscal year end.
BV is book value of equity at fiscal year end.
NI is income from continuing operations.
All variables, except for SALES_GRWTH and MKT_SHARE, are deflated by number of shares outstanding. YR_Y is an indicator variable that equals one if the observation is from fiscal year Y, and zero otherwise. Year-specific intercepts are untabulated.

reject the null hypothesis is not strong evidence, it is evidence inconsistent with investors perceiving brand value estimates as significantly less reliable than other components of book value of equity.

Table 7 presents findings from using simultaneous estimation techniques to estimate the relation between returns and changes in brand values. The equation specifying changes in brand values is:

$$\Delta \text{BRANDS}_{it} = \sum_{Y=92}^{96} \gamma_{0Y} \text{YR}_{Yit} + \gamma_1 \textbf{FACTORS}_{it} + \gamma_2 \text{RETURN}_{it} + \varepsilon_{4it}, \qquad (4)$$

where **FACTORS** includes advertising expense, ADV, brand operating margin, BR_MARGIN, firm sales growth, SALES_GRWTH and brand market share,

Table 7. Summary Statistics From Simultaneous Equation Estimation Treating Market Value of Equity and Brand Value Estimates as Jointly Determined Endogenous Variables. Fixed Year Effects Estimation for Sample of Firms with Brand Value Estimates From 1992 to 1996 Surveys, Reported in *Financial World* (1993–97)

$$RETURN_{it} = \sum_{Y=92}^{96} \beta_{0Y} YR_{Yit} + \beta_1 NI_{it} + \beta_2 \Delta NI_{it} + \beta_3 \Delta BRANDS_{it} + \varepsilon_{2i\Delta t}$$

Variable	Ordinary Least Squares			Variable	2nd Stage of 2-Stage Least Squares		
	Prediction	Coefficient	*t*-statistic		Prediction	Coefficient	*t*-statistic
NI	+	1.60	5.52	NI	+	1.12	2.87
ΔNI	+	0.14	0.67	Δ NI	+	−0.08	−0.32
Δ BRANDS	+	0.54	5.56	ΔBRANDS_PRD	+	1.59	2.74
Number obs.	404			Number obs.	404		
Adjusted R^2	0.19			Adjusted R^2	0.14		

RETURN is market-adjusted returns for the 12-month period beginning three months after the beginning of year *t*.
Δ BRANDS is the one-year change in the firm's total value of brand names.
NI is income from continuing operations; ΔNI is NI in year *t* minus NI in year *t* − 1.
ΔBRANDS_PRD is fitted value from estimation of ΔBRANDS on all exogenous variables in the system of equations, where the system comprises the returns equation specified above and $\Delta BRANDS_{it} = \gamma_0 + \gamma_1 FACTORS_{it} + \gamma_2 RETURN_{it} + \varepsilon_{3'it}$, where **FACTORS** include advertising expense, ADV, brand operating margin as reported by FW, BR_MARGIN, firm sales growth, SALES_GRWTH, measured as $(sales_{t-1}/sales_{t-(1+i)})^{1/i}$, where $3 \le i \le 5$ sales are obtained from Compustat, and brand market share, MKT_SHARE, calculated as the weighted average of the firm's sales from brands in a given industry divided by sales of all brand sales in that industry, as reported by FW, with weights equal to the firm's sales relating to brands in a particular industry compared with total firm sales from brands.
All independent variables, except for SALES_GRWTH and MKT_SHARE, are deflated by beginning of period price.
YR_Y is an indicator variable that equals one if the observation is from fiscal year Y, and zero otherwise. Year-specific intercepts are untabulated.

MKT_SHARE. All independent variables, except for SALES_GRWTH and MKT_SHARE, are deflated by market value of equity at the beginning of year *t*. We use the levels of these variables to explain annual changes in brand values because these variables change little year-to-year. Their primary role is to identify (4); we have no hypotheses relating to these variables.

The findings in Table 7 indicate that the Table 5 inferences relating to the significant positive relation between returns and changes in brand value estimates are not attributable to potential simultaneity bias. Specifically, the first set of results in Table 7 shows that our Table 5 OLS findings apply to the 404 firms for which we have complete data for estimating equation (4). More importantly, the second set of results shows that the coefficient on Δ BRANDS_PRD is significantly positive in the relation with contemporaneous returns. The coefficients on net income (change in net income) are significantly positive (insignificant) in both specifications.

5. Additional Analyses

5.1. Alternative Brand Proxies

The results in Table 4 indicate that FW brand value estimates are value-relevant, incremental to book value of equity and net income. The results in Table 6 indicate that much of the variation in the brand value estimates can be explained by variables that might be used to estimate brand values. Thus, to investigate whether the brand value estimates themselves provide power in explaining share prices incremental to these other variables, we estimate equation (1) after including the explanatory variables from (3) and interpret the additional variables as alternative proxies for brand values. Recall that these variables include advertising expense, ADV, brand operating, BR_MARGIN, firm sales growth, SALES_GRWTH, and brand market share, MKT_SHARE.

Table 8, Panel A, presents the results and reveals that BRANDS has a significantly positive relation with market value of equity, after controlling for these alternative brand value proxies (t-statistic = 3.22). Interestingly, the coefficients on all of the alternative proxies are insignificant, with the single exception of that on SALES_GRWTH, which is significantly positive, as predicted. These findings indicate that BRANDS reflects value-relevant information not reflected in these alternative proxies.

Two of the variables in the Table 8, Panel A, estimation specification are obtained from FW and are not available in firms' published financial statements. To investigate the possibility that brand value estimates are proxies for value-relevant information already reflected in firms financial statements, we estimate the relation using only financial statement variables. That is, we exclude MKT_SHARE and calculate MARGIN as the firm's gross margin, that is, sales minus cost of goods sold. The findings, reported in Table 8, Panel B, indicate that MARGIN is significantly positively associated with market value of equity, incremental to the other included variables, as predicted. SALES_GRWTH also is significantly positively related, as in the Panel A specification. Interestingly, ADV has a significantly negative relation with market value of equity, after controlling for brand value estimates and the other potential brand proxies. This suggests that investors view as an economic expense the component of advertising expense that is orthogonal to the brand value estimate and other included variables. More importantly for our research question, the findings also indicate that, as predicted, the coefficient on BRANDS is significantly positive (t-statistic = 4.75). This finding again indicates that brand value estimates reflect value-relevant information not reflected in these financial statement amounts.

Table 8. Summary Statistics from Fixed Year Effects Regression of Market Value of Equity on Brand Value Estimates, Book Value of Equity, Net Operating Income, and Other Potential Proxies for Brand Values. Sample of Firms with Brand Value Estimates from 1991 to 1996 Surveys, Reported in *Financial World* (1992–97)

Panel A: Including *Financial World* Variables				Panel B: Financial Statement Variables			
Variable	Prediction	Coefficient	*t*-statistic	Variable	Prediction	Coefficient	*t*-statistic
BV	+	0.62	8.32	BV	+	0.43	5.82
NI	+	5.35	12.75	NI	+	4.71	11.92
BRANDS	+	0.24	3.22	BRANDS	+	0.24	4.75
ADV	+	0.25	0.55	ADV	+	−0.85	−1.93
BR_MARGIN	+	0.26	0.58	MARGIN	+	0.68	7.78
SALES_GRWTH	+	22.82	3.27	SALES_GRWTH	+	27.42	4.17
MKT_SHARE	+	7.89	1.40				
Number obs.	487			Number obs.	489		
Adjusted R^2	0.58			Adjusted R^2	0.62		

BRANDS is the firm's total value of brand names.
BV is book value of equity at fiscal year end.
NI is income from continuing operations.
ADV is advertising expense.
BR_MARGIN is the brand operating margin as reported by FW. MARGIN is the firm's total sales minus cost-of-goods-sold.
SALES_GRWTH is sales growth, measured as $(sales_{t-1}/sales_{t-(1+i)})^{1/i}$, where $3 \geq i \geq 5$, and sales are obtained from Compustat.
MKT_SHARE is brand market share, calculated as the weighted average of the firm's sales from brands in a given industry divided by sales of all brand sales in that industry, as reported by FW, with weights equal to the firm's sales relating to brands in a particular industry compared with total firm sales from brands.
Dependent variable is market value of equity measured at fiscal year end.
All variables, except for SALES_GRWTH and MKT_SHARE, are deflated by number of shares outstanding.
Fixed-effects refers to estimation with fixed-year effects. The year-specific intercepts are untabulated.

5.2. Analysts Earnings Forecasts

Brand values arise from the present value of future cash flows, or earnings, expected to be generated by the firm's brand names. Although FW uses historical earnings from a brand to calculate brand value estimates, FW incorporates expectations about the future earnings generating potential of the brand through the brand strength multiple. (See the Appendix for descriptions of the brand strength multiple components.) Because of the link between asset values and expected future earnings, we conduct three additional analyses based on (1) that investigate whether the brand value estimates capture brand values incremental to analyst earnings forecasts, a proxy for expected future earnings.

First, we include as an additional explanatory variable in (1) the mean analysts' long-term earnings growth forecast, which we obtain from I/B/E/S International, Inc. Second, we include as an additional explanatory variable earnings per share multiplied by the mean analysts' long-term earnings growth forecast. Third, we include as additional explanatory variables the mean analyst one- and two-year ahead earnings forecasts and the long-term earnings growth forecast multiplied by the two-year ahead earnings forecast. Untabulated findings reveal that, although the coefficients on the analyst forecast variables often are significantly positive, as one would expect, in all three specifications the coefficient on BRANDS is significantly positive in the pooled and separate-year estimations. These findings suggest that the brand value estimates reflect value-relevant information beyond that reflected in expected future earnings as measured by analyst earnings forecasts.

5.3. Recognized Brand Assets

Thus far, we have implicitly assumed that sample firms do not recognize brand assets, which might not be the case for firms that acquire brands, that is, in a purchase business combination. To investigate the effects on our inferences of this assumption, we obtain from the sample firms' financial statements disclosures about recognized brand assets. Untabulated findings reveal that of the 435 available firm-year financial statements, only 91, or 21 per cent, relating to 35 firms mention that recognized intangible assets include purchased brands. Only 59 or 14 per cent of the firm-year observations disclose the recognized brand asset amount. Financial statements associated with more than three-quarters of firm-year observations, 344, do not mention brands in connection with recognized intangible assets.

Untabulated statistics also reveal that the amounts recognized by sample firms differ noticeably from the FW brand value estimates. For firms with available financial statements, the mean (median) ratio of recognized brand assets to FW brand value estimates is 0.12 (0.00), when we assign zero to recognized brand assets for firms not disclosing recognized brand assets. This ratio is particularly low when one considers the possibility that FW does not necessarily estimate values for all of a firm's brands. For the firm-year observations disclosing recognized brand assets, the mean (median) ratio is 0.56 (0.14), where the skewness is primarily attributable to one firm.[20]

We conduct two additional analyses to investigate the potential effects on our inferences of recognized brand assets. First, to the extent that brand assets are recognized by sample firms and, thus, included in BV, the coefficient on BRANDS in (1) represents the incremental coefficient on brand assets, relative to the coefficient on BV, not the coefficient on the asset itself. Thus, we estimate (1) after subtracting from BV recognized brand assets for firms that disclose recognized brand assets. Untabulated findings reveal that the coefficient on BRANDS is significantly positive, as predicted. We also estimate (1) after subtracting from BV goodwill and, for firms that disclose the recognized amount of brand assets, we also subtract recognized brand assets. We do this because it is possible that some firms recognize brands acquired in a purchase business combination as part of goodwill, not as a separate asset. Untabulated findings relating to this specification reveal that the coefficient on BRANDS is significantly positive, consistent with other specifications we report.

Second, we consider whether FW brand value estimates reflect brand values incremental to recognized brand assets. Although one can interpret (1) as providing this evidence, constraining the coefficient on recognized brands to equal that on other components of book value of equity potentially confounds the test. Thus, we estimate (1) after subtracting from BV recognized brand assets and including recognized brand assets as a separate explanatory variable. The untabulated findings reveal that the coefficient on recognized brand assets is insignificantly different from zero and the coefficient on BRANDS is significantly positive, as in Table 4. We also estimate this specification after subtracting from BV recognized brand assets and goodwill, and including the amount subtracted as an additional explanatory variable. The findings again reveal that the coefficient on recognized brand assets, including goodwill, is insignificantly different from zero and the coefficient on BRANDS is significantly positive.

5.4. Other Sensitivity Checks

We conduct several additional analyses to investigate the robustness of our findings. First, we examine the possibility that our results are driven by a small set of observations with a substantial level of brand values. To this end, we partitioned the sample into firms with ratios of brand values to total assets above and below the sample median. Untabulated results indicate that the association between brand value estimates and prices and returns are similar for the two subsamples.

Second, we investigate whether our inferences relate only to firms for which brands with values estimated by FW are large relative to the firms' operations. We investigate this by permitting the coefficient on BRANDS in (1) to vary for firms with ratios of brand sales per FW to total sales per Compustat above and below the sample median. Although the untabulated incremental coefficient for the above-median firms is positive, it is insignificantly different from zero, indicating that our findings do not relate only to firms whose brands represent a large fraction of their operations.

Third, we note that 68 per cent sample firms have only one brand for which FW reports an estimated value. We investigate whether the relation between market value of equity and brand value estimates differs for these firms by permitting the coefficient on BRANDS in (1) to vary for firms with multiple brands. Untabulated findings indicate that both the base and incremental coefficients on BRANDS are significantly positive, indicating that the relation is significant for all firms, but stronger for firms with multiple brands. This finding is consistent with brand value estimates reflecting more value-relevant information for firms with multiple brands, perhaps because net income and book value of equity capture single-brand values more directly than multiple brand values.

....

6. Summary and Concluding Remarks

Although brand names are important intangible assets of many firms, US GAAP does not permit firms to recognize internally developed brands as accounting assets. A major reason precluding accounting recognition is concern about whether brand values are reliably estimable. This paper provides evidence relating to the reliability of estimates of brand values by investigating whether share prices and returns reflect brand values estimated by *Financial World* (FW), based on the methodology developed by Interbrand, Ltd., an established brand valuation consulting firm.

We use a sample of 1204 brand value estimates collected from FW's annual surveys of brands relating to 1991–96 fiscal years to test the joint hypothesis that brand values are relevant for equity valuation of firms owning brands and FW brand value estimates are sufficiently reliable to be reflected in share prices. Our tests are based on estimating the association between the FW brand value estimates and share prices, incremental to book value of equity and net income, and the association between year-to-year changes in the brand value estimates and annual returns, incremental to net income and changes in net income. We find consistent evidence that brand value estimates are significantly associated with equity market values in both specifications, providing evidence in support of our hypothesis.

Because brand value estimates could be, at least in part, determined with reference to equity share prices, we also estimate a system of simultaneous equations that treats the brand value estimates and market value of equity as jointly determined endogenous variables. Findings from estimating these equations provide strong evidence that our inferences are not attributable to simultaneity bias. That is, the brand value estimates are significantly positively related to share prices and returns, even after controlling for potential simultaneity bias. Findings from this analysis are inconsistent with investors assessing brand value estimates as significantly less reliable than other components of book value of equity.

The simultaneous equation analysis also shows that brand value estimates are, as predicted, significantly positively associated with advertising expense, brand operating margin, and brand market share, although, contrary to predictions, they are not significantly positively associated with sales growth. Thus, we also investigate whether the brand value estimates are significantly related to market value of equity incremental to these additional factors, which could be viewed as alternative proxies for brand value, and find that they are. Thus, brand value estimates reflect value-relevant information beyond that reflected in these alternative measures associated with brand value. Additional analyses reveal that brand value estimates also reflect value-relevant information beyond that reflected in recognized brand assets and analysts' earnings forecasts.

Because brand values likely are relevant to investors, finding that estimates of brand values are reflected in share prices and returns calls into question concerns that estimates of brand values are unreliable. Whether their reliability is sufficient to warrant financial statement recognition is left to accounting standard-setters to determine.

Acknowledgments

We appreciate the helpful comments and suggestions by participants at the 1998 *Review of Accounting Studies* Conference, especially Jim Ohlson, the discussant, and workshop participants at the University of Alabama and Georgia State University, Baljit Sidhu, and an anonymous reviewer. We thank the editors of *Financial World* for helpful discussions, and I/B/E/S for use of analyst earnings forecast data. We also appreciate the research assistance of Hung-Ken Chien. Mary Barth and Ron Kasznik appreciate funding by the Financial Research Initiative, Graduate School of Business, Stanford University.

Appendix: Description of *Financial World*'s Brand Valuation Methodology

FW draws heavily on a brand value methodology developed by Interbrand Ltd., which is a London-headquartered consulting firm. FW began reporting estimated values for a small number of high profile brands (such as Budweiser, Coca-Cola, Heinz, and Marlboro) in September 1992. Over time, FW has expanded its coverage to include more brands across a broad set of industries. Key factors that guide FW's addition or deletion of brands in their annual survey are readership interest in the brand as assessed by FW or Interbrand, and availability of data to estimate brand profit and brand strength. Relating to readership, for example, FW has increased its coverage of brands of information technology firms (e.g. America Online, Dell Computer, and Netscape) beyond well-established brands that were covered in the early surveys (e.g. IBM, Intel, and Microsoft). Relating to data availability, FW does not publish brand value estimates for brands for which FW does not believe it has sufficient reliable information. For example, values for brands owned by Mars, Inc. (e.g. M&M's, Snickers, and Uncle Ben's) are not reported by FW because Mars Inc. is privately held and has a reputation for minimal public disclosure of financial information. Similarly, FW makes no attempt to estimate brand values owned by privately held firms where FW believes the information available is reliable (e.g. the Levi's brand of Levi Strauss).

A brand value reflects the product of two factors: net brand-related profits and a brand strength multiplier. We describe each below.

A.1. Net Brand-Related Profits

Net brand-related profits is the estimated after-tax operating income of a brand minus what could be earned on a basic nonbranded, that is, generic, version of the product. FW estimates the worldwide operating income of the brand by extensive discussions with the brand-owner firm's securities analysts and by its own analysis of the firm's financial statements, including segment disclosures. FW estimates the earnings of a nonbranded version of the product by estimating the amount of capital required to generate the brand's sales and assuming a generic version of the product would generate a 5 per cent net pre-tax return on that capital. The excess of the brand's estimated after-tax profits over the generic product's estimated after-tax profits is net brand-related profits.[21]

A.2. Brand Strength

FW obtains brand strength multiples for each brand directly from Interbrand. The Interbrand model of brand strength has seven components (see discussion in Guilding and Moorhouse, 1992):

1. Leadership *(maximum twenty-five points)*: The brand's ability to influence its market. To achieve a high leadership score, a brand must be a dominant force in its sector with a strong market share.

2. Stability *(maximum fifteen points)*: The ability of a brand to survive. Well-established brands that enjoy consumer loyalty will receive higher strength scores.

3. Market *(maximum ten points)*: The brand's trading environment. Changes in market growth, market stability, or in the level of competition are important factors, as are opinions on supplier or customer (buyer) power and demand elasticity.

4. Internationality *(maximum twenty-five points)*: The ability of the brand to cross geographic and cultural borders. It is difficult to affect the internationality score by any significant amount over a short time horizon. Plans for international expansion or the withdrawal from specified markets will, however, have an impact on profitability. International brands are almost always more valuable than national or regional brands, especially because

international brands usually benefit from marketing economies of scale and more robust sales, and because the brand is not dependent on one domestic market.

5. Trend *(maximum ten points)*: The ongoing direction of the brand's importance to its industry. Unlike other dimensions of brand strength, trend can change dramatically over a short time period. Trend will not only affect brand strength, but also may well affect the ability of the brand to improve or maintain profitability. Trend analysis indicates a brand's ability to remain contemporary and hence retain profitability.

6. Support *(maximum ten points)*: The effectiveness of the brand's communications. In the short-term, the level of support expenditures is an essential feature in the calculation of profitability. This support includes discretionary expenditures such as marketing support, which is made up of brand maintenance and brand development expenses. It is often difficult to determine a brand's support score because one needs to consider both quantity and quality support.

7. Protection *(maximum five points)*: The brand owner's legal title. This factor is generally an opportunity to express doubts or concerns over a brand's relative level of protection, for example, challenges to the trademark registration, rather than to appraise its absolute existence.

These components are weighted to develop a single brand strength measure, which ranges from 0 to 100. Each brand strength measure translates to a specific earnings multiplier—the higher the brand strength, the higher the multiplier. The brand strength multiplier can change each year, although the range remains similar from year-to-year. For example, in 1994 the range was 6–20 while in 1995 the range was 4.4–19.3.[22]

A.3. Illustrating the Interbrand Methodology

FW uses the Gillette brand name to illustrate its approach. In 1995 the Gillette brand was estimated to be worth $10.3 billion (FW, 1996):

'The blades and razor brand had $2.6 billion in 1995 sales and $961 million in operating earnings. First, we estimated how much capital was employed to produce the brand. To do so, we first determined the median ratio of capital employed to company sales for each industry. In the personal-care category, this was 0.38, or $38 of capital to produce $100 in sales. We estimated this ratio by the brand sales to estimate the capital employed to produce the brand. For Gillette this came to $988 million ($2.6 billion times 0.38)'.

'A generic brand on average should have a 5% profit on the capital employed to produce a product. So we multiplied this 5% by the capital employed to produce the brand, and we arrived at $49 million for Gillette'.

'After subtracting this $49 million from the brand's $961 million in earnings, we got the earnings that can be attributed to the Gillette brand name—$912 million. Keep in mind that we use the two-year weighted average of the earnings attributed to the brand'.

'We then applied the maximum corporate tax rate for the country where the brand's parent company is located (35% for US companies) to the two-year earnings average. For Gillette the calculated net income attributable to the brand was $575 million'.

'The final step was to multiply the brand's after-tax earnings figure by its strength multiple. Such multiples, in 1995, range from 4.4 to 19.3. For Gillette, one of the most prestigious names in the personal-care industry, this multiple was an impressive 17.9. The final brand value is $10.3 billion'.

Notes

1. Brand values also potentially are relevant to evaluating the performance of brand managers because the single most important asset a brand manager must manage is the brand itself. This study's motivation relates to external financial reporting and, thus, we do not focus on brand manager performance evaluation. See Foster and Gupta (1994) for a discussion of research challenges in this area.

2. Annual reports to shareholders of several of our sample firms contain statements highlighting their focus on brand management. For example, Time Warner states 'We believe that the surest way to create value for our shareholders is to develop, extend, and enhance the global brands that are Time Warner's alone' (1995 Annual Report).

3. FW articulates similar criticisms of US GAAP when presenting their annual survey of brand value. The following quotation is illustrative: 'Given the large and growing importance of brand equity, it is high time that the accounting profession took a second look at the topic. FW maintains that brand value can indeed be measured and that, in general, it does not depreciate over time like a factory or machine. . . . In FW's opinion, the conventions of historical cost introduce more distortions than they avoid, particularly in the field of brand equity' (1991 survey, FW, 1992).

4. For example, in the 1995 survey, FW (1996) reports value estimates for 14 Philip Morris brands, for example, Marlboro, Kraft, Maxwell House, Miller, and Kool-Aid, the aggregate value of which is $65.663 billion. The largest among these are Marlboro and Kraft, with estimated values of $44.614 billion and $5.742 billion, respectively.

5. Our sample does not include privately held or non US firms for which Compustat data are unavailable, even though FW reports estimates of brands for several such firms.

6. One reason for lack of two consecutive years of brand value estimates is the increase in FW's brand coverage over time. Another is that FW ceased reporting brand value estimates for sixty-three brands, most of which FW dropped after only one year of coverage, perhaps because of large decreases in estimated brand value.

7. Because FW focuses its reporting on brands with large estimated values, use of brand value estimates available in three consecutive years likely biases the graph against brands with large decreases in estimated brand value.

8. The returns analysis in Section 3.2 is designed to investigate whether these year-to-year changes in brand value estimates reflect changes in brand values.

9. See Section 5.3 for additional analyses relating to the possibility that book value of equity of some sample firms includes the cost of acquired brands.

10. Reliability is a matter of degree. Whether an estimate possesses sufficient reliability for accounting standard-setters to consider it reliable enough for financial statement recognition is a judgment for them to make. We provide evidence on the extent of reliability, not conclusions about whether the estimates are reliable 'enough' for recognition. Comparison of the coefficient on the brand value estimates with that on book value of equity provides some evidence on how the reliability of the estimates compares with that of recognized amounts.

11. Our inferences are unaffected by using share prices three months after year end.

12. Under this interpretation, Ohlson's (1995) model also suggests including in (1) the annual change in BRANDS, ΔBRANDS, consistent with viewing ΔBRANDS as an 'as

if' component of net income. Untabulated findings from including ∆BRANDS as an additional explanatory variable in (1) indicate that although its coefficient is significantly positive, as one might expect, its inclusion has little effect on the coefficients on the other variables. Note also that (1) is analogous to Ohlson (1995), (7), which is based on a particular linear information dynamics for net income. If net income does not follow this dynamic, then growth and/or expected future earnings are potential omitted variables. We include growth in the specification in Table 8 and report in Section 5.2 findings from additional analyses that consider analysts' forecasts of future earnings. In both cases, our inferences regarding BRANDS are unaffected.

13. Our inferences are unaffected if we use the amount reported in the prior year to calculate change in brand value. Our inferences also are unaffected if we include in (2) the change in ∆ BRANDS, although the associated data requirements result in loss of a substantial number of observations.

14. We define sales growth using Compustat rather than FW data because of data limitations. Our inferences regarding the value-relevance of brand value estimates are unaffected by using a one-year sales growth measure based on FW reported brand sales, although doing so substantially reduces the sample size. Our inferences also are unaffected by using Compustat data for all variables, and to using one-year lagged, rather than contemporaneous, advertising expense.

15. Including sales growth and brand market share as explanatory variables in (3) with other variables on a per share basis implicitly assumes that all variables are devoid of scale. To ensure our inferences are unaffected by this assumption, we estimated (3), using ordinary least squares (OLS) and as part of the simultaneous system, where the share-deflated variables are instead deflated by sales, which effectively is the deflator for SALES_GRWTH and MKT_SHARE. The untabulated findings are similar to those we report in Table 6, except that the insignificantly negative coefficient on SALES_GRWTH, reported in Panel A, is significantly negative in the revised specification.

16. The Z1-statistic is $(1/\sqrt{T}) \sum_{j=1}^{T} (t_j/\sqrt{k_j}/(k_j - 2))$, where T is the number of years, t_j is the t-statistic, and k_j is the degrees of freedom for year j (see Healy et al., 1987). The Z2-statistic is (mean t)/(std deviation $t/\sqrt{(T-1)}$ (see White, 1984; Bernard, 1987).

17. We use the term significant to denote p-values less than 0.05. Untabulated findings reveal that including BRANDS in (1) reduces the estimated coefficients on both BV and NI, by 9% and 11%, respectively. Our inferences are unaffected by estimating equation (1) using sales as a deflator, and undeflated, and including either number of shares outstanding or sales as an additional explanatory variable (Barth and Kallapur, 1996). All of our inferences are unaffected by using White (1980) heteroscedasticity-consistent standard errors to calculate test statistics.

18. Inspection of the untabulated separate-year regressions reveals that the difference between the coefficients on BRANDS and BV is decreasing over the sample period. In the 1993–96 regressions, the difference is 0.79, 0.29, 0.11, and 0, respectively. Untabulated regressions that also include ∆BRANDS reveal that the coefficient on ∆ BRANDS is significantly smaller than that on NI in the pooled regression and in all separate-year estimations. Unlike the coefficient on BRANDS, this difference in

coefficients is not shrinking over time, suggesting Δ BRANDS is estimated with more error than is BRANDS (Barth, 1994).

19. Note that the effectiveness of the two-stage estimation depends, in part, on whether the first-stage regression explains a significant portion of the variation in BRANDS. The untabulated adjusted R-squared of the first-stage regression of BRANDS on all of the exogenous variables is 0.57, suggesting the exogenous variables explain a substantial portion of the variation in brand value estimates.

20. For firms disclosing that recognized intangible assets include brands, but not disclosing separately the brand amount, we treat total intangible assets as if they relate to brands.

21. Prior to 1994, FW used the most recent year's brand operating income to calculate brand values. Starting with the 1994 survey (FW, 1995), it uses a two-year weighted average of the earnings attributed to the brand, with the most recent year weighted twice as much as the previous year. FW uses this averaging to prevent brand values from varying widely because of economic or short-term industry fluctuations that do not reflect variations in the value of the brand itself. Nonetheless, our separate-year estimation results reveal no discernible temporal pattern.

22. We reviewed the Letters to the Editor of *Financial World* subsequent to each annual survey to identify any specific criticism of the FW brand valuation methodology. The few letters that were published did not take issue with the methodology. For example: 'I have sent your article on brands to our clients. It is important reading for all of us'— Chief Executive Officer (CEO), J. Walter Thompson.

References

Aaker, D. A. (1991), *Managing Brand Equity* (New York: Free Press).

—— (1996), *Building Strong Brands* (New York: Free Press).

—— and Jacobson, R. (1994), 'The financial information content of perceived quality', *Journal of Marketing Research*, 31: 191–201.

Abdel-khalik, A. R. (1975), 'Advertising effectiveness and accounting policy', *The Accounting Review*, 50: 657–70.

Barth, M. E. (1994), 'Fair value accounting: Evidence from investment securities and the market valuation of banks', *The Accounting Review*, 69: 1–25.

—— and Clinch, G. (1998), 'Revalued financial, tangible, and intangible assets: Associations with share prices and non market-based value estimates', *Journal of Accounting Research*, 36: 199–233.

—— and Kallapur, S. (1996), 'The effects of cross-sectional scale differences on regression results in empirical accounting research', *Contemporary Accounting Research*, 13(2): 527–67.

—— and Kasznik, R. (1998), 'Share repurchase decisions and market reaction: Accounting-related and general information asymmetry and idle Cash', Working paper, Stanford University.

—— and Kasznik, R., and McNichols, M. F. (1998), 'Analyst coverage and intangible assets', Working paper, Stanford University.

—— and Landsman, W. R. (1995), 'Fundamental issues related to using fair value accounting for financial reporting', *Accounting Horizons*, 9: 97–107.

Bernard, V. L. (1987), 'Cross-sectional dependence and problems in inference in market-based Accounting research', *Journal of Accounting Research*, 25: 1–48.

Bublitz, B. and Ettredge, M. (1989), 'The information in discretionary outlays: Advertising, research, and development', *The Accounting Review*, 64: 108–24.

Easton, P. D. and Harrison, T. S. (1991), 'Earnings as an explanatory variable for returns', *Journal of Accounting Research*, 29: 19–36.

Financial World (1992), 'What's in a name? What the world's top brands are worth', September 1, 1992.

—— (1993), 'Who says brands are dead'? September 1, 1993.

—— (1994), 'Brands: what's hot. What's not', August 2, 1994.

—— (1995), 'Brands, the management factor', August 1, 1995.

—— (1996), 'Brands, blind faith', July 8, 1996.

—— (1997), 'Most valuable brands', September/October, 1997.

Foster, G. and Gupta, M. (1994), 'Marketing, cost management, and management accounting', *Journal of Management Accounting Research*, 6: 43–77.

Guilding, C. and Moorhouse. (1992), 'The case for brand value budgeting', in C. Drury (ed.), *Management Accounting Handbook* (London: ICAE).

Healy, P., Kang, S., and Palepu, K. G. (1987), 'The effect of accounting procedure changes on CEO's cash salary and bonus compensation', *Journal of Accounting and Economics*, 9: 7–34.

Hirschey, M. and Weygandt, J. J. (1985), 'Amortization policy for advertising and research and development expenditures', *Journal of Accounting Research*, 23: 326–35.

Keller, K. L. (1997), *Strategic Brand Management* (Upper Saddle River, New Jersey: Prentice Hall).

Ohlson, J. (1995), 'Earnings, book values, and dividends in security valuation', *Contemporary Accounting Research*, 12: 661–87.

Simon, C. J. and Sullivan, M. W. (1993). 'The measurement and determinants of brand equity: A financial approach', *Marketing Science*, 12(1): 28–52.

White, H. (1980), 'A heteroskedasticity-consistent covariance matrix estimator and a direct test for heteroskedasticity', *Econometrica*, 817–38.

—— (1984), *Asymptotic Theory for Econometricians* (Orlando, FL: Academic Press, Inc., Harcourt Brace Jovanovich).

Intellectual Human Capital and the Birth of US Biotechnology Enterprises

Lynne G. Zucker, Michael R. Darby, and
Marilynn B. Brewer

The number of American firms actively using biotechnology grew rapidly from nonexistent to over 700 in less than two decades, transforming the nature of the pharmaceutical industry and significantly impacting food processing, brewing, and agriculture, as well as other industries. Here we demonstrate empirically that the commercialization of this technology is essentially intertwined with the development of the underlying science in a way which illustrates the significance in practice of the localized spillovers concept in the agglomeration literature and of the tacit knowledge concept in the information literature. Indeed we present here strong evidence that the timing and location of initial usage by both new dedicated biotechnology firms (*'entrants'*) and new biotech subunits of existing firms (*'incumbents'*) are primarily explained by the presence at a particular time and place of scientists who are actively contributing to the basic science as represented by publications reporting genetic-sequence discoveries in academic journals.

By quantifying separable effects of individual scientists, major universities, and federal research support we provide specific structure to the role of universities and their faculties in encouraging local economic development through what are conventionally described in the literature as geographically localized knowledge spillovers.[1] Such localized knowledge spillovers may play fundamental roles in both economic agglomeration and endogenous growth (Paul M. Romer, 1986, 1990; Gene M. Grossman and Elhanan Helpman, 1991). However, our evidence, like the other literature cited here, specifically indicates localized effects without demonstrating that they can be characterized as spillovers (or externalities).

Section 1 lays out our basic hypothesis. The data are described in Section 2. Empirical results are reported and discussed in Section 3. A summary and conclusions section (Section 4) and Data Appendix complete the article.

----

1. The Hypothesis

Innovations are generally treated in the growth literature as a nonrivalrous good—freely useable by an unlimited number of potential users at a zero marginal cost (Richard R. Nelson and Romer, 1996). A complementary literature recognizes that some information requires an investment of considerable time and effort to master. The human capital developed by this investment is seen as earning a normal return on the cost of the investment, both direct costs and foregone earnings. We believe that some innovations, particularly a breakthrough 'invention of a method of inventing' (Griliches, 1957), may be better characterized as creating (rivalrous) human capital—intellectual human capital—characterized by natural excludability as opposed to a set of instructions for combining inputs and outputs which can be protected only by intellectual property rights. This natural excludability arises from the complexity or tacitness of the information required to practise the innovation (see Nelson, 1959; Kenneth J. Arrow, 1962; Nelson and Sidney G. Winter, 1982; and Nathan Rosenberg, 1982).

Based on both extensive interviews and empirical work summarized in Zucker and Darby (1996), we believe that, at least for the first ten or fifteen years, the innovations which underlie biotechnology are properly analysed in terms of naturally excludable knowledge held by a small initial group of discoverers, their coworkers, and others who learned the knowledge from working at the bench-science level with those possessing the requisite know-how. Ultimately the knowledge spread sufficiently widely to become part of routine science which could be learned at any major research university. After the initial 1973 discovery by Stanley Cohen and Herbert Boyer of the basic technique for recombinant DNA—the foundation of commercial biotechnology as well as of a burst of scientific innovation—the financial returns available to talented recombinant-DNA scientists first rose dramatically as the commercial implications became widely appreciated and then more gradually declined as more and more scientists learned the techniques, until knowledge of the new techniques *per se* earned only the normal return for the time required for a graduate student to master them. Further, mere knowledge of the techniques of recombinant DNA was not enough to earn these extraordinary returns; the knowledge was far more productive when embodied in a scientist with the genius and vision to continuously innovate and define the research frontier and apply the new research techniques in the most promising areas.

We hypothesize that entry of firms into biotechnology in a given year thus will be determined by the geographic distribution of stars and perhaps others then actively practising the new science as well as by the geographic distribution of economic activity. Stars are properly viewed as locationally (semi-) fixed since few star scientists who knew how to do recombinant DNA were willing to abandon their university appointments and laboratory teams to pursue commercial applications of biotechnology. The primary pattern in the development of the industry involved one or more scientist-entrepreneurs who remained on the faculty while establishing a business on the side—businesses which, where successful, resulted in millions or even billions of dollars for the professors who acquired early ownership stakes. Thus, we see the university as bringing about local industrial benefits by permitting its professors to pursue private commercial interests while their faculty appointments tie them to the area. In preliminary work not reported here, we tried to develop measures of local economic activity for industries, like pharmaceuticals, specifically impacted by the new technology, but these attempts never added significantly to the measures of general activity used in the empirical work below. The *local* availability of venture capital is widely believed to play a significant role in the birth of new biotech entrants (Martin Kenney, 1986; Joshua Lerner, 1994, 1995); so we also include that variable in our regressions.

2. The Data

Data have been collected in panel form for fourteen years (1976–89) and 183 regions (functional economic areas as defined by the US Department of Commerce, Bureau of Economic Analysis (BEA), 1992*b*). Frequently, the data are aggregates of data at the zip code or county level.[2] Lagged variables include data for 1975 in the unlagged form. See the Data Appendix for more details.

2.1. Firms

Our data set on firms was derived from a base purchased from the North Carolina Biotechnology Centre (NCBC) (1992) which was cleaned and supplemented with information in *Bioscan* (1989–93) and its precursor (Cetus Corp., 1988). We identified 751 distinct US firms for which we could determine a zip code and a date of initial use of biotechnology. Of these 751 firms, 511 were entrants 150 incumbents, and ninety (including eighteen joint ventures) could not be definitively classified. By 1990, fifty-two of the 751 firms had died or merged into other firms.

We then calculated the number of births in each region by year of initial use of biotechnology for all 751 firms as well as for their identified subcomponents of entrants and incumbents. We also have the stocks of surviving firms, entrants, and incumbents by region and year.

2.2. Scientists

Early in our ongoing project studying the scientific development and diffusion of biotechnology, we identified a set of 327 star scientists based on their outstanding productivity through early 1990. The primary criterion for selections was the discovery of more than forty genetic sequences as reported in *GenBank* (1990) through April 1990.[3] However, twenty-two scientists were included based on writing twenty or more articles, each reporting one or more genetic-sequence discoveries.[4] In the 1990s, sequence discovery has become routinized and is no longer such a useful measure of research success. These 327 stars were only three quarters of 1 per cent of the authors in *GenBank* (1990) but accounted for 17.3 per cent of the published articles, almost twenty-two times as many articles as the average scientist.

We collected by hand the 4061 articles authored by stars and listed in *GenBank* and recorded the institutional affiliation of the stars and their coauthors on each of these articles. These coauthors are called '*collaborators*' if they are not themselves a star. Some data on the stars and collaborators who ever published in the United States is given on the left side of Table 1, where the scientists are identified by the organization(s) with which they were affiliated on their first-such publication. The higher citation rate for firm-affiliated scientists is explored at length in Zucker and Darby (1996).

Figure 1 illustrates the time pattern of growth in the numbers of stars and collaborators who have ever published and the total number of firms using biotechnology in the United States. There was a handful of stars who published articles reporting genetic-sequence discoveries before the 1973 breakthrough, but even after 1973 their number increased gradually until taking off in 1980. The numbers of collaborators and firms lagged behind the growth in stars by some years.

To identify those scientists clearly working at the edge of the science in a given year, we term a star or collaborator as '*active*' if he or she has published three or more sequence-discovery articles in the three-year moving window ending with that year. As seen in the right side of Table 1, this stringent second screen provides an even more elite definition of star scientists as well as identifying some very significant collaborators. We count for each year the number of active stars and active collaborators who are affiliated with an organization in each region.

The locations of active stars and firms are both concentrated and highly correlated geographically, particularly early in the period. Figure 2 illustrates this pattern for the whole period by accumulating the number of stars who have

Table 1. Distribution of Star Scientists and Collaborators Who Have Ever Published in the United States

Organization Type[b]	Full Data Set		Ever Active in US[a]	
	Number of Scientists	Citations[c]/ Scientist/Years	Number of Scientists	Citations[c]/ Scientist/Years
Stars:				
University	158	85.5	108	110.8
Institute	44	63.0	26	98.7
Firm	5	143.7	1	694.3
Dual	0	NA	0	NA
Total	207		135	
Collaborators:				
University	2901	10.4	369	30.6
Institute	776	13.7	88	35.8
Firm	324	29.2	43	99.1
Dual	3	7.2	0	NA
Total	4004		500	

[a] Ever active in the United States means that in at least one three-year period beginning 1974 or later and ending 1989 or earlier, the scientist was listed on at least three articles appearing in our data set of 4061 articles which reported genetic-sequence discoveries and were published in major journals and that the affiliation listed in the last of the three articles was located in the United States.

[b] The organization type refers to the affiliation listed on their *first* publication with a US affiliation.

[c] Citation counts are for 1982, 1987, and 1992 for all articles in our data set (whenever published) for which the individual was listed as an author.

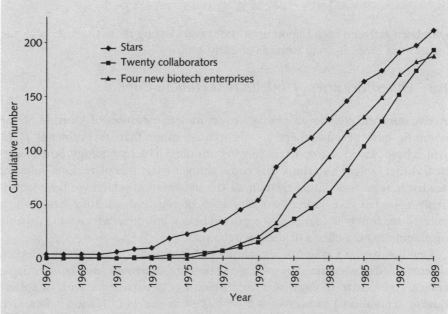

Fig. 1. Cumulative number of US stars, collaborators, and new biotech enterprises, 1967–89.

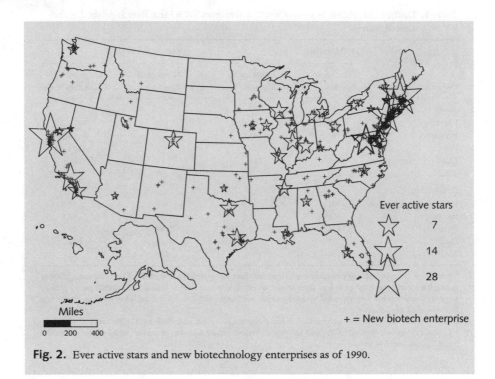

Fig. 2. Ever active stars and new biotechnology enterprises as of 1990.

ever been active in each region up to 1990 and plotting them together with the location of biotech-using firms as of early 1990.

2.3. Other Measures of Intellectual Human Capital

Active stars and collaborators may be incomplete measures of location of the scientific base because there are techniques other than recombinant DNA which have played an important role in commercial biotechnology. Some skeptical readers might also think that some simpler measures of regions' relevant academic resources would contain all the information which we have laboriously collected. We found two measures of regional scientific base which entered separately in regressions reported below, but none which were capable of eliminating the effects of the star scientists.

One measure is a count of the number of *'top-quality universities'* in a region where top quality is defined by having one or more *'biotech-relevant'* (biochemistry, cellular/molecular biology, and microbiology) departments with scholarly quality reputational ratings of 4.0 or higher in the 1982 National Research Council survey (Lyle V. Jones *et al.*, 1982). There are twenty such universities in the United States.[5] Our second measure, *'federal support'*, is the total number (in hundreds) of faculty supported by 1979–80 federal grants to all universities in each region for biotech-relevant research.[6] These variables take on the same value for a given region in each year.

2.4. *Other Variables*

Using listings in Stanley E. Pratt (1982), we measure *'venture capital firms'* as the number of such firms in a region legally eligible to finance start-ups in each year up to 1981. For later years, the number of firms is fixed at the number in 1981 to avoid possible simultaneity problems once the major wave of biotech founding began.[7] (While great bookstores spring up around great universities, the former should not be counted as causing the latter.)

Since entry of biotech firms would be expected to occur where there is other economic activity, particularly involving a highly skilled labour force, we also include *total employment* in all industries (in millions of persons) and *average wages* (measured by deflated average earnings per job in thousands of 1987 dollars) for each region and year.

Finally, an increase in the (all-equity) cost of capital, as measured by the *earnings-price ratio* on the Standard & Poor's 500 Index would reduce the net present value of entry and so should have a negative impact on birth of new firms, entrants or incumbents.

---

3. Empirical Results

We test our hypothesis using both the full panel data and by regressing the geographical distribution of the data in 1990 on values of the independent variables circa 1980. The former more fully exploit the available information while the latter avoid problems of possible simultaneity which might arise after 1980 when commercial biotechnology became a significant economic factor in some regions. All the regressions reported here, as well as an extensive sensitivity analysis noted below, were estimated in the poisson form appropriate for count variables with numerous zeroes using LIMDEP (William H. Greene, 1992: pp. 539–49), with the Wooldridge regression-based correction for the variance–covariance matrix estimates.[8] The poisson regressions estimate the logarithm of the expected number of firm births; so the signs and significance of coefficients have the usual interpretation. Although OLS regressions are inappropriate for our count dependent variables with most observations at zero and the rest tailing off through small positive integers, we reported broadly consistent results using that technique in an earlier version of the paper (Zucker *et al.*, 1994).

In our sensitivity analysis, we ran the same poisson regressions for entrants and incumbents defined both exclusive and inclusive of the arguable case of joint ventures. The results were generally very similar to the subcomponent regressions in Table 4. In other unreported poisson regressions, we found that eliminating those regions with no firms and no stars from the sample did not result in qualitatively different results.

3.1. The Long-Run Model

Because of concerns about possible simultaneity biases once the industry became a significant economic force, we begin our empirical discussion with models which relate the number of firms in each region at the beginning of 1990 to the distribution of intellectual human capital and other variables as of about 1980. These results provide something of an acid test of our approach.

In Table 2, we present cross-section poisson regressions across the 183 regions explaining the number of firms in each at the beginning of 1990 when our data

Table 2. Poisson Regressions on the Stock of Biotech—Using Firms at the Beginning of 1990 by Region

	(a)	(b)	(c)	(d)	(e)	(f)
Constant	0.911^{***}	0.644^{***}	0.468^{***}	-2.595^{***}	-2.718^{***}	-2.607^{***}
	(0.014)	(0.015)	(0.033)	(0.086)	(0.256)	(0.345)
Number stars active at any	0.567^{***}	0.587^{***}	0.466^{***}	—	0.877^{***}	0.649^{***}
time during 1976–80	(0.029)	(0.072)	(0.090)	—	(0.076)	(0.084)
Number collaborators active	-0.076^{***}	0.175^{***}	-0.183^{**}	—	-0.333^{***}	-0.261^{***}
at any time during 1976–80	(0.012)	(0.033)	(0.068)	—	(0.045)	(0.037)
(Number stars active at any	—	-0.028^{***}	-0.019	—	-0.049^{***}	-0.024^{*}
time during 1976–80)^2	—	(0.007)	(0.014)	—	(0.012)	(0.012)
(Number collaborators active	—	-0.005^{***}	0.002	—	0.007^{**}	0.001
at any time during 1976–80)^2	—	(0.001)	(0.003)	—	(0.003)	(0.002)
Number top-quality	—	—	1.388^{***}	—	1.594^{***}	0.442^{*}
universities in the region	—	—	(0.150)	—	(0.107)	(0.195)
Number faculty with federal	—	—	0.263	—	0.752^{***}	0.711^{***}
support in the region	—	—	(0.143)	—	(0.088)	(0.051)
Number venture capital	—	—	—	0.017^{***}	-0.045^{***}	-0.013^{**}
firms in the region in 1980	—	—	—	(0.002)	(0.003)	(0.004)
Total employment (all	—	—	—	0.222^{***}	-0.009	-0.213^{***}
industries) in the region in 1980	—	—	—	(0.019)	(0.043)	(0.049)
Average wages per job in	—	—	—	0.166^{***}	0.143^{***}	0.139^{***}
the region in 1980	—	—	—	(0.004)	(0.014)	(0.019)
Cumulative births of biotech	—	—	—	—	—	0.300^{***}
firms during 1976–80	—	—	—	—	—	(0.025)
Log-likelihood	-871.9	-707.3	-543.2	-753.9	-416.0	-350.7
Restricted log-likelihood	-1401.7	-1401.7	-1401.7	-1401.7	-1401.7	-1401.7

Notes: $N=183$. Standard errors (adjusted by Wooldridge, 1991 Procedure 2.1) are in parentheses below coefficients.
* Significantly different from 0 at the 5% level.
** Significantly different from 0 at the 1% level.
*** Significantly different from 0 at the 0.1% level.

set ends.[9] Column (a) restrains the analysis to only the numbers of stars and collaborators ever active in each region at any time up through 1980, while columns (b) and (c) add first their squares and then our other intellectual human capital variables. Column (d) considers alternatively other economic variables which might explain entry, and column (e) combines the variables in (c) and (d). Column (f) adds to this model the number of biotech firms existing in 1980.

Column (a) in Table 2 indicates that the number of stars and collaborators active through 1980 is a powerful predictor of the geographic distribution of biotech enterprises in 1990, since the log-likelihood increases to -871.9 compared to -1401.7 for a constant alone. It is the star scientists that contribute positively, with collaborators having a much smaller negative coefficient in this regression and most of the other long-run models discussed below. We had expected that the coefficient on collaborators would be much smaller than that on stars, but positive. We do obtain a positive coefficient on active collaborators when the squared terms are added in column (b), but that turns negative again upon addition of other variables in the remaining columns of Table 2.[10] (In the annual regressions discussed below, we generally estimate positive effects of active collaborators, but they are often statistically insignificant.)

We can offer two explanations for the generally negative sign on the number of active collaborators in the long-run regressions: (i) This coefficient reflects two partially offsetting influences; collaborators have a positive direct effect on the entry of firms but reduce the effect of stars who are devoting more of their time to training students and relatively less to starting their own firms. Training collaborators is surely a useful and rewarded activity—particularly for the academic stars—but it may take more of the stars' energy than it is worth if firm birth were the only criteria.[11] (ii) The sign and magnitude of the coefficient on collaborators may simply reflect significant multicollinearity among the intellectual human capital variables in the very early years. This is especially likely since when we examine the full cross-section/time-series results just below we obtain (we think more reliable) zero or positive coefficients on collaborators, so the puzzle largely disappears.

The full 'fundamentals' model (excepting the decade-lagged dependent variable) is presented in column (e) of Table 2, where all the coefficients are significant except that for total employment. Leaving aside the question of the negative collaborator coefficient, we note the strong, positive, separate effects of stars, top-quality universities, and federal research grants at universities on birth of firms in a given geographic region. The intellectual human capital variables alone increase the log-likelihood ratio from -1401.7 to -543.2 (see column (c)), with the final three variables bringing this quantity up to -416.0. As to the last three variables, the quality of the labour force, measured by average wages per job, seems much more relevant than its size. Surprisingly, to some observers, the number of venture capital firms in a region enters, but with a significantly negative sign. We interpret the negative sign as evidence that venture capitalists did play an active role in the formation of entrant firms, but they apparently resulted in fewer, larger firms being born in the areas in which they were more active.[12]

This sign of the coefficient of the number of venture capital firms in a region is robust in sensitivity experiments with other forms (not reported here) except for regressions which exclude the intellectual human capital variables such as in column (d). That regression looks good in terms of significance and expected sign pattern although it has a much lower explanatory power than the intellectual human capital variables alone (column (c)). Just below, we report very similar results in a cross-section/time-series context. Thus, it is certainly easy to see why the evidence for an important positive impact of venture capital firms on the birth of biotech firms may have appeared stronger in previous work than seems warranted based on fuller models: Since venture capital firms have developed around a number of great universities, their presence proxies for intellectual human capital in the absence of more direct measures; if they are the only variable indicating presence of great universities and their faculties, they enter positively even if their packaging activities result in a negative direct effect on births.

The decade-lagged dependent variable is added to the full fundamentals model in column (f) of Table 2. Doing so primarily has the effect of weakening the significance of the top-quality universities variable (but, see the annual model below) due to significant multicollinearity between the variables.[13] One interpretation of this positive coefficient on the lagged dependent variable is that agglomeration effects strengthen the impact of fundamentals on regional development. However, the statistical properties of poisson regressions with lagged dependent variables are somewhat problematic so such regressions and their estimated standard errors should be viewed cautiously.

In conclusion, the intellectual human capital variables play a strong role in determining where the US biotech industry developed during the 1980s. We have been able to identify particular star scientists who appear to play a crucial role in the process of spillover and geographic agglomeration over and above that which would be predicted based on university reputation and scientists supported by federal grants alone. The strong positive role of venture capital variable reported previously is not supported for firm births. Indeed, the data tell us that there were fewer firms founded, other things equal, where there were more venture capital firms. It is left to future research to explore whether firms which are associated with particular star scientists or were midwifed by venture capitalists are more successful than other firms.[14]

3.2. The Annual Model

We next report analogous poisson regressions exploiting the panel nature of our data set with observations for the 183 regions for each of the years 1976–89. Tables 3 and 4 report poisson regressions for this entire panel.

Column (a) of Table 3 reports the results using only the counts of stars and their collaborators active each year in each region. As with the long-run models in Table 2, examination of the data suggested that these effects particularly for stars—were nonlinear so we add squared values in column (b).

Table 3. Annual Poisson Regressions on the Birth of Biotech—Using Firms by Region and Year, 1976–89

	(a)	(b)	(c)	(d)	(e)	(f)
Constant	−1.591***	−1.918***	−2.148***	−4.447***	−4.491***	−4.687***
	(0.032)	(0.041)	(0.057)	(0.226)	(0.349)	(0.565)
Number stars active in the region and year	0.157***	0.529***	0.270**	—	0.361***	0.282**
	(0.020)	(0.051)	(0.088)	—	(0.080)	(0.103)
Number collaborators active in the region and year	0.043***	0.083*	0.047	—	0.013	0.032
	(0.013)	(0.035)	(0.049)	—	(0.047)	(0.052)
(Number stars active in the region and year)^2	—	−0.022***	−0.014*	—	−0.015**	−0.014
	—	(0.002)	(0.006)	—	(0.005)	(0.008)
(Number collaborators active in the region and year)^2	—	−0.001	0.000	—	0.000	0.001
	—	(0.001)	(0.001)	—	(0.001)	(0.002)
Number stars active in the region and year × DUMMY 1986–89	—	—	−0.219	—	−0.298**	−0.245
	—	—	(0.113)	—	(0.102)	(0.128)
Number collaborators active in the region and year × DUMMY 1986–89	—	—	0.117	—	0.115	0.027
	—	—	(0.067)	—	(0.064)	(0.081)
(Number stars active in the region and year × DUMMY 1986–89)^2	—	—	0.006	—	0.009	0.007
	—	—	(0.007)	—	(0.006)	(0.008)
(Number collaborators active in the region and year × DUMMY 1986–89)^2	—	—	−0.001	—	−0.001	0.001
	—	—	(0.002)	—	(0.002)	(0.002)
Number top-quality universities in the region in 1981	—	—	0.444***	—	0.472***	0.462***
	—	—	(0.125)	—	(0.095)	(0.109)
Number faculty with federal support in the region in 1979–80	—	—	0.625***	—	0.982***	0.930***
	—	—	(0.093)	—	(0.094)	(0.093)
Number venture capital firms in the region and year[a]	—	—	—	0.019**	−0.028***	−0.024**
	—	—	—	(0.007)	(0.006)	(0.008)
Total employment (all industries) in the region and year	—	—	—	0.173***	−0.081	−0.117*
	—	—	—	(0.051)	(0.048)	(0.055)
Average wages per job in the region and year	—	—	—	0.153***	0.125***	0.132***
	—	—	—	(0.010)	(0.016)	(0.017)
Earnings-price ratio (Standard & Poors 500) for year	—	—	—	−0.024	−0.026	−0.017
	—	—	—	(0.016)	(0.026)	(0.039)
Number firms active in the region at end of previous year	—	—	—	—	—	0.020
	—	—	—	—	—	(0.013)
Number firms active in all US at end of previous year	—	—	—	—	—	−0.000
	—	—	—	—	—	(0.000)
Births of biotech firms in the region for previous year	—	—	—	—	—	0.054
	—	—	—	—	—	(0.034)
Log-likelihood	−1677.0	−1429.1	−1274.3	−1669.5	−1202.3	−1184.6
Restricted log-likelihood	−2238.5	−2238.5	−2238.5	−2238.5	−2238.5	−2238.5

Notes: $N=2562$. Standard errors (adjusted by Wooldridge, 1991 Procedure 2.1) are in parentheses below coefficients.
[a] For years after 1981, the number of venture capital firms in a region is held constant at the 1981 level to avert simultaneity problems.
* Significantly different from 0 at the 5% level.
** Significantly different from 0 at the 1% level.
*** Significantly different from 0 at the 0.1% level.

Table 4. Annual Poisson Regressions on the Birth of Biotech—Using Entrants and Incumbents by Region and Year, 1976–89

	(a) Entrants	(b) Incumbents	(c) Entrants	(d) Incumbents	(e) Entrants	(f) Incumbents
Constant	−4.726***	−5.798***	−4.843***	−5.673***	−4.928***	−5.228***
	(0.284)	(0.563)	(0.409)	(0.902)	(0.669)	(1.285)
Number stars active in the	—	—	0.414***	0.323	0.351**	0.242
region and year	—	—	(0.095)	(0.165)	(0.124)	(0.169)
Number collaborators active	—	—	−0.006	0.000	−0.012	0.019
in the region and year	—	—	(0.053)	(0.105)	(0.059)	(0.101)
(Number stars active in the	—	—	−0.016**	−0.016*	−0.017	−0.015
region and year)^2	—	—	(0.006)	(0.008)	(0.009)	(0.011)
(Number collaborators	—	—	0.001	0.002	0.000	0.001
active in the region and year)^2	—	—	(0.002)	(0.003)	(0.002)	(0.003)
Number stars active in the region	—	—	−0.227*	−0.519*	−0.196	−0.456
and year × DUMMY 1986–89	—	—	(0.113)	(0.237)	(0.147)	(0.251)
Number collaborators active	—	—	0.096	0.233	0.011	0.144
in the region and year ×	—	—	(0.071)	(0.141)	(0.090)	(0.153)
DUMMY 1986–89						
(Number stars active in the	—	—	0.007	0.018	0.006	0.015
region and year × DUMMY	—	—	(0.007)	(0.010)	(0.010)	(0.013)
1986–89)^2						
(Number collaborators active in	—	—	−0.001	−0.004	0.001	−0.002
the region and year ×	—	—	(0.002)	(0.003)	(0.003)	(0.004)
DUMMY 1986–89)^2						
Number top-quality universities	—	—	0.440***	0.479*	0.410**	0.447
in the region in 1981	—	—	(0.110)	(0.205)	(0.126)	(0.238)
Number faculty with federal	—	—	0.973***	1.114***	0.932***	1.041***
support in the region in	—	—	(0.112)	(0.296)	(0.107)	(0.295)
1979–80						
Number venture capital firms in	0.023**	0.006	−0.029***	−0.027*	−0.024**	−0.024
the region and year[a]	(0.009)	(0.013)	(0.007)	(0.012)	(0.009)	(0.013)
Total employment (all industries)	0.128	0.296**	−0.110	−0.052	−0.149*	−0.078
in the region and year	(0.067)	(0.098)	(0.058)	(0.098)	(0.067)	(0.103)
Average wages per job in the	0.156***	0.139***	0.123***	0.113**	0.127***	0.114**
region and year	(0.012)	(0.024)	(0.018)	(0.039)	(0.020)	(0.040)
Earnings-price ratio (Standard &	−0.036	−0.033	−0.022	−0.056	−0.016	−0.082
Poors 500) for year	(0.021)	(0.043)	(0.031)	(0.070)	(0.046)	(0.092)
Number firms active in the region	—	—	—	—	0.023	0.024
at end of previous year	—	—	—	—	(0.015)	(0.025)
Number firms active in all US at	—	—	—	—	−0.000	−0.001
end of previous year	—	—	—	—	(0.000)	(0.001)
Births of biotech firms in the	—	—	—	—	0.037	0.055
region for previous year	—	—	—	—	(0.041)	(0.061)
Log-likelihood	−1265.1	−486.3	−945.9	−386.8	−935.8	−382.9
Restricted log-likelihood	−1628.7	−607.9	−1628.7	−607.9	−1628.7	−607.9

Notes: N=2562. Standard errors (adjusted by Wooldridge, 1991 Procedure 2.1) are in parentheses below coefficients.
[a] For years after 1981, the number of venture capital firms in a region is held constant at the 1981 level to avert simultaneity problems.
* Significantly different from 0 at the 5% level.
** Significantly different from 0 at the 1% level.
*** Significantly different from 0 at the 0.1% level.

Again, as the number of stars increases, their marginal contribution diminishes eventually passing through zero.

These nonlinearities might reflect the declining value over time of the intellectual human capital as we have measured it. Basically, as the knowledge diffuses we expect that more and more stars will result in less and less pay-off to anyone of them if he or she were to start a firm, and indeed stars are less likely to result in birth of firms after 1985 than before. This is illustrated in column (c) of Table 3 where we add four interaction terms in which these counts and their squares have been multiplied by a dummy DUMMY 1986–89 equal to 1 during 1986–89 and 0 otherwise, as well as the other intellectual human capital terms. During 1986–89 the positive effect of stars is sharply reduced while that of collaborators more than triples.[15] Nonetheless, we should view this inference cautiously since the significance values of the interaction terms for stars and collaborators with DUMMY 1986–89 fall between 0.10 and 0.05, except for stars in the full fundamentals model in column (e) where the stars interaction term is significant at the 0.01 level.

Thus, we see that (at least during the first decade of this industry) localities with outstanding scientists having the tacit knowledge to practice recombinant DNA were much more likely to see new firms founded and preexisting firms begin to apply biotechnology. There is some evidence that as knowledge about gene splicing diffused and the tacit knowledge lost its scarcity and extraordinary value, the training function of universities became more important relative to the attraction of great scientists to an area. It is interesting that the quadratic term for stars is negative, suggesting diminishing returns (or possibly just proportionately fewer, larger firms) rather than the increasing returns suggested by standard views of knowledge spillovers which posit uninternalized, positive external effects from university scientists.[16] In the same regression in column (c), we see that, beyond the identified stars and collaborators, university quality and federal support are also significant measures of intellectual human capital relevant to firm founding.

Column (d) of Table 3 leads to the same conclusions with panel data as found for the same column in Table 2: The economic variables enter significantly with the expected sign if the intellectual human capital variables are omitted from the regression. However, unlike the previous long-run case, we can now enter the earnings-price ratio.[17] Here this variable enters with the correct sign, but does not even reach the 0.10 level of significance.

Column (e) of Table 3 presents the annual full fundamentals model incorporating the intellectual human capital and other variables. The results for the intellectual human capital measures are robust while the sign of the venture capital variable turns significantly negative as in the long-run model and the employment variable becomes insignificant (and negative).

Column (f) of Table 3, analogously to Table 2, adds a lagged dependent variable to the full fundamentals model. We also included the one-year lagged regional and national counts of firms using biotechnology as dynamic influences reflecting local agglomeration effects and market competition effects, respectively. None of the three dynamic variables enter significantly although their signs are consistent with some geographic agglomeration.

Thus, taken as a whole the results summarized in Table 3 support the strong role of intellectual human capital variables in determining the development of the American biotech industry.

The role of the economic variables, particularly the number of venture capital firms in the region, is explored further in Table 4. This table presents representative results for births in the entrant and incumbent subcomponents of firm entry into biotechnology. We see in columns (a) and (b) that if only the economic variables are introduced we get all the expected signs at appropriate significance (except for employment in (a) and the earnings-price ratio in both), including a result consistent with conventional wisdom that the number of venture capital firms has a significantly positive effect on the birth of new firms but an insignificant effect on the birth of subunits of existing firms which would not normally be financed by venture capital firms. The full fundamentals model is reported in columns (c) and (d) for births of entrants and incumbents, respectively, which is to be compared to column (e) for all firm births in Table 3. Again, in the presence of intellectual human capital the simple economic story does not hold up: the coefficients of venture capital firms and total employment turn negative, significantly so in the former case. Similar results are obtained in the dynamic versions of the full model reported in columns (e) and (f) of Table 4. The robustness of the negative venture capital coefficient remains a puzzle for future work, particularly in view of Yolanda K. Henderson's (1989) evidence that, despite some significant localization, most investments by venture capitalists cross regional boundaries.

4. Summary and Conclusions

The American biotechnology industry which was essentially nonexistent in 1975 grew to 700 active firms over the next fifteen years. In this paper, we show the tight connection between the intellectual human capital created by frontier research and the founding of firms in the industry. At least for this high-tech industry, the growth and location of intellectual human capital was the principal determinant of the growth and location of the industry itself. This industry is a testament to the value of basic scientific research. The number of local venture capital firms, which appears to be a positive determinant when intellectual human capital variables are excluded from the regressions, is found to depress the rate of firm birth in an area, perhaps due to the role of these venture capital firms in packaging a number of scientists into one larger firm which is likely to go public sooner.

We conclude that the growth and diffusion of intellectual human capital was the main determinant of where and when the American biotechnology industry developed. Intellectual human capital tended to flourish around great universities, but the existence of outstanding scientists measured in terms of research productivity played a key role over, above, and separate from the presence of those universities and government research funding to them. We believe that our results provide new insight into the role of research universities and their top scientists as central to the formation of new high-tech industries spawned by scientific breakthroughs. By being able to quantitatively identify individuals with the ability both to invent and to commercialize these breakthroughs, we have developed new specificity for the idea of spillovers and in particular raised the issue of whether spillovers are best viewed as resulting from the nonappropriability of scientific knowledge or from the maximizing behavior of scientists who have the ability to appropriate the commercial fruits of their academic discoveries.

....

Appendix: Data

The data used are generally in panel form for fourteen years (1976–89) and 183 regions (functional economic areas as defined by the BEA). Frequently, the data are aggregates of data at the zip code or county level. Lagged variables include data for 1975 in the unlagged form. These data sets, part of our ongoing project on 'Intellectual Capital, Technology Transfer, and the Organization of Leading-Edge Industries: Biotechnology', will be archived upon completion of the project in the Data Archives at the UCLA Institute for Social Science Research. A full description of the data is available from the authors upon request.

A.1. Biotechnology Firms

The starting point for our firm data set covered the industry as of April 1990 and was purchased from NCBC (1991), a private firm which tracks the industry. This data set identified 1075 firms, some of which were duplicates or foreign and others of which had died or merged. Further, there were a significant number of firms missing which had exited prior to April 1990. For these reasons, an intensive effort was made to supplement the NCBC data with information from *Bioscan* (1989–93) and an industry data set provided by a firm in the industry which was also the ancestor of the *Bioscan* data set (Cetus Corp., 1988).

We generally counted entry of firms by adding up for each year and region the number of entrants founded and incumbents first using biotechnology. A few special cases should be noted: Where a firm enters the data set due to the merger of an entrant and another firm, we count it for the purposes of this paper as a continuation of the original entrant and not a new birth (the older entrant if two are involved). If firms already in the data set merge and one continues with the other(s) absorbed, the enterprise is counted as the continuing enterprise and not a new birth.

A.2. Scientists

Star scientists and their collaborators were identified as described in the text. Individual scientists are linked to locations through the institutional affiliations reported in their publications in the article data set. The discovery of genetic sequences is recognized by *GenBank*'s assignment to an article of a 'primary accession number' to identify each. The twenty-two additional stars added to the 315 with more than forty primary accession numbers thus had twenty or more articles with at least one primary accession number and 20–40 primary accession numbers total.

A.3. Articles

Our article data set consists of all 4061 articles in major journals listed in *GenBank* as reporting genetic-sequence discoveries for which one or more of our 327 stars were listed as authors. (A small number of unpublished papers and articles appearing in proceedings volumes and obscure journals were excluded to permit the hand coding detailed below.) All of these articles were assigned unique article ID numbers and collected by hand. For each article, scientist ID numbers are used to identify the order of authorship and the institutional affiliation and location for each author on each article. This hand coding was necessary because, under the authorship traditions for these fields, the head of the laboratory who is often the most prestigious author frequently appears last. Our stars, for example, were first authors on 18.3 per cent of the articles and last authors on 69.1 per cent of the 4031 articles remaining after excluding the thirty sole-authored articles.[18] Unfortunately, only first- and/or corresponding-author affiliations are available in machine-readable sources.[19]

The resulting authorship data file contains 19,346 observations, approximately 4.8 authors for each of the 4061 published articles. Each authorship observation gives the article ID number, the order of authorship, the scientist ID number of one of our stars and collaborators, and an institutional ID number for the author's affiliation which links him or her to a particular institution with a known zip code as of the publication date of the article.

A.4. Citations

We have collected data for 1982, 1987, and 1992 on the total number of citations to each of our 4061 published articles listed in the Institute for Scientific Information's *Science Citation Index* (1982, 1987, 1992). These citation counts are linked to the article and authorship data set by the article ID number. The citations were collected for articles if and only if they appeared in the article data set; so scientists are credited with citations only insofar as they are to the 4061 articles reporting genetic-sequence discoveries and published in major journals.

A.5. Universities

Our university data set consists of all US institutions listed as granting the Ph.D. degree in any field in the Higher Education General Information Survey (HEGIS), Institutional Characteristics, 1983–84 (US Department of Education, National Center for Education Statistics, 1985). Each university is assigned an institutional ID number, a university flag, and located by zip code based on the HEGIS address file. Additional information described in the text was collected from Jones et al. (1982) for those universities granting the Ph.D. degree in biochemistry, cellular/molecular biology, and/or microbiology which we define as 'biotech-relevant' fields.

A.6. Research Institutes and Hospitals

For those US research institutions and hospitals listed as affiliations in the article data set, we assigned an institutional ID number and an institute/hospital flag, and obtained an address including a zip code as required for geocoding. No additional information has been collected on these institutions.

A.7. Venture Capital Firms

We created a venture capital firm data set by extracting from the Pratt (1982) directory the name, type, location, year of founding, and interest in funding biotech firms. This information was extracted for all venture capital which were legally permitted to finance start-ups. This latter requirement eliminated a number of firms which are chartered under government programs targeted at small and minority businesses. This approach accounts includes founding date of firms appearing in the 1982 Pratt directory, excluding those firms that may have either entered thereafter or existed in earlier years but exited before the directory was compiled.

A.8. Other Economic Variables

Total employment and average earnings per job by region and year are as reported by the Bureau of Economic Analysis based on county level data in US Department of Commerce (1992b): Total employment is from Table K, line 010 (in millions of persons). Average earnings is from Table V, line 290 (wage & salary disbursements, other labour income, and proprietors income per job in thousands of current dollars), deflated by the implicit price

deflator for personal consumption expenditures. The annual data for the implicit price deflator for personal consumption expenditures were taken from US Department of Commerce
(1992a: 247, line 16) as updated in the July 1992 *Survey of Current Business* (p. 92, line 16). The
S&P 500 earnings-price ratio was taken from *CITIBASE* (1993), series FSEXP.

Notes

1. Zvi Griliches (1992) has surveyed the importance of R&D spillovers as a major source of
   endogenous growth in recent 'new growth theory' models and the difficult empirical
   search for their existence. Despite these difficulties, there have been a number of articles
   reporting evidence of geographic localization of knowledge spillovers, including Adam
   B. Jaffe (1989), Jaffe *et al.* (1993), and Edwin Mansfield (1995).
2. The BEA's functional economic areas divide all the counties in the United States into
   regions including one or more cities, their suburbs, and the rural counties most closely
   tied to the central city.
3. See Zucker *et al.* (1993). As will be obvious, much of the time between 1990 and the initial submission of this paper was spent in developing reasonable measures of intellectual
   human capital and in collecting and coding data necessary to locate the authors of the
   discoveries reported in the articles in question and to trace the diffusion process.
4. Scientists advised that some sequence discoveries are more difficult than others and thus
   merit an article reporting only one sequence. Therefore we included scientists with
   twenty or more discovery articles to avoid excluding scientists who specialized in more
   difficult problems.
5. The twenty universities were: Brandeis University, California Institute of Technology,
   Columbia University, Cornell University, Duke University, Harvard University, Johns
   Hopkins University, Massachusetts Institute of Technology, Rockefeller University,
   Stanford University, University of California–Berkeley, University of California—Los
   Angeles, University of California—San Diego, University of California—San Francisco,
   University of Chicago, University of Colorado at Denver, University of Pennsylvania,
   University of Washington (Seattle), University of Wisconsin–Madison, and Yale
   University.
6. We also tried a measure of biotech-relevant research expenditures as reported by the universities, but this variable was too collinear with the federal support variable to enter separately and appeared to be less consistently measured across universities.
7. Instrumental variables would provide a more elegant approach to this problem if suitable instruments had been found.
8. As discussed in Jerry Hausman *et al.* (1984), the poisson process is the most appropriate
   statistical model for count data such as ours. In practice, overdispersion (possibly due to
   unobserved heterogeneity) frequently occurs. Given the problems with resort to the negative binomial (A. Colin Cameron and Pravin K. Trivedi, 1990), Jeffrey M. Wooldridge
   (1991) developed a flexible and consistent method for correcting the poisson

variance–covariance matrix estimates regardless of the underlying relationship between the mean and variance. We are indebted to Wooldridge and Greene for advice in implementing the procedure in LIMDEP.

9. In an earlier version of this paper we included an alternative form of Table 2 (available from the authors upon request) in order to forestall interpretations that the results in Table 2 may reflect reverse causality. This alternative table reported regressions which explain the number of firms alive at the beginning of 1990 that were born after 1980. Nearly identical results were obtained, reflecting the fact that bulk of new biotechnology enterprises were founded after 1980.

10. In column (b) of Table 2 (and Table 3), the negative coefficient on the squared term indicates that as the number of stars or collaborators increases, their marginal contribution diminishes eventually passing through zero. For collaborators, in columns (c)–(f) of these tables the sign pattern reverses so that the partial derivative of the log probability of birth with respect to collaborators starts out negative, and increases as their number increases, eventually becoming positive.

11. In support of this explanation, we note that in our sensitivity analysis we tried regressions which substituted interaction terms multiplying the numbers of active stars and collaborators for the squared terms. In those regressions, we obtain significant positive coefficients on the numbers of stars and collaborators and a significant negative coefficient on their interaction.

12. This hypothesis was derived from anecdotal evidence, but note that the top nine of Ernst & Young's list of top-ten companies by 1993 market valuation (G. Steven Burrill and Kenneth B. Lee, Jr., 1994: 54) were located and founded in regions richly endowed with venture capital firms: Boston (3), San Francisco (3), Los Angeles (1), San Diego (1), and Seattle (1).

13. In the alternative version of Table 2 (see footnote 9 above), the coefficient on the lagged dependent variable was nearly as large as in Table 2, so the significant positive coefficient does not arise from firms born 1976–80 appearing in both the current and lagged dependent variables.

14. See Zucker et al. (1994) for our first effort to assess the determinants of success of firms after birth.

15. To compute the effects of stars in the 1986–89 period, we need to add the coefficients of the number of active stars and the coefficient of the same variable interacted with DUMMY 1986–89 and then do the same for the two terms involving the squared values of these variables. An analogous approach yields the effect of collaborators during 1986–89. We examined also interactions with dummy variables for 1976–80 and with a time trend. Since the coefficients were very small and statistically insignificant for interaction terms involving 1976–80 dummies, we believe the reported form more accurately reflects the time or diffusion dependence than a negative trend throughout the period.

16. We are indebted to Jeff Armstrong for this point.

17. The earnings-price ratio had to be dropped from these analyses because it is available only nationally over time.

18. This positional tradition holds across national boundaries: As a percentage of articles coauthored by their fellow nationals, American stars are 16.4% of first authors and

71.2% of last authors, compared to 21.2% and 63.1 per cent, respectively, for Japanese, and 19.7% and 69.2% for other nationalities.

19. The *Science Citation Index* lists up to six of the affiliations listed on the paper but only links the corresponding author to a particular affiliation.

....

References

Arrow, Kenneth J. (1962), 'Economic welfare and the allocation of resources for invention', in Richard R. Nelson (ed.) *The Rate and Direction of Inventive Activity: Economic and Social Factors*. National Bureau of Economic Research Special Conference Series, Vol. 13 (Princeton, NJ: Princeton University Press), 609–25.

Bioscan, Vols. 3–7 (Phoenix, AZ: Oryx Press), 1989–1993.

Burrill, G. Steven and Lee, Kenneth B., Jr. (1994), *Biotech 94: Long-Term Value, Short-Term Hurdles*. Ernst & Young's Eighth Annual Report on the Biotechnology Industry (San Francisco: Ernst & Young).

Cameron, A. Colin and Trivedi, Pravin K. (1990), 'Regression-based tests for overdispersion in the poisson model', *Journal of Econometrics*, 46(3): 347–64.

Cetus Corp. (1988), 'Biotechnology company data base', predecessor source for *Bioscan*. Computer printout, Cetus Corp.

CITIBASE: Citibank Economic Database (1993), *Machine-Readable Database*, 1946–June 1993 (New York: Citibank).

GenBank, Release 65.0 (1990), *Machine-Readable Database* (Palo Alto, CA: IntelliGentics, Inc.).

Greene, William H. (1992), *LIMDEP: User's Manual and Reference Guide, Version 6.0* (Bellport, NY: Econometric Software).

Griliches, Zvi (1957), 'Hybrid corn: An exploration in the economics of technological change', *Econometrica*, 25(4): 501–22.

—— (1992), 'The search for R&D spillovers', *Scandinavian Journal of Economics*, Supplement, 94: 29–47.

Grossman, Gene M. and Helpman, Elhanan (1991), *Innovation and Growth in the Global Economy* (Cambridge, MA: MIT Press).

Hausman, Jerry, Hall, Bronwyn H., and Griliches, Zvi (1984), 'Econometric models for count data with an application to the patents-R&D relationship', *Econometrica*, 52(4): 909–38.

Henderson, Yolanda K. (1989), 'Venture capital and economic development', Paper presented to the New England Advisory Council, Federal Reserve Bank of Boston, Boston, MA.

Institute for Scientific Information (1982, 1987, 1992), *Science Citation Index, ISI Compact Disc Editions, Machine-Readable Database* (Philadelphia: Institute for Scientific Information).

Jaffe, Adam B. (1989), 'Real effects of academic research', *American Economic Review*, 79(5): 957–70.

——, Trajtenberg, Manuel, and Henderson, Rebecca (1993), 'Geographic localization of knowledge spillovers as evidenced by patent citations', *Quarterly Journal of Economics*, 63(3): 577–98.

Jones, Lyle V., Lindzey, Gardner, and Coggeshall, Porter E. (eds) (1982), *An Assessment of Research-Doctorate Programs in the United States: Biological Sciences* (Washington, DC: National Academy Press).

Kenney, Martin (1986), *Biotechnology: The University-Industrial Complex* (New Haven, CT: Yale University Press).

Lerner, Joshua (1994), 'Venture capitalists and the decision to go public', *Journal of Financial Economics*, 35(3): 293–316.

—— (1995), 'Venture capitalists and the oversight of private firms', *Journal of Finance*, 50(1): 301–18.

Mansfield, Edwin (1995), 'Academic research underlying industrial innovations: Sources, characteristics, and financing', *Review of Economics and Statistics*, 77(1): 55 65.

Nelson, Richard R. (1959), 'The simple economics of basic scientific research', *Journal of Political Economy*, 67(3): 297–306.

—— and Romer, Paul M. (1996), 'Science, economic growth, and public policy', in Bruce L. R. Smith and Claude E. Barfield (eds) *Technology, R&D, and the Economy* (Washington, DC: Brookings Institution and American Enterprise Institute), 49–74.

—— and Winter, Sidney G. (1982), *An Evolutionary Theory of Economic Change* (Cambridge, MA: Harvard University Press).

North Carolina Biotechnology Center (1992), *North Carolina Biotechnology Center U.S. Companies Database, Machine-Readable Database* (Research Triangle Park, NC: North Carolina Biotechnology Center).

Pratt, Stanley E. (1982), *Guide to Venture Capital Sources*, 6th ed. (Englewood Cliffs, NJ: Prentice-Hall).

Romer, Paul M. (1986), 'Increasing returns and long-run growth', *Journal of Political Economy*, 94(5): 1002–37.

—— (1990), 'Endogenous technological change' *Journal of Political Economy*, 98(5): S71–S102.

Rosenberg, Nathan (1982), *Inside the Black Box: Technology and Economics* (Cambridge: Cambridge University Press).

U.S. Department of Commerce (1992a), *Bureau of Economic Analysis, Economics and Statistics Administration. National Income and Product Accounts of the United States, volume 2, 1959–88* (Washington, DC: U.S. Government Printing Office).

—— (1992b), *Regional Economic Information System, Version 1.3, CD-ROM, Machine-Readable Database* (Washington, DC: Bureau of Economic Analysis).

U.S. Department of Education (1985), *National Center for Education Statistics. Higher Education General Information Survey (HEGIS), Institutional Characteristics, 1983–84, Machine-Readable Database*, ICPSR 8291 (Ann Arbor, MI: Inter-University Consortium for Political and Social Research).

Wooldridge, Jeffrey M. (1991), 'On the application of robust, regression-based diagnostics to models of conditional means and conditional variances', *Journal of Econometrics*, 47(1): 5–46.

Zucker, Lynne G., Brewer, Marilynn B., Oliver, Amalya, and Liebeskind, Julia (1993), 'Basic science as intellectual capital in firms: Information dilemmas in rDNA biotechnology research', Working paper, UCLA Institute for Social Science Research.

—— and Darby, Michael R. (1996), 'Star scientists and institutional transformation: patterns of invention and innovation in the formation of the biotechnology industry', *Proceedings of the National Academy of Sciences*, 93(23): 12709–16.

Lynne G. Zucker et al.

——and Armstrong, Jeff (1994), 'Intellectual capital and the firm: The technology of geographically localized knowledge spillovers', National Bureau of Economic Research (Cambridge, MA) Working Paper No. 4946.

——Darby, Michael R., and Brewer, Marilynn B. (1994), 'Intellectual capital and the birth of U.S. biotechnology enterprises', National Bureau of Economic Research (Cambridge, MA) Working Paper No. 4653.

8 Science and Technology as Predictors of Stock Performance

Zhen Deng, Baruch Lev, and Francis Narin

Innovation and technological change are the main drivers of companies' productivity and growth. But public information on companies' efforts to innovate (namely, their investment in science and technology and the consequences of that investment) is generally scant and not timely. To alleviate this impediment to the valuation of companies' performance and prospects, we examined the ability of a new set of publicly available patent-related measures to reflect science- and technology-based companies' potential and growth. We tested the ability of the patent-related measures to predict stock returns and market-to-book ratios. Our empirical results indicate that patent measures reflecting the volume of companies' research activity, the impact of companies' research on subsequent innovations, and the closeness of research and development to science are reliably associated with the future performance of R&D-intensive companies in capital markets.

A widely held belief is that the economic and stock market boom of the past two decades in the United States has been propelled primarily by science and technology. Industrial research and development, new information technology, and scientific developments from universities, federal laboratories, and corporations generate a constant stream of innovations and productivity gains that enhance the performance of the economy and drive up stock prices. The links between R&D, technological change, and economic growth have been theoretically and empirically established at the national, industry, and corporate levels. In particular, empirical research has established that corporate R&D is strongly associated with subsequent gains in companies' productivity, earnings, and stock prices.[1]

Public information about companies' R&D activities is inadequate, however, for the purpose of investment analysis. A company's periodic R&D expenditures, the sole innovation-related item required to be disclosed in financial statements, is too coarse an indicator for valuation of the nature, quality, and expected benefits of its science and technology efforts. Companies generally do not disclose information on the extent of *basic research* (e.g. pharmaceutical R&D targeted at developing new drugs), which when successful, provides for substantial long-term growth, as distinct from *applied research* (e.g. a modification of an existing drug) or *process R&D*, which are generally characterized by a shorter duration of benefits. Moreover, investors cannot glean from R&D cost data the substantial differences in innovative capabilities that exist among companies.[2] Furthermore, various innovative activities, particularly of small companies, are not formally classified as R&D; hence, they are not reported separately to investors.

In search of timely and relevant indicators of companies' innovative capabilities and outcomes, we examined a set of new measures of companies' science and technology that are based on patent application citations (i.e. the references cited in the patent documents). We demonstrate on a sample of technology- and science-based companies that these measures are significantly associated, after control for conventional financial variables, with subsequent market-to-book ratios and stock returns. Accordingly, we believe that patent citations will prove to be useful indicators for investment research and analysis of R&D-intensive companies.

1. Patent Citations

The extensive documentation accompanying patent applications includes a wealth of information from which analysts can learn various aspects of the quality of companies' science and technology. Of particular relevance are the references cited in the patent documents that identify earlier inventions ('prior art') in the form of previous patents or scientific papers and articles relevant to the extant patent application. A new patent must satisfy three criteria: It must be novel, useful, and not obvious. It is the novelty requirement—namely, that the patent be different from all known prior art—that gives rise to the references cited on the front page of the patent application. These references allow the patent examiner to assess the novelty of the invention. Patent citations also play an important role in infringement litigation by delineating the property rights, or 'claims', of the patent (see Lanjouw and Schankerman, 1997). Appendix A contains an example of a real patent and its related citations.

Economists have in recent years examined the usefulness of patent citations as output measures of companies' innovative activities (R&D expenditures are an input measure). For example, Trajtenberg (1989, 1990) reported that the intensity of citations to a set of patents in subsequent patents ('forward citation') is related to the social gains from the examined patents. Lanjouw and Schankerman found that litigated patents are cited far more heavily in subsequent patent applications than nonlitigated patents, which suggests that citation intensity indicates patent value (i.e. frequently cited patents are worth defending). CHI Research, in cooperation with Eastman Kodak Laboratories, reported that highly ranked patents by Kodak's staff were more frequently cited than patents of lower rank (Albert *et al.*, 1991). Hall *et al.* (1998) provided evidence that the intensity of citations of companies' patents is contemporaneously associated with their market values. Prior evidence thus substantiates patent citations as indicators of the value of companies' science and technology.[3]

A typical US patent cites about eight earlier US patents, one or two foreign patents, and one or two nonpatent references, of which the majority are science references (citations to scientific papers, meetings, and similar documents representing basic scientific research). In the past decade, a slow but steady increase has occurred in the number of US and foreign patents, referenced by US patents—from approximately eight in 1985 to twelve in 1997. During that period, a more rapid increase has occurred in citations to science—from average of 0.3 per patent application in 1985 to two in 1997, with a tripling of citations to US scientific papers in the 1988–94 span (see Narin *et al.* 1997).

The fundamental idea underlying the economic analysis of patent citations is that a large number of forward citations indicates that the examined patent is an important invention that has led to numerous technological improvements. Therefore, a company whose patent portfolio contains a large number of oft-cited patents is generating innovative technology likely to yield important inventions and successful products. The expectation is, and this is the hypothesis underlying our empirical tests, that companies whose patents are frequently cited will tend to be more successful innovators and perform better in both the product/service and capital markets than companies whose patents are less frequently cited.

As an indicator of intensity of citation, we compared a company's citation record with the average citation record of all companies in CHI Research's US patent database. Specifically, the citation intensity indicator (termed hereafter 'citation impact') reflects the total number of forward citations in a given year to the company's patents issued in the most recent five years, divided by the average number of citations of all US patents in the CHI Research database in the corresponding years. For example, a citation impact measure of 1.10 indicates that the company's patents received in the past five years a total number of citations higher by 10 per cent than average.[4] The patent exhibited in Appendix A had a 2.81 citation impact value.

Basing a measure on forward citations creates a bias against recent patents (for this study, those registered in 1995 or 1996) because of the short period of time in which they could be cited (only 1997 and 1998). CHI, Research largely overcomes this 'recency bias' by basing the citation impact measure on the *citing* years rather than on the *cited* years. For example, the 1995 citation impact measure of Company X does not reflect citations in 1996–98 to the company's patents registered in 1995. Rather, the 1995 measure reflects citations in 1995 by all patents to Company X's patents registered during the preceding five-year period, 1990–94. CHI Research then standardizes the 1995 citation impact measure of Company X by dividing it by the total number of citations in all patents issued in 1995 to all patents issued during the 1990–94 period. A citation impact measure based on the citing years does not decay toward-the end of the sample period as do forward citation measures based on cited years.

Other attributes of patent citations may indicate additional aspects of the quality of companies' science and technology. One such attribute is the 'science link' of a company's patents, which indicates the number of references in the company's own patent applications to scientific papers, as distinct from references to previous patents. Science link indicates how close to science, or to basic research, the company's R&D activities are. (As indicated in the diagram and discussion in Appendix A, the patent in Appendix A has a science link indicator of 3.) Keep in mind that the science link indicator is based on citations to previous scientific papers and is thus a 'backward citation' indicator whereas the citation impact measure is based on forward citations. A patent's science link measure is technology dependent; the measure is generally high in biotechnology, which relies heavily on science, and modest in chemistry and electronics.

In general, companies that are innovating rapidly are more successful in product development and marketing than companies that are relying on old technologies. This phenomenon leads to another citation indicator—technology cycle time—which measures the median age of the US patents cited in the company's patents. For example, the technology cycle time of the patent in Appendix A is 6.7 years. A tendency to cite mature patents indicates that the company engages in old technology. Note that this measure also is backward looking and industry dependent. Technology cycle time is as short as three or four years in rapidly changing industries, such as electronics, and as long as fifteen years in slowly changing technologies, such as ship building. In drugs and medicine, the technology cycle time tends to be 8–9 years, which because it is in the middle range of the overall technology cycle distribution, implies that important advances in drugs and medicine are not coming from rapidly developing increments in technology but from basic scientific research.

In addition to the preceding three citation indicators, we included in our tests the number of a company's patents (patent count). This indicator of the number of US patents granted to the company during a given year supplies a measure of the volume of technological activity. Patent count includes only regular utility patents; categories such as design and reissued patents are excluded.[5]

Mergers, acquisitions, and divestitures pose a problem in tracing the patent record of a company. In the data-processing stage, CHI Research tries to identify the patents that were owned by partners to a merger so that a company's historical record of patents will reflect the R&D activities of the merged enterprises.

2. Data and Sample Statistics

Company-specific data on the four patent attributes we examined (patent count, citation impact, science link, and technology cycle time) were derived from CHI Research files. CHI Research compiles data for companies whose patenting activity is above a threshold—generally, ten or more patents registered in at least one year from 1985 to 1995. Because we required financial statement and stock market data for our analysis, we cross checked the companies in the CHI Research files with the Compustat database. This process yielded 411 companies in the Compustat population that were qualified to be in the CHI Research database.[6] Because we scaled some of the variables by book value (equity) in our empirical test, we deleted from the sample twenty-three companies with negative equity, yielding a final sample of 388 companies. The sample companies were grouped in four industries—chemicals, drugs, electronics, and 'other'.

The period we examined is 1985–95 (the stock performance data extend to 1996). Because of data limitations, the company-specific patent attributes we used are averages for the initial five-year period, 1985–89, and are yearly data for the subsequent six years, 1990–95. Of the 388 sample companies, 235 companies (61 per cent) had data for the entire 1985–95 period, ninety-two companies are missing one to three years of data, and sixty-one companies are missing five to seven years of data. Thus, although our sample contains a large number of companies that operated throughout the whole period, it also includes young companies that joined the sample during that period. Moreover, thirty-three of the sample companies were deleted from Compustat's main file during the 1985–95 period because of mergers, bankruptcies, and so on.[7] Thus, survivorship bias does not appear to pose a serious problem in our sample.

Table 1 provides summary statistics for the sample. The mean patent count is 107, but the large standard deviation (191) and the relatively low median (37) indicate a great deal of variability in patent counts among the companies and the presence in the sample of a few companies with large numbers of patents. The average citation impact, 1.09, indicates that the sample companies have a slightly higher number of citations (by subsequent patents) than the population, although the median sample company has a slightly lower-than-average citation impact (0.94). The mean science link, 0.89, indicates that the sample companies cited fewer than one scientific study on average per patent application.

Table 1. Sample Summary Statistics

Variable	Mean	Standard Deviation	Median
Patent count (number)	107.19	191.37	37.00
Citation impact	1.09	0.67	0.94
Science link	0.89	1.65	0.43
Technology cycle time (years)	9.76	3.44	9.50
R&D intensity (R&D to sales)	0.06	0.07	0.04
Spillover[a]	0.70	0.79	0.33
Size (capitalization, $ millions)	6893.00	11,214.00	2434.00
Return on equity (%)[b]	0.26	0.20	0.25
Annual stock return (%)[c]	0.15	0.32	0.12
Market-to-book ratio	2.91	2.05	2.35

Notes:
[a] The spillover measure for company i is the industry's weighted-average number of patents divided by R&D expenditures, excluding the patents and R&D of company i.
[b] Annual earnings divided by beginning-of-year book value of equity.
[c] Total annual stock return (dividends plus capital gains) from Compustat.

The sample mean is slightly above the average indicated by the mean science link of the CHI Research population, 0.75. The technology cycle time mean of 9.76 years is close to the population mean, 9.95 years.

In the 1985–95 period, an improvement occurred in all the indicators of patent activity in the sample. Between 1989 and 1995, the patent count increased from an average of 104.8 per company to 112.3 (a change of 7.2 per cent); the average citation impact measure increased from 1.08 to 1.13 (4.6 per cent); the average science link increased from 0.61 to 1.36 (123 per cent); and the technology cycle time decreased from 10.15 years in 1989 to 9.56 in 1995 (5.8 per cent).

The mean R&D intensity (R&D over sales) of the sample companies, 5.53 per cent (0.06 in Table 1), is higher than the mean R&D intensity of all Compustat companies engaged in R&D, which was 3.75 per cent in 1995 (Chan *et al.* 1998). The average market capitalization of the sample companies is $6.89 billion (median $2.43 billion), which is substantially larger than the average capitalization of the Compustat population—$1.66 billion in 1989–95.

Thus, the sample companies are relatively large and engage in above-average R&D activity, and nearly two-thirds of them operated throughout the 1985–96 period.

Table 2. Dow Chemical Company vs Its Industry

									Technology Cycle (years)	
	Patent Count		Patents per R&D		Citation Impact		Science Link			
Year	Dow	Industry	Dow	Industry	Dow	Industry	Dow	Industry	Dow	Industry
1989	455	115	0.52	0.35	0.70	0.80	0.84	0.92	10.6	10.0
1990	417	105	0.37	0.37	0.76	0.76	1.14	1.06	11.4	10.1
1991	378	121	0.33	0.44	0.74	0.67	1.34	0.81	10.5	10.1
1992	374	117	0.29	0.48	0.82	0.75	1.53	0.81	11.0	9.9
1993	346	111	0.28	0.62	0.85	0.81	1.70	0.97	10.7	9.7
1994	297	104	0.24	0.55	0.73	0.79	2.35	1.21	10.6	9.3
1995	263	105	0.33	0.43	0.77	0.81	2.75	1.45	9.6	10.2

Note: The patent count indicates patents approved in a given year. Patents per R&D is the ratio of number of patents to annual R&D expenditures in millions of dollars. 'Industry' comprises twelve large, diversified chemical companies that are similar to Dow. The numbers for the industry are medians.

3. Single-Company Illustration

To illustrate the analysis of patent attributes for a single company, Table 2 provides the attributes for the Dow Chemical Company and median values for the chemical industry. Dow generates a substantially larger number of patents per year than the median competitor, although Dow's patent count has been rapidly decreasing (it went from 455 in 1989 to 263 in 1995) whereas the industry median has been relatively stable. In terms of patents per R&D expenditures, since 1991, Dow has spent substantially more on an average patent than its competitors. Dow's citation impact measure (ranging between 0.70 and 0.85) matches the industry, which indicates that the effect of Dow's technology on subsequent innovations is similar to that of its competitors.

A different conclusion is reached when the *nature* of Dow's R&D is considered. The science link indicator for Dow starts (in 1989) below the industry level but rapidly increases thereafter, so that by 1995, the link for Dow is 2.75 vs 1.45 for the industry. By 1995, therefore, Dow's patents were including substantially more citations to scientific sources than its competitors' patents; thus, Dow's patentable research was 'closer to science' (basic research) than its competitors'.[8] Finally, Dow's technology cycle time is very close to the industry median, which indicates that the technological age of Dow's innovations cannot be distinguished from that of its competitors. In summary, Dow's innovative activities are distinct from its competitors along two dimensions—the scale of innovation (number of patents approved) and the closeness of its R&D to basic science.

4. Patent Attributes and Stock Performance

This section describes the first analysis and the subsequent multivariate analysis we carried out of the relationship between patent attributes and subsequent stock performance.

4.1. A First Pass

To gain an initial impression of the ability of patent attributes to predict future company performance as reflected in the stock market, we examined the correlations between the patent attributes and subsequent stock returns and between the attributes and market-to-book ratios (M/Bs). We found that citation impact and science link have substantially higher correlations with returns and M/Bs than do patent count and technology cycle time.[9] We thus focus at this stage of the analysis on citation impact and science link.

To enhance the stability of the annual patent attribute measures, we computed three-year averages of these indicators. The first averaging period, given data restrictions, was five years (1985–89); it was followed by five three-year periods—1989–91, 1990–92, 1991–93, 1992–94, and 1993–95. For each company and the six subperiods, we computed the subsequent annual stock return and the M/B; for example, for the 1993–95 period, the stock return is for 1996 and the M/B is for the end of 1996.

We then classified the companies within each of the four sample industries (chemicals, drugs, electronics, and other) into four groups according to the relative size of their citation impact and science link indicators: Low/low (below industry median by the two indicators), low/high (below median by citation impact and above median by science link), high/low (above median by citation impact and below median by science link), and high/high (above industry median by both patent indicators). We then computed the median (over the six subperiods) one-year ahead M/B and stock return for each industry subgroup.

For the chemical sector, Fig. 1 shows the one-year ahead M/Bs and stock returns for the four groups composed according to citation impact and science link. Companies with below-industry-median citation impact and science link indicators (the low/low group) had a subsequent median M/B of 2.099, whereas companies with above-median values of these indicators (the high/high group) had a 25 per cent larger one-year ahead M/B. The mixed companies had M/Bs between those of the low/low and high/high groups.

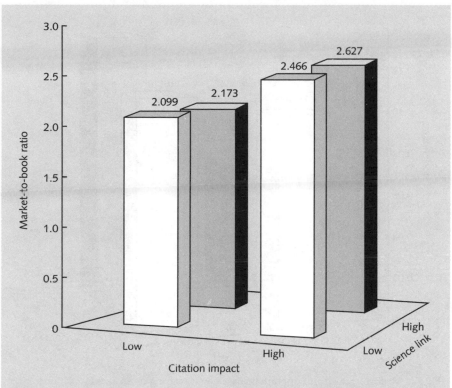

Fig. 1. Median *M/B*s of portfolios based on classifying companies by citation impact and science link in the previous three years: chemical companies.

Figure 2 also indicates that the one-year ahead median stock return of the low/low chemical companies was 9.9 per cent whereas the return of the high/high companies was 13.6 per cent—a 37 per cent difference.

Results for the remaining industries—drugs, electronics, and other—are not presented here but, with a few exceptions, duplicated the relationships presented for the chemical industry. The most notable exception was the drug industry, where the one-year ahead median return of the low/low group, at 20.3 per cent, was substantially *higher* than the return of the high/high group, 11.5 per cent.

4.2. Multivariate Analysis

Our correlation analysis indicates that most patent attributes are significantly associated with subsequent stock returns and market-to-book ratios. Patent

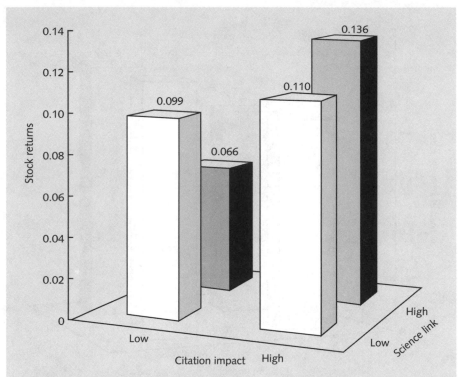

Fig. 2. Median stock returns of portfolio based on classifying companies by citation impact and science link in the previous three years: chemical companies.

attributes may proxy, however, for more-fundamental factors affecting companies' performance and investor perceptions. For example, Lev and Sougiannis (1996) found that companies' R&D intensity (R&D expenditures to sales) and their R&D capital (estimated from past R&D expenditures) are positively associated with stock returns and M/Bs. Because patent attributes are correlated with R&D intensity, the observed association between patent attributes and stock performance may simply proxy for the fundamental association between stock performance and R&D expenditures.[10] Therefore, we decided to perform a multivariate analysis combining the patent attributes with other variables known to be associated with stock performance in order to make inferences about the *incremental* predictive power of patent attributes.

Specifically, we ran the following pooled cross-sectional regressions:

$$M/B_{i,t+\tau} = \alpha_1 NPAT_{i,t} + \alpha_2 CIMP_{i,t} + \alpha_3 SL_{i,t} + \alpha_4 TC_{i,t} \\ + \alpha_5 RDINT_{i,t} + \alpha_6 SPIL_{i,t} + \alpha_7 E/B_{i,t} + \varepsilon_{i,t} \qquad (1)$$

and

$$R_{i,t+\tau} = \alpha_1 NPAT_{i,t} + \alpha_2 CIMP_{i,t} + \alpha_3 SL_{i,t} + \alpha_4 TC_{i,t} + \alpha_5 RDINT_{i,t}$$
$$+ \alpha_6 SPIL_{i,t} + \alpha_7 Size_{i,t} + \alpha_8 B/M_{i,t} + \varepsilon_{i,t}, \tag{2}$$

where

$M/B_{i,t+\tau}$ = company i's ratio of market value to book value of equity at one, two, and three years ($\tau = 1, 2, 3$) after fiscal year-end

$NPAT_{i,t}$ = company i's number of patents granted in year t, scaled by the book value (equity) of the company

$CIMP_{i,t}$ = the citation impact for company i—namely, the (standardized) number of forward citations of company i's patents—in year t

$SL_{i,t}$ = the science link indicator for company i in year t

$TC_{i,t}$ = the technology cycle time indicator for company i in year t

$RDINT_{i,t}$ = the R&D intensity for company i in year t

$SPIL_{i,t}$ = a spillover indicator, measured as the industry's weighted-average number of patents divided by R&D expenditures, excluding the patents and R&D of company i; this measure is intended to capture the impact of other companies' R&D activities on company i's performance

$E/B_{i,t}$ = the earnings-to-book ratio (ROE) of company i in year t

ε = an error term

$R_{i,t+\tau}$ = company i's stock return during one, two, and three years after fiscal year t

$Size_{i,t}$ = size of company i measured as total market value at the end of year t

$B/M_{i,t}$ = the company's ratio of book value to market value of equity at the end of fiscal year t

All the independent variables were averaged over a three-year period (except for the first subperiod, 1985–89, which was five years). The dependent variables—stock performance—were for one, two, and three years subsequent to the independent variables.

The form of (1)—for the M/B—was motivated by recent theoretical work on valuation models (e.g. Ohlson, 1995), in which the market value of the company is modeled as a function of book value, earnings, and other relevant information. The M/B is, accordingly, a function of earnings to book value and other information, represented in (1) by the various patent citation measures, together with R&D intensity and the spillover indicator. Equation (2)—for stock return—was motivated by the Fama and French (1992) model relating stock returns to lagged company size and the book-to-market-value ratio.[11] Here also, we added to the Fama–French independent variables the four patent citation indicators, R&D intensity, and the spillover variables. Because the regression equations were run on time-series and cross-sectional pooled data, we included in the regressions a time variable for the six base periods examined and industry dummy variables (chemicals, pharmaceuticals, or electronics).

Table 3 provides the regression estimates for the M/B and for stock returns for each of the three years subsequent to the base periods examined. Panel A of Table 3 indicates that three of the four patent indicators—number of patents (patent count), citation impact, and science link—are positively and significantly (at the 10 per cent level or better) associated with subsequent M/Bs in each of the three 'years ahead' examined. The fourth patent indicator—technology cycle—has the expected negative sign (the shorter the technology cycle, the better the market performance) but is statistically insignificant. The probable reason for the insignificance of the technology cycle indicator is its high correlation (multicollinearity) with several of the independent variables, particularly citation impact (-0.51 Pearson coefficient) and R&D intensity (-0.42 Pearson coefficient).[12] Of the control variables examined, R&D intensity and ROE are highly significant (at better than the 1 per cent level) in each year. The statistically significant industry dummies are drugs (positive) and electronics (negative). The explanatory power of the model is high, as indicated by the adjusted R^2 of 0.80.

Thus, from the M/B regressions, we can conclude that number of patents approved and the patent citation measures are strongly associated with investors' growth expectations as reflected by subsequent M/Bs.

The performance of the science link measure as reported in Fig. 1 is of special interest because it indicates the nature of the company's innovative activities, the closeness of its R&D to basic research. (Keep in mind that this measure is based on the number of citations in a company's patents to scientific studies and conferences, not citations of previous patents.) This information cannot be obtained from companies' financial reports. The association between the science link and investors' growth expectation is probably related to empirical findings (e.g. Griliches, 1995) indicating that the contribution of basic research to companies' productivity is substantially larger (some studies indicate a 3 : 1 ratio) than the contribution of applied research.

Panel B of Table 3 reports the stock return regression estimates (2). The citation impact measure is statistically significant in all three forward years; the patent count is significant in Year 2 but only marginally so in Year 3. When the stock return regressions were run for each of the four industries separately, the patent count and technology cycle measures were statistically significant (at the 5 per cent level) with the expected signs (negative for technology cycle time) for drug companies. The spillover measure in Fig. 2 is positive and significant (at the 2 per cent level) in Years 2 and 3, which suggests that other companies' R&D activities contribute positively, with a lag, to a given company's performance and stock market valuation. This relationship is a reflection of the well-documented phenomenon that the social return on R&D—that is, the benefits to enterprises other than the one conducting the research—is substantially

Table 3. Regression Results (Significance Levels of the Coefficients in Parentheses)

Years Ahead	Patent Count	Citation Impact	Science Link	Technology Cycle	R&D Intensity	Spillover	ROE	Size	Book to Market	Adjusted R^2
A. Market-to-book regressions										
One	1.144	0.413	0.067	−0.017	6.075	−0.394	4.6?			0.81
	(0.00)	(0.00)	(0.10)	(0.35)	(0.00)	(0.19)	(0.00)			
Two	0.719	0.579	0.124	−0.033	4.500	−0.037	4.605			0.80
	(0.01)	(0.00)	(0.02)	(0.12)	(0.00)	(0.91)	(0.00)			
Three	0.644	0.745	0.120	−0.028	4.848	−0.412	4.845			0.79
	(0.04)	(0.00)	(0.07)	(0.28)	(0.00)	(0.27)	(0.00)			
B. Stock return regressions										
One	0.069	0.040	0.004	−0.002	0.064	0.073		3.465	0.104	0.28
	(0.20)	(0.04)	(0.67)	(0.60)	(0.68)	(0.23)		(0.96)	(0.00)	
Two	0.248	0.073	−0.016	−0.001	0.517	0.253		2.660	0.211	0.38
	(0.01)	(0.07)	(0.36)	(0.92)	(0.09)	(0.02)		(0.86)	(0.00)	
Three	0.199	0.160	−0.027	−0.004	0.633	0.379		−1.954	0.303	0.42
	(0.14)	(0.01)	(0.37)	(0.72)	(0.16)	(0.02)		(0.42)	(0.00)	

higher than the private return on R&D (see Griliches). As in Fama and French, the book-to-market ratio is strongly associated with subsequent returns.

The association between patent attributes and subsequent stock returns is somewhat weaker than the association between patent attributes and M/Bs. The reason lies in the difference between the two market variables: Whereas the M/B indicates growth expectations irrespective of when the underlying information reached the market, the stock return reflects only new information, information unavailable to investors at the beginning of the return accumulation period. Thus, for example, a company's R&D intensity is highly associated with growth expectations (as reflected by the significance of R&D shown in Fig. 1) but is not associated with subsequent stock returns (as shown in Fig. 2) because stock prices fully reflect contemporaneously the information embedded in R&D intensity. Our finding that citation impact and, to some extent, patent count are associated with subsequent stock returns (as shown in Fig. 2) suggests, therefore, that the information conveyed by these measures is not fully reflected in stock prices in a timely manner. Such an outcome is not surprising; patent attributes are still rarely used in investment and security analysis. Overall, the multivariate analysis indicates that the examined patent attributes may contribute an important dimension to security analysis.

5. Conclusion

Science- and technology-based companies generally provide inadequate information to investors about their innovation-producing activities. The only innovation-relevant financial data required to be disclosed in corporate financial reports is the periodic R&D expenditures of the company. Missing, in particular, is information about the nature of the company's innovative activities (e.g. basic versus applied research) and their outcomes. Given these inadequate public disclosures, analysts may benefit from examining patent-related measures that reflect various qualitative aspects of companies' science and technology activities. Our empirical analysis indicates that most of the patent attributes we examined are statistically associated with subsequent stock returns and market-to-book ratios. The suggestion is that patent-based measures provide a useful tool for the investment analysis of technology- and science-based enterprises.

Acknowledgement

We are indebted to Bronwyn Hall for helpful comments and suggestions.

Appendix A: Example and Explanation of Patent Citations

This appendix contains a replication of a patent application, explanation and calculation of the patent impact variables, and a diagram of forward and backward citations (Fig. 3).

US Patent
US Patent Number: 5,278,955
Issue Date: 11 January 1994
Inventors: Forte, R.W.; Stokes, E.J.
Title: Open systems mail-handling capability in a multi-user environment
Assignee: International Business Machines Corporation (Armonk, NY)

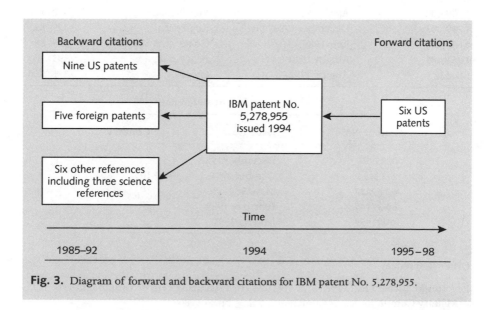

Fig. 3. Diagram of forward and backward citations for IBM patent No. 5,278,955.

Zhen Deng et al.

International Patent Classification (IPC): G06F 13/00
US Patent Office Classifications (USPOC): 395/200.36; 364/222.2; 364/240.8; 364/241.7; 364/242.94; 364/260.4; 364/260.9; 364/284; 364/284.3; 364/284.4; 364/DIG 1; 395/200.76; 395/500

Abstract:
A system and method is provided which allows users of an OSI mail-handling system the advantage of communicating with users of other mail-handling systems and utilizing the functionality associated with the OSI system. The functionality of a RFC-987 gateway is extended to provide, in addition to a straight conversion function, full OSI mail-handling functions. A conventional mail handler is extended to allow for both OSI mail and conventional mail originating from a user of any mail system to be processed, thus providing a common interface for mail system users. Further, the sendmail component has now been enabled to recognize OSI addresses and route the associated messages to the appropriate destination. Mixed mode addressing has also been extended to include OSI type addresses in an address string that may contain components from several different networks (e.g. TCP/IP, UUCP).

US Patent References

Patent No.	Issue Date	Inventors	USPOC
4,506,111	March 1985	Takenouchi *et al.*	179/2.A
4,648,061	March 1987	Foster	264/900
4,677,588	June 1987	Benjamin *et al.*	395/325
4,688,170	August 1987	Waite *et al.*	395/500
4,739,402	April 1988	Maeda *et al.*	358/147
4,790,003	December 1988	Kepley *et al.*	379/88
4,837,798	June 1989	Cohen *et al.*	379/88
4,951,245	August 1990	Bailey *et al.*	395/500
142,622	August 1992	Owens	395/500

Foreign Patent References

Patent No.	Issue Date	Country
0295904	December 1988	EP
2112454	October 1987	JP
62-69437	May 1988	JP
64-37145	February 1989	JP
2-001659	January 1990	JP

Other References

1. Verjinski, Richard D., 'PHASE, A Portable Host Access System Environment,' 1989 IEEE Military Communications Conference, vol. 3, pp. 806–809.

2. Tang, Debra, *et al.*, 'A Gateway between MHS (X.400) and SMTP.' Proceedings of the Computer Standards Conference, 1988-Computer Standards Evolution: Impact and Imperatives. IEEE Comput. Soc. Press, pp. 7 14.

3. Racke, Wilhem F., *et al.*, 'Extending an Existing Mail Service to Support X.400 Message Handling,' Proceedings of the Computer Networking Symposium, 1999. IEEE Comput. Soc. Press, pp. 245–253.

4. IBM TDB, 'Process Manager for a Personal Computer,' vol. 30, no. 6 (November 1987), pp. 10–15.

5. IBM TDB, 'Real Mail User Interface for In-Basket,' vol. 31, no. 10 (March 1989), pp.171–172.

6. IBM TDB, 'Service Processor Architecture and Microcode Algorithm for Performing Protocol Conversations Start/Stop, BSC, SDLC,' vol. 31, no 12 (May 1989), pp. 461–464.

Citations Received from Later Patents (Forward Citations)

Citing Patent	Issue Year	Title
5,781,902	1998	Method, computer program product, and system for extending the capabilities of an existing process to store and display foreign data.
5,742,845	1998	System for extending present open network communication protocols to communicate with nonstandard I/O devices directly coupled to an open network.
5,710,883	1998	Hypertext document transport mechanism for firewall-compatible distributed Worldwide Web publishing.
5,632,018	1997	Electronic mail system.
5,579,467	1996	Method and apparatus for formatting a communication.
5,550,984	1996	Security system for preventing unauthorized communications between networks by translating communications received in ip protocol to non-ip protocol to remove address and routing services information.

Discussion of Patent Indicators

This section provides the definitions of citation impact, technology cycle time, and science link. For elaboration, see www.chiresearch.com.

Citation Impact. Citation impact is a count of the citations received by a company's patents from the front pages of later patents (forward citations) normalized by dividing the forward citations by the average number of citations received by all patents issued the same year.

The citation impact of a company's patents for a particular year is calculated from the citations from all patents issued in that year to patents granted to the company in the preceding five years. For the preceding IBM patent example, we can calculate the citation impact of IBM for 1996 by focusing on citations to IBM patents issued in the 1991–95 period from all patents issued in 1996.

The IBM patent, issued in 1994, received two citations from 1996 patents (as well as one from 1997 and three from 1998). The average 1994 patent received 0.71 citations from 1996, so this IBM patent has an individual citation ratio of 2.81 (2/0.71). The citation impact of IBM's patents for 1996 is the average of these citation ratios for all IBM patents issued between 1991 and 1995 based on citations received from 1996 patents. The average number of citations received by patents in each of these years from 1996 patents will differ. The divisor will thus be different for each year between 1991 and 1995.

Technology Cycle Time. Technology cycle time reveals how quickly a technology is evolving. It is based on the median age of the US references (backward citations) cited on the front page of a patent, shown in the example section called 'US Patent References'.

The median is initially calculated from only the year of issue of both the citing and cited patents. In this example, the citing patent was issued in 1994, and the median issue year of the cited patents (i.e. the issue year of the five out of the nine US patents referenced in the IBM patent in chronological order) was 1988, a difference of six years. An algorithm to estimate the publication month of each cited patent is then added to the technology cycle time calculation. As a result of this refinement, the technology cycle time for this patent was calculated to be 6.7 years.

Science Link. Science link shows how strongly a patent is linked to scientific research. It is measured by the number of references (backward citations) to scientific journal papers and conference proceedings cited on the front page of a patent. In this example, the IBM patent offers six references to nonpatent literature, shown in the section titled 'Other References'. Only three of these references (1, 2, and 3), however, are to journals and conferences; the other three are to internal IBM publications. Hence, the science link value for this patent is 3. The overall Science link for IBM is calculated by taking the mean science link of all of its patents.

Notes

1. See Hall (1993), Griliches (1995), Lev and Sougiannis (1996), Nadiri and Kim (1996), and Coe and Helpman (1995).
2. See Teece *et al.* (1997) for a discussion of innovative capabilities.
3. See Griliches *et al.* (1987) for a survey of patent research in the 1980s.
4. Note that the citation impact measure we use includes self-citations—that is, citations of a company's patent in subsequent patent applications by the same company. We believe that self-citations are relevant to the assessment of a company's scientific strength because they indicate that the company continues to build on its earlier inventions by improving and enhancing them. In contrast, a company that had inventions in certain technological areas and later abandoned them (indicated by an absence of forward self-citations) is likely to have a scattered and ineffective scientific strategy.
5. 'Design patents' are not inventions but rather ornamental concepts. Reissued patents are granted when the original patent is defective. Because we include the original patent, considering the reissued patent would be double counting.
6. Not all R&D-intensive sectors patent significantly. For example, the level of patenting has been until recently relatively low in software companies, despite the high level of R&D (software development costs) in that industry. Software companies have typically relied on copyrights and trademarks to protect their property rights.
7. We obtained information on these companies from the Compustat Research file.
8. Interestingly, in a recent presentation to financial analysts, Dow distributed a comprehensive report ('A Strong Future on a Successful Past: The Dow Chemical Company Review for Financial Analysts Meeting, 1997') that stated at the beginning, 'Who we are: A diversified science-based chemicals, plastic, and ag-science company'. No quantitative data were in the report, however, to support the 'science-based' claim. Such data are provided by the science link indicator in Table 2.
9. For example, the Pearson correlation coefficients of citation impact and science link with the one-year-ahead M/B were, respectively, 0.14 and 0.22 (both statistically significant at the 1% level) whereas the correlations between patent counts and technology cycle and M/B were, respectively, 0.03 and -0.10.
10. For our sample, the Pearson correlation coefficient between R&D intensity and citation impact is 0.25 and between R&D intensity and patent count is 0.20; both coefficients are statistically significant at the 1% level.

11. The other variables in Fama–French—notably β and the earnings-to-price ratio—were not statistically significant.
12. The correlation between technology cycle and M/B is -0.10 (significant at the 1% level).

References

Albert, M., Avery, D., Narin, F., and McAllister, P. (1991), 'Direct validation of citation counts as indicators of industrially important patents', *Research Policy*, 20: 251–9.

Chan, L., Lakonishok, J., and Sougiannis, T. (1998) The stock, market valuation of research and development expenditures', Working paper. University of Illinois.

Coe, D. and Helpman, E. (1995), 'International R&D spillovers', *European Economic Review*, 39: 859–87.

Fama, E. and French, K. (1992), 'The cross-section of expected stock returns', *Journal of Finance*, 47(2): 427–65.

Griliches, Z. (1995), 'R&D and productivity: Econometric results and measurement issues', in Paul Stoneman (ed.) *Handbook of the Economics of Innovation and Technological Change* (Oxford, UK: Blackwell).

——Pakes, A. and Hall, B. (1987), 'The value of patents as indicators of inventive activity', in P. Dasgupta and P. Stoneman (eds) *Economic Policy and Technological Performance* (Cambridge, UK: Cambridge University Press), 97–124.

Hall, B. (1993), 'Industrial research during the 1980s: Did the rate of return Fall'? *Brookings Papers on Economic Activity Micro*, 2: 289–344.

——Jaffe, A. and Trajtenberg, M. (1998) 'Market value and patent citations: A first look', Working paper. University of California at Berkeley.

Lanjouw, J. and Schankerman, M. (1997), 'Stylized facts on patent litigation: value, scope and ownership', Working Paper No. 6297. National Bureau of Economic Research.

Lev, B. and Sougiannis, T. (1996), 'The capitalization, amortization, and value-relevance of R&D' *Journal of Accounting and Economics*, 21: 107–38.

Nadiri, I. and Kim, S. (1996), 'R&D, production structure and productivity growth: Comparison of the U.S., Japanese, and Korean manufacturing sectors', Working Paper No. 5506. National Bureau of Economic Research.

Narin, F., Hamilton, K., and Olivastro, D. (1997), 'The increasing link between U.S. technology and public science', *Research Policy*, National Bureau of Economic Research, 26: 317–30.

Ohlson, J. (1995), 'Earnings, book values and dividends in security valuation', *Contemporary Accounting Research*, 11: 661–87.

——Pisano, G., and Shuen, A. (1997), 'Dynamic capabilities and strategic management', *Strategic Management Journal*, 18(7): 509–33.

Trajtenberg, M. (1989), 'The welfare analysis of product innovations with an application to computed tomography scanners', *Journal of Political Economy*, 97: 445–79.

—— (1990), 'A penny for your quotes: Patent citations and the value of innovations', *Rand Journal of Economics*, 21: 172–87.

9 The Value Relevance of Trademarks[1]

Chandrakanth Seethamraju

1. Introduction

Intangibles research deals with the valuation, value relevance, and recognition of intangible assets on the financial statements. Under current GAAP, most intangible assets are not recognized in a firm's financial statements unless they are acquired and identifiable. This contrasts with research findings that show that information about unrecognized intangibles plays a significant role in determining and explaining firm value. For example, Lev and Sougiannis (1996) find that the value relevance of accounting information is limited in R&D intensive industries; Ittner and Larcker (1998) show that customer satisfaction measures are leading indicators of financial performance; and Barth *et al.* (1999) show that brand values as estimated by *Financial World* (1997) are value relevant.

This paper studies a hitherto unexamined intangible asset: internally generated and externally acquired trademarks. For internally developed trademarks, I determine whether the value of trademarks is on average measurable and material. Using data from a proprietary trademark database provided by CCH Trademark Research Corporation, I estimate the values of internally developed trademarks by means of a method based on the empirical relation of trademarks to overall sales. Using the Ohlson (1995) framework, I then test whether the resulting estimates of trademark values are reflected in the equity market values of the firms that own them.

I also test the value relevance of acquired trademarks by examining trademarks that are about to be recognized on the balance sheet as part of arms-length transactions. I use standard event study analysis on a sample of 187 announcements of trademark purchases, and arrive at two main findings. First, the stock market reaction to firms announcing that they are purchasing trademarks is positive and significant. This is what would be expected if purchased trademarks provided economies of scale, resulted in the firm gaining greater market share, or created barriers to entry. The mean size adjusted return for the three-day window centred on the announcement is 1.7 per cent. Firms that make quantitative disclosures about the purchase have a size-adjusted return that is 2.1 per cent greater than firms that make qualitative disclosures, most likely because providing quantitative information reduces the uncertainty about the impact of the purchase on financial performance. Second, the estimated values of internally developed trademarks are reliably associated in the cross-section with firms' equity market values, suggesting that the value estimates are measurable and useful to investors. They are also material: the mean estimated value of trademarks owned by firms in the sample is $580 million as compared to a mean book value of $1.7 billion. Taken together, these results suggest that financial reporting might be improved if firms provided better disclosures about trademarks in their financial statements.

Overall, this study makes two contributions to the academic literature on intangibles. First, I develop a new method to reliably measure the values of trademarks. The method could be straightforwardly applied to other intangibles. Second, I improve our understanding of the gap between market value and book value by focusing on an intangible asset that is not measured on financial statements, namely, internally developed trademarks.

The remainder of the paper is organized as follows. Section 2 briefly describes the institutional framework surrounding trademarks. Section 3 provides a literature review. Section 4 describes the sample and data. Section 5 deals with the research design and tests to establish value relevance. Section 6 provides the results for the tests of value relevance and describes the sample and tests used for the acquired trademarks event study. Section 7 concludes.

2. Institutional Background

The US Patent and Trademark Office (PTO) governs the registration of trademarks and other types of marks in the United States. All applications for registration of trademarks have to be filed with the PTO. The Trademark Act of 1946, also known as the Lanham Act, and the Trademark Manual of Examining Procedures (TMEP) govern the federal registration of trademarks.

2.1. Definitions

A trademark has been defined by the Federal Trademark Act Lanham Act (see 15 U.S.C. section 1127) of 1946 as:

'The term Trademark includes any word, name, symbol, or device, or any combination thereof: 1. Used by a person, or 2. Which a person has a bonafide intention to use in commerce and applies to register on the principal register establishes by this Act, to identify and distinguish his or her goods, including a unique product, from those manufactured or sold by others and to indicate the source of the goods, even if that source is unknown'.

Conceptually, trademarks are used to identify goods of all types. They can be thought of as marketing shorthand that induces a consumer to communicate which product he or she wants. Economides (1997) states that 'a trademark says little about the composition or specification of the good, instead it identifies the maker of the good. The buyer infers information about the features of the good through recalling his previous experience with the product'. Trademarks therefore aim to place a connection in the mind of the consumer between a product and its level of quality. The senate committee's recommendation on the law that became the Lanham Act (1946) partly described the purposes of trademarks as follows: 'Second, where the owner of a trademark has invested resources to present to the public the product, which he has developed, he is protected in his investment from its misappropriation by pirates and cheats'. There is a process of innovation that goes into creating a product and the trademark protects the innovation. This innovation could be in terms of quality or type of use, among others.

In summary, trademarks have two functions: legal protection from duplication and conveying a snapshot of the information regarding the characteristics of a product and its level of quality. These functions enable trademarks to generate economic benefits to the firm through sales. Trademarks can be thought of as assets whose economic value derives from the information that they contain. Trademarks are useful in valuation of firms both internally and externally. An indicator of acceptance of the value externally is the fact that financial institutions accept trademarks as security for loans. Internal valuation could be useful in the context of performance evaluation of managers.

2.2. Examples of Trademarks

Appendix A and Appendix B are examples of how a trademark is documented on the Federal Trademarks Register. Appendix A is an internally developed trademark of Apple Computer. There is no record of any assignments or sales transactions. There is a registration date (17 June 1986), registration number (1,397,471) and the class of goods/services (US cl: 26) under which this trademark is registered.

Appendix B is an example of an assigned trademark now owned by Apple Computer but not originally developed by them. There is similar data as the trademark in Appendix A, but in addition at the bottom there is a record of assignment. The original registrant was Carolina Engineering Laboratories in 1986. They assigned the trademark to Thomas M. O'Malley on 24 October 1990, and he in turn assigned the trademark to Apple Computer on 31 October 1990. The date of recording the assignment is 26 July 1991. A transaction of this kind is a business transaction or an arms-length transaction. A purchase of this trademark would appear on the balance sheet, either separately or if there were a number of assets included in the transaction and values were not assigned separately it would probably be included with goodwill.

2.3. Accounting for Intangible Assets and Trademarks

Under GAAP, recognized intangible assets must have certain characteristics:

1. *Identifiability.*   The intangible assets must be specifically identifiable like patents, trademarks, copyrights, etc.

2. *Manner of acquisition.*   The intangible assets can be internally or externally developed, and can be acquired singly or in groups or in business combinations.

3. *Determinate or indeterminate life.*   Patents are issued for a period of twenty years. Copyrights also expire within a definite period. Other intangible assets, such as organizational costs, secret processes, and goodwill, have no determinable life.

4. *Transferability.*   The rights to a patent or trademark can be separately identified and bought and sold.

Accountants worldwide have had to address the question of how best to incorporate intangible assets in the financial statements. In the United States, trademarks are rarely reflected on the firm's balance sheet because all expenditures in developing and registering a trademark, such as development and advertising costs, are required to be expensed when incurred. If, however, there is an arms-length purchase of a trademark, that trademark is carried on the balance sheet at historical cost if the amount specifically paid for it is discernible. If not, the costs of purchase will be embedded within goodwill.

2.4. International Accounting Standards

Some countries, such as Canada, Japan, Australia, and France require that purchased goodwill and trademarks be recognized as assets and amortized. Other countries (e.g. Germany and Italy) allow the trademark to be immediately written off against shareholders equity, or recognized as amortizable assets. In the United Kingdom, the Companies Act allows capitalization of brands on the balance sheet. Firms in the United Kingdom value the brands that they possess and report them on the balance sheet as assets that at present need not be amortized. This raises the need to accurately determine the life of a brand. In some cases, brands need substantial advertising expenditures to maintain their efficacy, suggesting that they are not as long lived as might be expected.

3. Literature Review

Aaker (1991) discussed the role of brands thus: 'A brand is a distinguishing name and/or symbol (such as a logo, trademark, or package design) intended to identify the goods or services of either one seller or a group of sellers, and to differentiate those goods or services from those of competitors. A brand thus signals to the customer the source of the product, and protects both the customer and the producer from competitors who would attempt to provide products that appear identical'. This description is similar to that of a trademark as discussed by the senate recommendation committee for the Lanham Act in section 2. Since it is difficult to distinguish between brands and trademarks, this study treats brands and trademarks as synonymous.

Keller (1997) lists the benefits of a brand name as greater loyalty from customers, less vulnerability to competitive marketing actions, less vulnerability to marketing crises, larger margins, more inelastic consumer response to price increases, more elastic consumer response to price decreases, greater trade cooperation and support, increases marketing communication effectiveness, possible licensing opportunities, and additional brand extensions.

Smith (1997: 88) states 'One of the most obvious economic effects of a trademark is that it might permit the owner to charge more than others for a product or service that is very similar to others in the market place. This is caused by enhanced market demand for the subject product or service. If this enhanced market demand for the product or service is brought about by the magnetism of the trademark, then the income stream represented by the premium price can be attributed to this asset'. In this view, the value of a trademark is attributable to the sales price premium it generates.

The intangibles research literature and literature investigating the role of nonfinancial value measures includes several empirical studies that have established the value relevance of intangible assets. Lev and Sougiannis (1996) develop a methodology to value R&D capital. They find that capitalization-and-amortization adjustments to reported earnings and book values are value relevant to investors. Lev and Zarowin (1999) advocate a proposal to comprehensively capitalize intangible investments and to introduce a systematic restatement of financial reports. Deng, Lev, and Narin (1999) find that patent statistics are associated with market value of firms owning them. Ittner and Larcker (1998) find that customer satisfaction measures are leading indicators of financial performance.

Hand (2002) finds that the NPVs of expenditures on personnel, advertising, and R&D expenses are consistently positive during the 1980s and 1990s. Hirschey and Weygandt (1985) find that advertising expenses are value relevant, indicating that advertising expense is a proxy for the development of valuable brand names. However, Bublitz and Ettredge (1989) conclude that the benefits from advertising expenditures are short lived, which is equivalent to recognizing them as current period expenses. Barth and Clinch (1998) provide evidence that recognized revalued intangible assets of Australian firms, a substantial proportion of which relate to brand names, are value relevant.

The accounting and marketing literature also includes several empirical studies that examine the relations between brand attributes and security prices and/or returns. For example, Barth *et al.* (1999) examine the value relevance of brand values and find that the brand values estimated by the business magazine *Financial World* are value relevant, controlling for equity book value and earnings. They also find that year-to-year changes in brand values are correlated with annual stock returns, controlling for net income and changes in net income. Aaker and Jacobsen (1994) find that returns are positively associated with changes in measures of brand quality, though the relationship is not statistically significant. Simon and Sullivan (1993) outline a technique for estimating a firm's brand equity, based on the firms' market value, and find that firms and industries with commonly known brand names have high estimates of brand equity.

3.1. Trademark Value Creation and Price Premium

Aaker (1991) states that the brand equity assets have the potential to provide a brand with a price premium. One way to observe the price premium is to examine the market prices of products, identify differences, and determine whether such differences are associated with different brands. If one establishes that a price premium is being charged, the value of the brand in that year is the sales volume multiplied by the price premium. Discounting expected future values of the price premium yields an estimate of the value of the brand.

Smith (1997) states 'One of the most obvious economic effects of a trademark is that it might permit the owner to charge more than others for a product or service that is very similar to others in the market place. This is caused by enhanced market demand for the subject product or service. If this enhanced market demand for the product or service is brought about by the magnetism of the trademark, then the income stream represented by the premium price can be attributed to this asset'. From this discussion, the valuation techniques described for trademarks have a basis in fundamental economics, with factors such as sales and the ability to compare the trademark in question to similar but nontrademarked product being key to valuation.

4. Sample and Data

This section deals with trademarks that are internally developed by firms and do not appear on the balance sheet. Using all firms with advertising expense data for the year 1995 on the 1998 COMPUSTAT tape in the following SIC codes, I develop a methodology to value trademarks and test if this value is impounded in firms' equity market values:

SIC code	Industry
2000–2099	Food products
2800–2899	Chemicals
4800–4899	Telecommunications
3570–3582 and 3672–3679	Electronics/Computers
2300–2399	Apparel

The industries above were chosen in order to represent a diverse cross section of industries with available advertising expense data. In consumer industries, such as food products and apparel, trademarks may be of greater importance, while in basic industries like chemicals they may matter less. I focus on advertising data because advertising expense has the potential to capture some or all of the brand value embodied in trademarks. There are 237 firms in these five industries with advertising expense data on COMPUSTAT for the year 1995. The trademark data for the sample of 237 firms is extracted from the CCH Trademark Research Corporation database. The period over which the analysis is performed is 1993–97.

Summary statistics for the overall sample in 1997 are reported in Table 1. In 1997 the average market value of firms in the sample was $8.6 billion, and the average book value was $1.7 billion. There is a high probability that sample firms have intangible assets beyond simply trademarks, since the average market to book ratio is 4.9. The average amount of recognized intangible assets is $511 million and the average number of internally developed trademarks owned by these firms was 60.4. Sample firms on average registered 7.5 new

Table 1. Summary Statistics for Sample Firms in 1997 ($N = 184$)

Variable[a]	Mean	Std. Dev	Minimum	Maximum
LEVEL	60.4	104.6	1	646
CHNG	7.5	13.6	0	78
BVAL	1732.6	4746.4	0.8	41,394
MKVAL	8567.9	23,738.0	0.8	164,758
MKBK	4.9	6.9	0.2	58
ADVEXP	224.6	642.5	0	5939
EMP	19.2	46.0	0.01	287
TOTASETS	4979.2	13,997.0	2.1	131,459
TRADEMARK	580.2	1729.1	0	13,811
INTAN	311.2	1739.0	0	16,554
NI	301.0	853.8	−1060.0	5601

[a] All variables are for the year 1997 and except for LEVEL, CHNG, EMP, and MKBK are in millions of dollars. LEVEL, CHNG, and MKBK are numbers and EMP is in thousands. LEVEL is the number of internally developed trademarks owned by firms at the end of the year. CHNG is the new trademarks registered during the year. BVAL is the book value of common equity at the end of the fiscal year. MKVAL is the market value at the end of the fiscal year. MKBK is the market to book ratio. ADVEXP is the advertising expense in the year deflated by book value. EMP is the number of employees at the end of the year. TOTASETS is the total assets of firms in the sample. TRADEMARK is the estimated market value of all internally generated trademarks. INTAN is the intangible assets recognized on the balance sheet. NI is the earnings after extraordinary items.

trademarks in 1997. The average estimated value of trademarks (based on the methods discussed later in the paper) is $580 million.

....

5. Research Design

5.1 Production Function for Sales

My first objective is to establish that trademarks provide economic benefits. I tackle this by assuming that the physical output measure that can be most directly related to the value contained in trademarks is sales. I use a Cobb–Douglas production function to assess the relation between sales and trademarks, where trademarks act both as an intermediate output of the firm's research and product development activity and as a direct input for sales. The value of a trademark can also be considered as being embodied in the premium price earned by the firm that is recognized in sales. The original Cobb–Douglas multiplicative function is transformed into a linear function by taking the natural logarithms of all variables:

$$\text{Log}(Q_t) = a + b_0 \log(C_t) + b_1 \log(L_t) + b_2 \log(TM_t) + b_3 \log(ADV_t) + \varepsilon_t, \qquad (1)$$

where Q is output, measured as sales, C is physical capital measured as fixed assets at end of year t, L is labour, measured as number of employees in year t, TM is the number of trademarks owned by a firm at the end of year t, and ADV is the advertising expense in year t. The parameters a, b_0, b_1, b_2, and b_3 are the regression coefficients.

I estimate (1) in two ways: in logarithms of contemporaneous variables (Table 2, Panel A) and after taking four-year differences in the logarithms of the explanatory variables (Table 2, Panel B). The latter approach approximates using the rate of growth in sales as the dependent variable. Both estimation methods include fixed industry and year effect dummies, and the data spans the years 1993–96. It should be noted that advertising and the number of trademarks may capture the same information or different dimensions of the same underlying intrinsic value. This is because firms communicate characteristics of a trademarked product through advertising. Trademarks and advertising may also be complements; without trademark protection, advertising expense might not provide benefits over a long period of time because anybody could duplicate the product and sell it without fear of facing lawsuits. On the other hand, trademarks alone are unlikely to have much value. Advertising expense is needed to communicate the attributes of the trademark to the public. In light of this, I use the log of advertising as a control variable, where the current year's advertising expense is a proxy for the advertising stock.

Panel A of Table 2 shows that in the contemporaneous model, the coefficient on the variable TM, the number of trademarks owned by a firm at its fiscal year end, is positive and significant even in the presence of advertising. In Panel B of Table 2 the results indicate that trademarks have only small incremental explanatory power over advertising in explaining cross sectional variation in long run growth in sales, suggesting that the protection afforded by trademarks results in realized economic benefits to the firm in the form of sales. This suggests that trademarks are value relevant and their value is incremental to advertising.

5.2. Valuation Methodology

In monetary terms, the value of trademarks is related to the price premium that the trademark permits the firm to earn. I use the coefficients on the variable TM from Model 2 in Panel A of Table 2 to estimate the incremental sales attributable to the trademarks registered in 1997. I then multiply the coefficient by the actual percentage change in number of trademarks in 1997, and by the sales in 1997. This computation results in the incremental sales attributable to new trademarks registered in the year 1997:

$$\text{INCSALE} = b_2 * \text{PCHTMRK}_{1997} * \text{SALES}_{1997}, \tag{2}$$

Table 2. Production Function Regressions Where Sales is the Output Measure

Independent Variable[a]	Model 1	Model 2
Panel A: Contemporaneous model where the dependent variable is ln(sales) (N = 890)		
Intercept	2.07**	1.75**
	(18.1)	(15.3)
TM	0.03**	0.06**
	(3.1)	(5.0)
L (Labour)	0.28**	0.29**
	(12.0)	(11.8)
C (Capital)	0.57**	0.67**
	(22.9)	(28.4)
ADV (Advertising)	0.12**	
	(9.3)	
Adjusted R-squared	96.7%	96.4%
Panel B: Growth model where the dependent variable is the four-year difference in ln(sales) (N = 531)		
Intercept	0.03	0.03
	(0.9)	(0.8)
ΔTM	0.05*	0.06*
	(2.6)	(2.7)
ΔL (Labour)	0.36**	0.37**
	(12.1)	(12.3)
ΔC (Capital)	0.40**	0.43**
	(12.8)	(14.0)
ΔADV (Advertising)	0.05**	
	(4.1)	
Adjusted R-squared	76.6%	75.5%

[a] ADV is the log of advertising expense for year t. TM is measured by the natural logarithm of the number of trademarks owned by a firm at time t. L is Labour measured as the natural logarithm of the number of employees in the firm at time t. C is the log of capital measured as fixed assets at time t. t-statistics are in parentheses.
* and ** denote statistical significance at the 5% and 1% levels, respectively.

where INCSALE is the incremental sales attributable to trademarks in 1997, $PCHTMRK_{1997}$ is the percentage change in trademarks in 1997, and $SALES_{1997}$ is the actual sales in 1997.

The variable INCSALE can be thought of as being the series of cash flows attributable to the trademarks. I assume that this cash flow lasts forever and that the appropriate discount rate is 10 per cent. Treating this as a perpetuity results in the estimated market value of all trademarks:

$$\text{TRADEMARK} = \text{INCSALE} \star (\text{LEVEL}/\text{CHNG})/0.10, \qquad (3)$$

where LEVEL is the total number of trademarks owned at fiscal year end 1997 and CHNG is the number of new trademarks registered by the firm in 1997. Using (3), the mean estimated value of the total portfolio of trademarks owned by firms in the sample is $580 million. Alternatively, if the life of the cash flows arising from the incremental sales due to the trademark is only five years, the total portfolio of trademarks owned by firms is valued at $220 million. Either way, these are economically material amounts.

5.3. Tests for Value Relevance

The analysis in Section 5.2 demonstrated that trademark values can be estimated and are economically material. I use these trademark value estimates in the next set of tests where the Ohlson (1995) model is employed to establish value relevance through the association between market value of equity and trademark value estimates.

Under the assumptions that the equity market value of the firm is the present value of future expected dividends and that accounting satisfies the clean surplus relation, firm value can be derived from book value and the present value of expected future abnormal earnings:

$$p_t = b_t + \sum_{\tau=1}^{\infty} R^{-\tau} E_t[x_{t+\tau}^a], \tag{4}$$

where p_t is the market value of the firm, b_t is the book value, R is the discount factor, x^a is the abnormal earnings, defined as accounting earnings minus the cost of capital and calculated as the discount rate times the book value at the beginning of the period. Scaling both sides by book value yields:

$$\frac{p_t}{b_t} = 1 + \sum_{\tau=1}^{\infty} R^{-\tau} \frac{E_t[x_{t+\tau}^a]}{b_t}. \tag{5}$$

Estimated trademark values are treated as information not reflected in financial statements, and therefore an additional explanatory variable.

Simplifying and substituting $PVAE_t$ for the term $\sum_{\tau=1}^{\infty} R^{-\tau} E_t[X_{t+\tau}^a]$, I empirically estimate the following regression equation:

$$\frac{p_t}{b_t} = \alpha_0 + \alpha_1 \frac{PVAE_t}{b_t} + \alpha_2 \frac{TRADEMARK_t}{b_t} + \eta_t, \tag{6}$$

where $TRADEMARK_t$ is the estimated value of trademarks in 1997, p_t is the market value of the firm in 1997, b_t is the book value, and $PVAE_t$ is the present value of future abnormal earnings.

I estimate $PVAE_t$ using analyst forecast data provided by IBES following the procedure described in Barth and Clinch (1998) and Deng (1999). Specifically, earnings in years $t+1$ and $t+2$ are measured as the first median consensus earnings forecast after actual earnings for year t are reported; earnings in years $t+3$ through $t+5$ are estimated based on analysts forecast of long term earnings growth rate. Abnormal earnings beyond year $t+5$ are assumed to be zero.

238

The cost of equity is assumed to be a constant 10 per cent. Future book values are estimated using the clean surplus relation $BV_{t+1} = BV_t + X_{t+1} - d_{t+1}$. Future dividends are estimated using the firms' most recent dividend payout ratio multiplied by future estimated earnings, unless earnings are negative, in which case dividends are estimated as 6 per cent of total assets. Equation (6) is also expanded to include advertising expense as a robustness check.

Following Ohlson (1995), I treat the variable TRADEMARK in (6) as part of 'other information' that determines current equity market value but is not yet reflected in financial statements. From this perspective, finding that $\alpha_2 > 0$ would be consistent with estimated trademark values capturing valuation-relevant information that is not reflected in current period earnings or the statistical projection of current period earnings into the future. Based on prior research, I predict that $\alpha_1 > 0$.

6. Results

Table 3 reports the results of estimating (6) and provides evidence that trademark value estimates are value-relevant. In the first column of Table 3 are the

Table 3. Regression Tests of the Association between Firms' Equity Market Values at the End of Fiscal 1997 and Analyst Forecast-based Estimates of the Present Value of Future Abnormal Earnings and the Value of their Trademarks

Independent Variable[a]	Model 1	Model 2	Model 3
Intercept	4.68**	1.99**	1.93**
	(10.2)	(4.1)	(3.9)
PVAE	1.41**	1.00**	1.02**
	(7.5)	(6.2)	(5.7)
TRADEMARK		1.36**	1.38**
		(8.8)	(7.6)
SALESGR			0.00
			(1.2)
ADV			−0.02
			(−0.0)
Adjusted R-squared	24.7%	48.1%	48.6%

[a] All variables are deflated by book value at end of the fiscal year 1997. PVAE is the present value of expected future abnormal earnings estimated by taking the present value of the difference between analysts' forecasts of earnings and cost of capital assumed to be 10% of the book value of equity at the beginning of the fiscal year. TRADEMARK is the trademark value estimates of new trademarks registered in 1997. ADV is the advertising expense in 1997. SALESGR is the growth rate in sales from 1996 to 1997.
* and ** denote statistical significance at the 5% and 1% levels, respectively.

results for the benchmark model where only abnormal earnings is included as an explanatory variable, from which it can be seen that the coefficient on the present value of expected future earnings, PVAE, is positive and statistically significant. In the second and third columns I expand the regression to include three additional explanatory variables: the estimated value of trademarks calculated assuming a perpetuity, TRADEMARK, advertising expense, ADV, and sales growth, SALESGR. The coefficient estimate on TRADEMARK is always positive and significant, indicating that trademark value estimates capture value-relevant information. In contrast, the coefficient estimates on ADV and SALESGR are both insignificantly different from zero. This suggests that current advertising does not capture trademark value over and above what is embedded within TRADEMARK. In unreported robustness tests, I repeated these same tests using the trademark value estimates based on a five-year life and obtained qualitatively similar results.

6.1. Abnormal Stock Returns Around the Announcement of Purchases of Trademarks

In this the event study section of the paper, I exploit a sample of firms that disclosed through press releases that they had purchased trademarks during the years 1993–98. I uncovered these firms via a comprehensive search on Lexis–Nexis that identified the names of the firms and the dates on which trademark purchase announcements were made. The key words used were 'Trademark or brand' and 'purchase', 'acquire', or 'buy', and the resulting sample consists of 290 transactions reported in the press during the years 1993–98. Further requiring that the announcing firm had sufficient stock price data to be included in an event study limited the sample to 187 announcements by 120 different firms. (In the tests using size-adjusted abnormal returns the number of firm announcements declines to 177.) Table 4 provides details on key financial measures of the sample firms. The mean market capitalization of firms purchasing trademarks is \$9.2 billion, while the mean book value is \$1.8 billion. The large gap between equity market and book values suggests the presence of substantial intangible assets. The mean book-to-market ratio is 0.37, and the mean annual sales are \$5.9 billion.

Raw returns $R_i(t)$ for each sample firm i on event day t were obtained from CRSP. The three-day cumulative raw return $R_i(-1, +1)$ centred on event day 0 represents the trademark purchase announcement return. Panel A of Table 5 provides summary statistics over the sample cumulative raw returns. For the three-day window centred on the trademark purchase announcement date, the mean raw return is 1.7 per cent and the median raw return is 0.4 per cent, each

Table 4. Summary Statistics for the Sample of Firms Involved in Purchases of Trademarks

Variable[a]	Mean	Median	Std. Dev.	Min.	Max.
SALES	5858.2	989.2	9559.9	2.5	35,284.0
MKVAL	9176.3	1248.9	18,142.3	6.0	88,610.9
BVAL	1788.3	368.0	3055.6	−29.6	12,359.0
BM	0.38	0.31	0.32	−0.83	1.69
ADV	383.9	1.3	832.0	0.0	3284.0
RND	158.1	0.0	424.7	0.0	2140.0
PE	29.2	18.2	0.04	−64.8	689.6
LBM	−1.2	−1.2	0.7	−3.4	0.34
LMKVAL	6.8	7.0	2.6	1.9	11.1
QAN	0.40	0.0	0.5	0.0	1.0

[a] SALES is the sales revenue of the firm in the year of announcement. MKVAL is the market value of the firm at the end of the year in which the purchase announcement was made. BVAL is the book value of the firm's common equity at the end of the fiscal year. BM is the ratio of the book value of common equity to the market value of common equity. ADV is the advertising expense in the year of the purchase announcement. RND is the research & development expenditure. PE is the price/earnings ratio. LBM is the natural logarithm of BVAL. LMKVAL is the natural logarithm of the equity market value of the firm. QAN is an indicator variable set to one if the announcement disclosure contains quantitative information, and zero otherwise.

Table 5. Summary Statistics for Stock Returns Around Announcements of Trademark Purchases

Return Measure	N	Mean (%)	t-statistic	Std. Dev. (%)	Median (%)	Min. (%)	Max. (%)
Panel A: Announcement period stock returns							
Raw returns	187	1.7	(3.5)	6.0	0.4	−11.8	19.2
Market-adjusted returns	187	1.5	(3.1)	6.5	0.4	−12.5	20.5
Size-adjusted returns	177	1.7	(3.0)	7.5	0.5	−12.5	18.9
Panel B: Differences in announcement period stock returns across two disclosure classifications							
Raw returns, QAN = 0[a]	113	1.1	(1.9)	6.4	0.3	−11.8	19.2
Raw returns, QAN = 1	74	2.5	(3.3)	6.5	0.8	−10.5	17.8
Market-adjusted returns, QAN = 0	113	0.7	(1.3)	6.7	0.3	−12.5	17.7
Market-adjusted returns, QAN = 1	74	2.5	(3.3)	6.6	0.6	−11.6	20.5
Size-adjusted returns, QAN = 0	107	0.8	(1.4)	6.4	0.4	−12.5	18.6
Size-adjusted returns, QAN = 1	70	2.9	(2.8)	8.8	0.8	−10.1	18.9

[a] QAN is an indicator variable which takes on the value 1 when the disclosure accompanying the announcement is quantitative in nature, 0 otherwise.

of which is significantly different from zero at the 1 per cent level. The mean market adjusted abnormal return is 1.5 per cent and the median market adjusted return is 0.4 per cent, with the former being significantly different from zero at the 1 per cent level and the latter at the 10 per cent level. The mean size adjusted abnormal return is 1.7 per cent and the median return is 0.5 per cent, both of which are significantly different from zero at the 1 per cent level. I conclude from this event study that investors react positively to the announcement by a firm that it is purchasing a trademark.

6.2. Factors Affecting Investor Reaction to Trademark Purchases

Next I examine the impact of voluntary disclosures on investors' reactions to purchases of trademarks. I propose that investors' expectations of the commercial success of the trademark purchased by the firm are determined by their assessment of success with which the trademark can be marketed, its perceived synergies with existing products (which could lead to benefits in terms of better market share and power), economies of scale in manufacturing and marketing, and the creation of barriers to entry.

With each of these factors, the purchasing firm has the option to disclose information about the economic prospects of the acquired trademark. Disclosures made by firms when announcing trademark purchases were both quantitative and qualitative. Quantitative disclosures typically included information on one or all of the following: the size of the market covered by the trademark in dollar or percentage terms, the future potential of that market, and the price at which the trademark had been purchased. I defined qualitative disclosures as announcements only that a trademark had been (or was going to be) purchased, and all other announcements that could not be classified as being quantitative.

I hypothesize that disclosure of quantitative (qualitative) information will (will not) reduce the uncertainty in investors' minds about the future prospects for the products represented by the trademark, resulting in a larger (smaller) stock price reaction at the trademark purchase announcement. I use an indicator variable QAN to capture the quantitative classification, where QAN is set to one for quantitative disclosures, and zero otherwise. Of the voluntary disclosures made by firms, 40 per cent were quantitative (Table 4). Appendix C provides an example of a quantitative trademark purchase announcement, and Appendix D provides an example of a qualitative disclosure.

I then split the sample into two subsamples based on QAN and test if the reaction by investors to the trademark purchase announcement is larger for the quantitative disclosure subsample than the qualitative disclosure subsample. The results are reported in Panel B of Table 5. I find that the mean raw return for qualitative disclosures (QAN = 0) is 1.1 per cent and the median is 0.3 per cent, neither of which is reliably different from zero. In contrast, the mean raw return for quantitative disclosures (QAN = 1) is 2.5 per cent and the median is 0.8 per cent. The former is significantly different from zero at the 1 per cent level, and the latter is significantly different from zero at the 5 per cent level. However, a test of the hypothesis that the subsample means are equal cannot be rejected.

The analysis above was repeated using market adjusted and size adjusted returns and the results are shown in Panel B of Table 5. The mean and median size-adjusted returns for QAN = 0 are 0.8 per cent and 0.4 per cent, respectively. The mean is not significantly different from zero while the median is significantly different from zero at the 10 per cent level. The mean and median size adjusted returns for QAN = 1 are 2.9 per cent and 0.8 per cent respectively, and both are significantly different from zero at the 1 per cent level. The test of the hypothesis that the subsample means are equal is rejected at the 5 per cent level. Results for market-adjusted returns are similar to the results for size adjusted returns. Overall I conclude that overall firms providing voluntary quantitative disclosures experience a size-adjusted return of 2.1 per cent greater than firms providing qualitative disclosures at the announcement of the purchase of a trademark.

7. Conclusions

In this study I have demonstrated in several ways that the values of internally developed trademarks are measurable, material, and value-relevant. I first tested the value relevance of trademarks within a production function framework and found that trademarks are incrementally informative in explaining output as measured by sales. The empirical association between trademarks and sales was then used as a basis to value the new trademarks registered by sample firms in 1997. I estimated that the mean value of registered trademarks in my sample firms was a material $580 million. Using Ohlson's (1995) accounting-based equity valuation framework, I then showed that the estimated values of new trademarks are associated with market values of the firms thereby leading to the conclusion that these values reflect value relevant information and are reflected in share prices. This suggests that firms might improve financial reporting by providing increased disclosures about trademarks in their financial statements.

I also showed that investors perceive the transactions involving acquired trademarks as reliably creating value on average. The stock market reacted positively to announcements of trademark acquisitions, most likely because investors believe that the purchased trademark will generate synergies from the firm's existing product line. Finally, I found that stock price reactions to announcements of trademark acquisitions are positively related to voluntary quantitative disclosures when provided in the announcement press release. This probably arises because quantitative disclosures reduce the uncertainty associated with future profit projections that utilize the acquired trademark.

Firms making positive disclosures enjoy, on average, a size adjusted return of 2.9 per cent greater than firms making qualitative disclosures.

Appendix A: Example of an Internally Generated Trademark

LASERWRITER
Status: REGISTERED
Gds/Svcs: Int'l. Cl.: 9 (US Cl.: 26)
              COMPUTER PRINTERS
              First Use: 12/14/1984   In Commerce: 12/14/1984
Reg. No.:   1,397,471 Registered: 06/17/1986
Serial No.:   73-543951   Filed: 06/20/1985   Published: 03/25/1986
Affidavits: 8 & 15 02/18/1992
Corresp.:   JILL R. SARNOFF
              APPLE COMPUTER, INC.
              20525 MARIANI AVE.
              CUPERTINO, CA 95014
Registrant: APPLE COMPUTER, INC. (CA CORP.)
              20525 MARIANI AVENUE
              CUPERTINO, CA 95014

Appendix B: Example of an Acquired Trademark

STYLEWRITER
Status: REGISTERED   Date: 11/17/1993
Gds/Svcs: Int'l. Cl.: 9 (US Cl.: 26)
              INTERFACE FOR MATING DOT MATRIX PRINTERS TO NEAR
              LETTER QUALITY PRINTERS
              First Use: 09/09/1985   In Commerce: 09/09/1985
Reg. No.:   1,399,269 Registered: 07/01/1986
Serial No.:   73-569136   Filed: 11/18/1985   Published: 04/08/1986
Affidavits: 8 & 15 11/17/1993

Corresp.:   JILL R. SARNOFF
               APPLE COMPUTER, INC.
               20525 MARIANI AVENUE
               CUPERTINO, CA 95014

Owner: APPLE COMPUTER, INC. (CA CORP.)
               10431 N. DEANZA BLVD.
               CUPERTINO, CA 95014

Registrant: CAROLINA ENGINEERING LABS (NC CORP.) CHARLOTTE, NC.
Assignments:

Assignee: APPLE COMPUTER, INC. (CA CORP.)
               10431 N. DE ANZA BLVD., CUPERTINO, CA 95014

Assignor: O'MALLEY, THOMAS M. (CITIZEN)

Recorded: 07/26/1991   Assigned: 10/31/1990   Reel/Fr.: 0804/0843

Action: ASSIGNS THE ENTIRE INTEREST AND GOODWILL

Assignee: O'MALLEY, THOMAS M. (CITIZEN)
               WILLIAN BRINKS OLDS HOFER GILSON & LIONE, 455 N.
               CITYFRONT PLAZA DR., CHICAGO, IL 606115599

Assignor: CAROLINA ENGINEERING LABS LTD. (SEE DOCUMENT FOR DETAILS)

Recorded: 07/26/1991   Assigned: 10/24/1990   Reel/Fr.: 0804/0840

....

Appendix C: Example of a Quantitative Disclosure at Trademark Purchase Announcement

Copyright 1998 Capital Cities Media Inc., July 20, 1998
HEADLINE: SARA LEE ACQUIRES LOVABLE BRANDS.
BODY: NEW YORK—Sara Lee Corp. has acquired the domestic trademarks of The Lovable Co. for $ 9.5 million and received the licensing rights for the marks in Canada. As reported, Sara Lee in early July put in a $ 4.7 million initial bid to acquire the trademarks of Lovable, which in March filed a chapter 11 petition to liquidate. Michael S. Haber, Lovable's counsel at Smith, Gambell & Russell, based in Atlanta, said the final price was driven up at an auction last week by 'spirited bidding' between Sara Lee and VF Corp., which owns Vanity Fair Intimates and several other intimate apparel businesses. The Warnaco Group in early July had put in a $ 4.6 million bid, but did not participate in the auction, according to Haber. The marks include Lovable and Celebrity and several others that serve the mass channel. Wal-Mart historically had been Lovable's largest customer; other major accounts were J.C. Penney Co.; Sears, Roebuck & Co.; Kmart Corp., and Victoria's Secret. 'We look forward to reviving the Lovable brands in North America', said a Sara Lee spokesman, adding that it was 'too early' to comment on specific plans for the brands. Sara Lee's innerwear stable includes Bali, Dim, Hanes Her Way, Just My Size, Playtex, and Wonderbra.

Appendix D: Example of Qualitative Disclosure at Announcement

Business Wire, November 10, 1997
DISTRIBUTION: Business Editors
LENGTH: 842 words
HEADLINE: Cherokee and Sideout Join Forces
DATELINE: VAN NUYS, Calif.
BODY: 10 Nov. 1997—Cherokee Inc. (Nasdaq:CHKE) Monday announced it has reached an agreement with Sideout Sport Inc. to purchase the worldwide rights to its various trademarks and existing licensing agreements. Financial terms of the acquisition were not disclosed. Robert Margolis, chairman, said, 'We have been looking to acquire additional brands to globally market our wholesale and retail direct licensing programs. Our objective was to locate a well-respected, emerging brand to market to the upper moderate sector in America as a compliment to our Cherokee business. Our global marketing team is making major inroads into world markets with the Cherokee brand. Sideout will also be a significant adjunct to this international growth strategy'.

Notes

1. I particularly wish to thank my thesis advisor Baruch Lev. Thanks also go to Kashi Balachandran, Joshua Livnat, Jim Ohlson, Stephen Ryan, Suresh Radhakrishnan, and Shyam Vallabhajosyula for their valuable help. Trademark Research Corporation provided access to Trademark registration data, and I/B/E/S provided earnings per share forecast data.

References

Aaker, David A. (1991), *Managing Brand Equity* (New York: Free Press).
—— and Robert, Jacobson (1994), 'The financial information content of perceived quality', *Journal of Marketing Research*, 31: 191–201.
Barth, M. E., Clement, M. B., Foster, G., and Kaznik, R. (1999), 'Brand values and capital market valuation', *Review of Accounting Studies*, 3–68.
—— and Clinch, G. (1998), 'Revalued financial, tangible and intangible assets: Associations with share prices and non market-based value estimates', *Journal of Accounting Research*, 36–199.
Bublitz, B. and Ettredge, M. (1989), 'The information in discretionary outlays: Advertising, research, and development', *The Accounting Review*, 64: 108–24.
Cameron and Trivedi, Pravin K., Count data models for financial data.

Deng, Zhen, Baruch Lev, and Franas Narin (1999), 'Science and technology as predictors of stock performance', *Financial Analysts Journal*, May/June, 20–32.

Deng, Zhen (1999), 'Patents, Citations and equity valuation', Working paper, Baruch College.

Economides, Nicholas (1997), *Trademarks*, New Palgrave dictionary of Economics and the Law, forthcoming

Financial World (1997), *Most Valuable Brands*. September/October 1997.

Hand, J. R. M. (2002), 'The profitability and the returns-to-scale of intangibles and recognized assets made by publicly traded US firms, 1980–2000', this volume.

Hirschey, M. and Weygandt, J. J. (1985), 'Amortization policy for advertising and research and development expenditures', *Journal of Accounting Research*, 23: 326–35.

Ittner, Christopher D. and Larcker, D. F. (1998), 'Are non-financial measures leading indicators of financial performance? An analysis of customer satisfaction,' *Journal of Accounting Research*, 36: 1–46.

Keller, K. L. (1997), *Strategic Brand Management* (New Jersey: Prentice Hall).

——— and Sougiannis, T. (1996), 'The capitalization, amortization and value-relevance of R&D', *Journal of Accounting and Economics*, 21: 107–38.

——— and Zarowin, P. (1999), 'The boundaries of financial reporting and how to extend them', *Journal of Accounting Research*, 37(2): 353–86.

Ohlson, James A. (1995), 'Earnings, book values, and dividends in equity valuation', *Contemporary Accounting Research*, 11(2): 661–87.

Simon, Carol, and Mary Sullivan (1993), 'The measurement and determinants of brand equity: A financial approach', *Marketing Science*, 12: 28–52.

Smith, Gordon V. (1997), *Trademark Valuation* (New York: John Wiley).

10 Profits, Losses, and the Nonlinear Pricing of Internet Stocks

John R. M. Hand

1. Introduction

Empirical research into the valuation of companies normally assumes that the relations between profitability and equity market values are linear in the cross section and stationary over time. The thesis of this paper is these assumptions can be dramatically flawed for intangible-intensive firms. The flaw arises because United States generally accepted accounting principles are biased in that they dictate that expenditures on internally developed intangibles such as R&D, branding, and human capital must be immediately expensed, rather than capitalized and amortized over time. As a result, if the intangible intensity of a firm is sufficiently high, seemingly perverse and counterintuitive nonlinear correlations emerge between firms' net incomes and equity market values, such as greater losses being associated with greater equity market values. This phenomenon has been modelled by Zhang (2000b), but has not been empirically tested.

In this paper I test the prediction that highly intangible-intensive firms will exhibit nonlinear and nonstationary relations between net income and equity market values. The sample I use is US Internet companies over the period 1997 : Q1–2000 : Q3 because of the immense role that intangibles play in their business strategies (Lev 2000, 2001). For Internet firms, the rents provided by physical assets are viewed as tiny beside those of intangible assets. In this sense, Internet firms typify the increasingly important role that intangibles play in creating competitive advantage in today's fierce and global markets (Boulton *et al.* 2000; Lev 2000, 2001; Zingales 2000).

In support of my central thesis, I show using rank regressions that accounting bias and dynamic business economics created nonlinear and nonstationary

248

relations between accounting information and the equity market values of Internet firms. I observe that while Internet firms' core profits (revenues less cost of sales, general and administrative expenses, selling and marketing costs, and R&D expenditures) are *positively* priced, core losses are *negatively* priced. The reason for the negative pricing of losses is not that the losses are due to poor operating performance, but instead reflect massive investments in intangible assets that accounting rules require be expensed into net income rather than be treated as assets and amortized over time.

To separate the impacts of accounting bias from those of business economics, I further investigate the pricing of the components of core income for positive and negative core income observations. I find that selling and marketing and R&D intangibles are priced as assets when income is negative, but more like expenses when income is positive. Since loss firms typically spend more than twice as much of their revenues on intangibles as do profit firms, this difference implies that the stock market only attributes future benefits to intangibles (i.e. prices them as assets) *when intangibles play the dominant role in the firm's business strategy*. Consistent with this hypothesis, when income is positive and the role played by intangibles is less critical, operating activity in the form of gross margin is more positively priced and important than when income is negative.

I also show that the pricing nonlinearities of Internet firms change systematically over time. Over time, the pricing of profits and losses becomes less dissimilar in that the pricing of profits becomes less positive and the pricing of losses becomes less negative. Also, the pricing of selling and marketing becomes less asset-like over time, while the pricing of R&D becomes more asset like. As accounting rules facing Internet firms changed little over the sample period, I hypothesize that the convergence in the pricing of profits and losses is due to decreasing economic differences among Internet firms as firms age and the sector matures. Consistent with this conjecture, I show that variation over time in the pricing of core income is related to variation over time in the pricing of gross margin, selling and marketing expenses, and R&D.

Taken together, my findings show that usual assumption that accounting information maps into equity market value in a linear and stationary manner is severely inappropriate for highly intangible-intensive firms, particularly those that are young and fast growing, where intangibles play the dominant role in the firm's business strategy. Therefore, valuation research that fails to take into account the nonlinearities that arise from the intersection of biased accounting, large intangibles, and business dynamics risks making dangerously flawed inferences. More generally, my results suggest that all empirical accounting-based valuation research should treat the pricing of intangibles differently to the pricing of recognized assets.

This paper also demonstrates that while legitimate doubts have been raised about the ability of US accounting rules to provide useful information to investors, especially in fast changing, intangible-intensive industries (Amir and Lev 1996; Lev and Zarowin 1999; Lev 2000, 2001), the expensing required of intangibles such as marketing and R&D transforms rather than eliminates the value relevance of accounting information. Indeed, it may be that rules that require intangibles to be expensed yields reported earnings that are of high, not low, quality. This is because expensing the costs of all internally developed intangibles removes managerial discretion and mitigates earnings management. Keeping income statements free of earnings management may therefore be particularly valuable to investors evaluating newly emerging, high-technology, high-growth sectors because it makes it harder for managers to hype their firm's stock (Lang and Lundholm 2000). Expensing also allows investors more comparable information across firms and across the lifecycle of any particular firm, as well as information that is arguably faster and cheaper to analyse.

The remainder of the paper proceeds as follows. Section 2 summarizes the extant literature on the pricing of intangible intensity and reported profits vs losses, and the pricing of Internet firms in particular. Section 3 describes the firms and data used, while Section 4 explains the methods employed to measure the value relevance of accounting information. Section 5 reports empirical results, and Section 6 concludes.

2. Theory and Empirical Evidence on the Pricing of Intangible-intensive Firms

2.1. The Pricing of Reported Profits vs Losses

The levels-based approach for assessing the value relevance of accounting information typically relies on or appeals to Ohlson's (1995) model in which equity value at time t is a linear function of book equity at time t, net income over period t, and net dividends over period t. This approach assumes that accounting is unbiased, and that the parameters describing the evolution of a given firm's abnormal earnings are stationary. Unbiased accounting here means that the revenues and expenses reported in firms' financial statements accurately reflect the underlying business economics on a timely basis. Recently, Zhang (2000b) shows analytically that the combination of accounting conservatism and growth in intangibles such as R&D and branding can in theory substantially affect the mapping of accounting data into equity value. In Zhang's model, when accounting is conservative the market-to-book ratio generally increases with return on equity when return on equity is positive. However, when return on equity is negative, the market-to-book ratio may also rise as return on equity becomes more negative, as if the market is rewarding more negative earnings, when in fact the negative pricing is due to the collision of conservative accounting and large expenditures that are subject to the conservative accounting, such as R&D, branding, and human capital.

Although this paper and that of Zhang (2000b) are not the first to propose and/or find that the pricing of losses may differ from that of profits, nor to probe the role played by conservative accounting in valuation, my study differs from prior work by proposing and testing a novel hypothesis that explicitly takes into account a firm's business economics and the restrictions imposed by accounting rules. This is that losses will be negatively priced when accounting is biased and intangibles dominate in the business strategy of a firm.[2]

I also investigate the pricing of the components of core income across observations where core income is positive vs negative. I do this to separate the impacts of accounting bias from those of business economics. If the negative pricing of losses is due to conservative accounting being applied to intangibles that are economically assets, not expenses, then expenditures on intangibles should be priced positively not negatively for loss firms. The same logic also applies to the pricing of intangibles when income is positive, unless the business economics of positive income firms are such that their expenditures on intangibles are economically less like assets and more like expenses. The pricing of the components of core income therefore provides a window into the market's perception of the business economics of firms' operating and investing activities that cannot be obtained by examining the pricing of core income alone.

2.2. The Pricing of Internet Firms

Given the speed with which Internet firms arose, academic accounting and finance research into the economics of the Internet and Internet firms is itself very recent. I briefly summarize what I see as the major papers in the literature.

Using ninety-five corporate name changes to Internet-related dotcom names during 1998 and 1999, Cooper et al. (2001) document a striking positive average stock price reaction to the announcement of a firm adding '.com' to its name. This 'dotcom' effect produces cumulative abnormal returns on the order of 74 per cent for the ten days surrounding the announcement day. The effect does not appear to be transitory in that there is no evidence of a postannouncement negative drift. Schill and Zhou (2001) compare investors' valuations of Internet carve-outs with those of the parent. They find several examples of parents whose value in holdings of carved-out Internet subs significantly violate the law-of-one-price by exceeding the market value of the entire parent over an extended period of time. Schwartz and Moon (2000) apply real option and capital budgeting theory to value Internet firms. Meulbroek (2000) finds that, in contrast to insider selling in the general population of firms, sales in Internet-based companies do not produce negative excess stock returns, suggesting that market participants do not on average interpret managers' sales as a sign of overvaluation.

Demers and Lev (2001), Hand (2001), Rajgopal *et al.* (2000), and Trueman *et al.* (2000) examine the univariate and partial value relevance of nonfinancial measures such as web traffic in the pricing of Internet stocks. As a group, their findings indicate that while one or more measures of web traffic are value relevant, current and expected future net income and its components are key to explaining equity market values.

Demers and Lev (2001) also examine the value relevance of the cash burn rate and the efficiency of business-to-consumer (B2C) Internet firms' stock prices to web traffic data. They conclude that cash burn is a significant value-driver, and that the reaction of Internet firms' stock prices to new web traffic data is not entirely consistent with strong form market efficiency. Demers and Lev further find that investors in B2C firms appeared to capitalize product development costs and advertising expenditures through the first quarter of 2000, but not in the second quarter of 2000. Trueman *et al.* (2001) examine the roles of analysts, past revenues and web traffic in forecasts of future revenues. They conclude that analysts significantly underestimate future revenues, and that historical revenue growth and web traffic helps explain, their errors. Finally, Hand (2002) estimates the Internet present values of expenditures on human capital, brand and R&D made by Internet firms, and tests whether such intangibles exhibit increasing returns-to-scale.

3. Sample Firms

3.1. Internet Firms

My sample of publicly traded Internet firms comes from www.internet.com. This website provides comprehensive information on the Internet industry, and the parent company that owns www.internet.com, namely internet.com Corp., is itself publicly traded on the NASDAQ. Among the free data that www.internet.com makes available is its InternetStockList™. Billed by www.internet.com as 'A Complete List of All Publicly Traded Internet Stocks', it consists of fifty major

Internet firms that comprise the more narrow Internet Stock Index (ISDEX™) also put out by www.internet.com plus a large number of smaller Internet firms.

The ISDEX™ is a widely recognized Internet stock index, being regularly quoted and referred to in financial media such as *The Wall Street Journal*, Reuters, Dow Jones Newswire and CNBC. For a firm to be included in the ISDEX™, www.internet.com relies primarily on the so-called 51 per cent test, the goal of which is to distinguish firms that would not exist without the Internet.[3] The 51 per cent test requires that 51 per cent or more of a firm's revenues must be judged to come from or because of the Internet. www.internet.com argues that this separates 'pure play' Internet companies from others who may have Internet products but which would and do exist without the Internet generating a majority of their revenue. Although no minimum market capitalization, trading volume or shares outstanding restrictions are imposed, the Internet firms included in the ISDEX™ are frequently the largest and most widely recognized companies in the e-commerce sector. www.internet.com estimates that ISDEX™ represents over 90 per cent of the capitalization of the Internet stock universe on an ongoing basis.[4]

My sample consists of the union of the firms on the InternetStockList™ at 11/1/99 and at 4/5/00, plus three firms no longer traded on 11/1/99 (Excite, Geocities, and Netscape). After eliminating foreign firms and firms with incomplete financial statement data, my sample covers 274 Internet firms that were publicly traded at the end of at least one fiscal quarter over the period 1997 : Q1–2000 : Q3 and which had complete income statement data at the end that quarter. Since there are less stringent definitions of an Internet company that would lead to a larger data set, my sample may underestimate the number of firms in the Internet sector.[5]

Figure 1 shows the behavior of the ISDEX™ Internet stock index, the NASDAQ and the S&P 500 over the period 4/1/1997 to 4/1/2002. Fig. 1 demonstrates that although many Internet firms reaped huge gains for their stockholders, they have also seen extreme price volatility.

3.2. Non-Internet Firms

The thesis of this paper is that the assumption of stable, linear relations between accounting data and equity market values that describe mature firms is inappropriate for intangible-intensive businesses such as Internet firms. I therefore compare and contrast some of the key economic characteristics of Internet firms against two groups of nonInternet firms: a random sample of publicly traded nonInternet firms and a sample of nonInternet firms that went public at the same time as Internet firms ('IPO-matched firms'). The former permits a contrast with typical publicly traded firms, while the latter controls for

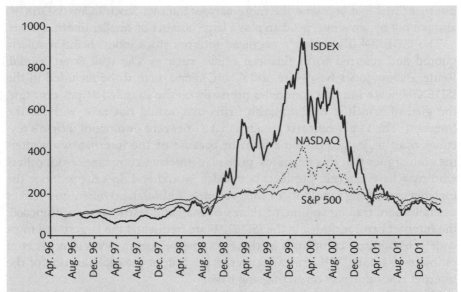

Fig. 1. Level of the ISDEX internet stock index vs the NASDAQ and S&P 500 (4/1/1996 to 4/1/2002; base = 100 set on 4/1/1996).

economy-wide conditions specific to the time period during which Internet firms emerged. The random sample of 274 firms is chosen from the set of all publicly traded companies listed on the NYSE, AMEX, and NASDAQ at 12/31/98. The set of IPO-matched nonInternet firms was identified via www.ipomaven.com, CRSP and www.ipocentral.com. To be included, the nonInternet firm had to go public within a few trading days of its Internet firm counterpart. Since Internet IPOs have tended to cluster in time, and I permitted a nonInternet IPO to be included only once, only 213 Internet firms had available nonInternet IPO-matches.

3.3. Comparisons Between Internet and NonInternet Firms

Table 1 reports summary statistics on a variety of economic characteristics across Internet and nonInternet firms on 12/28/1999. The data in Table 1 were recorded via the Internet directly from www.marketguide.com using Excel's dynamic external Web Query tool.[6]

Table 1 indicates that Internet firms are strikingly different from nonInternet firms. For example, panels A and B reveal that as of 12/28/99, the median Internet firm had ten times the market capitalization yet employed only 40 per cent the number of people as the median nonInternet firm ($865 million vs $87 million; 169 vs 417 employees). Relative to the median nonInternet firm, the median

Table 1. Economic Comparisons between Internet Firms and NonInternet Firms at 12/28/1999[a]

		Equity Market Value ($ mil.)	# of Employees at most recent FYE	Beta[b]	Actual $ EPS 1998[c]	Mean Forecast $ EPS 1999[d]	Mean Forecast $ EPS 2000[d]	Forecast Long-term EPS Growth[e]	# trading Days for Turnover of Float[f]	Actual 3-year Revenue Growth[g]
Panel A: Internet firms[h]	Min.	$13	6	0.40	−113.34	−8.95	−6.76	15%	3	−66%
	Median	865	169	2.55	−1.04	−0.87	−0.76	50	19	115
	Mean	5175	418	2.85	−2.36	−1.09	−0.90	55	24	179
	Max.	357,306	21,000	7.74	4.60	2.27	2.99	201	306	1000
	# obs.	261	254	78	244	239	235	198	251	125
	% < 0	0%	0	0	87%	83	73	0	0	4
Panel B: Random sample of nonInternet firms[i]	Min.	$1	2	−1.52	−12.79	−12.54	−1.75	0%	4	−61%
	Median	87	417	0.78	0.44	0.80	1.12	17	143	15
	Mean	2029	4521	0.86	0.41	0.88	1.31	20	193	30
	Max.	149,078	156,700	3.77	8.32	5.54	6.04	88	1450	897
	# obs.	274	270	270	268	187	165	140	238	262
	% < 0	0%	0	7	32%	18	8	0	0	16
Panel C: Firms that went public at same time as Internet firms[j]	Min.	$2	6	−0.82	−94.95	−3.71	−5.79	3%	4	−45%
	Median	418	344	1.20	0.04	0.40	0.58	30	71	36
	Mean	1511	1733	1.20	−0.85	0.19	0.44	32	129	93
	Max.	35,743	36,900	3.17	11.32	4.87	5.38	111	3550	1300
	# obs.	190	186	61	170	169	167	133	180	134
	% < 0	0%	0	2	49%	31	23	0	0	7

Notes: [a] Unless otherwise noted, data were taken from www.marketguide.com on 12/28/99 using a dynamic web data pull in Excel. Data definitions can be found at http://www.marketguide.com/mgi/HELP/glossary.html.

[b] The slope of the 60 month-regression line of the percentage price change of the stock relative to the percentage price change of the S&P 500. Not calculated if there is less than 24 months of data available. If unavailable from www.marketguide.com but available at www.stocksheet.com, then taken from www.stocksheet.com.

[c] Actual $ EPS 1998 data are taken from www.stocksheet.com and are for the firm's most recently completed fiscal year as of 12/28/99 (typically ended 12/31/98). EPS is defined as earnings per share from total operations (continuing plus discontinued operations) as taken from the 10-K, 10-Q, or preliminary statements. For firms that went public in 1999, actual $ EPS 1998 data reported by www.stocksheet.com are not on a pro-forma basis that would reflect the IPO. Further details on this definition can be found at http://www.stocksheet.com/definitions.html. This explains the huge negative outliers in panels A and C.

[d] Forecasts are for diluted EPS excluding extraordinary items and discontinued operations.

[e] Compound annual growth rate forecasted for EPS (excluding extraordinary items and discontinued operations) over the next five years.

[f] Public float divided by average daily trading volume. Average daily trading volume is total trading volume over the prior three months divided by 66.

[g] Revenue growth rates greater than 1000% have been set to 1000%.

[h] N = 271 firms listed on www.internet.com's InternetStockList ("Complete list of all publicly traded Internet stocks") on 11/1/99 plus 3 firms on earlier listings that were no longer traded on 11/1/99 (Excite, Geocities, and Netscape).

[i] Randomly selected from the set of all firms publicly traded at 12/31/98 on the NYSE, AMEX, and NASDAQ per CRSP.

[j] NonInternet firms that went public within a few trading days of the Net firms per CRSP, www.ipomaven.com and www.ipocentral.com.

Internet firm also has more than three times the beta risk (2.55 vs 0.78). The tenor of these comparisons also holds when Internet firms are contrasted with IPO-matched nonInternet firms (see panels A vs C).

The lack of reported profits for Internet companies is striking. As of 12/28/99, the past and expected future profitability of Internet firms is dramatically less than both nonInternet firms in general and IPO-matched nonInternet firms. Of Internet firms, 87 per cent reported a loss in fiscal 1998, as compared to 32 per cent for nonInternet firms in general and 49 per cent for IPO-matched nonInternet firms. As of 12/28/99, analysts forecast that Internet firms were 4.6 (9.1) times as likely to report a loss in fiscal 1999 (2000) as were typical nonInternet firms, and 2.7 (3.2) times as likely to report a loss in fiscal 1999 (2000) as were IPO-matched nonInternet firms.

While the lack of Internet firms' profitability is at odds with that of nonInternet firms, it is not unique historically. Amir and Lev (1996) report that over the period 1984 : Q1–1993 : Q4, 69 per cent of reported quarterly EPS of the fourteen independent cellular telephone companies were negative. They also report that the corresponding figure for forty-four biotechnology companies over the same period was 72 per cent. This compares to 77 per cent of Internet firms over the period 1997 : Q1–1999 : Q2 reporting negative EPS, suggesting that Internet firms may be no more unprofitable than have been other groups of firms in earlier technology-based, high-growth industries.

In contrast to the seemingly dismal picture of Internet firms' current profitability are analysts' forecasts that as of 12/28/99, the median Internet firm was expected to enjoy an earnings growth rate of 50 per cent over the next five years ('long-term growth rate in EPS'). This compares to 16 per cent for nonInternet firms and 30 per cent for IPO-matched nonInternet firms.[7] Such favourable expectations for the long-term profitability of Internet firms may stem in part from the dramatically higher revenue growth rates that Internet firms have experienced. The median Internet firm's most recent 3-year annual revenue growth rate is more than seven times that of nonInternet firms in general, and three times that of IPO-matched nonInternet firms.

4. The Value Relevance of Accounting Information for Internet Stocks

Zhang's (2000b) accounting-based pricing model forms the theoretical motivation behind my empirical tests. Since Zhang's model predicts that losses are more likely to be observed the more of a firm's revenue is spent on expenditures that are subject to conservative accounting, I lead up to my pricing tests by examining the intangible-intensity of firm-quarters in which core income is positive versus negative. I define core income as revenues less cost of sales, general and administrative expenses, selling and marketing costs, and R&D expenditures. Core income differs from net income because it excludes write-offs of purchased in-process R&D, merger, acquisition and investment costs, stock-based compensation, and income tax expense. I use this definition of income because it is less likely to contain transitory items, which Jan and Ou (1995) propose can cause the pricing of losses to be negative.

Table 2 reports the definitions of, and descriptive statistics for, the variables used in my regression tests. All financial statement data is collected from 424B1, 424B4, 10-Q and 10-K S.E.C. filings at www.sec.gov, while the market value of common equity is calculated from Compustat and/or www.yahoo.com. Beyond ensuring accuracy and consistency, hand-collection is necessary because Compustat does not provide the selling and marketing costs that Internet firms report on a quarterly basis, nor is Compustat data entirely up to date or complete. Because they are so large, about 90 per cent of Internet firms report selling and marketing costs separately from general and administrative expenses on their income statements.[8]

Internet firms are almost certainly more intangible intensive than nonInternet firms in general, and are perhaps the most intangible intensive of all firms. Since nonInternet firms rarely break out selling and marketing from general and administrative expenses in their SG&A, direct comparisons are not possible for all intangibles. However, some indications can be gleaned from figures reported by Amir and Lev (1996). They report that the median NYSE (OTC) firm spent about 20 per cent (27 per cent) of its revenues on SG&A over 1988–93, whereas the median independent cellular company spent 50 per cent. In contrast, the median ratio of just the selling and marketing component of SG&A for my sample of Internet companies is 51 per cent, and the median ratio of selling and R&D to sales is a whopping 71 per cent.

Panels B and C of Table 2 clearly show that intangible intensity is much higher for Internet firms with negative core income than Internet firms with positive core income. For example, firms with negative core income spend a median (mean) of 86 per cent (154 per cent) of revenues on selling, marketing and R&D, as compared to a median (mean) of 35 per cent (37 per cent) for firms with positive core income. Of the two, selling and marketing is by far the larger: firms with negative core income spend a median of 62 per cent of revenue on selling and marketing and 20 per cent on R&D, whereas firms with positive core income spend a median of only 27 per cent of revenue on selling and marketing and 10 per cent on R&D. This intangible intensity is the major reason why 80 per cent of my 1787 firm-quarters of available data have negative core income, and it strongly points toward intangibles playing a much more dominant role in the economics of such firms.[9]

257

John R. M. Hand

Table 2. Definitions and Descriptive Statistics for Regression Variables

Panel A: Variable definitions

Data are from 424B1, 424B4, 10-Q and 10-K S.E.C. filings at www.sec.gov, except MVE which is calculated from Compustat and/or www.yahoo.com.

MVE	= Market value of common equity at end of fiscal quarter
BV	= Book value of common equity at end of fiscal quarter
REV	= Net sales
COGS	= Cost of sales
GA	= General + administrative expenses
MKTG	= Selling + marketing expenses
RD	= Research + development costs
CI	= Core income ≡ REV − COGS − GA − MKTG − RD
P/R	= Price-to-sales (MVE ÷ REV)
RD/R	= RD-to-sales (RD ÷ REV)
M/R	= Selling and marketing-to-sales (MKTG ÷ REV)
RDM/R	= (RD + MKTG) ÷ REV
ROE	= Core return on equity (CI ÷ BV)
M/B	= Market-to-book ratio (MVE ÷ BV)

	MVE	BV	CI	REV	MKTG	RD	P/R	M/R	RD/R	MRD/R	ROE	M/B
Panel B: Means (in $ millions, unless % or ratios)												
CI > 0[a]	$15,536	884	51.4	219	45.5	25.2	80	27%	10%	37%	4.3%	16.2
CI < 0[b]	1639	215	−10.0	23	10.7	3.5	158	115%	39%	154%	−17.3%	12.9
t-test[c]	5.1	4.4	6.3	5.4	4.9	4.4	−3.5	−9.4	−11.9	−11.2	12.7	2.2
Panel C: Medians (in $ millions, unless % or ratios)												
CI > 0	$1433	154	3.6	35	9.1	2.6	39	27%	10%	35%	2.9%	9.6
CI < 0	399	64	−5.9	9	6.1	1.7	45	62%	20%	86%	−8.6%	5.9
Z-statistic[d]	12.2	10.3	29.1	17.8	6.4	4.1	−2.5	−20.4	−11.2	−20.0	29.1	9.0

Panel D: Descriptions of the components of net income for Internet firms

Revenues are typically, but not always, recognized on an Internet basis. When revenue arises from the sale of a physical product, cost of sales is the cost of the merchandise sold. When revenue comes from the sale of a service, cost of sales usually consists of salaries and personnel costs associated with content development, data analysis, testing and maintenance of the firm's website, and the direct costs of professional services.

General and administrative expenses comprise payroll and related expenses for executive, finance and administrative personnel, recruiting and professional fees, and corporate expenses.

Selling and marketing expenses include advertising and promotional expenditures, fulfillment costs, fees paid to establish and maintain strategic relationships with Internet companies, public relations, and all payroll and related costs for personnel engaged in marketing, selling, and fulfillment activities. Unlike the vast majority of publicly traded companies, Internet firms typically report general and administrative expenses separately from selling and marketing costs in their income statements.

R&D expense (which, if present, maybe labelled as R&D, product development, or technology and development) usually covers product development, such as the salaries and personnel costs associated with the content development, data analysis, testing, and enhancement of the firm's technology and services. Due to its imprecise nature, I exclude write-offs of purchased in-process R&D from R&D expense.

In all, the variables used in this study account for almost all the major income statement line items. The two exceptions are write-offs of purchased in-process R&D, merger, acquisition and investment costs, and stock-based compensation. Merger, acquisition, and investment costs typically consist of the amortization of goodwill and other purchased intangibles, equity in the income of affiliates, and other M&A charges. Stock-based compensation comprises the portion of acquisition-related consideration conditioned on the continued tenure of key employees, which must be classified as compensation expense rather than as a component of the purchase price under GAAP. Stock-based compensation also includes stock-based charges such as option-related deferred compensation recorded at the firm's IPO, and certain other compensation and severance arrangements.

Finally, due to the prevalence of losses, income tax expense is most often zero.

Notes:
[a] N = 353 firm-quarters in which Internet firms had CI > 0 and BV > 0.
[b] N = 1434 firm-quarters in which Internet firms had had CI < 0 and BV > 0.
[c] *t*-statistic testing for a difference in means, assuming unequal variances.
[d] Z-statistic on Wilcoxon 2-sample rank sums test for a difference in medians (Normal approximation).

4.1. Regression Methods

I assess the relations between accounting information and equity market values through quarter-by-quarter rank regressions. I use ranks rather than the raw data or the raw data deflated by shares, total assets, revenues or book equity for two reasons. First, scatter plots of raw or deflated data reveal the presence of significant numbers of extreme observations (regardless of the deflator). The rank transformation substantially mitigates the influence of outliers, thereby directly addressing scale bias as defined by Easton and Sommers (2000) in which regression coefficients are dominated by the largest firms in a sample. Second, deflation can create more problems than it solves. For example, in the cross section the number of shares is arbitrary and is therefore not a meaningful scalar. Total assets and book equity are problematic because they are highly affected by the degree and nature of accounting bias. As such, deflating by total assets or book equity may induce nonlinear relations into data that are in reality linear, rather than enable the researcher to more clearly observe the true underlying relations of interest. The cost of using ranks is that potentially useful cardinal information is ignored.

I do not include the book value of common equity as an independent variable in the regressions. While this may seem unusual from the perspective of the standard Ohlson (1995) equity valuation model, including book equity would make the results subject to the criticism for many Internet companies, the book value of equity and the market value of equity are almost mechanically linked. To illustrate this concern, suppose that two years after being founded, an Internet company has 100 shares outstanding and zero book equity ($50 of contributed capital offset by $50 of accumulated losses). Suppose further that the firm then goes public by selling 10 per cent of its existing shares to the public for $500. At that point its market value is $5000 and its book equity is $500. However, the book equity figure is entirely determined by and reflective of the IPO price. As a result, the inclusion of book equity for Internet companies runs the high risk of simply regressing current market value on lagged market value.[10]

5. Regression Results

5.1. Nonlinearities in Pricing

Table 3 reports the results of estimating rank regressions separately for each of the quarters in the period 1997 : Q1–2000 : Q3.[11] The only independent variable in panel A is core income, while the regressions in panel B have as independent

John R. M. Hand

Table 3. OLS Rank Regressions of Equity Market Values on Accounting Information for 274 Internet Firms (1997 : Q1–2000 : Q3).[a] Separate Regressions are Estimated at the End of Each Fiscal Quarter for Positive and Negative Core Income (CI) Observations.[b]

	CI > 0			CI < 0		
Quarter	#obs.	CI	Adj. R^2(%)	#obs.	CI	Adj. R^2(%)
Panel A: Sole independent variable is core income[c]						
97:1	8	0.88*	74	24	−0.44*	16
97:2	9	0.80*	59	30	−0.50*	22
97:3	12	0.83*	65	31	−0.65*	40
97:4	10	0.98*	95	40	−0.64*	40
98:1	12	0.80*	60	44	−0.69*	47
98:2	15	0.43	12	47	−0.69*	46
98:3	16	0.66*	40	56	−0.64*	40
98:4	19	0.84*	69	64	−0.52*	26
99:1	24	0.77*	57	83	−0.56*	31
99:2	28	0.66*	41	141	−0.48*	23
99:3	37	0.51*	24	206	−0.44*	19
99:4	36	0.44*	17	215	−0.32*	10
00:1	50	0.60*	35	199	−0.37*	13
00:2	48	0.60*	35	178	−0.39*	14
00:3	29	0.77*	58	78	−0.21*	3
Mean[d]		0.70	49		−0.50	26
t-statistic[d]		(16.7)			(−7.2)	

Panel B: Independent variables are the components of core income[e]

	Data: CI > 0							Data: CI < 0					
Quarter	#obs.	GM	GA	MKTG	RD	Adj. R^2(%)	Pr > F[f]	#obs.	GM	GA	MKTG	RD	Adj. R^2%	Pr > F
97:1	8	0.93	−0.11	0.26	−0.13	80	0.14	24	0.13	0.19	0.36	0.10	47	<0.01
97:2	9	1.21*	−0.53	0.36	0.03	94	0.01	30	0.13	0.07	0.58*	0.17	66	<0.001
97:3	12	0.80*	−0.44*	0.86*	−0.20	98	<0.001	31	−0.08	0.33	0.44*	0.35	68	<0.001
97:4	10	1.34	−0.23	0.09	−0.30	84	0.02	40	−0.05	0.29*	0.45*	0.39*	70	<0.001
98:1	12	0.61	−0.13	0.35	0.01	84	<0.01	44	−0.06	0.16	0.58*	0.29	63	<0.001
98:2	15	0.68	−0.22	0.03	0.25	−55	0.03	47	0.05	0.21	0.67*	−0.11	73	<0.001
98:3	16	1.15*	−0.15	−0.08	−0.08	−57	0.02	56	0.22*	0.06	0.57*	0.10	76	<0.001
98:4	19	1.68*	−0.28	−0.37	−0.41	82	<0.001	64	0.34*	0.17	0.28*	0.15	67	<0.001
99:1	24	0.85*	0.25	−0.22	−0.05	−67	<0.001	83	0.04	0.10	0.54*	0.24*	55	<0.001
99:2	28	0.93*	−0.11	0.01	−0.06	61	<0.001	141	0.06	0.17*	0.41*	0.32*	55	<0.001
99:3	37	0.73*	0.15	−0.12	−0.05	55	<0.001	206	0.03	0.23*	0.27*	0.42*	49	<0.001
99:4	36	0.44	0.18	−0.39	0.71*	67	<0.001	215	0.10	0.17*	0.21*	0.38*	36	<0.001
00:1	50	0.75*	−0.15	−0.11	0.33	70	<0.001	199	0.21*	0.30*	0.08	0.35*	46	<0.001
00:2	48	0.90*	−0.14	−0.29	0.37*	72	<0.001	178	0.29*	0.28*	0.15	0.26*	55	<0.001
00:3	29	1.09*	−0.44*	−0.23	0.33	70	<0.001	78	0.39*	0.18	−0.07	0.43*	49	<0.001
Mean		0.94	−0.16	−0.01	0.05	73			0.12	0.19	0.37	0.26	0.33	58
t-statistic[e]		(11.6)	(−2.7)	(−0.1)	(0.7)				(3.2)	(9.2)	(6.7)	(6.6)		

Notes:

[a] $N = 271$ firms listed on www.internet.com's InternetStockList ('Complete list of all publicly traded Internet stocks') on 11/1/99 plus 3 firms on earlier listings that were no longer traded on 11/1/99 (Excite, Geocities, and Netscape).

[b] Data are reranked each fiscal quarter and by the sign of core income.

[c] Core income CI ≡ REV − COGS − GA − MKTG − RD (see Table 2 definitions of regression variables). *Denotes a 2-tailed p-value of less than 0.10.

[d] Mean coefficient over the fifteen quarters. T-statistic is based on the time-series standard deviation of the fifteen coefficient estimates.

[e] See Table 2 for definitions of independent variables. Included but not reported is the variable DZRD = 1 if RD = 0, zero otherwise. The coefficient on DZRD is almost always insignificantly different from zero.

[f] Pr > F is the p-value pertaining to the F-statistic on the regression.

variables all the components of core income. Together, panels A and B reveal three nonlinearities in the pricing of accounting information for Internet firms.

The first, seen clearly in panel A, is that while core profits are reliably positively priced, core losses are reliably negatively priced. This finding is consistent with the central thesis of the paper, that the collision of conservative GAAP and the intangible intensity of Internet firms with negative core income spend on selling, marketing, and R&D intangibles leads to the counter-intuitive result that larger losses correlate with larger equity market values. Not surprisingly, however, the stock market unravels the conservatism of US GAAP in that it infers that the losses reported by Internet firms reflect large-scale investments in assets, rather than poor operating performance caused by high expenses.

The second nonlinearity concerns the pricing of selling and marketing and R&D intangibles. Panel B reveals that when core income is negative, selling and marketing and R&D expenditures are positively priced—that is, they are viewed by the market as assets. Across the fifteen quarters spanning 1997 : Q1–2000 : Q3 the mean coefficient on selling and marketing costs is 0.26 (t-statistic = 6.7) and the mean coefficient on R&D expense is 0.33 (t-statistic = 6.6). In contrast, when core income is positive, selling and marketing and R&D are priced more like expenses. Although not reliably negative, as would be required to be unambiguously priced as expenses, neither of the mean coefficient estimates is reliably positive. The mean coefficients on selling and marketing are −0.01 (t-statistic = − 0.1) and 0.05 (t-statistic = 0.7), respectively. Given the evidence in Table 2 that intangible intensity is at the median two and a half times higher for firms with negative core income than firms with positive core income, I infer from these results that the stock market only attributes future benefits to intangibles when intangibles play a dominant role in the firm's business strategy.[12]

The last nonlinearity I highlight concerns the pricing of gross margin. Panel B shows that when income is positive and therefore the role played by intangibles in the firm's business strategy is much smaller, operating activity in the form of gross margin is substantially more positively priced and economically important than when income is negative. Across the sample period, the mean coefficient on gross margin is 0.94 (t-statistic = 11.6) when core income is positive as compared to 0.19 (t-statistic = 3.2) when core income is negative.

5.2. Nonstationarity in the Mapping of Accounting Information into Equity Market Value

Table 4 reports the results of regressions that test for the presence of time trends in the coefficients on core income, gross margin, selling and marketing expenses, and R&D costs. Table 4 reveals that the nonlinearities documented in Section 5.1 do not remain constant over time, but change in a gradual but statistically

Table 4. OLS Trendlines Fitted to the Coefficients Mapping Accounting Information into Equity Market Value for 274 Internet Firms (1997 : Q1–2000 : Q3)[a]

Item	Core Income CI > 0				Core Income CI < 0			
	Intercept	Slope	Adj. R^2(%)	Pr > F[b]	Intercept	Slope	Adj. R^2(%)	Pr > F
Core income	0.86	0.02	24	0.04	−0.66	0.02	37	<0.01
	(11.1)	(−2.3)			(−10.8)	(3.0)		
Gross margin	1.05	−0.01	−3	0.46	−0.02	0.02	24	0.04
	(6.1)	(−0.8)			(−0.3)	(2.3)		
Selling and marketing	0.44	−0.06	47	<0.01	0.57	−0.03	39	<0.01
expenses	(7.4)	(−3.1)			(3.2)	(−3.7)		
R&D costs	−0.27	0.04	31	0.02	0.14	0.02	14	0.09
	(−2.0)	(2.7)			(1.8)	(1.8)		

Notes:

[a] $N = 271$ firms listed on www.internet.com's InternetStockList ('Complete list of all publicly traded Internet stocks') on 11/1/99 plus 3 firms on earlier listings that were no longer traded on 11/1/99 (Excite, Geocities, and Netscape).

[b] Pr > F is the *p*-value pertaining to the *F*-statistic on the regression. For each item, an OLS trendline is fitted by regressing the coefficient estimates reported in Table 3 on a time index (1997 : Q1 = 1, 1997 : Q2 = 2, ..., 2000 : Q3 = 15). Separate trendlines are estimated for positive and negative core income observations.

discernible manner. Most notably, over time the pricing of positive (negative) core income becomes less positive (negative), a pattern that is also followed by gross margin. In contrast, the pricing of selling and marketing expenses becomes less positive over time, while the pricing of R&D becomes more positive.[13]

Since accounting rules facing Internet companies remained virtually unchanged over the sample period, a natural explanation for the convergence in the pricing of profits and losses is that it reflects decreasing economic differences among Internet firms as the sector has matured. The analysis reported in Table 5 lends some support to this view. For example, one might expect that a maturing sector would see fewer differences in the pricing of gross margin over time as the profitability of operating activities become less diverse. Table 5 shows that variation over time in the pricing of core income is significantly positively related to variation over time in the pricing of gross margin, regardless of the sign of core income.

The behaviour of selling and marketing and R&D expenditures is less clear. On the one hand, the pricing of selling and marketing becomes less asset-like over time, and the pricing of R&D becomes more asset-like. Such changes are consistent with the 'land-grab' business model that governed Internet commerce in its early years transitioning to more of a 'product-development' business model. In the early years of Internet commerce within my sample period (1997 and 1998), Internet firms placed great emphasis on seizing market share through intense branding activities. With market shares or trajectories then mostly staked out, more recent years have seen less emphasis on branding and more emphasis on R&D in order to create new products that most profitably exploit the business opportunities provided by the Internet. What is harder to understand from Table 5 is why when core income is positive, variation over

Table 5. OLS Regressions Explaining the Variation Over Time in the Mapping of
Core Income into Equity Market Value for 274 Internet Firms
(1997 · Q1–2000 : Q3)[a]

GM	MKTG	RD	Adj. R^2 %	Pr > F[b]
Panel A: Mapping of positive core income into equity market value				
0.32			34	0.01
(2.9)				
	0.20		12	0.11
	(1.7)			
		−0.40	47	<0.01
		(−3.7)		
0.36	0.25		60	<0.01
(4.1)	(3.1)			
0.14		−0.30	47	<0.01
(1.1)		(−2.1)		
Panel B: Mapping of negative core income into equity market value				
0.61			33	<0.01
(2.8)				
	−0.52		40	<0.01
	(−3.2)			
		0.47	18	0.06
		(2.0)		
0.46	−0.42		58	<0.01
(2.6)	(−3.0)			
0.65		0.52	63	<0.01
(4.1)		(3.4)		

Notes:
[a] $N = 271$ firms listed on www.internet.com's InternetStockList ('Complete list of all publicly traded Internet stocks') on 11/1/99 plus 3 firms on earlier listings that were no longer traded on 11/1/99 (Excite, Geocities, and Netscape).
[b] Pr > F is the p-value pertaining to the F-statistic on the regression.
   The dependent variables are the coefficients on core income from fifteen quarter-by-quarter rank regressions of equity market value on core income. Separate regressions are estimated for positive and negative core income observations. The independent variables are the coefficients on gross margin (GM), selling and marketing (MKTG), and research and development (RD) from similar regressions of equity market value on GM, MKTG, and RD.

time in the pricing of core income is positively (negatively) related to variation over time in the pricing of selling and marketing (R&D), but that these relations reverse when core income is negative, where variation over time in the pricing of core income is negative (positive) related to variation over time in the pricing of selling and marketing (R&D).

5.3. Diversity Within the Internet Sector

Although I have treated the Internet sector as homogenous, it can be argued that the Internet sector is economically diverse. For example, at its www.wsrn.com website, Wall Street Research Net groups Internet firms into twelve categories: Advertising, Consultants and Designers, Content and Communities, E-Commerce

Enablers, E-Tailers, Financial Services, ISP/Access, Internet Services, Performance Software, Search and Portals, Security, and Speed and Bandwidth. To determine the extent to which the results thus far are peculiar to, or driven by, only a few subsectors, I estimated two pooled time series cross-sectional regression for each subsector. The first regressed the rank of equity market value on the rank of core income, while the second regressed the rank of equity market value on the ranks of the components of core income.

The (untabulated) results from regressing the rank of equity market value on the rank of core income by subsector show that the individual and average coefficient estimates tend strongly to be of the same sign and statistical significance as those reported in Table 3. When core income is positive (negative), nine out of eleven (ten out of twelve) estimated coefficients are positive (negative). The (untabulated) results from regressing the rank of equity market value on the ranks of the components of core income by subsector yield individual coefficient estimates on selling and marketing and R&D that are almost uniformly positive (negative) across subsectors when core income is positive (negative). When core income is positive (negative), one out of twelve (ten out of twelve) coefficient estimates on selling and marketing expenses are positive, and none out of twelve (seven out of twelve) coefficient estimates on R&D expense are positive. It is also the case that for every sector the median ratio of selling, marketing, and R&D expenditures to revenues is much greater when core income is negative than when core income is positive. The findings from this subsector analysis are therefore consistent with the argument made in Section 5.1 and the results reported in Table 3 that the negative pricing of losses arises because the losses are caused by huge investments in intangibles, not poor operating performance.

6. Conclusions

In this paper I have predicted and found that the pricing of accounting information for intangible-intensive firms such as Internet stocks is nonlinear in several ways. First, while profits are positively priced, losses are negatively priced. Based on the theory provided by Zhang (2000b), I argued that the negative pricing of losses occurs because the losses are caused by huge investments in intangible marketing and R&D assets, not by poor operating performance. Second, intangibles are only priced as assets when income is negative. When income is positive, intangibles are priced more like expenses. Since loss firms spend more than twice as much of their revenues on intangibles as do profit firms, this implies that the stock market only attributes future benefits to intangibles when intangibles play a dominant role in the firm's business strategy. Third, when income is positive and the role played by intangibles is therefore much smaller, operating activity in the form of gross margin is much more strongly positively priced than when income is negative. In addition to these results, I found that the pricing nonlinearities of Internet firms are not constant over time. Most notably, consistent with economic differences between firms decreasing as the Internet sector has matured, the pricing of profits has become less positive, while the pricing of losses has become less negative.

Taken together, my findings indicate that conventional assumption that accounting information maps into equity market value in a linear and stationary manner is inappropriate for young, rapidly growing, intangible/technology-intensive firms such as those in the Internet sector. Given that intangibles have and will likely continue to become more important for firms in general, rather than being limited to Internet firms, theoretical and empirical market-based accounting research should explicitly take accounting bias and business strategy into account. Without recognizing the nonlinearities that arise from the intersection of biased accounting, large intangibles and business strategy, market-based accounting research risks developing poor theoretical models and making poor empirical inferences.

This said, my study also demonstrates that while legitimate doubts have been raised about the ability of US accounting rules to provide useful information to investors, especially in fast changing, intangible-intensive industries (Amir and Lev 1996; Lev and Zarowin, 1999; Lev 2000, 2001), the expensing required of intangibles such as marketing and R&D transforms rather than eliminates the value relevance of accounting information. Indeed, it may be that rules that require intangibles to be expensed yields reported earnings that are of high, not low, quality. This is because expensing the costs of all internally developed intangibles removes managerial discretion and mitigates earnings management, an attribute that may be particularly valuable to investors evaluating newly emerging, high-technology, high-growth sectors. Expensing also allows investors more comparable information across firms and across the life-cycle of any particular firm, as well as information that is arguably faster and cheaper to analyse.

Notes

1. This work is supported by the Poole Family Fund. My thanks to Barbara Murray and Susie Schoeck for research assistance. The paper has benefited from the comments of M. Barth, W. Beaver, E. Demers, E. Maydew, K. Palepu, J. Ritter, S. Ryan, D. Shackelford, A. Smith, G. Waymire, and P. Wysocki, and seminars and conferences at the Federal Reserve Bank of Atlanta, U.C. Berkeley, the University of Chicago, Indiana University, New York University, and UNC Chapel Hill.

2. For example, Feltham and Ohlson (1995, 1996) and Zhang (2000*a*) model certain aspects of conservative accounting. Empirically, Jan and Ou (1995) report a negative univariate relation between price and losses over the period 1973–91. They attribute this to losses being more transitory than positive earnings. Hayn (1995), Berger *et al.* (1996), Burgstahler and Dichev (1997), and Barth *et al.* (1998) propose that the existence of abandonment and/or real options may lead to losses being priced differently to profits. Riffe and Thompson (1998), Collins *et al.* (1999), and Leibowitz (1999) all observe empirical indications of differential pricing between positive and negative income.

3. Other items examined include 'marketshare leadership (measured by revenues) and whether the firm represents the Internet diversity according to our seven subsections of the Internet industry enterprises'. These subsections are (1) e-tailers and e-commerce, (2) software, (3) enablers, (4) security, (5) content and portals, (6) high speed and infrastructure, and (7) ISPs and access.

4. Net stocks tend to be put onto www.internet.com's IPO Watch!™ list prior to their IPO, followed by the Internet IPO index (IPODEX™) immediately after they go public. After a month or two of 'seasoning', they then seem to become eligible to be added to the InternetStockList™. For example, on 12/27/99 there were forty-nine firms listed on IPO Watch!™, forty-eight on the IPODEX™, and 281 on the InternetStockList™.

5. For example, on 4/5/00 www.marketguide.com reported that its database of Internet companies numbered 685. However, they do not report how they define an Internet company. As a result, their list contains firms such as MCI/Worldcom and Microsoft that are arguably not Internet firms.

6. This allows one to copy a web page into an Excel worksheet. Selected items can then be located and saved.

7. A positive growth rate from a negative base figure is clearly problematic. Attempts to determine what analysts actually mean when they forecast positive EPS growths for firms with negative income were unsuccessful.

8. Where selling and marketing expenses were not broken out of aggregate SG&A in the firm's income statement, such observations were 'backfilled' by setting selling and marketing costs to revenues multiplied by the sample median value for the ratio of firms' selling and marketing expenses to revenues.

9. The market-to-book ratio is often seen as an indirect measure of the intangible intensity of a firm. However, panels B and C indicate that by this price-based measure, firms with positive core income are more intangible intensive than are firms with negative core income. I do not use the market-to-book ratio as my primary indicator of intangible intensity for two reasons. First, over the majority of the period 1997:Q1–2000:Q3, Internet stocks were viewed by most sophisticated market observers to be wildly overvalued (e.g. Perkins and Perkins, 1999). Such overvaluation might distort the ratio in unknown ways. Second, market value can include the value of expected future positive NPV projects. The direct, nonprice based measure of intangibles that I use, namely the ratio of expenditures on selling, marketing, and R&D to revenue, finesses both of these concerns.

10. Consistent with this viewpoint, book equity receives little or no attention in the financial press when it comes to evaluating Internet stocks. This is in sharp contrast to the attention paid to net income and its components.

11. The data used in the regressions are reranked every quarter, and within each quarter separately for positive and negative core income observations. In contrast, the data shown in Fig. 2 are ranked separately for positive and negative core income observations without first conditioning by calendar quarter.

12. The market also prices general and administrative expenses as an asset when core income is negative, but as an expense when core income is positive. One explanation for this is that firms with negative core income are younger, and therefore rely more crucially on the talent of senior management than do more mature firms. Since for Internet firms, a large part of general and administrative expense is the payroll and related costs for executives, it appears that the market views general and administrative expenses as having future benefits when the company is in the early stages of its life.

13. Not shown in Figs 3–6 is the pricing over time in general and administrative expenses. These do not exhibit any statistically reliable trends over time.

References

Amir, E. and Lev, B. (1996), 'Value-relevance of nonfinancial information: The wireless communications industry', *Journal of Accounting and Economics*, 22 (1–3): 3–30.

Barth, M. E., Beaver, W. H., and Landsman, W. R. (1998), 'Relative valuation roles of equity book value and net income as a function of financial health', *Journal of Accounting and Economics*, 25: 1–34.

Berger, P. G., Ofek, E., and Swary, I. (1996), 'Investor valuation of the abandonment option', *Journal of Financial Economics*, 42: 257–87.

Boulton, R. E. S., Libert, B. D., and Samek, S. M. (2000), *Cracking the Value Code: How Successful Businesses are Creating Wealth in the New Economy* (HarperBusiness), HarperCollins Publishers.

Burgstahler, D. C. and Dichev, I. D. (1997), 'Earnings, adaptation, and equity value', *The Accounting Review*, 72: 187–216.

Collins, D. W., Pincus, M., and Xie, H. (1999), 'Equity valuation and negative earnings: The role of book value of equity', *The Accounting Review*, 74: 29–61.

Cooper, M., Dimitrov, O., and Rau, P. R. (2001), 'A rose.com by any other name', *Journal of Finance*, 56(6): 2371–88.

Demers, E. and Lev, B. (2001), 'A rude awakening: Internet shakeout in 2000', *Review of Accounting Studies*, 6: 331–59.

Easton, P. D. and Sommers, G. A. (2000), 'Scale and scale effects in market-based accounting research', working paper, The Ohio State University.

Feltham, G. A. and Ohlson, J. A. (1995), 'Valuation and clean surplus accounting for operating and financial activities', *Contemporary Accounting Research*, 11: 689–732.

——(1996), 'Uncertainty resolution and the theory of depreciation measurement', *Journal of Accounting Research*, 34(2): 209–34.

Hand, J. R. M. (2001), 'The role of accounting fundamentals, web traffic, and supply and demand in the pricing of U.S. Internet stocks', *European Finance Review*, 5(3): 295–317.

John R. M. Hand

Hand, J. R. M. (2002), 'Evidence on the winner-takes-all business model: The profitability returns-to-scale of expenditures on intangibles made by U.S. Internet firms, 1995–2001', working paper, UNC Chapel Hill.

Hayn, C. (1995), 'The information content of losses', *Journal of Accounting and Economics*, 20: 125–53.

Jan, C. and Ou, J. (1995), 'The role of negative earnings in the valuation of equity stocks', working paper, New York University.

Lang, M. and Lundholm, R. J. (2000), 'Voluntary disclosure and equity offerings: Reducing information asymmetry or hyping the stock'? *Contemporary Accounting Research*.

Leibowitz, M. A. (1999), 'Market-to-book ratios and positive and negative returns on equity', *The Journal of Financial Statement Analysis*, Winter, 21–30.

Lev, B. and Zarowin, P. (1999), 'The boundaries of financial reporting and how to extend them', *Journal of Accounting Research*, 37: 353–85.

—— (2000), 'New math for a new economy', *Fast Company*, January–February.

—— (2001), 'Intangibles: Management, measurement, and reporting', Brookings Institute.

Meulbroek, L. K. (2000), Does risk matter? Corporate insider transactions in Internet firms', working paper, Harvard Business School.

Ohlson, J. A. (1995), 'Earnings, equity book values, and dividends in equity valuation', *Contemporary Accounting Research*, 661–87.

Perkins, A. B. and Perkins, M. C. (1999), *The Internet Bubble: Inside the Overvalued World of High-Technology Stocks* (New York, NY: Harper).

Rajgopal, S., Kotha, S., and Venkatachalam, M. (2000), 'The relevance of web traffic for Internet stock prices', working paper, University of Washington.

Riffe, S. and Thompson, R. (1998), 'The relation between stock prices and accounting information', *Review of Accounting Studies*, 2: 325–51.

Schill, M. J. and Zhou, C. (2001), 'Pricing in an emerging industry: Evidence from internet subsidiary carve-outs', *Financial Management*, 30(3): 5–34.

Schwartz, E. S. and Moon, M. (2000), 'Rational pricing of internet companies', *Financial Analysts Journal*, 56(3): 62–75.

Trueman, B., Wong, M. H. F., and Zhang, X.-J. (2000), 'The eyeballs have it: Searching for the value in Internet stocks', *Journal of Accounting Research*, 38: 137–70.

—— (2001), 'Back to basics: Forecasting the revenues of internet firms', *Review of Accounting Studies*, 6: 305–29.

—— (2000a), 'Conservative accounting and equity valuation,' *Journal of Accounting and Economics*, 29: 125–49.

—— (2000b), 'Conservatism, growth, and the analysis of line items in earnings forecasting and equity valuation', working paper, U.C. Berkeley.

Zingales, L. (2000), 'In search of new foundations', *Journal of Finance*, August: 1623–55.

## 11

Why Firms Diversify: Internalization vs Agency Behaviour

Randall Morck and Bernard Yeung

1. Introduction

Many corporations are diversified while many others are not. An extensive literature has developed around the issue of whether diversification adds to firm value or reduces it. Case studies can yield both results. For example, in 1978 IT&T did business in twelve different industries at the three digit SIC code level and had an average Tobin's q ratio of 0.57, while in the same year, 3M did business in eleven different industries and had a q ratio of 2.02. Did diversification hurt one firm and help the other, or did a company like 3M build shareholder value despite its diversification?

Systematic empirical investigations suggest that a diversification discount is the norm, especially in the United States[1]; see, for example, Montgomery and Wernerfelt (1988), Lang and Stulz (1994), Berger and Ofek (1995, 1996), John and Ofek (1995), Servaes (1996), and Denis *et al.* (1997). However, others show a diversification premium; for example, Rumelt (1982), Schipper and Thompson (1983), Matsusaka (1993), and Hubbard and Palia (1997).

There is also time dependence in the value of diversification. The value of diversification fell from the positive range in the 1960s and early 1970s, through the neutral range in the late 1970s, and into the negative range in the 1980s.[2] Now, in the late 1990s, suggestions are again emerging about value increasing diversification. For example, Prahalad (1998) refers to the recent wave of focus-increasing, size-reducing restructuring as 'corporate anorexia'. Moreover, high profile diversifying mergers like the distiller Seagram's 1998 takeover of the entertainment firm Polygram NV continue to occur.

Many economists have argued for a diversification premium on efficiency grounds. For example, Penrose (1959) argues for positive synergies from a resource-based perspective. Firms can benefit by expanding into related activities that share similar resources. Another argument (e.g. Scharfstein, 1997) is that large firms can pool financial resources and thus behave like internal banks for their business divisions. If internal financing involves less information asymmetry than external financing, firm diversification could be an efficient arrangement that commands a premium in firm value. In general, these arguments focus on the benefits of including more transactions within a corporate hierarchy.

There are also strong arguments that diversification reduces firm value. Bagwell and Zechner (1993) and Stein (1997) argue that highly diversified companies have more coordination problems and are subject to more influence costs. Morck et al. (1990) argue that diversification exacerbates agency problems between shareholders and managers. Jensen (1986) argues for a negative return to diversification due to free cash flow agency problem. Baumol (1959) argues that value decreasing corporate growth in scale and scope is common. In general, these arguments focus on the costs of including more transactions within a corporate hierarchy.

The arguments of Coase (1937) are thus critical to both sides. A firm's boundary should be drawn where the benefits of including an additional set of transactions within its hierarchy just match the costs of including it. Not all firms have set their boundaries right: some are too far out and some are too far in. Also, the factors that determine these Coasian costs and benefits change over time. When they change, optimal firm boundaries change, and value maximizing firms adjust their boundaries. During these transitions, we should observe many instances of value increasing diversification when 'overly tight' boundaries expand or value increasing divestitures when 'overly loose' boundaries shrink.[3] This is because firm boundaries should adjust in the right directions in a healthy economy.

In this paper we present evidence that diversification can add value for some firms and reduce value for others. We argue that the internalization theory of Caves (1971), Buckley and Casson (1976), Dunning (1977), Rugman (1980), and Helpman (1984) underlies positive corporate synergy. The synergy stems from the possession of information-based assets with large economies of scale and scope. Firms with such assets ought to have more expanded firm boundaries. They can add value by being larger and more diversified because of these economies of scale and scope in their information based assets. We use this perspective to decompose the value effect of diversification into a component related to the possession of information-based assets and a residual, which we interpret as the net value effect of internal capital allocation and agency concerns. We find that diversification adds value in firms with substantial information-based assets, but destroys value otherwise. We then conduct a 'follow up' study that reveals that the market for corporate control disciplines unwarranted diversification but encourages expansion to tap under-utilized information assets, perhaps explaining the time dependence discussed above.

We believe this to be an important insight because it addresses why some firms should control more resources while others should control fewer. The efficient allocation of resources is a fundamental concern in economics. Our results suggest what sort of firms ought to control more resources—firms with information-based assets. Moreover, our findings verify that the economy is, on average, pushing firms to adjust in the right directions. From a managerial perspective, our results suggest that a fundamental force for firm growth is the possession of information-based assets. This is consistent with the central role assigned to information-based assets in economy-wide growth by endogenous growth theories; for example, Schumpeter (1942), Romer (1986).

In Section 2, we present our theoretical thoughts. In Section 3 we present our empirical methodology, followed by our data in Section 4. In Section 5, we present and discuss our results and we conclude in Section 6.

2. Theoretical Arguments

The literature most explicitly identifies three considerations as determining whether diversification increases or reduces firm value. These are: (1) the benefits due to synergy, (2) the benefits of intra-firm capital allocation, and (3) the costs of greater organization and agency problems in more diversified organizations.

2.1. Synergy

The literature is vague as to exactly what a synergy is. Generally, synergy seems to mean value that results from decreased fixed costs after a merger. Since fixed costs are likely to be duplicated by firms operating in similar industries, papers generally presume that synergies arise from related mergers, but not from mergers across unrelated industries.

The difficulty here is in defining 'relatedness'. Relatedness can take place between businesses that appear to be distinctly unlinked to outside observers. Transportation and electronics are clearly different industries, but electronics is a large and rising component of the cost of an automobile. Entertainment and computer network technology are similarly becoming intertwined, and some of the most exciting advances in power transmission involve using new ceramics as superconductors.

Standard measures of relatedness can be quite problematic. These classifications often rely on how close industry classification codes are, for example, industries sharing identical three digit SIC codes are more related than industries that share only identical two digit SIC codes, which are in turn more related than industries that share only identical one digit SIC codes, etc. The proximity of the numerical values of industry classification codes is not always a true measure of business relatedness. The anecdotes in the previous paragraph clearly illustrate that business in distinctly different industry classification codes can be very related. Let us consider another example: the relatedness among male underwear, male work clothing, curtains and draperies, and cologne. Their industry classifications are, respectively, 2322, 2326, 2391, and 2844. Relying on industry classifications, one would think that male work clothing is more related to male underwear than cologne is. By the same token, one would expect that curtains and draperies are more related to male clothing than cologne is. Yet, higher end male underwear and cologne are closely related products whose values stem from company brand name image and marketing skills (e.g. the Calvin Klein products). Male work clothing and curtains and draperies, however, are not related to male underwear in this way.

Another practice is to define relatedness using historical correlation in business cash flow. The correlation allows researchers to conveniently pick up businesses that have complementary products and/or that use similar production inputs. The disadvantage of the approach is that it relies on historical data so that recent changes in business-relatedness are hard to identify. Moreover, not all businesses well correlated in this manner ought to be controlled by the same company. For example, while architecture firms and construction companies have highly correlated earnings, they are often not integrated and construction companies outsource architectural services. More fundamentally, the approach begs a deeper question: Why should businesses with more correlated cash flows be bundled in the same corporation?

2.2. *The Internalization Theory of Synergy*

We propose a different framework that directly addresses why some companies ought to have more divisions. Consider a company like 3M that possesses a wealth of knowledge in adhesive material. It profitably branches into businesses that can tap into its technological know-how, like stationary (e.g. stick up notes and adhesive tapes) and cassette tapes (attaching magnetic substances to plastic tapes). Honda has proven capability in transferring power to wheels; it owns divisions in cars, motorcycles, and lawnmowers. Accounting firms with a wealth of business intelligence branch into consulting. Companies that have products desired by an identical group of customers tend to merge together, for example, Citibank and Travelers. Companies with brand capital own divisions that can benefit from the same name recognition, for example, Calvin Klein and Sara Lee.

The commonality of these examples is that firms diversify into businesses, some of which appear to be unrelated, which nonetheless use some common information-based assets. This is the basis of the internalization theory of synergy, proposed by, for example, Caves (1971), Buckley and Casson (1976), Dunning (1977), Rugman (1980), Helpman (1984), and others.[4] According to the theory, information-based assets are the key prerequisite for the existence of synergy. Examples of information-based assets are production knowledge and skills, marketing capabilities and brand name, and superior management capabilities.

Information-based assets, once developed, can be applied repeatedly and simultaneously to multiple businesses and locations in a nonrivalrous manner to generate extra returns. In this respect, intangible assets are quasipublic goods with large economies of scale and scope. The question is how best to appropriate the value of these applications.

Arms-length transactions of information-based assets are often thwarted by market failure problems. Because these problems are well known, we shall be very brief here. First, information is often difficult to transmit, so it is often easier to give directions than to 'explain and teach' (see, e.g. Demsetz, 1988: 157–62).[5] Second, information asymmetry is an obstacle in the trading of information-based assets: the seller is interested in exaggerating the value of her assets while the buyer has little reasons to purchase it based on blind trust. The 'lemons' problem implies that a seller often cannot sell at a price commensurate with the actual quality of its asset. At the same time, giving the buyer enough information to let him estimate the value of an information-based asset often also gives him enough information to replicate the asset, leaving him with little incentive to pay. Weak property rights protection may forbid the use of contracts to mitigate the tendency to renege on promise to purchase. Third, the value of an information-based asset may stem from monopolistic possession. As more firms possess the asset, its value dissipates due to competition. A renter of information-based assets may behave opportunistically, for example by conducting unauthorized applications of the rented assets. The renter then gains at the expense of the asset owner. Fourth, the application of intangibles may entail specific investment. Ex post sunk investment the seller of the intangible assets may want to increase the rental fees while the buyer may want to decrease them. The parties have a hold-up problem to overcome. Fifth, the successful application of information-based assets may rely on a user's effort and maintenance and upgrading. Ownership prevents shirking and damage to the asset. For example, the renter of a brand name might damage it by selling inferior products under it for short-term profit, whereas the owner of the brand name would not.

One solution to these transactions costs is to internalize the markets for such information-based assets by bringing the buyers and sellers together within the same firm. In other words, the solution is to incorporate the additional application of information-based assets inside one corporate boundary. This suggests that diversification benefits stem from the economies of scale and scope of intangible assets, and that sheer size and diversification can augment the value of a firm that has substantial information-based assets. Indeed, an undiversified firm possessing such assets may be neglecting its shareholders by under-exploiting its information-based assets.

2.3. Internal Capital Market Argument and Agency Problems

The other main explanations for diversification benefits and costs are 'internal capital market' and 'agency problems'. Business needs financing, for example, to fund new investment, to bridge nonsynchronized cash inflows and outflows, and to cushion temporary troughs in income. External financing can be costly because of information asymmetry between corporate insiders and investors (Myers and Majluf, 1984), so internal financing is considered less expensive. Corporate diversification lets cash rich divisions with few positive NPV projects finance capital expenditures in cash poor divisions with better growth opportunities. Divisions in diversified firms consequently may be both less liquidity constrained in seizing investment opportunities and less averse to individual business unit volatility. Moreover, diversification and internal financing may mean better monitoring and more readiness to divest unprofitable investments (Gertner *et al.*, 1994). Of course, it has also been argued that the convenient availability of financing and the lack of scrutiny by outside investors can lead to agency problems (Jensen, 1986), including over-investment and the misallocation of capital. While it is unclear whether the creation of internal capital market definitely leads to value augmentation, the argument nevertheless implies that scale and scope *per se* should affect firm value.

Other arguments that suggest scale and scope *per se* augment firm value are possible. For example, a larger and more diversified firm can offer better career opportunities and greater job security. These benefits are attractive to managers, and are also conducive to both managers and employees investing in firm-specific human capital. Larger firms with a multitude of needs and a greater pool of heterogeneous managerial talent may be able to arrange better matches in job assignments. Firms that carry out a variety of activities may also be in a better position to discover new investment opportunities and so hold more real investment options. There is genuinely no shortage of arguments that scale and scope *per se* can add value.

On the other hand, agency problems and influence costs in diversified corporations are undoubtedly real and large. Diversified firms can be harder to manage than one-industry firms. They are also less transparent to investors. By reducing firm-specific risk, diversification makes it harder for the board and investors to notice incompetent management, and so might give bad managers undeserved job security, as well as the status and influence that go with managing a larger firm. In addition, since CEO compensation is often deliberately linked to earnings and share price performance, and is also observed to be strongly linked to sheer firm size (Jensen and Murphy, 1990), corporate expansion and diversification plausibly give managers larger and less risky incomes. Hence, managers might be inclined to pursue growth and diversification even if this destroys firm value. Further, recent empirical work shows that a sort of corporate socialism affects diversified firms: all divisions are entitled to their even share of the capital expenditure budget regardless of their actual investment opportunities. The importance of these agency issues is underscored by the findings of Palia (1998) that the diversification discount on firm value is reduced when a diversified firm has a CEO with a more performance sensitive compensation package, a higher level of insider ownership, and a smaller board.

The above arguments imply that corporate diversification and/or sheer size can add to firm value when a firm possesses enough information-based assets. That is, firms with more intangible assets should have a more expanded firm boundary. Diversification and size *per se* may positively affect firm value due to efficiency created by internal capital allocation (including human capital), and it may also negatively affect firm value due to agency problems and influence costs.

In the empirical work below, we decompose the impacts on firm value of diversification and sheer size into two components: one related to information-based assets, and another unrelated to them. We interpret the former as capturing the effect of increased diversification in the presence of intangibles (i.e. due to internalization) and the latter as capturing other effects of diversification—presumably including the effects due to agency problems, influence costs, internal financial, and human capital markets.

3. Methodology

In the cross sectional analysis we undertake, our methodology is to regress various measures of firms' Tobin's q ratios on control variables and on measures of

Randall Morck and Bernard Yeung

firm size and the extent of diversification. We are basically assuming that financial markets value firms efficiently. Thus, a firm's market value, the net present value of the cash flows its investors anticipate, is

$$V = PV(c_1, c_2, c_3, \dots) \tag{1}$$

The value of the firm's assets used to generate these cash flows is A. Tobin and Brainard (1977) define a firm's average q as its market value divided by the replacement value of its assets:

$$q = \frac{V}{A}. \tag{2}$$

A capital investment's net present value or NPV is the difference between the expected present value of its future cash flows and its cost. Since 'cost' for capital budgeting purposes and 'replacement cost' are analogous,

$$\text{NPV} = PV(c_1, c_2, c_3, \cdots) - A. \tag{3}$$

Tobin and Brainard (1977) therefore consider q to be

$$q = \frac{V}{A} = 1 + \frac{\text{NPV}}{A}, \tag{4}$$

where NPV is the combined net present values of all the firm's activities, its 'intangible edge', so to speak. Our regressions are of the form

$$q = \beta_0 + \beta_1 i_1 + \beta_2 i_2 + \beta_3 i_3 + \cdots + \beta_n i_n + \varepsilon, \tag{5}$$

where each i_j is a proxy for a given type of positive or negative NPV per dollar of tangible assets. Since the assets that make up A are usually tangible assets, the i_j can be viewed as proxies for intangible assets or liabilities. Abstracting from tax considerations and other market imperfections, β_0 should be one and the other coefficients should be either positive or negative as the ith variable proxies for an intangible asset or intangible liability. These intangibles should include information-based assets related to activities as well as firm scale or scope.

We are interested in the coefficients of variables that measure information-based assets, scope or scale, and interactions between information-based assets and scale or scope. We model our interaction terms as varying parameter coefficients. That is, we decompose the β_js that measure scope or scale into

$$\beta_j = \gamma_0 + \gamma_1 \times \text{information-based assets}, \tag{6}$$

so that our regressions become

$$q = \beta_0 + \beta_1 \begin{bmatrix} \text{information-} \\ \text{based assets} \end{bmatrix} + \beta_2 \begin{bmatrix} \text{scope or} \\ \text{scale assets} \end{bmatrix} + \cdots + \varepsilon$$

$$= \beta_0 + \beta_1 \begin{bmatrix} \text{information-} \\ \text{based assets} \end{bmatrix} + \left(\gamma_0 + \gamma_1 \begin{bmatrix} \text{information-} \\ \text{based assets} \end{bmatrix} \right) \begin{bmatrix} \text{scope or} \\ \text{scale assets} \end{bmatrix} + \cdots + \varepsilon$$

$$= \beta_0 + \beta_1 \begin{bmatrix} \text{information-} \\ \text{based assets} \end{bmatrix} + \gamma_0 \begin{bmatrix} \text{scope or} \\ \text{scale assets} \end{bmatrix}$$

$$+ \gamma_1 \begin{bmatrix} \text{information-} \\ \text{based assets} \end{bmatrix} \times \begin{bmatrix} \text{scope or} \\ \text{scale assets} \end{bmatrix} + \cdots + \varepsilon.$$

If the primary effect of firm scope or scale is to facilitate the internalization of markets for information-based assets, we expect γ_0 to be zero and γ_1 to be positive (and thus β_2 to be positive). If synergies unrelated to information-based assets add value (like internal capital market effects) then γ_0 should be positive. If expanded scope and scale amplify agency and influence cost problems and these overwhelm synergies unrelated to information-based assets, γ_0 will be negative. If the interplay of internalization and heightened agency and influence cost problems is paramount, γ_0 should be negative while γ_1 is positive.

Our way of identifying the positive internalization-based benefits of scale and scope is admittedly imperfect; but its weakness biases against finding positive results. The identifier is a positive γ_1, which indicates a positive relationship between firm value and scale and scope diversification motivated by internalization. To determine a priori the correct type of internalization motivated scale and scope expansion is notoriously unreliable for outside observers, as our arguments illustrate when we discuss the difficulties in using SIC classification codes and historical correlations in cash flow to identify synergies between lines of business. If firms with intangibles on average conduct the correct kind of scale and scope expansion, we should observe a positive γ_1. However, some firms may have conducted excess and/or inappropriate scale and scope expansion even though an internalization opportunity exists. If excess and inappropriate scale and scope expansion dominate, γ_1 would not show a positive internalization effect. Thus, these problems lessen the likelihood of finding a positive γ_1, and so render such a finding particularly noteworthy.

The second step in our empirical analysis is to ask whether corporate control transactions discipline unwarranted diversification and encourage under-diversified firms to diversify. To do this, we classify firms into those that should diversify and those that should not. We argue that a firm should diversify if its estimated coefficient on scope is positive, that is, if

$$\beta_j = \gamma_0 + \gamma_1 \times \text{information-based assets} > 0. \tag{8}$$

In other words, a firm should diversify if it has sufficient internalization potential to overcome the negative effect of increased agency and influence cost problems. In contrast, a firm should not diversify if it has insufficient information-based assets to overcome the negative effect of heightened agency and influence costs problems, that is, with

$$\beta_j = \gamma_0 + \gamma_1 \times \text{information-based assets} \le 0. \tag{9}$$

We then note which of our firms have and have not already diversified. This allocates our firms into four categories:[6]

	Already diversified	Not already diversified
Should be diversified	I	II
Should not be diversified	III	IV

This classification lets us ask which of our four categories of firms subsequently tended to expand. We can also ask which category of firms is most or least subject to market discipline in the form of hostile takeovers. Generally, do corporate control transactions discipline unwarranted diversification and encourage internalization? Answers to these questions serve as a further check to the validity of our results in step one. Moreover, if our results in step one are valid, they also serve to check whether or not the market for corporate control changes firms' levels of diversification in the correct manner.

4. Data

4.1. Cross-section Sample

We use 1978 data for our initial cross-sectional analyses for two reasons. First, 1978 is in a 'neutral' period when the value of average diversification appears to be in transition from positive to negative. Second, 1978 is prior to the beginning of the 1980s merger wave, so we can observe how the market for corporate control deals with different types of diversified firms.

Our basic sample of US manufacturing firms is from the NBER Financial Master File (Hall, 1988). This file contains market value based estimates of debts and assets, allowing us to construct q ratios that are adjusted for inflation, which was important in the late 1970s. We supplement this with data from Compustat, particularly from Compustat's Historical Industry Segment Research File to estimate line of business q ratios. Firms are in our sample if we can estimate inflation-adjusted q's for 1976, 1977, and 1978. Our data on the geographic locations of US firms' subsidiaries is from the National Register—International Directory of Corporate Affiliates (1980/81), which reports 1978/79 data. The intersection of available data from these sources yields a basic cross-section sample of 1277 US firms.

4.2. Scope and Scale Variables

To measure cross industry diversification, we use the number of three digit SIC codes in which the firm operates (n_3) and also the number of four digit SIC codes (n_4). These numbers are from Standard and Poor's Register of Corporations, which lists a primary four digit industry and up to twelve secondary four digit industries for each firm. For robustness check, we replace n_3 by the number of reported business segments (s_3) in each firm's accounting data that Compustat assigns to different three digit industries. Likewise, we replace n_4 by a four digit version of Compustat data. Finally, we also replace n_3 by n_2, the number of two digit SIC codes in which a firm operates. All the replacements do not qualitatively change our results. Our reported regression results are based on n_3.

To measure geographic diversification, we follow Morck and Yeung (1991) in using the number of foreign nations in which a firm has a subsidiary (nats). As a robustness check, we have repeated our analysis using the number of foreign subsidiaries the firm has. The results are almost identical to our reported results. To conserve space, we do not show them.

To measure sheer firm size, we use total sales (sales). Since the raw value of the variable would introduce substantial heteroskedasticity into regression errors, we also employ a dummy variable set to one if the firm is in the top 5 per cent of the sample by sales and to zero otherwise. As robustness checks, we also used the logarithm of sales, a rank transformation of sales, and an inverse normal of a rank transformation as well as dummies for the top one and ten per cent of the sample. We also tried similar size measures based on total assets rather than sales. All give qualitatively similar results. We use only the raw sales variable and the top 5 per cent dummy because the coefficients of these are easy to interpret and because they result in insignificantly higher R^2s. We use heteroskedasticity-consistent standard errors in regressions that include raw sales. Our three scale and scope measures are clearly collinear. We therefore rely on F-tests as well as t-tests when we claim statistical significance.

4.3. Tobin's q

The construction of Tobin's q is based on Linderberg and Ross (1981). We use an average for 1976–78. Our q's are adjusted to reflect market value estimates for debt, inventories, plant and equipment, and other factors according to Hall (1988).

The purpose of our analysis is to compare diversified to undiversified firms. To do this, we must define what we mean by a 'similar' undiversified firm. Several alternative approaches make economic sense. We first use $q-\mu_q$, the firm's q ratio minus the average q ratio of all firms in its core industry, as defined by Standard and Poor's Register of Corporations. Econometrically, the approach is equivalent to injecting industry dummies as independent variables to control for fixed industry effects while q itself is the dependent variable. In these regressions, the economic question we ask is whether venturing beyond a firm's core business adds value.

A problem with this approach is that different levels of intangibles are 'normal' in different industries. For example, the intangible asset of 'consumer loyalty' may be more important to automakers than to brick making firms. This means different industries have different mean q ratios. Comparing a one industry firm and a conglomerate based in the same core industry to the same benchmark core industry q may be inappropriate.

The solution is the 'chop shop' approach, pioneered by LeBaron and Speidell (1987), of using each firm's q ratio minus a weighted average of industry average q ratios based on undiversified firms. We follow Lang and Stulz (1994) in constructing this variable, but use two variants. The first $(q - q_{pps})$ uses industry segment sales to weigh pure play q_s, while the second $(q - q_{ppa})$ uses industry segment assets.[7] The weights are constructed using Compustat Industry Segment data. Asset weights make more theoretical sense, but Compustat industry segment assets seldom add up to total assets, leaving an overhead to allocate arbitrarily (we divide it proportionally by assets). Segment sales generally add up to total sales, so sales weights avoid this problem. We use inflation adjusted q ratios throughout our 'chop shop' calculations.

Unfortunately, an operational 'chop shop' approach relies on reported industry segment information, and firms have considerable accounting discretion in defining segments. Pacter (1993), Harris (1995), and Hayes and Lundholm (1996) argue that firms strategically increase the number of segments they report. In particular, when overall firm performance is poor top managers add segments so as to isolate poor performance in divisions not run directly by the head office. The ensuing bias in cross-terms is difficult to predict. Furthermore, in constructing such chop-shop qs, we find that a few industries contain no pure-play firms and we have to drop about 5.7 per cent of our sample firms. Omitting firms in these industries might risk omitting instances of the most natural synergies. Fortunately, Lang and Stulz (1994) demonstrate that the 'chop shop' methodology and an approach similar to our first alternative yield similar results.

None of our approaches is wholly satisfactory. We present cross-sectional empirical results using all our various q measures and argue that the consistency of our findings across these different definitions makes a spurious result unlikely.

4.4. Intangibles

We consider intangibles related to R&D and marketing, as these are most frequently connected with economies of scale (Helpman, 1984; Caves, 1986). Following Morck and Yeung (1991), we use research and development spending per dollar of tangible assets (rd/a) to proxy for production related intangibles and advertising spending per dollars of tangible assets (adv/a) to proxy for marketing related intangibles.[8] These variables are again averages for 1976–78. If a firm for which all other accounting data is available does not report R&D or advertising spending, or reports either to be 'nil', the variable in question is set to zero.

We are not able to proxy for intangibles related to superior management or other factors. That is certainly not the most desirable of situations. However, from a practical point of view, firms high on management skills are also high on the ability to produce and market. Hence, our production and marketing intangible proxies may also be capturing superior management. Concerned with the missing variable problem, we examine whether our regressions have a heteroskedasticity problem.

We deliberately omit proxies for 'growth' or 'past success'. It makes sense to include such variables when it is necessary to control for the present value of future growth opportunities in general. Since the purpose of our study is to explore the detailed nature of these growth opportunities, including such broad brush variables is inappropriate and would amount to 'double counting'.

4.5. Control Variables

We control for industry effects with either three digit or four digit primary industry dummies per Standard and Poor's Register of Corporations, Directors and Executives. Controlling for fixed industry effect is a necessity when the dependent variable is a firm's raw q. When the dependent variable is the chop-shop q, it is still useful to include industry dummies to control for remaining fixed effects. Our results based on the chop-shop q_s do not change qualitatively when industry dummies are omitted although the significance level drops slightly.

We also include a capital structure variable, long-term debt per dollar of tangible assets (d/a). This is also an average for 1976–78. We include this variable because intangible assets make poor collateral, so firms whose assets are more tangible may have higher leverage.

4.6. Follow Up Study Variables

We follow our cross section of firms from 1979 to 1985. We opt for this window on the grounds that it is long enough to allow the market for corporate control to function. Too short a window would give us too little M&A activity, while too long a window might let firm characteristics change too much. Also, we stop in 1985 because the market for corporate control changed qualitatively in the late 1980s, possibly due to state anti-takeover laws and the Tax Reform Act of 1986, among other things.[9] To the extent that our window is still too long, this should add noise and reduce the significance of our results. During this period, our sample firms complete 245 domestic acquisitions of publicly traded targets and 110 foreign acquisitions. Meanwhile, 34.5 per cent (441 firms) of our sample firms become take-over targets.

5. Results and Discussion

5.1. Cross-sectional Results

Table 1a displays univariate statistics and Table 1b displays bivariate statistics for our cross section variables. Note first that q is positively correlated with cross-country diversification, but negatively correlated with cross-industry diversification. Also, cross-industry diversification measures are negatively correlated with spending on intangibles, while geographic diversification measures are positively correlated with R&D spending. The observations suggest that geographic and cross-industry diversification is clearly economically significantly different.[10] This portends the possibility that geographic diversification is more synergistic from the internalization perspective, while cross-industry diversification is more fecund with value reducing problems. Note also that firm size is uncorrelated with q. Our measures of intangibles, R&D and advertising over assets, are positively correlated with q and debt is negatively correlated with q.

In Table 2, we display our multivariate cross-sectional regressions, which are of the form

$$q = \sum v_i + \beta_1 \text{Debt}/\text{Assets} + \beta_2 \text{R\&D}/\text{Assets} + \beta_3 \text{Advertising}/\text{Assets}$$
$$+ (\delta_0 + \delta_1 \text{R\&D}/\text{Assets} + \delta_2 \text{Advertising}/\text{Assets})$$
$$\times (\text{cross-industry diversification})$$
$$+ (\gamma_0 + \gamma_1 \text{R\&D}/\text{Assets} + \gamma_2 \text{Advertising}/\text{Assets})$$
$$\times (\text{geographic diversification})$$
$$+ (\eta_0 + \eta_1 \text{R\&D}/\text{Assets} + \eta_2 \text{Advertising}/\text{Assets}) (\text{firm size}) + \varepsilon, \quad (10)$$

where cross-industry diversification is the number of three digit industries the firm operates in, geographic diversification is the number of countries it operates in, and firm size is either sales or the rank transformation of sales. Three digit industry dummies v_i are also included.

First note that the results are consistent across our two definitions of q. We repeated the analysis using a third variant of q, an industry segment assets-based 'chop shop' q (not shown), and also obtained similar results.

Table 1a. Univariate Statistics

	Mean	Standard Deviation	Median	Minimum	Maximum
Scale and scope variables					
Number of 3-digit SIC segments (n3)	3.83	2.59	3	1	12
Number of 4-digit SIC segments (n4)	4.7	3.37	4	1	12
Number of reported 3-digit SIC segments (s3)	1.46	1.06	1	1	9
Number of foreign nations with a subsidiary (nats)	2.79	6.11	0	0	58
Sales (sales)	887	3469	146	0.08	63,221
Firm value measures					
Tobin's q (q)	0.84	0.55	0.68	0.109	3.93
Tobin's q—prim. ind. av. $(q - \mu_q)$	0	0.47	−0.06	−1.27	2.73
Tobin's q—sales weighted average of pure play q's $(q - q_{pps})$	−0.054	0.49	−0.11	−1.57	2.73
Tobin's q—asset weighted average of pure play q's $(q - q_{ppa})$	−0.053	0.49	−0.11	−1.21	2.62
Information-based intangible asset variables					
R&D spending per $ of tangible assets (rd/a)	0.024	0.040	0.009	0	0.359
Advertising spending per $ of tangible assets (adv/a)	0.023	0.056	0.001	0	0.772
Control variables					
Leverage per $ of tangible assets (d/a)	0.25	0.16	0.23	0	0.90

Notes: Sample size: 1277 firms for all variables except for $q - q_{pps}$ and $q - q_{ppa}$, for which only 1205 firms are available; bidder abnormal return, available for 242 bids; bidder return in foreign takeovers which exists for 110 bids; and capital expenditure growth, available for 773 firms.

Table 1b. Simple Correlation Coefficients

	Measures of Scope and Scale					Measures of Firm Value				Intangibles		Debt
	$n3$	$n4$	$s3$	nats	sales	q	$q - \mu q$	$q - q_{pps}$	$q - q_{pp}$	rd/a	adv/a	d/a
$n3$	1.00 (0.00)	0.94 (0.01)	0.23 (0.01)	0.16 (0.01)	0.11 (0.01)	−0.11 (0.01)	−0.08 (0.01)	−0.07 (0.01)	−0.07 (0.01)	−0.09 (0.01)	−0.08 (0.01)	0.05 (0.08)
$n4$		1.00 (0.00)	0.21 (0.01)	0.18 (0.01)	0.14 (0.01)	−0.11 (0.01)	−0.07 (0.01)	−0.06 (0.03)	−0.06 (0.04)	−0.10 (0.01)	−0.07 (0.01)	0.03 (0.25)
$s3$			1.00 (0.00)	<0.01 (0.01)	−0.01 (0.71)	−0.12 (0.01)	−0.11 (0.01)	−0.12 (0.01)	−0.11 (0.01)	−0.09 (0.01)	<0.01 (0.96)	0.05 (0.09)
Nats				1.00 (0.00)	0.34 (0.01)	0.15 (0.01)	0.09 (0.01)	0.10 (0.01)	0.10 (0.01)	0.11 (0.01)	0.03 (0.24)	−0.05 (0.05)
Sales					1.00 (0.00)	−0.01 (0.80)	0.01 (0.73)	0.02 (0.52)	0.02 (0.53)	0.01 (0.75)	−0.02 (0.48)	−0.10 (0.01)
q						1.00 (0.00)	0.86 (−0.01)	0.84 (0.01)	0.84 (0.01)	0.31 (0.01)	0.11 (0.01)	−0.09 (0.01)
$q - \mu q$							1.00 (0.00)	0.96 (0.01)	0.96 (0.01)	0.13 (0.01)	0.02 (0.53)	−0.11 (0.01)
$q - q_{pps}$								1.00 (0.00)	1.00 (0.01)	0.09 (0.01)	−0.001 (0.97)	−0.12 (0.01)
$q - q_{ppa}$									1.00 (0.00)	0.09 (0.01)	−0.001 (0.98)	−0.11 (0.01)
rd/a										1.00 (0.00)	0.09 (0.01)	0.05 (0.11)
adv/a											1.00 (0.00)	−0.06 (0.04)

Sample size: 1277 firms for all variables except for $q - q_{pps}$ and $q - q_{ppa}$, for which only 1205 firms are available. Numbers in parentheses are significance levels. Variables are as defined in panel A of this table.

Table 2. OLS Regression of Tobin's q on Scope and Scale Variables and Cross-terms of these with Proxies for Information-based Intangibles (R&D and Advertising Over Assets) Controlling for Intangibles Levels, Debt, and Three Digit Industry Codes. The Dependent Variable in Regressions 2.1–2.4 is q; in Regressions 2.5 and 2.8 it is q Relative to Segment Sales Weighted Averages of the qs of Undiversified Firms in the Industries in which the Firm Operates

	Inflation Adjusted q Ratio				Segment Sales 'Chop Shop' q Ratio			
	2.1	2.2	2.3[a]	2.4	2.5	2.6	2.7[a]	2.8
δ_0: Cross Industry Diversification number of three digit SIC segments (n3)	−0.030 (−4.08)	−0.028 (−3.76)	−0.027 (−4.38)	−0.027 (−3.67)	−0.030 (−3.82)	−0.028 (−3.55)	−0.028 (−4.11)	−0.027 (−3.47)
δ_1: Cross Industry Diversification × R&D over assets (n3 × RD/A)	0.61 (3.27)	0.40 (2.05)	0.42 (1.97)	0.40 (2.05)	0.61 (3.12)	0.42 (2.05)	0.43 (2.06)	0.42 (2.05)
δ_2: Cross Industry Diversification × Advertising over assets (n3 × Adv/A)	0.18 (1.26)	0.19 (1.39)	0.09 (0.67)	0.16 (1.12)	0.14 (0.94)	0.16 (1.08)	0.04 (0.23)	0.12 (0.81)
γ_0: Geographic Diversification number of foreign nations with a subsidiary (nats)		0.0001 (0.04)	0.0028 (0.58)	0.0011 (0.30)		0.0005 (0.13)	0.0031 (0.61)	−0.0015 (−0.38)
γ_1: Geographic Diversification × R&D over assets (nats × RD/A)		0.19 (2.85)	0.16 (1.79)	0.18 (2.75)		0.16 (2.36)	0.13 (1.37)	0.15 (2.27)
γ_2: Geographic Diversification × Advertising over assets (nats × Adv/A)		0.021 (0.51)	−0.007 (−0.13)	0.003 (0.06)		0.033 (0.78)	0.003 (0.05)	0.014 (0.31)
η_0: Firm Size (size is either sales or a 95th percentile dummy)			−0.00001 (−2.73)	−0.126 (−1.24)			−0.00001 (−2.72)	−0.125 (−1.18)
η_1: Firm Size × R&D budget over assets (size × RD/A)			0.0001 (0.81)	1.70 (0.69)			0.0001 (0.81)	1.73 (0.68)
η_2: Firm Size × Advertising budget over assets (size × Adv/A)			0.0005 (1.79)	3.20 (1.67)			0.0006 (2.06)	3.29 (1.68)
Firm Size Measure Used			Raw	Dummy			Raw	Dummy
β_2: R&D spending per $ of tangible assets (rd/a)	1.01 (1.64)	1.04 (1.69)	1.00 (1.31)	1.03 (1.67)	0.65 (1.03)	0.70 (1.10)	0.65 (0.90)	0.68 (1.07)
β_3: Advertising spending per $ of tangible assets (adv/a)	−0.50 (−1.15)	−0.60 (−1.30)	−0.48 (−0.87)	−0.48 (−1.04)	−0.54 (−1.21)	−0.70 (−1.45)	−0.56 (−0.99)	−0.58 (−1.18)
β_1: Leverage per $ of tangible assets (d/a)	−0.37 (−3.78)	−0.36 (−3.70)	−0.36 (−3.35)	−0.36 (−3.7)	−0.37 (−3.64)	−0.36 (−3.57)	−0.36 (−3.20)	−0.36 (−3.55)
v: three digit industry code dummies	Yes	Yes	Yes	Yes	Yes	Yes	Yes	Yes
R^2	0.297	0.308	0.311	0.310	0.098	0.110	0.116	0.113

Notes:

[a] White (1980) adjusted t-ratios are used for these regressions to control for heteroskedasticity induced by the raw sales variable.

Sample size is 1277 firms for regressions of q, 1205 firms for regressions of q2 qpp.. Numbers in parentheses are t ratios.

Observe that δ_0 is uniformly negative and statistically significant, implying that cross-industry diversification in the absence of information-based intangibles is related to lower share value. In contrast, δ_1 is consistently positive and statistically significant, indicating that cross-industry diversification adds to shareholder value in the presence of R&D related assets. Cross-industry diversification appears less able to add value through advertising related intangibles since δ_2 is insignificant, though its sign is consistently positive.

The regressions in Table 2 use the number of three digit industry codes to measure cross-industry diversification. Using the number of two digit codes, four digit codes, or using the number of industry segments reported all yield similar results. Our results using two digit codes to measure cross-industry diversification merit further mention since diversification across two digit codes is arguably the least related. Using two digit codes, the value of δ_0 is more negative than in Table 2, and remains highly significant. The magnitude δ_1 also rises, and remains statistically significant in all regressions except the analogue of 2.8; δ_2 remains very insignificant and its sign is occasionally negative. All other regression coefficients are not materially affected. If we accept the view that cross-industry diversification into two digit industries is very unrelated, it is unsurprising that δ_0 becomes more negative. However, the finding that δ_1 remains significantly positive adds credence to our internalization argument.

Geographic diversification also adds value mainly in the presence of R&D related intangibles, as γ_1 is consistently positive and significant. Both γ_0 and γ_2 are insignificant, suggesting that geographic diversification in the absence of R&D is valueless, but also innocuous. Similar results follow if we use the number of foreign subsidiaries, rather than the number of countries the firm operates in, to measure geographic diversification.[12]

An F-test rejects the hypothesis that δ_0 and γ_0 are equal. The higher γ_0 indicates that geographic diversification has higher noninternalization related positive synergies while value-reducing agency problems are more prevalent in cross-industry diversification.

Sheer firm size is first measured by total sales. Since including raw sales figures as an independent variable creates heteroskedasticity problems, Table 2 displays consistent standard errors as in White (1980) for these regressions. (The pattern of significance using ordinary standard errors is similar.) In the absence of information-based assets, large firm size is associated with depressed firm value, as η_0 is significantly negative in regressions 2.3 and 2.7. Firm size is correlated with added shareholder value if information-based assets are present, but here advertising related intangibles appear more important than R&D related intangibles. The estimate of η_2 is positive and significant while η_1 is insignificant.

Intriguingly, when we replace sales by its rank, the interaction terms both become insignificant and firm size becomes positively correlated with q.

Replacing sales by its logarithm generates intermediate results with coefficients between those of the raw and rank sales specifications. The rank transformation converts a highly skewed distribution (σ^3/σ^2, $\sigma = 11.9$) to a uniform distribution, reducing the importance of very large firms. The logarithmic transformation similarly pulls in the right tail, though less severely. Apparently, a very large firm size is needed to gain value from a big advertising budget. From this, we conclude that the absolute values of sales, not their relative values, matter; and that most of the explanatory power comes from very large firms whose squared deviations from mean sales are the largest.

Accordingly, we replace sales by a dummy variable set to one if a firm's sales place it in the largest 5 per cent and set to zero otherwise. Regressions using this dummy to measure size are shown in columns 2.4 and 2.8, and mimic the findings in 2.3 and 2.7, though the parameter estimate of η_0 is now insignificant. If we use the largest 1 per cent or the largest 10 per cent, we obtain qualitatively similar results with virtually identical R^2s. Using the top 25 per cent or the top 50 per cent produces results similar to those from the logarithm or rank transformed sales. As a further robustness check, we reproduced all the above calculations using total fixed assets rather than sales as the basic size measure and obtained qualitatively similar results.

5.2. Discussion

A 'first pass' interpretation of our results is that cross-industry diversification, geographic diversification, and sheer size creates value through the internalization of markets for information-based intangibles. However, cross-industry diversification and large size in the absence of such intangibles destroy value—presumably because of heightened agency problems that internal capital market benefits, even if they are present, cannot overcome.

Our findings do not contradict previous results in the literature. Our results say that cross-industry diversification is usually negative. Our regressions are of the form

$$q = (\delta_0 + \delta_1 R\&D/A + \delta_2 Adv/A)$$
$$\times(\text{cross industry diversification}) + \text{other terms.} \quad (11)$$

For cross-industry diversification to create value, it must be the case that

$$\delta_0 + \delta_1 R\&D/A + \delta_2 Adv/A > 0. \quad (12)$$

Assuming δ_2 to be zero since it is statistically insignificant, condition (12) reduces to

$$R\&D/A > -\delta_0/\delta_1. \quad (13)$$

287

If we take averages across all the specifications in Table 2, $-\delta_0/\delta_1$ is about 0.0621. (If we take averages across only regressions 2.3 and 2.7, $-\delta_0/\delta_1$ is 0.0647.) The mean of R&D/A from Table 1 is $\mu_{R\&D} = 0.0239$ and the standard deviation is $\sigma_{R\&D} = 0.0395$. Thus, $-\delta_0/\delta_1$ is roughly equal to the mean R&D spending plus one standard deviation (expressed as percentages of assets). In other words, only a small subset of firms whose

$$R\&D/A > \mu_{R\&D} + \sigma_{R\&D} \tag{14}$$

can add value through cross-industry diversification, and the majority of firms do not. Hence, researchers tend to find that cross-industry diversification is value decreasing on average.

We can use similar procedures to assess whether each firm should diversify geographically or not, and whether each firm should seek to achieve great size. We can classify our firms as to whether or not they should acquire each of our three dimensions of scope and scale; and whether they have already done so or not. Such classifications are shown in Table 3.[13]

Panel A of Table 3 shows that firms whose past diversification destroyed shareholder value outnumber by roughly ten to one firms whose diversification added to shareholder value. Indeed, having potential value decline from diversification is actually significantly correlated with being diversified ($t = 3.85$).[14] This is consistent with Lang and Stulz (1994), Berger and Ofek (1995, 1996), John and Ofek (1995), Servaes (1996), Stein (1997), Denis et al. (1997), Rajan et al. (1997), Shin and Stulz (1997), and Scharfstein (1997), and others. Our results suggest that cross-industry diversification is associated with value destruction in most cases because most diversified firms do not possess adequate intangible assets.

However, we can also reconcile this literature on value creating diversification with Rumelt (1982), Schipper and Thompson (1983), Matsusaka (1993), Hubbard and Palia (1997), and others, who find that cross-industry diversification can add value. In particular, our findings support the view of Matsusaka (1997) that specific synergies may exist between firms in different industries, and that diversifying firms are searching for these. Our results suggest that these synergies generally involve applying intangibles from one industry in another.

If we assume that the negative relationship of scale and scope variables with firm value is due to dominant agency and influence cost problems, the contrast between Panel A and the remaining panels in Table 3 suggests that these problems are less common in geographical diversification and horizontal expansion than in cross-industry diversification. Unlike cross-industry diversification, geographic diversification is significantly more prevalent ($t = 8.00$) among firms that possess intangibles that make such diversification an asset. Large size is also significantly more common ($t = 3.00$) among firms that possess intangibles that

Table 3. The Relationship between Value Enhancing Potential in Cross-Industry Diversification, Geographic Diversification and Sheer Size and Actual Cross Industry Diversification, Geographic Diversification and Firm Size. Panels Contain Numbers of Firms in Each Category.

Panel A		Firm is diversified across industries	
		Yes	No
Should be diversified across industries?	Yes	92	46
	No	919	220

Panel B		Firm is diversified across countries	
		Yes	No
Should be diversified across industries?	Yes	419	410
	No	125	323

Panel C		Is larger than industry average?	
		Yes	No
Should be larger than industry average?	Yes	115	199
	No	267	696

would render large size an asset. While the number of value destroying cross-industry diversification is ten times the number of value creating cross-industry diversification, the number of value creating geographic diversification is 3.5 times the number of value destroying geographic diversification. Indeed, unwarranted cross-industry diversification is 72 per cent of the sample while unwarranted geographical diversification and sheer size expansion are, respectively, only 10 and 21 per cent of the sample. The foreign direct investment literature emphasizes that local incumbents have a daunting home turf advantage over foreign entrants. Perhaps, the difficulties in breaking into foreign markets are a blessing in disguise; as they deter value decreasing geographic diversification.

5.3. Follow Up Study Results

We conduct a follow up study on whether the market for corporate control disciplines unwarranted diversification and encourages synergy-creating diversification as depicted in Table 3. We focus on the market for corporate control because it is a clear indicator of strategies designed to quickly alter

Randall Morck and Bernard Yeung

firms' boundaries in scope and scale. We follow the firms of our 1978 cross-section until 1985 (i.e. the window is from 1979 to 1985).[15] We note in Table 4 what sorts of corporate control transactions they become involved in.

Table 4. Successful Corporate Control Transactions Involving Firms in the Cross-Section Sample and Occurring between 1979 and 1985

Panel A		Is diversified across industries?		
		Yes	No	
Should be diversified across industries?	Yes	4.35	0.00	% launching takeovers
		4.35	6.52	% that are target of successful hostile takeover
		26.1	37.0	% that are target of successful friendly merger
		3.4	43.5	% that are target of successful control transaction
		(92)	(46)	Number of firms in subsample
	No	8.92	2.73	% launching takeovers
		10.70	6.36	% that are target of successful hostile takeover
		23.0	31.8	% that are target of successful friendly merger
		33.6	38.2	% that are target of successful control transaction
		(919)	(220)	Number of firms in subsample

Panel B		Is diversified across countries?		
		Yes	No	
Should be diversified across countries?	Yes	12.6	9.51	% launching foreign takeovers
		9.31	11.2	% that are target of successful hostile takeover
		22.9	28.8	% that are target of successful friendly merger
		32.2	39.0	% that are target of successful control transaction
		(419)	(410)	Number of firms in subsample
	No	11.2	4.02	% launching foreign takeovers
		12.0	7.13	% that are target of successful hostile takeover
		15.2	27.6	% that are target of successful friendly merger
		27.2	34.7	% that are target of successful control transaction
		(125)	(323)	Number of firms in subsample

Panel C		Is larger than industry average?		
		Yes	No	
Should be larger than industry average?	Yes	17.4	5.53	% launching takeovers
		2.36	3.30	% annual growth rate in inflation adjusted assets
		17.4	11.1	% that are target of successful hostile takeover
		15.7	32	% that are target of successful friendly merger
		33.0	41.2	% that are target of successful control transaction
		(115)	(199)	Number of firms in subsample
	No	17.2	5.03	% launching takeovers
		1.48	2.84	% annual growth rate in inflation adjusted assets
		13.5	5.89	% that are target of successful hostile takeover
		18.4	28.0	% that are target of successful friendly merger
		31.8	33.9	% that are target of successful control transaction
		(267)	(696)	Number of firms in subsample

Panel A of Table 4 shows that 8.92 per cent of the firms that should not have diversified across industries, but did anyway, undertook further cross-industry takeovers. In comparison, significantly fewer other firms, only 2.73 per cent, undertook diversifying takeover bids ($t = 3.82$). Surprisingly, none of the firms that should be diversified across industries, but are not, diversified via takeovers. This is significantly below the 7.47 per cent average rate across the other categories ($t = 1.93$). If our interpretation of our cross-section results holds, the market for corporate control is facilitating value destroying takeovers and failing to spur value creating ones here. Alternatively, the targets of these takeovers may possess the information-based intangibles the firm needs to turn its diversified structure into an asset.

However, 10.7 per cent of our 919 improperly diversified firms become the targets of hostile takeovers versus a significantly lower ($t = 2.65$) hostile takeover rate of 5.87 per cent among all other firms.[16] These improperly diversified firms are also significantly less likely than other firms to become the targets of friendly mergers (23 per cent vs 31.0 per cent, $t = 2.98$). In contrast, the 46 firms that should diversify across industries but have not are significantly more likely than other firms to become the targets of friendly takeovers (37 per cent vs 24.8 per cent, $t = 1.87$). These results are consistent with the market for corporate control targeting both excessively and insufficiently cross-industry diversified firms, via hostile and friendly takeovers, respectively.

Panel B of Table 4 shows that firms which have not diversified geographically, but should, are more likely than other firms to become friendly merger targets (28.8 per cent vs 23.5 per cent, $t = 2.02$). They are also more likely than other geographically undiversified firms to make a first foreign acquisition: 9.51 per cent do so versus 4.02 per cent ($t = 2.89$). Firms that have diversified geographically, but should not have, are not significantly more likely than other firms to become hostile takeover targets, but are significantly less likely to be friendly merger targets (15.2 per cent vs 26.3 per cent, $t = 2.72$). These results are consistent with the market for corporate control acting to correct a lack of geographic diversification when geographic diversification would add value, but not to correct excess geographic diversification.

Panel C shows that the 199 small firms with potential synergies from size expansion are less likely than other firms to carry out takeovers ($t = 1.61$). These firms' capital expenditure budgets are higher than those of other firms (3.30 per cent of assets vs 2.45 per cent for other firms), but the difference is statistically insignificant. Still, these 199 prime candidates for expansion are significantly more likely than other firms to become takeover targets (41.2 per cent vs 33.3 per cent, $t = 2.16$), and this is primarily due to more becoming friendly merger targets (32 per cent vs 24.3 per cent, $t = 1.75$). They are not significantly more likely than other firms to become hostile takeover targets. Again, friendly mergers appear to be used to capture unexploited synergies.

In contrast, the 267 firms with insufficient synergy producing intangibles to justify a large scale of operations have smaller capital budgets (1.48 per cent of assets vs 2.88 per cent for other firms) and this difference is statistically significant ($t = 2.01$). They are, however, more likely than other firms to launch takeover bids (17.2 per cent vs 6.53 per cent, $t = 5.28$). They are also much more likely than other firms to become hostile takeover targets (13.5 per cent vs 8.12 per cent, $t = 2.64$) and much less likely to become friendly merger targets (18.4 per cent vs 27.4 per cent, $t = 2.91$). However, large firms that should not be large are less likely than large firms that should be large to become hostile takeover targets and more likely to become friendly takeover targets. Hence, the success the market for corporate control in disciplining larger firms that should not be large is not clear-cut.

5.4. Conjecture

Previous studies show that markets valued diversification across industries more highly in earlier decades than now. Our findings suggest where to seek reasons for this change. If the value of diversification depends on a trade-off between its ability to add value by leveraging the use of information-based assets (and/or providing an internal capital market) and the value it costs by exacerbating agency problems, regime changes that affect this trade-off should affect the value of diversification. The following is therefore our conjecture.

In the 1970s, markets for information-based goods were less developed than now, especially outside the United States and a few other advanced economies. This made internalizing the markets for these assets essential to achieving their full value. Consequently, a very large scale and scope of operations was especially important—and valuable—for an innovating firm possessing considerable intangibles then. Thus, by investigating the value of internalization using 1978 data, we have stacked the cards in favour of finding a value premium associated with geographical and industry diversification for innovative firms possessing considerable intangibles. We conjecture that this internalization-related value premium should change over time as institutions change. In particular, the solidification of intellectual property rights protection makes licensing agreements, joint ventures and the like more realistic as alternative ways to increase the scale and scope of application of an intangible. Increased transparency due to better accounting standards, more sophisticated investors, and more competition by institutions for their savings may also have created a world in which agency problems are more obvious than they once were. Consequently, the evolution of this value premium over time is itself an interesting question. It seems plausible that these sorts of changes have encouraged firms to rely more arm's-length transactions to leverage the value of their intangibles, and that the value of internalization has consequently diminished.[17] Value-enhancing diversification, geographic and cross industry, may thus have become steadily rarer. In the limit, value-destroying diversification alone might remain.

Our findings echo theories about 'internal capital market synergy'. In the 1960s and early 1970s, financial markets and institutions were less developed than now, and regulations made external financing costly and time consuming. Head office financial management, acting as an internal bank, might have been an intangible asset then—adding value when applied across larger scales or broader scopes of operation. Now, with financial markets deregulated and better developed, centralized financing has less value and the trade-off has shifted. Reducing agency and influence cost problems might have come to dominate this trade-off, and increased focus is now in order. In countries with poorly developed financial systems and little protection for intellectual property, diversification across industries continues to add value (Khanna and Palepu, 1997).

5.5. Caveats

This research is suggestive in nature and clearly preliminary. We highlight some caveats. The notable feature of the regression results in Table 2 is that diversification is associated with higher firm value only for firms with adequate intangible assets, and is associated with lower firm value for other firms. Our interpretation, which what 'internalization' predicts, is that diversification *per se* is on average value decreasing, but that greater scale and scope operations are appropriate and value enhancing for firms possessing considerable intangible assets. We want to be cautious on the robustness of our interpretation. Moreover, we hasten to point out that our results do not imply a particular causality claim, though they do render some causality stories unlikely.

For example, it has been suggested that our result is consistent with higher q firms being more diversified and therefore less capital constrained, and that this accounts for their higher R&D spending. Contrary to the idea, Table 1*b* shows higher q firms to be less diversified across industries, and shows firms that are highly diversified across industries to spend less on R&D. Moreover, this causality chain does not explain why many diversified firms exhibit a diversification value discount while a minority of diversified firms does not.

One interpretation is that high q firms are more diversified first and then spend more on intangibles. Our cross-sectional regression will not shed light on the time sequence of diversification and investment on intangibles. In a study focusing only on geographic diversification, Mitchell *et al.* (1998) use a Granger causality test to show that firms tend to diversify geographically before they increase their spending on intangibles. However, they show that while the investment in intangibles is necessary to increase firm profits, geographic diversification alone is not. Moreover, Morck and Yeung (1992) show that the abnormal stock return on days when US firms announce foreign acquisition bids is positively related to past spending on intangibles. These results unambiguously suggest that greater scale and scope operations are value enhancing for firms possessing considerable intangible assets, which is what 'internalization' predicts.

Another spin on our findings is that they are consistent with low q firms that have few intangibles using diversification to search for a 'right' industry match (Matsusaka, 1997), while high q firms with copious intangibles find that their capabilities match with many industries and thus are more diversified.

Our results do not imply that sheer investment in R&D and advertising spending necessarily make size growth and diversification value enhancing. R&D and advertising spending can be excessive or misdirected. Also, poor management can squander such investment. We use R&D and advertising spending only to proxy for actual intangible assets related to production and marketing. If there were better proxies, we would prefer to use them. Using past R&D and advertising spending to proxy for production and marketing intangibles is a common practice that has generated consistent results. However, that merely means excessive or misdirected R&D and advertising spending is not common enough to render the proxies ineffective. Shooting for the proxies *per se* does not necessarily lead to true possession of the underlying intangibles.

We may have omitted other types of intangibles in our study. For example, we have not been able to capture management skills in this study. However, to the extent that firms possessing high management skills also possess high production and marketing skills, our production and marketing intangible proxies may have captured high management skills too. Omitting important intangibles leads to a missing variable problem that causes heteroskedasticity. We therefore use White's (1980) heteroskedasticity consistent t-tests wherever necessary.

In our follow-up study, our main claim is that firms that should not diversify, but have, are more likely to become hostile takeover targets; while firms that should be diversified, but have not, are more likely to become friendly takeover targets. To the extent that, in the early 1980s, hostile takeovers were a mechanism for increasing corporate focus, and friendly takeovers a way of achieving synergies, the market for corporate control is consistent with our assessment of which firms' boundaries should expand and which firms' boundaries should shrink.

However, to convincingly argue that the market for corporate control appropriately redefines firm boundaries, we need more information. For instance, we would like to check whether under-diversified firms are acquired by diversified firms and/or they experience active diversification after being taken over. Also, we would like to check whether firms with excess diversification are acquired by firms with high level of intangibles and/or they experience active divestiture after being taken over.

The existing literature, however, contains useful information. Mitchell and Lehn (1990) shows that firms that make value reducing acquisitions subsequently tend to become takeover targets themselves. Moreover, the subsequent acquirers then tend to divest the target's value decreasing acquisitions. Berger and Ofek (1996) find that diversification value discount increases the likelihood of being taken over. Furthermore, in a sub-sample of large diversified targets, a greater diversification discount is correlated with more extensive post-takeover divestiture activity, which generally results in divested divisions being operated as parts of focused firms. Daley *et al.* (1997) find that cross-industry spin-offs generate value for the divesting firm, but same industry spin-offs do not. This is associated with improved operating performance in the divesting firm following cross-industry spin-offs.

6. Conclusions

Our findings support the view that synergy derives, at least in part, from the wider application of information-based intangible assets, such as those stemming from investment in production and marketing skills. Because they are information-based, such assets can be profitably applied to multiple businesses and locations simultaneously. As they are nonrivalrous goods, their use in one place does not physically preclude their simultaneous use elsewhere. These assets thus have large returns to scale and scope. However, high transaction costs due to information asymmetry make capturing these returns difficult via arm's-length contracts. A solution for a firm to obtain value from expanding the application of its intangibles to other firms' operations is to 'internalize' the market for these intangibles by acquiring the productive assets of the other firms.

We find that cross-industry diversification is correlated with higher shareholder value if the diversifying firm has substantial information-based intangible assets. Otherwise, cross-industry diversification is correlated with lower shareholder value. Geographic diversification is also accompanied by increased share value when information-based intangibles are present, but has little relationship with value otherwise. Sheer firm size is related to depressed share values in the absence of intangibles, but to higher share values in their presence. Intangibles related to R&D seem most important in adding value to cross-industry and geographical diversification. Intangibles related to advertising seem most important in forging value from sheer firm size. From these findings, we infer that expanded scale and scope may add value in the presence of information-based intangible assets, but may destroy value otherwise.

To further validate our results, we conduct a follow up study on our sample firms. Firms with substantial intangibles, but that had not diversified across industries, diversified geographically, or become very large, were designated as having untapped diversification benefits. They were significantly more likely than other firms to become the targets of friendly takeovers. Friendly takeovers in the 1980s were seldom used as disciplinary devices, but instead appear to have been aimed at achieving synergies. From this, we conclude that synergy in a takeover is related to the target having substantial intangible assets while also being small or undiversified.

Firms that had initially been diversified across industries, but that had relatively few intangible assets, were designated as having unwarranted diversification. These firms were significantly more likely than other firms to become hostile takeover targets. Since hostile takeovers in the early 1980s were a means of increasing corporate focus, this suggests that the market for corporate control viewed diversification as a cause of low share value in these firms.

An interesting observation in our study is that, at the end of the 1970s, there was too little geographic diversification, in that many firms with adequate intangibles that should have diversified geographically did not. At the same time, there was too much cross-industry diversification in the sense that many firms without adequate intangibles were diversified across industries. The wave of foreign direct investment by US firms and the surge of foreign acquisition in the United States may be the market's response to the untapped geographic diversification potential. At the same time, our follow-up study suggests domestic hostile takeovers were a disciplinary response to unwarranted diversification.

We conclude that cross-industry diversification, geographic diversification, and firm size add value in the presence of intangibles related to R&D or advertising, but destroy value in their absence. This is consistent with synergy stemming from the internalization of markets for information-based assets. It is also consistent with the view that M&A synergies come from some matches, but not others. However, the requirement is not that the two firms must be in the same industry or country, but that one firm's operations can be improved by applying the R&D or advertising related intangibles of the other. This supports Livermore (1935), who found a similar relationship between intangible assets, like R&D or advertising, and superior post-takeover firm performance in the United States 'turn of the century' merger wave.

The corporate diversification problem is important because it addresses precisely why some firms should control more resources while others should control fewer. The efficient allocation of resources is a fundamental concern in economics. Our results suggest that firms with more information-based capabilities ought to control more resources. From a managerial perspective, the suggestion is that the development and possession of information-based capabilities is the critical element in value enhancing firm growth. From a macroeconomic perspective, this is consistent with information-based assets enhancing the productivity of other inputs, as in the endogenous growth models of Romer (1986) and others.

Finally, our results are a snapshot of a fluid trade-off. Faced with transactions difficulties in appropriating the value of intangibles, firms resort to 'internalize' the markets for their intangibles. But firms' ability to appropriate the value of intangibles via arm's-length transaction increases as property rights are better protected and as firms develop the skills to use contractual arrangement to protect their property rights. Furthermore, as the number of players in a market increases (as the market becomes 'deeper'), the market becomes a more effective disciplinary device to mitigate opportunistic behaviour. This further raises the reliability of arm's-length transactions. Licensing agreements and the like plausibly became more realistic options, and internalization less essential. Increased transparency due to better accounting standards, more sophisticated investors, and more competition for their savings may also more clearly expose agency problems. Thus, the value premium associated with internalization value is likely to change over time, and a steady decline seems plausible. That is, value-enhancing diversification may have become steadily more rare over time.

....

Notes

1. The literature is very voluminous. We shall therefore just list some examples without trying to be all-inclusive.

2. Jensen (1989) argues that diversification became bad only in the 1980s. Schipper and Thompson (1983) show that in earlier period announcement returns for diversifying acquisitions are positive. Matsusaka (1993) and Hubbard and Palia (1997) find that bidder announcement returns for diversifying acquisitions are positive in the 1960s. Morck et al. (1990) find that stock returns to diversifying takeovers are statistically indistinguishable from zero in the 1970s but become negative in the 1980s. Matsusaka (1993) suggests that his results are consistent with the hypothesis that in the earlier periods the market favored acquisitions intended to exploit managerial synergies. For thorough reviews, see Montgomery (1994) and Matsusaka (1997).

3. From this perspective, we ought not believe that diversification always creates or destroys value. A sub-optimal firm boundary is a disequilibrium phenomenon that should not last. Some may argue that diversification reflects a firm life cycle: start-ups are more focused and more mature firms are more diversified. The former is more likely to have a firm value premium and the latter is more likely to suffer from agency discount. While plausible, the idea cannot explain why a collection of equally mature and large firms show both diversification discount and premium. To explain the observations, the firm life cycle idea has to be combined with a theory on the determination of firm boundary.

4. See Caves (1986: ch. 1) for a more thorough and comprehensive overview of the economics presented here. The importance of the internalization theory of synergy has been empirically verified in the context of geographic diversification (Morck and Yeung, 1991, 1992). With some modifications, its logic should also apply to firms operating within a large country such as the United States.

5. In the business strategy literature, many types of intangibles are part of capabilities embedded in a business organization that cannot be easily identified and are often nonextractible from an organization so that arms-length transactions of these capabilities are impossible. See, for example, Teece *et al.* (1997) and Kogut and Zander (1992).

6. Type III firms are those with unwarranted diversification that is the focus of the diversification value discount literature. Type II firms experience under-investment. Under-investment can be due to a variety of reasons, for example, investment capital constraints.

7. Some industries do not have pure play firms. It is possible to infer their pure play q, however. Suppose industry A does not have pure play firms. Yet, there are firms operating in both industry A and B and industry B has pure play firms. We can then use these diversified firms = qs, their segment weights, and industry B's pure play q to infer industry A's pure play q. The procedure allows us to identify most industries' pure play q. We drop firms affected by industries for which we cannot infer their pure play qs. We lose 73 out of 1277 observations (5.7%). The problem with this procedure is that it assumes away any diversification discount for industries with no pure play firms. The advantage is that it allows us to keep most of the sample.

8. Using sales instead of total dollars of tangible assets to scale research and development and advertising spending does not affect our results.

9. See Mikkelson and Partch (1997).

10. The preliminary results are consistent with known empirical results. For example, Harris and Ravenscraft (1991), and Kang (1993) and others find generally positive bidder returns in foreign acquisitions. In contrast, Asquith *et al.* (1983) and others consistently report negative or zero event day returns for bidders in domestic acquisitions.

11. See Note 10.

12. The results are consistent with studies of the impact of international acquisition on firm value. Doukos and Travlos (1988), Morck and Yeung (1992), Kang (1993), and others find that bidder returns in foreign acquisitions tend to be positive, in contrast to the negative or zero returns that Asquith *et al.* (1983) and others find for bidders in domestic acquisitions. Consistent with this being due to internalization, Harris and Ravenscraft (1991) and others find that cross-border takeovers are more concentrated in R&D-intensive industries than are domestic acquisitions. Consistent with this reflecting internalization, Morck and Yeung (1991, 1992) find that geographic diversification adds value when the diversifying firm has substantial intangible, information-based assets, but destroys value otherwise. Harris and Ravenscraft (1991) also find that most international M&A activity is horizontal takeovers.

13. The classification is based on the average of the regression coefficients in regressions 2.3, 2.4, 2.7, and 2.8. (Using only regression coefficients in regression 2.3 and 2.7 yield similar results.) For each company, we construct an estimate as depicted in (12). We

recognize that some of these point estimates are not statistically significant. Keeping them in the sample adds noise to our classifications and thus to our follow-up study. The noise will make statistical significant results in our follow-up study less likely and thus finding such results is particularly noteworthy.

14. The t-ratio of 3.85 is from a t-test to reject the hypothesis that $b1 = 0$ in the OLS regression $d0 = b0 + b1.d1 + e$ where $d0$ is a dummy variable set to one if the relevant coefficients in Table 2 indicate, on average, that the firm should diversify, and set to zero otherwise; and where $d1$ is a dummy set to one if the firm is already diversified and to zero otherwise. A t-test to reject $b1 = 0$ is algebraically equivalent to an F-test in an ANOVA setting to reject the hypothesis that the fraction of diversified firms that should be diversified equals the fraction of undiversified firms that should be diversified. More complex χ^2 tests yield virtually identical confidence levels. This footnote applies to other t-tests we report subsequently.

15. The length of the follow up window, as we have discussed, is decided on the grounds that it is long enough to allow the market for corporate control to function. Too short a window would give us too little M&A activity, while too long a window might let firm characteristics change too much. Also, we stop in 1985 because the market for corporate control changed in the late 1980s due to state antitakeover laws and the Tax Reform Act of 1986.

16. Our result here is consistent with Berger and Ofek (1996) who show that diversification value discount attracts takeovers. One purpose of our follow-up study is to validate our regression result which supports that diversification augments (decreases) firm value when it is conducted by firms with sufficient (insufficient) intangibles. We identify improperly diversified firms as those that do not have sufficient intangibles to warrant diversification, which is our explanation for diversification value discount.

17. Christophe (1997) reproduces the 1970s findings of Morck and Yeung (1991), but finds that their result no longer exists in the 1980s, and concludes that this is due to increased exchange rate volatility. Without contradicting this, our findings suggest that better international intellectual property rights protection might be an additional factor.

....

References

Asquith, Paul R., R. F. Brunner, and David W. Mullins (1983), 'The gains to bidding firms from merger', *Journal of Financial Economics*, 11: 121–39.

Bagwell, Laurie Simon and Josef Zechner (1993), 'Influence costs and capital structure', *Journal of Finance*, 48(3): 975–1008.

Baumol, William (1959), *Business Behavior: Value and Growth* (Macmillian: New York).

Berger, Philip G. and Eli Ofek (1996), 'Bustup takeover of value-destroying diversified firms', *Journal of Finance*, 51(4): 1175–200.

——(1995), 'Diversification's effect on firm value', *Journal of Financial Economics*, 37(1): 39–65.

Buckley, Peter J. and Mark Casson (1976) *The Economic Theory of the Multinational Enterprise* (Macmillan: London).

Caves, Richard (1971), 'International corporations: The industrial economics of foreign investment', *Economica*, 38: 1–27.

——(1986), *Multinational Enterprise and Economic Activity* (Cambridge: University Press).

Coase, Ronald H. (1937), 'The nature of the firm', *Economica* 4: 386–405.

Christophe, Stephen (1997), 'Hysteresis and the value of the US Multinational Corporation', *Journal of Business*, 70(3): 435–62.

Daley, Lane, Vikas Mehrotra, and Ranjini Sivakumar (1997), 'Corporate focus and value creation: Evidence from spin-offs', *Journal of Financial Economics*, 45: 257–81.

Demetz, Harold (1988), 'The theory of the firm revisited', in Ch. 9, *Ownership Control and the Firm: the Organization of Economic Activity*, Vol. 1 (Cambridge, MA: Basil Blackwell Ltd). (1990 paper back edition).

Denis, David J., Diane K. Denis, and Atulya Sarin (1997), 'Agency problems, equity ownership, and corporate diversification', *Journal of Finance*, 52(1): 135–16.

Dunning, John (1977), 'Trade, location of economic activity and the MNE: A search for an eclectic approach', in B. Ohlin, P.-O. Hesselborn, and Wijkman, P. M. (eds) *The International Allocation of Economic Activity: Proceedings of a Nobel Symposium Held at Stockholm*, (London: Macmillan), pp. 395–418.

Gertner, Robert H., David Scharfstein, and Jeremy C. Stein (1994), 'Internal versus external capital markets', *Quarterly Journal of Economics*, 109(4): 1211–30.

——(1988), 'The manufacturing sector master file', Palo Alto N.B.E.R. technical paper, Stanford.

——(1993), 'The stock market's valuation of R&D investment during the 1980's', *American Economic Review*, 83(2): 259–64.

Harris, Mary Stanford (1995) 'Economic factors affecting managers' business segment reporting choices', unpublished manuscript, Pennsylvania State University.

Harris, Robert S. and Josef Zechner (1991) 'The role of acquisitions in foreign direct investment: Evidence from the U.S. stock market', *Journal of Finance*, 46(3): 825–44.

Harris, Robert and David Ravenscroft (1991), 'The role of acquisitions in foreign direct investment: Evidence from the U.S. stock market', *Journal of Finance*, 46: 825–44.

Hayes, Rachel M. and Russell Lundholm (1996), 'Segment reporting to the capital market in the presence of a competitor', *Journal of Accounting Research*, 34: 261–79.

Helpman, Elhanan (1984), 'A simple theory of international trade with multinational corporations', *Journal of Political Economy*, 92: 451–71.

Hubbard, R. Glenn and Darius Palia (1997), A re-examination of the conglomerate merger wave in the 1960s: An internal capital markets view', Columbia University.

Jensen, Michael C. (1989), 'Eclipse of the public corporation', *Harvard Business Review*, 67(5): 61–74.

——(1986), 'Agency costs of free cash flow, corporate finance, and takeovers', *American Economic Review*, 76(2): 323–29.

—— and Murphy Kevin J. (1990), 'Performance pay and top-management incentives', *Journal of Political Economy*, 98(2): 225–64.

John, Kose and Eli Ofek (1995), 'Asset sales and increase in focus', *Journal of Financial Economics*, 37(1): 105–26.

Kang, Jun-Koo (1993), 'The international market for corporate control: Mergers and acquisitions of U.S. firms by Japanese firms', *Journal of Financial Economics*, 34(3): 345–71.

Khanna, Tarun and Krishna Palepu (1997), 'Why focused strategies may be wrong for emerging markets', *Harvard Business Review*, 75(4): 41–51.

Kogut, Bruce and U. Zander (1992), 'Knowledge of the firm, combinative capabilities and the replication of technology', *Organization Science*, 3: 383–97.

Lang, H. P. Larry and Rene M. Stulz (1994), 'Tobin's q, corporate diversification, and firm performance', *Journal of Political Economy*, 102(6): 1248–8.

LeBaron, Dean and Lawrence S. Speidell (1987), 'Why are the parts worth more than the sum? "Chop Shop," a corporate valuation model', in Lynn E., Browne and Eric S. Rosengren (eds) *The Merger Boom* Conference Series, no. 31 (Boston: Fed. Reserve Bank).

Linderberg, B. Eric, and Stephen Ross (1981), 'Tobin's q ratio and industrial organization', *Journal of Business*, 54: 1–32.

Livermore, Shaw (1935), 'The success of industrial mergers', *Quarterly Journal of Economics*, 68–96.

Martin, J. Kenneth, and John J. McConnell (1991), 'Corporate performance, corporate takeovers, and management turnover', *Journal of Finance*, 46(2): 671–87.

Matsusaka, G. John (1997), 'Corporate diversification, value maximization, and organizational capabilities', University of Southern California.

——(1993a), 'Takeover motives during the conglomerate merger wave', *Rand Journal of Economics* Autumn, 24(3): 357–79.

——(1993b), 'Target profits and managerial discipline during the conglomerate merger wave', *Journal of Industrial Economics*, 41(2): 179–89.

Mikkelson, H. Wayne, and M. Megan Partch (1997), 'The decline of takeovers and disciplinary managerial turnover', *Journal of Financial Economics*, 44(2): 205–28.

Mitchell, L. Mark, and Kenneth Lehn (1990), 'Do bad bidders become good targets'? *Journal of Political Economy*, 98(2): 372–98.

Mitchell, Will, Randall Morck, Myles Shaver, and Bernard Yeung (1998), 'Causality between international expansion and investment in intangibles, with implications for financial performance and firm survival', in J.-F. Hennert (ed.) *Global Competition and Market Entry Strategies* (Elsevier: North-Holland).

Montgomery, Cythnia (1994), 'Corporate diversification', *Journal of Economic Perspectives*, 8(3): 163–78.

Montgomery, Cynthia and Birger Wernerfelt (1988), 'Tobin's q and the importance of focus in firm performance', *American Economic Review*, 78(1): 246–50.

Morck, Randall and Bernard Yeung (1991), 'Why investors value multinationality', *Journal of Business*, 64(2): 165–87.

——(1992), 'Internalization: An event study test', *Journal of International Economics*, 33: 41–56.

Morck, Randall, Andrei Shleifer, and Robert Vishny (1990), 'Do managerial objectives drive bad acquisitions', *Journal of Finance*, 45(1): 31–48.

Myers, C. Stewart, and Nicholas S. Majluf (1984), 'Corporate financing and investment decisions when firms have information that investors do not have', *Journal of Financial Economics*, 13(2): 187–221.

Pacter, Paul (1993), 'Reporting disaggregated information', *Financial Accounting Standards Board, 123-A*, FASB.

Palia, Darius (1998), 'Corporate governance and the diversification discount', University of Chicago, mimeo.

Penrose, E. T. (1959), The theory of the growth of the firm, Oxford University Press: Oxford.

Prahalad, C. K. (1998), 'Growth strategies', *Executive Excellence*, 15(1): 6–7.

Rajan, Raghu, Henri Servaes, and Luigi Zingales (1997), 'Conglomerate discount and inefficient investment', University of Chicago, working paper.

Rugman, Alan M. (1980), 'Internalization as a general theory of foreign direct investment', *Weltwirtschaftliches Archiv*, 365–79.

Rumelt, Richard P. (1982), 'Diversification strategy and profitability', *Strategic Management Journal*, 3(4): October, 359–69.

Romer, Paul M. (1986), 'Increasing returns and long run growth', *Journal of Political Economy*, 1002–37.

Scharfstein, David (1997), 'The dark side of internal capital markets II', MIT, working paper.

—— and Stein, J. (1998), 'The dark side of internal capital markets: Divisional rent-seeking and inefficient investment', MIT, working paper.

Schipper, Katherine and Rex Thompson (1983), 'Evidence on the capitalized value of merger activity for acquiring firms', *Journal of Financial Economics*, 11: 85–119.

Schumpeter, Joseph A. (1942), *Capitalism, Socialism and Democracy* (New York: Harper and Brothers).

Servaes, Henri (1996), 'The value of diversification during the conglomerate merger wave', *Journal of Finance*, 51(4): 1201–25.

Shin Hyun-Han and René M. Stulz (1997), 'Are internal capital markets efficient'? Ohio State University, working paper.

Stein, Jeremy C. (1997), 'Internal capital markets and the competition for corporate resources'. *Journal of Finance* 52(1): 111–33.

Teece, David J., G. Pisano, and A. Shuen, (1997), 'Dynamic capabilities and strategic management', *Strategic Management Journal*, 18.

Tobin, James and William Brainard (1977), 'Asset markets and the cost of capital', in R. Nelson and B. Balassa (ed.) *Economic Progress, Private Values and Public Policy: Essays in Honor of William Fellner* (Amsterdam: North Holland).

White, H. (1980), 'A heteroskedasticity-consistent covariance matrix estimator and a direct test for heteroskedasticity', *Econometrica*, 48: 817–38.

## 12

The Increasing Returns-to-scale of Intangibles[1]

John R. M. Hand

1. Introduction and Summary of Findings

During the 1990s, the US economy enjoyed its longest expansion ever. This success is most often attributed to a set of micro- and macroeconomic factors that have been labelled as the New Economy. Among these factors, many businesspeople and economists argue that in particular intangibles have over time come to play a more central role in creating value (Boulton *et al.*, 2000; Lev, 2000, 2001) because of the strong opportunities that successful investments in intangibles can provide for firms to obtain increasing profitability returns-to-scale (De Long, 1998; Shapiro and Varian, 1999; Lev, 2000; Noe and Parker, 2001; Hand, 2002*a*).

The goal of this paper is to determine the extent to which large-sample evidence confirms or denies this view. My method centers on estimating the ex post net present value (NPV) profitability of expenditures three key unrecognized intangibles—R&D, advertising, and personnel—for the universe of publicly traded US firms over the past two decades. I choose these intangibles over patents, customer service, and strategic alliances because they are more similarly defined and measured across firms and their costs are required to be disclosed when material. The proxies I use for investments in R&D, advertising, and personnel intangibles are the annual expenditures recorded by Compustat as having been made by firms on their R&D, advertising, and general and administrative activities, respectively.

I use the estimated NPVs to test four major predictions that arise from the hypothesis that intangibles and their potential to create increasing profitability

303

returns-to-scale now play a central role in creating value. First, if intangibles create value, then they will have nonnegative NPVs. Second, if intangibles today create more value than they did in the past, then their NPVs will on average have increased over time. Third, if intangibles result in increasing profitability returns-to-scale, then their NPVs per-dollar-of-investment will increase as the scale of the investment made in them increases. Fourth, if intangibles exhibit more intense profitability returns-to-scale today than they did in the past, then that should be apparent in the data.

I estimate the ex post NPV profitability of expenditures on intangibles using more than 61,000 firm-year observations over the period 1980–2000. Without imposing a particular coefficient lag structure, I regress current year dollar gross margin on current and lagged R&D, advertising, and general and administrative expenses and beginning of year total recognized assets. From the estimated regression coefficients, I compute the per-dollar-of-investment NPVs on recognized assets and R&D, advertising, and personnel intangibles by discounting the implied long-run impacts and then subtracting the $1 cost of the investment. This method is applied first to the entire sample on a year-by-year basis, and then by scale-of-expenditure groups where in each year observations are placed into one of six groups based on the absolute size of the firm's spending on R&D, advertising, or general and administrative expenses in that year.

My analysis yields four main findings. First, the NPVs of expenditures on R&D, advertising, and personnel have been consistently positive over the past twenty years. Over the period 1980–2000, I estimate that the mean yearly NPVs of $1 expenditures on R&D, advertising, and personnel were $0.35, $0.24, and $0.14, respectively. Of the sixty-three individual yearly NPV estimates (three per year for twenty-one years) some 81 per cent are reliably positive, and none are reliably negative. Second, the profitability of R&D increased more than threefold between 1980 and 2000, rising from $0.16 per dollar of investment in the 1980s to $0.51 in the 1990s, while the profitability of advertising and personnel intangibles remained unchanged, and the net current period return on tangible assets declined. The jump in the profitability of R&D in the 1990s is consistent with technology-driven innovation having been an important driver of the economic boom experienced by the United States over that same period (e.g. Boulton et al., 2000; Lev, 2001). Third, on average the NPV profitability of R&D and advertising increases as the scale of the expenditures made on those intangibles increases. In contrast, the NPV on personnel activities decreases with scale. Finally, the increasing profitability returns-to-scale of expenditures on both R&D and advertising have become more pronounced over time.

Overall, my findings support the view that R&D and advertising intangibles have emerged over the past twenty years to become a critical means by which firms today create value, and that one mechanism of value creation is that of increasing profitability returns-to-scale. I infer that the competitive environment for R&D and advertising-intensive businesses has become increasingly imperfect over the past two decades, in that firms that make the largest investments in R&D and advertising can create cost-based and/or network-derived barriers to entry, and thereby earn supra-normal rents.

The remainder of the study is as follows. Section 2 discusses the role of intangibles in creating value, particularly through increasing profitability returns-to-scale. Section 3 explains the sample selection process, and reports key descriptive statistics for the firms used in the study. Section 4 presents the regression model used to estimate the NPVs of expenditures on intangibles and recognized assets, and details the empirical results. Section 5 concludes.

2. The Role of Intangibles in Creating Value

2.1. What is an Intangible?

Under US GAAP, intangibles are the costs a firm incurs to develop internally or purchase noncurrent rights or economic benefits that are nonphysical and which are allowed to be recognized on the firm's balance sheet. Major examples of these kinds of recognized, on-the-balance-sheet intangible assets are purchased franchises, patents, trademarks, copyrights, leaseholds, and goodwill. In contrast, the economic definition of an intangible asset is much broader—economically, an intangible asset is *any* nonphysical item that has the ability or potential to provide a future economic benefit to the firm. The economic definition goes beyond GAAP to include the on-balance-sheet recognition of a variety of costs that GAAP mandates be immediately expensed as soon as they are incurred.

Of these economic but (from an accounting point of view) unrecognized intangibles, this study focuses on three: R&D, advertising, and personnel intangibles. I choose R&D, advertising, and personnel intangibles over prominent other unrecognized intangibles such as patents, customer service, and strategic alliances because R&D, advertising, and personnel intangibles are more similarly defined and measured across firms, and, importantly for R&D and advertising, their costs have typically been disclosed in financial reports when material. The proxies I use for investments in R&D, advertising, and personnel intangibles are the annual expenditures recorded by Compustat as having been made by firms on their R&D, advertising, and general and administrative activities, respectively.

R&D is clearly an intangible from an economic point of view because management only spends money on R&D because they expect to earn future cash inflows with a positive net present value. Advertising is a key component of brand intangibles. Advertising has been found to be an asset in the sense of having a positive impact on future profitability, although of over a shorter horizon than R&D (Ravenscraft and Scherer, 1982; Sougiannis, 1994). I select general and administrative expense as the proxy for personnel intangibles for three reasons. First, general and administrative expense directly contains management and administrative personnel salaries. Second, although under APB No. 15 and SFAS No. 123 the value of stock options granted to employees is almost never recognized in financial statements, I conjecture that the value of employee stock options is positively correlated with the salary cost component of general and administrative expense. As a result, the coefficients on general and administrative expense will to some extent capture the influence of the unrecognized and omitted value of employee stock option capital.[2] And third, general and administrative expense typically contains expenditures on brand beyond advertising, such as cost of customer acquisition and retention.

2.2. Increasing Profitability Returns-to-scale from Successful Intangibles

Appendix A summarizes the four main economic features that characterize investments in intangibles, of which increasing profitability returns-to-scale is the one addressed in this paper. Increasing profitability returns-to-scale is created by two sets of factors: supply side economies of scale, and demand side network effects. Supply side economies of scale occur when increased size leads to lower unit costs. This occurs with many intangible assets because intangible assets are typically nonrival in nature. Physical and financial assets are rival assets, meaning that if person A uses a plot of land to grow coffee, then person B cannot also use that land to grow tea. Rival assets have positive opportunity costs. Moreover, greater benefits can only be extracted from rival assets via increased marginal costs. If an entrepreneur starts a coffee plantation, he will begin by buying the best land he can. Then, as he expands production, he will have to buy less and less suitable land, and the marginal cost of his coffee production will rise. In contrast, intangibles are typically nonrival assets, where multiple users can employ the asset without any depreciating it. As a result, nonrival assets have low or zero opportunity costs beyond the initial investment made to create them. For example, when writing software, a firm incurs large fixed costs. However, once written, more of that software can be made at essentially zero marginal cost—merely the cost of copying the program onto a compact disk or emailing it to another user. Software also does not physically depreciate like tangible assets do.

Demand side network effects exist when the value of connecting to a network is increasing in the number of other people connected to it (Farrell and

Saloner, 1985; Brynjolfsson and Kemerer, 1996). Network effects can create positive feedback so that a customer base gets larger because existing customers attract new customers, even in the absence of expenditures by the company. The ideal result of such positive feedback is that the firm rapidly obtains a natural monopoly of its business space. Moreover, the staying power of that natural monopoly can be high because the firm's customers can become locked-in to using its products, and because the costs of switching to a competitor's products (even if a competitor exists) may be prohibitively high.

The combination of supply side economies of scale and demand side network effects can therefore lead to strategically successful intangibles exhibiting increasing profitability returns-to-scale, wherein the probability that a firm will earn monopoly profits on its intangible assets is increasing in the scale of its investment in those intangibles, and the speed with which it increases that scale. As such, it often pays for intangible-intensive firms to spend massively and rapidly so as to maximize the likelihood that they will benefit from both supply side economies of scale and demand side network effects, obtain a natural monopoly in their business space, and thereby extract the economic rents and profitability commensurate with that monopoly position. For obvious reasons, this strategy is also termed the winner-takes-all business model.

....

3. Firms and Data

Table 1 lists and defines the variables used in the study by their annual Compustat item numbers. Income statement variables are shown in panel A, balance sheet variables in panel B, and market-based variables in panel C. Per these variable definitions, general and administrative costs GA are computed as selling, general and administrative expense SGA less advertising ADV less research and development RD, where missing ADV and RD are first set to zero. Compustat includes RD in SGA when RD is broken out separately and is therefore nonmissing. Compustat also includes ADV in SGA. All variables are expressed in December 2000 dollars, using the CPI.

Panels A and B of Table 2 describe the Compustat firms used in the study across time and industries. The set of possible observations begins with all Compustat firms with nonmissing and nonnegative values for sales revenues, cost of sales, SG&A expense, end-of-fiscal-year market value of common equity, and beginning-of-year total assets. R&D and advertising expense are required to be nonnegative, and if missing are set to zero. Firms' equity market values were required to be greater than $1 million in December 2000 dollars. Since

Table 1. Variable Definitions per their Compustat Annual Data Item Numbers. All Variables are Converted into December 2000 Dollars using the CPI

Variable	Label	Compustat Annual Data Item(s)
Panel A: Income statement		
Revenue	REV	12 (net sales)
Revenue growth rate	REVGW	REV ÷ REV lagged one year
Cost of sales	COGS	41 (cost of sales)
Gross margin	GM	REV − COGS
Advertising expense	ADV	45 (advertising expense); zero if missing
R&D expense	RD	46 (R&D expense); zero if missing. RD includes write-offs of purchased in-process R&D, and sometimes excludes product development costs
SG&A expense	SGA	189 (selling, general, and administrative expense). Compustat includes RD in SGA when RD is broken out separately (and therefore RD is nonmissing). Compustat also includes ADV in SGA
G&A expense	GA	SGA − ADV − RD
Depreciation and amortization	DAM	125 (depreciation and amortization, from statement of cash flows or flow of funds statement)
Zero ADV dummy	ZADV	1 if ADV = 0; zero otherwise
Zero RD dummy	ZRD	1 if RD = 0; zero otherwise
Core net income	IBXD	237 (income before extraordinary items and discontinued operations)
Return on equity	ROE	IBXD ÷ BVE if BVE > 0; else set missing
Panel B: Balance sheet		
Total assets	TA	6 (total assets)
Total liabilities	TL	181 (total liabilities)
PP&E	PPE	8 (net property, plant, and equipment)
Book equity	BVE	60 (total common equity, else TA − TL)
Leverage	LEV	TL ÷ MVE
Panel C: Market-based		
Market value of equity	MVE	199 (fiscal year-end closing price) × 25 (common shares outstanding at fiscal year end)
Market-to-book ratio	MTB	MVE ÷ BVE if BVE > 0; else set missing

Compustat states that SG&A and advertising are unavailable for banks, utilities, life insurance or property and casualty companies, such firms are excluded.[3] Also excluded are firms with IPERMs on CRSP greater than 800,000 and firms with SIC codes outside those specified in Panel B. The first year of the data set is 1980 both because I choose to focus on the decades of the 1980s vs 1990s, and because although SFAS No. 2 was introduced in 1974, one of the regression models I employ requires seven years of lagged R&D.

Applying these restrictions yields 83,302 usable firm-year observations. The number of observations is large in every year, ranging from a low of 3057 in 1980 to a high of 5382 in 1997 (Table 2, Panel A). The number of firms in

Table 2. Number of Compustat Firms by Year and Industries, 1980–2000

Compustat Fiscal Year	# obs.[a]	Compustat Fiscal Year	# obs.
Panel A: Number of Compustat firms per year[b]			
1980	3057	1990	3626
1981	3130	1991	3627
1982	3418	1992	3755
1983	3471	1993	3978
1984	3641	1994	4343
1985	3626	1995	4600
1986	3618	1996	4995
1987	3749	1997	5382
1988	3810	1998	5341
1989	3701	1999	5144
		2000	3290
Total			83,302

Panel B: Industry composition

#	Industry (Primary SIC codes)	1980–89 # obs.	1980–89 % obs.	1990–2000 # obs.	1990–2000 % obs.
1.	Mining and construction (1000–1999)	1333	3.8	1815	3.8
2.	Food (2000–2111)	1141	3.2	1443	3.0
3.	Textiles, printing/publishing (2200–2780)	3176	9.0	3291	6.8
4.	Chemicals (2800–2824, 2840–2899)	1199	3.4	1567	3.3
5.	Pharmaceuticals (2830–2836)	825	2.3	1449	3.1
6.	Extractive industries (2900–2999, 1300–1399)	2885	8.2	2595	5.4
7.	Durable manufacturers (3000–3999, excl. 3570–3579, 3670–3679)	13,040	37.0	16,157	33.6
8.	Computers (7370–7379, 3570–3579, 3670–3679)	2424	6.9	5704	11.9
9.	Transportation (4000–4899)	1217	3.5	2171	4.5
10.	Retail (5000–5999)	5126	14.6	6864	14.3
11.	Services (7000–8999, excl. 7370–7379)	2855	8.1	4975	10.3
Total		35,221	100.0	48,081	100.0

Notes:
[a] Compustat states that SGA and ADV are not available for banks, utilities, life insurance, or property and casualty companies. As a result, such companies are excluded (defined as SIC codes 4900–4999, 6000–6411 and 6500–6999). Also excluded are a small number of observations with CRSP PERM numbers above 800,000 and observations with SIC codes outside those delineated in panel B.
[b] Sample is all Compustat firms with nonmissing GM, RD, ADV, GA, MVE, and TA lagged one year. Per the variable definitions in Table 1, GA is computed as SGA − ADV − RD, where missing ADV and RD are first set to zero. Further, REV, COGS, SGA, RD, ADV, TA, and MVE must be nonnegative, and MVE must be greater than $1 million in December 2000 dollars.

2000 is substantially less than that in 1999 because 2000 did not cover a full calendar year. Panel B demonstrates that consistent with tangible intensive businesses becoming less important over time, but intangible intensive becoming more important over time, the percentage of sample firms that are in the Textiles, Printing and Publishing, Extractive, and Durable manufacturers industries declined in the 1990s vs the 1980s, while the percentage of sample firms in the Pharmaceuticals and Computer industries increased.

Table 3 reports percentiles for the data over the full period 1980–2000. Percentiles pertaining to general variables appear in Panel A, while percentiles for variables intended to measure the absolute magnitude and relative intensity of expenditures on recognized assets and intangibles are shown in Panel B. Data in both panels reveal that most variables are highly right-skewed. Of firm-year observations, 97 per cent have positive gross margin GM but only 67 per cent have positive income before extraordinary items and discontinued operations IBXD. The median annual real revenue growth rate is 5.2 per cent, with 38 per cent of firm-year observations having negative real revenue growth.

Panel B indicates that R&D expense is positive in 46 per cent of firm-year observations, advertising is positive only 33 per cent of the time, and general

Table 3. Percentiles for Key Variables of Compustat Firms, 1980–2000[a]

Percentile	MVE	TA[b]	REV	GM	IBXD	GM ÷ REV	ROE	REVGW	LEV
Panel A: General variables (in millions of Dec. 2000 dollars or per cent)[c]									
99	$ 21,550	20,572	21,929	7891	1132	88%	420%	407%	16,828%
95	4204	4326	5156	1580	223	73	44	100	506
75	370	390	510	157	17	48	16	22	139
50	75	89	114	36	2.0	34	8.2	5.2	59
25	18	23	25	8.1	−1.4	23	−5.3	−6.8	23
5	3.3	4.5	2.1	0.4	−29	9.0	−117	−36.5	4.8
1	1.4	1.8	0	−1.5	−190	−38	−579	−72.0	1.3
% > 0	100%	100	99	97	66	98	70	62	100
# obs.	83,302	83,295	83,302	83,302	83,126	82,219	83,121	81,964	83,184

Percentile	RD	ADV	GA	RD ÷ REV[d]	ADV ÷ REV	GA ÷ REV	MVE ÷ BVE[e]	TA ÷ REV	DAM ÷ TA
Panel B: Intensity of tangibles and intangibles (in millions of Dec. 2000 dollars or per cent)									
99	$ 639	436	3534	96%	18%	334%	31	15,725%	28%
95	68	39	746	20	6.2	79	9.8	434	14
75	3.3	0.5	81	3.6	1.2	32	3.1	126	7.0
50	0	0	20	0	0	21	1.7	80	4.8
25	0	0	5.7	0	0	13	1.0	55	3.2
5	0	0	1.3	0	0	5.2	0.5	30	1.4
1	0	0	0.4	0	0	2.3	0.3	18	0.4
% > 0	46%	33	100	46	33	100	77[f]	100	100
# obs.	83,302	83,302	83,302	82,219	82,219	82,219	78,902	82,219	81,873

Notes:
[a] Variable definitions are per Table 1, and sample is that summarized in Table 2.
[b] Total assets at the beginning of the fiscal year.
[c] All variables are expressed in December 2000 dollars (translated using the CPI).
[d] Ratios defined using REV as the denominator are only computed when REV > 0.
[e] MVE ÷ BVE is only computed when BVE > 0.
[f] For MVE ÷ BVE only, the percentage figure denotes the percentage of observations where MVE ÷ BVE > 1.

and administrative expense is always positive. General and administrative expenses are large, being a median of 21 per cent of revenue, as are recognized assets at 80 per cent of revenue. The median firm depreciates and amortizes 4.8 per cent of its recognized asset base annually. Although not reported in Table 3, recognized intangibles comprise only a small portion of total assets. The median ratio of recognized intangibles to total assets is zero, and the 75th percentile is less than 5 per cent. Thus, recognized assets are almost always comprised of tangible assets. The median market-to-book ratio is 1.73 over the decades of the 1980s and 1990s. The mean market-to-book ratio is a much larger 4.11 as a result of substantial right-skewness in the distribution of the ratio.

··

4. Measuring the NPV Profitability of Expenditures on Intangibles

4.1. *NPV Profitability Regression Model*

Using the variable notations shown in Table 1, I estimate the NPV profitability of expenditures on R&D, advertising, and personnel intangibles through the following model:

$$GM_{it} = \mu + \sum_{j=0}^{K} \alpha_j RD_{i,t-j} + \sum_{j=0}^{K} \beta_j ADV_{i,t-j} + \sum_{j=0}^{K} \gamma_j GA_{i,t-j} + \theta TA_{i,t-1}$$

$$+ \sum_{q=1981}^{2000} \pi_q YEAR_{qit} + \sum_{r=1}^{10} \lambda_r SIC_{rit} + \sum_{j=0}^{K} \varphi_j ZRD_{i,t-j}$$

$$+ \sum_{j=0}^{K} \zeta_j ZADV_{i,t-j} + \varepsilon_{it}. \tag{1}$$

I hypothesize in (1) that a firm's gross margin is a linear function of current and K lagged values of research and development RD, advertising ADV, general and administrative costs GA, and beginning of year recognized assets TA. Equation (1) assumes that the most primitive incremental benefit of spending on an intangible is the creation of gross margin, not revenues, because when a sale is made a direct cost of sales is also necessarily incurred. In its most general form, the model includes year and industry intercept dummies as well as separate intercepts for current and lagged firm years in which R&D and advertising are zero.

Equation (1) adopts a fundamental rather than a market-based approach to estimating the profitability of intangibles. In a market-based approach, the market value of equity is assumed to capture the market's rational expectations of the future cash flows from expenditures on tangible and intangible investments (Hirschey, 1982; Sougiannis, 1994; Lev and Sougiannis, 1996; Aboody and Lev, 1998). There are two difficulties with the market-based method. First, the market-based approach presumes that the stock market is efficient. However, a substantial body of evidence in accounting and finance is inconsistent with this presumption, both in general and also for R&D in particular (Lev and Sougiannis, 1996; Chan et al., 2000; Chambers et al., 2002). Second, the market value of equity reflects the expected cash flow impacts of past and future expenditures on intangibles in addition to current expenditures. This makes it difficult to determine changes in the profitability of intangibles over time. For these reasons, I correlate current and lagged values of expenditures on intangibles with current period gross margin rather than correlating expenditures on intangibles with the market value of equity.

In contrast to prior work that has estimated the profitability of R&D intangibles, such as Sougiannis (1994), Lev and Sougiannis (1996), and Nissim and Thomas (2000), I impose no structure on the parameters on current and lagged expenditures on any intangible. Since current and lagged values of intangible expenditures tend to be highly collinear, reliable estimates of individual coefficient estimates are inherently difficult to obtain. For example, the mean correlation over the sample period of RD with RD lagged seven years is 0.86, while that of ADV with ADV lagged three years is 0.81. The favoured solution to this problem has been to assume that the coefficients on a given set of current and lagged variables such as R&D follow either a Koyck or an Almon lag pattern. However, this method can have two costs. First is the cost of misspecification— that is, assuming that the lag structure is second-order polynomial Almon when it is not.[4] Second, if a Koyck lag structure is estimated, then unless the same Koyck decay parameter is assumed for RD, ADV, and GA, the estimation becomes complex and is unlikely to yield plausible results because of the large number of cross-variable coefficient restrictions (Johnston, 1972: 299–300).

Because the goal of (1) is to estimate NPVs, and NPVs are linear combinations in the form of adjusted summations of the coefficient estimates, one does not need to impose a lag structure as long as a sufficient number of lags are included, that is, if K is sufficiently large.[5] Not imposing a structure on the parameters on current and lagged expenditures on intangibles finesses these costs without imposing a substantial penalty in their place. This is because although including only a relatively small number of lagged terms is almost certainly too conservative (with the true number of lags being larger than the number included), the high autocorrelations of expenditures on intangibles means that the coefficients on the lags that are included will substantially capture the impact of the omitted lags. That is, the high autocorrelations lead to omitted variable bias working in favour of estimating the impacts of intangibles on gross margin, not against it.

Using R&D as the prototypical intangible, the gross undiscounted benefit of $1 spent on R&D in (1) is taken to be $\sum_{j=1}^{K} \hat{\alpha}_j$. Strictly speaking, the effect of R&D in year t is the sum of the coefficient on current R&D, the lag 1 coefficient from year $t + 1$, the lag 2 coefficient from year $t + 2$, etc. However, following Sougiannis (1994), in approximation to this structure I assume that the lag j coefficient from year t adequately reflects the economics linking R&D expenditures in year t with gross margin in period $t + j$. To then arrive at the NPV of $1 spent on R&D, given that intangible expenditures are expressed in real terms, the $\hat{\alpha}$s must be discounted by a real discount rate R, and the expenditure of $1 must be subtracted. The NPV of $1 spent on R&D is therefore given by $\sum_{j=1}^{K} \hat{\alpha}_j R^{-j} - 1$ Similar expressions apply to ADV and GA.

Although the riskiness of recognized assets likely differs from that of unrecognized intangibles, and within unrecognized intangibles the riskiness of R&D differs from that of advertising, I use a uniform real weighted average annual cost of capital rate of $R = 1.06$.[6] When combined with the average inflation rate of 4.0 per cent over the period 1980–2000, the real annual discount rate of 6 per cent equates to a nominal weighted average annual cost of capital rate of 10 per cent. On the one hand, it would clearly be more accurate to apply a different discount rate to each intangible, and not doing so weakens the reliability of inferences derived from the empirical analysis. In particular, if the correct discount rate for R&D, advertising, and personnel intangibles is higher than 10 per cent, the profitability NPVs derived from my regressions may be overstated. On the other hand, knowing exactly what the correct discount rates are is very difficult to determine. My imperfect attempt to address these concerns is to adopt a weighted average discount rate of 10 per cent that exceeds the ex post mean historical rate across US firms as a whole of between 7 and 8 per cent.

In addition to estimating the parameters needed to gauge the NPV profitability of R&D, advertising, and general and administrative activities, (1) also estimates the current period gross return on recognized assets through the parameter θ. The parameter θ measures the incremental contribution made by recognized assets to the firm's current year gross margin after taking into account the gross margin generated by current and lagged R&D, advertising, and general and administrative activities. Since gross margin deliberately does not take account of the cost of debt or equity capital employed, I use total assets rather than operating assets alone. To arrive at the current period net return on recognized assets, denoted NR(TA), the current year cost of using the recognized assets must be subtracted from θ. I estimate this cost on both an aggregate or yearly basis using the median ratio of firms' depreciation and amortization expense DAM to beginning of year total assets:

$$NR(TA) = \theta - \text{median}\left\{\frac{DAM}{TA}\right\}. \tag{2}$$

It should be noted that NR(TA) is not the NPV of recognized assets in the way that NPV(RD) is for R&D, although it is part of it. Estimating the NPV of recognized assets would be complex, for example, due to the diversity in the economic lives of different classes of assets. As such, I do not pursue the NPV of recognized assets in this study. Not estimating the NPV of recognized assets will only bias the coefficients in (1) if the difference between NPV(TA) and NR(TA) is correlated with the included independent variables. The extent to which this is the case is unknown and is therefore a limitation of the study.

As noted by Lev and Sougiannis (1996) and Nissim and Thomas (2000), models such as (1) may raise simultaneity issues. A shock that raises the demand for a firm's products will typically increase both current gross margin and the marginal return to capital. Since the latter will also lead to increased investment in intangibles, recognized assets or both, expenditures on investment cannot be considered a truly exogenous variable and will be correlated with the error term, leading to inconsistent parameter estimates. While this is a valid concern, I expect the number of observations available for the estimation of (1) to be sufficiently large that concerns about parameter efficiency or consistency are minimal.

The methods outlined above aim to finesse the issue of taxes by estimating the value of pretax benefits arising from a \$1 pretax expenditure. An alternative approach would be to estimate the after tax benefits from spending \$1 after the tax shelter provided to the expenditure was accounted for. I choose the former approach because of the complexities that would be introduced by statutory tax rates for different kinds of expenditures changing over time, and the need to accurately estimate marginal tax rates for large numbers of firms.[7]

The variables in (1) are not deflated because heteroscedasticity in the error term should not bias the coefficient estimates. However, to avoid parameter estimates being unduly influenced by outliers, in each year the largest 1 per cent of GM, RD, ADV, GA and these same variables lagged one year are deleted. Unreported scatter plots of GM against RD, GA, ADV, and one-year lagged TA subsequent to this procedure indicate that it successfully excludes influential observations.[8]

4.2. Regression Results

4.2.1. Results for the Full Period 1980–2000, Not Conditioning on the Scale of Expenditures

The results of estimating (1) year-by-year over the full period 1980–2000 are given in Table 4. Panel A reports the gross benefits from \$1 spent on RD, ADV,

Table 4. Regressions Estimating the NPVs of $1 Spent on R&D, Advertising, and General and Administrative Intangibles, and the Current Period Net Return on $1 of Recognized Assets for Compustat Firms, 1980–2000.[a]

Panel A: Gross benefits of $1 expenditures (averages of twenty-one annual regressions, 1980–2000)

# Lags	$\sum_{j=0}^{K}\hat{\alpha}_j$	$\sum_{j=0}^{K}\hat{\beta}_j$	$\sum_{j=0}^{K}\hat{\gamma}_j$	$\hat{\theta}$	Avg. R_a^2	Avg. #obs.
$K=0$	$ 1.44[b]	$ 1.25	$ 1.15	$ 0.10	95.7%	3875
	(34.6)[c]	(19.1)	(96.2)	(17.9)	{3.1%}[d]	
$K=3$	1.16	1.27	1.10	0.12	96.3%	2937
	(15.7)	(23.1)	(89.7)	(21.4)	{2.1%}	
$K=7$[e]	1.03	1.29	1.10	0.12	96.5%	2001
	(11.0)	(22.5)	(87.5)	(21.4)	{2.4%}	

Panel B: Net benefits of $1 expenditures (averages of twenty-one annual regressions, 1980–2000)

# Lags	$\sum_{j=0}^{K}\hat{\alpha}_j R^{-j} - 1$	$\sum_{j=0}^{K}\hat{\beta}_j R^{-j} - 1$	$\sum_{j=0}^{K}\hat{\gamma}_j R^{-j} - 1$	$\hat{\theta} - \text{median}\left\{\dfrac{DAM_{it}}{TA_{i,t-1}}\right\}$
$K=0$	$ 0.44	$ 0.25	$ 0.15	$ 0.056[j]
	(10.6)	(3.8)	(12.5)	(9.0)
$K=3$	0.35	0.24	0.14	0.068
	(7.1)	(4.8)	(12.5)	(11.6)
$K=7$	0.31	0.27	0.14	0.069
	(5.7)	(5.4)	(11.7)	(11.8)

Notes:
[a] Variable definitions are per Table 1. Firms are indexed by i and years by t. Year dummies are denoted as YEAR, and SIC dummies are denoted as SIC. To mitigate any undue influence from outliers, in each year the largest 1 per cent of RD_t, ADV_t, GA_t, RD_{t-1}, ADV_{t-1}, and GA_{t-1} are deleted.
[b] Sum of coefficient estimates over K lags.
[c] Simple Fama–MacBeth t-statistic on the null that the sum of the parameters is zero.
[d] Average adjusted R^2 from the regression of GM on SIC dummies only.
[e] Denotes seven lags for RD but only three lags for each of GA and ADV.

Regression: $GM_{it} = \mu + \sum_{j=0}^{K}\alpha_j RD_{i,t-j} + \sum_{j=0}^{K}\beta_j ADV_{i,t-j} + \sum_{j=0}^{K}\gamma_j GA_{i,t-j} + \theta TA_{i,t-1}$

$$+ \sum_{r=1}^{10}\lambda_r SIC_{rt} + \sum_{j=0}^{K}\varphi_j ZRD_{i,t-j} + \sum_{j=0}^{K}\zeta_j ZADV_{i,t-j} + \varepsilon_{it}.$$

and GA intangibles and recognized assets TA. Panel B reports the corresponding NPVs. Inferences concerning the significance of coefficient estimates in the former approach are made using the Fama–MacBeth (1973) method of focusing on the means and simple t-statistics of the vector of yearly parameter estimates.[9] As discussed in Section 4.1, the very high autocorrelations of RD, ADV, and GA make it almost impossible to determine the true number of lags for each intangible. I practically address this issue by estimating several values of K, the number of lags, and determining the extent to which the resulting NPVs materially change as K changes.

Several findings warrant highlighting in Table 4. First, the number of lags chosen makes little difference to the NPVs reported in panel B.[10] I compromise between the number of observations used to estimate the parameters (which favours $K=0$) and prior work such as Sougiannis (1994) that concludes that R&D has up to a seven year lag (which favours $K = 7$) by choosing $K = 3$. Second, using $K = 3$, over the period 1980–2000, the mean NPVs of $1 expenditures on R&D, advertising, and general and administrative activities were $0.35, $0.24, and $0.14, respectively. The Fama–MacBeth t-statistics on the means of the yearly NPVs indicate that each mean is very reliably positive. Unreported tests confirm that the NPVs reported in panel B for $K = 3$ are also each reliably different from one another.

Taken together, these results appear strongly consistent with intangibles playing a central and economically profitable role in the creation of fundamental value during the past two decades. Of course, under perfect competition the NPV for both recognized assets and intangibles should be zero. The findings in Table 4 that all four NPVs are reliably positive might therefore point to one or more of several possibilities. First, the results may reflect the presence of imperfect competition, with expenditures on R&D and advertising intangibles providing greater barriers to entry and therefore higher fundamental profitability than recognized assets or personnel. This is the interpretation I favour. However, it might also be that either the regression model may be misspecified, or it might be that future cash flows from intangibles are not of similar risk and should not all be discounted at the same rate. The latter explanation would require that the riskiness of R&D expenditures exceed that of expenditures on advertising, and the riskiness of advertising expenditures exceed that of expenditures on personnel. This is certainly possible.

4.2.2. Individual Year Results, not Conditioning on the Scale of Expenditures

Table 5 reports the year-by-year NPVs estimated under the $K = 3$ lag specification. These are the underlying numbers that are averaged in panel B of Table 4. The NPVs are also presented visually in Fig. 1. The mean NPVs across the approximately equal subperiods 1980–87, 1988–1993, and 1994–2000 are reported in Panel A of Table 6, while Panel B of Table 6 tests for the presence of a linear time trend in the NPVs. Taken together, Tables 5 and 6 and Fig. 1 indicates that the NPV of $1 spent on R&D rose substantially, tripling from $0.16 in the 1980–87 to $0.51 in 1994–2000. Per panel B of Table 6, the t-statistic of 4.9 on the time-trend coefficient indicates that the increase is highly statistically significant. The jump in R&D profitability is consistent with arguments that R&D innovation was a key driver of the economic boom experienced by the US during the 1990s (Boulton et al., 2000; Lev, 2001).

In contrast to R&D, the profitability of advertising and general and administrative activities has either declined or remained unchanged over time. In 1980–87 the mean NPVs of advertising and general and administrative expenditures were $0.32 and $0.14, respectively, as compared to $0.12 and $0.14 in 1994–2000. The t-statistics of -0.8 and 1.0 on the time trends on NPV(ADV) and NPV(GA), respectively, indicate there is no statistic evidence of an increase or a decrease in the NPVs of ADV and GA over time. While the average NPV

Table 5. Mean Market-to-book Ratios, and Coefficients from Annual Regressions Estimating the NPVs of $1 Spent on R&D, Advertising, General and Administration, and the Current Period Net Return on $1 of Recognised Assets for Compustat Firms, 1980–2000[a]

Year	Mean $\left[\dfrac{MVE}{BVE}\right]$	# obs.	$\sum_{j=0}^{3} \hat{\alpha}_j R^{-j} - 1$[b]	$\sum_{j=0}^{3} \hat{\beta}_j R^{-j} - 1$	$\sum_{j=0}^{3} \hat{\gamma}_j R^{-j} - 1$	$\hat{\theta} - \text{median}\left\{\dfrac{DAM_{it}}{TA_{i,t-1}}\right\}$
1980	2.05	2344	$0.01	$-0.04	$0.04*	$0.13*
1981	1.77	2423	0.09	0.10	0.10*	0.10*
1982	1.99	2551	0.15	0.33*	0.19*	0.06*
1983	2.39	2625	0.26*	0.64*	0.14*	0.06*
1984	2.04	2778	0.06	0.44*	0.15*	0.08*
1985	2.34	2652	0.21*	0.24*	0.20*	0.05*
1986	2.74	2776	0.19*	0.40*	0.18*	0.04*
1987	2.43	2755	0.30*	0.26*	0.08*	0.09*
1988	2.45	2681	0.03	-0.00	0.05*	0.12*
1989	2.70	2766	0.35*	0.25*	0.08*	0.10*
1990	2.32	2844	0.61*	0.16*	0.14*	0.06*
1991	2.90	2903	0.69*	0.52*	0.14*	0.03*
1992	2.81	2963	0.43*	0.54*	0.21*	0.04*
1993	3.04	2993	0.51*	0.42*	0.17*	0.04*
1994	2.70	3043	0.72*	0.23*	0.15*	0.06*
1995	3.17	3192	0.25*	-0.14	0.08*	0.09*
1996	3.23	3469	0.26*	-0.16	0.11*	0.07*
1997	3.49	3618	0.64*	0.37*	0.12*	0.06*
1998	3.18	3781	0.44*	0.41*	0.14*	0.05*
1999	3.96	3947	0.51*	0.18	0.20*	0.05*
2000	3.00	2577	0.54*	-0.07	0.17*	0.07*
Mean	2.70	2937	$0.35*	$0.24*	$0.14*	$0.07*
Std. Dev.	0.54	437	0.22	0.05	0.23	0.03

Notes:
[a] Variable definitions are per Table 1. Firms are indexed by i and years by t. To mitigate any undue influence from outliers, in each year the largest 1 per cent of GM_t, RD_t, ADV_t, GA_t, RD_{t-1}, ADV_{t-1}, and GA_{t-j} are deleted. An asterisk denotes that the parameter or combination of parameters has a 2-tailed p-value < 0.05.

[b] $R = 1.06$ is the real annual weighted average cost of capital. It is computed using a real risk-free rate of 2.2% (avg. 1980–2000) and a market risk premium of 3.75%.

Regression: $GM_{it} = \mu + \sum_{j=0}^{3} \alpha_j RD_{i,t-j} + \sum_{j=0}^{3} \beta_j ADV_{i,t-j} + \sum_{j=0}^{3} \gamma_j GA_{i,t-j} + \theta TA_{i,t-1} + \sum_{m=1}^{10} \lambda_m SIC_{mit}$

$+ \sum_{j=0}^{3} \varphi_j ZRD_{i,t-j} + \sum_{j=0}^{3} \zeta_j ZADV_{i,t-j} + \varepsilon_{it}.$

of advertising is roughly double that of general and administrative activities, it is also clearly more volatile over time. Finally, the current period net return on a dollar of recognized assets fell from $0.076 in 1980–87 to $0.064 in 1994–2000 (the t-statistic on the time trend for NR(TA) of -1.9 is marginally indicative of a decline in the current period net return over time).

4.3. Profitability Returns-to-scale Tests

In this section I report the findings of tests aimed at determining whether and in what manner the NPVs of expenditures on intangibles and recognized assets

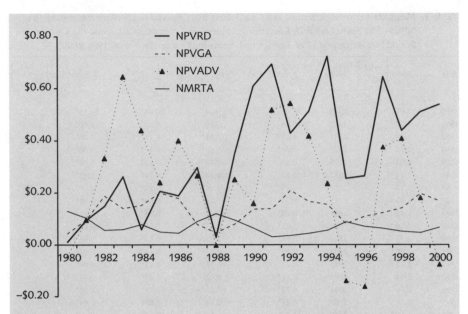

Fig. 1. NPVs of $1 spent on R&D (NPVRD), advertising (NPVADV), general and administrative activities (NPVGA), and the current period net return on recognized assets (NRTA), 1980–2000.

Table 6. Comparison of the NPVs of RD, ADV, and GA Intangibles and the Current Year Net Return on Recognized Assets of Compustat Firms, 1980–2000, by subperiod[a]

Period	NPV(RD)	NPV(ADV)	NPV(GA)	NR(TA)
Panel A: Means NPVs of intangibles and the current year net return on recognized assets[b]				
1980–86	$0.16	$0.30	$0.14	$0.076
1987–93	$0.44	$0.32	$0.13	$0.063
1994–2000	$0.48	$0.12	$0.14	$0.064

Panel B: Time trends in the NPVs of intangibles, the current year net return on recognized assets, and annual market-to-book ratios

Regression: $Y_t = \psi + \nu\, YEAR_t + \epsilon_t$, $YEAR_t = 1980, \ldots, 2000$

$Y =$	NPV(RD)	NPV(ADV)	NPV(GA)	NR(TA)
$\hat{\nu}$	0.025	−0.007	0.002	−0.002
t-statistic	4.3	−0.8	1.0	−1.9

[a] Variable definitions are per Table 1.
[b] Net present values NPV(RD), NPV(ADV), and NPV(GA), and the current period net return on recognized assets NR(TA), are those estimated and reported in Table 5.

exhibit increasing profitability returns-to-scale. Economists have suggested that a combination of demand side network effects and supply side economies of scale can lead to a strategically successful firm—particularly an intangible-intensive firm in the 1990s—holding a natural monopoly (De Long, 1998, 2000; Shapiro and Varian, 1999; Lev, 2000; Hand, 2002b). If expenditures on intangible assets exhibit increasing returns-to-scale, then the NPVs associated with expenditures on intangibles should be increasing in scale, and the more so over time if the 1990s was indeed an economic environment in which intangibles flourished.

4.3.1. Definition of Scale and Descriptive Statistics by Scale

Computing NPVs as a function of scale requires a definition of scale. Since the focus of the paper is on unrecognized intangibles rather than tangible assets, I define scale using the magnitude of real expenditures on RD, ADV or GA. Each year observations are placed into six scale-based groups as follows. If any variable $X_t \in \{RD_t, ADV_t, GA_t\}$ lies in its top 99th percentile or above, that firm-year observation is coded as being in the largest scale group, SCALE = 6. If any X_t is above its 95th percentile and less than or equal to its 99th percentile and the firm-year observation is not already in SCALE = 6, then it is put in group SCALE = 5. If any X_t is above its 90th percentile and less than or equal to its 95th percentile and the firm-year observation is not already in SCALE = 6 or 5, then it is put in group SCALE = 4. If any X_t is above its 75th percentile and less than or equal to its 90th percentile and not already in group SCALE = 6, 5 or 4, then it is put in SCALE = 3. If any X_t is above its 50th percentile and less than or equal to its 75th percentile and not already in SCALE = 6, 5, 4 or 3, then it is put in SCALE = 2. All remaining observations are placed in the smallest scale group SCALE = 1.

The resulting means and medians of the absolute and revenue-deflated variables RD, ADV, and GA in each scale group together with the market-to-book ratio, TA/REV and the annual depreciation rate applied to beginning of year total assets are reported in Table 7. As a given firm-year observation is placed into the highest of the three separate scale codings for RD, ADV, and GA, group SCALE = 6 has more than 1 per cent of total firm-year observations in it (actual = 2.5 per cent). Likewise, group SCALE = 5 has more than 4 per cent (actual = 8.1 per cent), group SCALE = 4 has more than 5 per cent (actual = 10.0 per cent), group SCALE = 3 has more than 15 per cent (actual = 27.8 per cent), and group SCALE = 2 has more than 25 per cent (actual = 30.1 per cent). Not surprisingly, therefore, group SCALE = 1 has less than 50 per cent of firm-year observations (actual = 21.5 per cent).

Table 7 reveals that the grouping procedure yields mean and median real magnitudes for RD, ADV, and GA that increase monotonically with SCALE. This is also the case for ADV ÷ REV but not for GA ÷ REV and RD ÷ REV, indicating that firms' absolute and relative intangible intensities usually differ.

Table 7. Means and Medians for Key Variables of Compustat Firms over the Period (1980–2000) when Data are Grouped by the Scale of Real Expenditures on RD, ADV, and GA Intangibles[a]

SCALE[b]		RD	ADV	GA	RD÷REV[c]	ADV÷REV	GA÷REV	MVE÷BVE[d]	TA÷REV	DAM÷TA
S = 1	Mean	$0	0	6.8	0	0	28%	2.5	189%	7.4%
(n = 852)	Median	0	0	5.1	0	0	18	1.5	95	5.2
per year)	% > 0	0%	0	100	1.9	1.6	100	69[e]	100	100
S = 2	Mean	$0.6	0.1	19	4.6%	0.6%	32%	3.0	123%	5.9%
(n = 1195)	Median	0.2	0	10	0.5	0	22	1.7	78	4.6
per year)	% > 0	57%	27	100	56	26	100	74	100	100
S = 3	Mean	$4.2	1.5	62	5.4%	1.3%	27%	2.7	106%	5.8%
(n = 1101)	Median	2.0	0	34	0.8	0	21	1.7	75	4.7
per year)	% > 0	57%	46	100	57	46	100	78	100	100
S = 4	Mean	$14	7.6	174	4.5%	2.0%	24%	2.7	90%	6.0%
(n = 397)	Median	5.7	2.3	118	0.8	0.8	21	1.9	74	4.8
per year)	% > 0	57%	55	100	56	54	100	83	100	100
S = 5	Mean	$57	34	566	3.8%	2.4%	20%	2.8	89%	6.1%
(n = 321)	Median	31	14	429	1.1	1.0	19	2.0	78	4.9
per year)	% > 0	60%	55	100	61	56	100	86	100	100
S = 6	Mean	$223	136	1702	4.3%	2.9%	19%	3.4	92%	5.4%
(n = 100)	Median	161	92	1615	2.1	1.3	19	2.3	86	4.8
per year)	% > 0	70%	57	100	74	60	100	91	100	100

[a] Variable definitions are per Table 1. All variables are expressed in December 2000 dollars (via the CPI).

[b] Each year observations are placed into six scale-based groups as follows. If any variable $X_t \in \{RD_t, ADV_t, GA_t\}$ lies in the top 99th percentile or above, that firm-year observation is coded as being in the largest scale group, SCALE = 6. If any X_t is above its 95th percentile and less than or equal to its 99th percentile and the firm-year observation is not already in SCALE = 6, then it is put in group SCALE = 5. If any X_t is above its 90th percentile and less than or equal to its 95th percentile and the firm-year observation is not already in SCALE = 6 or 5, then it is put in group SCALE = 4. If any X_t is above its 75th percentile and less than or equal to its 90th percentile and not already in group SCALE = 6, 5 or 4, then it is put in SCALE = 3. If any X_t is above its 50th percentile and less than or equal to its 75th percentile and not already in SCALE = 6, 5, 4 or 3, then it is put in SCALE = 2. All remaining observations are placed in the smallest scale group SCALE = 1.

[c] Ratios defined using REV as the denominator are only computed when REV > 0.

[d] MVE ÷ BVE is only computed when BVE > 0.

[e] For MVE ÷ BVE only, the percentage figure denotes the percentage of observations where MVE ÷ BVE > 1.

It should be noted that all the firm-year observations in group SCALE = 1 have zero RD and zero ADV, meaning that it is not possible to estimate the NPVs for R&D and advertising for the smallest group, SCALE = 1.

4.3.2. Estimates of NPVs on Intangibles and on Recognized Assets, by Scale

The results of estimating equation (1) on a pooled basis over the entire period 1980–2000 by SCALE using $K = 3$ are reported in Table 8. The NPV estimates for RD, ADV, and GA are also plotted by SCALE in Fig. 2. From Table 8 and Fig. 2, several findings stand out. First, expenditures on R&D exhibit increasing returns-to-scale in that their NPVs are larger the larger is the scale of the R&D expenditure. Moreover, although the NPV is reliably negative at the smallest level of scale, the NPV is reliably and strongly positive at the two largest levels of scale. To be consistent with economically sensible increasing profitability returns-to-scale, the former is not necessary to have observed, but the latter is.

Second, expenditures on advertising also exhibit increasing returns-to-scale in that their NPVs are larger the larger is the scale of the advertising expenditure.

Table 8. Estimates of the NPVs of RD, ADV, and GA Intangibles and Recognized Assets TA for Compustat Firms, 1980–2000, when Data are Grouped by the Scale of Real Expenditures on RD, ADV, and GA Intangibles[a]

Scale	$\sum_{j=0}^{3}\hat{\alpha}_{j}R^{-j} - 1$[b]	$\sum_{j=0}^{3}\hat{\beta}_{j}R^{-j} - 1$	$\sum_{j=0}^{3}\hat{\gamma}_{j}R^{-j} - 1$	$\hat{\theta} - \text{median}\left\{\dfrac{\text{DAM}_{it}}{\text{TA}_{i,t-1}}\right\}$[b]	Adj. R^2	#obs.[g]
S = 1	n.a.[c]	n.a.[c]	0.46[d]	0.031	51.2%	11,792
(smallest scale)			(<0.001)[e]	(<0.001)	{1.6%}[f]	
S = 2	−1.04	−2.22	0.31	0.050	73.2%	18,336
	(<0.01)	(0.19)	(<0.001)	(<0.001)	{17.8%}	
S = 3	0.19	−0.27	0.22	0.058	82.8%	17,960
	(0.15)	(0.24)	(<0.001)	(<0.001)	{14.9%}	
S = 4	0.25	0.38	0.19	0.053	87.3%	6962
	(0.09)	(0.08)	(<0.001)	(<0.001)	{14.5%}	
S = 5	0.62	0.15	0.14	0.059	90.1%	5440
	(<0.001)	(0.18)	(<0.001)	(<0.001)	{10.9%}	
S = 6	0.57	0.82	0.10	0.056	90.6%	1191
(largest scale)	(<0.001)	(<0.001)	(<0.001)	(<0.001)	{9.0%}	

[a] Variable definitions are per Table 1. Firms are indexed by i and years are indexed by t.
[b] Median{DAM ÷ TA} is the median ratio of depreciation and amortization to beginning of year over the period 1980–2000 for the scale group.
[c] In the smallest scale group $S = 1$ all values for RD and ADV are zero.
[d] Discounted sum of coefficient estimates over K lags. Discount rate $R = 1.06$ is one plus the yearly real weighted average cost of capital, and is computed using real risk-free rate of 2.25% (avg. 1980–2000) and a market risk premium of 3.75%
[e] Simple Fama–MacBeth t-statistic on null of zero.
[f] Average adjusted R^2 in the regression of GM on SIC dummies only.
[g] Average number of observations over the estimation period 1980–2000.

Regression: $\text{GM}_{it} = \mu + \sum_{j=0}^{3}\alpha_{j}\text{RD}_{i,t-j} + \sum_{j=0}^{3}\beta_{j}\text{ADV}_{i,t-j} + \sum_{j=0}^{3}\gamma_{j}\text{GA}_{i,t-j} + \theta\text{TA}_{i,t-1}$

$\qquad + \sum_{q=1981}^{2000}\pi_{q}\text{YEAR}_{qit} + \sum_{r=1}^{10}\lambda_{r}\text{SIC}_{rit} + \sum_{j=0}^{3}\varphi_{j}\text{ZRD}_{i,t-j} + \sum_{j=0}^{3}\zeta_{j}\text{ZADV}_{i,t-j} + \varepsilon_{it}.$

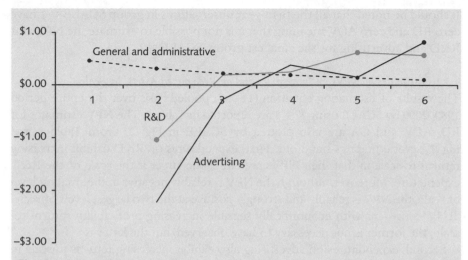

Fig. 2. NPVs of $1 spent on R&D, advertising, and general and administrative activities, 1980–2000, by SCALE of expenditure (1 = smallest, 6 = largest). A circle denotes an NPV that is reliably different from zero.

Although the NPV is reliably positive at only the largest level of scale, the pattern of advertising NPVs as a function of scale is consistent with increasing profitability returns-to-scale.

Third, although expenditures on GA have reliably positive NPVs at all levels of scale, unlike the *increasing* profitability returns-to-scale observed for R&D and advertising, the magnitudes of the NPVs for expenditures on general and administrative activities are *decreasing* as scale increases. This somewhat surprising result indicates that to the extent that general and administrative expenses do truly proxy for personnel intangibles, although personnel intangibles create value no matter how large the scale of expenditure, they create the most value for small firms (since small firms are very likely the ones that spend the least dollars on personnel intangibles). This suggests that either human capital is disproportionately valuable in small firms, or it is equally valuable across all sizes of firms, but as firms get larger there emerge large costs that offset the benefits that are created. For example, it is often claimed that small firms provide the most flexible, unconstrained work environments, whereas in large firms it is hard to create an entrepreneurial atmosphere.

Finally, the current period net return on recognized assets is reliably positive at all levels of scale, but is not systematically increasing or decreasing in scale. This is what would be predicted if indeed recognized assets yield a competitive rate of return because for recognized assets there are very close substitutes available, competing away abnormal profitability.

Table 9 summarizes the results of estimating (1) by SCALE and with $K = 3$ separately for the subperiods 1980–1986, 1987–1993, and 1994–2000. The results in Table 9 suggest that the returns-to-scale relations shown in Table 8 and Fig. 2 for R&D (advertising) intangibles are strongly (mildly) more present in the

Table 9. Comparisons of the NPVs of Expenditures on RD, ADV, and GA Intangibles and the Net Current Period Return on Recognized Assets TA for Compustat Firms, 1980–86 vs 1987–93 vs 1994–2000. Data are Grouped Each Year by the Scale of Real Expenditures on RD, ADV, and GA Intangibles[a]

Mean NPV[b]	NPV(RD)	NPV(ADV)	NPV(GA)	NR(TA)	# obs.
Panel A: Smallest scale intangible expenditures, SCALE = 1[c]					
1980–86	n.a.[d]	n.a.[d]	$0.64*	$0.030*	3279
1987–93	n.a.	n.a.	0.62*	0.002*	3567
1994–2000	n.a.	n.a.	0.36*	0.042*	4946
Panel B: SCALE = 2					
1980–86	$−1.00	$−2.38	$0.37*	$0.046*	5394
1987–93	0.13	−1.97	0.28*	0.045*	6317
1994–2000	−1.05	−0.69	0.31*	0.051*	6625
Panel C: SCALE = 3					
1980–86	$−0.03	$−0.23	$0.29*	$0.044*	5680
1987–93	0.28	−0.57	0.17*	0.067*	5916
1994–2000	0.06	−0.28	0.24*	0.058*	6364
Panel D: SCALE = 4					
1980–86	$−0.58*	$0.55	$0.25*	$0.054*	2011
1987–93	0.27	0.30	0.23*	0.046*	2124
1994–2000	0.44*	0.10	0.17*	0.057*	2827
Panel E: SCALE = 5					
1980–86	$0.32*	$−0.13	$0.19*	$0.060*	1472
1987–93	0.97*	0.27	0.12*	0.055*	1659
1994–2000	0.48*	0.70	0.14*	0.064*	2309
Panel F: Largest scale intangible expenditures, SCALE = 6					
1980–86	$0.06	$0.48*	$−0.00	$0.087*	313
1987–93	0.70*	0.76*	0.02	0.066*	322
1994–2000	0.62*	0.89*	0.19*	0.037*	556

Notes:

[a] Variable definitions are per Table 1. Asterisk denotes that the mean or t-statistic has a 2-tailed p-value < 0.05.

[b] Yearly NPVs and θ_t are those estimated and reported in Table 5.

[c] Each year observations are placed into six scale-based groups as follows. If any variable $X_t \in \{RD_t, ADV_t, GA_t\}$ lies in the top 99th percentile or above, that firm-year observation is coded as being in the largest scale group, SCALE = 6. If any X_t is above its 95th percentile and less than or equal to its 99th percentile and the firm-year observation is not already in SCALE = 6, then it is put in group SCALE = 5. If any X_t is above its 90th percentile and less than or equal to its 95th percentile and the firm-year observation is not already in SCALE = 6 or 5, then it is put in group SCALE = 4. If any X_t is above its 75th percentile and less than or equal to its 90th percentile and not already in group SCALE = 6, 5 or 4, then it is put in SCALE = 3. If any X_t is above its 50th percentile and less than or equal to its 75th percentile and not already in SCALE = 6, 5, 4 or 3, then it is put in SCALE = 2. All remaining observations are placed in the smallest scale group SCALE = 1.

[d] In the smallest scale group SCALE = 1, all values for ADV and RD are zero.

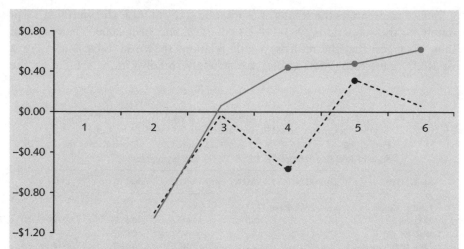

Fig. 3. NPVs of $1 spent on R&D as a function of the scale of the expenditure on R&D (1 = smallest, 6 = largest) over 1980–87 (dashed) and 1994–2000 (thick solid). A circle denotes an NPV that is reliably different from zero.

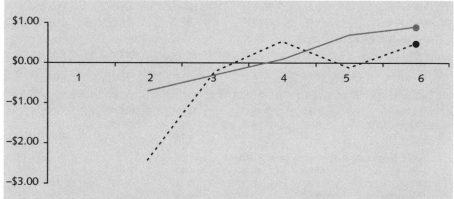

Fig. 4. NPVs of $1 spent on advertising as a function of the scale of the expenditure on advertising (1 = smallest, 6 = largest) over 1980–87 (dashed) and 1994–2000 (thick solid). A circle denotes an NPV that is reliably different from zero.

subperiods 1987–93 and 1994–2000 than in 1987–1993. This is consistent with the hypothesis that R&D and advertising—but particularly R&D—intangibles have become more important to creating value over time. Figures 3 and 4 makes a similar point by visually comparing the NPVs of R&D and advertising, respectively, as a function of SCALE for the 1980–1987 vs the 1994–2000 subperiods.

For example, in Fig. 12.3 (4) the NPV of R&D (advertising) is highest in the 1994–2000 subperiod in four (three) of the five scale groups.

5. Conclusions

The goal of this paper has been to determine the extent to which large-sample evidence confirms or denies the view that intangibles have over time come to play a more central role in creating value, particularly because of the opportunities that successful investments in intangibles provide for firms to generate increasing profitability returns-to-scale. My method centered on estimating the ex post NPV profitability of expenditures three key unrecognized intangibles— R&D, advertising, and personnel—for the universe of publicly traded US firms over the past two decades. I chose these intangibles over patents, customer service, and strategic alliances because they are more similarly defined and measured across firms and their costs are required to be disclosed when material. The proxies I used for investments in R&D, advertising, and personnel intangibles are the annual expenditures recorded by Compustat as having been made by firms on their R&D, advertising, and general and administrative activities, respectively.

I used the estimated NPVs to test four major predictions that arise from the hypothesis that intangibles and their potential to create increasing profitability returns-to-scale now play a central role in creating value. First, if intangibles create value, then they will have nonnegative NPVs. Second, if intangibles today create more value than they did in the past, then their NPVs will on average have increased over time. Third, if intangibles result in increasing profitability returns-to-scale, then their NPVs per-dollar-of-investment will increase as the scale of the investment made in them increases. Fourth, if intangibles exhibit more intense profitability returns-to-scale today than they did in the past, then that should be apparent in the data.

My analysis yielded four main findings. First, the NPVs of expenditures on R&D, advertising, and personnel have been consistently positive over the past twenty years. Over the period 1980–2000, I estimated that the mean yearly NPVs of $1 expenditures on R&D, advertising, and personnel were $0.35, $0.24 and $0.14, respectively. Of the sixty-three individual yearly NPV estimates (three per year for twenty-one years) some 81 per cent are reliably positive, and none are reliably negative. Second, the profitability of R&D increased more than threefold between 1980 and 2000, rising from $0.16 per dollar of investment in the 1980s to $0.51 in the 1990s, while the profitability of advertising and personnel intangibles remained unchanged, and the net current period return on tangible assets declined. The jump in the profitability of R&D in the 1990s is consistent with technology driven innovation having been an important driver of the economic boom experienced by the United States over that same period (e.g. Boulton *et al.*, 2000; Lev, 2001). Third, on average the NPV profitability of R&D and advertising increases as the scale of the expenditures made on those intangibles increases. In contrast, the NPV on personnel activities decreases with scale. Finally, the increasing profitability returns-to-scale of expenditures on both R&D and advertising have become more pronounced over time.

Overall, my findings support the view that R&D and advertising intangibles have indeed emerged over the past twenty years to become a critical means by which firms today create value, and that one mechanism of value creation is that of increasing profitability returns-to-scale. It appears that the competitive environment for R&D and advertising-intensive businesses has become increasingly imperfect over the past two decades, in that firms that make the largest investments in R&D and advertising can create cost-based and/or network-derived barriers to entry, and thereby earn supra-normal rents.

Appendix A: Economic Features Characterize Investments in Intangibles

A key hypothesis tested in this paper is that investments in intangibles have emerged over the past twenty years to become a critical means by which firms today create value, and that the value creation mechanism is increasing profitability returns-to-scale. This appendix summarizes the four main economic features characterize investments in intangibles, of which increasing profitability returns-to-scale is one (Lev, 2001; Hand, 2002*a*,*b*).

A.1. A Nonstandard Risk-return Profile

Per Figure A.1, the probability distribution of the return on investment (ROI) for tangible assets can be modelled as bell-shaped around a perfectly competitive ROI. This is because there are usually very close substitutes for tangible assets, competing away abnormal profitability. In contrast, the ROI probability distribution for intangibles is decreasing in ROI. The most likely outcome is that the investment will be a complete loss—an unlikely outcome for tangible assets. At the same time, however, the probability of a monopolistic and very large ROI is material and far higher than for an investment in tangible assets due to the lack of close substitutes.

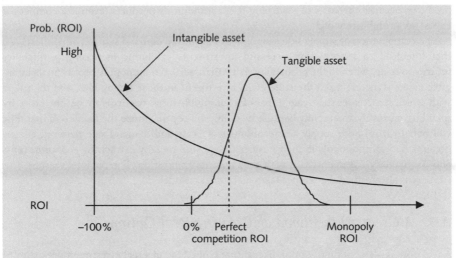

Fig. A.1. Model of probability distribution of the ROI for tangible vs intangible assets.

A.2. Increasing Profitability Returns-to-scale for Successful Intangibles

Increasing profitability returns-to-scale is created by two sets of factors: supply side economies of scale, and demand side network effects. Supply side economies of scale occur when increased size leads to lower unit costs. This occurs with many intangible assets because intangible assets are typically nonrival in nature. Physical and financial assets are rival assets, meaning that if person A uses a plot of land to grow coffee, then person B cannot also use that land to grow tea. Rival assets have positive opportunity costs. Moreover, greater benefits can only be extracted from rival assets via increased marginal costs. If an entrepreneur starts a coffee plantation, he will begin by buying the best land he can. Then, as he expands production, he will have to buy less and less suitable land, and the marginal cost of his coffee production will rise. In contrast, intangibles are typically nonrival assets, where multiple users can simultaneously use the asset without either depreciating it. As a result, nonrival assets have low or zero opportunity costs beyond the initial investment made to create them. For example, when writing software, a firm incurs large fixed costs. However, once written, more of that software can be made at essentially zero marginal cost—merely the cost of copying the program onto a compact disk or emailing it to another user. Software also does not physically depreciate like tangible assets do.

Demand side network effects exist when the value of connecting to a network is increasing in the number of other people connected to it (Farrell and Saloner, 1985; Brynjolfsson and Kemerer, 1996). Network effects can create positive feedback so that a customer base gets larger because existing customers attract new customers, even in the absence of expenditures by the company. The ideal result of such positive feedback is that the firm rapidly obtains a natural monopoly of its business space. Moreover, the staying power of that natural monopoly can be high because the firm's customers become locked-in to using its products, because the costs of switching to a competitor's products (even if a competitor exists) are prohibitively high.

The combination of supply side economies of scale and demand side network effects can therefore lead to strategically successful investments exhibiting increasing profitability returns-to-scale, wherein the probability that a firm will earn monopoly profits on its intangible assets is increasing in the scale of its investment in those intangibles, and the speed with which it increases that scale. It pays for intangible-intensive firms to 'bet-the-farm' by spending massively and rapidly because by doing so they maximize the likelihood that they will benefit from both supply side economies of scale and demand side network effects, obtain a natural monopoly in their business space, and thereby extract the economic rents and profitability commensurate with that monopoly position. For obvious reasons, this strategy is also termed the winner-takes-all business model.

A.3. A Greater Likelihood of Creating Real Options

A real option is an option or option-like feature embedded in a real investment opportunity. In many investment project settings, the firm has one or more options to make strategic changes to the project during the project's life. For example, a firm may have the option to abandon a project during its life, which amounts to a put option on the remaining cash flows associated with the project. These strategic options, which are known as real options, are typically ignored in standard discounted cash flow analysis where a single expected present value is computed. Ignoring the value of real options can lead to dramatically underestimation of the value of firm's real investments.

Noe and Parker (2001) argue that large expenditures early in the winner-take-all competition produce valuable strategic real options in later periods. For example, Amazon.com's intense, first-mover push into selling books online created expansion options that leveraged the company's investment into customer list intangibles. Whether Amazon succeeded or failed in the online book space, its massive and rapid expenditures on branding, R&D, information technology, and human expertise intangibles created for itself the option to move into CDs, toys, electronics, tools, travel and the like (were those areas to become financially attractive) rapidly and with low cost. Noe and Parker demonstrate analytically that the winner-take-all structure of high-fixed-cost, low-marginal-cost, markets for information goods ensures that market participation and the investment strategy are highly stochastic. If a firm chooses to participate in a particular Internet business space, it is optimal for it to act very aggressively through advertising that reduce the probability of entry of other firms. Such large expenditures on branding, R&D, and other intangibles both create real options and magnify the returns and risks associated with them.

A.4. Unusual Costs

Although intangibles have high potential returns, they come with two kinds of unusual costs. First, physical and financial assets have well-defined property rights that exclude others from enjoying their benefits. Intangibles do not. Nonowners can rarely be precluded from enjoying some of the benefits of investments made in the intangibles. For example, the benefits from employee training and the ideas employees get as a result of working for a firm cannot be removed from the employee should he or she decide to leave. The high-tech world is replete with examples of key employees leaving to form a new firm that eventually dominates that same industry. Although patents give bestow legal rights to an idea or product, competitors can and do infringe patents, meaning that large costs may need to be incurred to protect a patent. Second, unlike tangible assets, intangibles tend not to have organized, competitive markets in which they can be bought and sold. This creates a private cost, namely an intangible owned by a firm is less valuable because of its lack of tradability. It also creates costs to society in general, since markets perform vital economic and social functions. The lack of markets for intangibles arises because of fuzzy property rights, low marginal costs of production, and difficulties in contracting on the benefits accruing from the intangible. Although recent years have seen significant improvements in the ability to trade intangibles, for example, through patent licensing, mergers and acquisitions, joint ventures, and strategic alliances, trading in intangibles lacks transparency because details of licensing deals and alliances are rarely made public

....

Notes

1. My thanks to A. Ahmed, M. Alles, D. Harris, M. Harris, E. Maydew, D. Shackelford, T. Sougiannis, and participants at Syracuse University, the Duke/UNC Fall camp, and the 12th Annual Conference on Financial Economics and Accounting for comments.
2. Consistent with the hypothesis that employee stock options are unrecognized assets, Bell *et al.* (2002) find that the disclosed pro-forma cost of employee stock options is positively correlated with both current equity market value and future abnormal earnings for computer software firms.
3. Defined as SIC codes 4900–4999, 6000–6411, and 6500–6999.
4. For example, Maddala (1977: 368–9) notes that 'It has been found that incorrect restrictions [on the parameters in a lag structure] result in biased estimation of key parameters'.
5. This approach is similar to but less restrictive than the form-free method of Hatanaka and Wallace (1980), used by Ravenscraft and Scherer (1982). A short summary of the latter method as applied to R&D can be found in the appendix of Sougiannis (1994).
6. Because gross margin GM is computed before taking into account the cost of debt or equity capital, the annual discount rate I employ of $R = 1.06$ is one plus the real weighted average cost of capital. It is arrived at using a real risk-free rate of 2.25% (average over 1980–2000) and a risk premium of 3.75%.
7. Sougiannis (1994) reports finding similar results among four benefit measures: after tax earnings before advertising and R&D expense, pretax earnings, operating income, and gross margin.
8. In contrast, scatter plots of gross margin deflated by revenues, total assets or book equity against similarly scaled independent variables suggest that deflation creates significantly greater numbers of influential observations.

9. Test statistics are not adjusted for any autocorrelation in the coefficient estimates as with only twenty-one years of data, autocorrelations will be imprecisely estimated (Fama and French, 1998).

10. The reader may be concerned that the parameter estimates obtained for, say, R&D when $K = 0$ being little different from those obtained when $K = 7$ lead to the counter-intuitive inference that all the benefits of R&D are felt in the year the investment is made. This is not the case because when $K = 0$ the single coefficient on RD will be upward biased relative to its true value due to the high positive autocorrelation of RD (Maddala, 1977: 156).

....

References

Aboody, D. and Lev, B. (1998), 'The value relevance of intangibles: The case of software capitalization', *Journal of Accounting Research*, 36 (Supplement): 161–91.

Bell, T. B., Landsman, W. R., Miller, B. L., and Yeh, S. (2002), 'The valuation implications of employee stock option accounting for computer software firms', *The Accounting Review*, 77(4): 971–96.

Boulton, R. E. S., Libert, B. D., and Samek, S. M. (2000), *Cracking the Value Code: How Successful Businesses are Creating Wealth in the New Economy*, HarperBusiness.

Brynjolfsson, E. and Kemerer, C. F. (1996), 'Network externalities in microcomputer software: An econometric analysis of the spreadsheet market', *Management Science*, 42: 1627–47.

Chambers, D., Jennings, R., and Thompson, R. B. (2002), 'Excess returns to R&D-intensive firms', *Review of Accounting Studies*, 7(2/3): 133–158.

Chan, L. K. C., Lakonishok, J., and Sougiannis, T. (2000), 'The stock market valuation of research and development expenditures', Working paper, University of Illinois at Urbana-Champagne.

De Long, J. B. (2000), 'The two faces of the internet economy', *Fortune*, 2: 62–6.

Fama, E. F. and French, K. R. (1998), 'Taxes, financing decisions, and firm value', *Journal of Finance*, 53: 819–43.

—— and MacBeth, J. D. (1973), 'Risk, return, and equilibrium: Empirical tests', *Journal of Political Economy*, 81: 607–36.

Farrell, J. and Saloner, G. (1985), 'Standardization, compatibility, and innovation', *Rand Journal of Economics*, 16: 442–55.

Hand, J. R. M. (2002a), 'The new economy: Pricing of equity securities', in D. Jones (ed.) *Handbook of Economics in the Electronic Age*, Forthcoming.

—— (2002b), 'Evidence on the winner-takes-all business model: The profitability returns-to-scale of expenditures on intangibles made by U.S. internet firms, 1995–2001', Working paper, UNC Chapel Hill.

Hatanaka, M. and Wallace, T. D. (1980), 'Multicollinearity and the estimation of low-order moments in stable lag distributions', in J. Kmenta and T. D. Wallace (eds), *Evaluation of Econometric Models* (New York: Academic Press), pp. 323–89.

Hirschey, M. (1982), 'Intangible capital aspects of advertising and R&D expenditures', *Journal of Industrial Economics*, 30(4): 375–90.

Johnston, J. (1972), *Econometric Methods* (New York: McGraw-Hill).

Lev, B. (2000), 'New math for a new economy', *Fast Company*, January–February.

—— (2001), 'Intangibles: Management, measurement, and reporting', Brookings Institution Press.

—— and Sougiannis, T. (1996), 'The capitalization, amortization, and value-relevance of R&D', *Journal of Accounting and Economics*, 20: 107–38.

Maddala, G. S. (1977), *Econometrics* (New York: McGraw-Hill).

Nissim, D. and Thomas, J. (2000), 'R&D costs and accounting profits', Working paper, Columbia University.

Noe, T. H. and Parker, G. (2001), 'Winner take all: Competition, strategy, and the structure of returns in the internet economy', Working paper, Tulane University.

Ravenscraft, D. and Scherer, F. M. (1982), 'The lag structure of returns to research and development', *Applied Economics*, 14: 603–20.

Shapiro, C. and Varian, H. (1999), *Information Rules* (Boston, MA: Harvard Business School Press).

Sougiannis, T. (1994), 'The accounting based valuation of corporate R&D', *The Accounting Review*, 69: 44–68.

III. THE ADVERSE CONSEQUENCES OF THE INFORMATIONAL DEFICIENCIES OF INTANGIBLES

## 13

Off-balance Sheet R&D Assets and Market Liquidity

Jeff P. Boone and K. K. Raman

1. Introduction

By requiring that corporate research and development (R&D) spending be immediately expensed, Statement of Financial Accounting Standards (SFAS) No. 2 (FASB, 1974: para. 2) potentially creates a mismatch between costs and subsequent benefits. Potentially, these off-balance sheet (unrecorded) R&D benefits could generate ex ante inequity in the capital markets in the form of an information gap (asymmetry) between informed investors and other investors. The prior literature (e.g. Brennan and Subrahmanyam, 1995: 361) indicates that trading by informed investors (i.e. investors with access to private information or the analytical ability to extract private information from publicly available data) can impose 'significant liquidity costs on other market participants due to adverse selection'.

The purpose of our paper is to examine the information asymmetry effects associated with off-balance sheet (unrecorded) R&D assets. In particular, our study seeks to examine a potential harm (lower market liquidity) associated with the current accounting treatment for R&D expenditures.[1]

Lev and Sougiannis (1996: 134) indicate that R&D capitalization would provide investors with 'statistically reliable and economically relevant information'. However, usefulness is a necessary but not a sufficient condition for financial reporting regulation (Lev, 1988: 2). Rather, regulators (such as the Securities and Exchange Commission) have a mandate to maintain public confidence in the securities markets as a level playing field by mitigating information asymmetry or ex ante inequity (Levitt, 1998: 79).

As noted by Glosten and Milgrom (1985: 72–4), information asymmetry can lead to adverse economic consequences in the form of higher bid-ask spreads. Higher spreads have been shown empirically to be associated with higher stock returns (which implies a higher cost of capital), a finding consistent with the notion that investors have to be compensated for holding less liquid stocks (Amihud and Mendelson, 1986b: 246). We utilize the adverse selection component of the spread and the quoted depth as observable proxies for information asymmetry.

In this paper, we utilize intraday stock transactions data to measure the average adverse selection component of the bid-ask spread and the quoted depth during 1995 and 1996 for our sample firms. Our approach is based on theoretical models which indicate that the market maker (dealer) is not in the business of conducting private information search and is therefore at a disadvantage relative to information motivated traders; consequently, faced with the adverse selection risk associated with information asymmetry the market maker's defensive reaction is to *increase* the adverse selection component of the spread and *decrease* the quoted depth (Lee *et al.*, 1993: 371).

We perform and report results from three tests. First, we compare the average adverse selection component of the spread (ASCS) and the quoted depth for our sample of R&D-intensive firms with the ASCS and depth for non-R&D-intensive firms. Second, for R&D-intensive firms we examine the association between the ASCS (and depth) and the magnitude of off-balance sheet R&D assets. Finally, we investigate the association between the *change* in the ASCS (and the *change* in depth) for these R&D-intensive firms from 1995 to 1996 and the *change* in the magnitude of unrecorded R&D assets. After controlling for the factors that prior research (e.g. Chung *et al.*, 1995: 1031; Stoll, 1978: 1170) indicates are associated with the market maker's adverse selection risk, our overall results suggest that: (1) the ASCS is higher for R&D-intensive firms than for non-R&D-intensive firms, (2) the ASCS (and depth) for R&D-intensive firms is significantly associated with the magnitude of off-balance sheet R&D assets, and (3) the change in ASCS is associated with the change in the magnitude of off-balance sheet R&D assets.

The rest of our paper is organized as follows. In Section 2, we review the role of financial reporting regulations in promoting a level playing field (ex ante equity) and prior research on R&D including the value relevance and magnitude of off-balance sheet R&D assets. Section 3 discusses hypotheses, methodology, and research design, and Section 4 describes empirical findings. Section 5 presents our concluding remarks.

2. Background

2.1. Financial Reporting Regulation and Ex ante Equity

Lev (1988: 2) notes that in a multiperson setting of diverse users with varying preferences, endowments, and objectives, usefulness is *not* an adequate basis for accounting regulation. Rather, the public interest criterion applied by accounting regulators (such as the Financial Accounting Standard Board (FASB) and the SEC) is that of equity in the capital markets defined as ex ante equity or equality of opportunity, that is, equal access to value relevant information (Lev, 1988: 11). Differential access to information allows informed investors to increase their wealth at the expense of uninformed investors and is perceived by the US Congress and the SEC to be unfair (Beaver, 1998: 34). Similarly, Hakansson (1977: 396) and Shefrin and Statman (1992: 42) suggest that the notion of equal access to information is the main reason for bringing private information into the public domain through disclosure regulation.[2]

Lev and Zarowin (1999: 377) suggest that capitalization and amortization of R&D spending would permit management to better convey current performance to investors and reveal private information about company prospects via accrual choices such as the R&D amortization period. However, useful accounting information generally involves an appropriate trade-off between relevance and reliability. Capitalization of R&D would permit managers to exercise judgment as to what expenditures to capitalize and the amortization period, allowing for additional discretion that could be abused by opportunistic managers to massage or bias reported results (Lev and Zarowin, 1999: 379). Consequently, financial analysts may be motivated to do additional analysis in an attempt to undo management's judgement and apply consistent rules across firms.[3]

From a different perspective, informed investors may be currently privy to nonpublic information about R&D assets (obtained through private information search). If so, mandatory capitalization and amortization of R&D spending and disclosure of R&D assets on the balance sheet could render their private information moot. For example, Elliott and Jacobson (1991: 58) observe that '[Informed] investors and their representatives may not see it in their interests to have information-era disclosures universally available, because they sell and use their personally developed information on the value of securities'.

2.2. Prior Research

Prior accounting research on R&D is relatively sparse (Elliott et al., 1984; Hirschey and Weygandt, 1985; Bublitz and Ettredge, 1989; Chan et al., 1990; Wasley and Linsmeier, 1992; Sougiannis, 1994). Basically, these studies document the stock market's reaction to firms' R&D announcements and investor cognizance of R&D outlays. More recently, Chan et al. (2001) report a positive association between the ratio of R&D spending to sales and stock return volatility. They suggest that the higher volatility is due to investor uncertainty about the future payoffs from R&D spending. Separately, Barth et al. (2001) provide evidence that analyst coverage is significantly greater for firms with larger R&D spending, and Aboody and Lev (2000: 2765) indicate that intangibles created by R&D spending allow corporate insiders to trade on the information and gain at the expense of outside investors.

While prior research has generally used the ratio of R&D spending to sales as a proxy for R&D assets, Lev and Sougiannis (1996: 125) estimate directly the magnitude of firm-specific R&D assets using financial statement data and also adjust reported earnings for the capitalization and amortization of R&D outlays. Although the major tenet of SFAS No. 2 (FASB, 1974: para 41) is that a 'direct relationship between R&D costs and specific future revenue generally has not been demonstrated', Lev and Sougiannis (1996: 110) attempt to establish an empirical connection between R&D spending and subsequent earnings. They (1996: 114) note that firms incur R&D expenditures both to develop new knowledge as well to develop absorptive capacity (i.e. the capacity to recognize, assimilate, and take advantage of the knowledge of other firms within the same industry or related industries). Because competitors' ability to copy, imitate, or invent around proprietary know-how including patents can vary by industry, the useful life (and the amortization rate) of the benefits of the new knowledge and innovation derived from R&D spending can also be expected to vary by industry (Lev and Sougiannis, 1996: 114).

Lev and Sougiannis (1996: 112) obtain estimates of firm-specific R&D assets by estimating the empirical relationship between annual R&D expenditures since 1975 (when SFAS No. 2 became effective) and subsequent annual operating income for a large cross-section of R&D-intensive firms. The length of the statistically significant lagged R&D coefficients provides estimates of the average duration (useful life) of R&D benefits, and was found to vary by industry (from nine years in chemicals and pharmaceuticals to five years in scientific instruments) (Lev and Sougiannis, 1996: 120). The unrecorded R&D assets at year-end for each sample firm are then obtained by cumulating the unamortized portion of annual R&D spending for each year since 1975 (Lev and Sougiannis, 1996: 123). Also, earnings (adjusted for the R&D capitalization) were obtained by taking the reported earnings, adding the expensed R&D outlay, and subtracting the R&D amortization (Lev and Sougiannis, 1996: 122).

As one would expect, the adjustments to reported earnings and book values were material with average earnings and book values of stockholders equity (for all firms and years) underestimated by about 20.55 and 22.2 per cent, respectively (Lev and Sougiannis, 1996: 123). Lev and Sougiannis (1996: 128) report that these adjusted values were significantly associated with contemporaneous stock prices (measured three months after the fiscal year-end) and returns (measured over a twelve month time frame from −9 to +3 months surrounding the fiscal year-end), indicating the value relevance of the R&D capitalization process for investors. They (1996: 134) conclude that the association between R&D outlays and subsequent earnings is both 'statistically reliable and economically meaningful' (in direct contradiction to the premise of SFAS No. 2) and that the association is recognized by investors.

As described in Section 3, we evaluate SFAS No. 2 from the perspective of the market microstructure. Our capital market analysis is complementary to, albeit different from, the prior research by Lev and Sougiannis (1996).

3. Hypotheses and Model Development

3.1. Observable Effects of Information Asymmetry

By *not* according recognition to R&D assets, SFAS No. 2 potentially exacerbates information asymmetry by allowing informed investors to exploit their relative advantage in assessing the performance of R&D-intensive firms. Prior market microstructure research (Bagehot, 1971: 13; Lee et al., 1993: 371; Brennan and Subrahmanyam, 1995: 362) addresses the adverse selection risk faced by the market maker (dealer) and suggests that information asymmetry is associated with reduced market liquidity (*higher* bid-ask spreads and *lower* quoted depths). As discussed below, in this study we focus on the adverse selection component of the spread and the quoted depth.

According to the market microstructure literature (Bagehot, 1971: 13; Copeland and Galai, 1983: 1468; Glosten and Milgrom, 1985: 73), the role of the market maker (dealer) is to provide liquidity or immediacy by standing ready to trade at his/her declared bid and ask quotes which straddle the perceived equilibrium price. The sellers and buyers who trade with the market maker can be liquidity motivated (i.e. seek to convert securities into cash and vice versa) or information motivated (i.e. possess private information). The dealer is not thought to do any private information search (such as analysing the financial statements of the companies in whose shares he/she trades) and is viewed as relatively uninformed (Kim and Verrecchia, 1994: 44). Hence, although the dealer gains from liquidity motivated traders (because of the bid-ask spread) he or she loses to information motivated traders (due to adverse selection) (Glosten and Milgrom, 1985: 72). Thus, individuals with private information profit at the expense of the market who, in turn, profits from those who are liquidity motivated (Copeland and Galai, 1983: 1468). To survive in the business, the dealer's gains from transacting with the liquidity motivated must exceed the losses from transacting with the information motivated (Bagehot, 1971: 13). Normally, the dealer cannot distinguish ex ante between the two types of transactors, and dealers' inventories typically decrease (increase) before an increase (decrease) in the equilibrium price suggesting a loss due to the lag in adjusting the bid-ask spread (Stoll, 1976: 372).

Understandably, market makers undertake defensive measures to protect themselves against losses sustained in trading with those who possess private information (Bagehot, 1971: 13). A widening of the spread enables the dealer to earn additional profits in transactions with liquidity motivated traders to offset the higher losses in transactions with information motivated traders (Glosten and Milgrom, 1985: 72). Similarly, reducing the quoted depth (i.e. offering to trade a fewer number of shares at each quoted price) protects the market maker by reducing the maximum loss that he/she can sustain on a single trade with an informed trader (Lee *et al.*, 1993: 371). For R&D-intensive firms, the absence of public information about R&D assets can be expected to put market makers on the defensive since informed traders may have private information about the magnitude of such off-balance sheet assets. As noted by Lee *et al.* (1993: 371), faced with informed trading, the market maker can *increase* spread as well as *reduce* depth, that is, both spread and depth can be adjusted to actively manage the risk of loss to informed traders. Consistent with Lee *et al.* (1993: 371), we utilize spread and depth as dependent variables in our analysis as discussed below.

The market microstructure literature (e.g. Bagehot, 1971: 13; Stoll, 1976: 372) identifies the spread as the market maker's compensation for shouldering three different types of costs: inventory holding costs, order processing costs, and adverse selection costs attributable to transacting with information motivated traders. The inventory holding and order processing costs reflect the costs to the dealer of having to carry an adequate inventory of stocks to trade on demand (i.e. provide immediacy) and the clerical costs of processing those trades (Bagehot, 1971: 13). The adverse selection costs reflect the losses sustained by the market maker in transactions with informed traders (Copeland and Galai, 1983: 1468). Since the focus of our study is the association between adverse selection costs and off-balance sheet R&D assets, we focus on the adverse selection *component* of the spread rather than the *total* spread. We analyse the adverse selection component of the spread (rather than the total spread) since it is a more focused measure of the effects of adverse selection that is less influenced by extraneous factors such as the market maker's inventory holding and order processing costs. Hence, in this study we examine the association between the adverse selection component of the spread (and quoted depth) and unrecorded R&D assets. As discussed later in this section, our methodology for measuring the adverse selection component of the spread is based on Huang and Stoll (1996) and utilizes intraday stock transactions data.

3.2. Hypotheses

As discussed previously, Lev and Sougiannis (1996: 128) document a cross-sectional association between the stock returns of R&D-intensive firms and the pro forma earnings and book values obtained by making adjustments to reported accounting numbers to reflect a capitalize-and-amortize method of accounting for R&D expenditures. Also, as noted previously, the adjustments to reported earnings and book values of stockholders equity were material (Lev and Sougiannis, 1996: 123). These findings suggest that market makers in R&D-intensive firms potentially face a greater risk of adverse selection and trading losses to informed investors. Consequently, as part of their defensive response, market makers can be expected on average to *increase* the adverse selection component of the spread and *lower* the quoted depth for R&D-intensive firms.

The notion that financial statement data (such as R&D expenditures) are largely anticipated by market participants in advance of their officials release and that there is no specific point in time at which these data are impounded in the stock price is well established in the accounting literature (Ball and Brown, 1968: 169). Consistent with this notion and as discussed previously, Lev and Sougiannis (1996: 128) examine annual stock returns for their sample of R&D-intensive firms beginning nine months before and ending three months after the end of the fiscal year. In our study, we utilize a similar twelve month time frame to compute the average adverse selection component of the spread (ASCS) and the quoted depth. Keeping in mind that a *higher* spread or a *lower* depth is consistent with reduced market liquidity, our first hypothesis, stated in the alternative form, is as follows:

H1. Market liquidity is lower for R&D-intensive firms than for non-R&D-intensive firms.

Prior research in accounting suggests that the association between the equilibrium price of a stock and accounting data (such as earnings) is also one of magnitude (Beaver *et al.*, 1979: 339). In other words, the magnitude of accounting numbers represents pertinent information, consequently, to ignore magnitude would be to throw away valuable information. Hence, to the extent that unreported R&D assets constitute value relevant information, the magnitude of the off-balance sheet R&D assets can be expected to be relevant in assessing the market maker's adverse selection risk and potential trading losses to informed investors. Consequently, the magnitude of off-balance sheet R&D assets can be expected to be associated with the magnitude of the effects of informed trading on the adverse selection component of the spread and quoted depth. Our second hypothesis, stated in the alternative form, is as follows:

H2. For R&D-intensive firms, there is a negative association between market liquidity and the magnitude of off-balance sheet R&D assets.

The analysis of R&D-intensive firms by Lev and Sougiannis (1996: 128) suggests that private information about the magnitude of off-balance sheet R&D assets at fiscal year-end is revised on an ongoing basis from one year to the next as informed investors update their expectations of current year R&D

expenditures, and that the revised information is impounded in valuations (prices) also on an ongoing basis. To the extent that off-balance sheet R&D assets reflect information asymmetry between informed investors and others, it is to be expected that as estimates of off-balance sheet R&D assets are revised (up or down) from one year to the next by informed traders the adverse selection risk faced by the market maker will also change in the same direction with associated consequences for the adverse selection component of the spread and depth. In our study, keeping in mind that a *higher* spread or a *lower* depth is consistent with reduced liquidity, we hypothesize that the change in market liquidity from one year to the next is associated with the change in the magnitude of unrecorded R&D assets. Our third and final hypothesis, stated in the alternative form, is as follows:

H3. For R&D-intensive firms, the change in market liquidity from one year to the next is negatively associated with the change in the magnitude of off-balance sheet R&D assets.

3.3. Model Development

We estimate three different models, corresponding to our three hypotheses, as follows:

$$\text{ML} = f(\text{VOL, VAR, MV, PRC, EARNVAR, GROWTH, RISK, INSTPER,} \\ \text{INSIDPER, NASDAQ, MMCNT, NUMANAL, ANEFF, RDI}), \quad (1)$$

$$\text{ML} = f(\text{VOL, VAR, MV, PRC, EARNVAR, GROWTH, RISK, INSTPER,} \\ \text{INSIDPER, NASDAQ, MMCNT, NUMANAL, ANEFF, OBSRDA}), \quad (2)$$

$$\Delta\text{ML} = f(\Delta\text{VOL, }\Delta\text{VAR, }\Delta\text{MV, }\Delta\text{PRC, }\Delta\text{INSTPER, }\Delta\text{INSIDPER, }\Delta\text{MMCNT,} \\ \Delta\text{NUMANAL, }\Delta\text{ANEFF, }\Delta\text{OBSRDA}), \quad (3)$$

where ML is market liquidity and is measured by the ASCS and the quoted depth (DEPTH). The two dependent variables are defined in Table 1. The control variables (VOL through ANEFF) and the test variables RDI and OBSRDA are also defined in Table 1. To control for industry effects, these models also include dummy variables corresponding to the two-digit SIC codes for our sample firms. The variables with the 'Δ' prefix denote the dependent and independent variables in the change form.

3.3.1. Dependent Variables

3.3.1.1. The adverse selection component of the spread. Our approach for measuring the ASCS is based on Huang and Stoll (1996: 326) and is defined as the difference between the *effective* half-spread and the *realized* half-spread. Since the spread applies to a round trip transaction (two trades), Huang and Stoll (1996: 322) utilize half-spreads to measure the market maker's loss to informed investors per trade. Also, since a large fraction of actual trades takes place inside

Table 1. Definition of Variables

Dependent variables

$ASCS_{it}$	The average adverse selection component of the spread for firm i during year t, calculated by measuring the excess of the effective half-spread over the realized half-spread per share on each transaction for firm i, deflating by the midpoint of the quoted bid and ask prices at the time of the transaction, and averaging across all transactions during the year. The effective half-spread is $\mid p_{ij} - m_{ij} \mid$, where p_{ij} is the price at which jth transaction in firm i's stock is executed and m_{ij} is the midpoint of the bid and ask quotes in firm i at that time. The realized half-spread is $(p_{ij+\tau} - p_{ij})$ if the jth transaction in firm i's stock occurs at the bid quote and $-(p_{ij+\tau} - p_{ij})$ if the jth transaction in firm i's stock occurs at the ask quote, where p_{ij} is the price at which the jth transaction is executed and $p_{ij+\tau}$ is the transaction price of the first trade occurring at least 5 min after the jth transaction.
$DEPTH_{it}$	The average quoted depth for firm i during year t, that is, the sum of the number of hundred share lots that the market maker is willing to trade at the quoted bid price and the quoted ask price.
$\Delta ASCS_i$	Change in $ASCS_{it}$ from 1995 to 1996.
$\Delta DEPTH_i$	Change in $DEPTH_{it}$ from 1995 to 1996.

Independent variables

VOL_{it}	The average number of stock trades occurring daily in firm i during year t.
VAR_{it}	The average variance in daily stock returns for firm i during year t.
MV_{it}	The average market value of common equity for firm i during year t (in millions of dollars).
PRC_{it}	The average of the midpoint of the quoted bid and ask prices on each transaction for firm i during year t.
$EARNVAR_i$	The coefficient of variation in the earnings of firm i over the five-year period 1990–94, calculated as the standard deviation of annual earnings from continuing operations divided by the absolute value of the mean.
$GROWTH_i$	The five year sales growth for firm i, calculated as $(sales_{1994} / sales_{1989})^{1/5} - 1$.
$RISK_i$	The systematic risk (beta) of the common stock of firm i, calculated using monthly returns over the five-year period ending 31 December 1994.
$INSTPER_{it}$	The average percentage of shares owned by institutional investors in firm i during year t.
$INSIDPER_{it}$	The average percentage of shares owned by corporate officers and other legally-defined corporate insiders in firm i during year t.
$NASDAQ_{it}$	Dummy variable assigned a value of 1 if the stock of firm i is traded on Nasdaq during year t; 0 otherwise.
$MMCNT_i$	The average number of market-makers for firm i during year t.
$NUMANAL_{it}$	The average number of sell-side analysts following firm i during year t.
$ANEFF_{it}$	The average number of firms followed by firm i's analysts during year t (i.e. the sum of the number of firms covered by firm i's analysts in a particular year divided by the number of analysts covering the firm that year).
RDI_i	Indicator variable for R&D-intensive firm: equal to 1 for firms in the Lev and Sougiannis two-digit SIC groups (SIC 28, 35–38); 0 otherwise.
$OBSRDA_{it}$	The magnitude of unrecorded (off-balance sheet) R&D assets for firm i during year t obtained by cumulating the unamortized portion of firm i's annual R&D spending since 1975, scaled by the firms's total assets (reported total GAAP assets plus unrecorded R&D assets). The industry-specific (i.e. two-digit SIC group-specific) amortization rate of R&D assets is taken from the parameters reported in Table 3 of Lev and Sougiannis (1996).
ΔVOL_i	Change in VOL_{it} from 1995 to 1996.
ΔVAR_i	Change in VAR_{it} from 1995 to 1996.
ΔMV_i	Change in MV_{it} from 1995 to 1996.
ΔPRC_i	Change in PRC_{it} from 1995 to 1996.
$\Delta INSTPER_i$	Change in $INSTPER_{it}$ from 1995 to 1996.
$\Delta INSIDPER_i$	Change in $INSIDPER_{it}$ from 1995 to 1996.
$\Delta MMCNT_i$	Change in $MMCNT_{it}$ from 1995 to 1996.
$\Delta NUMANAL_i$	Change in $NUMANAL_{it}$ from 1995 to 1996.
$\Delta ANEFF_i$	Change in $ANEFF_{it}$ from 1995 to 1996.
$\Delta OBSRDA_i$	Change in $OBSRDA_{it}$ from 1995 to 1996.

Note: Yearly average are calculated for the twelve month period beginning nine months before and ending three months after the fiscal year-end.

the quoted spread (Lee and Ready, 1991: 739), the *effective* spread accounts for trades inside the posted quotes and is a more accurate reflection of a trader's execution costs than the *quoted* spread (Huang and Stoll, 1996: 324). The *realized* spread (which measures the market maker's realized revenues on the basis of the post-trade price reversal) is the average difference between the price at which a market maker sells at a given point in time and the price at which he/she buys at an earlier point in time (Huang and Stoll, 1996: 326). On average, a market maker does not realize the *effective* spread since prices typically reverse, that is, move against him or her (falling after a dealer buy and rising after a dealer sale) due to adverse information possessed by informed traders. Hence, the *realized* spread is generally less than the *effective* spread and the excess of the effective half-spread over the realized half-spread provides an estimate of the market maker's average loss per share on a transaction with information motivated traders. To survive in the business, the market maker has to recover this loss (by widening the total spread) in transactions with liquidity motivated traders. Hence, according to Huang and Stoll (1996: 327), the market maker's loss to informed traders represents the adverse selection (information) component of the spread.

We follow Huang and Stoll (1996: 324) and define: (1) the effective half-spread as $|p_{ij} - m_{ij}|$ where p_{ij} is the trade price at which the jth transaction in firm i's stock is executed and m_{ij} is the midpoint of the bid and ask quotes in firm i at that time, and (2) the realized half-spread as $(p_{ij+\tau} - p_{ij})$ if the jth transaction in firm i's stock occurs at the bid quote and $-(p_{ij+\tau} - p_{ij})$ if the jth transaction in firm i's stock occurs at the ask quote, where p_{ij} is the trade price at which the jth transaction is executed and $p_{ij+\tau}$ is the trade price on the first transaction occurring at least 5 min after the jth transaction. Huang and Stoll (1996: 328) choose 5 min as the period of time necessary for an offsetting trade to occur and demonstrate that their empirical results are insensitive to the use of alternative time periods. For each firm in our sample, we calculate the average adverse selection component of the spread by taking the excess of the effective half-spread over the realized half-spread per share on each stock transaction, scaling (deflating) by the midpoint of the quoted bid and ask prices at the time of the trade and averaging across all transactions during the twelve month period (-9 to $+3$ months) surrounding the firm's fiscal year-end. The *greater* the adverse selection component of the spread (variable ASCS), the *lower* the market liquidity.

3.3.1.2. Quoted depth. Lee *et al.* (1993: 371) suggest that faced with informed trading, the market maker can *increase* spread as well as *reduce* depth, that is, the number of shares the market maker is willing to trade at each quote. For example, by reducing the quoted depth, that is, by offering to trade a fewer number of shares at each quoted price, the market maker can reduce the maximum loss that he/she can incur on a single trade. Consistent with Lee *et al.* (1993: 371) and other things being equal, the *lower* the depth (variable DEPTH), the *lower* the market liquidity.

3.3.2. Control Variables

Our control variables are based on prior research (e.g. Chung *et al.*, 1995: 1031; Easley *et al.*, 1996: 1428) and include trading volume (VOL), return volatility (VAR), the market value of the firm's equity (MV), the stock price (PRC), earnings variability (EARNVAR), sales growth (GROWTH), systematic risk (RISK), percentage of stock ownership by institutions and insiders (INSTPER and INSIDPER), listing on the Nasdaq stock market (NASDAQ), the number of market makers (dealers) in the stock (MMCNT), number of analysts following the firm (NUMANAL), and analyst effort (ANEFF). These variables are defined in Table 1.

3.3.2.1. Model with ASCS as the dependent variable. Easley *et al.* (1996: 1428) suggest that the probability of informed trading is higher in low volume stocks. The higher the probability of informed trading, the greater the market maker's potential adverse selection costs (Easley *et al.*, 1996: 1405). Hence, we include the number of stock trades (VOL) as a control variable and predict a negative sign for this variable.

The greater the variability (volatility) in the stock price, the greater the market maker's anticipated losses to informed traders since the probability of obtaining larger deviations between the price based on public information and the price based on private (asymmetric) information is greater for firms with more volatile stocks (Brennan and Subrahmanyam, 1995: 370). Hence, consistent with Brennan and Subrahmanyam (1995: 370), we include the return variance variable (VAR) as a control variable in our model and predict a positive association with the adverse selection component of the spread.

Larger firms are thought to have lower levels of information asymmetry (Chung *et al.*, 1995: 1031). Prior research (e.g. Chung *et al.*, 1995: 1031) demonstrates that the size of the firm, as measured by the market value of equity, is negatively associated with spreads. We include the market value of equity (MV) as a control variable in our model and predict a negative sign for this control variable.

Stoll (1978: 1170) notes that the price of the stock is related to the relative spread (i.e. the dollar spread divided by price) since price is a proxy for inventory holding and order processing costs. Hence, we include the PRC as a control variable and (based on prior research, e.g. Stoll, 1978: 1170) predict a negative sign for this variable. Also, Yohn (1998: 180) has shown that spreads are related to earnings variability. Hence, the coefficient of variation in earnings over the previous five years (EARNVAR) is included in our model as a control variable and is predicted to have a positive sign. In addition, we control for sales growth (GROWTH) and systematic risk (RISK) since these characteristics may be related to spreads. These two control variables are both expected to have positive signs.

Chiang and Venkatesh (1988: 1047) provide evidence that firms with greater institutional and insider ownership have larger spreads. Hence we include the percentage of institutional and insider ownership (INSTPER and INSIDPER) as control variables and predict a positive sign for both. Also, prior research (e.g. Stoll, 1978: 1170) suggests that: (1) firms listed on the Nasdaq stock market have higher spreads, and (2) spreads are negatively related to the number of competing market makers (dealers). For this reason, we include in our model a dummy variable (NASDAQ) to control for Nasdaq listing and a variable (MMCNT) to control for the number of competing market makers. Variable NASDAQ (MMCNT) is expected to have a positive (negative) sign.

Finally, Yohn (1998: 178) has shown that spreads are negatively related to analyst following. In our model, we control for the number of analysts following a firm (variable NUMANAL) which is expected to have a negative sign. In addition, consistent with Barth et al. (2001), we include a proxy for analyst effort (ANEFF) based on the notion that analyst effort is related positively to private information search and information asymmetry. Based on Barth et al. (2001), variable ANEFF is defined as the average number of firms followed by the firm's analysts and is based on the concept that the fewer the firms in total covered by a firm's analysts, the greater the effort in covering the firm. Variable ANEFF is computed by summing the number of firms covered by a firm's analysts in a particular year and dividing it by the number of analysts covering the firm that year. As an example, if a firm is followed by three analysts who cover 16, 20, and 30 firms, respectively, ANEFF equals 22. Since ANEFF is decreasing in analyst effort, it is predicted to have a negative sign.

3.3.2.2. Model with DEPTH as the dependent variable. Although Lee et al. (1993: 371) discuss the quoted depth as a measure of market liquidity and as a dependent variable, they do *not* discuss control variables associated with depth. For completeness, we include in our model all the control variables discussed previously. To our knowledge, there is no prior research to suggest the expected signs for these control variables. Hence, we do not predict the signs of the control variables in the model with DEPTH as the dependent variable.

3.3.3. Test Variables

The test variables are the indicator variable RDI and the magnitude of unrecorded (off-balance sheet) R&D assets (OBSRDA). We discuss the test variables in connection with the three models presented earlier. In model 1, keeping in mind that a *higher* spread or a *lower* depth is consistent with reduced market liquidity, we hypothesize that ASCS (DEPTH) is higher (lower) for

R&D-intensive firms than for non-R&D-intensive firms. The test variable RDI is an indicator variable equal to 1 for R&D-intensive firms, and 0 otherwise. Consistent with Lev and Sougiannis (1996: 114), a firm is defined as R&D-intensive (RDI = 1) if it belongs to the two-digit SIC groups 28 and 35–38, and non-R&D-intensive (RDI = 0) otherwise. A positive (negative) sign is predicted for RDI in the model with ASCS (DEPTH) as the dependent variable.

In model 2, we hypothesize a positive (negative) association between ASCS (DEPTH) and the magnitude of off-balance sheet R&D assets (OBSRDA). The dollar value of unrecorded R&D assets is estimated using the Lev and Sougiannis (1996: 123) methodology. In particular, we use the industry-specific amortization rates for R&D assets reported in Table 3 of Lev and Sougiannis (1996: 121) and annual R&D spending since 1975 to calculate the unamortized balance of a firm's unrecorded (off-balance sheet) R&D assets. To capture the economic significance of R&D assets (OBSRDA), we scale the estimated off-balance sheet R&D assets by the sum of the firm's reported total GAAP assets and the estimated off-balance sheet R&D assets.[4] As discussed previously, the greater the magnitude of OBSRDA, the greater the adverse selection risk and potential trading losses faced by the market maker *vis-à-vis* information motivated traders. Hence, a positive (negative) sign is predicted for OBSRDA in the model with ASCS (DEPTH) as the dependent variable.

In model 3, the dependent and independent variables are in the change (Δ) form and measure the change from 1995 to 1996. Firm-specific characteristics (such as earnings variability, sales growth, systematic risk, and Nasdaq listing, as proxied by variables EARNVAR, GROWTH, RISK, and NASDAQ, respectively) which remain essentially unchanged between 1995 and 1996 are not included in model 3 to avoid full rank problems. The predicted signs for the remaining control variables in the change form (ΔVOL through ΔANEFF) are the same as the signs predicted for the corresponding control variables in the level form models 1 and 2. As discussed previously, an increase in the magnitude of off-balance sheet R&D assets is hypothesized to increase the adverse selection risk and trading losses faced by the market maker. Hence, we predict a positive (negative) sign for ΔOBSRDA in the model with ΔASCS (ΔDEPTH) as the dependent variable.

3.3.4. Sample and Data

As noted previously, consistent with Lev and Sougiannis (1996: 114), a firm was identified as R&D-intensive if it belonged to the two-digit SIC groups 28 and 35–38. We estimate the average adverse selection component of the spread (and depth) using the intraday stock transactions Trade and Quotations (TAQ) database provided by the New York Stock Exchange. The TAQ database covers exchange-listed firms as well as Nasdaq NMS firms. Eliminating firms for which complete data for the various dependent and independent variables were unavailable, our analysis is based on: (1) a sample of 158 R&D-intensive firms (based on the Lev and Sougiannis (1996: 114) two-digit SIC code classification), and (2) a sample of 487 non-R&D-intensive firms that had no reported R&D spending.

The TAQ database provides a time-dated record of each transaction executed and each quote revision issued for exchange-listed and Nasdaq NMS securities. We used the following conventions in constructing the time-series of daily quotes and trades. First, we eliminated the first transaction of each trading day to avoid the effects caused by overnight news arrival as well as special features associated with the opening procedure (Brennan and Subrahmanyam, 1996: 445). Second, because the TAQ dataset does not explicitly classify a transaction as either a buy or a sell, we compare the trade price to the prevailing bid and ask quotes and classify the transaction as a customer buy (sell) if it was executed at the market maker's quoted ask (bid) price. For trades executed within the quoted spread (i.e. within the bid and ask quotes), we use the tick test to classify the trade as a buy or sell (Lee and Ready, 1991: 735). We also apply the data screens used by Brennan and Subrahmanyam (1996: 447) and Huang and Stoll (1996: 320) to eliminate instances of likely coding errors in the data. Finally, as suggested by Lee and Ready (1991: 734), we delay all quotes by 5 seconds in order to minimize the problem of quotes being recorded ahead of trades.

4. Empirical Findings

4.1. Descriptive Statistics

Table 2 provides descriptive statistics (mean and standard deviation) for the dependent and independent variables for the R&D-intensive and non-R&D-intensive firms. As shown in panel A, for R&D-intensive firms in 1995, variable ASCS which represents the market maker's adverse selection costs (as measured by the average of the excess of the effective half-spread over the realized half-spread on each trade scaled by the midpoint of the bid and ask quotes at the time of that transaction) has a mean value of 0.0022 or 0.22 per cent of share price. The comparison number for the non-R&D-intensive firms is lower at 0.0019 or 0.19 per cent of share price. Similarly, for the R&D-intensive firms in 1995, variable DEPTH (which represents the average quoted depth) has a mean value of 6839 shares, while the comparison number for the non-R&D-intensive firms is slightly higher at 7313 shares. We do not test for differences in the means of these variables, since any univariate comparison could potentially be muddied by concurrent differences in the control variables discussed below.

Table 2. Descriptive Statistics

| | R&D-intensive Firms | | | | | Non-R&D-intensive Firms | | | | |
| | 1995 | | | 1996 | | 1995 | | | 1996 | |
Variable	n	Mean	S.D.	Mean	S.D.	n	Mean	S.D.	Mean	S.D.
ASCS	158	0.0022	0.0013	0.0019	0.0013	487	0.0019	0.0012	0.0018	0.0012
DEPTH	158	68.3871	83.2493	68.1930	81.1779	487	73.1254	80.2896	78.1780	85.3472
VOL	158	86.0509	94.4773	115.7889	110.1915	487	49.2889	54.0162	59.6500	65.1828
VAR	158	0.0003	0.0004	0.0002	0.0003	487	0.0002	0.0003	0.0002	0.0003
MV	158	2165.9500	3758.5200	2437.4600	3895.7600	487	1844.5700	2952.6800	2059.4900	3210.1000
PRC	158	22.8695	16.0247	27.0881	17.4268	487	23.1643	13.2815	24.8222	15.0189
EARNVAR	158	1.2663	1.6461	1.2663	1.6461	487	0.9257	1.4454	0.9358	1.4607
GROWTH	158	0.1155	0.1283	0.1155	0.1283	487	0.0954	0.1042	0.0947	0.1043
RISK	158	1.3029	0.5100	1.3029	0.5100	487	0.9361	0.4994	0.9344	0.4980
INSTPER	158	0.4429	0.2130	0.4569	0.2103	487	0.4392	0.2058	0.4383	0.1983
INSIDPER	158	0.1068	0.1223	0.1045	0.1229	487	0.1029	0.1268	0.1038	0.1308
NASDAQ	158	0.5570	0.4983	0.5570	0.4983	487	0.3889	0.4880	0.3873	0.4876
MMCNT	158	8.7273	9.6048	8.3201	9.2417	487	5.5473	8.2276	5.3142	7.9985
NUMANAL	158	11.5127	10.2266	11.4873	10.3547	487	11.9342	9.1352	12.0225	9.5802
ANEFF	158	21.0570	6.9433	20.9214	6.7784	487	26.4814	9.6742	25.3154	9.3161
OBSRDA	158	0.2387	0.3134	0.2208	0.2868	NA	NA	NA	NA	NA

Note: OBSRDA is not applicable (NA) for non-R&D-intensive firms.

As reported in Table 2, in 1995, the mean number of daily stock trades (VOL) for the R&D-intensive firms was 86 relative to 49 for the non-R&D-intensive firms. The mean return variance (VAR) for the R&D-intensive firms was 0.0003 relative to 0.0002 for the other (non-R&D-intensive) firms. The mean market value of equity (MV) for the R&D-intensive firms was about $2.2 billion, while the comparison number for the other firms was $1.8 billion. The average share price (PRC) for the R&D-intensive firms was $22.87 while the price for the non-R&D-intensive firms was quite similar at $23.16.

In 1995, the coefficient of variation in reported earnings over the preceding five years (EARNVAR) for the R&D-intensive firms was somewhat higher (1.27) than for the other firms (0.93). The growth rate in sales over the preceding five years (GROWTH) for the R&D-intensive firms was also somewhat higher (12 per cent) than for the non-R&D-intensive firms (9.5 per cent). The systematic risk (beta) over the preceding five years was slightly higher (1.30) for the R&D-intensive firms than for the other firms (0.94). Institutional ownership of outstanding shares was 44.3 per cent for the R&D-intensive firms and a slightly lower 43.9 per cent for the non-R&D-intensive firms. By contrast, insider ownership was 10.7 per cent for the R&D-intensive firms and a slightly lower 10.3 per cent for the other firms. Approximately 56 per cent of the R&D-intensive firms were trading on NASDAQ, while only 39 per cent of the non-R&D-intensive firms were so traded. The average number of market makers (MMCNT) for the R&D-intensive firms was 8.73 while the comparison number for the other firms was lower at 5.55. Similarly, the average number of analysts (NUMANAL) following R&D-intensive firms was 11.5 while the comparison number for the non-R&D-intensive firms was 11.9. Finally, the mean value of ANEFF (as measured by the average number of firms followed by a firm's analysts) was 21 for R&D-intensive firms and 26 for other firms. Since a *higher* value of ANEFF implies *lower* analyst effort, these statistics suggest that analyst effort was greater on average for R&D-intensive firms (a finding consistent with Barth et al., 2001). In our regression analysis (discussed below), we control for these concurrent differences in our test of Hypothesis 1, that is, whether market liquidity is lower for R&D-intensive firms than for non-R&D-intensive firms.

Table 2 also presents the mean values of variable OBSRDA (off-balance sheet R&D assets scaled by total assets) for 1995 and 1996 for the R&D-intensive firms. For example, the mean value for OBSRDA in 1995 is 0.2387 which indicates that on average the unrecorded (off-balance sheet) R&D assets constituted 23.87 per cent of the R&D-intensive firm's total assets. OBSRDA is test variable in our regression analysis (discussed below) of Hypothesis 2, that is whether for R&D-intensive firms, there is a negative association between market liquidity and the magnitude of off-balance sheet R&D assets.

For brevity, we do not present Pearson correlation matrices. However, the Pearson pairwise correlations indicated that OBSRDA was significantly correlated with the dependent variables ASCS and DEPTH with the expected signs, that is, off-balance sheet R&D assets were correlated *positively* with the adverse selection component of the spread (ASCS) and *negatively* with quoted depth (DEPTH). In our multivariate test of Hypothesis 2, we examine whether OBSRDA has an incremental effect on ASCS and DEPTH after controlling for the other independent variables in our model.

Given the large number of control variables included in our analysis, it was not surprising that some of the Pearson pairwise correlations among the control variables (e.g. between variables VAR and MV, VAR and PRC, MV and PRC, MV and NUMANAL, and NASDAQ and MMCNT) were rather high. However, the Pearson pairwise correlations between the test variable OBSRDA and the control variables were quite low. Below, in our discussion of regression results, we report a heuristic test known as the variance inflation factor (VIF) as an indicator of whether or not collinearity is a problem in interpreting our regression results.

4.2. Regression Results

4.2.1. Hypothesis 1

Table 3 presents the regression estimates using ordinary least squares for model 1 with ASCS (the average adverse selection component of the spread) and DEPTH (the average quoted depth) as the dependent variables.[5] To sharpen the contrast between R&D-intensive firms and non-R&D-intensive firms (and consistent with Lev and Sougiannis, 1996: 114, footnote 10), in Table 3 we include only those R&D-intensive firms for which R&D spending (as a proportion of sales) is greater than the sample median. In Table 3, the VIF (variance inflation factor) represents a collinearity diagnostic. This diagnostic measure is computed for each independent variable and is the reciprocal of one minus the R^2 when the particular explanatory variable is regressed on all the other explanatory variables. The prior literature suggests that a VIF close to 10.0 or higher is indicative of a collinearity problem (e.g. Neter *et al.*, 1996, 387).

In the regressions with ASCS as the dependent variable, despite high VIFs for some of the control variables (e.g. the variance in daily stock returns (VAR), the market value of equity (MV), listing on Nasdaq (NASDAQ), and the number of market makers (MMCNT)), our regression results yield estimates with predicted signs that are consistent with the prior literature (e.g. Brennan and Subrahmanyam, 1995: 370; Chung *et al.*, 1995: 1031) and imply plausible relationships between ASCS and the control variables. In the regression with DEPTH as the dependent variable, as noted previously, we do not predict the signs of the control variables since prior research has *not* examined these relationships. Still, many of the control variables are significant and the model has good explanatory power.

Table 3. Ordinary Least Squares Regression Analysis Results Testing Hypothesis 1 (level form—Model 1) (Sample Includes R&D-intensive Firms and Non-R&D-intensive Firms)

| | Dependent Variable = ln(ASCS) | | | | | Dependent Variable = ln(DEPTH) | | | | |
	Predicted Sign	Year 1995 Coef/t-stat	VIF	Year 1996 Coef/t-stat	VIF	Predicted Sign	Year 1995 Coef/t-stat	VIF	Year 1996 Coef/t-stat	VIF
Intercept	?	-3.409*** / -13.104	0	-2.950*** / -11.761	0	?	4.447*** / 16.355	0	4.630*** / 15.806	0
ln(VOL)	-	-0.054*** / -1.679	6.0	-0.046* / -1.581	6.5	?	0.298*** / 8.845	6.0	0.327*** / 9.563	6.5
ln(VAR)	+	0.189*** / 5.927	17.4	0.258*** / 7.640	23.2		0.139*** / 4.192	17.4	0.171*** / 4.333	23.2
ln(MV)	-	0.002 / 0.070	8.8	0.034 / 1.372	10.3	?	0.228*** / 8.619	8.8	0.202*** / 6.973	10.3
ln(PRC)	-	-0.233*** / -4.049	7.1	-0.195*** / -3.415	9.3	?	-0.609*** / -10.142	7.1	-0.564*** / -8.890	9.3
ln(EARNVAR)	+	0.035*** / 2.239	1.5	0.043*** / 3.028	1.5	?	-0.009 / -0.562	1.5	-0.019 / -1.139	1.5
GROWTH	+	-0.049 / -0.311	1.5	0.095 / 0.659	1.5	?	-0.376** / -2.274	1.5	-0.345** / -2.055	1.5
RISK	+	0.068** / 1.819	1.9	0.044* / 1.294	1.9	?	-0.111*** / -2.827	1.9	-0.109*** / -2.748	1.9
INSTPER	+	0.249*** / 2.559	1.9	0.245*** / 2.744	1.9	?	0.279*** / 2.743	1.9	0.254*** / 2.432	1.9
INSIDPER	+	0.360*** / 2.530	1.5	-0.076 / -0.593	1.6	?	-0.193 / -1.299	1.5	-0.053 / -0.352	1.5
NASDAQ	+	0.219 / 1.217	38.3	0.349** / 2.007	42.4	?	0.498*** / 2.645	38.3	0.214 / 1.051	42.4
ln(MMCNT)	-	-0.201*** / -3.449	30.0	-0.301*** / -5.560	30.1	?	-0.738*** / -12.104	30.0	-0.698*** / -11.052	30.1

	Pred. sign	Coeff.		VIF	Coeff.		VIF	Pred. sign	Coeff.		VIF	Coeff.		VIF
ln(NUMANAL)	–	0.010			–0.005			?	0.253***			0.269***		
		0.281	4.5		–0.139	4.4			6.537	4.5		7.085	4.4	
ln(ANEFF)	–	–0.022			–0.038			?	0.040			0.117**		
		–0.402	2.0		–0.800	1.7			0.694	2.0		2.110	1.7	
RDI	+	0.104*			0.142**			–	–0.017			0.008		
		1.279	4.3		1.817	4.6			–0.205	4.3		–0.083	4.6	
Adj. R^2		0.668			0.745				0.845			0.845		
Model F		18.35***			26.23***				47.79***			48.04***		
No. obs.		578			578				578			578		

Note: *, **, *** denote significance levels at the 0.10, 0.05, 0.01 level, respectively. Significance levels based on a one-tailed test when the sign of the coefficient is predicted; two-tailed otherwise. The F-test of the overall model is based on a nondirectional test.

Model 1: $\ln(y_j) = \alpha_j + \beta_1\ln(VOL) + \beta_2\ln(VAR) + \beta_3\ln(MV) + \beta_4\ln(PRC) + \beta_5\ln(EARNVAR) + \beta_3GROWTH + \beta_6RISK + \beta_4INSTPER + \beta_8INSIDPER + \beta_9NASDAQ + \beta_{10}\ln(MMCNT) + \beta_{11}\ln(NUMANAL) + \beta_{12}\ln(ANEFF) + \beta_{13}RDI + \epsilon.$

The model includes industry dummies for each two-digit SIC code (which allows the intercept α_j to vary across industries) and is estimated cross-sectionally across the sample consisting of R&D-intensive firms with R&D spending/sales ratio greater than the sample median value and other (non-R&D-intensive) firms. Y_j denotes either ASCS or DEPTH. For brevity, industry-specific intercepts are not reported.

Our main interest is in the test indicator variable RDI which is equal to 1 if the firm belongs to the two-digit SIC codes (28, 35–38) identified by Lev and Sougiannis (1996: 114) as R&D-intensive, and 0 otherwise. As discussed previously, SFAS No. 2 (FASB, 1974, para. 12) potentially exacerbates the level of information asymmetry for R&D-intensive firms by mandating that the intangible assets associated with R&D spending remain off-balance sheet. Since the market maker's defensive response to adverse selection risk is to *increase* the spread or *lower* the depth, we hypothesized that RDI would be significant with a positive (negative) sign in the regression with ASCS (DEPTH) as the dependent variable.

In the regression with ASCS as the dependent variable, RDI is significant in both 1995 and 1996 with the predicted positive sign. In the regression with DEPTH as the dependent variable, RDI is not significant (although is has the predicted negative sign). Since a *higher* spread, other things being equal, is consistent with *lower* market liquidity, the overall results in Table 3 provide some evidence consistent with Hypothesis 1, that is, that market liquidity is lower for R&D-intensive firms than for non-R&D-intensive firms.

4.2.2. Hypothesis 2

Table 4 presents the regression estimates using ordinary least squares for model 2 and our sample of R&D-intensive firms with ASCS (the average adverse selection component of the spread) and DEPTH (the average quoted depth) as the dependent variables. Once again, there is collinearity among some of the control variables as indicated by the high VIFs (close to or in excess of 10) for variables VAR (variance in daily stock returns), MV (the market value of the firm's equity), NASDAQ (listing on the Nasdaq), and MMCNT (the number of market makers). In the regressions with ASCS as the dependent variable, the results yield parameter estimates with anticipated signs that are consistent with the prior literature (e.g. Easley *et al.*, 1996: 1428; Chung *et al.*, 1995: 1031) and imply plausible relationships between ASCS and the control variables. In the regressions with DEPTH as the dependent variable, as discussed previously, we do not predict the signs for the control variables. Still, the model has good explanatory power as indicated by the number of control variables that are significant and the overall adjusted R^2.

Our main interest is in the accounting test variable OBSRDA. In Table 4, the *highest* VIF for this test variable is only 2.1. Hence, in Table 4, collinearity does not appear to be a problem in interpreting our empirical findings regarding the statistical significance of OBSRDA. As discussed previously, unrecorded R&D assets potentially exacerbate information asymmetry and increase the market maker's adverse selection risk with regard to informed traders. Also as noted previously (and consistent with Beaver *et al.*, 1979: 339), to the extent that the magnitude of accounting numbers constitutes value relevant information,

Table 4. Ordinary Least Squares Regression Analysis Results Testing Hypothesis 2 (level form—Model 2)

	Dependent Variable = ln(ASCS)					Dependent Variable = ln(DEPTH)				
	Predicted Sign	Year 1995 Coef/t-stat	VIF	Year 1996 Coef/t-stat	VIF	Predicted Sign	Year 1995 Coef/t-stat	VIF	Year 1996 Coef/t-stat	VIF
Intercept	?	−4.365*** / −8.205	0	−2.695*** / −5.038	0	?	4.002*** / 8.353	0	5.397*** / 10.352	0
ln(VOL)	−	−0.069 / −1.200	7.5	−0.022 / 0.497	5.2	?	0.320*** / 6.176	7.5	0.315*** / 7.326	5.2
ln(VAR)	+	0.163*** / 2.927	21.6	0.311*** / 5.540	25.6	?	0.057 / 1.133	21.6	0.201*** / 3.685	25.6
ln(MV)	−	0.029 / 0.643	10.9	−0.020 / −0.470	11.2	?	0.168*** / 4.148	10.9	0.184*** / 4.460	11.2
ln(PRC)	−	−0.246*** / −2.567	8.7	−0.037 / −0.416	8.7	?	−0.699*** / −8.096	8.7	−0.591*** / −6.893	8.7
ln(EARNVAR)	+	0.066*** / 2.447	1.4	0.048** / 1.997	1.3	?	−0.023 / −0.949	1.4	−0.036 / −1.517	1.3
GROWTH	+	0.317 / 1.211	1.8	0.372* / 1.567	1.7	?	−0.188 / −0.797	1.8	−0.078 / −0.339	1.7
RISK	+	0.086* / 1.424	1.5	0.038 / 0.703	1.5	?	−0.105* / −1.923	1.5	−0.116** / −2.189	1.5
INSTPER	+	0.187 / 0.958	2.7	0.033 / 0.176	2.9	?	0.108 / 0.616	2.7	0.038 / 0.205	2.9
INSIDPER	+	0.382* / 1.439	1.6	0.024 / 0.097	1.7	?	−0.293 / −1.224	1.6	−0.412* / −1.708	1.7
NASDAQ	+	0.430 / 1.106	58.6	−0.090 / −0.255	58.3	?	1.374*** / 3.921	58.6	0.031 / 0.091	58.3

Table 4. Continued

		Dependent Variable = ln(ASCS)						Dependent Variable = ln(DEPTH)				
		Year 1995		Year 1996				Year 1995		Year 1996	
	Predicted Sign	Coef/t-stat	VIF	Coef/t-stat	VIF		Predicted Sign	Coef/t-stat	VIF	Coef/t-stat	VIF
ln(MMCNT)	−	−0.284**		−0.248**			?	−1.048***		−0.711***	
		−2.318	45.5	−2.291	41.7			−9.500	45.5	−6.741	41.7
ln(NUMANAL)	−	−0.034		0.005			?	0.320***		0.362***	
		−0.516	6.2	0.091	4.8			5.349	6.2	6.900	4.8
ln(ANEFF)	−	−0.038		−0.050			?	0.047		0.004	
		−0.427	1.2	−0.616	1.2			0.592	1.2	−0.048	1.2
OBSRDA	+	0.233**		0.267***			−	−0.187**		−0.245**	
		2.145	1.8	2.285	2.1			−1.909	1.8	−2.148	2.1
Adj. R^2		0.724		0.782				0.909		0.911	
Model F		20.59***		27.87***				75.53***		77.62***	
No. obs.		158		158				158		158	

Notes: *, **, *** denote significance levels at the 0.10, 0.05, and 0.01 level, respectively. Significance levels based on one-tailed test when the sign of the coefficient is predicted; two-tailed otherwise. The F-test of the overall model is based on a nondirectional test.

Model 2: $\ln(y_j) = \alpha_t + \beta_1\ln(\text{VOL}) + \beta_2\ln(\text{VAR}) + \beta_3\ln(\text{MV}) + \beta_4\ln(\text{PRC}) + \beta_4\ln(\text{EARNVAR}) + \beta_5\text{GROWTH} + \beta_6\text{RISK} + \beta_7\text{INSTPER} + \beta_8\text{INSIDPER} + \beta_9\text{NASDAQ} + \beta_{10}\ln(\text{MMCNT}) + \beta_{11}\ln(\text{NUMANAL}) + \beta_{12}\ln(\text{ANEFF}) + \beta_{13}\text{OBSRDA} + \epsilon$.

The model includes industry dummies for each two-digit SIC code (which allows the intercept α_t to vary across industries) and is estimated cross-sectionally across the sample consisting of R&D-intensive firms only. Y_j denotes either ASCS or DEPTH. For brevity, industry-specific intercepts are not reported.

the magnitude of unrecorded R&D assets can be expected to be pertinent in assessing the market maker's adverse selection costs and potential trading losses to informed traders. Our hypothesis was that the market maker's defensive response in terms of the *increase* in the adverse selection component of the spread (ASCS) or the *decrease* in the average quoted depth (DEPTH) for R&D-intensive firms would be associated with the magnitude of off-balance sheet R&D assets. The results reported in Table 4, for both 1995 and 1996, provide clear support for our hypothesis: variable OBSRDA is significant with the predicted positive (negative) sign in the regressions with ASCS (DEPTH) as the dependent variable. Since a *higher* spread or a *lower* depth is consistent with reduced market liquidity, the results reported in Table 4 are consistent with Hypothesis 2, that is, for R&D-intensive firms, there is a negative association between market liquidity and the magnitude of off-balance sheet R&D assets.

4.2.3. Hypothesis 3

Table 5 presents the regression estimates using ordinary least squares for model 3 for our sample of R&D-intensive firms with the *change* in the average adverse selection component of the spread (ΔASCS) and the *change* in the average quoted depth (ΔDEPTH) from 1995 to 1996 as the dependent variables. In this model, the independent variables are also in the change form. In Table 5, collinearity does not appear to be a problem in interpreting the regression results since all the VIFs are well below ten. In the regressions with ΔASCS as the dependent variable, the results generally yield estimates with predicted signs and imply plausible relationships between the change in ASCS and the change in the control variables (albeit with less overall explanatory power than for the level form ordinary least squares (OLS) regressions reported in Table 4). In the regressions with ΔDEPTH as the dependent variable (Table 5), we do not predict the signs of the control variables as discussed previously. However, these regressions have low overall explanatory power as indicated by the adjusted R^2 of only about 2 per cent.

Our main interest is in the accounting test variable ΔOBSRDA. As discussed previously, the Lev and Sougiannis (1996: 128) results suggest that private information about the magnitude of off-balance sheet R&D assets at fiscal year-end are revised on an ongoing basis from one year to the next as informed investors update their expectations of current year R&D expenditures, and that the revised information is impounded in valuations (prices) also on an ongoing basis. Also, to the extent that off-balance sheet R&D assets reflect information asymmetry between informed investors and others, it is to be expected that as estimates of off-balance sheet R&D assets are revised (up or down) from one year to the next by informed traders the adverse selection risk faced by the market maker will also change in the same direction with associated consequences for the adverse selection component of the spread and the quoted depth.

Jeff P. Boone and K. K. Raman

Consistent with the notion that the magnitude of accounting data constitutes relevant information, we hypothesized that the change in the average adverse selection component of the spread (and the average quoted depth) from one year to the next is associated with the change in the magnitude of unrecorded R&D assets. In Table 5, in the regressions with ΔASCS as the dependent variable, ΔOBSRDA is significant with the predicted positive sign.[6] However, in the regression with ΔDEPTH as the dependent variable, ΔOBSRDA is not significant.

As noted previously, OBSRDA is based on the Lev and Sougiannis (1996: 123) methodology and (1) represents a direct estimate of the dollar magnitude of unrecorded R&D assets for each firm in our sample, and (2) incorporates variations in the useful life (amortization rate) of R&D assets across industries. Thus, ΔOBSRDA represents a direct estimate of the *change* in the magnitude of

Table 5. Ordinary Least Squares Regression Testing Hypothesis 3 (Change Form—Model 3)

	Dependent Variable = Δln(ASCS)			Dependent Variable = Δln(DEPTH)		
	Predicted Sign	Coef/t-stat	VIF	Predicted Sign	Coef/t-stat	VIF
Intercept	?	−0.036		?	0.159**	
		−0.301	0		2.321	0
Δln(VOL)	−	−0.031		?	0.021	
		−0.412	1.6		0.488	1.6
Δln(VAR)	+	0.187***		?	0.051*	
		3.347	1.5		1.805	1.5
Δln(MV)	−	−0.042*		?	−0.006	
		−1.392	4.4		−0.339	4.4
Δln(PRC)	−	0.084		?	−0.031	
		1.173	4.4		−0.772	4.4
ΔINSTPER	+	0.317*		?	−0.098	
		1.331	1.1		−0.727	1.1
ΔINSIDPER	+	−1.076		?	−0.155	
		−0.585	1.1		−0.656	1.1
Δln(MMCNT)	−	0.170		?	0.046	
		0.788	1.1		0.374	1.1
Δln(NUMANAL)	−	−0.100		?	0.014	
		−1.081	1.2		0.267	1.2
Δln(ANEFF)	−	−0.055		?	0.011	
		−0.436	1.1		0.155	1.1
ΔOBSRDA	+	0.452***		−	0.003	
		2.244	1.2		0.030	1.2
Adj. R^2		0.186			0.019	
Model F		4.60***			1.31	
No. obs.		158			158	

Notes: *, **, *** denote significance levels at the 0.10, 0.5, and 0.1 level, respectively. Significance levels based on a one-tailed test when the sign of the coefficient is predicted; two-tailed otherwise.
The F-test of the overall model is based on a nondirectional test.
Model 3: Δln(y_j) $= \alpha_i + \beta_1\Delta$ln(VOL) $+ \beta_2\Delta$ln(VAR) $+ \beta_3\Delta$ln(MV) $+ \beta_1\Delta$ln(PRC) $+ \beta_7\Delta$INSTPER $+ \beta_8\Delta$INSIDPER $+ \beta_{10}\Delta$ln(MMCNT) $+ \beta_{11}\Delta$ln(NUMANAL) $+ \beta_{12}\Delta$ln(ANEFF) $+ \beta_{13}\Delta$OBSRDA $+ \epsilon$.
This model is estimated cross-sectionally across a sample consisting of R&D-intensive firms only. Y_j denotes either ASCS or DEPTH, and Δ denotes the change in the variable from 1995 to 1996.

unrecorded R&D assets, that is, the change in the unamortized portion of all prior R&D spending.

In Table 5, ΔOBSRDA is significant with the expected *positive* sign in the regression with ASCS as the dependent variable. At the same time, there is *no* evidence that ΔOBSRDA is significantly associated with DEPTH. As discussed previously, a *higher* spread (with no offsetting change in depth) is consistent with reduced market liquidity. Hence, the overall results in Table 5 provide some evidence consistent with Hypothesis 3, that is, for R&D-intensive firms, the change in market liquidity from one year to the next is negatively associated with the change in the magnitude of off-balance sheet R&D assets.

In contrasting the results reported in Tables 4 and 5, recall that the model tested in Table 4 was in the *level* form while the model tested in Table 5 is in the *change* form. As pointed out by Landsman and Magliolo (1988: 587), the decision to estimate a cross-sectional relationship in the level or change form is driven by the set of economic and econometric assumptions that form our maintained hypotheses, such as the inter-temporal stability of the slope coefficients, the nature of any correlated omitted variables, measurement error, and residual correlation; thus, the issue of econometric appropriateness of changes versus levels models is indeterminate. In our study, for completeness, we examined both the level and change forms of our model. Although the results from the change form model were weaker, collectively the results in Tables 4 and 5 provide some evidence consistent with our hypotheses that (for R&D-intensive firms) market liquidity is negatively associated with the magnitude of off-balance sheet R&D assets.[7]

4.2.4. Additional Analysis

As an alternative explanation for our findings, a reviewer suggested that the negative association between market liquidity and the magnitude of off-balance sheet R&D assets may simply reflect higher investor uncertainty for R&D-intensive firms. The reviewer suggested that SFAS No. 2 (FASB, 1974, para. 13) requires only one item of information (R&D spending) to be disclosed as a single aggregate item, and that it may be the limited disclosure (and not the expensing rule itself) that increases uncertainty in this case. Similarly, Chan *et al.* (2001) suggest that inadequate disclosure in the financial statements about the nature of a firm's R&D activities exacerbates uncertainty about future prospects and imposes a cost to investors in the form of higher stock return volatility. Thus, in the context of our study, the test variable OBSRDA (the magnitude of unrecorded R&D assets) may simply be capturing the higher uncertainty about future payoffs from R&D spending.

As suggested by the reviewer, we reran our regression analyses using the ratio of R&D spending to sales (instead of OBSRDA) as the test variable. For brevity, these results are not presented in our paper. The R&D spending variable was significant in model 2 (the level form model) at the 0.05 level (one-tail) for both 1995 and 1996; however, the change in R&D spending variable was not significant in model 3 (the change form model). Since the capitalized R&D variables (OBSRDA and its change) are more significant than the R&D spending variables, the results suggest that our test variables (and by implication the Lev and Sougiannis (1996: 112) amortization rates) are more strongly associated with impaired market liquidity than the reported R&D spending variables. As suggested by the reviewer, these findings point to a possible need for additional disclosures about a firm's R&D activities which we address in Section 5.

5. Concluding Remarks

In this study, we examined the association between market liquidity (as measured by the adverse selection component of the spread and depth) and off-balance sheet R&D assets. Specifically, we compared market liquidity during 1995 and 1996 for a sample of R&D-intensive firms and other firms. In addition, for R&D-intensive firms, we utilized the Lev and Sougiannis (1996: 112) methodology to estimate the magnitude of firm-specific unrecorded R&D assets and examined the association between: (1) market liquidity and off-balance sheet R&D assets during 1995 and 1996, and (2) the change in market liquidity from 1995 to 1996 and the change in off-balance sheet R&D assets.

Our overall results suggest that the market maker's adverse selection costs are higher for R&D-intensive firms than for non-R&D-intensive firms. For R&D-intensive firms, there is a negative association between market liquidity and the magnitude of off-balance sheet R&D assets. In our analysis (which included both the level and change forms), our test variables were generally significant (had explanatory power) over and above the control variables discussed in the prior literature (e.g. Chung et al., 1995: 1031; Easley et al., 1996: 1428) as potential determinants of the marker's adverse selection risk. Our research design does not allow us to pinpoint the exact causal mechanism that is responsible for the apparent heightened information asymmetry in the equities market for R&D-intensive firms. Still, our findings suggest that the current accounting treatment of R&D spending may be associated with potential harm (diminished market liquidity) and that additional disclosures in the financial statements relating to the nature and future outcomes of a firm's R&D activities (rather than just the amount of R&D spending as a single aggregate item of disclosure as currently required by SFAS No. 2 (FASB, 1974, para. 13)) may help and may mitigate information asymmetry and improve market liquidity for R&D-intensive firms.[8]

Overall, our findings contribute to a growing literature that documents empirical associations between R&D intensity and capital market effects such as analyst coverage (Barth *et al.*, 2001), return volatility (Chan *et al.*, 2001), and gains to insider trades (Aboody and Lev, 2001: 2765). When juxtaposed against these findings, our results provide additional evidence suggesting possible deficiencies in the extant financial reporting for R&D-intensive firms.

Acknowledgements

Authors' names are in alphabetical order. We gratefully acknowledge the helpful comments and suggestions of the anonymous reviewers and workshop participants at Mississippi State University, the University of Nebraska, the 1998 Conference on Intangibles at New York University, and the University of North Texas. Professor Raman gratefully acknowledges summer research support provided by the Department of Accounting at the University of North Texas.

Notes

1. We thank an anonymous reviewer for pointing out that the potential harm, that is, the economic costs and social costs, associated with how accountants treat R&D spending has not been satisfactorily addressed in the prior literature. On the subject of unrecorded R&D assets, Rimerman (1990: 82) notes that these 'intangible, unmeasured assets have great importance in an economy increasingly dependent on expertise, data and technology, an economy in which an expanding service sector does not rely on fixed assets as the primary generator of revenue' (p. 82). Similarly, Swieringa (1998: 47), a former member of the Financial Accounting Standards Board, suggests that the current financial accounting model (which is reflective of traditional organizations that invest heavily in tangible fixed assets) in increasingly outdated in the context of increased investments in intangible, knowledge-based assets.
2. Lev (1988: 12) notes that depression-era regulations were relaxed or outright abolished in many industries (such as trucking, airlines, financial services, telecommunications) during the 1980s. Still, financial reporting regulations have not only retained their support but have continued to expand not only in the United States but in all market economies (Lev, 1988: 12). He suggests that the universality of disclosure regulation can only be understood in the context of the underlying equity justification (Lev, 1988: 12).
3. Potentially, the need for additional analysis to undo management's judgement could be obviated by requiring the continued disclosure of R&D expenditures as currently mandated by SFAS No. 2 (FASB, 1974: para. 13).

4. Thus, OBSRDA incorporates direct estimates of the dollar magnitude of firm-specific R&D assets and takes into account variations in the useful life (amortization rate) of R&D assets across industries.

5. Consistent with theory and prior research (Stoll, 1978: 1170; Brennan and Subrahmanyam, 1995: 370), all dependent and control variables (except GROWTH, RISK, INSTPER, INSIDPER, and NASDAQ) enter the model in natural log form. Variables GROWTH, INSTPER, and INSIDPER are percentage measures and should therefore bear a linear relationship with the log of the dependent variable (thus requiring no log transformation). Variables RISK and NASDAQ are not logged since the former already exhibits a very restricted range of variation (which would be further compressed by log-transformation) while the latter is a dummy variable. Also, for all the regressions reported in this paper, the null hypothesis of homoscedasticity could not be rejected at the 0.10 level in a nondirectional White (1980) test.

   Also, for each of the regressions in Tables 3–5 we evaluated the sensitivity of our results to influential observations by calculating the studentized residual for each observations (Belsley et al., 1980: 20), eliminating observations with studentized residuals in excess of the absolute value of two, and reestimating the regressions. The findings of these alternative analyses were similar to those discussed in the paper indicating that our results were not being affected by influential outliers.

6. Beaver (1968: 91) notes that changes in trading volume and return variance could in themselves represent the effects of a change in the level of information asymmetry. By controlling for changes in trading volume and return variance in our model, our regression tests for the accounting variable ΔOBSRDA are conservative.

7. In general, explanations for weaker results in the change form may include: (1) measurement error in the test variable accentuated by differencing which permits the measurement error to dominate and push the coefficients in the change form model towards zero (Landsman and Magliolo, 1988: 598), (2) inflated standard errors in the change form model induced by differencing and consequent reduction in the power of the test (Landsman and Magliolo, 1988: 594), or (3) inter-temporal coefficient instability (Landsman and Magliolo, 1988: 594).

8. As noted by Barth (2000: 9 and 18), data and methodology limitations often mean that the question motivating the research differs from the question actually addressed by the research, and thus the research speaks to the motivating question only indirectly. A key task of the researcher is to craft research questions and develop research designs that provide insights into the motivating question. Our study accords with Barth (2000: 9 and 18) observation in as much as it is motivated by the question of whether the expensing of R&D spending exacerbates information asymmetry in captial markets, yet is forced by limitations of data and methodology to actually address the research question of whether there are detectable associations between proxies for information asymmetry and the magnitude of off-balance sheet R&D assets. (Directly addressing the motivating question would require an experiment where the researcher would randomly assign some firms to a treatment group of firms which expense R&D and assign others to a control group of firms which capitalize R&D spending, and obtain market microstructure data for both groups. For understandable reasons, such an experiment is not practical and consequently such experimental data are unavailable.)

However, our research question and research design do provide insight into the motivating question as follows. If the required expensing of R&D spending actually exacerbates information asymmetry in capital markets, we should expect to observe a cross-sectional association between our proxies for information asymmetry and R&D-intensive as proxied by the magnitude of unrecognized R&D assets. Alternatively, if no association exists between the proxies for information asymmetry and R&D intensity, it would be difficult to argue that the required expensing of R&D exacerbates information asymmetry. Does an association between the proxies for information asymmetry and R&D intensity imply that the required expensing of R&D is the cause of the heightened information asymmetry? Not necessarily, since the association could be caused by other factors that are correlated with R&D intensity such as, for example, the higher outcome uncertainty that is attendant with R&D spending. Regardless of the exact causal mechanism that produced the associations that we document in our study, our results suggest that the current accounting treatment of R&D spending may be associated with diminished market liquidity and that expanded financial disclosure may mitigate information asymmetry and improve market liquidity for R&D-intensive firms.

References

Aboody, D. and Lev, B. (2000), 'Information asymmetry R&D and insider gains', *The Journal of Finance*, 55(6): 2747–66.

Amihud, Y. and Mendelson, H. (1986a), 'Liquidity and stock returns', *Financial Analysts Journal*, 42(3): 43–8.

—— (1986b) 'Asset pricing and the bid-ask spread', *Journal of Financial Economics*, 17(3): 223–49.

Bagehot, W. (1971), 'The only game in town', *Financial Analysts Journal*, 27(2): 12–14, 22.

Ball, R. and Brown, P. (1968), 'An empirical evaluation of accounting income numbers', *Journal of Accounting Research*, 6(1): 159–78.

Barth, M. (2000), 'Valuation-based accounting research: Implications for financial reporting and opportunities for future research', *Accounting and Finance*, 40(1): 7–31.

—— Kasznik, R., and McNichols, M. (2001), 'Analyst coverage and intangible assets', *Journal of Accounting Research*, 39(1): 1–34.

Beaver, W. (1968), 'The information content of annual earnings announcements', *Journal of Accounting Research*, 6(3): 67–92.

—— (1998), *Financial Reporting: An Accounting Revolution*, third ed. Upper Saddle River, NJ: Prentice-Hall.

—— Clark, R., Wright, W. (1979), 'The association between unsystematic security returns and the magnitude of earnings forecast errors', *Journal of Accounting Research*, 17(2): 316–40.

Belsley, D., Kuh, E., and Welsch, R. (1980), *Regression Diagnostics, Identifying Influential Data and Sources of Collinearity*, New York: Wiley.

Brennan, M. and Subrahmanyam, A. (1995), 'Investment analysis and price formation in securities markets', *Journal of Financial Economics*, 38(3): 361–81.

—— (1996), 'Market microstructure and asset pricing: On the compensation for illiquidity in stock returns', *Journal of Financial Economics*, 41(3): 441–64.

Bublitz, B. and Ettredge, M. (1989), 'The information of discretionary outlays: advertising, research and development', *The Accounting Review*, 64(1): 108–24.

Chan, L., Lakonishok, J., and Sougiannis, T. (2001), 'The stock market valuation of research and development expenditures', *The Journal of Finance*, 56, 2431–56.

Chan, S., Martin, J., and Kensinger, J. (1990), 'Corporate research and development expenditures and share value', *Journal of Financial Economics*, 26(2): 255–76.

Chiang, R. and Venkatesh, P. (1988), 'Insider holdings and perceptions of information asymmetry', *The Journal of Finance*, 43(4): 1041–8.

Chung, K., McInish, T., Wood, R., and Wyhowski, D. (1995), 'Production of information, information asymmetry, and the bid-ask spread: Empirical evidence from analysts' forecast', *Journal of Banking and Finance*, 19(6): 1025–46.

Copeland, T. and Galai, D. (1983), 'Information effects and the bid-ask spread', *The Journal of Finance*, 38(5): 1457–69.

Easley, D., Kiefer, N., O'Hara, M., and Paperman, J. (1996), 'Liquidity, information, and infrequently traded stocks', *The Journal of Finance*, 51(4): 1405–36.

Elliott, J., Richardson, G., Dyckman, T., and Dukes, R. (1984), 'The impact of SFAS No. 2 on firm expenditures on research and development replications and extensions', *Journal of Accounting Research*, 22(1): 85–102.

—— and Jacobson, P. (1991), 'US accounting: A national emergency', *Journal of Accountancy*, 172(5): 54–8.

Financial Accounting Standards Board (FASB) (1974), 'Statement of Financial Accounting Standards No. 2. Accounting for research and development costs', Financial Accounting Standards Board, Stamford, CT.

Glosten, L. and Milgrom, P. (1985), 'Bid-ask and transaction prices in a dealer market with heterogeneously informed traders', *Journal of Financial Economics*, 14(1): 71–100.

Hakansson, N. (1977), 'Interim disclosure and forecasts: An economic analysis and a framework for choice', *The Accounting Review*, 52(2): 396–416.

Hirschey, M. and Weygandt, J. (1985), 'Amortization policy for advertising and research and development expenditures', *Journal of Accounting Research*, 23(1): 326–35.

Huang, R. and Stoll, H. (1996), 'Dealer versus auction markets: A paired comparison of execution costs on NASDAQ and the NYSE', *Journal of Financial Economics*, 41(1): 313–57.

Kim, O. and Verrecchia, R. (1994), 'Market liquidity and volume around earnings announcements', *Journal of Accounting Economics*, 17(1): 41–68.

Landsman, W. and Magliolo, J. (1988), 'Cross-sectional capital market research and model specification', *The Accounting Review*, 63(4): 586–604.

Lee, C. and Ready, M. (1991), 'Inferring trade direction from intraday data', *The Journal of Finance*, 46(2): 733–46.

—— Mucklow, B. (1993), 'Spreads, depths, and the impact of earnings information: An intraday analysis', *Review of Financial Studies*, 6(2): 345–75.

Lev, B. (1988), 'Toward a theory of equitable and efficient policy', *The Accounting Review*, 63(1): 1–22.

—— and Sougiannis, T. (1996), 'The capitalization, amortization, and value-relevance of R&D', *Journal of Accounting and Economics*, 21(1): 107–38.

—— and Zarowin, P. (1999), 'The boundaries of financial reporting and how to extend them', *Journal of Accounting Research*, 37(2): 353–86.

Levitt, A. (1998), 'The importance of high quality accounting standards', *Accounting Horizons*, 12(1): 79–82.

Neter, J., Kutner, M., Nachtsheim, C., and Wasserman, W. (1996), *Applied Linear Statistical Models* (Chicago, IL: Irwin).

Rimerman, T. (1990), 'The changing significance of financial statements', *Journal of Accountancy*, 169(4): 79–83.

Shefrin, H. and Statman, M. (1992), 'Ethics Fairness Efficiency and Financial Markets. The Research Foundation of the Institute of Chartered Financial Analysts', Charlottesville, VA.

Sougiannis, T. (1994), 'The accounting based valuation of R&D', *The Accounting Review*, 69(1): 44–68.

Stoll, H. (1976), 'Dealer inventory behavior: An empirical investigation of NASDAQ stocks', *Journal of Financial and Quantitative Analysis*, 11(3): 359–80.

—— (1978), 'The pricing of security dealer's service: An empirical study of NASDAQ stocks', *The Journal of Finance*, 33(4): 1153–72.

Swieringa, R. (1998), 'Accounting research and policy making', *Accounting and Finance*, 38(1): 29–49.

Wasley, C. and Linsmeier, T. (1992), 'A further examination of the economic consequences of SFAS No. 2', *Journal of Accounting Research*, 30(1): 156–64.

White, H. (1980), 'A heteroscedasticity-consistent covariance matrix estimator and a direct test for heteroscedasticity', *Econometrica*, 48(4): 817–38.

Yohn, T. (1998), 'Information asymmetry around earnings announcements', *Review of Quantitative Finance and Accounting*, 11(2): 165–82.

## 14

Information Asymmetry, R&D, and Insider Gains

David Aboody and Baruch Lev

Researchers have documented that 'corporate insiders', defined by the 1934 Securities and Exchange Act as corporate officers, directors, and owners of 10 per cent or more of any equity class of securities, gain from trading in the securities of their firms.[1] However, the specific *sources* of information leading to insider gains in particular and to information asymmetry in general have not been comprehensively investigated. An identification of the sources of insiders' information contributes to our knowledge in various ways. For example, researchers often use proxies for the extent of information asymmetry, such as the number of analysts following a firm, the number of competing traders, or insiders' and institutional ownership (e.g. Stoll, 1978; Brennan and Subrahmanyam, 1995). Additional information asymmetry proxies are firm size and volume of trade (Chari *et al.*, 1988), financial analysts' forecast errors of earnings, and the volatility of abnormal stock returns (e.g. Krishnaswami and Subramaniam, 1999). Such proxies are obviously noisy, reflecting, in addition to information asymmetry, numerous firm and market attributes. Identification of the major sources or firm-specific drivers of information asymmetry will suggest more precise (less noisy) measures of asymmetry. For policy research concerned with the social consequences of insider gains and information asymmetry, identification of the sources of insiders' information will suggest means (e.g. enhanced disclosure of specific information) of mitigating harmful consequences.[2]

We investigate the insider gains issue from the perspective of a specific source of information asymmetry—research and development (R&D). Investment in R&D is a major productive input in a large number of firms, particularly those operating in the technology and science-based sectors. R&D,

however, differs from other capital and financial inputs (e.g. property, plant, and equipment, inventory, or project financing) along several important dimensions related to information asymmetry. First, many R&D projects, such as radically new drugs under development or software programs, are *unique* to the developing firm, whereas most capital investments, such as commercial property or airplanes, share common characteristics across firms within an industry. Consequently, investors can derive little or no information about the productivity and value of a firm's R&D from observing the R&D performance of other firms (e.g. not much can be learned about Merck's drug development program from an FDA approval of a Pfizer drug), whereas, for example, the average store performance of one retailer provides valuable information on the performance of other retailers. Second, while most physical and financial assets are traded in organized markets, where prices convey information about asset productivity and values, there are no organized markets for R&D and hence no asset prices from which to derive information. Third, accounting measurement and reporting rules treat R&D differently from other investments: While these rules mandate the marking-to-market in quarterly and annual reports of most financial investments, and the periodic recognition of value impairment (the decrease of market value below cost) of physical assets, thereby providing investors with updated information about changes in asset values, R&D is immediately expensed in financial statements, so that no information on value and productivity changes of R&D is reported to investors.

Given the relative scarcity of public information about firms' R&D activities, and the importance of these activities to the operations and profit potential of technology and science-based companies, we hypothesize that R&D contributes to information asymmetry between corporate insiders and outside investors and that some of the former will exploit this asymmetry to gain from insider trading.[3] Indeed, we find from comprehensive data on corporate officers' share trading from 1985 to 1997 that insider gains in firms conducting R&D (R&D firms) are substantially larger than insider gains in firms with no R&D activities (No-R&D firms). These differences in insider gains are both statistically and economically significant, and hold after controlling for various known risk factors. We also find that investors' reaction to the public disclosure of insiders' trade (about a month, on average, after the trade) is stronger for R&D firms than for No-R&D firms, corroborating our hypothesis that R&D activities enhance information asymmetry, and that this asymmetry is not eliminated by insiders' trade and investors' information search. We thus identify R&D as a major contributor to information asymmetry.

The paper is organized as follows. In Section 1 we develop our hypothesis and in Section 2 we describe the sample and summary statistics. Section 3 presents the estimation equations and reports empirical findings on the association between insider gains and firms' R&D intensity. In Section 4 we examine investors' reaction to the public disclosure of insider trades, and in Section 5 we present robustness tests. Section 6 concludes the study.

---

1. Information Asymmetry, R&D, and Insider Gains

All corporate investments create information asymmetries because managers can continually observe changes in investment productivity on an *individual* asset basis (e.g. aircraft utilization—load factor—at the route level), whereas outsiders obtain only highly aggregated information on investment productivity at discrete points of time. The extent of information asymmetry associated with R&D, however, is larger than that associated with tangible (e.g. property, plant, and equipment) and financial investments because of the relative uniqueness (idiosyncrasy) of R&D. Thus, for example, a failure of a drug under development to pass Phase I clinical tests, or of a software program to successfully complete an alpha (technological feasibility) test in a particular company are unique events not shared by other pharmaceutical or software companies. In contrast, a downturn in demand for commercial properties, for example, will exert a strong common effect on the property values of all real estate companies operating in a given geographical region. Similarly, interest-rate changes will affect systematically the values of bond and stock portfolios of companies. Thus, we argue, the relative uniqueness of R&D investments makes it difficult for outsiders to learn about the productivity and value of a given firm's R&D from the performance and products of other firms in the industry, thereby contributing to information asymmetry.[4]

The absence of *organized markets* in R&D further contributes to information asymmetry. Whereas investors can derive considerable information from prices of traded tangible and financial assets concerning their values at the firm level (e.g. inferring from changes in commodity prices about swings in values of firms' inventories), there is no direct price-based information on firm-specific changes in the value and productivity of R&D.[5] Some information on R&D can, of course, be inferred from stock prices of R&D-intensive companies, yet such information is noisy, given the multiple activities of R&D firms (e.g. manufacturing, services).

Accounting rules exacerbate the information asymmetries associated with R&D. Most financial assets have to be marked-to-market in quarterly and annual financial reports, and impairments in the values of tangible assets (i.e. when expected future benefits fall short of book values) have to be routinely reported in financial statements. Similarly, inventories and accounts receivable have to be written down in financial reports to market values. Thus, investors are periodically informed about changes in the values of most tangible and financial assets. In contrast, R&D expenditures are uniformly expensed in financial reports and therefore no information is required to be provided to outsiders about changes in the productivity and value of R&D. Even major R&D events, such as when a drug under development successfully passes clinical tests, are not routinely reported to investors.

Empirical evidence is consistent with a relatively large information asymmetry associated with R&D. For example, Barth *et al.* (2001) report that analyst coverage (number of analysts following a firm) is significantly larger for firms intensive in R&D relative to firms with lower or no-R&D, presumably because of the private information concerning R&D activities. Furthermore, analysts' *efforts* and, presumably, costs of analysing firms vary positively with R&D intensity.[6] Similarly, Tasker (1998a) reports that R&D-intensive companies conduct more conference calls with analysts than low (or no) R&D firms, implying a stronger investors' demand for information about the R&D activities of firms.[7]

Is all the private R&D-related information shared in a timely manner with outsiders through the information search of analysts and investors, so that in equilibrium there are no substantial information asymmetries left? Kyle's (1985) model of a single informed trader with many uninformed (noise) traders and a market maker addresses this question and indicates that in equilibrium: (1) 'The informed trader trades in such a way that his private information is incorporated into prices *gradually*' (p. 1316, emphasis ours), and (2) 'not all information is incorporated into prices by the end of trading' (p. 1326). The main conclusion of the model is that, while much of the insider's information gets gradually incorporated in prices through his/her trades, the *insider makes positive profits* by exploiting his monopoly power optimally in a dynamic context...' (p. 1315, emphasis ours).[8]

Particularly relevant to our hypothesis concerning R&D-related information asymmetry and the consequent insider gains is Kyle's (1985) conclusion that insiders' profits are proportional to $(\Sigma_0 \sigma_u)^{1/2}$, where Σ_0 is the variance of the liquidation value of the risky asset. We know from Kothari *et al.* (1998) that: '...R&D investments generate more uncertain future benefits than investment in tangible assets. Specifically, in a regression of future earnings variability on investment in R&D, PP&E (property, plant, and equipment) and other determinants of earnings variability like firm size and leverage, we find that the coefficient on R&D is about three times as large as that on PP&E' (p. 3). Thus, the documented larger variability of earnings and, by implication, firms' liquidation value associated with R&D should, according to Kyle (1985), enhance the gain of insiders in R&D firms, relative to insiders in No-R&D firms with lower variability of earnings.

369

Kyle's second (1989) model is particularly relevant to our case, because it allows uninformed investors to acquire private information. Among the conclusions of this model are: (1) 'thus, while uninformed speculators break even on average, informed speculators make money "at the expense" of noise traders . . .' (p. 337), (2) 'with imperfect competition, prices never reveal more than one-half the private precision of informed speculators' (p. 334), and (3) 'in order for the large market model to reveal any private information, private information must be cheap enough so that a large number of speculators find it profitable to purchase it' (p. 344). Thus, even with endogenous information acquisition, insiders are expected to gain from insider trading.

Given the importance of R&D in firms' productivity and growth, it is reasonable to expect investors and analysts to acquire private R&D-related information from managers, as the evidence discussed above indicates. However, because such information is costly, requiring among other things a significant investment in scientific knowledge (e.g. understanding genome research in biochemistry) and a considerable time investment (e.g. analysing financial reports, participating in conference calls), optimal information acquisition by outsiders will generally fall short of completely exhausting insiders' information. Stated differently, in equilibrium the marginal value of acquired information will equal marginal cost, but this does not necessarily imply that the *total* R&D information possessed by managers will be quickly incorporated in prices, leaving managers with no opportunities to gainfully trade on inside information. Indeed, our evidence (Section 4) indicates a significant market reaction to the *disclosure* of insiders' trades (twenty-five days, on average, subsequent to the actual trades), a reaction that is more pronounced for R&D than for No-R&D companies, implying that almost a month after trade by insiders and the extensive information search by outsiders, prices still did not fully reflect all of insiders' private information.

We accordingly hypothesize in this study that the R&D activities of firms create unique information asymmetries and that officers of R&D companies will gainfully exploit these asymmetries by trading the shares of their firms.

---

2. Data Sources and Sample Characteristics

The insider trading data analysed in this study were obtained from CDA/Investnet. The database contains all purchase and sale transactions made by insiders and reported to the SEC from January 1985 through December 1997.[9] We focus on 323,949 open market purchase and sale transactions that were conducted by *officers* of firms, as officers are a priori presumed to have inside information on R&D.[10] We delete 732 duplicate transactions and change of control transactions where the number of shares exchanged exceeded 20 per cent of the total shares outstanding. We also delete 2334 companies with 31,417 officer transactions that could not be located on the CRSP database, and 1459 firms with 29,897 transactions that were not found on COMPUSTAT. Finally, we delete 8865 insider transactions because of missing data on R&D in COMPUSTAT, resulting in a final sample of 253,038 transactions related to 10,013 firms.

Table 1 provides sample statistics by type of insider transaction and year. Of the 10,013 sample firms, 3818 are classified as R&D firms and 6195 are classified as No-R&D firms; the latter are those for which COMPUSTAT does not report any R&D expenditures during the period from 1985 to 1997. Consistent with prior studies, the total number of sale transactions (165,949; 81,539 for R&D and 84,410 for No-R&D firms) is almost twice the number of purchase transactions (87,089). The difference between purchase and sale transactions (number and value), however, is substantially larger for R&D firms (23,008 vs 81,539) than for No-R&D firms (64,081 vs 84,410), reflecting the pervasiveness of stock options and awards (included in sales but not in purchases) in R&D companies. The number and volume of insider transactions has increased continuously during the period from 1985 to 1997, and the increase in transaction values for R&D firms has been proportionately larger than for No-R&D firms. The three transaction measures—number of transactions, number of shares, and total value of transactions—are highly correlated. In the tests reported below we use the number of shares transacted. Replication of the tests with dollar value of transactions yielded very similar results to those derived from the number of shares.

Panel B of Table 1 reports mean and median market-adjusted returns (raw return minus the return on a value-weighted NYSE/AMEX/Nasdaq index) for three intervals subsequent to insider transactions: From transaction date to one day before the transaction's filing with the SEC (an average of twenty-five days in our sample) and six and twelve months following the transaction. The excess return data indicate that, on average, insider share purchases were followed by positive returns in each interval, whereas share sales were followed by negative returns. Thus, insiders in both R&D and No-R&D companies tend to buy shares ahead of good news and sell ahead of bad news. However, both the mean and median excess returns of R&D firms are significantly higher for purchase and lower for sale transactions than returns of firms without R&D activities. Thus, for example, the mean market-adjusted return from transaction to SEC filing date of insider purchases in R&D firms was 3.0 per cent vs 0.9 per cent for share purchases in No-R&D firms. Note that the 3.0 per cent excess return for R&D firms is economically large, given that the mean interval between transaction and filing dates is twenty-five days only. For insider sales, the mean

Table 1. Distribution of Insider Transactions and Market-Adjusted Returns, January 1985–December 1997

Panel A: Transaction data

	Jan. 1985–Dec. 1989		Jan. 1990–Dec. 1993		Jan. 1994–Dec. 1997		1985–1997	
	R&D	No-R&D	R&D	No-R&D	R&D	No-R&D	R&D	No-R&D
No. of transactions								
No. of purchases	7027	17,124	7004	21,794	8,977	25,163	23,008	64,081
No. of sales	18,255	21,585	28,018	29,150	35,266	33,675	81,539	84,410
Total no. of transactions	25,282	38,709	35,022	50,944	44,243	58,838	104,547	148,491
No. of shares (millions)								
No. of shares purchased	51.1	150.4	110.4	246.7	150.5	329.3	312.0	726.4
No. of shares sold	222.0	383.7	392.6	567.6	572.4	869.9	1187.0	1821.2
Total no. of shares traded	273.1	534.1	503.0	814.3	722.9	1199.2	1499.0	2547.6
Value of transactions ($ millions)								
Val. of shares purchased	366.7	2257.8	311.4	1599.2	699.8	2855.7	1377.9	6712.7
Val. of shares sold	3386.2	5213.6	8544.8	10,725.4	16,190.5	18,489.4	28,121.5	34,428.4
Total val. of shares traded	3752.9	7471.4	8856.2	12,324.6	16,890.3	21,345.1	29,499.4	41,141.1

Panel B: Return data

	R&D Firms				No-R&D Firms			
	Purchases		Sales		Purchases		Sales	
	Mean	Median	Mean	Median	Mean	Median	Mean	Median
Market-adjusted return from transaction to SEC filing date	3.0%	0.7%	−0.5%	−0.2%	0.9%	0.07%	−0.1%	−0.1%
Market-adjusted return over six months following the transaction date	9.61%	1.0%	−4.1%	−7.1%	3.56%	0.2%	−3.8%	−4.6%
Market-adjusted return over twelve months following transaction date	8.56%	1.93%	−10.0%	−14.0%	2.47%	0.36%	−8.6%	−9.2%

Note: All means and medians in Panel B are significantly different from zero at the 1% level and significantly different between R&D and No-R&D firms at the 5% level. Market adjusted returns are the raw returns minus the return on a value weighted NYSE/AMEX/Nasdaq index. No-R&D firms are those for which COMPUSTAT does not report R&D expenditures in any quarter during 1985–97.

market-adjusted return over the transaction-filing interval for R&D firms was −0.5 per cent vs −0.1 per cent for No-R&D firms.

The post-transaction returns generally increase from the first interval (transaction to SEC filing date) to the second interval (six months following trade), and further increase for the third interval (twelve months following trade). During six months following trade, excess mean returns from share purchases for R&D firms were 9.61 per cent vs 3.56 per cent for No-R&D firms. All the differences between mean (median) returns of R&D vs No-R&D firms in Table 1 are statistically significant at the 5 per cent level.

The return data in Table 1 are consistent with our hypothesis: Insider gains in R&D-intensive companies are substantially higher than insider gains in No-R&D companies. However, the underlying individual transaction data are not independent (there are multiple transactions per firm), and the returns over the six and twelve months intervals are overlapping. Moreover, firm attributes (e.g. risk, size) related to R&D may affect the documented returns, in addition to the hypothesized information asymmetry differences.

Accordingly, the return data in Table 1 should be viewed as descriptive and tentative, and we proceed below to aggregate insider transactions by firms, considering only no overlapping return intervals and controlling for known risk factors.

3. Insider Gains and R&D

We wish to examine the association between insider gains and information asymmetry as proxied by the firm's R&D intensity. To accomplish this we construct four monthly calendar-time portfolios conditional on the firms' R&D activities and the type of insiders' transactions (purchase or sale). The four portfolios are: (1) RD_p, for firms engaged in R&D whose insiders were 'net purchasers' of shares in a given month during the period from 1985 to 1997 (a net purchaser firm-month is one where the number of shares purchased by the firm's officers during the month exceeded the number of shares sold); (2) RD_s, for firms engaged in R&D whose insiders were 'net sellers' of shares (i.e. number of shares sold by insiders during the month exceeded purchases); (3) $NORD_p$, for firms without R&D whose insiders were net purchasers; and (4) $NORD_s$, for firms without R&D whose insiders were net sellers of shares.[11]

We calculate returns for each of the four portfolios as follows. For each calendar month (January 1985–November 1997, a total of 155 months) we compute a *firm-specific* mean raw return from the transaction dates of insiders' trades to one day prior to the filing date of those transactions with the SEC. These firm-specific transaction-to-reporting returns are averages over all the individual insider trades that occurred during the month. We then compute calendar-time equally weighted portfolio returns over all the firms with insider transactions in a given month, classified into the four portfolios described above, namely firms with and without R&D, where insiders during the month were net stock purchasers or net sellers.[12] We thus focus on portfolio returns over the transaction-to-SEC filing period, during which information asymmetry is presumably large. The public disclosure of insiders' trade substantially decreases information asymmetry, as evidenced by investors' reaction to this information (Section 4).

David Aboody and Baruch Lev

To examine the extent to which insiders in R&D firms gain more than those in No-R&D firms, we employ an intercept test using the three-factor model of Fama and French (1993). The dependent variable is the difference between calendar-time portfolio returns of R&D and No-R&D firms ($RD_{pt} - NORD_{pt}$). For example, for our first month, January 1985, RD_{pt} is the average return for all R&D firms whose officers were net purchasers of shares during January 1985, over the transaction-to-filing interval. $NORD_{pt}$ is the average return for all firms without R&D whose officers were net purchasers of shares during January 1985, over the transaction-to-filing interval. The regression is run over 155 observations—individual months during January 1985–November 1997. The independent variables are the three factors: Market return, size, and book-to-market. The regression is thus:

$$RD_{pt} - NORD_{pt} = \alpha_p + \beta_p (R_{mt} - R_{ft}) + \delta_p \, SMB_t + \sigma_p \, HML_t + \epsilon_p, \qquad (1)$$

where

$RD_{pt} - NORD_{pt} =$ return from going long on a portfolio of firms that engage in R&D and short on a portfolio of firms that do not engage in R&D, in months where insiders were net purchasers of shares. The return interval is between transaction date and one day prior to SEC filing date—twenty-five days on average.

$R_{mt} - R_{ft} =$ the market excess return in month t.

$SMB_t =$ the difference between month t return on a value-weighted portfolio of small stocks and one of large stocks.

$HML_t =$ the difference between month t return on a value-weighted portfolio of high book-to-market stocks and one of low book-to-market stocks.[13]

An identical regression to (1) was run for portfolios of insider *sales*: $RD_{st} - NORD_{st}$.

Panel A of Table 2 presents the univariate raw returns for the four portfolios examined. Consistent with prior research, we observe for all trades positive stock returns subsequent to insiders' share purchases and negative returns subsequent to insiders' sales. As hypothesized above, both the mean and median returns on the R&D portfolios are significantly higher than returns on the No-R&D portfolios when insiders purchased shares and lower when they sold shares. Investing long in a portfolio of R&D firms whose insiders purchased shares and short in a portfolio of No-R&D firms whose insiders purchased shares ($RD_t - NORD_t$) yields a mean (median) return of 0.92 per cent (1.66 per cent) over an average of twenty-five days between transaction and SEC filing dates.[14] The insider sales portfolios yield a differential mean (median) return of -0.60 per cent (-0.70 per cent) over the same interval in favor of R&D firms.

374

Table 2. Returns from Going Long on Insider Trading in R&D Firms and Short on No-R&D Firms

Panel A: Univariate returns

	Insider Purchases			Insider Sales		
	Mean	Median	# > 0	Mean	Median	# > 0
Firms with R&D	5.49%***	4.64%***	136	−1.26%***	−1.17%***	57
Firms without R&D	4.57%***	3.82%***	133	−0.66%***	−0.44%**	67
$RD_t - NORD_t$	0.92%***	1.66%***	96	−0.60%***	−0.70%***	53

Panel B: Three-factor model

	α	$RM_t - RF_t$	SMB_t	HML_t	Adjusted R^2Insider
Insider Purchases					
$RD_t - NORD_t$	0.011**	−0.129	0.491**	−0.364	0.056
t-statistic	(2.40)	(−1.01)	(2.65)	(−1.56)	
Insider Sales					
$RD_t - NORD_t$	−0.005*	0.088	0.232**	−0.072	0.043
t-statistic	(−1.85)	(1.24)	(2.24)	(−0.55)	

Notes: *, **, and *** denote significance at the 10, 5, and 1 per cent levels, respectively.
Panel A presents mean and median percentage raw returns earned on portfolios formed as follows: For each month between January 1985 and November 1997 we calculate, for each sample firm, the mean raw return from the insider transaction date to one day prior to the SEC filing date, over all insider transactions during the month. We calculate the mean returns separately for firms with and without R&D, and for firms where insiders were net purchasers during the month (i.e. share purchases exceeded sales) and firms where insiders were net sellers during the month. # > 0 indicates number of months (out of 155) when the mean return was positive. In Panel B, the intercept (α) of the Fama–French three-factor model in (1) is presented. It is the estimated intercept from a time series regression (155 observations) of the portfolio returns of firms with R&D minus the portfolio return of firms without R&D (RD − NORD) on the market excess return (RM − RF), a zero-investment size portfolio (SMB), and a zero-investment book-to-market portfolio (HML).

Panel B of Table 2 presents estimates from the Fama–French three-factor model in (1).[15] As hypothesized, the estimated intercepts from time-series regressions of the difference in return between firms with R&D and those without R&D (RD − NORD) on the three systematic factors are significantly positive when insiders purchased shares (0.011, $t = 2.40$), and significantly negative when insiders sold shares (−0.005, $t = -1.85$). The estimated intercepts are close to the univariate returns in Panel A: 0.0092 for purchases and −0.006 for sales. Given that the average interval over which these returns were gained was twenty-five days, the estimated gains are economically meaningful as well, particularly for stock purchasers.

An additional test is performed to gain insight into the association between R&D *intensity* and insider gains. First, we divide the sample into three groups: Firms without R&D expenditures, firms with R&D intensity (R&D over sales) below the sample median (low R&D), and firms with R&D intensity above the sample median (high R&D). We then run the three-factor model (1) for return differences between Low and No-R&D, High and No-R&D, and High and Low R&D portfolios. These regressions are run separately for net purchasers and net sellers of shares. Following are the estimated α coefficients and t-values from these regressions:

	α coefficient	t-value
A. *Insider Purchases*		
Low R&D minus No-R&D	0.002	0.388
High R&D minus No-R&D	0.021	3.446
High R&D minus Low R&D	0.019	2.997
B. *Insider Sales*		
Low R&D minus No-R&D	−0.004	−1.643
High R&D minus No-R&D	−0.006	−1.783
High R&D minus Low R&D	−0.002	−0.510

The estimated α coefficients indicate that for insider purchases of shares, the differential gain between R&D and No-R&D firms is mainly due to *high* R&D-intensity firms, as indicated by the estimated α for High R&D minus No-R&D (0.021), which is ten times larger than the estimated α of Low R&D minus No-R&D (0.002). For insider sales, the increase in insider gains in R&D firms (relative to No-R&D) is more monotonic in R&D intensity, as indicated by an estimated α of −0.004 for Low R&D minus No-R&D and α of −0.006 for High R&D minus No-R&D firms.

The analysis reported in this section thus indicates that insiders in R&D firms gain from trade in their firms' shares significantly more than insiders in No-R&D firms, and that for share purchases the gain differential is mainly attributed to firms with high (above median) R&D intensity.

··

4. Investors' Reaction to the Disclosure of Insider Trades

Section 16(a) of the 1934 Securities Act requires insiders to report their preceding month's trades to the SEC no later than the tenth day of each month. An examination of investors' reaction to the *public disclosure* of insiders' trades offers an opportunity to investigate several important issues. In particular:

(1) Is R&D a significant driver (cause) of information asymmetry? If, as hypothesized above, R&D contributes to information asymmetry, it is reasonable to expect investors to react more strongly to the disclosure of insider trades in R&D firms than in No-R&D firms. The reason: Given the relative

scarcity of public information about firms' research and product development activities, insider trades in R&D companies convey, on average, more information to the market than insider trades in No-R&D firms.

(2) Is insiders' private information fully and quickly revealed to investors by financial analysts' search efforts and by insiders' own trade activities? In the case of such efficient information revelation, there should be no unusual investor reaction to the public disclosure of insiders' trades. If, however, insiders' private information is not fully revealed to the market (thereby creating gain opportunities), the public disclosure of their trades should trigger investor reaction.

Our test results (below) indicate that R&D activities do contribute to information asymmetry and that not all of insiders' private information is revealed before the public disclosure of their trades. Table 3 presents raw returns for three disclosure intervals: The day the trade information was filed with the SEC (day 0);[16] the cumulative return over the day of filing and the subsequent trading day (0, +1); and the three-day cumulative return beginning with the day of filing (0, +1, +2). We include days +1 and +2 in the analysis because the SEC may disclose insiders' filings after trading hours of day 0 or on the following day.

As reported in Table 3, for each of the three disclosure intervals the mean returns are positive when insider purchases were disclosed and negative when insider sales were disclosed, for both R&D and No-R&D firms. Thus, consistent with Kyle (1985, 1989), despite analysts' search activities and insiders' own trades, not all of insiders' private information is revealed to investors prior to trade disclosure. However, the reaction to disclosure of insider trades in R&D firms is significantly stronger than the reaction to firms without R&D. When insiders' purchases of shares were disclosed, the mean market reaction on day 0 for R&D firms was 0.31 per cent vs 0.15 per cent for No-R&D firms (the difference is significant at the 1 per cent level). When insiders' sales of shares were disclosed, the mean market reaction on day 0 for R&D firms was −0.15 per cent vs −0.10 per cent for No-R&D firms.[17] The reaction to insider trade disclosure increases with the interval length, indicating that not all of the filed information is disclosed to investors on the filing date.[18]

The *volume* of trade surrounding the disclosure of insider transactions is another indication of information revelation. We find that for R&D firms where insiders sold shares the mean (median) volume of shares traded (deflated by outstanding shares) on day 0 was 0.74 per cent (0.34 per cent), whereas for No-R&D firms the mean (median) volumes were 0.41 per cent (0.19 per cent). The differences between those means (medians) are statistically significant at the 1 per cent level. For insider purchases in R&D firms, the mean (median) volume of shares traded (deflated by outstanding shares) on day 0 was 0.44 per cent (0.28 per cent), whereas for No-R&D firms, the mean (median) volume was 0.25 per cent (0.10 per cent). The differences between those means (medians) are also statistically significant at the 1 per cent level. We document

Table 3. Investors' Reaction to the Disclosure of Insider Trades

	Insider purchases			Insider sales		
	Mean	Median	# > 0	Mean	Median	# > 0
Day 0						
Firms without R&D	0.15%***	0.00%	35.6%	−0.10%*	0.00%***	39.3%
Firms with R&D	0.31%***	0.01%*	55.5%	−0.15%*	−0.01%***	38.4%
Days (0, +1)						
Firms without R&D	0.24%***	0.00%*	44.3%	−0.19%***	0.00%***	45.1%
Firms with R&D	0.40%***	0.01%*	55.1%	−0.34%***	−0.01%***	44.4%
Days (0, +1, +2)						
Firms without R&D	0.39%***	0.00%*	47.7%	−0.28%***	0.00%***	46.9%
Firms with R&D	0.58%***	0.02%*	58.8%	−0.47%***	−0.01%***	42.2%

Notes: * and *** denote that the means or medians of the R&D and No-R&D firms are significantly different from each other at the 10% and 1% levels, respectively.

Day 0 is the date when the filing on insider transactions was received by the SEC. Days (0, +1) refers to the cumulative raw return over day 0 and the following trading day. Days (0, +1, +2) is the three-day return. There are 29,689 sale transactions for No-R&D firms and 24,166 sale transactions for firms with R&D. There are 24,961 purchase transactions for No-R&D firms and 9262 purchase transactions for R&D firms. The total number of insider transactions here is smaller than in Table 1, because multiple transactions per firm reported to the SEC on the same day are considered here as one transaction. All mean and median returns are significantly different from zero at the 1% level. # > 0 indicates the percentage of individual returns that are positive.

similar, yet larger differences in volume of trade between R&D and No-R&D firms as we expand the interval to one and two days following the SEC filing date.

Based on the evidence, we conclude that investors react more strongly to the public disclosure of insider trades in R&D firms compared with firms without R&D activities, consistent with the hypothesis that R&D contributes to information asymmetry. Stated differently, there is more private information in R&D companies than in companies without R&D and observing insider trades (even with a time lag) is one means of narrowing the information gap. Furthermore, investors' significant reaction to insider trade disclosure, made on average twenty-five days after the actual trade, indicates that not all of the insiders' private information is revealed through their own trade or analysts' search activities.

5. Robustness Tests

5.1. Trade Intensity and R&D

If R&D enhances information asymmetry and managers exploit this asymmetry we would expect heavier insider trade activity in R&D firms than in firms without R&D, as the formers' officers attempt to gain from unique private information. The heavier activity of insiders in R&D firms may be reflected in more *frequent* trade and/or more *intensive* trade (relative to shares outstanding). Indeed we find that insiders in R&D firms trade relatively frequently: The mean (median) number of insider trades for R&D firms over the sample period was 17.1 (11) per firm, compared with 15.3 (9) for No-R&D firms.[19] We also find that the intensity of insider trades, measured in various ways, is higher for R&D firms than for firms without R&D. For example, when we measure trade intensity by the ratio of the number of shares traded by insiders in each transaction to the firm's outstanding shares, we find the mean (median) of that ratio for R&D firms to be 0.07 per cent (0.03 per cent), whereas for firms without R&D it is 0.06 per cent (0.02 per cent); the differences for both mean and median are statistically significant at the 1 per cent level. Furthermore, the correlation between R&D intensity and insider trade intensity is 0.112 (*p*-value of 0.0001). When insider trade intensity is measured as the ratio of the number of shares traded by an insider to the *individual's* total share holdings, we find the mean (median) intensity in R&D firms to be 22.4 per cent (8.5 per cent) vs 21.5 per cent (6.5 per cent) in No-R&D firms (the differences are once more significant at the 1 per cent level). The correlation between this intensity measure and the firm's R&D intensity is 0.066, significant at the 1 per cent level.[20]

The heavier trade activity of insiders in R&D firms documented here raises the question whether our findings in Section 3 (R&D officers gain more from inside trading than their counterparts in No-R&D firms) are due to trade intensity differences, rather than to information asymmetry. To examine this question we construct a sample of insider trades *matched* by trade size and run the three-factor regressions (1) on this sample. Specifically, for each sample month (1985–1997) we rank the *combined* R&D and No-R&D samples (separately for stock purchases and sales) by dollar value of transaction, and select adjacent R&D and No-R&D trades, where the difference in trade value was smaller than 10 per cent. These pairs of value-matched transactions are inputs into the three-factor regression.[21]

The regression estimates of these trade-size-controlled insider transactions are somewhat stronger than those in Panel B of Table 2. The intercept estimate for insider purchases is 0.011 ($t=2.00$), nearly identical to the α estimate in Table 2, and the intercept estimate for insider sales is -0.007, $t=-2.27$ (compared with -0.005, $t=-1.85$ in Table 2). We conclude, therefore, that the difference in insider gains between R&D and No-R&D firms is not induced by differences in size (value) of trades; rather managers of R&D firms exploit the relatively large information asymmetry associated with R&D.

5.2. Insider Gains and Changes in R&D Expenditures

Research indicates that changes in firms' R&D expenditures, once disclosed, are positively associated with stock returns (e.g. Chan *et al.* 1992; Lev and

Sougiannis, 1996; Aboody and Lev, 1998). Insiders, aware of changes in R&D budgets ahead of investors, are therefore expected to act on such information, increasing share purchases prior to disclosure of R&D increases and selling more than usual ahead of disclosure of R&D decreases. This conjecture is examined here.

Firm-specific changes in R&D expenditures are computed as the percentage change in a given quarter's R&D relative to R&D expenditures in the preceding quarter (there is no seasonality in quarterly R&D expenditures and therefore adjacent quarters are used in the change computation). During the sample period (1985–97), quarterly R&D expenditures increased (decreased) in 63.1 per cent (36.9 per cent) of the sample cases. Because many of the quarterly R&D changes are rather small (R&D time series are generally stable), we rank the firm-specific R&D changes by size and focus the analysis on the upper (relatively large R&D increases) and lower (large R&D decreases) quartiles.

For firms in the upper quartile of R&D changes, insiders purchased over the sample period a total of 40.0 million shares and sold a total of 91.4 million shares ahead of the disclosure of R&D increases in quarterly reports.[22] This purchase-to-sales ratio of 0.44 is substantially *larger* than the overall sample purchase-to-sales ratio (Table 1) for R&D companies—0.26 (312 to 1187 million shares)—suggesting enhanced insider purchases prior to an R&D increase announcement. For the bottom quartile of firms ranked by R&D changes (relatively large R&D decreases), insiders purchased 9.6 million shares and sold 138.9 million shares ahead of the quarterly report. The ratio of purchase-to-sales ahead of R&D decreases—0.07—is substantially *smaller* than the sample mean (0.26). It appears, therefore, that insiders increase share purchases ahead of disclosing R&D increases and enhance the sale of shares ahead of R&D decreases.[23]

We also perform a portfolio analysis conditional on the direction of R&D changes. Specifically, we form calendar-time portfolios for each sample month (1985–97, 155 months in total) of firms that have experienced an increase in R&D and those whose R&D has decreased. We do this separately for firms where insiders were predominantly purchasing shares during the month (RDP_t) and firms in which insiders were predominantly sellers of shares (RDS_t). For each firm, an average return (over all insider transactions during the month) is computed from the date of an insider transaction to one day prior to filing with the SEC, similarly to the returns analysed in Table 2. The Fama–French three-factor model is used to estimate excess returns (α), where the dependent variable is the difference between returns from share purchases and returns from the sale of shares ($RDP_t - RDS_t$), for firms that *increased* R&D expenditures (i.e. going long on firms in which insiders were net purchasers and short on firms in which insiders were net sellers). For firms that have *decreased* R&D, the dependent variable is the difference between returns from insider sales minus returns from insider purchases ($RDS_t - RDP_t$).

Panel B of Table 4 presents estimates of the three-factor model, conditional on foreknowledge (prior to public disclosure) of the change in R&D expenditures. It is evident from the α coefficients that for R&D *increases* (top row of Panel B), going long on firms in which insiders were net purchasers of shares and short on firms where insiders were net sellers yielded an excess return of 4.2 per cent over an average of twenty-five days between transaction and SEC filing date. For firms that have *decreased* R&D, the opposite strategy would have yielded an excess return of 2.2 per cent. Both excess returns are highly statistically significant.

Note that the estimated excess returns (α) in Table 4 (4.2 and -2.2 per cent) are substantially larger than those in Table 2 (1.1 and -0.5 per cent), indicating extra gains obtained by insiders possessing private information about future *changes* in R&D budgets, relative to the gains based on the 'average information' possessed by insiders.

Finally, Panel A of Table 4 presents mean (median) returns to insider trading in the expected direction (e.g. purchasing during an R&D increase), as well as to 'contrarians'—insiders that purchased shares ahead of an R&D decrease announcement and those that sold shares ahead of an R&D increase. The contrarians' mean gain from purchasing shares during a period of an R&D decrease (0.88 per cent) is substantially lower than that of insiders who purchased during

Table 4. Returns Earned on Portfolios Formed on the Basis of Changes in R&D Expenditures

Panel A: Univariate returns

	Insider Purchases			Insider Sales		
	Mean	Median	# > 0	Mean	Median	# > 0
Increase in R&D	5.55%***	4.74%***	129	1.53%***	1.37%***	98
Decrease in R&D	0.88%***	0.70%*	88	−1.28%***	−0.60%***	68

Panel B: Three-factor model

	α	$RM_t - RF_t$	SMB_t	HML_t	Adjusted R^2
R&D increases					
$RDP_t - RDS_t$	0.042***	−0.211	0.135	0.023	0.006
t-statistic	(8.33)	(−1.59)	(0.70)	(0.09)	
R&D decreases					
$RDS_t - RDP_t$	−0.022***	0.053	0.034	0.034	0.001
t-statistic	(−5.23)	(0.48)	(0.21)	(0.17)	

Notes: * and *** denotes significance at the 10% and 1% levels, respectively.
Panel A presents percentage raw returns earned on portfolios formed as follows: For each month between January 1985 and November 1997 we calculate, for each firm engaged in R&D, the raw return for each insider transaction from the transaction date to one day prior to the SEC filing date. We then calculate firm-specific mean (median) returns for firms in which insiders were net purchasers and for firms in which insiders were net sellers of shares. We compute returns separately for firms that increased R&D and those that decreased R&D expenditures. These mean (median) returns are reported in Panel A. # > 0 refers to number of months (out of 155) in which returns were positive. In Panel B, the estimated coefficients of the three-factor Fama–French regressions are presented. The dependent variable for R&D increases is the difference in excess returns (over the interval between transaction and filing date) between a portfolio of firms in which insiders were net purchasers of shares (RDP_t) and a portfolio of firms in which insiders were net sellers of shares (RDS_t). For R&D decreases, the dependent variable is reversed: $RDS_t - RDP_t$.

R&D increases (mean return of 5.55 per cent). The contrarians who sold shares during R&D increases saw share prices gain 1.53 per cent, on average, after they sold their shares. We can only speculate that those contrarians were motivated by liquidity or portfolio diversification needs.

6. Concluding Remarks

We examine insiders' gain from trade focusing on a specific source of information asymmetry—firms' R&D activities. R&D is unique (firm-specific) relative to other forms of capital. It is not traded in organized markets and disclosure in corporate reports about the productivity and value of R&D activities is deficient relative to the disclosure of tangible and financial assets. Accordingly, we hypothesize, R&D activities contribute substantially to the information asymmetry between managers and investors, and the former will tend to exploit this asymmetry to gain from insider trade.

We corroborate the hypothesis by providing evidence that insider gains in R&D-intensive companies are significantly larger than insider gains in firms not engaged in R&D. The R&D-related gains are both statistically and economically meaningful. We also find that investors' reaction to the public disclosure of insider trades is significantly stronger for R&D companies than for No-R&D companies, implying a larger information asymmetry in R&D firms, and that the R&D-related private information is not fully revealed prior to the public disclosure of insiders' trade. Finally, we report that insiders appear to time their transactions according to the direction of change in R&D expenditures, which is known to trigger investor reaction upon disclosure.

In this study we do not join the debate about the social consequences of insider trading. Some consider insider trading beneficial to market efficiency, and the loss to outside investors negligible, given the large volume differences between inside and outside investors (Jeng et al. 1999). Others, including Congress and the SEC (which have, over the last six decades, constructed an elaborate system of civil and criminal laws designed to restrict insider trading and the consequent profits), are obviously concerned with the consequences of insider trading. Such concerns extend beyond the direct loss to outside investors, to include, for example, adverse effects on managers' incentives (e.g. Fried, 1998). For those concerned with the consequences of insider gains, our study points at an important and fast-increasing source of private information leading to such gains—firms' R&D activities. Improved disclosure about R&D operations, such as the capitalization of development costs when products successfully pass technological feasibility tests (e.g. Aboody and Lev, 1998 for software companies) and the timely release of information about planned changes in R&D expenditures may be considered as means for mitigating the R&D-related information asymmetry and the consequent insider gains.

Notes

1. Estimates of the gains from insider trading vary widely: Early studies (e.g. Lorie and Niederhoffer, 1968; Jaffe, 1974; Finnerty, 1976) report abnormal gains ranging from 3% to 30%, for holding periods of up to three years. Seyhun (1986), using data on insider trading reported to the SEC during 1975–81, finds more modest gains to insiders: Over 300 days subsequent to trade, the average risk-adjusted gains were 4.3% for stock purchasers and 2.2% for sellers. Most of these gains occurred during the first 100 days after trade. In a subsequent study, Seyhun (1992) documents for the period from 1975 to 1989 average abnormal returns to insiders of 2.6 per cent for six months after stock purchases, and 5.3% for six months following sales. Jeng et al. (1999), using value-weighted portfolio schemes for the period from 1975 to 1996, report for a one year holding period insider gains on purchases of roughly 0.4% abnormal returns per month and insignificant abnormal returns for sales.

2. See Fried (1998) for a summary of the debate about the social consequences of insider gains and the effectiveness of securities regulations aimed at limiting these gains. The spectrum of opinions about social consequences ranges from viewing insider trading as desirable (e.g. it enhances market efficiency) to viewing insider gains as detrimental to firms (increase cost of capital, distort managerial incentives) and eroding investors' confidence in the integrity of capital markets. See also Jeng et al. (1999), who conclude that under the current regulatory system outsiders are not significantly disadvantaged when trading with insiders.

3. A perspective on the importance of R&D as a productive input can be gained from the fact that in 1997 total R&D spending in the United States was $210 billion, compared with $215 billion invested by manufacturing firms in property, plant, and equipment. The increasing importance of R&D is also reflected by its faster growth rate compared with other major inputs. For example, over the period from 1970 to 1997, the average annual growth rate of R&D was 8.0%, whereas the growth rate of capital investment (property, plant, and equipment) was 6.8 % (see Economic Report of the President, 1997 and National Science Foundation/SRS: Research and Development Performance by Sector).

4. The uniqueness of R&D is widely recognized in economics and finance research. Thus, for example, Titman and Wessels (1988: 5) postulate that asset uniqueness is a determinant of corporate capital structure and measure uniqueness by R&D intensity, arguing that R&D 'measures uniqueness because firms that sell products with close substitutes are likely to do less research and development since their innovations can be more easily duplicated. In addition, successful research and development projects lead to new products that differ from those existing in the market'.

5. Griliches (1995: 77) notes: 'A piece of equipment is sold and can be resold at a market price. The results of research and development investments are by and large not sold directly . . . the lack of direct measures of research and development output introduces an inescapable layer of inexactitude and randomness into our formulation'. Such randomness and inexactitude are obviously less severe to insiders than to outsiders.

6. Analysts' efforts were proxied by Barth *et al.* (1998) by the number of other firms followed by a given firm's analysts. Assuming that analysts have a common capacity limit and expend efforts up to that capacity, the smaller the number of firms an analyst follows, the larger, on average, the efforts spent analysing those firms.

7. Tasker (1998b) also reports that the majority of questions raised by analysts in conference calls involve R&D-related issues, such as the content of the company's product pipeline.

8. Kyle's (1985) predictions are sensitive to the number of informed traders. For example, Back *et al.* (1999) conclude: 'Competition may or may not lead to greater "efficiency" of prices. Whether the market price reflects private information more quickly when there are competing informed traders depends on how the information is distributed among the agents. Indeed, in this model, it is never the case that the market is *always* more efficient when information is distributed among competing traders than when the information is possessed by a single trader' (p. 30). 'A somewhat surprising result is that, beyond some date, the market would have learned more from a monopolist informed trader than from competing traders, regardless of the correlation of the competitors' signals' (p. 2). 'The relatively large amount of private information remaining near the end of trading leads to an extreme adverse selection problem' (p. 3).

9. The enforcement of the Securities and Exchange Act of 1934 was considerably strengthened by the Insider Trading Sanctions Act of 1984 (see Bainbridge, 1998), providing a reason to start the sample period in 1985.

10. The database we use includes several types of transactions we did not consider because it is not clear to what extent they are motivated by inside information. These transactions include: Acquisition of stocks through company plans, gifts of stocks, acquisitions through dividend reinvestment plans and under employee benefit plans. Examples of nonofficer insiders we exclude from the sample are various trustees and owners without managerial capacity.

11. In the large majority of sample firm-month cases, insider trades were either all sales or all purchases.

12. We replicate our tests with value-weighted portfolio returns and obtain very similar results to those of the equally weighted returns.

13. The construction of these variables is described in Fama and French (1993). We thank Ken French for providing us the data for the independent variables in (1).

14. Such an investment strategy cannot, of course, be implemented by outsiders who are not informed about insiders' transactions in real time.

15. We obtain similar results with a four-factor model, where the fourth factor is a return momentum (see Carhart, 1997).

16. This date is defined in our database as the date when the filing was received by the SEC.

17. Repeating the analysis of Table 3 using value-weighted mean returns slightly increases the significance of the results, whereas using size-adjusted returns slightly decreases the significance of the results.

18. We also calculate the correlation between the firms' R&D intensity (R&D to sales), as a proxy for information asymmetry, and the market reaction to trade disclosure on day 0. The correlation coefficient is 0.039 (p-value of 0.001) for insider purchases and −0.019 (p-value of 0.001) for insider sales.

19. The means and medians mentioned here are significantly different at the 1 per cent level between R&D and No-R&D firms.

20. We also find that the mean (median) number of shares traded in each insider transaction was 7102 (4000) shares for firms with R&D activities and 5693 shares (2000 shares) for firms without R&D expenditures. Similarly, the value of shares traded was significantly higher for firms with R&D than for No-R&D firms: The mean (median) value of shares traded in each transaction was $164,764 ($50,000) for firms with R&D vs $140,399 ($24,200) for firms without R&D expenditures. Moreover, the number and value of trades is higher in R&D firms than in No-R&D firms for *both* sale and purchase transactions.

21. The value match was close: The mean (median) transaction value is $215,648 ($48,000) for R&D firms and $214,526 ($47,787) for No-R&D firms.

22. The computation of shares purchased and sold by insiders is made for every fiscal quarter t, in 1985–97. The public disclosure of the change in R&D expenditures in quarter t, relative to $t − 1$, was made in quarter t financial report, released in quarter $t + 1$.

23. The mean (median) number of shares per insider transaction is also consistent with the direction of R&D changes. For R&D *increases*, the mean (median) number of shares in purchase transactions were 17,019 (5000) vs 15,912 (2500) for sale transactions. For R&D *decreases*, the mean (median) number of shares in purchase transactions were 10,003 (1000) versus 29,000 (15,000) for sale transactions.

....

References

Aboody, David and Baruch Lev (1998), 'The value-relevance of intangibles: The case of software capitalization', *Journal of Accounting Research*, 36 supplement: 161–91.

Back, Kerry, Henry Cao, and Gregory Willard (1999), 'Imperfect competition among informed traders', Working paper, Washington University.

Bainbridge, Stephen (1998), 'Insider trading', *Encyclopedia of Law and Economics*.

Barth, Mary, Ron Kasznik, and Maureen McNichols (2001), 'Analyst coverage and intangible assets', 39(1): 1–34.

Brennan, Michael and Avanidhar Subrahmanyam (1995), 'Investment analysis and price information in securities markets', *Journal of Financial Economics*, 38: 361–81.

Carhart, Mark (1997), 'On persistence in mutual fund performance', *Journal of Finance*, 52: 57–92.

Chan, Su, John Kesinger, and John Martin (1992), 'The market rewards promising R&D and punishes the rest', *Journal of Applied Corporate Finance*, 5: 59–66.

Chari, V. V., Ravi Jagannathan, and Aharon Ofer (1988), 'Seasonalities in securities returns: The case of earnings announcements', *Journal of Financial Economics*, 21: 101–21.

Fama, Eugene and Kenneth French (1993), 'Common risk factors in returns on stocks and bonds', *Journal of Financial Economics*, 33: 3–56.

Finnerty, Joseph (1976), 'Insiders and market efficiency', *Journal of Finance*, 31: 1141–48.

Fried, Jesse (1998), 'Reducing the profitability of corporate insider trading through pretrading disclosure', *Southern California Law Review*, 71: 303–92.

Griliches, Zvi (1995), 'R&D and productivity: Econometric results and measurement issues', in Paul Stoneman (ed.), *Handbook of the Economics of Innovation and Technological Change* (Oxford, Blackwell).

Jaffe, Jeffrey (1974), 'Special information and insider trading', *Journal of Business*, 47: 410–28.

Jeng, Leslie, Andrew Metrick, and Richard Zeckhuser (1999), 'The profits to insider trading: A performance-evaluation perspective, Working paper 6913, National Bureau of Economic Research.

Kothari, S. P., Ted Laguerre, and Andrew Leone (1998), 'Capitalization versus expensing: Evidence on the uncertainty of future earnings from current investment in PP&E and R&D, Working paper, University of Rochester.

Krishnaswami, Sudha and Venkat Subramaniam (1999), 'Information asymmetry, valuation, and the corporate spin-off decision, *Journal of Financial Economics*, 53: 73–112.

Kyle, Albert (1985), 'Continuous auctions and insider trading', *Econometrica*, 6: 1315–35.

—— (1989), 'Informed speculation with imperfect competition', *Review of Economic Studies*, 56: 317–56.

Lev, Baruch and Theodore Sougiannis (1996), 'The capitalization, amortization and value-relevance of R&D', *Journal of Accounting and Economics*, 21: 107–38.

Lorie, James and Victor Niederhoffer (1968), 'Predictive and statistical properties of insider trading, *Journal of Law and Economics*, 11: 35–51.

Seyhun, Nejat (1986), 'Insiders' profits, costs of trading, and market efficiency', *Journal of Financial Economics*, 16: 189–212.

—— (1992), 'The effectiveness of the insider-trading sanctions', *Journal of Law and Economics*, 35: 149–82.

Stoll, Hans (1978), 'The pricing of security dealer services: An empirical study of NASDAQ stocks, *Journal of Finance*, 33: 1153–72.

Tasker, Sarah (1998a), 'Bridging the information gap: Quarterly conference calls as a medium for voluntary disclosure', *Review of Accounting Studies*, 3: 137–67.

—— (1998b), 'Technology company conference calls: A small sample study', *Journal of Financial Statement Analysis*, 4: 6–14.

Titman, Sheridan and Roberto Wessels (1988), 'The determinants of capital structure choice', *Journal of Finance*, 43: 1–19.

The Stock Market Valuation of Research and Development Expenditures

Louis K. C. Chan, Josef Lakonishok, and
Theodore Sougiannis

The market value of a firm's shares ultimately reflects the value of all its net assets. When most of the assets are physical, such as plant and equipment, the link between asset values and stock prices is relatively apparent. In modern economies, however, a large part of a firm's value may reflect its intangible assets, such as brand names. Under generally accepted US accounting principles, many types of intangible assets are not reported in firms' financial statements. When a firm has large amounts of such intangibles, the lack of accounting information generally complicates the task of equity valuation.

One type of intangible asset, business research and development (R&D) activity, has lately been the subject of much attention. In part, the interest reflects recent widespread technological change, together with the dazzling growth of science- and knowledge-based industries, which are especially active in R&D. For example, at year-end 1999, the technology sector and the pharmaceuticals industry together account for roughly 40 per cent of the value of the S&P 500 index. Equally strikingly, the amount of R&D spending in some major technology industries is larger than their earnings. Finally, firms are required by US accounting standards to disclose their R&D expenditures in their financial statements, unlike many other kinds of spending on intangible assets.

The rise in the importance of technology-oriented companies raises the question of whether their stock market values reflect their intangible R&D capital. In an efficient market, the stock price impounds the value of a firm's R&D capital (along with other intangible assets), so there is no association between

R&D intensity and future stock returns. On the other hand, many R&D-intensive firms have few tangible assets. Instead, their prospects are tied to the success of new, untested technologies and hence are highly unpredictable. Large expenditures are usually required at the outset, and the outcome of many research projects is far from assured. The benefits, if any, are likely to materialize only much later, and the life-cycles of resulting products may be quite short. Finally, accounting information about a firm's R&D activity is generally of limited usefulness. Firms have some leeway in identifying what counts as an R&D cost and all of a firm's R&D spending is reported as one aggregate item. More important, as a result of the expensing convention for R&D, some yardsticks commonly used by investors, such as price-earnings ratios and market-to-book ratios, may be misstated. In particular, many R&D-intensive companies may appear to be priced at unjustifiably high multiples, so they appear to be 'expensive' by such criteria.

These complications raise the possibility that stock prices do not fully incorporate the value of R&D capital. Some authors (Porter, 1992; Hall, 1993; Hall and Hall, 1993) suggest that investors have short time horizons so they fail to anticipate the rewards from long-term investments such as R&D. Underpricing may also arise if investors mechanically accept firms' financial statements at face value without adjusting for the long-term benefits of R&D (the 'functional fixation hypothesis' in the accounting literature). This may be the case if investors, for example, value an R&D-intensive firm at a fixed multiple of its reported book value. Certainly, investors' ardor for technology stocks in recent years reflected their belief that R&D-intensive technology stocks are undervalued.

In contrast, many observers have suggested that investors overestimate the benefits from R&D, so valuations attached to R&D-intensive technology stocks are excessive. There is wide coverage of technology firms by the popular media and intensive marketing efforts devoted to these stocks by the investment industry. As a result, the market may be overly optimistic about the technological breakthroughs that are touted by R&D-intensive firms (such as a biotechnology firm's promise to deliver a cure for cancer). Further, if it is the case that many firms' R&D investments are not profitable (as Jensen, 1993 suggests) but investors systematically overlook this possibility, overvaluation may arise.

Accounting variables are widely used by the investment community in determining a firm's cost of capital. In this respect, failing to incorporate the value of a firm's intangible assets can affect its cost of capital. For example, bond covenants are generally tied to reported earnings or the book value of equity and assets. Since these accounting numbers do not reflect intangible assets, R&D-intensive firms may appear to be more highly leveraged than is the case and may face a higher cost of debt. Additionally, the ratio of book-to-market values is widely used as a measure of a firm's growth opportunities. If lenders and investors disregard a firm's intangible assets in assessing the book-to-market ratio, they may misstate its growth opportunities, and thereby the systematic risk, of an R&D-intensive firm.[1]

This paper documents the importance of firms' R&D capital, and investigates whether the stock market appropriately accounts for the value of R&D expenditures. Section 1 provides evidence on the importance of R&D spending, and gauges the impact of expensing R&D on standard valuation measures such as earnings yields and book-to-market ratios. We also report measures of the stock of R&D capital. Section 2 discusses whether measures of R&D intensity, including R&D spending relative to sales or relative to market value of equity, are related to future stock returns. Section 3 checks whether our results are robust to a variety of risk-adjustment procedures, including controls for confounding effects due to firm size, book-to-market, and past returns. Also in this section we extend our analysis to another important form of intangible capital, advertising expenditures. The lack of accounting disclosure about firms' R&D, in addition to having possible effects on stock prices, may also influence the level of investors' uncertainty. Accordingly, in Section 4 we explore whether the volatility of stock returns is related to R&D. A final section contains the summary and conclusions.

Although many investors are enamored with technology stocks and believe them to be superior investments, the historical evidence suggests otherwise. The average return on stocks that do R&D is comparable to the return on stocks with no R&D. The absence of any differences is consistent with the notion that the market price on average incorporates fully the benefits of R&D spending. The strongest signs of an association between R&D intensity and future returns come from stocks with high R&D relative to market value of equity (that tend to have experienced poor returns in the past). Excess returns for this category of stocks average 6.12 per cent per year over the postformation period. The market apparently gives insufficient credit to past losers who are spending heavily on R&D. Such firms probably face strong pressures to cut R&D and improve earnings. Their reluctance to do so, however, may reflect their managers' confidence that future prospects are not so bleak. Nonetheless, the market tends to overlook such signals (just as it tends to discount other indicators of managers' optimism such as stock repurchases and insider trades).[2] Our exploratory investigation of the effects on stock returns of another important intangible asset, advertising, uncovers very similar patterns as with R&D.

Although R&D intensity in general and stock returns are unrelated, this does not imply that the current accounting treatment of R&D is fully informative, or that there are no costs from the limited disclosure of such activity. We provide some evidence that R&D intensity is positively associated with return volatility. Insofar as the association reflects, at least in part, investors' lack of information about firms' R&D activity, there may be benefits from more detailed disclosure about R&D in accounting statements.

1. The Importance of R&D Spending

1.1 *Measures of R&D Intensity*

Table 1 provides summary statistics on R&D expenditures (total outlays, representing the amount charged against income under current US accounting procedures), and the estimated stock of R&D capital. R&D Spending is expressed relative to either total sales, earnings (net income), total dividends, or book value of equity. The stock of R&D capital is compared to the book value of equity. In each of these ratios, we aggregate separately the items in the numerator and denominator. The virtue of this procedure (compared to calculating

Table 1. Intensity of Research and Development Activity for all Firms doing R&D and for Selected Industries

| Year | Sales | R&D Expenditures as Per cent of | | | R&D Capital as Per cent of Book Value |
		Earnings	Dividends	Book Value	
Panel A: All Firms doing R&D					
1975	1.70	36.1	84.1	4.13	10.55
1980	1.78	34.4	87.6	5.08	12.55
1985	3.01	83.7	145.8	8.11	21.25
1990	3.40	79.4	148.9	9.59	25.76
1995	3.75	65.3	165.2	10.88	28.73

| SIC | Industry | R&D Expenditure as Per cent | | | | R&D Capital as Per cent of Book Value |
		Sales	Earnings	Dividends	Book Value	
Panel B: Selected industries						
737	Computer programming, software, and services	16.6	207.1	2833.0	27.5	54.9
283	Drugs and pharmaceuticals	11.9	92.2	192.0	21.1	53.3
357	Computers and office equipment	7.1	159.3	1242.4	21.0	55.9
38	Measuring instruments	5.6	89.8	276.9	13.0	36.6
36	Electrical equipment excluding computers	4.9	58.2	242.2	10.3	25.6
48	Communications	3.7	98.1	80.2	13.7	36.4
37	Transportation equipment	3.6	125.5	297.5	16.6	46.1

Note: For selected fiscal years from 1975 to 1995, total R&D expenditure and R&D capital are calculated for all firms doing R&D (Panel A) and firms classified into industries based on SIC codes (Panel B). The sample is all domestic firms listed on NYSE, AMEX, and Nasdaq with data on the COMPUSTAT files. The reported statistics are the ratios of R&D totals (either for all R&D firms or for an industry) to total values of the base variable (either for all R&D firms or for an industry). The base variables are: sales, earnings, dividends, and book value of equity. The selected industries comprise at least ten firms each, and are ranked by R&D expenditures relative to sales.

the average of the ratios across firms) is that it is insensitive to outlier cases where a firm has very low or no earnings, for example. An added advantage is that the calculation corresponds directly to the result of a capitalization-weighted portfolio investment strategy.[3]

Each firm's R&D capital is estimated from its past history of R&D expenditures as follows. The existing literature suggests no consensus on estimates for the useful life of expenditures and the amortization rate. Lev and Sougiannis (1996) estimate the impact of current and past R&D spending on earnings across a variety of industries. These estimates thereby measure the proportion of past spending that is still productive in a given year. Based on their estimates, we adopt the following tractable approximation of the stock of R&D capital, RDC_{it} for firm i in year t based on current and past R&D expenditure (RD_{it}):

$$RDC_{it} = RD_{it} + 0.8 * RD_{it-1} + 0.6 * RD_{it-2} + 0.4 * RD_{it-3} + 0.2 * RD_{it-4}. \quad (1)$$

Effectively we assume that the productivity of each dollar of spending declines linearly by 20 per cent a year. Our assumed capital amortization rate turns out to be close to the one used (15 per cent) in a highly influential database compiled on R&D activity by the National Bureau of Economic Research (see Hall et al., 1988).[4]

In panel A, R&D spending has grown sharply in importance. As a percentage of sales, R&D expenditures stood at 1.70 per cent in 1975 and more than doubled by 1995 to 3.75 per cent.[5] As R&D intensive firms tend to pay little or no dividends, R&D expenditures are as much as 1.65 times cash dividends to shareholders. R&D capital represents an important intangible asset that is not represented on firms' balance sheets, accounting for fully 29 per cent of the book value of common equity in 1995.[6] This number suggests that many technology-oriented stocks would appear less expensive if their intangible R&D assets were added to their book values.[7]

R&D spending is heavily concentrated in technology and science-oriented industries. As an illustration, panel B of Table 1 breaks out several industries (defined by two-digit or three-digit SIC codes) of particular interest and ranks them by 1995 R&D spending relative to industry sales. By far the highest ratio of spending is found in industry 737 (computer programming, software, and services).[8] R&D costs in this industry represent about 17 per cent of sales and two times earnings. Next in the industry ranking is the drugs and pharmaceuticals industry (SIC codes beginning with 283), where R&D is about 12 per cent of industry sales. Perhaps the recent popular impression that heavy R&D spending is associated with superior stock price performance stems in large part from the success of a few large, well-known companies drawn from these industries, such as Microsoft and Merck, over our sample period.

As a percentage of earnings, R&D expenditures vary from 58 per cent in industry 36 to 207 per cent in industry 737. The stock of R&D capital is also large relative to the accounting book value of equity. The magnitude of these figures suggests that expensing R&D costs may distort conventional valuation yardsticks such as price-earnings or price-to-book ratios.

1.2 The Impact of Expensing R&D Costs

To explore further the impact on commonly used valuation measures, we compare earnings under the current practice of immediately expensing R&D spending with 'adjusted earnings' calculated using an estimate of R&D expense.[9] Similarly we compare the book value of common equity with a measure of book value ('adjusted book value') that adds to the accounting book value the value of R&D capital.

The results in Table 2 for R&D-intensive industries highlight the potential distortions from immediately expensing R&D. The amortization adjustment is

Table 2. The Impact of Expensing Research and Development Spending on Earnings and Book Value for Selected Industries

SIC	Industry	Earnings as Per cent of Market Value	Adjusted Earnings as Per cent of Market Value
Panel A: Earnings			
737	Computer programming, software, & services	1.93	4.28
283	Drugs & pharmaceuticals	3.67	4.79
357	Computers & office equipment	4.46	5.73
38	Measuring instruments	4.11	4.53
36	Electrical equipment excluding computers	5.44	6.43
48	Communications	2.49	2.98
37	Transportation equipment	5.99	7.21
Panel B: Book value of equity			
737	Computer programming, software, and services	14.54	22.52
283	Drugs and pharmaceuticals	16.05	24.06
357	Computers and office equipment	33.65	52.46
38	Measuring instruments	28.40	38.81
36	Electrical equipment excluding computers	30.76	38.64
48	Communications	17.84	24.33
37	Transportation equipment	45.22	66.05

Note: For fiscal year 1995, earnings net of R&D expenditure and earnings net of R&D expense ('adjusted earnings') are calculated for all domestic firms listed on NYSE, AMEX, and Nasdaq with data on the COMPUSTAT files and who are engaged in R&D spending. Firms are classified into industries based on SIC codes. For each industry, total unadjusted and adjusted earnings for the industry are expressed as a percentage of the industry's market value of equity (Panel A). Book value of equity and book value of equity including R&D capital are also calculated for the industry and expressed as a percentage of the industry's equity market value (Panel B). The selected industries comprise at least ten firms each, and are ranked by 1995 R&D expenditure relative to sales.

especially striking for industry 737 (computer programming, software, and services). In panel A, the 1995 price-earnings ratio using reported earnings for this industry is 51.8 whereas the ratio based on adjusted earnings is less than half this amount (23.4). Similarly, the industry's price-to-book ratio comes down from 6.9 to 4.4 when R&D capital is accounted for in Panel B. Arguably, our assumption of a five-year life for R&D expenditures may be too long, given the short product cycles in the software industry. In the drugs and pharmaceuticals industry (industry 283), on the other hand, five years may not be long enough. Even in this industry, however, the amortization adjustments to earnings and book value are quite dramatic. With the adjustment, the price-earnings ratio comes down from 27.2 to 20.9, and the price-to-book ratio changes from 6.2 to 4.1.

In summary, R&D activity represents a significant and growing portion of firm resources. In several industries that are highly R&D intensive, the practice of immediately expensing R&D outlays can have a substantial distortionary effect on earnings and book values. If investors mechanically arrive at valuations based on such reported earnings or book values, the degree of mispricing can be substantial.

2. R&D Activity and Stock Returns

To see if the stock market correctly recognizes the expected future benefits from R&D spending, this paper implements an investment strategy based on R&D intensity. We first measure R&D intensity as R&D expenditures relative to sales. This variable is widely used in practice as an indicator of how much resources a firm devotes to R&D (see, e.g. the *Value Line Investment Survey*). Our second measure of intensity, the ratio of R&D expenditures to the market value of equity, is more in keeping with many indicators that are widely used in financial economics. In particular, scaling R&D by equity market value lets this intensity measure be interpreted in the same way as conventional indicators such as earnings- or book-to-price ratios. Sorting by R&D relative to market tends to highlight stocks that have large R&D spending and at the same time relatively depressed market values.

We take all domestic common stocks listed on the New York and American Stock Exchanges and on Nasdaq. Portfolios are formed at the end of April each year, based on the most recently available accounting information (assuming a four-month delay between the end of a firm's fiscal year and the release of its financial statements).[10] Eligible stocks are ranked by a measure of R&D intensity and assigned to one of five portfolios. Since we focus on valuation effects over longer horizons, we calculate equally weighted annual buy-and-hold returns over each of the three years following portfolio formation.[11] In addition, the tables report several characteristics of each portfolio.

2.1. Portfolio Results Based on R&D Relative to Sales

Table 3 provides results for portfolios sorted by R&D intensity relative to sales. Although it is commonly thought that firms doing R&D, such as technology companies, provide superior stock price performance, the raw return (Panel A) of firms that carry out R&D is on average no different from those of firms without R&D. Averaging over all the five groups of stocks doing R&D, for example, the mean annual return in the three years following portfolio formation is 19.65 per cent, compared to 19.50 per cent for firms without R&D. Put another way, run-of-the-mill cement and utility stocks on average did as well as highly-touted technology stocks. The similarity between the average returns of stocks with and without R&D is consistent with the hypothesis that the market on average correctly values any future benefits from research spending.

When we look within the group of firms engaged in research activity, there is little if any relation between R&D relative to sales and future returns in Panel A. Raw returns are roughly the same across the five portfolios. Over the three postformation years, for example, the most R&D-intensive portfolio, quintile 5, earns an average annual return of 19.52 per cent, compared to the overall average of 19.65 per cent per year for all R&D firms.

Firms with a high rank by R&D relative to sales tend to be glamour stocks, with lower ratios of book-to-market equity, sales-to-price, dividends, and earnings-to-price (Panel D). On this basis, earlier research (Chan et al., 1991; Fama and French, 1992; Lakonishok et al., 1994) raises the presumption that these stocks have historically earned comparatively low returns. Yet, as Panel A indicates, their average returns are similar to those of the other portfolios. It would thus appear that one set of glamour stocks, namely highly R&D-intensive stocks, do not have the relatively poor returns that usually accompanied glamour investing.

Panels B and C take the differences across portfolios in their value-glamour orientation into account. We follow the general approach in the literature and control for size and book-to-market effects.[12] Specifically, in Panel B each stock in a portfolio is assigned a control portfolio based on its ranking by size and by book-to-market. There are a total of thirty control portfolios, corresponding to

Table 3. Returns and Characteristics of Portfolios Classified by R&D Expenditure Relative to Sales

	1 (Low)	2	3	4	5 (High)	Non-R&D
Panel A: Returns before and after portfolio formation						
Average annual return over 5-year period before portfolio formation	0.1982	0.1904	0.2038	0.2066	0.2254	0.2025
First year after portfolio formation	0.1911	0.2068	0.2114	0.2157	0.1815	0.1987
Second year after portfolio formation	0.1738	0.1936	0.2013	0.1970	0.1971	0.1916
Third year after portfolio formation	0.1806	0.1898	0.2014	0.1984	0.2071	0.1947
Average annual return over 3-year period after portfolio formation	0.1818	0.1967	0.2047	0.2040	0.1952	0.1950
Panel B: Excess returns after portfolio formation						
First year after portfolio formation	−0.0058	0.0121	0.0185	0.0317	0.0016	−0.0018
Second year after portfolio formation	−0.0116	0.0092	0.0208	0.0254	0.0327	0.0036
Third year after portfolio formation	−0.0066	0.0043	0.0198	0.0235	0.0391	0.0060
Average annual return over 3-year period after portfolio formation	−0.0080	0.0085	0.0197	0.0269	0.0245	0.0026
Panel C: Excess returns based on adjusted book value						
First year after portfolio formation	−0.0063	0.0095	0.0154	0.0265	−0.0034	−0.0018
Second year after portfolio formation	−0.0130	0.0073	0.0165	0.0185	0.0245	0.0036
Third year after portfolio formation	−0.0075	0.0020	0.0155	0.0173	0.0310	0.0060
Average annual return over 3-year period after portfolio formation	−0.0089	0.0063	0.0158	0.0208	0.0174	0.0026
Panel D: Characteristics of portfolios						
Average number of firms	237.8	238.0	238.3	238.3	238.6	1856.5
R&D to sales	0.0046	0.0136	0.0289	0.0571	0.2262	0.0000
R&D to market value	0.0130	0.0321	0.0569	0.0807	0.1088	0.0000
Book-to-market	0.8997	0.8511	0.8001	0.7033	0.5408	0.9008
Adjusted book-to-market	0.9850	0.9754	0.9796	0.9396	0.8178	0.9008
Sales-to-market	3.1756	2.5879	2.3021	1.7118	1.0297	2.7738
Earnings-to-price	0.0800	0.0759	0.0684	0.0537	0.0058	0.0797
Dividend yield	0.0258	0.0243	0.0208	0.0153	0.0057	0.0257

Table 3. Continued

	1 (Low)	2	3	4	5 (High)	Non-R&D
Return on equity	0.1088	0.1090	0.1069	0.0983	0.0183	0.1060
Log Size	4.6863	4.6456	4.5959	4.5396	4.2323	4.4437
Panel E: Average annual growth rates after portfolio formation						
Annual earnings growth over 5 postformation years	0.0728	0.1083	0.1084	0.0772	0.1424	0.1015

Note: At the end of April each year from 1975 to 1995, all stocks are ranked by their R&D expenditure relative to sales, and assigned to one of five equally sized portfolios. Stocks with no R&D expenditures are assigned to a separate portfolio. The sample includes all NYSE, AMEX, and Nasdaq domestic primary issues with coverage on the CRSP and COMPUSTAT files. In Panel A, each portfolio's average annual buy-and-hold return is reported over the five years prior to portfolio formation; over each year from one to three years after portfolio formation; and averaged over the three postformation years. Panel B reports each portfolio's average return in excess of the equally weighted return on a control portfolio of stocks matched by firm size and book-to-market in the first through third postformation years. Panel C reports excess returns based on control portfolios matched by firm size and adjusted book equity (book equity plus the value of R&D capital) relative to market equity. Panel D reports characteristics of the portfolios: the average number of component stocks; the ratios of R&D expenditures to market value of equity and to sales; book value and adjusted book value of equity relative to market value of equity; sales relative to market value of equity; earnings relative to market value of equity; annual dividends divided by market value of equity; return on equity (earnings divided by the prior year's book value of equity); and the natural logarithm of market value of equity in millions of dollars. Panel E provides the annual growth rate in earnings for each portfolio over the five-year period following portfolio formation, using the procedure described in the Appendix.

five possible ranks by book-to-market and six possible ranks by size. The ranking by book-to-market is based on quintile breakpoints over all stocks. The breakpoints for size are based on NYSE issues only. The size categories are as follows: Groups 1–4 correspond to the largest four quintiles, respectively, of market capitalization; group 5 is the next-to-smallest decile and group 6 is the bottom decile. The additional breakdown of the bottom quintile of firms reflects the fact that many of the stocks who are active in R&D are small. Further, since the breakpoints for the size classification are based on NYSE stocks only, the bottom quintile comprises numerous firms. Each stock's return is measured net of the buy-and-hold return on its control portfolio.

If investors recognize that a firm's assets should include its intangibles, then firms should be matched on the basis of size and adjusted book-to-market ratios, where book equity values are adjusted to incorporate the value of R&D. This is done in Panel C, which otherwise follows the same procedure as Panel B.[13]

Stocks that are highly R&D intensive tend to earn positive excess returns in the postformation period, although the excess returns are generally not large. In Panel B, for instance, the mean excess return on the highest-ranked portfolio is 2.45 per cent per year over the three postformation years.[14] Including R&D capital in book equity knocks the average excess return over the postformation period down to 1.74 per cent in Panel C.[15]

Panel E of Table 3 looks directly at the future operating performance of the different portfolios. The details behind the calculations are provided in the Appendix. The average annual growth rate in earnings over the five post-formation years is virtually the same for stocks with R&D and without R&D (the means across all stocks with R&D and all stocks without R&D are 10.18 and 10.15 per cent, respectively).[16] The growth rate of earnings is notably higher only in the case of the most R&D-intensive stocks (quintile portfolio 5). For this quintile, the average growth rate for earnings is 14.24 per cent. The high growth rate is partly due to the fact that these stocks on average have the lowest base-year earnings (relative to price) of all the portfolios.

One important lesson from Table 3 thus seems to be that simply doing R&D by itself does not, on average, give rise to differential stock price performance. Since R&D-intensive stocks tend to be glamour stocks with relatively low book-to-market ratios (even after their book equity values are adjusted to include R&D capital), they might be presumed to earn below-average returns. Rather, Table 3 says that within the set of such glamour stocks, there are some stocks with large R&D spending whose returns are not lower than average. Putting these together gives rise to our result that a glamour stock that is highly active in R&D earns a slightly higher return than other glamour stocks.

2.2. Portfolio Results Based on R&D Relative to Market Value

Table 4 reports results for portfolios sorted by R&D expenditures relative to market value of equity. In general, the two measures of R&D intensity are correlated (Panel D). However, many firms that are highly R&D intensive relative to sales (such as pharmaceutical firms) do not rank highly on the basis of R&D relative to market equity. Rather, the portfolio of stocks ranked highest by R&D relative to market tends to be populated by stocks with poor past returns (or 'losers'). Over the five years prior to portfolio formation, the average annual return of stocks ranked in the top quintile by R&D relative to market is only 9.89 per cent (Panel A of Table 4). In comparison, stocks with no R&D have an average return over the same period of 20.25 per cent per year. Additionally, the earnings of stocks in quintile 5 are depressed, as reflected by their average earnings-to-price ratio or their average return on equity, which are the lowest in the table.

The stocks in the top quintile portfolio perform well in the years following portfolio formation. High R&D firms earn on average a return of 26.47 per cent in the first subsequent year, compared to 19.87 per cent for stocks with no R&D. The superior performance continues over the three postformation years. The average annual rate of return over the three postformation years is 26.19 per cent for the top R&D quintile and the spread between the two extreme quintiles (11.08 per cent per year on average over this period) is also large. The rebound for extreme past losers echoes the pattern uncovered by DeBondt and Thaler (1985). Firms with a history of poor performance may be subject to the kinds of extrapolative biases noted in the earlier literature. In particular, the market may discount too heavily the possibility of their future recovery. La Porta et al. (1997), for example, find a pattern of positive price reactions for value stocks around future earnings announcement dates, supporting the hypothesis that investors are too pessimistic about these firms.

In the case of stocks with high R&D intensity relative to market value, however, there is more to the story than just the subsequent recovery of past losers. Even after adjusting for size and book-to-market (Panels B and C), their returns are still high.[17] In Panel B, over the postformation period, quintile portfolio 5 has an average excess return of 6.12 per cent per year, yielding a mean spread of 7.83 per cent per year between the extreme quintiles.[18] Excess returns based on adjusted book-to-market ratios (Panel C) tell a similar story.[19]

One possible explanation for the excess returns on firms with high R&D to market equity draws from related evidence that the market underreacts to managers' signals (see e.g. Ikenberry et al., 1995; Loughran and Ritter, 1995; Lakonishok and Lee, 2001). Despite their poor performance, the firms in the top quintile portfolio spend a large portion of sales (in excess of 11 per cent) on

Table 4. Returns and Characteristics of Portfolio Classified by R&D Expenditure Relative to Equity Market Value

	1 (Low)	2	3	4	5 (High)	Non-R&D
Panel A: Returns before and after portfolio formation						
Average annual return over 5-year period before portfolio formation	0.2924	0.2460	0.2095	0.1687	0.0989	0.2025
First year after portfolio formation	0.1582	0.1782	0.1927	0.2135	0.2647	0.1987
Second year after portfolio formation	0.1401	0.1658	0.1869	0.2198	0.2534	0.1916
Third year after portfolio formation	0.1551	0.1677	0.1923	0.1975	0.2677	0.1947
Average annual return over 3-year period after portfolio formation	0.1511	0.1706	0.1906	0.2103	0.2619	0.1950
Panel B: Excess returns after portfolio formation						
First year after portfolio formation	−0.0177	−0.0040	0.0051	0.0161	0.0585	−0.0018
Second year after portfolio formation	−0.0220	−0.0023	0.0125	0.0353	0.0552	0.0036
Third year after portfolio formation	−0.0116	−0.0038	0.0140	0.0139	0.0699	0.0060
Average annual excess return over 3-year period after portfolio formation	−0.0171	−0.0034	0.0105	0.0218	0.0612	0.0026
Panel C: Excess returns based on adjusted book value						
First year after portfolio formation	−0.0182	−0.0063	0.0014	0.0105	0.0542	−0.0018
Second year after portfolio formation	−0.0231	−0.0035	0.0078	0.0284	0.0464	0.0036
Third year after portfolio formation	−0.0122	−0.0060	0.0100	0.0076	0.0611	0.0060
Average annual excess return over 3-year period after portfolio formation	−0.0178	−0.0053	0.0064	0.0155	0.0539	0.0026
Panel D: Characteristics of portfolio						
Average number of firms	237.8	238.0	238.3	238.3	238.6	156.5
R&D to sales	0.0210	0.0461	0.0660	0.0838	0.1137	0.0000
R&D to market value	0.0068	0.0188	0.0358	0.0644	0.1655	0.0000
Book-to-market	0.5832	0.6626	0.7020	0.7934	1.0523	0.9008
Adjusted book-to-market	0.6106	0.7290	0.8168	0.9850	1.5540	0.9008
Sales-to-market	1.6223	1.8656	1.9622	2.2467	3.1035	2.7738
Earnings-to-price	0.0651	0.0666	0.0618	0.0590	0.0311	0.0797
Dividend yield	0.0196	0.0200	0.0189	0.0179	0.0155	0.0257

Table 4. Continued

	1 (Low)	2	3	4	5 (High)	Non-R&D
Return on equity	0.1252	0.1129	0.0966	0.0779	0.0288	0.1060
Log size	5.0420	4.7837	4.6911	4.4042	3.7802	4.4437
Panel E: Average annual growth rates after portfolio formation						
Annual earnings growth over 5 postformation years	0.0730	0.0641	0.0644	0.0985	0.1713	0.1015

Note: At the end of April each year from 1975 to 1995, all stocks are ranked by their R&D expenditure relative to the market value of equity, and assigned to one of five equally sized portfolios. Stocks with no R&D expenditures are assigned to a separate portfolio. The sample includes all NYSE, AMEX, and Nasdaq domestic primary issues with coverage on the CRSP and COMPUSTAT files. In Panel A, each portfolio's average annual buy-and-hold return is reported over the five years prior to portfolio formation; over each year from one to three years after portfolio formation; and averaged over the three postformation years. Panel B reports each portfolio's average return in excess of the equally weighted return on a control portfolio of stocks matched by firm size and book-to-market in the first through third postformation years. Panel C reports excess returns based on control portfolios matched by firm size and adjusted book equity (book equity plus the value of R&D capital) relative to market equity. Panel D reports characteristics of the portfolios: the average number of component stocks; the ratio of R&D expenditures to market value of equity and to sales; book value and adjusted book value of equity relative to market value of equity; sales relative to market value of equity; earnings relative to market value of equity; annual dividends divided by market value of equity; return on equity (earnings divided by the prior year's book value of equity); and the natural logarithm of market value of equity in millions of dollars. Panel E provides the annual growth rate in earnings for each portfolio over the five year period following portfolio formation, using the procedure described in the Appendix.

R&D. Their managers' willingness to maintain R&D spending represents a vote of confidence that the firms' future opportunities might improve. Their beliefs are all the more credible because R&D spending directly depresses earnings, so their choice is not without pain. The growth rates in Panel E of the table support the extent of the regained profitability for the top quintile of R&D-intensive stocks. For this group, earnings over the five years following portfolio formation grow by 17.13 per cent, compared to 10.15 per cent for firms with no R&D.

The nature of the investor clientele for R&D-intensive technology companies may be an additional factor in determining stock prices. In particular, R&D-intensive firms who are past losers tend to be sold off by growth-oriented investors. Many value investors, on the other hand, stay away from technology stocks in general because they do not view such stocks as part of their natural investment domain. Additionally, value investors may not be drawn to technology stocks because they tend to look expensive under conventional criteria. The upshot is that there may be potentially more severe underpricing when R&D-intensive stocks experience poor performance.

Table 5 provides further evidence for the hypothesis that past losers who are spending heavily on R&D tend to be undervalued. This table uses a two-way sort to capture the influence of past return as well as R&D intensity. Since we

Table 5. Excess Returns of Portfolios Classified by R&D Intensity, and by Past Three-year Return

Classification by		Excess Return in Year after Portfolio Formation			Average Excess Return over Three Post-Formation Years
R&D relative to Sales	Past Three-year Return	First Year	Second Year	Third Year	
1 (Low)	1 (Low)	0.0085	−0.0120	−0.0172	−0.0069
	2 (High)	−0.0164	−0.0180	−0.0081	−0.0142
2	1	0.0282	0.0178	0.0028	−0.0069
	2	−0.0004	−0.0065	0.0029	−0.0014
3	1	0.0477	0.0173	0.0094	0.0248
	2	−0.0071	0.0172	0.0176	0.0092
4	1	0.0492	0.0357	0.0253	0.0368
	2	0.0177	0.0085	0.0106	0.0122
5 (High)	1 (Low)	0.0219	0.0482	0.0618	0.0440
	2 (High)	−0.0150	0.0120	0.0062	0.0010

Note: At the end of April each year from 1975 to 1995, all stocks with R&D expenditures are ranked by R&D expenditures relative to sales, and assigned to one of five equally sized portfolios. The sample includes all NYSE, AMEX, and Nasdaq domestic primary issues with coverage on the CRSP and COMPUSTAT files. Within each of the five portfolios, stocks are further ranked by their compound rates of return over the prior three years and subdivided into two equally sized groups. The table reports each portfolio's average excess return over each of the first three years following portfolio formation, and over all three postformation years. In measuring excess returns, each stock is matched with a control portfolio of stocks based on size and book-to-market and then past three-year return. The difference is calculated between the stock's annual buy-and-hold return and the return on the control portfolio.

directly condition on past return, R&D intensity is measured relative to sales. Within each of the portfolios sorted by R&D intensity, we assign a stock to one of two equally sized groups, depending on its rate of return over the three years prior to portfolio formation. Since previous research suggests that past return helps to predict future return, each stock's return is measured net of the return on a control portfolio matched on size, book-to-market and, furthermore, past three-year return. Equally weighted excess returns on each portfolio are reported in the table.

The two-way classification successfully teases out the firms that earn excess returns within each quintile by R&D relative to sales. The abnormal performance is concentrated in stocks with relatively low past returns. Notably, past losers in the highest ranked R&D portfolio earn an average return of 4.40 per cent per year over the postformation period after controlling for size, book-to-market, and past return. The results suggest that any mispricing of R&D stocks is more likely to be associated with firms with poor past performance.

3. Additional Results

3.1. Alternative Risk Adjustment Procedures

It is possible that any excess returns earned by R&D-intensive stocks reflect risk differentials (beyond what is picked up by our control portfolio procedures). In this section, we check for this possibility by applying a variety of risk-adjustment procedures. The procedures include a version of the Fama and French (1993, 1996) multifactor model to adjust for risk sensitivities; Fama and MacBeth (1973) cross-sectional regressions that account for differences in firm characteristics; Sharpe ratios; and performance across up and down markets. Since the sort by R&D relative to market equity shows the strongest traces of abnormal performance, we focus on this measure of R&D intensity.

Stocks that are highly ranked by R&D to market equity generally have low past returns, so their subsequent returns may be confounded by the reversals generally experienced by past losers. Further, past returns over an intermediate horizon of less than a year may be another factor that predicts future returns (see Chan et al., 1996). To control for these effects, in addition to size and book-to-market, in Table 6 we estimate time series regressions of the form

$$R_{pt} - R_{ft} = a_p + b_p[R_{Mt} - R_{ft}] + s_p \mathrm{SMB}_t + h_p \mathrm{HML}_t + w_p \mathrm{WML}_t + d_p \mathrm{UMD}_t + \varepsilon_{pt}. \quad (2)$$

Table 6. Factor Model Regressions for Monthly Returns (in Per Cent) on Portfolios Sorted by R&D Relative to Market Equity

	Portfolio	a	$t(a)$	b	$t(b)$	s	$t(s)$	h	$t(h)$	w	$t(w)$	d	$t(d)$	R^2
First year after portfolio formation	1 (Low)	−0.14	−1.99	0.98	57.66	0.68	20.40	−0.09	−2.74	−0.03	−0.97	−0.02	−1.11	0.96
	2	0.05	0.71	0.96	53.87	0.74	21.09	−0.10	−2.89	−0.07	−2.36	−0.06	−2.52	0.96
	3	0.16	1.86	1.01	47.54	0.76	18.26	−0.10	−2.38	−0.08	−2.34	−0.09	−3.53	0.95
	4	0.26	2.91	1.02	46.51	0.81	18.93	−0.11	−2.53	−0.18	−5.13	−0.08	−2.76	0.95
	5 (High)	0.55	4.44	1.04	34.15	0.96	16.08	−0.10	−1.70	−0.32	−6.63	−0.10	−2.73	0.92
Second year after portfolio formation	1	−0.10	−1.51	0.96	58.86	0.61	19.85	−0.07	−2.25	−0.07	−2.68	−0.07	−3.83	0.97
	2	0.04	0.62	0.95	52.43	0.75	22.08	−0.06	−1.88	−0.04	−1.61	−0.09	−4.15	0.96
	3	0.21	2.58	1.00	48.47	0.71	18.37	−0.09	−2.28	−0.11	−3.49	−0.09	−3.49	0.95
	4	0.39	4.02	1.00	40.92	0.79	17.21	−0.16	−3.49	−0.15	−4.15	−0.10	−3.39	0.94
	5	0.52	4.45	1.02	34.61	0.93	16.80	−0.16	−2.91	−0.30	−6.75	−0.05	−1.44	0.93
Third year after portfolio formation	1 (Low)	−0.04	−0.52	0.93	49.70	0.62	17.72	−0.05	−1.32	−0.07	−2.30	−0.07	−2.99	0.96
	2	0.04	0.54	0.95	46.15	0.66	17.08	−0.01	−0.28	−0.06	−1.82	−0.07	−2.80	0.95
	3	0.26	3.09	0.97	45.28	0.63	15.72	−0.14	−3.46	−0.15	−4.69	−0.10	−3.72	0.95
	4	0.19	2.08	1.02	43.77	0.79	18.14	−0.10	−2.26	−0.14	−3.96	−0.18	−3.18	0.95
	5 (High)	0.53	4.61	1.01	34.83	0.89	16.37	−0.23	−4.17	−0.29	−6.43	−0.00	−0.13	0.93

Note: At the end of April each year from 1975 to 1995, all stocks are ranked by R&D expenditure relative to market value of equity, and assigned to one of five equally sized portfolios. Stocks with no R&D expenditures are assigned to a separate portfolio. The sample includes all NYSE, AMEX, and Nasdaq domestic primary issues with coverage on the CRSP and COMPUSTAT files. Estimated coefficients, t-statistics, and adjusted R^2 are reported for the model:

$$R_{pt} - R_{ft} = a_p + b_p [R_{MT} - R_{ft}] + s_p SMB_t + h_p HML_t + w_p WML_t + d_p UMD_t + \varepsilon_{pt}$$

where $R_{pt} - R_{ft}$ is the monthly return on portfolio p in excess of the Treasury bill rate in month t, $R_{MT} - R_{ft}$ is the excess return on the value-weighted market index, SMB, and HM$_{-t}$ are the returns on the Fama and French (1993) factor-mimicking portfolios for size and book-to-market, respectively. WML$_t$ is the difference between the returns in month t on portfolios of past winners and losers, where winners (losers) are the top (bottom) quintile of stocks ranked by past return beginning sixty months and ending twelve months ago. UMD$_t$ is the difference between returns on portfolios of past winners and losers, where winners (losers) are the top (bottom) quintile of stocks ranked by past return beginning seven months and ending one month ago. The model is estimated using monthly returns from each of the first three years following portfolio formation.

The model is estimated using monthly returns from each of the first three years following portfolio formation. Here $R_{pt} - R_{ft}$ is the monthly return on portfolio p in excess of the Treasury bill rate in month t, $R_{Mt} - R_{ft}$ is the excess return on the value-weighted market index, and SMB_t, HML_t are the returns on the Fama and French (1993) factor-mimicking portfolios for size and book-to-market, respectively. The factors WML_t and UMD_t pick up the effect of long-term and intermediate-term past returns (measured over nonoverlapping horizons), respectively. Each is the difference between the returns in month t on a portfolio of past winners and a portfolio of past losers. Past winners (losers) are defined to be the stocks ranked in the top (bottom) quintile by their past returns beginning five years ago and ending one year ago in the case of WML_t. For UMD_t, past winners and losers are defined by past return beginning seven months and ending one month ago.[20]

The factor model (2) also helps to remedy one drawback to excess returns based on control portfolios matched by size and book-to-market ratio. In particular, the matching procedure for control portfolios relies on measured book values that do not include the value of intangible assets, or alternatively requires assumptions about the amortization rate for R&D. Additionally, if technology stocks always behave like growth stocks regardless of their book-to-market ratios, the adjustment based on matching portfolios may be misleading.

The evidence in Daniel and Titman (1997) suggests an alternative to using factor loadings as a stock's risk exposures. In particular, firm characteristics such as size, book-to-market, and past returns may yield better risk measures. To implement this approach, we estimate annual cross-sectional regressions of stock returns on firm size (in logarithms), adjusted book-to-market ratio, R&D intensity relative to market, and past returns. The estimated coefficients are then averaged over time. The results from the factor model and the model using firm attributes turn out to be qualitatively similar; so, for the sake of brevity, we concentrate on the factor model adjustment.

Given their poor past performance, stocks with high R&D relative to market tend to have comparatively large negative loadings on WML and, in the first year, on UMD in Table 6. Even after controlling for the five factors, there are notable differences in alphas across the quintile portfolios. In particular, the alpha for the top quintile portfolio is large and statistically significant in each of the three postformation years. Over the first postformation year, the excess performance for the top quintile is 0.55 per cent per month.[21] The spread between the extreme quintiles' alphas is 0.69 per cent per month in the first year (or an annualized spread of 8.28 per cent). The spread continues to be large in the second and third postformation years as well (they are 7.44 and 6.84 per cent per year, respectively).[22] To sum up, our earlier findings are not sensitive to how we adjust for size and book-to-market effects. Further, the abnormal performance of stocks with high R&D to market is not solely driven by return reversals associated with past losers.

Other measures of risk-adjusted performance also suggest that the large returns on the portfolio with high R&D intensity relative to market are not entirely due to risk. The Sharpe ratio of the top quintile portfolio, for example, is 0.85 (based on annual returns over the first postformation year). The corresponding Sharpe ratio for the market index is 0.53. If risk is measured as potential losses during down markets, the top quintile portfolio is also not very risky. For example, across all down-market months (where the return on the market is below the Treasury bill rate) the average return on the top quintile portfolio over the Treasury bill rate is −2.60 per cent per month. The corresponding average for the market index is −3.25 per cent per month. In up markets, the average return over the T-bill rate is 5.32 and 3.28 per cent per month for the top quintile portfolio and the market, respectively.[23]

3.2. Advertising and Stock Returns

Although the promise of technological breakthroughs has pushed R&D capital into the limelight, there are other forms of intangible capital as well. In this subsection, we provide an exploratory analysis of another common form of investment in intangible capital, namely, advertising. Like research and development spending, advertising expenditures have some elements of long-term investment (although the effective lifetime of advertising expenditures may be comparatively shorter). Advertising expenditures are also expensed. Empirically, advertising represents a smaller component of aggregate sales or earnings compared to R&D. Advertising makes up about 0.9 per cent of total 1995 sales of all firms, whereas R&D accounts for almost twice as much (1.7 per cent). Our objective here is to see if the patterns uncovered in our analysis of R&D extend to advertising.

Table 7 provides results for portfolios sorted by advertising expenditures relative to market value of equity.[24] The number of firms that do advertising is roughly the same as those doing R&D (about 1200 firms on average each year report nonzero expense for either advertising or R&D). For the firms engaged in advertising, their average return over the three postformation years (20.46 per cent) is slightly higher than that of firms without advertising (18.95 per cent). The difference may reflect the fact that firms who do advertising tend to be concentrated in certain industries.[25]

The results for advertising expenditures relative to market essentially agree with our findings for R&D relative to market. For example, over the three years

Table 7. Returns and Characteristics of Portfolios Classified by Advertising Expenditure Relative to Equity Market Value

	1 (Low)	2	3	4	5 (High)	Non advertising
Panel A: Returns before and after portfolio formation						
Average annual return over	0.3146	0.2286	0.1978	0.1769	0.1402	0.1981
5-year period before portfolio formation						
First year after portfolio formation	0.1651	0.1958	0.2179	0.2246	0.2276	0.1946
Second year after portfolio formation	0.1491	0.1945	0.2113	0.2045	0.2321	0.1886
Third year after portfolio formation	0.1648	0.1972	0.2189	0.2196	0.2491	0.1854
Average annual return over	0.1597	0.1958	0.2160	0.2162	0.2363	0.1895
3-year period after portfolio formation						
Panel B: Excess returns after portfolio formation						
First year after portfolio formation	−0.0103	0.0037	0.0215	0.0266	0.0187	−0.0028
Second year after portfolio formation	−0.0085	0.0168	0.0272	0.0150	0.0295	0.0036
Third year after portfolio formation	0.0042	0.0189	0.0325	0.0264	0.0447	0.0000
Average annual excess return over	−0.0049	0.0131	0.0271	0.0227	0.0310	0.0003
3-year period after portfolio formation						
Panel C: Characteristics of portfolios						
Average number of firms	231.6	231.7	232.0	232.2	232.3	1887.7
Advertising to sales	0.0162	0.0181	0.0252	0.0342	0.0666	0.0000
Advertising to market value	0.0049	0.0159	0.0341	0.0707	0.2011	0.0000
Book-to-market	0.4723	0.6429	0.7804	0.9191	1.1760	0.8757
Sales-to-market	1.0028	1.5605	2.1899	3.1984	4.9396	2.5053
Earnings-to-price	0.0414	0.0629	0.0659	0.0715	0.0731	0.0758
Dividend yield	0.0096	0.0152	0.0190	0.0219	0.0231	0.0261
Log size	4.5883	4.5264	4.5185	4.4813	3.8427	4.5434

Note: At the end of April each year from 1975 to 1995, all stocks ranked by their advertising expenditure relative to the market value of equity, and assigned to one of five equally sized portfolios. Stocks with no advertising expenditures are assigned to a separate portfolio. The sample includes all NYSE, AMEX, and Nasdaq domestic primary issues with coverage on the CRSP and COMPUSTAT files. In Panel A, each portfolio's average annual buy-and-hold return is reported over the five years prior to portfolio formation; over each year from one year to three years after portfolio formation; and averaged over the three postformation years. Panel B reports each portfolio's average return in excess of the equally weighted return on a control portfolio of stocks matched by firm size and book-to-market in the first through third postformation years. Panel C reports characteristics of the portfolios: the average number of component stocks; the ratios of advertising expenditures to market value of equity and to sales; book value of equity relative to marker value of equity; sales relative to market value of equity; earnings relative to market value of equity; annual dividends dividend by market value of equity; and the natural logarithm of market value of equity in millions of dollars.

following portfolio formation, the firms in quintile portfolio 5 have an average excess return of 3.10 per cent per year. Advertising-intensive firms with poor past performance also face strong pressures to cut costs. When such firms keep investing in their franchise value through advertising despite these pressures, they are more likely to represent cases of relative undervaluation. Nonetheless, these cases are overlooked by the market.

4. R&D and Return Volatility

Our results suggest that, on average, a firm that does R&D earns a rate of return that is no different from a firm without R&D. Nonetheless, R&D may have effects on firms' financial performance beyond average stock returns. Although there are other sources of information about R&D activity beyond firms' financial statements, the lack of accounting disclosure suggests that investors may not be fully informed about this vital activity. One consequence may be a high degree of uncertainty surrounding an R&D-intensive firm's future prospects. As a result, the volatility of returns may rise with R&D spending, thereby imposing real costs on investors and possibly affecting the cost of capital for R&D-intensive firms.

The empirical issue is whether there is any association between R&D and return volatility. Higher volatility may be a consequence of the nature of the business in technology-based industries (where R&D spending is mainly concentrated). In addition, many R&D-intensive firms tend to be smaller and younger firms, so there may be an association on this account. Accordingly, we estimate a cross-sectional regression of the form

$$\sigma_{it}=\gamma_{0t}+\gamma_{1t}\text{LNSIZE}_{it}+\gamma_{2t}\text{LNAGE}_{it}+\gamma_{3t}\text{RDS}_{it}+\sum_{j=1}^{L}\phi_{jt}\text{IND}_{ijt}+\varepsilon_{it} \qquad (3)$$

at the end of April each year over the sample period, using all available stocks (doing R&D or not). The regression relates each stock's return volatility Σ_{it} (the standard deviation of monthly returns based on the subsequent twelve months) to the following variables: the firm's stock market capitalization (in logarithms), LNSIZE_{it}; the firm's age (in logarithms), LNAGE_{it}; as well as its R&D intensity relative to sales, RDS_{it}. To capture volatility associated with business conditions in the technology sector, the regression also includes dummy variables for industries IND_{ijt}. The industry classifications are based on two-digit SIC codes and, specifically, include the technology industries considered in Table 2 (some of which are based on three-digit SIC codes). Then we average the estimated coefficients from the cross-sectional regressions over all portfolio-formation years and use the time series standard deviation of the coefficients to calculate t-statistics.

The average coefficient for R&D intensity is 0.0963 with a t-statistic of 6.49. The stocks ranked in the top quintile by R&D relative to sales have an average R&D intensity of about 23 per cent (see Table 3). Compared to firms with no R&D, therefore, the regression model predicts that monthly return volatility for highly R&D-intensive companies is larger by about 2.21 per cent, everything else being equal. Since the average monthly volatility of returns for companies with R&D is about 13 per cent, the impact of R&D intensity is economically important. The coefficients for the other variables in (3) generally conform to intuition. In short, insofar as the limited disclosure of R&D contributes to higher return volatility, there may be a cost associated with the present accounting treatment of R&D.

....

5. Summary and Conclusions

In modern economies many firms have large amounts of intangible assets such as investments in R&D. Under generally accepted accounting principles in the United States, however, such intangibles are generally not recorded on financial statements. Since R&D spending is treated as a current expense, there can be potentially large effects on many firms' financial statements. This paper addresses the question of whether stock prices appropriately incorporate the value of firms' R&D investments.

The high level of spending on R&D suggests that large distortions can arise from expensing rather than capitalizing R&D costs. If investors fail to adjust standard valuation measures such as price-to-earnings or price-to-book ratios for the long-term benefits of R&D, potentially severe mispricing can arise.

Our evidence does not support a direct link between R&D spending and future stock returns. In the three-year period following portfolio formation, stocks doing R&D have an average return of 19.65 per cent per year, and stocks doing no R&D have an average return of 19.50 per cent. Thus it does not appear that, historically, a highly touted technology stock on average outperformed a more mundane cement company. This finding is consistent with the hypothesis that the stock price incorporates investors' unbiased beliefs about the value of R&D.

For firms engaged in R&D, the evidence on an association between R&D intensity measured relative to sales and future returns is not strong. The clearest evidence that high R&D plays a distinctive role arises from stocks with high R&D relative to the market value of equity. Their average excess return over the following three years is 6.12 per cent per year. Stocks ranked highly by R&D relative to market equity generally tend to be past losers. Firms that spend heavily on R&D despite poor past performance and pressures to cut costs represent instances where managers are relatively optimistic about the firms' future prospects. However, the market tends to discount this information and appears to be sluggish in revising its expectations. Our findings are not sensitive to how returns are adjusted for effects due to size, book-to-market, and return reversal effects. Further, we obtain similar results for spending on another type of intangible asset, advertising.

Although the historical record reveals little difference between the average stock price performance of R&D stocks and stocks with no R&D, this may not be the end of the story. We provide evidence that R&D intensity is associated with return volatility, after controlling for firm size, age, and industry effects. Even if market prices on average incorporate the future benefits from R&D, the lack of accounting information on such an important intangible asset may impose real costs on investors through increased volatility.

Appendix: Growth Rates of Portfolio Earnings

This Appendix describes how we construct measures of operating performance for a portfolio. In the text, we report returns based on a buy-and-hold strategy, where the composition of the portfolio is revised each year. In parallel with this strategy, we calculate growth rates in portfolio earnings, based on the ideas in Givoly and Lakonishok (1993), as well as Ikenberry and Lakonishok (1993). The procedure is as follows (see also the description in Chan, et al., 2000). In year t, we select stocks for a portfolio and we track the earnings on this portfolio from years $t - 5$ to $t + 5$. In the base year $t - 5$ we invest one dollar in each of the selected stocks. For the ith firm in the base year, we are entitled to the proportion $1/V_{i,t-5}$ of its earnings, where $V_{i,t-5}$ is the market value of firm i's equity in year $t - 5$ and $E_{i,t-5}$ is its total earnings available to common shareholders that year. Accordingly, the base level (at year $t - 5$) of portfolio p's earnings, $e_{p,t-5}$, per dollar invested, is given by

$$e_{p,t-5} = \frac{1}{N_{t-5}} \sum_{i=1}^{N_{t-5}} \frac{E_{i,t-5}}{V_{i,t-5}} \tag{A1}$$

where N_{t-5} is the number of firms in the portfolio available for investment.

In each subsequent year τ, where $t - 5 < \tau \leq t + 5$, the earnings on the buy-and-hold portfolio, per dollar originally invested in the base period, is given by

$$e_{p,\tau} = \frac{1}{N_{t-5}} \sum_{i=1}^{N_\tau} \frac{\Pi_{l=5}^{t-\tau+1}(1+r_i[t-l,t-l+1])E_{i,\tau}}{V_{i,\tau}}. \tag{A2}$$

The amount held in stock i in year τ is given by its compound return $\Pi_{l=5}^{t-\tau+1}[1+r_i(t-l,t-l+1])$ from the base year to the given year, where $r_i[t-l, t-l+1]$ is the return on the stock between years $t - l$ and $t - l + 1$. For each year τ relative to the portfolio formation year, this procedure gives a time series of annual portfolio earnings per dollar originally invested. Finally, we average each time series to yield eleven average values for portfolio earnings; these serve as the inputs for calculating the geometric average growth rates over the years preceding and following portfolio formation. These directly measure the operating performance of portfolios obtained from a buy-and-hold strategy and hence correspond to the returns reported in the text. Additionally the earnings for the portfolio as a whole are much less likely to be negative or very low in any given year.

Since firms entering a portfolio in a formation year t are not required to exist through the entire period from years $t - 5$ to $t + 5$, one further modification to the above procedure is necessary. As new firms enter the portfolio in year τ leading up to the formation year ($t - 5 < \tau \leq t$), the total amount held in the portfolio $\sum_{i=1}^{N_\tau} \Pi_{l=5}^{t-\tau+1}[1+r_i[t-l, t-l+1])$ is equally divided across the new number of stocks. Thereafter the dollar value held in each stock is calculated based on this revised amount. Similarly, as a stock drops out of the portfolio in year τ following the portfolio formation year ($t, \tau \leq t + 5$), we liquidate the position in the stock and equally prorate the proceeds across the remaining stocks. The subsequent value of each holding is compounded from this revised amount.

Notes

1. See, for example, Berk *et al.* (1999) for a discussion of how a firm's expected return and risk dynamics are affected by its asset base and growth options in an equilibrium model.
2. See, for example, Ikenberry *et al.* (1995) for evidence on the stock price effects of share repurchases, and Lakonishok and Lee (2001) for evidence on insider trading.
3. All financial information are taken from the COMPUSTAT Active and Research files. R&D expenditure is annual data item 46; sales is annual data item 12; net income is annual data item 172; dividends to common equity are measured as annual data item 21; book value of common equity is annual data item 60. Market value of common equity (price per share times number of shares outstanding) is from the CRSP Stock Return files.
4. In additional unreported work, we assumed a 10% amortization rate. The results are qualitatively unaffected.
5. It has been argued that the growth in R&D may be overstated to the extent that firms relabel other expenses as R&D in order to qualify for tax credits (see, e.g., the literature surveyed in Hall and van Reenen, 1999). From the standpoint of investors evaluating the benefits from R&D, such reallocation further complicates the valuation problem.
6. Note that the estimated capital stock is based on the actual outlays incurred, so the capital is valued at cost. Assuming some rate of return on R&D over the cost of capital would lead to an even larger intangible asset.
7. Not all firms carry out R&D: On average about 40% of firms report some value for R&D expenditures. Nonetheless, even when the comparison is relative to the entire set of US firms, the importance of R&D outlays is impressive; For example, expenditures in 1995 are about 81% of all firms' dividends.
8. Under current accounting rules, software research costs are expensed, as in other industries, but the costs of development for software are capitalized. Development refers to the translation of research findings into plans or designs for new products or processes. In general, firms are not required to report separately their expenses for research

and for development. A brief perusal of the financial statements of several large, well-known software companies suggests, however, that in many cases, effectively all their software R&D costs are expensed as incurred (at least over our sample period). For example, Microsoft's balance sheet indicates that all R&D costs are expensed and that the development portion is not material. Netscape and Symantec report similarly. For 1994, Lotus charged $159 million of R&D costs to operations and capitalized $36 million of development costs. It reported that capitalized software costs were amortized on a straight-line basis over the specific product's economic life, generally three years.

9. Corresponding to (1), R&D expense RE_{it} is the periodic amortization of the R&D capital stock:

$$RE_{it} = 0.2*(RD_{it-1} + RD_{it-2} + RD_{it-3} + RD_{it-4} + RD_{it-5}).$$

10. The sample is not limited to firms whose fiscal years end in December. In the case of firms with fiscal years not ending in December, their accounting data will be less up-to-date as of the portfolio formation date, given our assumed publication delay. However, most firms in the R&D sample (roughly 59% of the observations) have fiscal years that end in December.

11. When a stock is delisted in the course of a year after portfolio formation, we pick up the CRSP delisting return if it is available. Thereafter we splice the stock's return with the return on the value-weighted market index until the next portfolio formation date. Our analysis of long-horizon returns for a large sample of firms over an extended period differentiates us from other related studies. For example, Chan *et al.* (1990) look at returns on days around announcements of R&D plans for ninety-five firms from 1979 to 1985.

12. For evidence that size and book-to-market are important factors for stock returns, see Fama and French (1992) and Chan *et al.* (1998).

13. Adjusted book-to-market ratios, with R&D capital included, spread out returns even more than the unadjusted book-to-market variable. Sorting all stocks (with and without R&D) by adjusted book-to-market ratios into ten portfolios produces an average spread in size-adjusted returns of 5.9% between the extreme deciles in the first subsequent year, compared to 5.1% based on unadjusted ratios. The adjusted ratio produces larger spreads every year compared to the unadjusted ratio up to five years following portfolio formation.

14. When we measure returns over longer horizons in order to give investors enough time to correct any initial mispricing, the excess returns are similar in magnitude.

15. The excess returns in Panels B and C are also not large relative to their standard errors. For example, in Panel B the highest-ranked quintile portfolio has a t-statistic of 0.96 for the average annual excess return over the three postformation years (where the standard error is adjusted for serial correlation induced by overlapping observations).

16. Note, however, that our calculation of growth rates differs from the usual measure of growth in earnings per share. In particular our calculated growth rates reflect how much earnings an investor is entitled to per dollar of initial investment. Further we assume a buy-and-hold investment strategy, so the growth rates include the

reinvestment of dividends. The average dividend yield is 1.84% for R&D stocks and 2.57% for stocks with no R&D.

17. The results in Fama and French (1996) suggest that once size and book-to-market are controlled for, long-term past losers do not earn excess returns. Lev and Sougiannis (1996), using a procedure different from ours, also find that R&D relative to market equity predicts future returns. They use the Fama and MacBeth (1973) methodology and estimate cross-sectional regressions of stock returns on beta, size, book-to-market, leverage, earnings yield, and the ratio of R&D capital to market equity. The coefficient on the R&D variable is positive and statistically significant.

18. The t-statistic for the average excess return on the top quintile portfolio over the three postformation years is 2.68. Excess returns over the five years following portfolio formation are of comparable magnitude.

19. Earlier research suggests that anomalous patterns in returns are typically more pronounced for small stocks. This turns out to be so for R&D relative to market as well. Over the three postformation years, the average excess return is 9.89% per year for the highest-ranked R&D portfolio of firms in the bottom decile of market capitalization.

20. For details on the construction of WML_t and UMD_t, see Chan et al. (1998).

21. In comparison, the alpha for R&D quintile portfolio 4 is lower. Note, however, that in the top quintile portfolio R&D spending as a fraction of market value is much higher than in the other groups, averaging 16.55% (see Panel D of Table 4).

22. It might be argued that abnormal performance shows up because the factor model does a poor job of describing the returns on stocks making up the top quintile portfolio based on R&D to market. However, Fama and French (1996) find no evidence of abnormal performance from a three-factor model applied to small stocks with high book-to-market ratios, or to extreme past losers. Hence, it is not likely that the alphas in Table 6 reflect a misspecified factor model.

23. Our analysis controls for all the sources of risk that have been uncovered in the empirical literature, using a variety of methodologies. There is always a possibility, however, that some (yet to be identified) source of risk has been omitted. As a consequence, the persistence of excess returns may be an indication of misspecification of the asset pricing models.

24. As is the case with R&D relative to sales, the sort by advertising to sales does not produce notable differences in future returns across portfolios. Accordingly, for the sake of brevity, these results are omitted.

25. Compared to the set of firms doing R&D, the firms engaged in advertising, for example, include a larger number of financial institutions, securities firms, media and broadcasting companies, and firms in consumer goods industries.

....

References

Berk, Jonathan B., Richard C. Green, and Vasant Naik (1999), 'Optimal investment, growth options, and security returns', *Journal of Finance*, 54: 1553–607.

Chan, Louis K. C., Yasushi Hamao, and Josef Lakonishok (1991), 'Fundamentals and stock returns in Japan', *Journal of Finance*, 46: 1739–64.

—— Narasimhan, Jegadeesh, and Josef Lakonishok (1996), 'Momentum strategies', *Journal of Finance*, 51: 1681–713.

—— Jason, Karceski, and Josef Lakonishok (1998), 'The risk and return from factors', *Journal of Financial and Quantitative Analysis*, 33: 159–88.

—— —— —— (2000), 'New paradigm or same old hype in equity investing'? *Financial Analysts Journal* 56: 23–36.

Chan, Su Han, John D. Martin, and John W. Kensinger (1990), 'Corporate research and development expenditures and share value', *Journal of Financial Economics*, 26: 255–76.

Daniel, Kent and Sheridan Titman (1997), 'Evidence on the characteristics of cross-sectional variation in stock returns', *Journal of Finance*, 52: 1–33.

DeBondt, Werner F. M. and Richard Thaler (1985), 'Does the stock market overreact'? *Journal of Finance*, 40: 793–805.

Fama, Eugene F. and Kenneth R. French (1992), 'The cross section of expected stock returns', *Journal of Finance*, 47: 427–65.

—— (1993), 'Common risk factors in the returns on stocks and bonds', *Journal of Financial Economics*, 33: 3–56.

—— (1996), 'Multifactor explanations of asset pricing anomalies', *Journal of Finance*, 51: 55–84.

—— and James MacBeth (1973), 'Risk, return and equilibrium: Empirical tests', *Journal of Political Economy*, 81: 607–36.

Givoly, Dan and Josef Lakonishok (1993), 'Earning growth and the firm-size anomaly', in B. John Jr. Guerard, and Mustafa N. Gultekin, (eds) *Handbook of Security Analyst Forecasting and Asset Allocation* (Greenwich, CT: JAI Press).

Hall, Bronwyn H. (1993), 'The stock market's valuation of R&D investment during the 1980's', *American Economic Review*, 83: 259–64.

—— and Robert E. Hall (1993), 'The value and performance of U.S. corporations', *Brookings Papers on Economic Activity*, 1: 1–34.

—— and John van Reenen (1999), 'How effective are fiscal incentives for R&D'? A review of the evidence, NBER working paper 7098.

—— Clint, Cummins, Elizabeth, S. Laderman, and Joy, Mundy (1988), 'The R&D master file documentation', NBER technical working paper 72.

Ikenberry, David and Josef Lakonishok (1993), 'Corporate governance through the proxy contest: Evidence and implications', *Journal of Business*, 66: 405–35.

—— —— and Theo Vermaelen (1995), 'Market underreaction to open market share repurchases', *Journal of Financial Economics*, 39: 181–208.

Jensen, Michael C. (1993), 'The modern industrial revolution, exit, and the failure of internal control systems', *Journal of Finance*, 48: 831–80.

Lakonishok, Josef and Inmoo Lee (2001), 'Are insiders' trades informative'? *Review of Financial Studies*, 14: 79–111.

—— Andrei Shleifer, and Robert W. Vishny (1994), 'Contrarian investment, extrapolation, and risk', *Journal of Finance*, 49: 1541–78.

LaPorta, Rafael, Josef Lakonishok, Andrei Shleifer, and Robert Vishny (1997), 'Good news for value stocks: Further evidence on market efficiency', *Journal of Finance*, 52, 859–74.

Lev, Baruch and Theodore Sougiannis (1996), 'The capitalization, amortization, and value-relevance of R&D', *Journal of Accounting & Economics*, 21: 107–38.

Loughran, Tim and Jay R. Ritter (1995), 'The new issues puzzle', *Journal of Finance*, 50: 23–51.

Porter, Michael E. (1992), 'Capital disadvantage: America's failing capital investment system', *Harvard Business Review*, 70: 65–82.

16 Why Does Fixation Persist? Experimental Evidence on the Judgement Performance Effects of Expensing Intangibles

Joan L. Luft and Michael D. Shields

1. Introduction

Both managerial and financial accounting research examine whether individuals fixate on accounting or can 'see through' or 'unscramble' the effects of alternative accounting methods (see reviews by Wilner and Birnberg, 1986; Libby *et al.*, forthcoming; Kothari, forthcoming). Our study addresses a key question that remains unresolved in prior studies: Will opportunities to learn eliminate fixation?

A number of studies, both archival and experimental, suggest that fixation results from lack of experience or relevant data, and therefore opportunities to acquire this experience or data—that is, to learn—should eliminate it (Gupta and King, 1997; Waller *et al.*, 1999; Chen and Schoderbek, 2000). Experiments in which student subjects have opportunities to learn sometimes reduce or eliminate fixation on accounting (Gupta and King, 1997; Waller *et al.*, 1999). Professional financial analysts, however, continue to display fixation when predicting stock prices based on accounting information, although they presumably have opportunities to learn about the relation between accounting data and stock prices on the job, before participating in the experiment (Hopkins, 1996; Hirst and Hopkins, 1998; Hopkins *et al.*, 2000). The absence of learning opportunities for financial analysts *within* the experiments remains problematic, however, especially because some of the accounting methods on which the experiments focus are relatively rare or novel (Lipe, 1998).

In this study we test whether capitalization vs expensing of intangibles expenditures results in fixation even when individuals have opportunities to learn. Accounting for intangibles is a particularly valuable context for testing the persistence of fixation. First, it has broad practical implications for both financial and managerial accounting. Aboody and Lev (1998) and Chan *et al.* (1999) suggest that requirements to expense intangibles for external reporting result in mispricing of some firms' stock. Even though GAAP requires firms to expense most expenditures for intangibles, a number of firms capitalize these expenditures for internal reporting out of concern that expensing can mislead managers (Stewart, 1991; Tully, 1993, 1998).

Second, individuals with business training and experience might reasonably be expected to see through the expensing of intangibles. Expensing vs capitalizing intangibles is more widely publicized and conceptually simpler than most of the other accounting issues for which fixation has been demonstrated: debt-equity swaps (Hand, 1990), deferred tax asset adjustments (Chen and Schoderbek, 2000), accounting for mandatorily redeemable preferred stock (Hopkins, 1996), and reclassification adjustments in comprehensive income for unrealized gains or losses in marketable securities (Hirst and Hopkins, 1998; Maines and McDaniel, 2000). By choosing a simple and familiar accounting issue, we provide a setting in which learning *not* to fixate should be relatively easy.

Subjects in our experiment receive data on intangibles expenditures (spending on a quality-improvement program) and gross profits at twenty similar manufacturing plants. In these data, the effect of the intangibles expenditures on profits in the current and two succeeding periods is too small to be statistically significant, but the effect on profits three periods in the future is large and statistically significant. The experiment tests whether subjects learn the lagged effect of quality-improvement expenditures on profits from these data, and whether they learn it equally well when the firm capitalizes expenditures (classifies them as investments in assets) or expenses them. The statistical predictive ability of the expenditure data is identical whether the expenditures are expensed or capitalized, and subjects' incentives to learn the relation are identical in both conditions.

When the firm capitalizes expenditures (investment condition), subjects learn the relation between intangible expenditures and profits relatively well. With expensed expenditures (expense condition), subjects do not learn the relation as well; on average, they underestimate the strength of the lagged relation by about half and make significantly greater prediction errors than do subjects in the investment condition. When they use what they have learned about the effect of intangibles on profits to predict new cases, subjects in the expense condition predict less consistently across cases and exhibit less consensus across individuals than do subjects in the investment condition. Moreover, subjects in the expense condition display less insight into their own judgement processes when asked to explain how they made their predictions.

These results do not occur because subjects naively believe that expensing means the expenditures have no future benefits. We verify in a pre-experiment question that all subjects expect intangibles expenditures to affect profits in future periods, even when the firm immediately expenses the intangibles. Moreover, nearly all subjects in the expense condition detect the three-period lagged effect of expenditures on profits in the data they receive. Compared to subjects in the investment condition, however, they make greater errors in estimating the *magnitude* of the lagged expenditure–profit effect, and they incorporate it much less effectively into their judgements, as their lower judgement consistency, consensus, and self-insight demonstrate.

These results show that learning is not necessarily a quick remedy for fixation on accounting, *because accounting can influence the learning process itself.* This finding is consistent with psychological theories of the learning process presented in Section 2. This study adds to the repertory of explanations of how fixation occurs—and even persists despite apparent user sophistication about accounting (i.e. subjects' awareness of the potential future benefits of intangibles) and opportunities to eliminate fixation through learning.

The remainder of the paper proceeds as follows: Sections 2–4 present the hypothesis motivation, design, and results of an experiment that tests the effects on judgement of capitalizing vs expensing expenditures on intangibles. Section 5 discusses the study and its implications for future research.

2. Hypothesis Motivation

A wide range of individuals in an organization, from top management to lower-level employees with small-scale spending authorization, make decisions about expenditures on intangibles. Individuals' judgements about the effects of intangibles expenditures on profits are key inputs into these decisions. This section describes what individuals must learn to perform well in this judgement task, how they learn it, and how we expect accounting classification to affect the learning process.

2.1. What Must Individuals Learn?

Expenditures on intangibles affect current and future profits through two pathways, which we designate the *accounting-calculation effect* and the *indirect economic-causal effect.* As an example of the accounting-calculation effect, if the firm expenses a $10,000 expenditure on employee training, then the expenditure reduces current profits by $10,000 and has no accounting-calculation effect on future profits. If the firm capitalizes the expenditure and amortizes it over four periods, it reduces profits by $2500 each period. Knowledge of basic accounting rules enables individuals to identify the magnitude and timing of these accounting-calculation effects.

The effect of training-program expenditures on profits includes not only these simple calculations, but also changes in revenue and/or operating costs resulting from changes in employee behaviour after the training. When the expenditure yields a positive return, the indirect economic-causal effect[1] exceeds the accounting-calculation effect, and errors in estimating the economic-causal effect can affect profit predictions significantly. Individuals may develop prior beliefs about the magnitude and timing of indirect economic-causal effects based on their experience with other training programs or information about others' experience. However, individuals can estimate the actual profit effects of particular expenditures only by observing the relevant expenditures and profits, and then inferring the relation between them from these observations. Neither prior beliefs nor knowledge of accounting rules necessarily yield the same results as estimation of these indirect economic-causal relations from the data.

Field research has documented that managers use accounting reports to modify and refine their beliefs about the relations between their actions (e.g. expenditure choices) and profits. In a large-scale field study of nonfinancial managers' use of accounting data, McKinnon and Bruns (1992: 206) found that managers use periodic accounting reports to test and modify their mental models of key causal relations underlying firm performance.

As managers review their success as reported in accounting reports, they are continuously at work, testing and perfecting their mental model of the relationship between activities and success as measured by the management accounting system . . . In this way, part of the accounting model is incorporated by managers into their own models. Managers learn to associate actions with organizational performance and success.

This observation is consistent with the claim that managers can use reports from performance measurement systems to test and modify the beliefs about cause-and-effect relations embedded in a firm's strategy and action plan—for example, the relation between employee-training expenditures and profits in a human-capital-intensive firm (Kaplan and Norton, 1996a: 65).

Regressions of profits on expenditures capture both accounting-calculation and indirect economic-causal effects of these expenditures simultaneously. Although managers sometimes use such formal statistical analysis, subjective estimation is common in practice (McKinnon and Bruns, 1992; Kaplan and

Norton, 1996b).[2] Such subjective estimation is a difficult inferential task, however, especially when individuals must assess lagged effects such as the effect on future profits of spending on quality, customer satisfaction, research and development, or employee training. Prior experimental research provides evidence that, as time lags between reported cause and effect increase, individuals are less able to detect causal relations and use them in judgements and decisions (Sterman, 1989a,b; Diehl and Sterman, 1995). Little is known, however, about how accounting affects individuals' ability to detect lagged relations and use them appropriately in judgement.

2.2. Accounting and the Learning Process

This section uses basic psychology research about learning under uncertainty to predict how accounting classifications affect the learning process. We expect this effect to occur under the following two conditions only: (1) detecting expenditure–profit relations in the data and using them appropriately in judgement requires considerable cognitive processing effort: the relations are not so strong or salient that they are immediately transparent; (2) the amount of potentially relevant data available is large enough, relative to individuals' cognitive information-processing resources, that not all data receive the maximum possible processing. In other words, the setting is such that attention and subjective processing effort are scarce resources (Birnberg and Shields, 1984; Simon, 1990).

These conditions have two possible alternative consequences. One is that individuals will spread limited attention roughly equally across all potentially relevant relations in the data, resulting in learning that is imperfect, but no more imperfect for one relation than for another. The second possibility is that individuals will allocate attention *unequally* across potentially relevant relations in the data; thus, they may not learn equally well relations that are equally strong in the data. Research in psychology, summarized below, provides evidence consistent with the second view.

Suppose individuals must estimate the relation between Y (e.g. current profits) and multiple X_i's (expenditures on a particular type of intangible in current and prior periods). Anyone, or all, of the X_i's may affect Y, but the existence and magnitude of the relation are uncertain *ex ante*. In subjective estimation (unlike multiple regression), individuals tend to examine X_i–Y relations one at a time rather than simultaneously, probably because of limited working memory (Brehmer, 1979; Klayman, 1988). Individuals use a variety of subjective strategies to estimate X_i–Y relations, some more effort-intensive and more nearly optimal than others (Hutchinson and Alba, 1997). In particular, individuals tend to allocate more attention and use more effort-intensive processing for the X_i–Y

relations they examine earlier; they tend to give less scrutiny to X_i-Y relations that they examine later, resulting in significantly larger estimation errors (Brehmer, 1974, 1979; Klayman, 1988). The order in which individuals examine X_i-Y relations is therefore key to judgement accuracy.

The order in which individuals examine X_i-Y relations often depends on domain knowledge (prior beliefs) activated by data labels or referents (Muchinsky and Dudycha, 1975; Sniezek, 1986; Broniarczyk and Alba, 1994). For example, suppose Y is total costs, X_1 is customer satisfaction, and X_2 is productivity. If individuals believe that productivity has a strong effect on total costs and that customer satisfaction has a weak effect, then they are likely to examine the productivity-total cost relation first and more carefully, and therefore to estimate it more accurately than the customer satisfaction-total cost relation. When individuals are unsure of the X_i-Y relation in the data, perhaps because they have not examined the data intensively and lack strong prior beliefs about the relation, they tend to systematically underweight X_i, rather than systematically overweight it or weight it in a random but unbiased way (Sniezek, 1986; Broniarczyk and Alba, 1994). These processes are partly conscious and deliberately controlled, but also partly unconscious (Brehmer, 1979; Broniarczyk and Alba, 1994).

We expect individuals to attend earlier and more intensively to the lagged expenditure–profit relation when the firm capitalizes rather than expenses the expenditure. First, individuals may interpret a firm's decision to expense vs capitalize an intangibles expenditure as a signal about the expected timing of the benefits from the expenditure, and may therefore deliberately direct more attention to lagged relations.[3] Second, the expense classification may automatically direct attention to the current-period relation, and individuals may therefore examine lagged relations less closely without being aware how unequally they are allocating their attention. In addition, the expense classification suggests a negative effect on profits; when individuals expect the wrong sign for a relation, they often estimate the magnitude of the relation less accurately (Muchinsky and Dudycha, 1975; Sniezek, 1986).

Subjects in our experiment receive data on gross profits and expenditures on a quality-improvement program (employee training, etc.) at twenty similar manufacturing plants. We ask them to use these data to learn how quality-program expenditures affect gross profits. We then ask them to use what they have learned to predict gross profits at an additional twenty plants, given information on quality-program expenditures at these plants. The expenditures are classified either as expenses or as investments in assets. When the expenditures are classified as expenses, we expect individuals to allocate less attention to lagged effects; therefore they should learn this relation less accurately and be less certain of the strength of the lagged effect on profit, and therefore should tend to underestimate it. Because the lagged effect is an important determinant of profits in our experimental setting, we expect individuals' profit predictions to be less accurate when the intangibles are classified as expenses.

H1a: Individuals' profit predictions will be less accurate when expenditures on intangibles are expensed than when they are capitalized.

Our experimental design allows us to partition individuals' prediction errors into several components that can have different causes and different practical consequences. Appendix A shows a two-step breakdown of mean squared prediction error (MSE). The first step is the partition shown in Panel A (Theil, 1966; Lee and Yates, 1992):

$$MSE = (\overline{Y}_s - \overline{Y}_e)^2 + (S_{Ys} - S_{Ye})^2 + 2(1 - r_a)S_{Ys}S_{Ye}, \tag{1}$$

where $\overline{Y}_s$ (s = subject) is the mean of individuals' profit predictions, $\overline{Y}_e$ (e = environment) is the mean of actual profits, S_{Ys} and S_{Ye} are their corresponding standard deviations, and r_a is the Pearson correlation between the predicted and actual profits.

The three components of the partition represent different judgement errors. The first is *bias*: overall optimism or pessimism in predictions. If classifying the expenditures on intangibles as investments causes individuals to predict higher profits on average, regardless of the exact magnitude and timing of the quality expenditures, then the bias measure will capture this effect.

The second component of the partition is *variability*. Individuals' judgements may vary more or less around the mean than the actual outcomes do, perhaps because individuals tend to overreact or underreact *generally* to information provided. For example, an individual who uses the mean value of profits as the prediction for each case would exhibit no bias but extreme underreaction to the information available. If individuals expect quality expenditures to have more (or less) effect on profits when they are classified as investments, regardless of the timing of the expenditures, then the variability measure will capture this effect.

The third component is a function of r_a, which the psychology literature calls *achievement* (Lee and Yates, 1992; Cooksey, 1996), magnified by variability in actual and predicted outcomes. If individuals fail to identify the *relative* importance of different lags in the expenditure–profit relation or fail to use this knowledge consistently in their predictions—for example, if individuals expect contemporaneous effects of intangibles expenditures to be large and lagged effects to be small when in fact the converse occurs—then r_a will capture this effect.

We predict fixation will persist in this experiment because we expect individuals in the expense condition to underestimate the strength of the lagged effect of intangibles expenditures on profits, relative to individuals in the investment condition. This implies that r_a will be smaller when intangibles are expensed, and that the difference in r_a across experimental conditions will be the principal source of difference in prediction error.

H1b: Individuals' profit-prediction achievement (r_a) will be lower when intangibles are expensed than when they are capitalized.

Our explanation of expense vs investment effects does not imply that individuals' predictions will be more optimistic or pessimistic on average or more (or less) responsive to all intangible-expenditure information. Therefore we do not hypothesize differences in the bias or variability of individuals' profit predictions.

Panels B and C in Appendix A show how to decompose r_a further to identify sources of difference in achievement. This decomposition, the so-called lens model (Tucker, 1964; Lee and Yates, 1992), is based on comparisons between two regression models of the relation between intangibles expenditures and profits. Regressing *actual profits* on actual expenditures, using the data that individuals receive to learn the expenditure–profit relation, creates an environmental model ((2), Panel B). Regressing an *individual's profit predictions* on the expenditures individuals receive as a basis for prediction creates a policy-capturing model for that individual. If the individual's subjective analysis of the learning data leads to the same inferences about expenditure–profit relations as a statistical (regression) analysis, and if the individual consistently applies these inferences in making predictions, then the two models will be the same.

The lens-model equation below identifies potential sources of low achievement (r_a) in terms of correlations between the environmental and policy-capturing models:

$$r_a = R_e G R_s + C(1-R_e^2)^{1/2}(1-R_s^2)^{1/2}. \tag{4}$$

Panel C of Appendix A shows how we calculate the components of this equation. R_e (environmental predictability) measures the accuracy with which a statistical model predicts profits, using the data available to individuals. If the relation between profits and intangibles expenditures is deterministic, then R_e equals 1.0. The less of the variation in actual profits that the intangibles-expenditure data can explain, the lower R_e is.[4] G, which the psychology literature refers to as *matching* (Lee and Yates, 1992; Cooksey, 1996), captures the similarity in the relative magnitudes of the coefficients between an individual's policy-capturing model ((3), Appendix A) and the environmental model ((2), Appendix A).[5] R_s (*consistency* or cognitive control) captures the degree to which individuals use the same model without error from prediction to prediction. If unmodeled relations exist in the underlying data (e.g. if nonlinearities or interactions exist in the data but the statistical model employed is linear additive), then C captures the extent to which individual judgement incorporates these relations.

In our study, R_e is identical across conditions by design, and no nonlinear relations exist in the underlying data ($C = 0$). Therefore only two of the lens-model measures, matching (G) and consistency (R_s), can differ across conditions. We predict that expensing the intangibles expenditures will reduce matching, because individuals will underweight the lagged effect of intangibles on profits to a greater degree in the expense than in the investment condition.

H2a: Matching (G) in individuals' profit predictions will be lower when intangibles are expensed than when they are capitalized.

H2b: In predicting profits, individuals will underweight the significant lagged effect of intangibles expenditures more when these expenditures are expensed than when they are capitalized.

Matching is important in practice because it indicates an understanding of the relative magnitudes of contemporaneous and lagged effects of intangibles expenditures. Consistency (R_s) is also important in practice, for two reasons. First, individuals' judgements about the effect of various expenditures on future profits often affect resource allocation decisions. Inconsistency in these judgements can impair resource allocation even if *average* judgement (as captured by G) is good. For example, individuals who make inconsistent judgements will sometimes overestimate future profits from a given type of expenditure and therefore overspend, while at other times they will underestimate future profits from the same expenditure and thus underspend. Second, efficient contracting requires the contracting individuals to be predictable: principals can design contracts to induce agents to take the actions the principals desire only if principals can predict how agents will respond to the incentives offered (Baiman, 1982, 1990; Sunder, 1999). Our consistency measure is an indicator of predictability. Thus, when individuals' judgements (and the actions that depend on these judgements) are inconsistent, contracts will not necessarily have the effect principals intend.

Sniezek (1986) shows that individuals make more consistent judgements when the label or referent of the data (in our case, 'investment' vs 'expense') prompts them to examine important relations in the data early in the judgement process. In contrast, when individuals focus most of their attention on a relation that proves to be unimportant, they are likely to feel uncertain that they have a good basis on which to make judgements (profit predictions). They may therefore try multiple judgement strategies across cases, resulting in inconsistent judgements. In our setting, this is likely to occur when individuals allocate more attention to looking for a current-period expenditure–profit relation that is, in fact, a poor basis for profit prediction. In contrast, when they allocate more attention to learning the more predictive lagged effect, they should be more certain they have a good basis for profit prediction and thus should be more likely to use that basis consistently, rather than alternating among different judgement strategies. In consequence, we expect judgements to be less consistent when intangibles expenditures with future value are expensed than when they are capitalized.

H2c: Individuals' profit predictions will be less consistent (lower R_s) when intangibles are expensed than when they are capitalized.

We also expect the accounting classification to affect consensus and self-insight. Consistent with prior literature (Ashton, 1985; Stewart *et al.*, 1997), we define *consensus* as similarity in predictions across individuals. Low judgement consensus implies time-consuming discussion (and perhaps additional data collection and analysis) when individuals must establish agreement before making expenditure decisions. Low consensus can also imply costly conflict and, in the extreme, impasse and failure to make expenditures that would benefit the organization.

We expect the investment classification to lead to higher consensus. We expect individuals in the investment condition to be more successful in detecting and using the strong lagged effect of intangibles expenditures on profits, which is present in the data all individuals see. This common basis for prediction should lead to higher consensus. In the expense condition, in contrast, we expect individuals to be less successful in finding a satisfactory basis in the data for predicting profits. They must rely more on idiosyncratic prediction strategies and prior beliefs that vary across individuals, resulting in lower judgement consensus.

H3: Individuals' profit-prediction consensus will be lower when intangibles are expensed than when they are capitalized.

Consistent with prior literature, we define *self-insight* as the degree to which individuals' *ex post* explanations of how they made judgements correspond to how they actually made judgements (Cook and Stewart, 1975). The lower individuals' self-insight, the less accurately they explain the basis of their judgements and therefore the more difficult and costly it is likely to be to resolve disagreements among individuals about the profits they expect from a given set of expenditures.

Self-insight can be low because only part of the judgement process is conscious. When individuals explain how they made judgements, part of their explanation is an account of their consciously directed thought processes, and part is their best guess about processes that are unobservable and/or difficult to recall accurately (Nisbett and Wilson, 1977). Absent complete knowledge of their own judgement processes, individuals tend to report judgement processes they think would be reasonable under the circumstances (Nisbett and Wilson, 1977).[6] Thus, if they believe an expense should have a strong effect on contemporaneous profits, then they will tend to report *ex post* that they weighted current-period expenditures heavily in the expense condition—even if they did not in fact do so. We expect that in the expense condition individuals will *not* in fact consistently place heavy weights on current-period expenditures. As predicted above, they will tend to be uncertain and to predict inconsistently. Thus when intangibles are expensed, individuals' actual use of information in predicting profits will correspond poorly with their *ex post* explanations. In the investment condition, in contrast, individuals are likely to believe an investment should have a strong lagged effect on profits, and therefore they will tend to report *ex post* that they weighted the lagged effect heavily in predicting profits. If, as predicted, they actually weight the lagged effect heavily in predictions, then correspondence between their actual and reported use of data will be high.

H4: Individuals' self-insight into their profit predictions will be lower when intangibles are expensed than when they are capitalized.

3. Design of Experiment

3.1. Subjects

Thirty-one MBA students who had completed a course in management accounting and six undergraduates who had completed a course in cost accounting volunteered to participate in this experiment. *Full-time managerial experience* (not including other work experience) ranged from zero to ten years (mean of thirty-five months for MBA students and four months for undergraduates). We asked subjects with managerial experience to estimate the percentage of time they had spent on budgeting (mean = 12 per cent), forecasting and planning (32 per cent), making spending decisions (15 per cent), advising on or recommending spending decisions (12 per cent), and quality programs (9 per cent). Because *t*-tests revealed no significant ($p < 0.05$), differences between these two subject groups on the means of any of the variables collected (except for work experience and number of accounting and math courses completed), the tests described below pool data from both subject groups.[7] We paid subjects performance-contingent compensation, as described below.

3.2. Task

Subjects received information about twenty similar manufacturing plants. The plants made the same product and were built to the same design, using similar technology and production scale. All plants participated in a quality-improvement initiative, which included employee training, process and quality engineering, and preventive maintenance. Internal accounting reports classified spending on this program as either a quality-improvement expense or an investment (the experimental treatment). In the investment condition, the firm capitalized the expenditures and straight-line amortized them, deducting the amortization expenses in computing gross profits. In the expense condition, the firm subtracted the entire amount of the expenditures in calculating gross profits in the quarter during which the spending occurred.

An introductory page in the experimental materials told subjects that because the plants were so similar, the effect on quarterly gross profits of a dollar of spending on the quality-improvement program was roughly the same across plants. However, because the program was new, the firm was still learning how the program affected quarterly gross profits and what the optimal level of spending was. Local managers had some freedom to experiment with different quality-improvement spending levels. There were no seasonal variations in the data and no significant external shocks or unusual internal events that would have altered or masked the effects of quarterly quality-improvement expenses on quarterly gross profits. Therefore, if the quality-improvement program had a significant effect on quarterly gross profits, then it should be detectable in the data.

After reading this introduction, each subject received expenditure data for twenty plants for the just-completed quarter (t), expenditure data for the preceding three quarters ($t-1$, $t-2$, and $t-3$), and actual gross profit for quarter t. This is the learning data set. Table 1 shows the learning data subjects received, which was identical across experimental conditions except for the word 'expense' or 'investment' in the column heading.

The advantage of providing identical expenditure and profit data to subjects in both conditions is enhanced experimental control; but the disadvantage is that the underlying revenue-generating and expense-calculation processes were not identical in the two conditions. Profit at t in the investment condition included amortization expense from the expenditure at $t-3$, but profit at t in the expense condition did not. Therefore, in order for profit to be equal in the two conditions, revenues at t must also be larger in the investment condition. Net cash flow at $t-3$ was also likely to be higher in the investment condition.

We chose to allow a difference across conditions in underlying (unobservable) revenue and expense processes, rather than in the observed data subjects used in learning and judgement. The difference in unobservable processes, if it had any effect, worked against finding support for the study's hypotheses. If subjects tried to disentangle the revenue and expense effects, rather than simply to relate expenditures to total profits as required by the experimental task, then profit prediction would be more difficult in the investment condition. (The multiple-period amortization requires more calculation steps and is complicated by uncertainty about the length of the intangible asset's life.) This effect biases against finding the predicted superior judgement in the investment condition.

After studying the learning data without a calculator, subjects received a set of expenditure data from another twenty similar plants (the judgement data set) and predicted gross profits for these plants based on the quality-improvement expenditure data. As in the learning data, the expenditures were classified as either investments or expenses. Subjects could retain and refer to the learning data when they examined the new data set and made their judgements.

The presentation format of the judgement data was identical to that in Table 1, except that the profit column was blank. The experimental materials told

Table 1. Experimental Materials: Learning Data

| | Actual Quality Improvement[a] | | | | Actual Gross |
Plant	3 Quarters Ago	2 Quarters Ago	Previous Quarter	Quarter Just Completed	Quarter Just Completed
A	$1.368 M	$1.890 M	$0.795 M	$0.984 M	$21.976 M
B	$0.900 M	$2.933 M	$1.647 M	$1.534 M	$12.562 M
C	$0.997 M	$0.886 M	$0.247 M	$2.337 M	$18.544 M
D	$1.542 M	$2.439 M	$2.146 M	$1.440 M	$24.734 M
E	$1.995 M	$1.065 M	$0.984 M	$1.449 M	$26.174 M
F	$0.959 M	$1.135 M	$1.170 M	$2.261 M	$16.181 M
G	$2.032 M	$2.080 M	$1.275 M	$1.277 M	$27.841 M
H	$0.888 M	$0.853 M	$0.798 M	$1.886 M	$19.354 M
I	$1.144 M	$0.567 M	$0.669 M	$1.287 M	$17.480 M
J	$2.301 M	$1.552 M	$1.082 M	$1.826 M	$25.622 M
K	$1.294 M	$2.206 M	$2.277 M	$0.793 M	$22.972 M
L	$1.540 M	$0.644 M	$2.357 M	$1.163 M	$20.897 M
M	$1.078 M	$0.247 M	$1.498 M	$0.649 M	$22.246 M
N	$0.001 M	$1.718 M	$1.709 M	$1.590 M	$ 9.125 M
O	$1.319 M	$2.183 M	$1.020 M	$0.214 M	$18.915 M
P	$1.115 M	$1.665 M	$0.634 M	$0.789 M	$22.628 M
Q	$0.733 M	$2.018 M	$1.611 M	$0.973 M	$13.750 M
R	$2.255 M	$1.517 M	$1.444 M	$0.022 M	$27.757 M
S	$1.398 M	$0.281 M	$1.140 M	$0.749 M	$22.065 M
T	$2.580 M	$0.631 M	$1.339 M	$1.488 M	$27.332 M

Notes:

[a] For subjects assigned to the investment condition, 'investment' was inserted in the blank. For subjects assigned to the expense condition, 'expense' was inserted in the blank.

Subjects received these data as a basis for learning the effect of quality improvement expenditures on gross profits at twenty similar manufacturing plants.

subjects that quality expenditure data were available in a timely fashion, but that the accounting department took up to fifteen business days to finalize profit calculations. The managers in the firm, however, wanted an estimate of quarterly gross profits immediately at the end of the quarter, so each subject's job was to predict quarterly gross profits using the quarterly quality spending data.

A computer program created both learning and judgement data sets from a model with specified population means, variances, and correlations.[8] Table 2 shows statistical properties of the data subjects received. Parameters specified in the model were identical for both learning and judgement data sets, but as Table 2 shows, sampling variation resulted in slight differences between the learning and judgement data sets in the sample means and correlations. None of the differences between learning and judgement data was statistically significant ($p < 0.05$).

Gross profits at time t had (1) a negative but insignificant correlation with spending at t, (2) no significant correlation with spending at $t - 1$ or $t - 2$, and (3) a strong positive correlation with spending at $t - 3$. The expense at t was small enough relative to gross profits that its contemporaneous effect was swamped by other sources of variation in gross profits; but the effect on gross profits at $t - 3$ was substantially larger and thus dominated the noise. The three-period lag this study employed was consistent with archival data from manufacturing. Ponemon *et al.* (1994), using data from forty-seven paper and pulp mills, show the strength of the relation between prevention expenditures and failure-cost reductions (i.e. profit increases) peaking at about eight months

Table 2. Parameters of Experimental Data

	Gross Profit	Quality Spending			
Quarter	t	t	$t - 1$	$t - 2$	$t - 3$
Learning data					
Mean	$20,907,800	$1,238,000	$1,292,100	$1,425,500	$1,372,000
S.D.	$5,222,000	$609,600	$560,000	$766,300	$617,900
Pearson correlations					
Gross profit	−0.27	−0.02	−0.17	0.90*	
Quality spending$_t$			−0.23	−0.12	−0.18
Quality spending$_{t-1}$				0.30	0.01
Quality spending$_{t-2}$					−0.12
Judgment data					
Mean	$20,688,800	$1,187,900	$1,133,800	$1,513,900	$1,503,300
S.D.	$5,164,700	$547,600	$476,700	$626,500	$628,700
Pearson Correlations					
Gross Profit		−0.36	0.17	0.07	0.95*
Quality spending$_t$			−0.33	0.09	−0.28
Quality spending$_{t-1}$				−0.03	0.13
Quality spending$_{t-2}$					0.04

* Correlation differs significantly from zero ($p < 0.05$).

after the expenditure for internal failure cost reductions and thirteen months after the expenditure for external failure cost reductions. In an analysis of annual quality data from twelve plants of a Fortune 500 firm, Ittner et al. (2001) find a significant effect of prior years' quality-improvement (prevention) expenditures on current-year defects (which in turn affect current-year profits via nonconformance costs), but no significant effect of current-year quality-improvement expenditure on current-year defects.[9]

3.3. Independent Variable

The accounting treatment was a between-subjects variable. In the learning and judgement data, we classified quarterly quality-improvement expenditures as either an investment or an expense.

3.4. Dependent Variables

We used each subject's gross profit predictions to develop the dependent variables. We measured judgement accuracy (H1a) for each subject as the mean absolute error of the subject's gross profit predictions:[10]

$$\sum_j |Y_{sj} - Y_{ej}| / 20, \quad j = 1, \ldots, 20,$$

where Y_{sj} is the subject s's profit prediction for plant j, and, Y_{ej} is the actual profit for plant j.

Appendix A shows the calculation for judgement achievement (r_a), matching (G), and consistency (R_s), the dependent measures for H1b, H2a, and H2c, respectively. The measure for H2b was the difference between standardized coefficients on intangibles expenditures at $t-3$ in the environmental model and subjects' policy-capturing models (standardized values of $b_{st-3} - b_{et-3}$ in the models shown in Appendix A).[11]

We used two measures of judgement consensus (H3). One, used frequently in lens-model studies (Ashton, 1985, 1992; Stewart et al., 1997), was the mean of the Pearson correlations between the judgements of each pair of subjects in an experimental condition. The second was the variance of the coefficients in subjects' policy-capturing models (β_s's in (2), Appendix A).

Also consistent with prior literature (Cook and Stewart, 1975), we measured self-insight (H4) as the correlation between two sets of gross profit predictions: (1) predictions based on the policy-capturing model estimated for each subject ($\hat{Y}_s$ in Appendix A) and (2) predictions based on the weights that subjects supplied ex post when we asked how important each of the four periods of expenditure data was in making their predictions. If they correctly reported the relative impacts of the four periods of expenditure data on their predictions, the self-insight measure would equal 1.0. To the extent that the relative weights they reported differed from the relative weights in their policy-capturing models, the measure would be smaller.

3.5. Procedure

We randomly assigned each subject to one of the two treatment conditions (expense or investment). Subjects self-paced their way through the experimental materials in a lab setting. The first section of the materials, which subjects completed and returned before seeing the rest of materials, collected information on subjects' prior beliefs about the effect on gross profits of spending on a quality-improvement program in a manufacturing facility. The description of this program (which included employee training, process improvement, etc.) was the same as the description that appeared subsequently in the main task of the experiment. Subjects estimated the profit impact of a given level of spending on the quality program in the quarter of the expenditure and in each of several subsequent quarters. We told subjects in the investment condition that the expenditures were capitalized, and subjects in the expense condition that they were expensed.

This estimate captured two factors that we needed to control in the hypothesis tests. One was subjects' prior beliefs about the benefits of spending on quality programs. The other was subjects' beliefs about the signaling value of the accounting classification. If they believed that management was conveying credible information about the timing of the program's benefits by classifying expenditures as expenses or investments, their initial estimate would incorporate this belief.

The experimental materials then described the compensation system for the experiment. Subjects' payment depended on the accuracy of their profit predictions and could range from $6 to $20. We used a quadratic loss function because we assessed the accuracy of subjects' judgements relative to the best-possible judgements, that is, predictions from an OLS model based on a quadratic loss function. We calculated a squared error measure for each subject summed over his or her twenty judgements: Σ (your judgement − best possible judgement)^2. Cash payment was inversely related to the magnitude of the error measure.

After learning about the compensation system, subjects examined the learning and judgement data and accompanying instructions, and made their profit predictions. After they turned in these materials, subjects allocated 100 points across the four periods of quality-expenditure information, indicating their

relative importance to subjects' judgements.[12] The next section of the experimental materials asked questions related to the just-completed judgement task
(how difficult it was, how familiar, etc.). The final section asked the subjects to
identify, in retrospect, what they were thinking about quality–profit relations as
they made their predictions. Eight response alternatives (including an 'other'
category) identified possible causal relations with different temporal (contemporaneous, lag) and directional (increase, decrease) properties and causal mechanisms (see Appendix B). Subjects allocated 100 points across these alternatives
based on how important each had been to their thinking when they predicted
profits. They also provided demographic data (work experience, education
level, etc.).

4. Results

Hypothesis 1a posited that individuals' profit predictions would be less accurate
when the intangibles expenditures were expensed than when they were capitalized. Table 3 shows the mean absolute error in subjects' profit predictions in
the expense and investment conditions and the key components of the mean
squared error partition. Consistent with H1a, subjects' mean absolute error
was about 25 per cent larger in the expense condition ($4.81 million vs
$3.94 million), and this difference was significant ($t = 1.98$, one-tailed $p < 0.03$).[13]

Table 3. Judgement Accuracy Mean Absolute Error, Bias, Variability, and Achievement

	Expense (n = 18) Mean (S.D.)	Investment (n = 19) Mean (S.D.)	t-statistic (two-tailed p)
Mean absolute error in gross profit predictions	$4.81 (1.22)	$3.94 (1.43)	1.98 (0.06)
Mean gross profit prediction	$19.64 (2.42)	$19.65 (2.88)	0.01 (0.99)
Standard deviation of predictions	$4.59 (2.13)	$4.59 (1.89)	0.00 (0.99)
r_a (achievement)	0.34 (0.40)	0.68 (0.21)	3.19 (0.01)

The first row shows mean absolute errors in subjects' predictions of gross profits when expenditures on
intangibles were classified as expenses and as investments. The three following rows show means of key elements in the partition of mean squared error shown in Appendix A, Panel A: the mean and standard deviation of subjects' profit predictions and r_a (achievement). Measures are in millions of dollars except for r_a,
which is a correlation measure. The t-test for r_a is performed on Fisher Z-transformations of subjects' r_a.

As described in Section 2, there were three possible sources for difference in mean squared error (and thus in mean absolute error) across conditions: bias, variability, and achievement (r_a). Bias occurred if the mean predicted profit differed systematically from the mean actual profit. Subjects' mean profit predictions ($19.64 million in the expense condition and $19.65 million in the investment condition) were not significantly different from actual profits in the judgement data set ($20.7 million) in either condition ($t = 0.63$, $p < 0.54$, expense; $t = 0.61$, investment). Mean profit predictions were almost identical in the two experimental conditions ($t = 0.01$, $p < 0.99$) and thus cannot account for differences across conditions in prediction error. Classifying the intangibles expenditures as expenses rather than investments did not lead subjects to make more optimistic or pessimistic predictions overall.

Variability errors would have occurred if the standard deviation of predicted profits differed from the standard deviation of actual profits. The mean of the standard deviation of subjects' predictions ($4.59 million in each condition, Table 3) was not significantly different from the standard deviation of actual profits in the judgement data set ($5.16 million, Table 2) in either condition ($t = 1.13$, $p < 0.28$, expense; $t = 1.32$, $p < 0.21$, investment). The mean standard deviations of subjects' predictions were quite similar across conditions ($t = 0.000$, $p < 0.99$). Thus, differences in variability cannot account for differences across conditions in prediction error. Classifying the expenditures as expenses rather than investments did not, in general, cause subjects to overreact or underreact to the expenditure data. Subjects in both conditions clearly learned from the data they received, because they generated profit predictions with means and standard deviations that closely matched the learning data set.

Hypothesis 1b predicted that achievement would be lower in the expense than in the investment condition. This difference in achievement is the principal source of difference in prediction error across conditions, since bias and variability are nearly identical in expense and investment conditions. Consistent with H1b, Table 3 shows that mean r_a was significantly lower in the expense condition (0.34) than in the investment condition (0.68; $t = 3.19$, $p < 0.01$).

Hypothesis 2a predicted that matching would be lower when intangibles were expensed than when they were capitalized. As the first row in Table 4 shows, the mean level of matching (G) was significantly lower in the expense (0.52) than in the investment condition (0.85; $t = 2.33$, $p < 0.03$), supporting H2a.

G measured the simultaneous effect of all four coefficients in each subject's policy-capturing model and did not indicate what was specifically wrong with subjects' models in the expense condition. Rows two to five of Table 4 show mean differences between the standardized coefficient (β_e) on each quarterly spending variable in the environmental model ((1), Appendix A) and the corresponding standardized coefficient in subjects' predictive models (β_s) ((2) in Appendix A) in each condition. The accounting classification of expenditures

Table 4. Comparison of Subjects' Policy-Capturing Models with:
(1) Environmental Model (Matching) and (2) Subjects' Predictions (Consistency)

	Expense (n = 18) Mean (S.D.)	Investment (n = 19) Mean (S.D.)	t-statistic (two-tailed p)
Matching (G)	0.52	0.85	2.33
	(0.57)	(0.17)	(0.03)
$\beta_{st} - \beta_{et}$	0.14	0.19	0.52
	(0.29)	(0.28)	(0.61)
$\beta_{st-1} - \beta_{et-1}$	0.14	0.15	0.41
	(0.23)	(0.20)	(0.69)
$\beta_{st-2} - \beta_{et-2}$	0.21	0.24	0.27
	(0.29)	(0.24)	(0.79)
$\beta_{st-3} - \beta_{et-3}$	−0.48	−0.14	2.86
	(0.46)	(0.22)	(0.01)
Consistency (R_s)	0.69	0.86	2.40
	(0.26)	(0.15)	(0.02)

Matching (G) measures the similarity between subjects' policy-capturing models and an environmental model (see Appendix A for definitions of measures and models). $\beta_{st} - \beta_{et}$ is the difference between the standardized coefficient on contemporaneous intangibles expenditure in subjects' policy-capturing models and the corresponding coefficient in the environmental model (and similarly for $t - 1$, $t - 2$, and $t - 3$). Consistency (R_s) measures the degree to which subjects use the same model without error in multiple predictions.

on intangibles did not affect the accuracy of subject-model coefficients on *contemporaneous* intangibles expenditures ($\beta_{st} - \beta_{et}$) ($t = 0.52$, $p < 0.61$), nor on expenditures at $t - 1$ and $t - 2$ ($t = 0.41$, $p < 0.69$ and $t = 0.27$, $p < 0.79$, respectively). Consistent with H2b, however, mean errors in subject-model coefficients for the three-period lag ($\beta_{st-3} - \beta_{et-3}$) were significantly greater when intangibles expenditures were classified as expenses (−0.48) than when they were classified as investments (−0.14; $t = 2.86$, $p < 0.01$).[14] Expensing the intangibles caused subjects to significantly underestimate the strength of this important positive lagged effect.[15]

The last row in Table 4 shows results for consistency (R_s). As predicted in H2c, subjects' mean level of consistency was lower in the expense condition (0.69) than in the investment condition (0.86; $t = 2.40$, $p < 0.02$).

Hypothesis 3 predicted lower judgement consensus in the expense condition than in the investment condition. As Table 5 shows, mean pairwise correlations between subjects' predictions were lower in the expense condition ($r = 0.19$) than in the investment condition ($r = 0.58$). We did not perform statistical tests of this difference, however, because the correlations were not independent (each subject's predictions were correlated with the predictions of all other subjects in his or her experimental condition). Individual subjects' policy-capturing models

Table 5. Judgement Consensus and Self-Insight

	Expense (n = 18)	Investment (n = 19)	Expense vs Investment Tests
Consensus: Mean pairwise correlations between subjects' gross profit predictions	0.19	0.58	NA
Consensus: Variance of β_{st-3}	0.21	0.05	$F = 4.57$ ($p < 0.01$)
Self-insight mean (S.D.)	0.47	0.85	$t = 2.08$ ($p < 0.05$)
	(0.60)	(0.18)	

See Appendix A, Panel C for calculation of measures.

provided an alternative measure of consensus. Variation in subjects' models (β_s's) created variation in predictions (lack of consensus). (Table 4 reports standard deviations of β_s's.) The variance of β_{st-3} was significantly greater in the expense condition than in the investment condition, indicating less consensus about the key predictor of profits in the expense condition (0.21 vs 0.05; $F = 4.57$, $p < 0.01$). Variances of β_{st}, β_{st-1}, and β_{st-2} did not differ significantly across conditions: F's < 1.50, p's > 0.10. These results supported H3.

Hypothesis 4 predicted that self-insight would be lower in the expense condition than in the investment condition. The last row in Table 5 shows the self-insight measure, which captured the similarity between the relative weights on expenditure variables in subjects' policy-capturing models and the relative weights subjects provided *ex post*. Mean self-insight was significantly lower in the expense condition (0.47) than in the investment condition (0.85; $t = 2.08$, $p < 0.05$), consistent with H4.

4.1. Supplementary Analyses

The distributions of most of the judgement performance measures were somewhat skewed. We therefore performed nonparametric (Mann-Whitney U) tests of the hypotheses. Results did not differ qualitatively from the parametric results reported above. We also tested all hypotheses with a reduced sample, omitting the six undergraduate subjects, using both parametric and nonparametric tests. Results were qualitatively similar except for the nonparametric test of self-insight, which did not reach conventional levels of significance (one-tailed $p < 0.16$).

4.1.1. Prior Beliefs
We have argued that subjects' profit predictions differed in the expense and investment conditions because subjects processed the learning data differently in the two conditions. One potential alternative explanation was that profit predictions differed because subjects in the investment condition had prior

beliefs more closely resembling the underlying relations in the learning data than did subjects in the expense condition. A related alternative was that subjects believed the accounting classification provided a credible signal about the magnitude and timing of the profit impacts of expenditures on quality improvement, and that this belief directly affected their profit predictions, independent of the way they processed the learning data. For example, subjects in the expense condition might have accurately estimated the three-period lagged effect in the learning data, but discounted it in judgement because of a belief that the accounting classification signaled a minimal lagged effect.

We controlled for both of these alternatives by performing analyses of covariance on the six key dependent measures: mean absolute error, achievement (r_a), matching (G), error in subjects' β_{st-3} coefficients, consistency (R_s), and self-insight. The covariates in these analyses were subjects' pre-experiment estimates of the contemporaneous and future effects on gross profits of quality-program expenditures, classified as either investments or expenses.[16] The covariates were at least marginally significant (one-tailed $p < 0.10$) in the analyses of mean absolute error, achievement, matching, and the error in-the $t-3$ coefficient, but not in the analyses of consistency and self-insight. The signs of the coefficients on the covariates were intuitively plausible. When subjects expected the *lagged* effect to be large, the $t-3$ coefficients in their policy-capturing models were larger, their achievement and matching scores were higher, and their mean absolute error was smaller. When they expected the *current*-period effect to be large, their $t-3$ coefficients were smaller, their achievement and matching scores were lower, and their mean absolute error was greater.

After controlling for the effects of these prior beliefs, however, the effect of the accounting classification remained significant (two-tailed $p < 0.05$) for each of the dependent variables examined. This result indicated that the judgement differences between expense and investment conditions were not due solely to prior beliefs about quality expense and investment, independent of what subjects inferred from the learning data set.

4.1.2. Attention Directing

The self-insight results suggested the limitations of retrospective reports, but also indicated that these reports were informative; the self-insight measure was significantly positive (one-tailed $p < 0.05$) for thirty-two of the thirty-seven subjects. Subjects' retrospective reports of their judgement processes (see Appendix B) further supported our claim that the expense and investment classifications focused attention on different subsets of the learning data. The investment classification focused individuals' attention more on future-period effects (explanations 5–7 in Appendix B), whereas the expense classification focused their attention more on current-period effects (explanations 1–4 in Appendix B). On average, subjects in the investment condition assigned 28.2

more points to future-period explanations than to current-period explanations, while subjects in the expense condition assigned 12.5 *fewer* points to future-period than to current-period explanations. This difference in point assignment between investment and expense conditions was significant ($t = 2.91, p < 0.01$).

---

5. Discussion and Future Research

Prior research has questioned whether individuals will learn to see through accounting when significant learning opportunities are available (Wilner and Birnberg, 1986; Lipe, 1998), but evidence on learning has been limited. Our experiment shows that opportunity to learn is not necessarily a quick remedy for accounting fixation, because accounting can affect the allocation of attention and thus can influence the learning process itself. We do not suggest that people are *incapable* of overcoming fixation and learning to make correct inferences from accounting data. With fewer competing demands on attention, additional cues to direct attention to important relations, or incentives that increase total attention, individuals might allocate enough attention to a lagged expense-profit relation to predict profits more accurately. However, all else equal, people can arrive at accurate predictions more quickly and easily when accounting is closer to economic reality. This means learning at lower cost in terms of data, attention, and effort (lower out-of-pocket compensation costs for effort and lower opportunity costs of directing attention away from other issues). In some settings there may also be competitive-advantage benefits to learning key economic relations more quickly.

Our results also contribute to understanding what it means to be a sophisticated user of accounting information. Early fixation studies see a lack of accounting-calculation knowledge as the reason for judgement biases: 'If outputs from different accounting methods are called by the same name, such as profit, cost, etc., *people who do not understand accounting* will tend to neglect the fact that alternative methods may have been used to prepare the outputs' (Ijiri *et al.*, 1966: 194, emphasis added; see Ball 1972, 1 for a similar argument). In this view, individuals should not fixate if they have sufficient knowledge of relevant accounting rules.

More recent studies have emphasized the importance of category knowledge about indirect economic-causal effects of accounting; for example, experienced analysts know that decreases in stock price typically accompany one category of financing (new equity issues) but not another (new debt issues) (Hopkins, 1996). Individuals who possess this knowledge may appear more sophisticated than those who do not; but they are also *more* likely to display fixation when encountering an atypical instance of the category, such as a hybrid security classified as debt or equity (Hopkins, 1996; Libby *et al.*, forthcoming). Additional encounters with atypical instances could help individuals refine their category knowledge and deal appropriately with atypical members of a category, however. In this view, the sophistication required to avoid fixation on accounting would consist of refined category knowledge that clearly distinguishes atypical from typical instances and supports correct expectations about the behavior of atypical instances.

Our study suggests that the requirements of user sophistication can be even more demanding; a clear understanding of atypical instances in principle is not always sufficient to eliminate fixation in practice. Intangibles are an atypical expense in that they affect future-period profits, whereas typical expenses do not. Our subjects understand this, as shown in their responses to the pre-experiment question about the effect of an intangibles expense on future profits. Subjects in the expense condition expect a lagged effect on profits—but their performance in estimating this effect and using it in judgements is still significantly worse than that of subjects in the investment condition.

Subjects in the expense condition perform relatively poorly because they look less closely at the most important data, *not* because they draw erroneous conclusions from the data at which they do look closely. (Table 4 showed that subjects in the expense condition do *not* overestimate the current-period effects of the expenditures, compared to subjects in the investment condition.) This attention-allocation story may help to explain the findings of prior research about the effectiveness of learning opportunities in reducing fixation. For example, in Waller *et al.* (1999), fixation diminishes rapidly with opportunities to learn, perhaps because the experimental setting poses no significant attention-allocation problem. Subjects in that experiment receive cost information on a single product, choose a price for the product, and then learn the profit they make, which is a deterministic function of price. Thus, subjects in Waller *et al.* (1999) must learn a deterministic relation between one X (price) and one Y (profit), rather than a probabilistic relation between four X_i's (four periods of expenditures) and one Y (profit), as in our experiment. The likelihood that subjects will not closely examine data on the right X_{i-Y} relation is presumably minimal when there is only one X_i.[17] Similarly, in Gupta and King (1997) subjects must learn to estimate costs for three products by observing the relation between their cost estimates (X_i) and aggregate profits (Y); the more accurate their estimates are, the higher their profits. Learning is slower when subjects must estimate three X_i-Y relations (because the accounting system provides inaccurate data on all three) than when they must estimate only two (because the accounting system estimates one product cost correctly).

Joan L. Luft and Michael D. Shields

One potentially important difference between our experiment and Waller et al. (1999) and Gupta and King (1997) is the way we presented the learning data. Subjects in Waller et al. (1999) and Gupta and King (1997) decided on prices or cost estimates in *each* trial of the experiment before seeing the actual profit outcome. In the learning phase of our experiment, subjects learned profit outcomes of intangibles expenditures without having to make predictions first. Some psychologists have argued that requiring predictions or decisions during the learning phase should promote learning because it creates greater involvement; others have argued that it should reduce learning because it inhibits integration of learning data across cases or causes anchoring on initial judgements, which are likely to be inaccurate because they are made on the basis of very little data (Klayman, 1988; Well et al., 1988; Broniarczyk and Alba, 1994). Experiments have found, however, that requiring case-by-case predictions during the learning phase makes no difference to performance in the subsequent judgement phase, other things equal (Well et al., 1988; Broniarczyk and Alba, 1994). It seems unlikely, therefore, that our experimental results are driven by absence of prediction requirements during the learning phase.

Broniarczyk and Alba (1994) also find, however, that simultaneous presentation of all the learning cases (as in our experiment) leads to poorer learning than does a sequential presentation that requires subjects to examine each case for some time before they can see the next. These two presentation formats correspond to different real-world tasks—for example, examining reports from a dozen similar business units for a given period simultaneously vs examining reports from a given unit over time. Our experimental setting corresponds to the first situation, and the results may not be fully generalizable to the second.

Another limitation to the generalizability of this paper's results is that our experimental setting does not include actions some firms take to aid potentially faulty judgement. Our subjects made their judgements alone; the opportunity to discuss the data with others might mitigate or exacerbate the performance deficits observed in the expense condition. Our subjects also make their judgements without the aid of formal statistical methods that might help overcome judgement biases. Task-properties feedback leads to better judgement performance than outcome information alone (Bonner and Walker, 1994); and in tasks like ours, task-properties feedback is defined as statistical information such as correlations and regression coefficients (Balzer et al., 1989). Some firms provide statistical models of the drivers of financial performance to employees as substitutes for subjective estimation, but many do not; the efficacy of statistical models is a contested issue (Kaplan and Norton, 1996b; Ittner and Larcker, 1998), and individuals' willingness to rely on such models instead of their own subjective judgement is an open question.

When individuals make subjective estimates, other attention-directing devices can counter accounting methods' tendency to lead managers to misallocate attention. For example, additional nonfinancial data may prompt closer examination of lagged relations by drawing attention to the link from expenditure at one point in time to increased revenues or decreased operating costs at later times by way of intermediate-period improvements in quality, productivity, customer satisfaction, etc.

The usual limitations of laboratory research suggest caution in assuming that our results will replicate fully in natural settings. The task and data are simplified and stylized, and some subjects have limited work experience—although many have relevant experience, and experience differences did not drive results. Sufficient specialized experience can provide knowledge about intangibles that eliminates the judgement task represented in this experiment; that is, it can create settings in which there is no longer significant *ex ante* uncertainty about the timing of benefits from intangible expenditures. In many important settings, however, individuals lack this specialized knowledge because they are facing new situations and must learn from observing available data. For many expenditures on 'softer' intangibles such as employee training and process improvement, it is far from clear how soon firms should expect to reap benefits from a particular new initiative, or how long additional benefits will persist. Even experienced managers depend on accounting data to infer the timing and magnitude of these effects.

....

Appendix A: Prediction Error and Lens Model Statistics

Panel A: Partition of Mean Squared Prediction Error

$$\text{MSE} = (\overline{Y}_s - \overline{Y}_e)^2 + (S_{Ys} - S_{Ye})^2 + 2(1 - r_a)S_{Ys}S_{Ye}, \tag{1}$$

where:

MSE $= \sum_j (Y_{sj} - Y_{ej})^2 / 20, j = 1, \ldots, 20;$
$Y_{sj} =$ subject s's gross profit prediction for plant j;
$Y_{ej} =$ actual (environmental) gross profit for plant j;
$\overline{Y}_s = \sum_j Y_{sj} / 20;$
$\overline{Y}_e = \sum_j Y_{ej} / 20;$
$S_{Ys} =$ standard deviation of Y_s;
$S_{Ye} =$ standard deviation of Y_e;
$r_a = r(Y_e, Y_s).$

Panel B: Modelling the Environment and the Individual
Learning data subjects received
$Y_{ei} =$ actual (environmental) gross profit at plant i in quarter t, $i = 1, \ldots, 20.$
$X_{it}, X_{it-1}, X_{it-2}, X_{it-3} =$ quality expenditure at plant i in quarter t, $t-1$, etc.

Joan L. Luft and Michael D. Shields

Judgement data subjects received
X_{jt}, X_{jt-1}, X_{jt-2}, X_{jt-3} = quality expenditure at plant j in quarter t, $t-1$, etc., $j = 1, \ldots, 20$.
Predictions and outcomes
Y_{sj} = subject s's prediction of gross profit for plant j in quarter t.
Y_{ej} = actual (environmental) gross profit for plant j in quarter t.

Environmental model
Estimated by regressing Y_{ei} on X_{it-1}, X_{it-2}, and X_{it-3}:

$$\hat{Y}_e = a_e + b_{1e}X_t + b_{2e}X_{t-1} + b_{3e}X_{t-2} + b_{4e}X_{t-3}. \tag{2}$$

Individual policy-capturing model
Estimated separately for each subject by regressing Y_{sj} on X_{jt},[a] X_{jt-1}, X_{jt-2}, and X_{jt-3}

$$\hat{Y}_s = a_s + b_{1s}X_t + b_{2s}X_{t-1} + b_{3s}X_{t-2} + b_{4s}X_{t-3}. \tag{3}$$

Panel C: Lens Model Equation and Measures

$$r_a = R_eGR_s + C(1-R_e^2)^{1/2}(1-R_s^2)^{1/2}, \tag{4}$$

where:
r_a (achievement)	$= r(Y_e, \hat{Y}_s)$;
R_e (environmental predictability)	$= r(Y_e, \hat{Y}_s)$;
G (matching)	$= r(\hat{Y}_e, \hat{Y}_s)$;
R_s (consistency)	$= r(Y_s, \hat{Y}_s)$;
C (residual achievement)	$= r(d_{Ye}, d_{Ys})$;
d_{Yej}	$= Y_{ej} - \hat{Y}_{sj}$;
d_{Ysj}	$= Y_{sj} - \hat{Y}_{sj}$.

Additional measures:

$$\text{Self-insight} = r(\hat{Y}_s, \hat{Y}_w),$$

where $\hat{Y}_w = b_{1w}X_t + b_{2w}X_{t-1} + b_{3w}X_{t-2} + b_{4w}X_{t-3}$ and b_w is the weight provided by subject s in a post-experiment question.

$$\text{Consensus (pairwise)} = r(Y_{sm}, Y_{sn}),$$

where m and n are the individual subjects, $m \neq n$. Pairwise correlations are averaged to provide consensus measures for larger groups.

[a] Note that, consistent with prior literature (Libby, 1981; Lee and Yates, 1992; Cooksey, 1996), we use the *judgement* data to estimate subjects' policy-capturing models, but use the *learning* data to estimate the environmental model. Although subjects *reveal* their policy-capturing models through use of the judgement data, they *estimate* their models from the learning data. The appropriate measure of the quality of their subjective estimation is therefore a statistical model estimated from the learning data.

Appendix B: Retrospective Thoughts about How Quality-Improvement Expenditures Affect Profits

Please try to remember how you thought quarterly quality-improvement expenses affect quarterly gross profits *when you made your quarterly gross profit predictions*. Allocate 100 points across the following factors, based on *how important you thought they were* when you made your predictions. Enter zero for any explanations that did *not* occur to you when you were making your predictions. [*Mean responses for expense (E) and investment (I) conditions are shown in the two right-hand columns.*]

		Means	
		E	I
1.	Increased quality-improvement expenses in the current quarter *decrease* profits in *that quarter* because they are subtracted from revenues in the profit calculation.	14.6	13.7
2.	Increased quality-improvement expenses in the current quarter *decrease* profits in *that quarter* because they cause temporarily disruptive and costly changes in products and/or operating processes.	14.6	9.5
3.	Increased quality-improvement expenses in the current quarter *increase* profits in *that quarter* because improved quality makes the product more attractive to customers and increases that quarter's sales revenues.	12.8	1.8
4.	Increased quality-improvement expenses in the current quarter *increase* profits in *that quarter* because they make the operating processes more efficient and reduce product costs that quarter.	13.9	1.6
5.	Increased quality-improvement expenses in the current quarter *increase* profits in *future quarters* because the product gradually becomes more attractive to customers, as they become aware of the improvement.	20.0	20.3
6.	Increased quality-improvement expenses in the current quarter *increase* profits in *future quarters* as the full effect of increased operating efficiencies is gradually realized.	19.2	31.1
7.	Increased quality-improvement expenses in the current quarter *decrease* profits in *future quarters* because they take money away from other, more profitable investments your firm could make.	4.2	3.4
8.	Other (explain):	0.8	18.2

Notes

1. We call the economic-causal effects of expenditures 'indirect' because they occur only through some intervening process. An employee training expense decreases current profit through the accounting-calculation effect, regardless of whether the training has any effect on employee behaviour; but the expense affects future profit only through the intervening process of behaviour changes.

2. Individuals may use subjective approaches because they believe statistical analysis is too costly, the data quantity or quality is not sufficient to support reliable formal statistical analysis, or they believe they can outperform statistical models.

3. This argument assumes that individuals believe that information they do not possess has influenced the firm's choice between capitalizing and expensing the intangible expenditure.

4. R_e is the square root of the environmental model's unadjusted R^2.

5. Because G is a correlation measure, it does not capture differences between the models with respect to intercepts or to absolute magnitudes of the coefficients. If an individual's policy-capturing model is $\hat{Y}_s = 5 + 10X_1 + 5X_2$ while the environmental model is $\hat{Y}_e = 1 + 2X_1 + X_2$, then predictions from the two models would be perfectly correlated and G would be 1.0, even though the individual's predictions are quite inaccurate. The inaccuracy would be fully captured in the first two components of the MSE partition, however, and therefore would not also be included in r_a or its components. (The individual's predictions would display optimism in the bias measure and overreaction in the variability measure.) In contrast, if the individual's policy-capturing model is $\hat{Y}_s = 5 + 1X_1 + 2X_2$—that is, if the relative weights on X_1, and X_2 differ from those in the environmental model—G would be substantially lower.

6. Although the self-reports of judgement processes that Nisbett and Wilson (1977) recount appear to be sincere, some self-reports probably also reflect an element of impression management. Individuals may report weights that they believe will make them appear knowledgeable or rational.

7. The groups differed in one respect consistent with the difference in experience: Prior beliefs about the effect of quality expenditures on profit were more diverse among undergraduate subjects. The variance in prior beliefs was significantly greater for undergraduates than for MBAs (Levene's $F = 32.82$, $p < 0.00$ for prior beliefs about current-period effects; $F = 30.81$, $p < 0.00$ for prior beliefs about the sum of the next three periods' lagged effects). Although more experienced subjects exhibited more consensus *before* they saw the learning data, there was no difference across subjects groups in post-learning consensus. Variance in the $t - 3$ lagged coefficient was a principal drive of low consensus (see Table 4); but this variance was not significantly greater for undergraduates than for MBAs ($F = 1.17$, $p > 0.05$).

8. The process was similar to using a random number generator to create samples from a distribution of a single random variable with a specified mean and variance; but it was more complex in that it created data for five variables (four quarters of expenditures and one quarter of gross profits) with specified correlations among them.

9. Other key characteristics of the experimental data set included the lack of serial correlation among the X_i's and the strength of the X–Y relation. See Ponemon et al. (1994) for an illustration of quality costs that fluctuate markedly, with no apparent pattern, from period to period. The relation between quality expenditures and gross profits was stronger in the experimental materials than it was likely to be in the natural environment, to allow subjects a reasonable chance to detect the quality–profit relation even in the expense condition. This choice did not bias toward finding the expected results; if expense-condition subjects had difficulty identifying the lagged relation even when it was relatively easy to see, then they were unlikely to perform better when it was difficult to see.

10. We also calculated and tested mean squared prediction error (MSE), since the partitioning described in Section 2 applies to MSE, not to mean absolute error. See footnote 13 for results. We used mean absolute prediction error as the primary dependent variable because it was more nearly normally distributed and more interpretable.

11. The psychology literature often uses standardized coefficients because they facilitate comparisons across judgement tasks with differently scaled predictors (Cooksey, 1996).

12. The psychology literature elicits subjects' perceptions of the relative importance of different predictors in a variety of ways (e.g. allocating 100 points, asking for ratings on Likert scales). Results for self-insight hypotheses are not sensitive to elicitation methods, however; Cook and Stewart (1975) find that seven methods of eliciting these perceptions yield qualitatively the same results in tests of self-insight.

13. Mean *squared* prediction error was also significantly larger in the expense condition. Because the distribution of MSE was strongly influenced by extreme errors and highly skewed, we performed a t-test on ln(MSE) and a Mann-Whitney test on MSE (one-tailed $p < 0.06$ for both tests). Mean *absolute* prediction error was also somewhat skewed, although less than MSE; we therefore also performed a Mann-Whitney test on mean absolute error, which yielded similar results (one-tailed $p < 0.01$).

14. Analysis of unstandardized coefficients led to qualitatively similar inferences. We also obtained qualitatively similar results with a MANOVA on all four coefficients, which allows for the potential within-individual correlations of the four coefficients.

15. An alternative analysis pooled all subjects' profit predictions and estimated the following regression: $Y_{sj} = a + b_1 X_{jt} + b_2 X_{jt-1} + b_3 X_{jt-2} + b_4 X_{jt-3} + Z + b_5 ZX_{jt} + b_6 ZX_{jt-1} + b_7 ZX_{jt-2} + b_8 ZX_{jt-3}$, where Y_{sj} = profit prediction by subject s for plant j, X_{jt} = expenditure at plant j at time t, and $Z = 0$ in expense condition, 1 in investment condition. The adjusted R^2 of the pooled regression was 0.32 ($F = 37.74$, $p < 0.001$). The experimental condition significantly affected subjects' use of the expenditure data at $t - 3$; b_8 was significantly positive ($t = 3.90$, $p < 0.001$). Consistent with the analysis in Table 4, the experimental condition did not affect subjects' use of the expenditure data at t, $t - 1$, or $t - 2$; b_5, b_6, and b_7 were not significantly different from zero (t's < 0.60, p's > 0.54).

16. The future-quarter prior-belief estimate was the sum of the profit effects subjects estimated for the first, second, and third quarters after the expenditure. We obtained the same qualitative results using the estimated effect for the third quarter after the expenditure and the sum of all future quarters' estimated effects. Subjects' mean (standard deviation) estimate of the effect of $1 of expenditure on the quality program was $1.58 ($8.44) for the current quarter and $1.61 ($6.71) for the next three quarters.

17. Subjects actually choose a price-quantity combination in Waller *et al.* (1999), but quantity errors are rare; the learning that takes place in the study is predominantly reduction in pricing error.

References

Aboody, D. and Lev, B. (1998), 'The value relevance of intangibles: The case of software capitalization'; *Journal of Accounting Research*, 36(supplement): 161–91.

Ashton, A. H. (1985), 'Does consensus imply accuracy in accounting studies of decision making'? *The Accounting Review*, 60(2): 173–85.

Ashton, R. H. (1992), 'Effects of justification and a mechanical aid on judgment performance', *Organizational Behavior and Human Decision Processes*, 52: 292–306.

Baiman, S. (1982), 'Agency research in managerial accounting: A survey', *Journal of Accounting Literature*, 1: 154–213.

——(1990), 'Agency research in managerial accounting: A second look', *Accounting, Organizations and Society*, 15(4): 341–71.

Ball, R. (1972), 'Changes in accounting techniques and stock prices', *Journal of Accounting Research*, 10 (Supplement): 1–38.

Balzer, W. K., Doherty, M. E., and O'Connor, R. (1989), 'Effects of cognitive feedback on performance', *Psychological Bulletin*, 106 (November): 410–33.

Birnberg, J. G. and Shields, M. D. (1984), 'The role of attention and memory in accounting decisions', *Accounting, Organizations and Society*, 9(3/4): 365–82.

Bonner, S. E. and Walker, P. L. (1994), 'The effects of instruction and experience on the acquisition of accounting knowledge', *The Accounting Review*, 69(1): 157–78.

Brehmer, B. (1974), 'Hypotheses about relations between scaled variables in the learning of probabilistic inference tasks', *Organizational Behavior and Human Performance*, 11: 1–27.

—— (1979), 'Preliminaries to a psychology of inference', *Scandinavian Journal of Psychology*, 20: 193–210.

Broniarczyk, S. M. and Alba, J. W. (1994), 'Theory vs. data in prediction and correlation tasks', *Organizational Behavior and Human Decision Processes*, 57(1): 117–39.

Chan, L. K. C., Lakonishok, J., and Sougiannis, T. (1999), 'The stock market valuation of research and development expenditures', Working paper, National Bureau of Economic Research.

Chen, K. C. W. and Schoderbek, M. P. (2000), 'The 1993 tax rate increase and deferred tax adjustments: A test of functional fixation', *Journal of Accounting Research*, 38(1): 23–44.

Cook, R. L. and Stewart, T. R. (1975), 'A comparison of seven methods for obtaining subjective descriptions of judgmental policy', *Organizational Behavior and Human Decision Processes*, 13(1): 31–45.

Cooksey, R. W. (1996), *Judgment Analysis: Theory, Methods, and Applications* (San Diego, CA: Academic Press).

Diehl, E. and Sterman, J. D. (1995), 'Effects of feedback complexity on dynamic decision making', *Organizational Behavior and Human Decision Processes*, 62(2): 198–215.

Gupta, M. and King, R. R. (1997), 'An experimental investigation of the effect of cost information and feedback on product cost decisions', *Contemporary Accounting Research*, 14(1): 99–127.

Hand, J. R. M. (1990), 'A test of the extended functional fixation hypothesis', *The Accounting Review*, 65(4): 740–63.

Hirst, D. E. and Hopkins, P. E. (1998), 'Comprehensive income reporting and analysts' valuation judgments', *Journal of Accounting Research*, 36 (supplement): 47–75.

Hopkins, P. E. (1996), 'The effect of financial statement classification of hybrid financial instruments on financial analysts' stock price judgments', *Journal of Accounting Research*, 34 (Supplement): 33–50.

—— Houston, R. W. and Peters, M. F. (2000), 'Purchase, pooling, and equity analysts' valuation judgments', *The Accounting Review*, 75(3): 257–81.

Hutchinson, J. W. and Alba, J. W. (1997), 'Heuristics and biases in the "eyeballing" of data: The effects of context on intuitive correlation assessment', *Journal of Experimental Psychology: Learning, Memory, and Cognition*, 23(3): 591–621.

Ijiri, Y., Jaedicke, R. K., and Knight, K. E. (1996), 'The effects of accounting alternatives on management decisions', In R. K. Jaedicke, Y. Ijiri, and O. Nielsen (eds), *Research in Accounting Measurement* (New York, NY: American Accounting Association).

Ittner, C. D. and Larcker, D. F. (1998), 'Innovations in performance measurement: Trends and research implications', *Journal of Management Accounting Research*, 10: 205–38.

—— Nagar, V., and Rajan, M. (2001), 'An empirical examination of dynamic quality-based learning models', *Management Science*, 47(4): 563–78.

Kaplan, R. S. and Norton, D. P. (1996a), 'Linking the balanced scorecard to strategy', *California Management Review*, 39(1): 53–79.

—— (1996b), *The Balanced Scorecard: Translating Strategy into Action* (Boston, MA: Harvard Business School Press).

Klayman, J. (1988), 'On the how and why (not) of learning from outcomes', In B. Brehmer and C. R. B. Joyce (eds) *Human Judgment: The SJT View* (New York, NY: Elsevier Science Publishers).

Kothari, S. P. (2001), 'Capital markets research in accounting', *Journal of Accounting and Economics*, 31(1–3): 105–231.

Lee, J-W. and Yates, J. F. (1992), 'How quantity judgment changes as the number of cues increases: An analytic framework and review', *Psychological Bulletin*, 112(2): 363–77.

Libby, R. (1981), *Accounting and Human Information Processing* (Englewood Cliffs, NJ: Prentice Hall).

—— Bloomfield, R. and Nelson, M. W. (2002), 'Experimental research in financial accounting', *Accounting, Organizations and Society*, 27(8): 775–810.

Lipe, M. G. (1998), 'Discussion of comprehensive income reporting and analysts' valuation judgments', *Journal of Accounting Research*, 36 (Supplement): 77–83.

Maines, L. A. and McDaniel, L. S. (2000), 'Effects of comprehensive-income characteristics on non-professional investors' judgments: The role of financial-statement presentation format', *The Accounting Review*, 75(2): 179–208.

McKinnon, S. M. and Bruns, W. J. (1992), *The Information Mosaic* (Boston, MA: Harvard Business School Press).

Muchinsky, P. M. and Dudycha, A. L. (1975), 'Human inference behavior in abstract and meaningful environments', *Organizational Behavior and Human Performance*, 13: 377–91.

Nisbett, R. E. and Wilson, T. D. (1997), 'Telling more than we know: Verbal reports on mental processes', *Psychological Review*, 84: 231–59.

Ponemon, L., Carr, L., and Wendell, J. (1994), 'The validity of quality costs: An empirical study of mills in the paper and pulp industry', *Advances in Management Accounting*, 3: 213–36.

Simon, H. A. (1990), 'Information technologies and organizations', *The Accounting Review*, 65(3): 658–67.

Sniezek, J. (1986), 'The role of variable labels in cue probability learning tasks', *Organizational Behavior and Human Decision Processes*, 38(2): 141–61.

Sterman, J. D. (1989a), 'Misperceptions of feedback in dynamic decision making', *Organizational Behavior and Human Decision Processes*, 43(3): 301–35.

——(1989b), 'Modeling managerial behavior: Misperceptions of feedback in a dynamic decision making experiment', *Management Science*, 35(3): 321–39.

Stewart III, G. B. (1991), *The Quest for Value* (New York, NY: Harper).

Stewart, T. R., Roebber, P. J., and Bosart, L. F. (1997), 'The importance of the task in analyzing expert judgment', *Organizational Behavior and Human Decision Processes*, 69(3): 205–19.

Sunder, S. (1999), Common knowledge and accounting. Plenary address, Accounting, Behavior and Organizations Research Conference. Available at http://www.som.yale.edu/faculty/sunder/ABOPresentation.

Theil, H. (1996), *Applied Economic Forecasting* (Amsterdam, The Netherlands: North-Holland).

Tucker, L. R. (1964), 'A suggested alternative formulation in the developments by Hursch, Hammond, and Hursch and by Hammond, Hursch, and Todd', *Psychological Review*, 71: 528–30.

Tully, S. (1993), 'The real key to creating wealth', *Fortune*, (September 20): 38–50.

—— (1998), 'America's greatest wealth creators', *Fortune*, (November 9): 193–204.

Waller, W. S., Shapiro, B., and Sevcik, G. (1999), 'Do cost-based pricing biases persist in laboratory markets'? *Accounting, Organizations and Society*, 24(8): 717–39.

Well, A. D., Boyce, S. J., Morris, R. K., Shinjo, M., and Chumbley, J. I. (1988), 'Prediction and judgment as indicators of sensitivity to covariation of continuous variables', *Memory and Cognition*, 16(3): 271–80.

Wilner, N. and Birnberg, J. (1986), 'Methodological problems in functional fixation research: Criticism and suggestions', *Accounting, Organizations and Society*, 11(1): 71–82.

IV. THE NEED FOR SOLUTIONS

17 The Growing Intangibles Reporting Discrepancy

Margaret Blair and Steven Wallman

'Given that no company can establish a monopoly on brains, how do you keep the people that make it work? There are no tangible assets to divest. There is intellectual property and that's about it—and a building'.

Attorney Lloyd Cutler,
commenting on the proposed breakup of Microsoft
(*Washington Post*, 29 April 2000, p. A1)

The US economy, like the economies of most industrial countries, is increasingly one in which the 'products' that firms provide are not simply physical goods but are services or experiences. Even the physical goods we buy are greatly enhanced in their value to us by the technology embedded in them or by the brand image they carry. Indeed, market services and intangible goods now account for more than two-thirds of gross domestic product (GDP) in the United States.[1]

A critical difference between an economy that is based on the production, trade, and consumption of physical goods and an economy that involves extensive trade in services, experiences, technology, and ideas is that the former can be readily measured. It is extremely difficult to measure the volume of trade in the latter in any units other than the price paid for them. Likewise, it is difficult to quantify the investment and expenditure of resources required to produce intangible goods or to assess whether expenditures on the inputs into the production of intangibles are well spent. How does one measure the capacity of an economy to exchange services, experiences, technology, and ideas?[2] How does one measure national wealth in this kind of an economy? How does one know whether the economy is growing or shrinking, whether productivity is increasing and how fast, whether one company is performing better than another, or whether our citizens are better off this year than they were last year? Perhaps most important, how do we know whether we are, individually or as a nation,

Market services and intangible goods account for more than two-thirds of US GDP. Some day-to-day examples:

Services	Embedded Technology in
Financial or legal advice	Extra memory or
Insurance	computing power
Education	Anti-lock car brakes
Nursing	The latest allergy
Child care	medications
Physical therapy	Reduced cholesterol
Hotel stays	mayonnaise
Catering	Vitamin-enriched cereals
Internet connections	High-performance fibers
Telephone and cable	in athletic wear
connections	
Air travel	

Experiences	Brand Images
Concerts	Nike footwear
Movies	Coca-Cola
Sports events	Rolex watches
Restaurant meals, from	Starbucks coffee
elegant cuisine to	Tommy Hilfiger denim
'fast' food	pants
Sky diving	Ralph Lauren bed
Bungee jumping	linens
Cruises	

making investments that will increase productivity and economic wealth in the years ahead?

This report is about the vast uncertainty around such questions and its implications both for public policy and for the allocation of investment resources by the private sector. In particular, it focuses on the problem of providing accurate and useful information about the intangible inputs into such an economy—the ideas, special skills, organizational structures and capabilities, brand identities, mailing lists and data bases, and the networks of social, professional, and business relationships that make it possible for hundreds of millions of people to exchange services, experiences, technology, and ideas.[3]

1. The Importance of Intangibles

Intangibles is a difficult term to define. One reason for the lack of consensus about a definition is that the elements of what could or should be regarded as intangibles depend on whether one is talking about accounting concepts or measures of national income and wealth or how to develop and manage the nonphysical inputs into a business. For purposes of this analysis, the task force adopted the following broad definition: intangibles are nonphysical factors that contribute to, or are used in, the production of goods or the provision of services or that are expected to generate future productive benefits to the individuals or firms that control their use.[4]

Historically, intangibles have not been treated as part of national wealth, nor have they generally been accounted for as part of the assets of firms. In 1911 Irving Fisher defined economics as 'the science of wealth' and defined wealth as 'material objects owned by human beings'.[5] These definitions have formed the basis of the measurement conventions used in the national accounts. Similarly, business accounting was developed to keep track of transactions that enhance or diminish the assets of firms. Here again, the convention has been that only physical items or intangibles purchased in arms-length transactions (such as patents) should count as assets, whereas other inputs have to be counted as services and treated as transitory.

Yet intangibles are important in the production, marketing, and distribution of physical goods as well as the delivery of services. Intangibles are not the same as services, but they are linked, and the delivery of highly skilled services and professional services involves substantial inputs of intangibles. How important have intangibles become? This report grew out of the concern that data on the role of intangibles in the economy is seriously inadequate. But even the indirect evidence gives strong reason to believe that the economic importance of intangibles is growing rapidly.

1.1. Role of Services in the Economy

Services have increased steadily as a share of measured total output in the United States, from 22 per cent of GDP in 1950 to about 39 per cent in 1999.[6] Intangibles such as skills and professional knowledge, organizational capabilities, reputational capital, mailing lists and other collections of data, are important factors in the provision of many services.

1.2. Value of Financial Claims

Although investments in intangibles such as R&D, brand name development, and software systems are generally not recorded as part of the book value of corporations (unless they were purchased externally), outside investors recognize their worth and tend to place high value on firms with high levels of these sorts of investments. In the past twenty years, there has been a rapid increase in the total value of financial claims and securities issued by the corporate sector (debt plus equity), despite low growth in tangibles; only a small part of this increase can be accounted for by purchases of physical capital or even by inflation in the value of existing physical capital. Economist Robert Hall has analysed the rather large discrepancy that has developed in the past decade between the value assigned to firms by the financial markets and the value recorded on their books. He concludes that this empirical discrepancy can only be reconciled with financial theories about how stocks are valued if 'corporations own substantial amounts of intangible capital not recorded in the sector's books or anywhere in government statistics'. He has since named this unrecorded intangible capital 'e-capital'.[7]

Hall's analysis is based on aggregate economic data for all nonfarm, nonfinancial corporations, but the same conclusion seems almost inescapable if one looks at the balance sheets of even a few individual firms. As of early August 2000, for example, the market value of Walt Disney Co. stock totaled around $83 billion, and the firm also had about $34 billion in outstanding liabilities, for a total market capitalization of $117 billion. But on the books the firm had only $43.7 billion in assets. This total included some $11.3 billion worth of recognized intangible assets. Apparently the financial markets thought that Disney had closer to $85 billion worth of intangibles—almost eight times the recognized book value of such assets. Similarly, Sprint Corp. had a total market capitalization of $60.2 billion in early August 2000, compared with $39 billion in book assets, which included $9.6 billion in recognized intangibles. Here again, the financial markets apparently thought that Sprint had nearly $31 billion worth of intangibles, more than three times what its balance sheet showed. The remarkable bull market in stocks—and especially the huge run up in technology and Internet stock prices—over the past decade cooled somewhat in the last few months of 2000, but not nearly enough to change the analysis. In fact, equity prices would have to fall by two-thirds or more, across the board, for the significant discrepancy between market value and book value to disappear.[8]

Cross-sectional evidence on firms also suggests that some significant part of the discrepancy between market value and book value is due to investments in intangibles.[9] The discrepancy is greatest in firms that are known to have been investing most heavily in certain kinds of intangible complements to computers. Erik Brynjolfsson and Shinkyu Yang, for example, find a strong correlation between the total value of computers in a corporation and the implicit value assigned to the intangibles in that corporation by the stock market. 'It is not that the market values a dollar of computers at $10', Robert Hall observes about this finding. 'Rather, the firm that has a dollar of computers typically has another $9 of related intangibles'.[10] Likewise, Timothy Bresnahan, Brynjolfsson, and Lorin Hitt find that firms that invest heavily in computer technology get the greatest boost in productivity if they invest simultaneously in human capital—upgrading the skills of their work force—and in organizational capital, specifically, by restructuring work to devolve decisionmaking authority downward and outward within the firm to rank and file employees.[11]

Other studies have found that firms in key growth industries (the high-tech, life sciences, and business services sectors) tend to have high ratios of R&D spending to sales, and, in turn, firms with high levels of spending on R&D tend to have high ratios of market value to book value.[12] Studies also show that the firms that make the greatest investments in the education and training of their work force have above average productivity and financial performance.[13] Taken together, these findings suggest that stock prices, although they are an extremely noisy signal, probably have at least some validity as an indicator of the growing role of intangibles in the economy.

1.3. Anecdotal Evidence from Firms

Another indication that intangibles are among corporations' most important investments is the accumulating anecdotal evidence from firms themselves. The Conference Board, for example, has produced two major studies that reveal substantial corporate interest in developing new and better measures of performance that go beyond financial measures alone. The most recent study reports that companies are developing indicators to measure 'activities and processes . . . such as the development of intellectual capital, and improving customer satisfaction and retention as well as workplace practices . . . In many cases, these "intangibles" provide the best indicator of a company's potential for growth'. It also cites evidence that institutional investors are interested in knowing more about these intangible investments.[14] Interest in these issues has exploded in the past few years and months, and the major accounting and consulting firms are pouring resources into projects to help their clients develop better business models and better measures of performance.[15]

Human capital investments have come to be seen by many corporate executives as a source of competitive advantage. This intuition is confirmed by research over the past ten to fifteen years demonstrating that investments in bundles of innovative work practices (sometimes called high-performance work systems) in areas such as training, job design, selection, staffing, employee involvement, labour-management cooperation, and incentive compensation positively impact firm performance.[16] The reputation of the chief executive officer (CEO) has also been shown to be important to business success.[17] In their advertising, companies are increasingly emphasizing their technical leadership, the speed and quality of their service, and the sophistication, commitment, and skills of their employees. Yet factual information about investments in intangible resources is conspicuously lacking from most companies' annual reports and 10-K filings.[18]

2. Measurement Difficulties

One major reason why good, hard data on the importance of intangible assets in the economy are not available is that intangibles are inherently difficult to measure, quantify, and account for. Because one cannot see, or touch, or weigh intangibles, one cannot measure them directly but must instead rely on proxies, or indirect measures, to say something about their impact on some other variable that can be measured. Just as one cannot answer the question 'How satisfied are the company's customers?' in the same one-dimensional way as one can answer 'How many hamburgers did the company sell?' one cannot measure how much customer loyalty a firm's advertising campaign created in the same way as one can measure how much office space the firm added with its new building. To be sure, assigning value to many *tangible* assets may require considerable subjective judgment, but while valuing tangibles can be difficult, valuing *intangibles* is generally a much more complex proposition.

2.1. Accounting Rules

Accounting rules are designed to record what happens in specific transactions and thereby track the flows of assets into and out of a corporation. Under the accounting principles used in the United States and in most developed countries, for resources to be considered assets they must be well defined and distinct from other assets, the firm must have effective control over them, it must be possible to predict the future economic benefits from them, and it must be possible to determine whether their economic value has been impaired (for example, through depreciation or depletion) and to what extent.[19] These criteria mean that the term *assets* is generally interpreted to mean property, plant, and equipment; financial assets; and purchased identifiable intangible assets, such as patents, trademarks, and mailing lists.

To be sure, accountants have long understood the need to recognize some assets that do not fit neatly into any of these categories. 'Purchased goodwill' is one of the few additional categories recognized in the United States, however.[20] When company A acquires company B, for example, A adds B's net assets (assets minus liabilities) to the net assets on its own balance sheet. If B has $500 million worth of property, plant, and equipment, financial, and other identifiable assets and zero liabilities on its books, those assets will be added to the books of A. But suppose that A has paid $750 million for B. How does it account for the additional $250 million that are not reflected in B's book value? If possible, A would first 'write-up', or assign a higher value—based on appraisals—to the acquired hard assets. Then it would assign a value to any specific intangibles that could be identified and valued. Finally, A would add the remaining amount (say $200 million) to its books as goodwill. Goodwill, rather than referring to specific assets, is just a catch-all residual category, a label given to the going concern value of assets in the target company over and above those that can be kicked, or counted, or weighed, or valued with some precision.

Other than purchased goodwill, accounting rules generally require that internal expenditures on such intangible assets as R&D, training, advertising, and promotion be 'expensed', that is, treated as expenses in the period in which they are incurred and charged against current earnings. This implies that the inputs paid for by those expenses are used up in production in the period in which the expenses are incurred, and that such expenditures do not create any asset that will provide an input into future production.

Within the accounting profession, there has been growing debate over whether this treatment is appropriate, especially for R&D. A number of scholars have argued that expenditures on R&D should be treated as investments, just like expenditures on new plant or equipment. When a company spends money on a new warehouse, for example, the expenditures are not treated as expenses in the current period but are recorded as a reduction in cash assets and an addition to the plant and equipment assets of the firm. In each subsequent period, the company records a charge against current earnings to reflect the fact that some of the value of the asset has been used up or worn out. This accounting treatment is called 'capitalizing' the expenditure, and the subsequent periodic charges against earnings are called 'depreciation'. Thus the debate over the accounting treatment of R&D is a question about whether R&D ought to be understood as a current cost of doing business, and therefore expensed, or it should be capitalized, on the theory that the expenditures are adding an asset to the firm.[21]

Indeed, there is disagreement among prominent accounting standards bodies worldwide about how to record R&D expenditures. The International Accounting Standards Committee (IASC) requires that research be expensed, but development costs that meet certain criteria must be capitalized. In the United Kingdom, the Accounting Standards Board (ASB) requires expensing of research but permits development to be capitalized. And in Japan, the accounting profession permits capitalization of research, development, and a range of other internally generated intangibles. In the United States, however, the Financial Accounting Standards Board requires full expensing of R&D, except for the final development stages of potential software products.[22]

If measuring, quantifying, and accounting for R&D assets is difficult, human capital poses even greater challenges. To be sure, the accounting treatment is well defined and not particularly controversial: wage and nonwage labour costs are expensed in the same accounting period as the labor services are performed, unless the costs are associated with the building of fixed assets or the manufacture of products that are added to asset inventories. In these cases, labour costs are expensed as the assets produced by the labour services are sold or depreciated.

To the extent that such costs are associated with ongoing operations, this makes sense. The costs of labour services are reported either in the same period as the services are provided or in the period in which the products generated by the services are sold or used up. But to the extent that some of the expenditures on labour (such as for training, team building, and reorganization) generate benefits in future periods, this accounting treatment produces a distortion. Because such expenditures never show up on the company's balance sheets as an asset, they are not managed in the same way as other assets, and the firm can only guess at the rate of return it gets on them. When a firm is acquired and the acquiring firm adds goodwill to its books, that goodwill may reflect the value of a skilled work force in the acquired company. Yet this is not transparent. Moreover, in future periods the acquiring firm must take a charge against its earnings for depreciation of the goodwill, even if it is simultaneously recording the expenses associated with investments in maintaining the asset through training or updating the know-how, competences, and skills of the workers.

A final reason why the traditional accounting model has not been very helpful in providing information about intangible assets to business managers is that accounting rules are designed to record and track discrete and sequential transactions and to show their cumulative effect. The value created by investments in intangibles is rarely tied to discrete transactions, however. Rather, it is often highly contextual and dependent on complementary investments in other intangibles. The value of a brand, for example, may depend on patent rights to some underlying technology as well as expenditures on advertising or other reputation-enhancing activities. Furthermore, the process of creating valuable intangible assets is not always linear or direct. A 'failure' in an R&D program might lead to insights that interact with the findings from another program and end up creating value in unexpected ways.[23] And value can be destroyed in similarly unexpected and indirect ways.[24]

2.2. Other Measures

If accounting models do not generally produce good measures of intangibles, are there other measures that do? So far the answer appears to be maybe, for some assets, in some situations, and for some purposes.

For example, stock and bond prices provide a measure of the value that financial markets place on the financial claims (debt plus equity) of individual corporations. This value can be viewed as a claim on the aggregate value of the physical and financial assets of those corporations plus the value of the intangible assets, or the going concern value, in those corporations. Thus, as indicated above, one can look at the difference between the market value of the financial claims against a corporation and the value of its tangible assets and come up with a measure of the financial market's estimate of the value of that firm's intangible assets.

A few companies and creative financial institutions have also been attempting to 'securitize' the income streams from bundles of intangible assets, especially intellectual property, by using financial instruments such as asset-backed securities (ABSs). These are debt securities for which the issuing companies have pledged the cash flow (often enhanced by third-party guarantees) from some collection of assets or some subset of the firm's business. ABSs backed by financial assets, such as receivables, have been issued for many years, but only in the past five or six years have firms and financial institutions put together a significant number of deals based on intellectual property.[25] Implicit in the fact that the lending institutions are willing to buy the securities backed by these assets is the notion that it is possible to estimate the value of the pledged intangible assets.[26]

These measures of securitized intangibles may be a useful indicator of how important intangibles have become in individual firms. And the aggregate difference between the value of financial claims and the value of tangible assets says something about their importance in the economy as a whole. But such measures have serious drawbacks for other purposes. The market prices of financial assets are notoriously volatile and noisy indicators of underlying value. They also provide only an aggregated measure and give no hint about the nature of the specific assets, resources, or other factors that produce that value, let alone the factors that might enhance or diminish that value. Hence financial asset prices, by themselves, are currently of limited use to managers for day-to-day decisions about investing in or using intangibles and preserving or enhancing their value.

Although the implicit information in ABS issues is, perhaps, useful at the level of individual firms, intellectual property ABSs have so far only been issued in private placements to financial institutions, and there is no public market in these instruments. Moreover, the details of such transactions are usually confidential. Thus, although such transactions suggest that certain intangible assets can be valued, the information on value that they yield is not shared as well as it might be with other investors or the market as a whole.[27]

As noted in the previous chapter, however, there is empirical evidence that expenditures on certain kinds of intangibles development, especially R&D, are generally reflected in higher stock prices.[28] This suggests that participants in financial markets are somehow gathering and interpreting information about intangibles, even if that information is not formally reported by companies in their public documents or otherwise widely shared with investors.

In attempting to get behind the aggregate story told by stock prices, a number of companies, organizations, and individuals have developed measures for internal use. These have been used to help measure and monitor nonfinancial perform-ance and to show the linkages among the intangible factors that contribute to that performance, as well as the link between nonfinancial and financial per-formance.[29] Some of these measures have gained a certain prominence and have apparently proved to be useful management tools in individual companies. None, however, is being used consistently by a large enough group of firms to provide useful cross-sectional or time-series data, or even reasonable benchmarks that one company could use to compare its performance with that of another. So far, at least, the information generated by these efforts is still ad hoc and situation specific. As the Strategic Organizational Issues subgroup of the task force con-cluded, 'companies have no coherent, consistent or regular approaches to repres-enting, managing, and valuing their intangibles . . . Investment decisions in the area of intangibles seem more a matter of faith than fact'.[30]

3. Consequences of Poor Measurement

What harm, if any, comes from the fact that there is currently no way to quant-ify or, in many cases, even articulate and describe in clear comparable terms the factors that lead to better business performance? It is known, in general, that education and training are important in producing a skilled work force; that innovation is important; that market share is valuable; and that brands, reputation, and image are important factors in gaining market share. Does it matter that it seems hard to be more specific? It is the job, the creative act, if you will, of management to make resource allocation decisions and to engage employees, business partners, and other participants in value-creating activities. Does it matter that this creative process is still fundamentally quite mysterious?

The task force believes that not being able to identify and measure the intan-gible inputs into wealth creation creates substantial costs for society. Although many of these costs are unavoidable, this project has been motivated by the belief that one could know more than is known, and that because of the high costs of not knowing, it is worth expending resources to learn. Below, we briefly review some of the costs of not knowing.

3.1. National Accounts

In the United States, large amounts of data on the performance of the economy are collected and developed each year by the federal government (and the governments of other countries). Much of the data for the national accounts are developed by aggregating up from individual or firm-level data or projecting from survey data to produce measures such as GDP, corporate profits, personal savings, aggregate capital stock, productivity, and inflation. The national accounts are used in setting a variety of policies. In 1999 and 2000, for example, the Federal Reserve Board was concerned about the rapid growth rate of measured GDP, the low unemployment rate, and the high capital utilization rate, fearing that an overheated economy might lead to increased inflation. So the Fed increased interest rates in hopes of slowing down economic activity. Was this the right response, or was the US economy now capable of higher sustained levels of economic growth without inflation?

In the early 1990s, many policymakers were concerned about projected deficits in the federal budget and took actions (in the form of tax increases and spending cuts) to reduce those deficits. But the US economy performed far better in the 1990s than anyone might have hoped six or eight years earlier, and by 2000 the federal budget was producing substantial surpluses. Why were the forecasts so far off the mark? And today policymakers are concerned about the ability of the economy to provide for millions of retiring baby boomers in the near future. What kinds of investments are needed today to boost productivity ten, twenty, or thirty years down the road? These and other serious questions of public policy cry out for a better understanding of the role of intangible assets in the economy.[31]

There is good reason to believe that the failure to account adequately for investments in intangibles results in the understatement of GDP, of corporate profits, and of personal savings because accounting systems that treat investments in intangibles as expenses thereby overstate the costs of producing current output. Leonard Nakamura has argued, for example, that if corporate expenditures on R&D had been capitalized instead of expensed, measured corporate profits would have been higher in recent years, and stock prices in 1999 relative to these adjusted profits would not have been seriously out of line with historic experience, nor seen as a matter of policy concern.[32] Measured GDP would also have been higher if R&D had been capitalized. To the extent that expenditures on other kinds of intangibles (such as marketing, human resource development, and software development) were increasing as a share of GDP in the 1990s, the same argument would apply; measured profits and output would have been even higher, and price-earnings ratios would seem more reasonable by historic standards.

More generally, it seems likely that the failure to understand the role of intangible assets in the aggregate economy will lead repeatedly to misdiagnoses of economic problems and inappropriate policy responses.

3.2. Capital Markets

It is widely accepted that stock prices tend to incorporate some information about intangibles. However, a variety of disclosure problems stem from the lack of transparency of the information and the process by which investors learn about and act on this information. These problems likely increase the cost of capital and reduce the perceived fairness of the capital markets to individual investors.[33]

The requirements for disclosure of key corporate financial information in the United States are among the most extensive and stringent in the world. Corporations are required to file detailed financial information with the Securities and Exchange Commission when they first register their securities for public trading, and they must provide a full and detailed update annually, condensed interim reports every quarter, and immediate updates in the case of extraordinary events. These extensive disclosure requirements are a central part of a corporate governance and financial system that, more than any other in the world, has encouraged small investors to invest in corporate equities. The result has been a powerful engine for turning personal savings into investments, investments into technical advances, and technical advances into economic growth. But the effectiveness of disclosure requirements at ensuring good corporate governance and performance is being eroded, because as intangibles become more important relative to tangible assets, this required disclosure reveals less about the real assets and sources of value inside a firm.

Baruch Lev argues, for example, that commonly used performance measures, such as return on equity or return on total assets, become much less useful in intangibles-intensive firms, because 'major investments are missing from the denominator'.[34] Likewise, the human capital assets of firms—their reserve of skills, competencies, and know-how and the resources being expended to renew and expand them—are beyond the spectrum of information that is typically available to investors. The lack of clear, quantifiable, and comparable information about intangibles-intensive companies tends to encourage selective disclosure of inside information to key investors, making it easier for people with inside information to gain at the expense of outsiders and small investors.

In fact, by the summer of 2000 the SEC had become so concerned about the tendency of listed firms to make selective disclosures that it approved a new regulation requiring companies to release material market-moving information to all investors simultaneously. Under Regulation FD, if a company purpose-fully or inadvertently discloses selective information, in a phone call from an analyst, for example, the company must publicly release and publicize this information within twenty-four hours.[35] Critics argue that this will simply dis-courage companies from releasing any information that is not required, rather than encouraging them to issue more information more widely and more fairly.[36] While selective release of information might make small investors more cautious than they would be otherwise, a reduction in information is likely to make all investors more cautious. However, if the capital markets demand more information, and this is provided universally, as Regulation FD intends, then all investors will benefit as measures and information now provided only selectively become more transparent.

Against this, it might be noted, as of the close of 2000, even after significant decreases in valuations in the technology sector, many 'dot-com' and other high-tech companies were commanding high price-earnings ratios. Since many of these companies have virtually no assets except for their intangibles (a con-cept, a copyright perhaps, and the willingness of a cadre of eager twenty-eight-year-olds to work fourteen hours a day, seven days a week for stock options), it is hard to make the case that intangibles-intensive firms cannot get capital, or even that the cost of capital is too high. But, at least for the time being, investor sentiment has grown more cautious of this sector and support could weaken further. More comprehensive and more reliable information about intangibles in such companies would help reduce the problems of information asymmetry and the associated costs in market volatility for the sector as a whole.[37] Moreover, better information would lead to better decisions about which spe-cific companies and ideas should be funded and which should not. This, in turn, would help to restore overall market confidence.

3.3. Industries

At the level of specific industries, lack of good data on intangibles and their contribution to productivity and performance may lead to a misallocation of resources, both within firms and between firms in the same industry. As eco-nomist Joseph Stiglitz notes, 'If we are going to know what are high-return activities and we want our resources to be allocated towards high-return activities, we have to have accurate ways of measuring what those returns are'.[38]

One of the factors that could lead to a misallocation of resources within an industry is the perfectly reasonable tendency of investors to compare the performance of individual companies against their industry peers. But the validity of this approach depends on whether the industry benchmarks used in such a comparison are good indicators of future performance. Comparisons of asset levels, investment rates, or profit rates without some adjustment for investments in intangibles are likely to be very misleading. Data on expenditures on training, patent citations, number of Ph.D.s on the staff, share of revenues from new products, new product development times, or other indicators of the firms' investments in intangibles could provide more insight into the relative performance of companies—if such data were available.

3.4. Companies

Other significant costs arising from the lack of good knowledge about the role of intangible assets in the economy are those that affect individual companies. Today, good management practice demands greater sophistication about the contribution of intangibles to the strategic performance of a company. Managers need to know which activities to encourage, what kinds of investments to make, and what kinds to avoid to improve overall performance. They also need to be able to communicate a strategic vision to employees throughout the firm, a game plan for how to achieve that vision, and a set of interim goals and measurements that will provide feedback on their progress. Although good management has always involved elements of intuition and gut instinct, managers themselves concede that their poor understanding of the role of intangibles makes it harder for them to judge the performance of individual employees or teams within the firm, as well as the true costs and benefits of a large share of their business activity.

One indication that some firms consider the costs of not knowing substantial is the energy they are devoting to the development of internal nonstandard and nonfinancial measures of performance. Examples of such measures observed by members of the task force include profitable revenue growth, market share, product acquisition costs, market requirements and specifications, time to break even in profits, time from conception to market for new products, competitor responses, schedule slip rates, per cent of revenue created by products that have been in the market less than some given amount of time, and number of new products created on each technology platform. Some companies also face external pressure to develop and provide information on what might be called 'social performance', such as environmental performance, workplace safety, and wages and working conditions in factories run by subcontractors. In these areas, not knowing may not seem like a problem until something goes seriously wrong and the company is suddenly faced with law-suits or substantial reputational costs.[39]

3.5. Taxation

Another public policy problem that is exacerbated by the growing importance of intangible assets in the economy is the problem of identifying a fair, useful, and feasible basis for assessing tax liabilities and collecting taxes. This issue has already arisen in a highly public way in the controversy over whether online commercial transactions ('e commerce') ought to escape sales taxes at the state level. When an individual buys a washing machine in an appliance store, it is relatively easy to identify the jurisdiction in which the transaction took place for sales tax purposes. But when an individual buys an online subscription to an electronic magazine, downloads it at work in Washington, DC, and reads it at home in Maryland, the rules about which jurisdiction, if any, may tax that transaction and who is supposed to collect the tax and pass it along to the tax-ing authorities become much less clear.

Leaving aside e-commerce, intangible assets raise a number of tax policy concerns similar to those raised in the context of financial accounting. For example, should the costs of creating an intangible asset be deducted when incurred or depreciated over an expected useful life of the asset? How does one determine the appropriate transfer prices for exchanges of intellectual property rights, licenses, and other intangibles among international subsidiaries of a corporation when there is no comparable public market for these goods? If tangible assets are subject to state and local property taxes, is it appropriate also to levy these taxes on intangible assets? More broadly, how does the tax treatment of intangible assets affect the efficient allocation of resources in the economy?

....

Notes

1. Microsoft Corp., "Microsoft_2000," annual report (www.microsoft.com/msft/ar00/balance.htm [January 2001]). Market capitalization is based on market value of equity (5.283 billion shares outstanding, at $60 per share) plus $10.8 billion in liabilities.
2. See S. L. Mintz, "Seeing Is Believing: A Better Approach to Estimating Knowledge Capital," *CFO*, February 1999, pp. 29–37, discussing "knowledge capital" measurement methodol-ogy developed by Professor Baruch Lev of New York University. Mintz estimates that as of May 31, 1998, Merck had more than $48 billion in knowledge capital, and Pfizer had nearly $24 billion.

3. See, for example, "Retail Link Is on the Cutting Edge," *Business and Industry*, vol. 15 (May 1998), p. 70, for a discussion of the software used to manage Walmart's so-called vendor managed inventory system.

4. For an example involving Ford Motor Co., see Keith Bradsher, "Can Motor City Come up with a Clean Machine?" *New York Times*, May 19, 1999, p. C1. Image may also be a critical factor for Microsoft in its court battle with the antitrust authorities.

5. Charles Goldfinger, "Intangible Economy and Its Implication for Statistics and Statisticians," *International Statistical Review*, vol. 65 (August 1997), pp. 191–220, citing Conseil Economique et Social (CES), "Les Leviers Immateriels de l'Action Economique" (Paris, May 1994).

6. See Barry P. Bosworth and Jack E. Triplett, "Numbers Matter," Policy Brief 63 (Brookings, July 2000), for a discussion of the problems of measuring productivity in the service sector.

7. One of the task force co-chairs took an early lead in addressing these issues. See Steven M. H. Wallman, "The Future of Accounting and Disclosure in an Evolving World: The Need for Dramatic Change," *Accounting Horizons*, vol. 9 (September 1995), pp. 103–16.

8. Leandro Canibano and Paloma Sanchez, "Measuring Intangibles to Understand and Improve Innovation Management," research proposal, Universidad Autonoma, Madrid, 1998, note that the adjective *intangible* can accompany various concepts, such as assets, investments, resources, or other phenomena. The transformation of the adjective into a noun is suggestive of the absence of a broadly accepted definition. Numerous definitions and classifications have been proposed, particularly during the past decade. See also Ulf Johanson and others, "Human Resource Costing and Accounting versus the Balanced Scorecard: A Literature Survey of Experience with the Concepts," working paper (Stockholm University School of Business, 1999). Some analysts have limited the definition of intangibles to those factors over which legal rights have been clearly assigned, such as patents, copyrights, and brands. See Baruch Lev, *Intangibles: Management, Measurement, and Reporting* (Brookings, 2001); Leonard Nakamura, "Intangibles: What Put the *New* in the New Economy?" Federal Reserve Bank of Philadelphia *Business Review* (July–August 1999), pp. 3–16. We use a broader definition in order to include factors such as organizational features, individual knowledge and skills, or networks of business relationships, over which property rights may not be well defined.

9. Cited in Nakamura, "Intangibles," p. 11.

10. Bureau of Economic Analysis, National Income and Product Accounts, table 1.1 (www.bea.doc.gov/bea/dn1.htm [January 2001]).

11. Robert E. Hall, "The Stock Market and Capital Accumulation," Working Paper 7180 (Cambridge, Mass.: National Bureau of Economic Research, June 1999), quote is from p. 4; Robert E. Hall, "E-Capital: The Link between the Stock Market and the Labor Market in the 1990s," *Brookings Papers on Economic Activity, 2:2000*, pp. 73–118. Lev, *Intangibles*, finds that for firms in the S&P 500 index, the average ratio of market value of equity to net book value had risen from a little over 1 in the late 1970s to more than 6 by the late 1990s. Hall, using a conceptually similar but methodologically different approach, finds that the ratio of the market value of all financial claims (debt plus equity) on corporations to the reproduction cost of property, plant, and equipment had risen from around 0.8 in the mid-1970s to nearly 1.8 in the mid-1990s. By the end of 1999, the ratio exceeded 2. Hall's findings suggest that the current high levels of this ratio are similar to or slightly above levels reached in the mid-1960s, but by Lev's measure the current levels are unprecedented.

12. Authors' calculations based on the 1999 annual reports of Walt Disney Co. (disney.go.com/investors/annual99/dis99ar55.html [January 2001]) and Sprint Corp. (ww3.sprint.com/sprint/annual/99/delivering/shareholders/shareholders.html [January 2001]) and stock price quotations from the *Wall Street Journal*, August 3, 2000. The extraordinary volatility and dramatic movements in equity prices in the second half of 2000, especially in the Internet stock sector, demonstrate the need for far greater transparency in understanding the drivers of wealth production, especially in the high-tech and knowledge-based industries. Otherwise, as we argue below, one can expect to see continued high volatility as the markets attempt to calibrate values with too little information.

13. Bronwyn H. Hall, "Innovation and Market Value," in Ray Barrell, Geoffrey Mason, and Mary O'Mahoney, eds., *Productivity, Innovation and Economic Performance* (Cambridge University Press, 2000), finds that the market value of the modern manufacturing corporation is strongly related to its knowledge assets.

14. Erik Brynjolfsson and Shinkyu Yang, "The Intangible Costs and Benefits of Computer Investments: Evidence from Financial Markets" (Sloan School of Management, Massachusetts Institute of Technology, April 1999); Hall, "The Stock Market and Capital Accumulation," p. 28.

15. See Timothy F. Bresnahan, Erik Brynjolfsson, and Lorin M. Hitt, "Technology, Organization, and the Demand for Skilled Labor," in Margaret M. Blair and Thomas A. Kochan, eds., *The New Relationship: Human Capital in the American Corporation* (Brookings, 2000), pp. 175–78.

16. In 1996 the average ratio of R&D spending to sales of electronics, drugs, software, and biotech companies were, respectively, 6.1 percent, 12 percent, 17.8 percent, and 41 percent, compared with an overall average for manufacturing of around 4 percent; see Baruch Lev, "R&D and Capital Markets," *Bank of America Journal of Applied Corporate Finance*, vol. 11 (Winter 1999), pp. 21–35. On the link between R&D spending and market-to-book ratios, see Hall, "Innovation and Market Value"; Baruch Lev and Theodore Sougiannis, "Penetrating the Book-to-Market Black Box: The R&D Effect," *Journal of Business Finance and Accounting*, vol. 26 (April–May 1999); Bronwyn Hall, Adam Jaffe, and Manual Trajtenberg, "Market Value and Patent Citations: A First Look," Working Paper 7741 (Cambridge, Mass.: National Bureau of Economic Research, 2000); Brynjolfsson and Yang, "The Intangible Costs and Benefits of Computer Investments." Louis K. C. Chan, Josef Lakonishok, and Theodore Sougiannis, "The Stock Market Valuation of Research and Development Expenditures," working paper (University of Illinois at Urbana-Champaign, June 1999) find that stocks of R&D-intensive firms tend to outperform stocks of firms with little or no R&D, but they interpret this to mean that the market fails to give such firms sufficient credit for the value of their R&D investments.

17. See Sandra A. Black and Lisa M. Lynch, "Human-Capital Investments and Productivity," *American Economic Review*, vol. 86, no. 2 (1996), pp. 263–67; Laurie J. Bassi and others, "Profiting from Learning: Do Firms' Investments in Education and Training Pay Off?" white paper (Alexandria, Va.: American Society for Training and Development, September 2000).

18. Carolyn Kay Brancato, "New Corporate Performance Measures," Report 1118-95-RR (New York: Conference Board, 1995), quotes are from p. 9; Carolyn Kay Brancato,

"Communicating Corporate Performance: A Delicate Balance," Special Report 97-1 (New York: Conference Board, 1997).

19. Cap Gemini Ernst & Young's Center for Business Innovation has sponsored several major research reports in the last few years on the correlation between intangibles and market value or financial results; see, for example, *Measures that Matter* (Cambridge, Mass., March 1997); *Managing the Success of the IPO Transformation Process* (Cambridge, Mass., June 1998); *The Value Creation Index* (Cambridge, Mass., June 2000). It also co-published a book with the Organization for Economic Cooperation and Development (OECD) entitled *Enterprise Value in the Knowledge Economy: Measuring Performance in the Age of Intangibles* (Cambridge, Mass.: Center for Business and Innovation, December 1997). PricewaterhouseCoopers has developed a new business reporting model called "ValueReporting"; see Robert Eccles and others, *The ValueReporting Revolution: Moving Beyond the Earnings Game* (Wiley, 2001). And in August 2000, Arthur Andersen gave a $10 million grant to the Massachusetts Institute of Technology's Sloan School of Management to develop a "New Economy Value Research Lab." See Steffan Heuer, "The Bean Counters Strike Back," *The Standard*, August 21, 2000.

20. See Jeffrey Arthur, "Effects of Human Resource Systems on Manufacturing Performance and Turnover," *Academy of Management Journal*, vol. 37 (June 1994), pp. 670–87; Laurie Bassi and Mark VanBuren, "Valuing Investments in Intellectual Capital," *International Journal of Technology Management*, vol. 18, nos. 5, 6, 7, 8 (1999), pp. 414–32; Brian E. Becker and Mark A. Huselid, "High Performance Work Systems and Firm Performance: A Synthesis of Research and Managerial Applications," *Research in Personnel and Human Resources* (forthcoming); Marvin L. Bouillon, B. Michael Doran, and Peter F. Orazem, "Human Capital Investment Effects on Firm Returns," *Journal of Applied Business Research*, vol. 12 (Winter 1995); Huselid, "The Impact of Human Resource Management Practices on Turnover, Productivity, and Corporate Financial Performance," *Academy of Management Journal*, vol. 38, no. 3 (1995), pp. 635–72; and Casey Ichniowski and Kathryn Shaw, "The Impact of HRM Practices on Performance: An International Perspective," working paper (Department of Labor, December 1996).

21. A study by Burson-Marsteller, a public relations firm, found that CEO reputation has a significant impact on the overall reputation of a firm. In a survey of 1,400 corporate stakeholders in 1999, the company found that 88 percent said they would buy stock on the basis of the CEO's reputation, 87 percent said they would recommend a company as a good joint venture partner on that basis, 81 percent said they would believe in a company under media pressure on that basis, and 80 percent said they would recommend a company as a good place to work on that basis. See Burson-Marsteller, "Maximizing CEO Reputation" (www.ceogo.com/research/research011.html [January 2001]).

22. See Laurie J. Bassi and others, "Measuring Corporate Investments in Human Capital," in Margaret M. Blair and Thomas A. Kochan, eds., *The New Relationship: Human Capital in the American Corporation* (Brookings, 2000).

23. See Financial Accounting Standards Board, "Elements of Financial Statements," Statement of Financial Accounting Concepts 6 (December 1985).

24. For purposes of the national accounts, statisticians at the Department of Commerce have also begun recognizing "software" as a separate asset category.

25. In corporate accounting, special rules and categories are applicable in certain industries. In the oil industry, for example, oil companies may choose between "successful efforts"

and "full cost" accounting approaches when recording expenditures associated with searching for oil and gas. If oil or gas is found, the search costs associated with a particular discovery may be capitalized ("successful efforts"), while all other exploration costs are immediately expensed. Alternatively, companies may choose to expense all exploration costs immediately. Similarly, film production companies are permitted to "capitalize" some of the costs of making a film for book accounting purposes, and then take a depreciation charge in each subsequent year over the expected commercial life of the property. And some accountants have begun recognizing "in-process R&D" as a separate category of assets in accounting for corporate acquistions.

26. See Jorgen Mortensen, Clark Eustace, and Karel Lannoo, "Intangibles in the European Economy" (Brussels: Center for European Policy Studies, March 1997), p. 22.

27. A recent study commissioned by the European Commission examined changes underway in the approach to R&D inside firms. See "The Intangible Economy: Impact and Policy Issues," Report of the European High Level Expert Group on the Intangible Economy (Brussels: European Commission, 2000), pp. 8–10.

28. In the summer of 2000, a small company called Emulex saw its stock price collapse from $103 per share to $45 per share in fifteen minutes when Bloomberg News posted a press release saying that the firm's chief executive had resigned, net earnings would be restated, and the SEC had begun an investigation into its accounting practices. The price recovered quickly once it was widely published that this information was not true. See Alex Berenson, "On Hair-Trigger Wall Street, A Stock Plunges on False News," *New York Times*, August 26, 2000, p. A1. See also Charles J. Fombrun, *Reputation: Realizing Value from the Corporate Image* (Harvard Business School Press, 1996).

29. One of the earliest known examples of ABS financing was a $100 million bond issue by Dow Chemicals in 1994, backed by its patent portfolio. In 1999, Formula 1 issued a $1.4 billion bond backed by its intellectual property rights in contracts covering event staging and performance rights and media, broadcast, and advertising rights. For more details, see Clark Eustace, "Intellectual Property and the Capital Markets," working paper (London: City University Business School, May 2000), appendix 4.

30. However, see also Ronald J. Mann, "Secured Credit and Software Financing," Law and Economics Working Paper 99-014 (University of Michigan, 1999), on the difficulties of using software as collateral for debt finance.

31. See Eustace, "Intellectual Property and the Capital Markets," p. 10.

32. See Hall, "Innovation and Market Value"; Lev and Sougiannis, "Penetrating the Book-to-Market Black Box"; Hall, Jaffe, and Trajtenberg, "Market Value and Patent Citations"; and Brynjolfsson and Yang, "The Intangible Costs and Benefits of Computer Investments."

33. Examples include the "balanced scorecard" developed by Robert Norton and David Kaplan (David P. Kaplan and Robert S. Norton, "Putting the Balanced Scorecard to Work," *Harvard Business Review* [September–October 1993]); the "dashboard" model developed by the Conference Board (Brancato, "Communicating Corporate Performance"); the "Navigator" model developed by Skandia Corp. (Skandia Corp., "Intellectual Capital Report," supplement to *Annual Financial Report* [Stockholm: various years] and Leif Edvinsson and Michael Malone, *Intellectual Capital* [Harpers, 1997]); the ValueReporting model developed by PricewaterhouseCoopers (PricewaterhouseCoopers, *ValueReporting Forecast 2000* [2000]); the "employee-customer profit chain" model developed at Sears, Roebuck (see J. Anthony Rucci, Steven P. Kirk, and Richard T. Quinn, "The

Employee-Customer Profit Chain at Sears," *Harvard Business Review* [January–February, 1998]); and the annual *Report to Society* developed by Shell UK as a mechanism for tracking and disclosing nonfinancial performance information.

34. See the report of the task force's Strategic Organizational Issues subgroup (www.brookings.edu/es/research/projects/intangibles/intangibles.htm).

35. See Bosworth and Triplett, "Numbers Matter," for a discussion of the policy problems that result from faulty data on productivity in the service sector. The federal agencies responsible for compiling macroeconomic performance statistics are well aware of the measurement problems arising from poor information about intangibles and other aspects of the New Economy. See Economics and Statistics Administration, *Digital Economy 2000* (Department of Commerce, June 2000).

36. See Nakamura, "Intangibles." Nakamura's research predated most of the truly egregious run-up in the stock prices of "dot.com" companies in the second half of 1999. Many of these companies had no profits and would not have had profits even if their R&D expenditures had been capitalized. But as of this writing, stock prices in the dot.com sector have undergone a substantial correction. If financial markets had access to better information about the intangible assets in these companies, prices might never have become so volatile in the first place.

37. See Chan, Lakonishok, and Sougiannis, "The Stock Market Valuation of Research and Development Expenditures."

38. Lev, *Intangibles*.

39. See Securities and Exchange Commission, "Selective Disclosure and Insider Trading," Release 33-7881, August 15, 2000 (www.sec.gov/rules/final/33-7881.htm). The rule took effect on October 23, 2000.

Challenges From the New Economy for Business and Financial Reporting

Wayne S. Upton, Jr

1. Introduction

This Special Report examines the much-heralded new economy and some implications for business and financial reporting. There are hundreds, if not thousands, of articles, studies, and consultants' reports that discuss the new economy, intellectual capital, and intangible assets. Most decry what they consider accounting's failures, and many offer (usually proprietary) solutions.

No paper of reasonable length could catalog all of this research into intellectual capital, human capital, knowledge management, and intangible assets. Instead, this Special Report is a sampler. It describes some notable proposals, examines the accounting and reporting issues, and explores some possible approaches that might improve business and financial reporting. It also provides a background for examining projects that standard setters might undertake and proposes some possibilities.

Two assertions dominate articles and papers about the intersection between the new economy on one hand and business and financial reporting on the other. First, the economy of 2000 is fundamentally different from the economy of 1950 and before. Second, traditional financial statements do not capture—and may not be able to capture—the value drivers that dominate the new economy. Those assertions have attracted a considerable following. Accounting bodies, standard setters, academics, and government regulators in Europe and all of the English-speaking countries have conducted studies and issued reports. To date, there has been little change in financial reporting.

Wayne S. Upton, Jr

The problem that confronts businesses, users of business reporting information, standard setters, and regulators is how best to understand and communicate the difference between the value of a company (usually expressed as the market capitalization) and the accounting book value of that company. One might simply attribute the entire difference to some ill-defined notion of 'intangibles' and be done with the exercise. But that approach is circular and provides little feedback information to users of financial and business reporting information. There must be more going on and more that can be said. We can observe the market capitalization of a traded stock and observe the accounting book value. We do not know exactly why they are different, but we can make some reasonable speculations. A company's market capitalization might be decomposed along the lines below:

1.		Accounting book value	$ XXX
2.	±	Market assessments of differences between accounting measurement and underlying value of recognized assets and liabilities	XXX
3.	±	Market assessments of the underlying value of items that meet the definition of assets and liabilities but are not recognized in financial statements (e.g. patents developed through internal research and development)	XXX
4.	±	Market assessments of intangible value drivers or value impairers that do not meet the definition of assets and liabilities (e.g. employee morale)	XXX
5.	±	Market assessments of the entity's future plans, opportunities, and business risks	XXX
6.	±	Other factors, including puffery, pessimism, and market psychology	XXX
7.		Market capitalization	$ XXXX

In a perfect world, financial statements would include all items that meet the definition of assets and liabilities and provide decision-useful information about their values (items 1, 2, and 3). Business reporting outside of financial statements and notes would provide information and metrics about other value drivers and impairers of value and about plans, opportunities, and risks (items 4 and 5). The last adjustment (item 6) might be labelled with the admonition found on old maps—here abide monsters! This Special Report examines issues and implications posed by three propositions about what some see as accounting's failure to keep pace with a changing economy.

Proposition 1—Traditional financial statements focus on the entity's ability to realize value from existing assets and liabilities. Proponents argue that financial statements are largely backward-looking. A new financial reporting paradigm is needed to capture and report on the entity's creation of value. This paradigm would supplement, or might replace, existing financial statements.

Proposition 2—The important value drivers in the new economy are largely nonfinancial and do not lend themselves to presentation in financial reports. However, a set of measures could be developed that would allow investors and creditors to evaluate entities and compare them with one another.

Proposition 3—The importance of intangible assets is the distinguishing feature of the new economy. By and large, existing financial statements recognize those assets only when they are acquired from others. Accounting standard setters should develop a basis for the recognition and measurement of internally generated intangible assets.

The three propositions also imply a fourth, rarely stated, alternative. Some maintain that existing business and financial reporting is adequate to the purpose for which it is intended. Those who hold this view maintain that changes, especially mandated changes, will do more to harm the usefulness and credibility of reporting than to improve its usefulness. While unpopular with advocates of the new economy, this fourth proposition demands equal attention.

Merchant banker John Rutledge, apparently a supporter of the fourth proposition, offers the following comments:

The most troubling idea of the IC [intellectual capital] generation is to tinker with financial statements, so companies full of smart people who don't make profits look more attractive to investors. Some want to include the capitalized value of workers' ideas on the balance sheet. Some want to include cultural factors, such as the gender composition of the workforce, as if it is somehow a driver of the profitability of a company. And some want to use measurements of intellectual capital to influence the credit markets or public policy. Anyone who has ever attended a Mensa meeting can see the fallacy of this idea. There is a big difference between smart and *effective*, and I'll take an effective person over a *smart* one any day.[1]

Mr. Rutledge goes on to say:

Monkeying with financial statements, for almost any reason, is a terrible idea. Investors have 500 years of practice interpreting financial statements while learning to understand, project, get comfortable with, and value our more than $60 trillion in total assets.

471

In doing so, they have developed methods to adjust for many of the anomalies (for example, amortization of goodwill, which can only be defined by describing what it is not) that emerge from our archaic double-entry bookkeeping practices from time to time. Scrambling the financial data we use to make such judgments would render these methods less useful. It also would throw up a cloud of uncertainty large enough to make owning assets more risky, and therefore less valuable. Giving people more information is fine: They can make their own judgments. Tinkering with the balance sheet is not a good idea. Although intellectual capital is important (who would doubt that people who know how to do things are more successful than people who don't?), it should be left off the balance sheet. Balance sheets are for *stuff*, the stuff that George Carlin talks about, not people or ideas. People aren't assets because you can't own them, at least not in this country (I'm neglecting alimony here); you can only rent them. Ideas are not assets because, partly due to the fact that the people who generate them can't be owned, you can't keep them bottled up for very long. (Except for the secret formula for Coke, that is.) If you want to measure the value of people and their ideas, you need to look at cash flows, not assets. Balance sheets measure the value of things you own; cash flows measure the value of things you rent. Unless we return to conditions in the antebellum South, this will remain true no matter how many computers we have on our desktops or how fast they run.

2. A Problem of Terminology

This chapter avoids the use of popular terms like *knowledge capital, human capital*, and *intellectual capital* except when describing others' use of the terms. Those terms appear frequently in discussions about the new economy, but with meanings so diverse as to render them useless as descriptions of anything recognizable as capital. For example, some writers use the term *intellectual capital* to refer to the entire difference between a company's market capitalization and its accounting book value. Others use the term in a far more restrictive sense to refer to particular competencies or intangible assets. At least initially, this Special Report adopts traditional accounting terminology.

1. *Assets* are defined in the FASB Concepts Statements and the International Accounting Standards Committee *Framework for the Preparation and Presentation of Financial Statements* (the IASC *Framework*).

2. *Intangible assets* are (surprise) those that are neither tangible nor financial instruments. This report limits its use of the term *intangible asset* to items that potentially satisfy the definition of an asset. Items that fail the definition of an asset may be important elements of business success, and Chapter 3 examines the use of nonfinancial metrics to provide information about those items. Chapter 4 examines whether the existing definition of *assets* or existing

recognition criteria should be modified to accommodate greater recognition of intangible items.

3. *Nonfinancial disclosures* and *metrics* include index scores, ratios, counts, and other information not presented in the basic financial statements.

4. *Financial reporting* includes the basic financial statements and accompanying notes.

5. *Business reporting* encompasses the broader universe of information provided by business enterprises, including management's discussion and analysis, information provided in the annual report, presentations to analysts, fact books, and business information provided on the company's website.

---

3. Is There Really a New Economy?

Descriptions of the new economy vary from one writer to the next, and the reader often shares chagrin over the rhetoric. Often, these descriptions say as much about the writer's predilections as they do about the new economy. Yet, we need to understand just what new economy promoters are talking about. Distinguishing characteristics of the new economy are variously described as:

- Knowledge, knowledge capital, know-how, and intellectual capital.
- The Internet.
- Technology.
- Information.
- Intangible assets.
- Knowledge sharing and new forms of organization.
- Network effects.
- Globalization.

One venture capitalist described the perceived disconnect between financial reporting and the new economy this way:

At the time that Henry Ford developed his mass production system, the skill of the workers involved in production was not an important concern. As a matter of fact, one of the benefits that Ford envisioned for his system was that it would permit him to deskill work and thus make workers as interchangeable as the parts from which his cars were constructed. He was so successful in reaching this goal that in one year he hired 50,000 workers to fill 15,000 production line jobs—an annual employee turnover rate of greater than 300%. In this case, the old accounting system was still accurate for determining the value of workers to the company.[2]

The author went on to say:

> Clearly, worker skills, the investment in employee training, and intellectual capital were not much of an issue for Henry Ford. As these assets were not of significant value, it made little difference whether they were reconciled for in the books. Today things are very different. It is impossible to operate a production system efficiently and produce high quality products if employees turn over every four months. Companies make large investments in training workers and the most productive companies value the knowledge and skills of a dedicated work force above all else.

Those passages reflect the popular view that the means of production have shifted from tangible assets to intangible, especially knowledge, assets. But those passages and others like them do not stand up well to examination. Consider Ford Motor Company in the 1920s, beginning with workforce.

After introducing the assembly line, Ford faced the employee turnover described above. His response was to increase the hourly pay of workers. Within months, the turnover rate declined sharply and the workforce stabilized. Today, some might call that an investment in the workforce. Perhaps Ford tried to eliminate the need for knowledge content in the jobs of assembly workers, but modern management theory also might argue that he did not eliminate important knowledge. Assembly workers typically hold 'unofficial' knowledge about what techniques work and the best way to do a job.[3] Consider, for example, the effect on production when workers decide to protest by doing their tasks 'by the book'.

But the focus on production workers ignores the significant knowledge input to a Model T. Ford still needed the skills of engineers, metallurgists, paint chemists, and a host of others that today we call 'knowledge workers'. No doubt, those specialists helped Ford develop both patentable and proprietary technologies. The Ford assembly line would today be lauded as a 'business model' asset. The Ford brand name was the most recognized in the industry. Customer satisfaction was high. The same intangible value drivers attributed to the new economy were an important, if unrecognized, part of the early success of Ford Motor Company.

Nobel laureate economist Milton Friedman's example of a common wood pencil is even more apt. Very few people know how to make a pencil. Most do not even know where or how to acquire the necessary materials. From this perspective, knowing *how* to make a pencil is far more important than the inventory and equipment required to assemble one. Yet, the common pencil (sometimes called a 'generic word processor') predates computers by several decades.

In a recent *New York Times* column, economist Paul Krugman of the Massachusetts Institute of Technology offered this summation in a discussion of the British television series *1900 House*:

On one side of this debate are the enthusiasts who proclaim the onset of the digital age more important than the Industrial Revolution, the biggest thing since bread, never mind the slicing. On the other side are economists and historians who compare our current roster of new technologies with the transforming technologies of the late 19th and early 20th centuries, and find our latest gizmos relatively trivial by comparison. The economic boom that has swept the United States during the second Clinton administration has made the arguments of the enthusiasts more plausible, but '1900 House' seems to me to be a reminder that the technoskeptics still have the better case.[4]

It is popular to say that the economy is different today and that 'old fashioned' accounting is inadequate. There may have been a shift between the relative values of tangible and intangible inputs to the means of production. Certainly balance of numbers, both in people and money, seems to have shifted. The percentage of workers who get their hands dirty to earn a living continues to shrink. Some statistics suggest that this shift has produced a dramatic (and perhaps unsustainable) increase in productivity in the US economy. On the other hand, it may be that our perceptions have shifted and we recognize something that was always there. If so, the 'old accounting system' was no more adequate to Ford in 1920 than to Lucent or Cisco in 2000.

Labels seldom help to solve problems. Labelling certainly does not help here. We may have a new economy, or our new tools may have given us an appreciation of factors that were always important. It does not much matter which. The more important question is how to improve business and financial reporting.

4. Some Notable Efforts to Come to Grips with the Problem

A comprehensive survey of the hundreds of articles and projects dealing with business reporting in the new economy is beyond the scope of this Special Report. The Brookings Institution's *Project on Understanding Intangible Sources of Value* (described later in this chapter) includes an extensive annotated bibliography that is available for download from the Brookings website.[5] Some notable efforts that focus on business and financial reporting and some of their relevant findings are summarized below.

5. American Institute of Certified Public Accountants

In 1991, the American Institute of Certified Public Accountants (AICPA) formed a Special Committee on Financial Reporting (the Special Committee). While not directly concerned with the reporting implications of the new economy, the Special Committee's 1994 report[6] touched on a number of topics discussed in this chapter. In its introduction, the Special Committee observed:

Increased competition and rapid advances in technology are resulting in dramatic changes. To survive and compete, companies are changing everything—the way they are organized and managed, the way they do work and develop new products, the way they manage risks, and their relationships with other organizations. Winners in the marketplace are the companies that are focusing on the customer, stripping away low-value activity, decentralizing decision making, reducing the time required to perform key activities, and forming new alliances with suppliers and customers—even competitors. They are setting the pace for others that must, in turn, reexamine their businesses in light of the increased competition.

In response to increased competition and changes in their businesses, companies also are changing their information systems and the types of information they use to manage their businesses. For example, they are developing new performance measures often designed to focus on activities that provide long-term value and competitive advantage, including non-financial measures such as product development lead time and financial measures such as economic value added.

Can business reporting be immune from the fundamental changes affecting business? [page 2]

In summarizing the Special Committee's recommendations, the report said:

To meet users' changing needs, business reporting must:

(a) Provide more information with a forward-looking perspective, including management's plans, opportunities, risks, and measurement uncertainties.

(b) Focus more on the factors that create longer term value, including non-financial measures indicating how key business processes are performing.

(c) Better align information reported externally with the information reported to senior management to manage the business. [page 5]

Interestingly, the Special Committee identified several of the topics discussed in this Special Report as 'lower priority issues'. The Special Committee described those topics as follows:

Standard setters should defer considering issues that have low priority according to the current evidence of users' needs. The Committee's study identified the following five areas that standard setters should not devote attention to at this time:

1. Value-based accounting model.
2. Accounting for intangible assets, including goodwill.

3. Forecasted financial statements.
4. Accounting for business combinations.
5. Alternative accounting principles. [page 125]

6. Financial Accounting Standards Board—Business Reporting Research Project

In February 1996, the FASB issued an Invitation to Comment, *Recommendations of the AICPA Special Committee on Financial Reporting and the Association for Investment Management and Research*, to solicit views on recommendations made to standard setters in both the AICPA report and a similar paper published by the Association for Investment Management and Research (AIMR). Issue 1 of the Invitation to Comment asked: 'Should the FASB broaden its activities beyond financial statements and related disclosures to also address the types of nonfinancial information that would be included in a comprehensive business reporting model?'

Overall, respondents had mixed views about FASB involvement with non-financial information. Some respondents opposed FASB standard setting for the disclosure of nonfinancial information. Other respondents suggested that the Board be selective and initially limit its efforts to focusing on operating data and performance measures and reasons for changes in such data and key trends. Others suggested that the FASB take a primary leadership role in developing a comprehensive business-reporting model similar to the one developed by the Special Committee.

At a public Board meeting on 29 January 1998, the Board decided to undertake a research project on business reporting. The Board formed a Steering Committee to conduct the project and instructed the Steering Committee to:

- Study present practices for the voluntary disclosure of certain types of business information that users of business reporting might find helpful in making investment decisions.
- Develop recommendations for ways to coordinate generally accepted accounting principles (GAAP) and Securities and Exchange Commission (SEC) disclosure requirements and to reduce redundancies.
- Study present systems for the electronic delivery of business information and consider the implications of technology for business reporting in the future.

The Steering Committee issued its report *Improving Business Reporting: Insights into Enhancing Voluntary Disclosures*, in 2001.[7] That report described the findings of working groups that studied voluntary disclosures of business information in ten industries. The report describes a framework for providing voluntary disclosures that includes five elements:

- Identify the aspects of the company's business that are especially important to the company's success. These are the critical success factors for the company.
- Identify management's strategies and plans for managing those critical success factors in the past and going forward.
- Identify metrics (operating data performance measures) used by management to measure and manage the implementation of their strategies and plans.
- Consider whether voluntary disclosures about the company's forward-looking strategies and plans and metrics would adversely affect the company's competitive position and whether the risk of adversely affecting competitive position exceeds the expected benefit of making the voluntary disclosure.
- If disclosure is deemed appropriate, determine how best to voluntarily present that information. The nature of metrics presented should be explained, and those metrics should be consistently disclosed from period to period to the extent that they continue to be relevant. [page 13]

---

7. Canadian Institute of Chartered Accountants

The Canadian Institute of Chartered Accountants (CICA) has been working on a new-economy project since 1994. The *Canadian Performance Reporting Initiative* (CPRI) has touched on a variety of topics discussed throughout this Special Report. The initial document to emerge from the CICA project was titled *Performance Measures in the New Economy*, authored by Robert I. G. McLean.[8] This report was published by the Premier's Council (Ontario) in 1995. Quoted below are a series of conclusions from chapter 1 of that report:

- The most important finding from the interviews and research conducted in preparing this report is that the need for better performance measures than are provided by the existing accounting model is being recognized not just by accounting theorists, but by chief executive officers, and by senior officials in Canada's major banks. Furthermore, a number of leading companies are actively experimenting with new performance measurement systems focusing on knowledge-intensive activities.
- In addition to the pragmatic concerns registered by business executives, a strong theoretical case can be made that the current accounting model does not adequately reflect economic reality for knowledge-intensive businesses.

- This is, however, not easily remedied, since accounting adequately for knowledge-based businesses will ultimately require the invention of a new accounting model.
- We are currently at a fairly early stage in the exploration of alternative approaches to measuring, managing, and valuing people skills, information, and technological capabilities. Some of these experiments are briefly documented in this report.
- The last paradigm shift in accounting involved a change in emphasis from valuing assets to measuring income, and took place over about a 50-year period in North America beginning in the late 19th century. The new accounting model, when fully developed, will likely place equal emphasis on both asset valuation and income measurement. However, in the early years, there will likely be experimentation with supplementary measures focusing on valuation of knowledge assets. It is likely that events will force the pace of this next paradigm shift, such that it will take place over a period of 15 to 20 years.
- The new accounting model will likely incorporate both accounting for knowledge-based businesses as well as green accounting.
- Influential organizations contacted all expressed interest in participating in a process to explore these issues further. These include: the Auditor General of Canada; the Society of Management Accountants of Canada; Statistics Canada; the Institute of Chartered Accountants of Scotland.
- Leadership by the CICA would be an important factor in accelerating the process of exploration, experimentation, research, and standard setting.

The CPRI has spawned a number of projects (some of which are discussed elsewhere in this chapter) including:

- Integrated performance reporting.
- Intellectual capital management.
- Shareholder value creation.
- Environmental performance measurement and reporting.
- Total value creation.

8. Brookings Institution

The Brookings Institution's *Project on Understanding Intangible Sources of Value* is a follow-on to an earlier conference on intangible assets sponsored by the US Securities and Exchange Commission. The project description includes the following passage:

The purpose of this project is to help initiate a national discussion about better ways of measuring, monitoring and reporting on critical intangible sources of wealth, both inside firms, and in the national accounts, and to assess work already underway to develop better measures of intangibles. It will also report what is currently known about the level and the measurement investments in intangibles, how decisions are made about making such investments, and the extent to which investment decisions are influenced by the methods of measurement. The report will also consider how public policies (e.g. regulations, reporting requirements, and tax rules) affect the development of better measures, and affect decision-making in the private sector where actors try to develop better measures. Finally, it will recommend policy changes that could help eliminate or reduce unnecessary or unwarranted adverse distortions.

On 24 October 2000, Brookings announced preliminary release of two reports. The first report, *Unseen Wealth: Report of the Brookings Task Force on Understanding Intangible Sources of Value*, presents the work of the Brookings task force.[9] The report recommends that the US government establish a federally funded Center for the Study of Business, Technology, and Innovation. The report proposes that the center conduct a three-part pilot project to:

- Capture a base of cost data on intangible investments.
- Develop a framework of value indicators.
- Develop a new generation of business models.

The report proposes that 100–150 companies participate in the pilot project and that they provide data on a confidential basis.

Unseen Wealth also makes several recommendations about financial reporting, including:

1. Debate about the capitalization or expensing of research and development costs 'is focused on the wrong problem'. In this view, investors want information about the value (not the cost) of internally generated intangibles and 'it is irrelevant whether such information is incorporated into the regular financial statements of companies or whether it is presented in some other format, such as in the footnotes in the management discussion and analysis, or in some other supplementary disclosure format'. (page 46)

2. The financial reporting model should 'begin to move toward a value-based system of accounting for corporate assets—both tangibles and intangibles—that would supplement the current cost-based system'. (page 47)

3. Disclosure of 'value drivers' should be expanded and the disclosure should be provided at the same level of the business as are segment disclosures.

4. The Securities and Exchange Commission should expand safe-harbour protections to include disclosures about intangible value drivers.

The second report, *Intangibles: Management, Measurement, and Reporting*, was authored by New York University Professor Baruch Lev for the Brookings project.[10] Professor Lev's disclosure proposal is discussed at greater length in chapter 3 of this Special Report. Other portions of his analysis are cited throughout this Special Report.

Also on 24 October Brookings and the American Enterprise Institute announced release of *The GAAP Gap: Corporate Disclosure in the Internet Age*.[11]

9. Danish Agency for Development of Trade and Industry

In 1998, the Danish Agency for Development of Trade and Industry published a study of *Intellectual Capital Accounts* developed with the cooperation of ten companies.[12] This study describes intellectual capital accounts in four categories:

- *Human resources*. This category covers statements about the composition, management and satisfaction of the human resources.
- *Customers*. This category covers statements about the composition, management and satisfaction of the customers.
- *Technology*. This category typically covers statements about the scope, function and application of the IT system.
- *Processes*. This category typically covers statements about the scope, equipment and efficiency of the business activities.

The 'accounts' described in the Danish study are not accounts in the normal bookkeeping sense. They are a collection of nonfinancial performance measurements.

10. Netherlands Ministry of Economic Affairs

In 1999, the Netherlands Ministry of Economic Affairs published *Intangible Assets, Balancing Accounts with Knowledge*.[13] The Netherlands ministry asked four accounting firms to develop models for the presentation of information about intangible assets.

1. KPMG proposed a 'dashboard' that portrays scores assigned to attributes of an entity's core competencies.

2. Ernst and Young proposed a reconciliation approach that begins with market capitalization and then deducts the fair values of tangible assets (net of liabilities) and identified intangible assets. The residual is characterized as the fair value of remaining intellectual capital.

3. PricewaterhouseCoopers proposed a disclosure approach that combined information about expenditures with nonfinancial performance metrics.

4. Walgemoed proposed expanded recognition of identifiable intangible assets on the face of the balance sheet, with those assets measured based on traditional accumulation of cost notions.

11. Organization for Economic Cooperation and Development

In June 1999, the Organization for Economic Cooperation and Development (OECD) sponsored a Symposium on Measuring and Reporting Intellectual Capital: Experience, Issues, and Prospects.[14] The symposium chairman observed:

In a subsequent policy and strategy forum, a broad range of stakeholders from companies, governments, trade unions, accountants, standards setters, and the academic community addressed the question of how to facilitate development of internal and external company reporting of intellectual capital. Forum chairman, Stuart Hornery, chairman of Lend-Lease Corporation, drew the following conclusions:

1. The process of value creation in companies is changing. There is a need for better information on intellectual capital, its relation to tangible capital, and its role in value creation. Financial data are evolving, but, alone, present insufficient information.

2. International organisations, governments, standards setters and other stake holders should encourage experimentation that would lead to general principles or guidelines for reporting key indicators of intellectual capital and information on value creation. They should systematically monitor and evaluate the results of such experimentation.

3. There is broad support for the creation of a framework for voluntary compilation at the enterprise level of a number of key indicators using all possible approaches, including company benchmarking. The framework for reporting should focus on areas that matter most to company performance.

4. Employees, suppliers, and customers are involved increasingly in the value creation process. Improvements in reporting should aim to inform them better.

5. There is a need for better understanding of the innovations in reporting. New approaches are moving towards Internet based real-time reporting; greater availability of information means that more information about a company comes from multiple sources. As a result, more internal information is available externally.

6. Businesses are concerned that disclosure of information on intellectual capital and value creation should be useful to business, as well as stakeholders. Many are actively experimenting. It is, however, too early to consider mandatory changes in rules affecting such disclosure. Any requirements need to be mindful of costs and benefits.

12. Institute of Chartered Accountants in England and Wales

In March 2000, the Institute of Chartered Accountants in England and Wales (ICAEW) published a study authored by Charles Leadbeater titled, *New*

Measures for the New Economy.[15] After an analysis of the need for and difficulties in developing new measures and new markets for intangible assets, Leadbeater proposes three alternative approaches that he labelled incremental, radical, and hybrid, with the following descriptions:

The incremental approach seeks gradually to fill in values for the intangible assets which traditional balance sheets overlook. Traditional financial accounts would remain the focus of corporate reporting but they would be augmented by relevant, robust information on intangibles. This approach would involve accounting procedures used routinely in corporate acquisitions to value intangibles as well as quasi-market valuations yielded by techniques such as real options.

The radical approach is to devise entirely new balance sheets for companies—Intellectual Capital Balance Sheets—which put intangible assets at the heart of the accounts. Financial information is included but as a measure of success and as a resource for investment. The generation and deployment of intangible assets forms the core of these new models. The best known of these new balance sheets is the intellectual capital report by Swedish insurance company Skandia. Another Swedish approach is the intangible asset monitor developed by management consultant Karl Erik Sveiby. . . .[16]

In some ways the hybrid approach is the most radical. It would involve far more sweeping changes, not just to the way managers and accountants value intangibles but also the value placed upon them by society as a whole. An underlying assumption of the debate about intangibles is that there should be an accounting solution to the difficulties of valuing them. This may involve gradual or radical reform but it would essentially involve accountants in drawing up a balance sheet for a company.

13. Securities and Exchange Commission

In an October 1999 speech to the Economic Club of New York, SEC Chairman Arthur Levitt announced the formation of a task force chaired by Jeffrey Garten, dean of the Yale University School of Management. Chairman Levitt described the group as follows:

The dynamic nature of today's capital markets creates issues that increasingly move beyond the bright line of black and white. New industries, spurred by new services and new technologies, are creating new questions and challenges that must be addressed. Today, we are witnessing a broad shift from an industrial economy to a more service based one; a shift from bricks and mortar to technology and knowledge.

This has important ramifications for our disclosure and financial reporting models. We have long had a good idea of how to value manufacturing inventory or assess what a factory is worth. But today, the value of R&D invested in a software program, or the value of a user base of an Internet shopping site is a lot harder to quantify. As intangible assets continue to grow in both size and scope, more and more people are questioning whether the true value—and the drivers of that value—is being reflected in a timely manner in publicly available disclosure.

These questions may have some merit. Groups, past and present including one sponsored by the FASB, have worked on variations of this issue. Nevertheless, I have asked Professor Jeffrey Garten, Dean of Yale's School of Management to assemble a group of leaders from the business community, academia, the accounting profession, standard setting bodies, and corporate America to examine expeditiously whether our current business reporting framework can more effectively capture these momentous changes in our economy. But let me be quite clear: The work of this group is not an invitation to delay any initiative currently underway, especially those involving business combinations. These projects must be evaluated on their own merits.

The Garten task force expects to issue its report in 2001.

14. Observations

The several efforts described in this chapter highlight attempts to engage the 'new-economy problem' or the 'intangibles problem' by focusing to differing degrees on the three propositions outlined on page 3. The table below summarizes how they approached the problem:

Agency	New Paradigm	New Metrics	Intangible Assets
American Institute of Certified Public Accountants—Special Committee on Financial Reporting		X	
Financial Accounting Standards Board—Business Reporting Research Project		X	
Canadian Institute of Chartered Accountants—Canadian Performance Reporting Initiative	X	X	
Brookings Institution— Understanding Intangible Sources of Value		X	X
Danish Agency for Development of Trade and Industry— Intellectual Capital Accounts		X	

Netherlands Ministry of Economic Affairs—Intangible Assets, Balancing Accounts with Knowledge	X	X
Organization for Economic Cooperation and Development	X	
Institute of Chartered Accountants in England and Wales—New Measures for the New Economy	X	X

Notes

1. John Rutledge, 'You're a Fool If You Buy into This', *Forbes ASAP* (April 1997).
2. William Davidow, 'Accounting Systems Are Completely Wrong', *Red Herring* (January 1995).
3. For an excellent discussion of how workers share knowledge, see John Seely Brown and Paul Duguid, 'Practice Makes Process', ch. 4 in *The Social Life of Information* (Boston: Harvard Business School Press, 2000).
4. Paul Krugman, 'Turn of the Century', *New York Times* (18 June, 2000).
5. http://www.brook.edu/es/research/projects/intangibles/intangibles.htm.
6. AICPA, *Improving Business Reporting—A Customer Focus* (New York: AICPA, 1994). Available online at http://www.rutgers.edu/Accounting/raw/aicpa/business/ main.htm.
7. (Norwalk: FASB, 2001). Available online at http://www.fasb.org.
8. Robert I. G. McLean, *Performance Measures in the New Economy* (Toronto: CICA, 1995). Available online at http://cpri.matrixlinks.ca/Archive/PMNE/PerfMeasNE.html.
9. Washington: Brookings Institution, 2000. Available online at http://www.brook.edu/es/research/projects/intangibles/tf.htm.
10. Washington: Brookings Institution, awaiting publication. December 2000 draft available online at http://www.stern.nyu.edu/~blev/.
11. Robert E. Litan and Peter Wallison (Washington: AEI-Brookings Joint Center for Regulatory Studies, 2000). Available online at http://www.aei.brookings.org/publications/default.asp.
12. Danish Trade and Industry Development Council, *Intellectual Capital Accounts—Reporting and Managing Intellectual Capital* (Copenhagen: September 1997). This work was done in cooperation between the Danish Agency for Trade and Industry and the researchers, Professor Jan Mouritsen, Copenhagen Business School and BDO-professor

Per Nikolaj Buck, The Aarhus School of Business. Available online at http://www.efs.dk/publikationer/rapporter/engvidenregn/all.html.

13. Netherlands Ministry of Economic Affairs, *Intangible Assets, Balancing Accounts with Knowledge* (The Hague: Ministry of Economic Affairs, 1999). Available at http://info.minez.nl/nieuwskiosk/publicaties/publicatietonen.phtm?vosnr=25B19A.

14. Copyright OECD, June 1999. The symposium program, speeches, and background materials can be viewed online at http://www.oecd.org/dsti/sti/industry/indcomp/act/Ams-conf/symposium.htm.

15. Charles Leadbeater, *New Measures for the New Economy* (London: Institute of Chartered Accountants in England and Wales, March 2000). Available at http://www.icaew.co.uk/institute/cbp/document.asp?WSDOCID=3669. Extracts from *New Measures for the New Economy* by Charles Leadbeater reproduced with the permission of the Centre for Business Performance of the Institute of Chartered Accountants in England and Wales.

16. The Skandia and Sveiby proposals are discussed elsewhere in this Special Report.

The Boundaries of Financial Reporting and How to Extend Them

Baruch Lev and Paul Zarowin

Introduction

In this study we investigate the usefulness of financial information to investors in comparison to the total information in the marketplace.[1] Our evidence indicates that the usefulness of reported earnings, cash flows, and book (equity) values has been deteriorating over the past twenty years. We document that this deterioration in usefulness, in the face of both increasing investor demand for relevant information and persistent regulator efforts to improve the quality and timeliness of financial information, is due to *change*. Whether driven by innovation, competition, or deregulation, the current reporting system does not adequately reflect the impact of change on firms' operations and economic conditions. The large investments that generally drive change, such as restructuring costs and R&D expenditures, are immediately expensed, while the benefits of change are recorded later and are not matched with the previously expensed investments. Consequently, the fundamental accounting measurement process of periodically matching costs with revenues is seriously distorted, adversely affecting the informativeness of financial information.[2] We validate our conjecture, that business change is an important factor responsible for the deterioration in the informativeness of financial information, first by providing evidence that the rate of change experienced by US business enterprises has increased over the past twenty years, and then by linking the increased rate of change with the decline in the usefulness of financial information.

We extend our inquiry by considering the accounting for innovative activities of business enterprises—the major initiator of change in developed economies.

These activities, mostly in the form of investment in intangible assets such as R&D, information technology, brands, and human resources, constantly alter firms' products, operations, economic conditions, and market values. We argue that it is in the accounting for intangibles that the present system fails most seriously to reflect enterprise value and performance, mainly due to the mismatching of costs with revenues. We demonstrate the adverse informational consequences of the accounting treatment of intangibles by documenting a positive association between the rate of business change and shifts in R&D spending, and an association between the decrease in the informativeness of earnings and changes in R&D spending.

Having linked the increasing importance of intangible investments, through their effect on the rate of business change, to the documented decline in the usefulness of financial information, we address the normative question of what can be done to arrest this decline. We advance two proposals; a comprehensive capitalization of intangible investments and a systematic restatement of financial reports. The first proposal expands on a practice currently used in special circumstances (e.g. software development costs), while the second proposal implies a radical change in current accounting practices.

1. The Decreasing Usefulness of Financial Information

We use statistical associations between accounting data and capital market values (stock prices and returns) to assess the usefulness of financial information to investors. Such associations reflect the consequences of investors' actions, whereas alternative usefulness measures, such as those based on questionnaire or interview studies, reflect investors' opinions and beliefs. Furthermore, empirical associations between market values and financial data allow for an assessment of the incremental usefulness of accounting data relative to other information sources (e.g. managers' voluntary disclosures or analysts' recommendations).

1.1. The Weakening Returns–Earnings Relation

Our first analysis examines the usefulness of reported earnings, using the following cross-sectional regression to estimate the association between annual stock returns and the level and change of earnings:

$$R_{it} = \alpha_0 + \alpha_1 E_{it} + \alpha_2 \Delta E_{it} + e_{it}, \quad t = 1977\text{--}96, \tag{1}$$

where R_{it} is the firm i's stock return for fiscal year t, E_{it} the reported earnings before extraordinary items (Compustat item #58) of firm i in fiscal year t, and ΔE_{it} the annual change in earnings: $\Delta E_{it} = E_{it} - E_{i,t-1}$, proxying for the surprise element in reported earnings.

Both E_{it} and ΔE_{it} are scaled by firm i's total market value of equity at the beginning of year t. Our sources of data are the 1996 versions of the Compustat (both Current and Research Files) and CRSP databases.

Table 1 presents estimates of regression (1) for each of the years, 1978–96 (1977 is 'lost' due to the first differencing of earnings). The 'total sample', containing 3700–6800 firms per year, includes all Compustat firms with available data. The 'constant sample' is 1300 firms with data in each of the twenty years examined. Panel A of Table 1 shows that the association between stock returns and earnings, as measured by R^2, has been declining throughout the 1977–96 period: from R^2s of 6–12 per cent in the first ten years of the sample to R^2s of 4–8 per cent in the last ten years.[3] A regression of the annual R^2s in panel A on a Time variable indicates (panel B) that the decrease is statistically significant (the estimated Time coefficient is -0.002, $t = -2.97$).

A different perspective on the informativeness of earnings is provided by the combined earnings response coefficient (ERC), defined as the sum of the slope coefficients of the level and change of earnings ($\alpha_1 + \alpha_2$ in regression (1)). This measure reflects the average change in the stock price associated with a dollar change in earnings. A low slope coefficient suggests that reported earnings are not particularly informative to investors, perhaps because they are perceived as transitory or subject to managerial manipulation. In contrast, a high slope coefficient indicates that a large stock price change is associated with reported earnings, reflecting investors' belief that earnings are largely permanent. It has been shown (e.g. Lev, 1989) that the estimated slope coefficient is a function of the precision of earnings. The estimated slope coefficients (ERCs) in Table 1 (fourth column from left) have been decreasing over 1977–96, from a range of 0.75–0.90 in the first five years of the sample, to 0.60–0.80 in the last five years. A regression of the yearly ERCs on Time (panel B) confirms that the ERC's decline is statistically significant (the estimated coefficient of Time for the total sample is -0.011, $t = -3.04$). The evidence on the declining slope coefficients of earnings complements the inferences based on declining R^2s. While the declining R^2s in Table 1 might be driven by an increase in the relative importance of nonaccounting information, with no change in the informativeness of earnings on a stand-alone basis, the declining slope coefficients indicate a deterioration in the value relevance of earnings to investors, irrespective of the effects of other information sources.

To assess whether the documented weakening of the returns-earnings association is due to the addition of new firms to the Compustat database (and hence to our sample), we replicated the analysis with a 'constant sample'

Baruch Lev and Paul Zarowin

Table 1. The Association Between Earnings and Stock Returns: Estimates from Yearly Cross-sectional Regressions of Annual Stock Returns on the Level and Change of Reported Earnings

Panel A: Equation (1): $R_{it} = \alpha_0 + \alpha_1 E_{it} + \alpha_2 \Delta E_{it} + e_{it}$

Year	Total Sample[a]			Constant Sample[a]	
	Number of observations	R^2	ERC	R^2	ERC
1978	3689	0.115	0.907	0.167	1.689
1979	3851	0.072	0.865	0.114	1.368
1980	4141	0.059	0.768	0.092	1.367
1981	4347	0.119	0.909	0.173	1.648
1982	4822	0.066	0.755	0.099	1.190
1983	4751	0.053	0.711	0.070	0.939
1984	5074	0.111	0.753	0.245	1.177
1985	5057	0.109	0.701	0.159	0.936
1986	5048	0.076	0.633	0.169	1.067
1987	5318	0.069	0.646	0.107	0.988
1988	5350	0.074	0.575	0.079	0.609
1989	5206	0.082	0.657	0.117	0.872
1990	5162	0.070	0.537	0.135	0.788
1991	5007	0.061	0.663	0.104	0.851
1992	5245	0.061	0.635	0.062	0.534
1993	5501	0.050	0.719	0.064	0.717
1994	6532	0.064	0.671	0.098	0.826
1995	6791	0.056	0.826	0.124	1.081
1996	6593	0.037	0.610	0.031	0.418

Panel B: Time regressions: $R_t^2 = a + b(\text{Time}_t) + c_t;$ $t = 1978 - 96$. $\text{ERC}_t = a + b(\text{Time}_t) + c_t;$ $t = 1978 - 96$

(t-value in parentheses)

	a	b	R^2
Total sample			
R^2	0.285	−0.002	0.30
	(4.00)	(−2.97)	
ERC	1.688	−0.011	0.31
	(5.25)	(−3.04)	
Constant sample			
R^2	0.470	−0.004	0.16
	(2.80)	(−2.11)	
ERC	5.353	−0.050	0.64
	(7.08)	(−5.76)	

Note: [a] The total sample includes all firms with the required data on Compustat's Current and Research Files. The constant sample includes about 1300 companies with the required data for the 20-year sample period, 1977–96.

Variable definitions for panel A: R_{it} is the annual stock return of firm i in fiscal year t, E_{it} and ΔE_{it} are the level and change of annual earnings of firm i in fiscal year t, and ERC_t is the combined slope coefficients or 'earnings response coefficient', the sum of the estimated regression coefficients of and E_{it} and ΔE_{it}. Both E_{it} and ΔE_{it} are scaled by market value of equity at the beginning of t.

Variable definitions for panel B: R_t^2 and ERC are the estimated coefficients of determination (adjusted R^2) and earnings response coefficients (ERC), presented in panel A, and Time_t is a time year variable, 1978–96.

of 1300 firms that operated throughout the sample period. This sample is clearly subject to a survivorship bias, while the total sample that includes firms from the Compustat Research File (i.e. deleted, bankrupt, or merged companies) is not subject to such a bias. The estimates reported in the right two columns of Table 1 indicate that the declining returns-earnings association is not the result of new firms joining the sample; both the R^2s and slope coefficients of the constant sample have been decreasing over time. The regressions on Time, reported in panel B, indicate that the decreases in R^2 and ERCs of the constant sample are even more pronounced than those of the total sample.

To summarize, our findings indicate that the cross-sectional association between stock returns and reported earnings, our measure of the usefulness of earnings to investors, has declined over the past twenty years. Our measure is not sensitive to changes over time in the quality of analysts' earnings forecasts because we do not measure the reaction to an earnings announcement, which is determined in part by the extent of earnings surprise. Rather, our analysis reflects the consistency between the information conveyed by earnings and that which affected investors' decisions during the entire year.

1.2. The Cash Flows–Returns Relation

Cash flows are often claimed to be more informative than earnings because they are less subject to managerial manipulation than accrual earnings, and because they are less affected by questionable accounting rules, such as those that require the expensing of investments in intangibles. To probe this claim we estimate the following cross-sectional regression for each sample year (1977–96):

$$R_{it} = \beta_0 + \beta_1 CF_{it} + \beta_2 \Delta CF_{it} + \beta_3 ACC_{it} + \beta_4 \Delta ACC_{it} + e_{it}, \quad (2)$$

where R_{it} is the firm i's stock return for fiscal year t, CF_{it} and ΔCF_{it} are the cash flow from operations and the yearly change in cash flow from operations, respectively.

ACC_{it} and ΔACC_{it} are the annual reported accruals and the change in annual accruals, where accruals equal the difference between reported earnings and cash flow from operations.

The four independent variables in (2) are scaled by the beginning-of-year market value of equity. Regression (2) thus estimates the association between annual stock returns, on the one hand, and operating cash flows plus accounting accruals (the difference between earnings and cash flows), on the other hand. Table 2 reports yearly coefficient estimates of this regression.

Our results indicate that the association between operating cash flows (plus accruals) and stock returns, as measured by R^2, is not appreciably stronger than the association between earnings and returns (R^2s in Table 19.1). As to the

Baruch Lev and Paul Zarowin

Table 2. The Association Between Cash Flows and Stock Returns: Estimates from Yearly Cross-sectional Regressions of Annual Stock Returns on Operating Cash Flows + Accruals

Panel A: Equation (2): $R_{it} = \beta_0 + \beta_1 CF_{it} + \beta_2 \Delta CF_{it} + \beta_3 ACC_{it} + \beta_4 \Delta ACC_{it} + e_{it}$

		Total Sample			Constant Sample	
Year[a]	Number of observations	R^2	ERC		R^2	ERC
1979	3276	0.074	0.750		0.074	0.772
1980	3432	0.052	0.574		0.065	0.797
1981	3571	0.124	0.853		0.187	1.857
1982	3945	0.059	0.560		0.091	1.112
1983	3948	0.041	0.536		0.068	0.869
1984	4169	0.111	0.679		0.240	1.169
1985	4163	0.092	0.573		0.146	0.918
1986	4098	0.063	0.515		0.122	0.939
1987	4361	0.052	0.518		0.114	0.916
1988	4361	0.064	0.496		0.110	0.447
1989	4232	0.078	0.642		0.134	1.014
1990	4179	0.058	0.472		0.124	0.823
1991	4097	0.042	0.467		0.054	0.434
1992	4321	0.052	0.548		0.057	0.535
1993	4543	0.048	0.666		0.090	0.991
1994	4953	0.071	0.685		0.136	0.928
1995	5142	0.051	0.704		0.163	0.949
1996	4953	0.036	0.416		0.029	0.288

Panel B: Time regressions: $R_t^2 = a + b(Time_t) + c_t$; $t=1979-96$. $CFRC_t = a + b(Time_t) + c_t$; $t=1979-96$
(t-value in parentheses)

	a	b	R^2
Total sample			
R^2	0.242	−0.002	0.16
	(2.77)	(−2.04)	
CFRC	1.159	−0.006	0.04
	(2.62)	(−1.28)	
Constant sample			
R^2	0.241	−0.001	0.00
	(1.13)	(−0.61)	
CFRC	3.424	−0.029	0.15
	(2.72)	(−2.03)	

Note: [a] The time series for cash flows starts with 1979 since the number of observations for 1977 (required for the cash flow change of 1978) was unusually low. The total sample includes all firms with the required data on Compustat's Current and Research Files. The constant sample includes about 1000 companies with the required data on Compustat for the 19-year sample period (1978–96).

Variable definitions for panel A: R_{it} is the annual stock return of firm i in fiscal year t, CF_{it} and ΔCF_{it} are the level and change of cash flows from operations of firm i in fiscal year t, and ACC_{it} and ΔACC_{it} is the level and change of accruals (earnings minus cash flows from operations) of firm i in fiscal year t. CF_{it}, ΔCF_{it}, ACC_{it}, and ΔACC_{it} are the scaled by market value of equity at the beginning of t. CFRC is the combined slope coefficients of the cash flow variables; $\beta_1 + \beta_2$ in (2).

Variable definitions for panel B: R_t^2 and $CFRC_t$ are the derived from panel A. $Time_t$ is a time year variable, 1979–96.

pattern of temporal association, the R^2s of both the total and constant samples in Table 2 decrease over the period examined, although only the former is statistically significant at the 0.05 level (see the Time coefficients in panel B of Table 2).

1.3. From Stock Returns to Prices

Following Ohlson (1995), it has become popular in accounting research to examine the relevance of financial data by regressing stock prices on earnings plus book value:

$$P_{it} = \alpha_0 + \alpha_1 E_{it} + \alpha_2 BV_{it} + e_{it}, \quad t = 1977\text{–}96, \tag{3}$$

where P_{it} is the share price of firm i at end of fiscal year t, E_{it} the earnings per share of firm i during year t, BV_{it} the book value (equity) per share of firm i at end of t, and e_{it} the other value-relevant information of firm i for year t, independent of earnings and book value.

Table 3. The Association Between Stock Prices and Book Values + Earnings Estimates from Yearly Cross-Sectional Regressions of Stock Prices on Earnings + Book Values

Panel A: Equation (3): $P_{it} = \alpha_0 + \alpha_1 E_{it} + \alpha_2 BV_{it} + e_{it}$

Year	R^2	Year	R^2
1977	0.923	1987	0.993
1978	0.932	1988	0.837
1979	0.796	1989	0.525
1980	0.866	1990	0.538
1981	0.867	1991	0.780
1982	0.867	1992	0.469
1983	0.899	1993	0.546
1984	0.832	1994	0.558
1985	0.887	1995	0.560
1986	0.874	1996	0.618

Panel B: Time regressions: $R_t^2 = a + b(\text{Time}_t) + c_t;\ t = 1979\text{–}96$
(*t-value in parentheses*)

Total sample	a	b	R^2
R^2	2.649	−0.022	0.57
	(7.09)	(−5.07)	

P_{it}, E_{it}, and BV_{it} are the share price at the end of fiscal year t, earnings per share, and book value per share, respectively, of firm i in fiscal year t. The sample includes all firms with the required data on Compustat's Current and Research Files, an average of 5500 firms per year.
   R^2 is the adjusted R^2 from panel A. Time$_t$ is a year variable, 1977–96.

As indicated in Table 3, the association between stock prices and earnings + book value, as measured by R^2, decreased during 1977–96, from R^2 levels of 0.90 in the late 1970s, to 0.80 in the 1980s, and to 0.50–0.60 in the 1990s. A regression of the yearly R^2s on a Time variable (panel B) yields a negative and statistically significant Time coefficient (-0.022, $t = -5.07$). The estimates reported in Table 3 pertain to the total sample. We obtained similar results for the constant sample (1130 firms per year): the estimated coefficient of Time from a regression of annual R^2 on Time is: -0.016 ($t = -4.04$). This finding of decreasing value relevance of earnings + book value is consistent with our previous results derived from the returns-earnings and returns-cash flow relationships.

---

2. Business Change and the Deterioration of Financial Statement Usefulness

We contend that the increasing rate of change experienced by business enterprises, coupled with biased and delayed recognition of change by the accounting system, is the major reason for the documented decline in the usefulness of financial information. Empirical support for this contention is provided in this section. We first document the increasing rate of change affecting business enterprises and then explore the implications of business change for the usefulness of accounting information.

2.1. Measuring Business Change

While surveys of executives, investors, and policymakers generally support a perception that the business environment is changing at an ever-increasing rate (e.g. Deloitte and Touche, 1995), there is little empirical support for this view. We document the pattern of business change for our sample companies by ranking them on two indicators of value: book value of equity at fiscal year-end and market value of equity at year-end. We then classify the sample firms for each year and value indicator into ten equal-sized portfolios based on the rank of book value or market value.

We measure the rate of business change by the frequency and magnitude of portfolio switches, namely, firms moving over time from one value portfolio to another. Specifically, we measure firm j's 'absolute rank change' by its movement across portfolios from year t-1 to year t. For example, if firm j is in book value portfolio 1 in 1977 and moved to portfolio 4 in 1978, its rank change

Table 4. The Increasing Rate of Business Change: Mean Absolute Values of Yearly Rank Changes (MARC) Experienced by Firms Classified into Ten Portfolios by Market and Book Values

Panel A: Yearly measures of change (MARC)

Market Value Portfolios				Book Value Portfolios	
Year	MARC Measure	Year	MARC Measure	Year	MARC Measure
—	—	1978	0.404	1978	0.179
—	—	1979	0.384	1979	0.181
—	—	1980	0.429	1980	0.240
—	—	1981	0.545	1981	0.276
—	—	1982	0.568	1982	0.294
1964	0.309	1983	0.624	1983	0.374
1965	0.308	1984	0.583	1984	0.317
1966	0.418	1985	0.550	1985	0.382
1967	0.416	1986	0.588	1986	0.410
1968	0.487	1987	0.539	1987	0.390
1969	0.434	1988	0.516	1988	0.324
1970	0.499	1989	0.500	1989	0.237
1971	0.443	1990	0.565	1990	0.309
1972	0.432	1991	0.528	1991	0.387
1973	1.113	1992	0.587	1992	0.409
1974	0.547	1993	0.584	1993	0.487
1975	0.490	1994	0.517	1994	0.401
1976	0.422	1995	0.526	1995	0.417
1977	0.385	—	—	1996	0.536

Panel B: Time regressions

Regression: $MARC(Indicator)_t = a + b(Time_t) + c_t$; $t = 1964\text{–}96$ (t-values in parentheses)

Dependent Variable	a	b	R^2
MARC (Market value), 1964–95	0.0026 (0.03)	0.0062 (5.33)	0.48
MARC (Market value), 1978–95	−0.0693 (−0.31)	0.0069 (2.63)	0.25
MARC (Book value), 1978–96	−0.8357 (−4.54)	0.0138 (6.44)	0.69

Sample firms are classified in each year into ten portfolios according to their market value of equity (MV) and alternatively by their book value of equity (BV). MARC indicates the average frequency of firms switching value portfolios from the past year to the current year, as well as the number of portfolios switched (i.e. magnitude of switch) by each firm. $MARC_t = \{\Sigma |DEC_{it} - DEC_{i,t-1}|\}/N_t$, where DEC_{it} and $DEC_{i,t-1}$ = decile rank (of book value or market value) for firm i in years t and $t-1$, N_t = number of firms in year t, and Σ means summation over all firms in t. The observations for the market value portfolios are all firms on the CRSP Daily File with share price and number of shares at the end of years t and $t-1$, an average of 4000 firms per year. The observations for the book value portfolios are all firms on Compustat's Current and Research Files with book value of equity at end of years t and $t-1$, an average of 5800 firms per year.

MARC$_t$ is the yearly mean absolute rank change in panel A. Time$_t$ is a year variable.

measure is 3. For each year and value indicator, we calculate a yearly 'mean absolute rank change' (MARC) that reflects the aggregate portfolio switches experienced by all the sample firms in that year. Our change measure will be low (zero at the limit) when portfolio membership is stable, whereas when firms bounce a lot from year to year across portfolios, the change measure will be high.

Table 4 presents the yearly MARC measures for the sample companies. Data for market value rankings are derived from the CRSP database (1963–95) and those for book value rankings are derived from Compustat (1977–96). The generally increasing MARC measures in panel A for both market and book value classifications indicate that the frequency of firms switching across portfolio rankings has increased over the past 20–30 years. For market value rankings, the change measures increase from 0.3–0.4 in the 1960s to 0.5–0.6 in the 1990s. For book value rankings, the change measures increase almost monotonically from 0.2–0.3 in the late 1970s and early 1980s to 0.4–0.5 in the 1990s.

We argue that the increasing rate of business change over the past two or three decades and the deficient accounting treatment of change have contributed to the documented decline in the usefulness of financial information. Essentially, while the accounting system is primarily based on the reporting of discrete, transaction-based events, such as sales, purchases, and investments, the impact of change on business enterprises is rarely triggered by specific transactions. Change, internally (e.g. product development) or externally (e.g. deregulation) driven, often affects enterprise value long before revenue or expense transactions warrant an accounting record. Investors generally react to the impact of change on business enterprises in real time, hence the increasing disconnection between market and accounting values.

Business change is primarily driven by increased competition and innovation. In contrast to the delayed reaction of the reporting system to deregulation, when change is driven by competition and innovation, the accounting system front loads the costs and delays the recognition of benefits. For example, restructuring costs, such as those for employee training, production reengineering, or organizational redesign, are immediately expensed, while the benefits of restructuring, in the form of lower production costs and improved customer service, are recognized in later periods. Consequently, during restructuring, the financial statements reflect the cost of restructuring, but not its benefits, and are therefore largely disconnected from market values that reflect the expected benefits along with the costs. Similarly, the immediate expensing of investment in innovation (e.g. R&D)—the major change-driver in technology and science-based companies—is both biased and inconsistent. Costs of innovation are recognized up front, while benefits are recorded in subsequent periods. To complicate things further, the accounting for intangibles is beset by inconsistencies. For example, a firm that develops an instrument for internal use will expense all development costs, but if the firm buys a similar instrument, it will be capitalized.

2.2. *Change and the Value Relevance of Earnings*

Our firm-specific change measure (the 'absolute rank change') is based on the frequency and extent of over time movement of firms among portfolios formed by ranking on book value and market value of equity. To link this change measure to the documented temporal decrease in the informativeness of earnings, we first compute for each sample firm the across time its absolute rank change, reflecting the number of times the firm switched book value portfolios during 1977–96, as well as the extent of such switches. To standardize the firm-specific measure, we scale it by the number of years the firm existed in the sample. For example, if firm j was in the top book value portfolio during 1977–83, the second (next to top) portfolio in 1984–91, and the fifth portfolio from 1992 to 1996, its rank change indicator is 0.20 (one point for the single rank switch in 1984 plus three points for the three-rank switch—from portfolio 2 to 5—in 1992, divided by the twenty years of the firm in the sample).

We classify the sample firms into two groups: stable and changing companies. The first group includes the No Change firms (about 1000), namely, those that remained in the same portfolio during the entire sample period (1977–96). The second group—the Change firms—includes the remaining sample (ranging from 3000 in the early sample years to 5500 in the mid-1990s). Alternatively, we classify firms into Low Change firms with a firm-specific 'absolute rank' change indicators (including, of course, the No Change firms) and High Change—the remaining sample.

Next, we examine the yearly cross-sectional returns-earnings regression (1) separately for the stable and changing firms. If change decreases the informativeness of earnings, the regression's R^2 and combined slope coefficients (ERC) should be larger for stable firms (a stronger returns-earnings association) than for changing ones. Furthermore, given our evidence that the rate of change of business enterprises increased during the past twenty years, that increase clearly affected the changing firms more than stable ones. Thus, we predict that the rate of decrease of R^2 and ERC over 1977–96 should be higher for changing firms than for stable ones. Results in Table 5 support both expectations.

Panel A of Table 5 reports yearly estimates of R^2s and combined slope coefficients for the four change classifications of firms, and panel B reports means and medians of the nineteen yearly estimates. The data corroborate our first expectation: both the means and medians of the yearly R^2 and ERC are larger for No Change firms than for Change firms (e.g. mean R^2 of

Baruch Lev and Paul Zarowin

Table 5. Business Change and Earnings Informativeness: Estimates from Annual Regressions of Stock Returns on the Level and Change of Annual Earnings for Firms Classified by the Rate of Business Change

Panel A: Yearly estimates of regression (1): Returns on earnings

	No Change		Change		Low Change		High Change	
Year	R^2	ERC	R^2	ERC	R^2	ERC	R^2	ERC
1978	0.11	1.28	0.12	1.17	0.13	1.36	0.12	1.15
1979	0.16	1.96	0.09	1.02	0.15	1.85	0.09	1.01
1980	0.05	0.79	0.08	1.07	0.06	0.90	0.09	1.09
1981	0.26	1.69	0.11	1.03	0.28	1.81	0.10	1.00
1982	0.08	1.05	0.09	1.12	0.10	1.20	0.09	1.10
1983	0.09	1.11	0.07	1.01	0.07	1.02	0.07	1.03
1984	0.23	0.77	0.16	1.13	0.23	0.91	0.15	1.10
1985	0.13	0.93	0.14	1.08	0.17	1.05	0.14	1.07
1986	0.12	1.23	0.12	1.04	0.15	1.24	0.11	1.03
1987	0.03	0.65	0.07	0.87	0.04	0.75	0.07	0.86
1988	0.08	1.05	0.12	0.94	0.07	0.91	0.12	0.94
1989	0.14	1.14	0.10	0.96	0.11	1.23	0.10	0.96
1990	0.12	0.83	0.10	0.89	0.10	0.96	0.10	0.89
1991	0.08	0.99	0.09	0.96	0.11	1.11	0.09	0.95
1992	0.16	1.53	0.09	0.95	0.15	1.58	0.09	0.93
1993	0.12	1.68	0.08	1.06	0.11	1.49	0.08	1.07
1994	0.22	1.80	0.10	1.05	0.17	1.47	0.10	1.06
1995	0.10	1.22	0.06	1.01	0.12	1.43	0.06	1.00
1996	0.07	1.41	0.06	0.96	0.06	1.27	0.06	0.96

Panel B: Means and medians of annual R^2 and ERC by change group (1977–96)

	R^2		ERC	
Change Group	Mean	Median	Mean	Median
No change	0.124	0.116	1.22	1.14
vs				
Change	0.097	0.095	1.02	1.02
Significance of difference	$p = 0.09$		$p = 0.03$	
Low change	0.124	0.114	1.24	1.23
vs				
High change	0.096	0.093	1.01	1.02
Significance of difference	$p = 0.06$		$p = 0.01$	

Panel C: Regressions of yearly R^2 and ERC (from panel A) on Time (t-values in parentheses)

Dependent Variable	Intercept	Time	R^2
No change			
R^2	0.204	−0.001	0.00
	(0.88)	(−0.35)	
ERC	0.514	0.008	0.00
	(0.37)	(0.50)	
Change			
R^2	0.256	−0.002	0.11
	(2.86)	(−1.78)	

Table 5. Continued

Dependent Variable	Intercept	Time	R^2
ERC	1.636	−0.007	0.21
	(6.31)	(−2.39)	
Low change			
R^2	0.330	−0.002	0.00
	(1.49)	(−0.93)	
ERC	1.180	0.001	0.00
	(1.02)	(0.05)	
High change			
R^2	0.246	−0.002	0.12
	(3.01)	(−1.84)	
ERC	1.585	−0.007	0.18
	(6.14)	(−2.23)	

Firms classified as *No change* did not switch book value ranking during 1977–96, while *Change* firms are the rest of the sample. Firms classified as *Low change* have an 'absolute rank change' indicator (defined in Section 2.2) ≤ 0.10, while *High change* firms are the rest of the sample. ERC is the combined slope coefficients or 'earnings response coefficient', namely, the sum of the estimated regression coefficients of level and change of earnings. The sample includes all firms with the required data on Compustat's Current and Research Files, an average of 4000 and 700 firms per year for the *Change* and *No change* groups, respectively, and an average of 3700 and 1000 firms per year for the *High change* and *Low change* groups, respectively.

0.124 vs 0.097 and mean ERC of 1.22 vs 1.02). Similarly, the R^2 and ERCs of the Low Change firms are larger than the association measures of the High Change firms. To determine the statistical significance of the difference in means of change groups we regressed the R^2 and ERCs of the combined change and No Change groups (and also of the combined Low and High Change groups), that is, thirty-eight observations in each regression, on a 0–1 dummy variable reflecting membership in a change group. The significance levels of the dummy variables, all lower than 0.10, are reported in panel B of Table 5. Thus, the rate of business change is negatively associated with the informativeness of earnings, as measured by the extent of the returns-earnings association.

Panel C of Table 5 presents estimates from regressions of the yearly R^2 and ERCs (reported in panel A) on a Time variable. The data confirm our second expectation that the temporal decline in the returns-earnings association is more pronounced for changing than for stable enterprises. The four coefficients of Time in the R^2 and ERC regressions for both the No Change and the Low Change groups are not statistically significant (see t-values in parentheses), and the R^2s of those four regressions equal zero, indicating essentially no deterioration over time in the returns-earnings association of stable companies. In contrast, the four Time coefficients of both the Change and High Change groups are all negative and statistically significant, and the four R^2s of these

Time regressions range between 0.11 and 0.21, indicating that the association between returns and earnings of changing firms has declined over the past twenty years. The significance levels of the differences in Time coefficients between the No Change and Change groups (and the Low and High Change groups) were determined by running a regression on the combined observations of the two groups with a dummy variable for group membership. P-levels of the dummy variable are: R^2 regression (No Change vs Change) $= 0.09$, ERC regression (No Change vs Change) $= 0.03$, R^2 (Low vs High Change) $= 0.06$, and ERC (Low vs High Change) $= 0.01$.

To summarize, we have argued that the increasing rate of business change coupled with the ineffectiveness of the accounting system in reflecting the consequences of change contributed significantly to the temporal decline in the value relevance of accounting information. We have empirically established this link by providing evidence that the rate of change experienced by business enterprises increased over the period 1977–96, and that the informativeness of earnings is negatively related to the rate of business change.

3. Intangibles, Innovation, and Change

Intangible investments, R&D in particular, are generally considered as the major driver of business change, creating new products, franchises, and improved production processes. However, while some intangible investments trigger change, others are just aimed at preserving the status quo. Thus, applied research, defined as 'spending aimed at learning more about the technology process a firm is already using, or about a good that it is already producing' (Jovanovic and Nyarko, 1995), is generally intended to sustain an existing competitive position, not to change the firm's operations. In contrast, basic research, defined as 'spending directed towards processes not yet in use, or goods not yet produced' (Jovanovic and Nyarko, 1995) is clearly aimed at initiating change.[4] Given these disparate intentions and consequences of R&D, the level or intensity (R&D spending to sales) of R&D is not necessarily associated with change and the consequent loss of informativeness of financial data. From an accounting measurement perspective, too, the level of R&D expenditures does not necessarily affect the informativeness of earnings. Thus, if the rate of R&D spending is constant over time, reported earnings are invariant to the accounting treatment of R&D; earnings will be the same whether R&D is capitalized and amortized or immediately expensed.

To examine this conjecture, we split our sample period, 1976–95, into three subperiods and compute for each sample firm the average R&D intensity

(R&D to sales) in the 'recent period' (1989–95) relative to the average R&D intensity in the 'early period' (1976–83). Sample firms were then classified by the direction of change in R&D intensity into four categories: Low–Low firms, with R&D intensity of 0.01 or lower in both the early and recent periods; High–High firms, with R&D intensity exceeding 0.01 in both periods; Low–High firms, with R&D intensity below 0.01 in the early period and above 0.01 in the recent period; and High–Low firms, the converse of Low–High. We then reestimated the cross-sectional returns on earnings (level and change) regression (1) for each of the four groups of firms for every year, 1976–95. The average yearly regression estimates of R^2 and the combined slope coefficients (ERCs), over the early sample period (1976–83) and the recent period (1989–95), are reported in Table 6.

The main diagonal of Table 6 reports mean regression estimates for stable R&D companies: Low–Low and High–High. The mean R^2s of both groups decreased from the early (1976–83) to the recent (1989–95) period: from 0.137 to 0.099 for Low–Low, and from 0.156 to 0.126 for High–High companies. These decreases in average R^2s for both groups, however, are statistically insignificant (at the 0.05 level). The average ERCs of the Low–Low and High–High groups also decreased between the two periods: from 1.44 to 0.820 for Low–Low ($t = -6.28$) and from 1.94 to 1.14 ($t = -3.45$) for High–High. Consistent with the findings of other authors (e.g. Collins et al., 1997), the R^2s and ERCs of the High–High subsample-companies intensive in R&D are larger than those of the Low–Low companies, confirming our earlier contention that high yet stable R&D spending does not induce a weak earnings-returns relation. The lower-left panel of Table 6 presents results for Low–High companies, those characterized by an increasing rate of R&D expenditures. As indicated in the table, the median R&D intensity of these companies increased from 0.4 per cent during 1976–83 to 1.8 per cent in 1989–95. These firms experienced a sharp decline over the sample period in the returns-earnings R^2 from 0.233 to 0.126 ($t = -2.03$) and in the combined ERC from 2.17 to 1.06 ($t = -2.29$). In contrast, High–Low firms, whose R&D intensity decreased from a median of 1.6–0.3 per cent, experienced a borderline significant increase in the association between returns and earnings: the R^2 of these firms increased from 0.080 to 0.178 ($t = 1.54$, $p = 0.15$) and the ERC increased from 0.75 to 1.29 ($t = 1.61$, $p = 0.13$).

To complete the linkages between the declining usefulness of earnings and the rate of business change, which is partially driven by R&D increases, we analyse now the association between the rate of business change and the change in R&D expenditures. Specifically, we show that fast-changing firms experienced a larger increase in R&D-intensity than stable companies. Thus, for the No Change and Change groups, and for the Low Change and High Change groups, as previously analysed in Table 5, we examine the annual average

R&D intensity. We expect that the average R&D intensity of changing firms is higher than that of stable firms and, more important, that the rate of increase in R&D intensity of changing firms is higher than that of stable companies.

The data in Table 7 confirm both expectations. First, the mean R&D intensity (over the 1978–96 period) of the Change group is larger than the intensity of the No Change group (0.030 vs 0.015; $t = 5.2$; $p = 0.01$), and the mean R&D intensity of the High Change group is larger than that of the Low Change group (0.032 vs 0.013; $t = 6.3$, $p = 0.01$). To examine the second expectation, we regress for each of the four change groups the yearly mean R&D intensity of the group on Time. Results (presented in Table 7) indicate that the rate of increase in R&D intensity during 1978–96 was substantially larger for changing firms than for stable ones: The Time coefficients of the Change and High Change groups, 0.0021 and 0.0022, are 5–7 times larger than the Time coefficients of the No Change and Low Change groups, 0.0004 and 0.0003, respectively. To determine the significance of the differences in the estimated time coefficients, we regressed the mean R&D intensity on Time, combining the No Change and Change groups (and the Low and High Change groups),

Table 6. R&D Change and Earnings Informativeness Estimates from Returns-Earnings Regressions (1) for Firms Classified by the Direction of Change in their R&D Intensity from the Early Sample Period (1976–83) to the Recent Sample Period (1989–95). Arrows in Each Panel Indicate the Change in the Measure (R^2 or ERC) from the Early to the Recent Period

Recent Sample Period (1989–95)	Early Sample Period (1976–83)	
	Low R&D	High R&D
Low R&D		
MED R&D	$0.000 \rightarrow 0.000$	$0.016 \rightarrow 0.003$
Mean R^2	$0.137 \rightarrow 0.099$	$0.080 \rightarrow 0.178$
Mean ERC	$1.440 \rightarrow 0.820$	$0.750 \rightarrow 1.290$
#	1259	67
High R&D		
MED R&D	$0.004 \rightarrow 0.018$	$0.034 \rightarrow 0.044$
Mean R^2	$0.233 \rightarrow 0.126$	$0.156 \rightarrow 0.126$
Mean ERC	$2.170 \rightarrow 1.060$	$1.940 \rightarrow 1.140$
#	96	455

Low R&D are firms with an R&D intensity <0.01 (1% of sales) and High R&D firms are those with R&D intensity ≥ 0.01. MED R&D is the median R&D intensity (R&D over sales) in the early and recent periods of firms in the panel. Mean R^2 is the mean over 1976–83 and 1989–95 of adjusted R^2 of the yearly returns on earnings cross-sectional regression (1). Mean ERC is the mean of combined slope coefficients ($\alpha_1 + \alpha_2$ in (1)) over 1976–83 and 1989–95. # is the number of firms.

using a 0/1 dummy for group membership. Both differences in Time coefficients, between No Change vs Change and Low vs High Change, are significant
at the 0.01 level. Note also the large differences in R^2s in Table 7: the Time variable explains almost perfectly the temporal variation in R&D intensity for
changing firms (R^2: 0.92 and 0.91), while for stable companies, Time provides
only a partial explanation for the temporal variance in R&D intensity (R^2: 0.23
and 0.31).

To summarize, we have provided evidence supporting the following phenomena and relationships: (i) the rate of change experienced by US business
enterprises has increased over the past twenty years, (ii) the increasing rate of
business change is associated with a decline in the informativeness of earnings,
(iii) an increase in R&D intensity is associated with a decline in earnings informativeness, and (iv) an increase in the rate of business change is associated with an
increase in R&D intensity. This evidence, we believe, supports the view that the
documented decline in the usefulness of financial information was mainly
caused by the increasing pace of change affecting business enterprises and the
inadequacy of the accounting system in reflecting the consequences of change.
Among change-drivers, innovation, generally brought about by investment in
R&D, is an important factor in the declining usefulness of financial information. We next discuss two proposals for enhancing the usefulness of financial
reports.

4. Improving the Usefulness of Financial Information

We discuss two proposals aimed at enhancing the usefulness of financial information. The first—capitalization of intangibles—extends a practice currently used in
limited circumstances, while the second, a systematic restatement of financial
reports, calls for a substantial modification of current reporting practices.

4.1. The Capitalization of Intangible Investments

We believe that the almost universal expensing of intangible investments in the
United States is inconsistent with the FASB's conceptual framework (Statement
of Financial Accounting Concepts No. 6) and with empirical evidence. The
conceptual framework defines an asset as: 'probable future economic benefit

Table 7. Firms' Rate of Change and their R&D Intensity Estimates from Regressions of Yearly Average R&D Intensity on Time for Firms Grouped by Rate of Business Change (*t*-values in parentheses). Regression: Mean R&D intensity$_t = a + b(\text{Time}_t) + e_t$, $t = $ 1978–96

| Change Group | Mean R&D Intensity | Coefficient Estimates | | |
		a	b	R^2
No Change	0.015	−0.0174	0.0004	0.23
vs		(−1.38)	(2.55)	
Change	0.030	−0.1490	0.0021	0.92
		(−12.15)	(14.61)	
Low Change	0.013	−0.0138	0.0003	0.31
vs		(−1.57)	(3.03)	
High Change	0.032	−0.1567	0.0022	0.91
		(−11.37)	(13.71)	

The classification of firms into the four change groups is described in Section 2. The sample includes all firms with the required data on Compustat's Current and Research Files, an average of 4000 and 700 firms per year for the *Change* and *No change* groups, respectively, and an average of 3700 and 1000 firms per year for the *High change* and *Low change* groups, respectively. The sample is the same as that used for Table 5.

obtained or controlled by a particular entity as a result of past transactions or events . . . assets . . . may be intangible, and although not exchangeable they may be usable by the entity in producing or distributing other goods or services. . . . anything that is commonly used to produce goods or services, whether tangible or intangible and whether or not it has a market price or is otherwise exchangeable, also has future economic benefit' (FASB, 1985*b*, paras 25, 26, 173). Surely, the recognition of intangible investments with attributable future benefits as assets is within the boundaries of GAAP. Objections to capitalization center on the uncertainty associated with the benefits of intangibles: 'The uncertainty (e.g. about R&D) is not about the intent to increase future economic benefits but about whether and, if so, to what extent they succeeded [sic] in doing so' (FASB, 1985*b*, para. 175).

Given the uncertainty concerns, it makes sense to recognize intangible investments as assets when the uncertainty about benefits is considerably resolved. It is well known that as projects under development advance, from formulation of the initial idea through increasingly demanding feasibility tests (e.g. alpha and beta tests) to the final product, the uncertainty of commercial success continually decreases. Accordingly, a reasonable balance between relevance and reliability of information would suggest the capitalization of intangible investment when the project successfully passes a significant technological feasibility test, such as a working model for software or a clinical test for a drug.

Accordingly, we propose the capitalization of all intangible investments with attributable benefits that have passed certain prespecified technological feasibility tests. We depart from the software capitalization standard (SFAS No. 86) by proposing that once capitalization commences (post feasibility test), all the project related, previously expensed R&D should also be capitalized. Given that the uncertainty about the project's viability has been substantially reduced, we see no reason for a different accounting treatment of pre- and post feasibility R&D.

Note that our capitalization proposal, which is conditioned on the achievement of technological feasibility, differs substantially from a mechanical capitalization (accumulation) of all past expenditures on intangibles, which can easily be replicated by investors from successive income statements. The proposed capitalization allows management to convey important inside information about the progress and success of the development program. Indiscriminate capitalization of all past R&D expenditures does not provide such information.

How will the reporting deficiencies discussed in previous sections be alleviated by the proposed capitalization of intangibles? First, such capitalization will improve the periodic matching of costs and benefits, particularly for firms with high growth rates of intangible investment. This will lead to reported earnings that more meaningfully reflect enterprise performance than currently measured earnings. Second, the capitalized intangibles will be reported on corporate balance sheets, placing intangible assets on a common footing with tangible assets. The amortization and write-offs of these assets will convey valuable information about managers' assessment of the expected benefits of intangibles.[5]

On the downside, capitalization of intangibles obviously increases the possibilities of earnings management. However, in contrast to other means of earnings management, such as the early recognition of revenues or an exaggerated restructuring charge, intangibles' capitalization is clearly and separately disclosed in the financial reports, allowing skeptical investors to easily reverse the capitalization. Thus, at best, intangibles' capitalization is a vehicle for managers to share with investors information about the progress and success of innovation-producing activities. At worst, capitalization can be reversed, thereby returning the financial reports to their current (full expensing) status.

4.2. Restated Financial Reports

Change, we have argued, and the inadequacies of its reflection by the current accounting system are mainly responsible for the deterioration in the usefulness of financial information. However, the consequences of change (e.g. the benefits of a corporate reorganization or of a significant drug development) are generally uncertain, and it is this uncertainty that is often invoked to justify the immediate expensing of change-related investments. The capitalization of technologically feasible intangible investments proposed above provides a reasonable balance between relevance and reliability of financial information, but this procedure is restricted to products under development. Other change-drivers, such as corporate reorganization or industry deregulation, cannot be accounted for by the proposed capitalization. We accordingly propose a new accounting procedure—the systematic restatement of financial reports to accommodate those change-drivers and other uncertainties affecting the quality of financial information.

Consider, for example, a corporate restructuring where a significant investment is made in efficiency-enhancing and revenue-generating mechanisms, such as extensive employee training, reorganization of divisions and production lines, and acquisition of technology and know-how (e.g. in-process R&D). Current accounting rules require the immediate expensing of such outlays (e.g. restructuring charges), given the uncertainty of their benefits. Such an expensing, however, understates current earnings and book values and overstates subsequent earnings, if the planned efficiencies materialize. We propose that as the expected consequences of the reorganization materialize, both the current and previous financial statements will be restated to reflect the capitalization of the restructuring charges (i.e. reversing their previous expensing) and the amortization of the capitalized amount over the expected duration of benefits. Such a restatement will correct both the understatement of earnings in the restructuring period and the overstatement of earnings in subsequent periods.

Consider once more the example of the telecommunications deregulation which, beginning in the late 1980s, opened the local telephone markets to competition. The regional telephone companies belatedly reacted to their loss of monopoly and to the new regulatory system that no longer assured asset values by writing off $26 billion of assets during 1994–95. Thus, throughout the early 1990s the earnings and book values of the telephone companies were overstated (reflecting inflated asset values), while the 1994–95 earnings were understated, given the massive write-offs. By our proposal, upon the write-off in 1995, a telephone company would have restated its 1990–94 financial reports to reflect a gradual write-off of asset values according to the realized impact of competition and consequent loss of asset values that has been experienced during that period. Thus, the 1995 report would be spared the nonrecurring massive loss, which in most cases is ignored by investors anyway, and the preceding reports would reflect the actual consequences of deregulation.

The logic underlying the proposed restatements is that while financial statements purportedly report the consequences of past events, they are crucially dependent on assumptions about future outcomes (e.g. accounts receivable that will default, contingencies that will materialize, or the actual depreciation pattern of assets). As future events evolve and uncertainty is resolved, our understanding of the past is increasingly improved. Shortly after quarter-end, for example, our knowledge about the quarterly results is fuzzy, whereas two years, say, after quarter-end our uncertainty about the quarterly results is greatly reduced.[6] Similarly, at launch, the expensing of R&D for a new drug may seem reasonable, yet when the drug receives FDA approval the past expensing is clearly inappropriate. Why then not restate past reports as uncertainty is resolved and one can better measure the past performance of the firm?

We believe the systematic restatement of past reports is essential, given the contextual role of financial information (Finger et al., 1996). Financial reports not only convey new information to investors, they also provide a rich history or context for interpreting current information and events. In fact, evidence presented in this and other studies indicates a deterioration in the amount of new information (timeliness) conveyed by key financial statement items, leaving the contextual function of financial reports to play an increasing role in investors' decisions.

Although not extensively researched, some evidence indicates the importance of the contextual role of accounting. For example, Barth et al. (1999) report that investors' reaction to an earnings surprise is conditioned on the sequence and signs of past surprises. Thus, an earnings increase following past increases is associated with a larger stock price change than an earnings increase following earnings decreases. Similarly, Lev et al. (1998) report that investors' reaction to an FDA drug approval depends, among other things, on the past operating success of the developing company. The evidence presented above that the returns-earnings R^2s of firms with the full 20-year history are substantially larger than the R^2s of firms with shorter historical records (Tables 1 and 2) is also consistent with a contextual role of financial information. Finally, the findings of Petroni et al. (1997) that revisions of reserve estimates of insurance companies extending as far back as ten years are significantly associated with investors' reaction to current information is consistent with both the contextual role of financial data and the value relevance of restatements.

If historical financial data affect the interpretation of new signals, then a continuous improvement of such history, in the form of a better matching of revenues with costs achieved by the proposed restatement of past reports, should improve investors' decisions. The restated data, reflecting the continuous resolution of uncertainty, will portray more realistic patterns of earnings, growth, and profitability (e.g. ROE) than the originally reported data.

A natural reaction to the proposed restatement is that the revised information will no longer be relevant to decision makers and might even confuse them by presenting several different earnings numbers pertaining to a given accounting period. We doubt the validity of these concerns. First, a restatement of past reports is currently a GAAP requirement in the case of acquisitions accounted for by the pooling method, without documented harm to investors. More importantly, and closer to our proposal, key macroeconomic variables, such as the gross domestic product (GDP) and the industrial production index, are routinely revised over several years after the initial estimates are released.[7] For example, the first estimate of quarterly GDP is released toward the end of the month following the quarter. This 'advance estimate' of GDP is based on judgmental assumptions and incomplete data on GDP components. The advance estimate of GDP is revised by the 'preliminary GDP estimate' which is released toward the end of the second month following the quarter. The 'final GDP estimate' for the quarter is released toward the end of the third month and is based on replacement of preliminary with comprehensive data and on changes in definitions and estimations. Following the final GDP estimate, the Bureau of Economic Analysis (BEA) schedules annual revisions of GDP, usually released in July, to improve the accuracy of GDP estimates as new information is obtained. The BEA also revises the entire history of the quarterly data series every five years in what is known as a benchmark revision.

Note the close resemblance of early estimates of macroeconomic data based on incomplete information to quarterly financial reports, which are similarly based on estimates and incomplete data. Regarding the concern with the usefulness of revised data and the confusion they can cause, a survey of the economic literature dealing with revisions of macroeconomic data (e.g. Mankiw and Shapiro, 1986; Diebold and Rudebusch, 1991) does not support such concerns. The evidence indicates that revisions are useful in conveying new information that cannot be forecasted by the early estimates.

5. Conclusions

We have documented in this study a systematic decline in the usefulness of financial information to investors over the past twenty years, as manifested by a weakening association between capital market values and key financial variables-earnings, cash flows, and book values. We have identified a major reason for the usefulness decline—the increasing rate and impact of business change and the inadequate accounting treatment of change and its consequences and linked change empirically to loss of informativeness of financial data. Of the various change-drivers, we have focused on intangible investments, thereby completing the linkage: intangibles → business change → loss of value relevance of financial information.

Notes

1. We assume that the major objective of financial reporting is the provision of decision-relevant information to investors, as stated in the FASB's Statement of Financial Accounting Concepts No. 1.
2. It is not change *per se* that distorts financial reporting, rather it is the increased uncertainty generally associated with change (e.g. uncertainty about the consequences of a substantial restructuring, product development, or deregulation). If the consequences of change were perfectly predictable, the accounting system would have no problem matching costs with revenues. The uncertainty associated with change provides the justification or excuse for the immediate expensing of practically all change-related outlays.
3. All R^2s reported in this study are adjusted R^2s.
4. The pharmaceutical industry provides an example of these two types of R&D. Basic research is aimed generally at developing New Molecular Entities, which are entirely new drugs capable of drastically changing the firm's product mix and competitive position. Applied pharmaceutical R&D, the development of 'me too' drugs, is aimed at modifying existing drugs or changing the route of administration, thereby essentially preserving the firm's competitive position.
5. Indeed, Aboody and Lev (1998) find that the amortization of capitalized software is negatively and significantly associated with stock returns. Write-offs were also found value relevant by Healy *et al.* (2002).
6. Ijiri (1989: ch. 7) elaborates on this important idea, that understanding the past requires improved information about the future, and quotes the British mathematician Raymond Smullyan: 'To know the past, one must first know the future'.
7. For example, on 31 July 1998, the Bureau of Economic Analysis of the US Department of Commerce announced that the seasonally adjusted estimate of real GDP growth for the second quarter of 1998 was an annualized 1.4%. In addition, the July press release contained revised estimates for the real GDP series (and components) from the first quarter of 1995 until the first quarter of 1998. The revision showed an increase in the estimated average year-over-year real GDP growth from 2.9% to 3.3% for the period from 1995 to 1997.

References

Aboody, D. and B. Lev (1998), 'The value relevance of intangibles: The case of software capitalization', *Journal of Accounting Research*, 36 (Supplement): 161–91.

Barth, M., J. Elliott, and M. Finn (1999), 'Market rewards associated with patterns of increasing earnings', *Journal of Accounting Research*, 37: 387–413.

Deloitte and Touche (1995), *Survey of American Business Leaders* (New York: Deloitte & Touche).

Diebold, F. and G. Rudebusch (1991), 'Forecasting output with the composite leasing index: A real-time analysis', *Journal of the American Statistical Association*, 86: 603–10.

Financial Accounting Standards Board (1985*b*), 'Statement of financial accounting concepts no. 6: Elements of financial statements', Stamford, Conn.: FASB.

Finger, C., B. Lev, and A. Rose (1996), 'The contextual role of financial reports', Working paper, New York University.

Healy, P., S. Myers, and C. D. Howe (2002), 'R&D accounting and the tradeoff between relevance and objectivity', 40(3): 677–710.

Ijiri, Y. (1989), 'Momentum accounting and triple-entry bookkeeping: Exploring the dynamic structure of accounting measurements', American Accounting Association, studies in accounting research, no. 31. Sarasota, Fla.: American Accounting Assn.

Jovanovic, B. and Y. Nyarko (1995), 'Research and productivity', Working paper, University of Pennsylvania.

Lev, B. (1989), 'On the usefulness of earnings and earnings research: Lessons and directions from two decades of empirical research', *Journal of Accounting Research* (supplement) 27: 153–92.

Lev, B. and T. Sougiannis (1996), 'The capitalization, amortization, and value relevance of R&D', *Journal of Accounting and Economics*, 21: 107–38.

——, S. Radhakrishnan, and C. Seethamraju (1998), 'FDA drug approvals and the formation of investors' Beliefs', Working paper, New York University.

Mankiw, G. and M. Shapiro (1986), 'News or noise: An analysis of GNP revisions', *Survey of Current Business*, May 20–25.

Ohlson, J. (1995), 'Earnings, book values and dividends in security valuation', *Contemporary Accounting Research*, 11: 661–87.

Petroni, K. and J. Anthony (1997), 'Accounting estimation error disclosures and firm valuation', *Journal of Accounting, Auditing and Finance*, 257–281.

Baruch Lev

1. Introduction

Investors, and often managers too, are deprived of intangibles-related information on essential business capabilities and performance characteristics.[1] Examples of important, yet not disclosed, performance indicators follow:

1. *The utilization of intellectual property.* Firms generally develop only a small fraction of the patents and know-how they possess into products or services, resulting in an underutilization of intellectual property. Effective managers license unused patents or develop know-how in collaboration with others. Information on the extent of the utilization of intellectual property— in the form of a breakdown of patents into three categories (under development, licensed, and in collaboration) as well as the volume of licensing revenues—provides an important indication of the effectiveness of the firm's management of knowledge.

2. *Bringing new products to the market.* The ability to commercialize innovations (such as convincing physicians to use a new drug or medical instrument) is often as important as the scientific or technological ability to generate the innovation. However, reliable indicators of innovation and commercialization capabilities are rarely available to investors. The highly aggregated sales figures publicly disclosed are too coarse to indicate these capabilities. 'Innovation revenues' (a measure indicating the per cent of total revenues from recently introduced products or services) is an effective indicator of the firm's innovation capacity and ability to bring products expeditiously to the market. This measure, however, is not widely disclosed, or even used internally by managers.

3. *Internet involvement.* Early experience indicates that Internet-based supply and distribution channels lead to considerable benefits and cost savings.[2] The extent and rate of increase of the firm's Internet activities is thus an important leading indicator of future revenue growth and efficiency gains. However, rarely if ever do investors receive systematic information on firms' Internet activities (per cent of online sales of total revenues, cost of online activities), despite the fact that such data are readily available and its disclosure not competitively harmful.

The above are but a few examples of crucial intangibles-related managerial capabilities and performance measures—managing knowledge, commercializing new products, utilizing the Internet—that are not disclosed to investors and often are not even utilized effectively by managers and board members. True, ultimately managerial capabilities and the quality of corporate assets will be reflected by sales and earnings figures but only ultimately and in a highly aggregated manner. An effective information system provides early indications of things to come and enables decision makers to identify specific performance drivers.

Given that information (particularly on the disclosure-challenged intangibles) is essential to managers, investors, and policymakers, I devote this chapter to proposing a comprehensive information system highlighting the performance and capabilities of modern business enterprises. Since some of the proposed information is not transaction based and is of a nonfinancial nature (regarding quality of patents, products in the pipeline, and so on), the system extends well beyond the confines of traditional accounting and can be considered a satellite information system to the current one.

---

2. The Objectives of the Proposed System

Current proposals for improving the information available on knowledge-intensive enterprises are either silent about the objectives of the proposed information or set general and vague targets such as the improvement of resource allocation or the leveling of the playing field between investors and information-privileged analysts or managers. Such objectives, while desirable, are too general and nebulous to guide the construction of a complex information system aimed at reflecting the value and contribution of elusive assets, such as intangibles. We need an operational objective for designing an improved information system.

The objective of the information system proposed below is the facilitation of two of the major forces characterizing modern economies: the democratization and the externalization of decision making processes both within organizations and in capital markets. By democratization and externalization I mean, respectively, the growing participation of individuals in capital markets and the increasing need to engage external entities in the management of businesses. Let me elaborate.

The democratization of capital markets is reflected in the increasing role of individual investors in these markets. No longer content with holding indexed funds, individual investors increasingly wish to perform their own investment analyses and structure built-to-order portfolios. Thus while professional financial analysts and investment advisers still play a central role in capital markets, millions of individual investors are becoming their own analysts. A large number of financial websites attempt to cater to the needs of these new 'analysts', but what the sites provide are mainly voluminous data with very little relevant information. Particularly missing is information on intangibles (such as investment in and productivity of alliances), because these sites basically compile and manipulate publicly available information such as financial statement data, analysts' earnings forecasts, and so on, which are devoid of meaningful information about intangible or knowledge assets.

The externalization of managerial decision making processes may be more subtle but not less real and fundamental than the democratization of capital markets. In the industrial-era vertically integrated corporation, decision making authority was largely centralized and confined within the boundaries of the organization. Managers had in house most of the information they needed. In contrast, in the modern corporation an increasing number of important decisions are shared with entities residing outside the legal confines of the corporation: customers, alliance partners, suppliers of outsourced services, and so on.

Merck, for example, is currently a partner in more than a hundred R&D alliances and joint ventures. Thus important R&D decisions that were previously made exclusively and privately inside Merck are now being made jointly with a large number of outsiders. Cisco Systems outsources most of its production and assembly activities, leading to crucial production and delivery decisions being shared with outsiders. Dell's computer configuration decisions (product design) are largely being made by its customers (the built-to-order concept), Wal-Mart's suppliers make most of its inventory and supply decisions, and the design of open-source software programs (like Linux) is constantly improved by an informal association of code writers (with a final decision authority given to a committee). Such externalization of decision making, of course, fundamentally differs from the intrafirm decentralization of decision making, common to the industrial-era corporations, and increases significantly the scope of information required by managers and investors.

The democratization—externalization (a mouthful) process—evolving both in capital markets and in 'the real economy' (business enterprises) creates new constituencies and enhanced demand for relevant information. Individual investors now need access to the detailed and nuanced information that has thus far been the exclusive domain of financial analysts and investment advisers. Filling this need would level the playing field. But more important, it would make capital markets more competitive and enhance the ability of investors to monitor managers' activities: both important economic objectives of public policy. The networked corporation, with its alliance members, suppliers and customers, subcontractors, and public institutions (e.g. universities cross-licensing patents with business enterprises), needs timely information about its partners and is called to provide information about itself to network partners (e.g. on its scientific and commercialization capabilities).

This then is the major objective of the information system proposed below: to provide the needs of the emerging constituencies—primarily individual investors and the myriad partners to the networked corporations—enabling these constituencies to make and execute decisions at the level of professional investors and managers.

3. The Fundamentals of the Proposed Information System

An analysis of frequently asked questions in conference calls between managers and financial analysts, of surveys of voluntary disclosures by corporations, and polls of decision makers indicates that the information most relevant to decision makers in the current economic environment concerns the enterprise's value chain (business model, in analysts' parlance).[3] This is also the information that the accounting system by and large does not convey in a timely manner. By value chain, I mean the fundamental economic process of innovation, that is vital to the survival and success of business enterprises. It starts with the discovery of new products or services or processes, proceeds through the development phase of these discoveries and the establishment of technological feasibility, and culminates in the commercialization of the new products or services. The value chain—the lifeline of innovative and successful business enterprises—is depicted in Fig. 1.

Note that the nine detailed information boxes of the figure represent a broad cross section of economic sectors and technologies. The intention is to provide a comprehensive representation of relevant information items. Specific

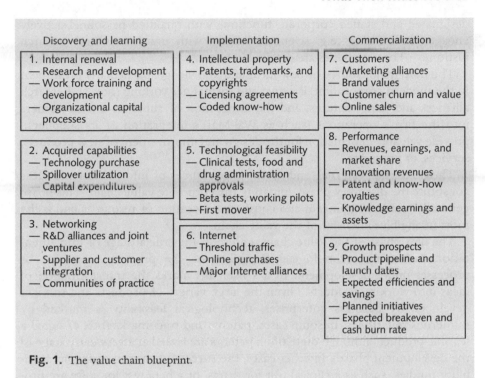

Fig. 1. The value chain blueprint.

companies are represented by a subset of items. For example, information box 4 is irrelevant for companies without patents, and the Internet-related information in boxes 6 and 7 will be missing for companies without online activities.

The value chain of businesses generally starts with the discovery of new ideas for products, services, or processes (consider Cisco's online product installation and maintenance system). Such ideas can emanate from the firm's internal R&D operation or from employees' networks (communities of practice), such as Xerox's Eureka system—which shares information and experience among its technicians—or from R&D intranet systems (box 1). Increasingly, knowledge and ideas are obtained from the outside, embedded in acquired assets. For many companies, the acquisition of technology and in-process R&D now matches or surpasses in value internal R&D.[4]

Knowledge is also acquired by learning from and imitating (reverse engineering) others' innovations. This process—termed by economists R&D spillovers—refers to the benefits to organizations or nations from the innovative activities of others. Effective and systematic organizational learning requires specific capacity to learn (adaptive capacity), as operationalized by a specially designated and staffed corporate function, with qualified personnel actively engaged in learning (e.g. scientists liaising with universities and research institutes). These activities are detailed in box 2.

The third major source of new ideas and knowledge, particularly prominent in the modern corporation, is active and formal networking (box 3). Research alliances and joint ventures, and the integration of suppliers and customers into the firm's operations (such as Wal-Mart's integration of its suppliers), provide valuable information for the design and improvement of new products, services, or processes.[5]

These internal, external, and networking sources of information and ideas constitute the discovery phase, initiating the corporate value chain. This phase generally requires significant and consistent allocation of resources and is the most intangibles-intensive of the value chain.

The next phase of the value chain represents the crucial stage of implementation—achieving technological feasibility of the products, services, or processes under development. In a sense, this marks the transformation of ideas into working products. Given the large variety of products and services developed by business enterprises, technological feasibility is marked by numerous milestones. In some cases, patents and trademarks (box 4) signal a feasible product (although quite often patents are issued at a very early stage of the development phase). In other cases, the successful passing of formal feasibility hurdles, such as a clinical test for drugs, or a beta test for software programs, is the mark of feasibility (box 5). Technological feasibility and readiness for commercialization requires, of course, an adequate labour force, in terms of both quantity and quality, and appropriate work practices, such as incentive based pay.

Increasingly, Internet and intranet technologies offer quantitative measures to indicate technological feasibility (box 6). For example, online operations that gain a reasonable number of visitors (indicated by such frequently used traffic measures as 'reach')—and even more important, repeat visitors—clearly exhibit a degree of technological feasibility of network operations.[6] J. C. Penney, for example, recently had 1.3 million unique visitors a month (repeat visitors are counted only once) to its website—more than any other retailer of apparel and home furnishings.[7] This is clearly an indication of a successful website.[8]

Technological feasibility marks a particularly important phase of the value chain, bringing with it a substantial reduction in the risk associated with products and services under development. Thus information on technological feasibility provides investors and managers important risk gauges.

The final phase of the value chain, commercialization, signifies the successful realization of the innovation process. Ideas, transformed into workable products and services, are in turn brought expeditiously to the market to generate sales and earnings. When such earnings exceed the cost of capital, value is created. That is what a business enterprise is all about.

Customers are naturally the focal point of the commercialization phase of the value chain (box 7). Brand value, manifested by a large market share or the ability to charge a premium price (e.g. the difference between the price of Bayer aspirin and a generic product) is an important commercialization indicator. Successful marketing alliances with leading companies (e.g. a small biotechnology company marketing a drug with Pfizer) are indicators of potential sales growth. For Internet operations, repeat and satisfied buyers, as well as high volume per online customer, bode well for the operation. These and other matters are valuable customer-related indicators of the commercial viability of the innovative process.

Box 8 provides important performance indicators, which are currently outside obligatory disclosure by generally accepted accounting principles (GAAP). Foremost among such measures is 'innovation revenues', indicating the share of revenue from recently introduced (within three to five years) products. This important indicator of innovation capabilities, and particularly of the firm's success at bringing products quickly to the market, is a reliable predictor of operational success and shareholder value creation.[9] Also reflecting top-line success are indicators of market share for the firm's products and the effectiveness of the firm's online distribution activities and marketing alliances.

Bottom-line (profitability) measures (box 8), not routinely disclosed, include indicators highlighting the economic profitability of the enterprise, such as the value added of operations (earnings minus a charge for the cost of equity capital) and the recently introduced measure of knowledge earnings, indicating the contribution of intangible assets to productivity.[10]

Finally, box 9 provides essential forward-looking information. This is the only component of the proposed value chain blueprint that is not factually based. It informs on the product pipeline, crucial for estimating the growth prospects of pharmaceutical and software companies, among others. It provides managers' estimates about the expected efficiencies from restructuring activities and expected growth of market share. For money-losing enterprises (frequent in Internet, biotechnology), it also provides an estimate of time to break even and the cash burn rate (months of operations supported by current liquid assets). All of these information items are frequently and persistently sought from management in conference calls.[11]

This is then an outline of the proposed information system—the value chain blueprint—that is aimed at providing a comprehensive and in-depth portrayal of the enterprise's capabilities and success in creating economic value. The focus is on innovation, and information on intangibles (R&D, patents, brands, alliances, networking) obviously plays a prominent role in this information system.

4. The Blueprint Criteria

The value chain blueprint provides an information system for use in both internal decision making and disclosure to investors. Specific blueprint indicators should satisfy three criteria to ensure maximal usefulness. First, they should be quantitative. Qualitative aspects of the value chain (such as employee work practices, patent cross-licensing) may be provided in an annex. Second, they should be standardized (or easily standardizable), meaning that they can be compared across firms for valuation and benchmarking purposes. Third and most important, they should be confirmed by empirical evidence as relevant to users (generally by establishing a significant statistical association between the measures and indicators of corporate value such as stock return and productivity improvement).

These three criteria for choice of the specific blueprint indicators ensure that the proposed information system satisfies current needs of users (e.g. comparability within an industry) and is scientifically robust (empirical research support). For concreteness sake, I provide several examples of operationalizing the blueprint criteria.

Voluminous empirical evidence indicates that, on average, investment in R&D, information technology, and customers pays off in terms of increased productivity and enhancement of market values of companies. This supports the disclosure (box 1, Fig. 1) of periodic R&D expenditures, meaningfully classified (e.g. R&D aimed at new products, the improvement or maintenance of existing products, and process R&D).[12] Data relating to customer acquisition costs (particularly relevant for Internet companies) should be disclosed separately from advertising and marketing expenses, given that empirical evidence has established a statistical association between customer acquisition costs and market values.[13]

Box 4 of the blueprint conveys information on the firm's intellectual property-intangibles secured by legal rights. The number of patents, trademarks, and copyrights registered during the period, as well as patent renewals, provides the rudimentary information. Empirical research indicates that various attributes of patents, such as the number of citations to the firm's patent portfolio contained in subsequent patents (forward citations), are important indicators of the quality of the firm's science and technology.[14] These quality measures are in turn linked to market values of corporations. Data on patents and their attributes thus meet the three blueprint criteria: they are quantifiable, they are standardized (available from various vendors),[15] and they are supported by research as value drivers.

Of particular importance are data on royalties received from the licensing of patents and know-how (box 8). Investors place higher value on such royalties than on most other components of income, probably due to the long-term nature of licensing agreements involved. Furthermore, royalties help investors in valuing the prospects of the R&D expenditures of companies. Evidence indicates that the R&D expenditures of firms with substantial royalty income are accorded higher market valuations than the R&D of companies lacking royalties, probably because the existence of customers for the firm's patents attests to the superior value of its R&D.[16]

The above examples demonstrate the key attributes of the blueprint component indicators: quantifiability, standardizability, and scientifically based linkages to value.

5. An Example

The proposed information system covers the relevant information for a wide variety of enterprises, but a typical company generally will have a parsimonious set of ten to twelve key value chain indicators. For example, I would expect a biotechnology company to report the following twelve items in its value chain blueprint.

For the discovery and learning phase:

1. Investment in internal and acquired R&D, classified by type of R&D (basic, applied), reported for the past three to five years.

2. Investment in alliances and joint ventures; total number of such alliances; classification into active and dormant ventures (including data on the volume of investments of alliance partners).

3. Investment in information technology, both internal and acquired.

Informing on the implementation stage:

1. Number of new patents granted and the various attributes of (such as citations to) the company's patent portfolio; trademarks and copyrights granted, if any.

2. Cross-licensing of patents and royalty income from patent licensing.

3. Results of clinical tests and US Food and Drug Administration (FDA) approvals.

4. Employee retention data and work force structure (such as ratio of scientists and R&D personnel to total employees); 'hot skills'.

5. Employees who are star scientists (prestigious award winners).[17]

And finally, the biotechnology company will have five categories related to commercialization:

- Innovation revenues (per cent of revenue from recent products).
- Revenues from alliances, joint ventures, patent licensing.

519

- Cash burn rate (length of operations on current resources).
- Product pipeline; expected launch dates of new products; products off patents.
- Expected market potential for major new products.

As noted earlier, the proposed value chain blueprint is aimed at internal (managers, board members) as well as external (investors, suppliers, policymakers) purposes. The difference—and the devil—lies in the details. At the internal (managerial) level, for example, data on the investment in and productivity of alliances would be provided at the individual alliance or joint venture level. For external reporting purposes, aggregate data on the number of alliances and the total investment in them, along with a breakdown of alliances into operating (including revenues from alliances) and dormant ventures, will suffice.

6. What About Accounting?

It is widely recognized that the current accounting system does not convey relevant and timely information about the value chain (business model).[18] Investment in discovery and learning, both internal and acquired, is usually expensed immediately in financial reports, with most expenditures (on employee training, software acquisitions, and web-based distribution systems, for example) not even separately disclosed to investors. The transaction-based accounting system ignores the implementation stage of the value chain (an FDA drug approval, a patent granted, or a successful beta test of a software product), although considerable value creation or destruction, as well as risk reduction, generally occurs during this stage. And even the commercialization stage of the value chain, which generates recordable costs and revenues, is reported in a highly aggregated manner, defying attempts to evaluate the efficiency of the firm's innovation process (the assessment of return on R&D or technology acquisition, the success of collaborative efforts, or the firm's ability to expeditiously bring products to the market).

Some of the limitations of accounting-based information are rooted in the structure of accounting, which essentially reflects legally binding transactions with third parties (sales, purchases, borrowing funds, stock issues). In the industrial and agricultural economies, most of the value of business enterprises was created by transactions—the legal transfer of property rights. In the current, knowledge-based economy, much of value creation or destruction precedes, sometime by years, the occurrence of transactions. The successful development of a drug, for example, creates considerable value, but actual transactions (sales) may take years to materialize. This is, by the way, the major reason for the growing disconnect between market values and financial information.[19]

Viewed from this perspective, the proposed information system, which focuses on the fundamental phases of the value chain (the business proposition of the enterprise), precedes and complements accounting-based information. The special emphasis of the proposed value chain blueprint on intangible investments clearly distinguishes it from current financial reports. Accounting, in a sense, provides a final reality check on the proposed system of value creation or destruction as products, services, or processes move along the value chain.

7. Standardizing Information on Intangibles

I propose that an appropriate accounting policymaking body, preferably the FASB with strong encouragement and oversight by the SEC, take upon itself the major task of standardizing intangibles-related information.

By standardization I mean creating a coherent structure of information and defining the individual information items composing the information structure. By information structure I mean a comprehensive set of interrelated reports on value chain (business model) development, with special emphasis on intangible investments and assets. This reporting construct would complement the conventional one (balance sheet, income statement) by providing systematic and standardized information on innovation and intangible investments.

The individual items that make up the information structure—expenditures oil customer acquisition, Internet traffic measures, or innovation revenues—require careful definition (such as what goes into customer acquisition costs). Valuation criteria must be clearly specified (Should customer acquisition costs be amortized? And how?).[20]

I strongly believe that if a coherent, well-defined, and decision-relevant system is developed to reflect the major attributes of intangible assets and their role (along with other assets) in the overall value creation process of the enterprise, most managers will respond by disclosing voluntarily some or all of the information. The reason for my optimism is that the availability of a new disclosure structure, endorsed by the major accounting policymaking institutions—and perhaps by other influential bodies (the large accounting firms)—will initiate the information revelation process discussed in Chapter 4. Enterprises with good news (high innovation revenues, successful alliances) will start disclosing—in effect, motivating others to join ranks. No news is bad news in capital markets; silence is penalized.

8. Synopsis

The key to achieving substantial improvement in the disclosure of information about intangibles, both within businesses and to capital markets, is the construction of a comprehensive and coherent information structure that focuses on the essential—the value creation (innovation) process of the enterprise—and places intangible assets in their proper role within this structure.

While focusing on what information yields functionality through disclosure, it is equally important to clarify what does not. In particular, managers should not be expected to disclose values of intangibles (e.g. the market value of a patent or the worth of key employees). The determination of asset and enterprise value is better left to outsiders, such as financial analysts.

In my opinion, the way to induce the release of meaningful information about intangibles is for policymakers to establish a comprehensive information standard. Standards have previously worked wonders towards enhancing production and widespread participation in networks.[21] A standard blueprint, such as the one outlined above, portraying the innovation process of businesses and focusing on the intangible investments generating the process, will drive a larger number of companies to provide new and useful information, internally and externally.

Notes

1. The title of this chapter follows that of a 1902 essay by Leo Tolstoy on poverty (material, not informational).
2. For example, 'the companies that have gone furthest' in the use of the Internet for business-to-business transactions 'claim to save astonishing amounts. GE plans to cut 15 per cent from its cost base of $100 billion in both 2001 and 2002'. See Economist, November 11, 2000, p. 6 of e-management survey.
3. For conference calls see, for example, Tasker (1998); for voluntary disclosures, see FASB (2000); for polls see, for example, Eccles and others (2001: ch. 7).
4. Deng and Lev (1998).
5. For more on Internet alliances, see Elfenbein and Lerner (2000).
6. For a discussion of traffic measures, see Demers and Lev (2000).
7. 'Penney Wise', Forbes, September 4, 2000, p. 72.
8. The ultimate test, of course, is the extent of purchases by website visitors, an aspect of its commercial success.
9. Crepon et al. (1998).

10. Regarding value added, FASB (2000) indicates that some companies already provide information on economic value contributed by operations. Regarding knowledge earnings, see annual ranking of companies by this measure published in CFO magazine (most recently, April 2001) and Fortune (April 2001).
11. Tasker (1998).
12. Currently, most companies disclose just total R&D expenditures.
13. See, for example, Demers and Lev (2000).
14. See, for example, Deng et al. (1999), Hall et al. (2000).
15. Investors can purchase the patent data on their own, but obviously, if the reporting company will acquire the patent data and disclose it to investors, considerable costs will be saved relative to individual investors acquiring the information.
16. Gu and Lev (2000).
17. Darby et al. (1999) have established a statistical association between star scientists and the value of biotechnology companies.
18. Evidence the Senate hearings on this issue, the public committee set up in 2000 by the Securities and Exchange Commission to examine the adequacy of reported information to investors, FASB (2000), and such research findings as Lev and Zarowin (1999).
19. Lev and Zarowin (1999).
20. This is obviously not the place to delve into the details of the standard setting task, but given the extent and pervasiveness of intangibles, it clearly is a major endeavor. However, the extensive experience of accounting policymakers in setting standards for financial information will come in handy.
21. See Shapiro and Varian (1999) on the importance of standards (e.g. a computer operating system in the development of markets and technologies).

References

Crepon, B., E. Duguet, and J. Mairesse (1998), 'Research, innovation, and productivity: An econometric analysis at the firm level', Working paper 6696, Cambridge, MA: National Bureau of Economic Research.

Darby, M., Q. Liu, and L. Zucker (1999), 'Stakes and stars: The effect of intellectual human capital on the level and variability of high-tech firms' market values', Working paper 7201, Cambridge, MA: National Bureau of Economic Research.

Demers, E. and B. Lev (2000), 'A rude awakening: Internet shakeout in 2000', Working paper, University of Rochester, Simon School of Business.

Deng, Z. and B. Lev (1998), 'Flash-then-flush': The valuation of acquired R&D-in-process', Working paper, New York University, Stern School of Business.

——and F. Narin (1999), 'Science and technology as predictors of stock performance', Financial Analysts Journal, 55: 20–32.

Baruch Lev

Eccles, R., R. H. Herz, E. M. Kelganis, and D. M. H. Philips (2001), *The Value Reporting Revolution* (New York: Wiley).

Elfenbein, D. and J. Lerner (2000), 'Links and hyperlinks: An empirical analysis of Internet portal alliances', Working paper, Harvard University, School of Business.

Financial Accounting Standards Board (2000), 'Business Reporting Research Project', Steering Committee Report, first draft.

Gu, F. and B. Lev (2000), 'Markets in intangibles: Patent licensing', Working paper, New York University, Stern School of Business.

Hall, B., A. Jaffe, and M. Trajtenberg (2000), 'Market value and patent citations: A first look', Working paper 7741, Cambridge, MA: National Bureau of Economic Research.

Lev, B. and P. Zarowin (1999), 'The boundaries of financial reporting and how to extend them', *Journal of Accounting Research* (supplement) 37: 353–85.

Shapiro, C. and H. Varian (1999), *Information Rules* (Harvard Business School Press).

Tasker, S. (1998), 'Technology companies conference calls: A small sample study', *Journal of Financial Statement Analysis*, 4: 6–14.

Index

Index

Index

Index

Index

Index

Index